The Handbook of Design for Sustainability

THE HA
OF DES
SUSTAIN

NDBOOK
IGN FOR
ABILITY

Edited by
Stuart Walker and Jacques Giard

Managing Editor: Helen L. Walker

B L O O M S B U R Y
LONDON · NEW DELHI · NEW YORK · SYDNEY

Bloomsbury Academic

An imprint of Bloomsbury Publishing Plc

50 Bedford Square	1385 Broadway
London	New York
WC1B 3DP	NY 10018
UK	USA

www.bloomsbury.com

First published 2013

British Library Cataloguing-in-Publication Data
A catalogue record for this book is available from the British Library.

ISBN: 978-0-8578-5852-8

Library of Congress Cataloging-in-Publication Data
The handbook of design for sustainability / edited by Stuart Walker and Jacques Giard.
pages cm
Includes bibliographical references and index.
ISBN 978-0-85785-852-8 — ISBN 978-1-47250-311-4
1. Sustainable design.   I. Walker, Stuart, 1955- editor of compilation.
II. Giard, Jacques, editor of compilation.
NK1520.H25   2013
720'.47—dc23
2013005682

Typeset by Apex CoVantage, LLC
Printed and bound in Great Britain

CONTENTS

ILLUSTRATIONS AND TABLES

FIGURES

TABLES

CONTRIBUTORS

Craig Badke's doctoral research investigates the complex social relationships we have with technology within the context of sustainability. It employs critical design exploration as a tool of inquiry into the conceptual nature of objects and how they co-shape our practices and moral understandings of the built environment. His work is aimed at developing a critical understanding of the social and cultural contexts related to the production and consumption of material culture and their implications for how we think about and approach design. He has taught graduate courses in design criticism, history, and theory, critical explorations in sustainable design, and product design studios. His paper "Designers Anonymous," coauthored with Stuart Walker, received an IDSA Best Paper Award.

Gijs Bakker is a designer, lecturer, educator, and exhibition curator. Over his career, spanning nearly five decades, he has frequently served as a jury member for international design competitions and consulted for major design firms. Until 2010 he headed the IM master's course and from 2010–2012 he was the dean of the three master's programs at the Design Academy Eindhoven. He is represented by numerous galleries, and his work has been acquired by many public and private collections worldwide. In addition to being the cofounder of both Droog design and the Chi ha paura...? Foundation, Gijs has undertaken many prestigious design commissions. Several major retrospectives of his work have been mounted. Most recently, the exhibit *Gijs Bakker and Jewelry*, traveled from the Stedelijk Museum's Hertogenbosch to the Pinakothek der Moderne (Munich) as well as several other important institutions. The exhibition also included a publication by Arnoldsche of Bakker's work.

Tracy Bhamra is professor of sustainable design and dean of Loughborough Design School, Loughborough University, United Kingdom. Her research lies in the area of design for sustainability, its application and effectiveness. This research has involved collaboration with multinational as well as small- and medium-sized companies from the automotive, electrical and electronic, textile and clothing, and energy generation industry sectors. Her book *Design for Sustainability: A Practical Approach* was published by Gower in 2007.

Janis Birkeland (BA, Bennington; MArch, Univeristy of California Berkeley; JD, University of California Hastings Law; PhD, University of Tasmania) is professor of sustainable design at the University of Auckland. Janis worked as an urban designer and city planner; additionally, she has worked as a registered architect and lawyer, in San Francisco. After moving to Australia, she turned to academia. Her previous position was professor of architecture at the Queensland University of Technology. She has run many tertiary and professional development units on sustainable systems and has written over 100 papers and has given over 100 invited talks on this area. Her books are *Design for Sustainability* (2002) and *Positive Development* (2008). She is currently developing and testing eco-retrofitting modules that provide ecosystem services as well as environmental and building services.

Albert Borgmann is regents professor of philosophy at the University of Montana. He has an MA in literature from the University of Illinois (Urbana) and a PhD in philosophy from the University of Munich. Since 1970 he has taught at the University of Montana. His special area is the philosophy of society and culture with particular emphasis on technology. Among his publications are *Technology and the Character of Contemporary Life* (University of Chicago Press, 1984), *Crossing the Postmodern Divide* (University of Chicago Press, 1992), and *Real American Ethics* (University of Chicago Press, 2006).

Lynne Blair is a senior lecturer in the School of Computing and Communications at Lancaster University. She has a background in formal specification and verification, utilizing techniques such as process algebra, automata, and logic-based techniques for distributed multimedia systems. A particular focus has been the study of interactions that occur in software systems and in aspect-oriented software development, including the development of dynamically adaptive systems through aspect-oriented techniques. More recently, she has started to build links between recent computer science developments and work undertaken during an MA in theology (a creative career detour!). This work addresses the more human aspects of computing such as personal and social implications of our digital economy on community values and integrity, and environmental implications of recent Web developments.

Christopher T. Boyko is a senior research associate in ImaginationLancaster at Lancaster University. With Rachel Cooper, he coedited *Designing Sustainable Cities* (2009) and has published peer-reviewed journals articles about the impact of design on non-communicable diseases for the *Journal of Health Communication* (2011), and on reconceptualizing density for *Progress in Planning* (2011). He also cowrote a state-of-science review on the impacts of the physical environment on mental wellbeing for the UK Government Office for Science's *Foresight Programme on Mental Capital and Wellbeing*. His research interests include sustainability, urban design, public space, environmental psychology, and wellbeing.

Jonathan Chapman is reader in design, and course leader of the MA sustainable design program at the University of Brighton. Author of *Emotionally Durable Design: Objects, Experiences & Empathy* (Earthscan, 2005), his work engages issues of design, ecology, and the human condition. In 2008 he stood before the House of Lords to present formal evidence as part of their Enquiry into Waste Reduction. Described in *New Scientist* as a "mover and shaker," Chapman's work has received extensive critical acclaim, including from CNN International, *New Statesman, The Telegraph, New York Times, The Independent,* and *New Scientist* and has been featured on BBC Radio 4.

Anne Chick is professor of design at the University of Lincoln, United Kingdom, and visiting professor in the faculty of environmental design at the University of Calgary, Canada. Her recent research has been in mapping the various fields of design for sustainability. She has published widely in this area, and her most recent book, co-authored with Dr. Paul Micklethwaite, Kingston University, United Kingdom, is *Designing for Sustainable Change: How Design and Designers Can Drive the Sustainability Agenda* (AVA Publishing, 2011). *Design Week* identified her as one of the top twenty influential individuals in sustainable design in 2009.

Rachel Cooper, OBE, is professor of design management and codirector of ImaginationLancaster at Lancaster University as well as Chair of the Lancaster Institute for the Contemporary Arts. She has authored several books in the design field, including *The Design Agenda* (1995), *The Design Experience* (2003), *Designing Sustainable Cities* (2009), and *The Handbook of Design Management* (2011). She is editor of *The Design Journal* and president of the European Academy of Design. Her research interests cover design management, design policy, design in the built environment, and design against crime.

Tim Cooper is professor of sustainable design and consumption at Nottingham Trent University. A former economist in the construction industry, he developed an interest in the lifespan of consumer durables as a researcher at the New Economics Foundation in the early 1990s before moving to Sheffield Hallam University, where he worked for fifteen years. His current research interests are multidisciplinary, embracing design, consumer behavior, public policy, and environmental ethics. He continues to specialize in product longevity within the broad field of sustainable consumption and is contributing editor of *Longer Lasting Products* (Gower, 2010). A former specialist adviser to the House of Commons Environment Committee, his research has been funded by the European Commission, Council of Europe, and several UK government bodies, as well as by industry. He has acted as research evaluator for the Research Council of Norway, Irish Environmental Protection Agency, and Belgian Federal Science Policy Office.

Aidan Davison is senior lecturer in the School of Geography and Environmental Studies at the University of Tasmania. The author of *Technology and the Contested Meanings of Sustainability* (SUNY, 2001), he pursues interdisciplinary enquiry into political and cultural questions of sustainability. His research interests include the significance of practical moral philosophy of technology for environmentalism, the centrality of paradox and ambivalence in the project of sustainable development, the political ecology of post-dualist accounts of nature, and everyday experience of suburban nature.

Christopher Day studied architecture and sculpture in London. Committed to eco-architecture and an ecological lifestyle since 1970, he has received four design awards including a Prince of Wales Award and National Eisteddfod first prize. He pioneered a listening-based consensus design method, used in over fifty projects, and has worked in nineteen countries. His books include *Places of the Soul* (1990), *Spirit and Place* (2002), *Consensus Design* (2002), *Environment and Children* (2007), *A Haven for Childhood* (1990), and *Dying: or Learning to Live* (2010). Translations are in German, Italian, Russian, Thai, Czech, Greek, and Welsh. Currently disabled and unable to speak, he consensus-designs from a wheelchair and gives (silent) lectures.

Dennis P. Doordan is coeditor of *Design Issues* and associate dean for research and scholarship in the School of Architecture at the University of Notre Dame. He has published books and articles on a wide variety of topics dealing with modern and contemporary architecture and design. His research interests include political themes in architecture and design, the impact of new materials, and the history of design. He is coeditor of the anthology *The Designed World. Images, Objects, Environments* (2010).

John Ehrenfeld retired in June 2009 as executive director of the International Society for Industrial Ecology. His continuing research focuses on sustainability. He is the author of *Sustainability by Design* (2009). He retired in 2000 as the director of the Massachusetts Institute of Technology (MIT) Program on Technology, Business, and Environment. In June 2009, the International Society for Industrial Ecology awarded him its Society Prize. In October 1999, the World Resources Institute honored him with a lifetime achievement award. He holds a BSc and ScD in chemical engineering from MIT and is author or coauthor of over 200 papers and other publications.

Kate Fletcher is a designer-researcher, consultant, and writer in fashion and sustainability. Her work, in business, education, policy, and research has been at the forefront of design for sustainability ideas and research practice in fashion for the last fifteen years. She advises and participates in fashion and sustainability initiatives around the globe including the UK's All Party Parliamentary Group on Ethics and Sustainability in Fashion. She is reader in sustainable fashion at London College of Fashion where her latest project explores the "craft of use." She has over fifty publications in the field, is author of *Sustainable Fashion and Textiles: Design Journeys* (2008) and coauthor of *Fashion and Sustainability: Design for Change* (2012).

Avi Friedman studied architecture and town planning in Italy, Israel, and Canada. In 1988, he founded the Affordable Homes Program at McGill University in Montreal, Canada. He is known for his housing innovation and in particular for the Grow Home and the Next Home designs, both townhouses that have been replicated internationally. He has published extensively in academic and trade publications and has authored ten books, including *Sustainable Residential Development* (2007) and *Homes Within Reach* (2005).

He is also a practicing architect and the recipient of numerous awards, including the Manning Innovation Award and the United Nations World Habitat Award. In the year 2000, he was selected by *Wallpaper* magazine as one of ten people from around the world "most likely to change the way we live."

Tony Fry is professor of design futures at Griffith University, Queensland College of Art, Brisbane. Tony also directs an indigenous culture–based creative industry research project in Timor-Leste. He is the author of nine books and numerous other publications. Tony was the former director of the EcoDesign Foundation in Sydney and has been the member of many award-winning design teams. His current research interests focus on urban nomadism, community formation, and the future of the city; the relation of design and history (rather than design history); and design, the prehistorical and animality.

Alastair Fuad-Luke is professor of practice, emerging design practices, at the School of Arts, Design and Architecture, Aalto University, Helsinki, Finland. He has contributed to the international debate about design(ing) for sustainability since the late 1990s, focusing on eco-design, slow design, codesign, and, more recently, design activism. His current work explores the societal impacts of design for positive development. In 2010 he was awarded the European Environmental Design prize by DIMAD, Spain, for his multiple editions of *The Eco-Design Handbook* (2009), and has written several other books including his most recent, *Design Activism: Beautiful Strangeness for a Sustainable World.*

Jacques R. Giard is professor of industrial design in The Design School at Arizona State University (ASU). Prior to his appointment at ASU, he was director of the School of Industrial Design at Carleton University, Ottawa, Canada. He received his undergraduate education in furniture design in Montreal (1969), did graduate studies in industrial design (engineering) in Birmingham, United Kingdom (1971), and earned a PhD from Concordia University in Montreal (1987). Before becoming a design educator, he had extensive professional experience in Canada with various design consultancies and manufacturers. He is the author of *Design FAQs* (2005), a university textbook on basic design, and *Designing: A Journey Through Time* (2009). He has had over forty articles and papers published in various journals and magazines in North America and Europe. He was national president of the Association of Canadian Industrial Designers and a member of the organizing committee for the ICSID 97 Congress, The Humane Village.

Ricardo J. Hernandez holds a BSc in industrial engineering from the Colombian School of Engineering, which was followed by an MSc in industrial engineering from the University of the Andes, Bogotá, Colombia, and a master research in industrial engineering major area product and process design from the National Institute Polytechnic of Grenoble, France. Currently he is a PhD student at Loughborough University undertaking research in sustainable product service systems (PSS) supported by design and ICT.

Bran Knowles is a PhD student at Lancaster University's HighWire Doctoral Training Centre, being supervised by Stuart Walker and Lynne Blair. Her previous education includes a bachelor's degree from The University of Chicago in comparative human development—an interdisciplinary program spanning psychology, anthropology, sociology, and biology—an MFA and MSc, both from the University of Dundee, and an MRes in digital innovation from Lancaster University. Throughout it all, her interest has been in human wellbeing in contemporary society.

JohnPaul Kusz is president of JPKusz, providing product and business development strategies dedicated to eliminating the negative environmental consequences of commerce to businesses, nongovernment organizations, and academic institutions. He has taught for over ten years as an adjunct professor at the Illinois Institute of Technology at both the Institute of Design and the Stuart School of Business, where he cofounded the Center for Sustainable Enterprise in 2000. His current research is focused on the development of "sustainable" product, business, and system models, exploring how to generate social and technical innovations that move us toward a more viable future. He has authored over forty-five articles on the potential of design to mitigate environmental impacts, including contribution to one of the first policy-oriented publications on the issue of design for the environment: *Green Products by Design, Choices for a Cleaner Environment* (U.S. Congress, Office of Technology Assessment, 1992).

Dorothy Mackenzie is a marketing and communications professional based in London, who has worked for the last twenty-five years at the interface between brands and sustainability. She has written a range of books and reports around this theme, including *Design for the Environment* (1991) and *Corporate Reputation–Does the Consumer Care?* (1992), and she spoke at Sustainable Brands 2010 in Monterey, California. Her appointments have included the UK Government's Advisory Committee on Business and the Environment and the Prince of Wales' Business and the Environment Programme. She chaired the leading environmental think tank Green Alliance and has sat on the boards of the Design Council and the Royal Society of Arts. She started her career in advertising, followed by new product development, design, and brand strategy. She cofounded and now chairs the London operations for Dragon Rouge, a global design and innovation consultancy.

Alexander Manu is a strategic innovation practitioner, international lecturer, and author. He works with executive teams in Fortune 500 companies in industries as diverse as consumer packaged goods, media, advertising, mobile communications, gaming, lotteries, and manufacturing. He lectures around the world on innovation, imagination, transformation change agents, and strategic foresight. He is a senior partner at InnoSpa International Partners, teaches at the Rotman School of Management, is a professor at the OCAD University in Toronto, and is a visiting lecturer at the Wallace McCain Institute for Entrepreneurship. He is also the author of *Disruptive Business* (2010), *Everything 2.0* (2008), *The Imagination Challenge* (2006), *ToolToys* (1995), and *The Big Idea of Design* (1999), as well as numerous articles published in national and international periodicals.

Ezio Manzini has been working in the field of design for sustainability for more than two decades. Most recently, his interests have focused on social innovation. He launched and currently coordinates DESIS: an international network on design for social innovation and sustainability (http://www.desis-network.org). Throughout his professional life, he has explored design potentialities in different fields, such as, in the 1980s, design of materials; in the 1990s, strategic design; and, over the last ten years, service design. He has taught and directed design research in several design schools including the Politecnico di Milano, where he has also coordinated the Unit of Research DIS—Design and Innovation for Sustainability, the doctorate in design, and, recently, DES: the Centre for Service Design in the INDACO (industrial design, arts, communication and fashion) department.

Anne Marchand is a product design professor at the Université de Montréal. She holds a PhD in environmental design from the University of Calgary (2008). Her research interests include issues related to sustainable consumption, alternative visual, and material cultures, localization in the design and production of goods, and research-through-design as a valid scientific research method. She is also conducting action research projects with First Nations communities in Québec, Canada, to support cultural, economic, and social empowerment through the creation of contemporary products.

Freya Mathews is adjunct professor of environmental philosophy and coordinator of the Environmental Culture and Sustainability Research Cluster at Latrobe University, Australia. Her books include *The Ecological Self* (Routledge, 1991), *For Love of Matter: a Contemporary Panpsychism* (SUNY, 2003), and *Reinhabiting Reality: Towards a Recovery of Culture* (SUNY, 2005). She has published over fifty articles and chapters in the area of environmental philosophy.

Richard Mawle is a researcher in sustainable design at the Loughborough Design School, Loughborough University, United Kingdom. His research focuses on product design practice and how this might be modified to reduce the environmental impact of consumer goods. This includes looking at practical ways to improve product life spans and investigating the frequent absence of a sustainable design agenda in product design briefs.

Shashank Mehta, senior faculty, industrial design at the National Institute of Design, Ahmedabad, India, is a mechanical engineer and product designer. He has worked with small- and large-scale industries and also with the crafts and social sectors. He has worked extensively in the area of technology and design fusion, sustainability, and indigenous innovations; he has authored various articles and research papers and has widely lectured on these subjects. Mehta has successfully anchored international workshops with the specific focus on "design for development" for participants from various developing countries.

Anna Meroni is professor at the INDACO (industrial design, arts, communication and fashion) department of Politecnico di Milano, an education and research center in design. She investigates services from the perspective of strategic social innovation, with a specific emphasis on community-centered design. Her main research areas are food systems and innovative housing for sustainable lifestyles. She is codirector of the master in strategic design and a visiting professor and scholar in schools and universities around the world. She is active in the launch and promotion of the international network DESIS, Design for Social Innovation and Sustainability.

Chris Ryan is professor and director of the Victorian Eco-innovation Lab at the University of Melbourne. In the early 1990s, he directed a large program to develop a methodology for design for sustainability in Australia that became EcoReDesign. He has worked with a range of European research groups. He was professor and director of the International Institute for Industrial Environmental Economics in Lund, Sweden (1997–2002). He wrote the "2002 UNEP Global Status Report on Sustainable Consumption." His most recent edited book is *Design for Sustainability—A Step-by-Step Approach* (UNEP, 2009). His current research focuses on sustainable urban development and low-carbon living.

Maria Cecilia Loschiavo dos Santos is a philosopher and professor of design at the School of Architecture and Urbanism, University of São Paulo, where she does basic research into design and society, defining fundamental relationships between design and urban poverty, homelessness, and displacement. Santos's current research is about discarded products, design, homelessness, and collectors. She is deeply committed to design and social responsibility issues, and serves as scientific consultant for Brazilian research agencies. She is also a scholar of the National Council for Scientific and Technological Development (CNPq).

John Ralston Saul, a champion of freedom of expression, was elected president of PEN International in 2009. An award-winning essayist and novelist, he has had a growing impact on political and economic thought in many countries. Declared a "prophet" by *TIME* magazine, he is included in the prestigious *Utne Reader's* list of the world's 100 leading thinkers and visionaries. His works have been translated into twenty languages in thirty countries. His most recent book is *The Collapse of Globalism and the Reinvention of the World* (2005). He is widely known for his philosophical trilogy—*Voltaire's Bastards* (1992), *The Doubter's Companion* (1994), and *The Unconscious Civilization* (1997).

Deborah Schneiderman is an associate professor of interior design in the School of Art and Design at Pratt Institute, and a registered architect and LEED Accredited Professional. She received her MArch in architecture from SCI-Arc and her BS in design and environmental analysis from Cornell University. Before becoming a design educator, she founded deSc architecture/design/research with a focus in environmentally sustainable design. Her research explores sustainable built environments, the integration of sustainability into the design curriculum, and sustainability and prefabrication. Recent publications include "A Pre- and Post-Evaluation of Integrating Sustainability Curriculum by Inserting Okala Modules Into an Interior Design Materials and Methods Course" in *The International Journal of Sustainability in Higher Education* (2012), the chapter "Integrating Sustainability into Design Curriculum" in *Sustainability at*

Universities—Opportunities, Challenges and Trends (2009), edited by Walter Leil Filho, and her book *Inside Prefab: The Ready-made Interior* (2012).

Louise Schouwenberg studied psychology at Radboud University Nijmegen, sculpture at the Gerrit Rietveld Academy, Amsterdam, and philosophy at University of Amsterdam and Erasmus University, Rotterdam. After a career as a visual artist, her focus from 2000 has been art and design theory. She writes for national and international art and design magazines and has contributed to a range of books, including *Hella Jongerius—Misfit* (Phaidon, 2010) and *Robert Zandvliet. I Owe You The Truth In Painting 1650–2012* (Nai Publishers, 2012). She has been an adviser with various organizations and has worked as a curator for exhibitions on the cutting edge between design and visual arts. Currently she is conducting research on Dutch design and contributing to the renovation plan of the Delegates' Lounge, UN headquarters, New York. In 2010 she was appointed head of the master's program in contextual design at the Design Academy Eindhoven, and lector (professor) in design theory.

Helen L. Walker, managing editor of this volume, is an independent language consultant with a master's degree in education and sustainability. She has taught languages at all levels from kindergarten to university undergraduates in the United Kingdom, the Middle East, and North America. She lectures and runs workshops on educational methods, particularly language immersion, and is an associate member of the Society for Editors and Proofreaders (SfEP).

Stuart Walker is head of design and codirector of the ImaginationLancaster creative research lab at Lancaster University and visiting professor of sustainable design at Kingston University, United Kingdom. Formerly, he was associate dean at the faculty of environmental design, University of Calgary, Canada. His research papers have been published and presented internationally, and his propositional designs have been exhibited at the Design Museum, London, across Canada, and in Rome. His books include *The Spirit of Design* (Earthscan, 2011), *Enabling Solutions,* with Ezio Manzini and Barry Wylant (University of Calgary Press, 2008), and *Sustainable by Design* (Earthscan, 2006).

John Wood is emeritus professor of design at Goldsmiths, University of London, which he joined in 1978 as deputy head of the fine art department. In 1989, he helped to start a new department of design by pioneering a holistic design degree that was founded on strong ethical and ecological principles. In 1995, he launched the first MA program in design futures. Both degrees incorporated meta-design principles that are shareable and extensible. His most recent book *Designing for Micro-Utopias* (Gower, 2007) is one of several hundred publications that seek to reconcile ethical, environmental, and philosophical aspects of design. Wood has cofounded several international networks, including the Metadesigners Network http://metadesigners.org/, the Writing-PAD Network, and the "Attainable Utopias" Network. He is also cofounder and coeditor of the *Journal of Writing in Creative Practice (Intellect)* and a performing founder member of the cult band Deaf School.

Lou Yongqi is the vice dean of the College of Design and Innovation of Tongji University, China, and visiting professor at the School of Art and Design, Aalto University in Finland. His main research focus is sustainable design and innovation. He plays an active role in promoting collaborations on interdisciplinary sustainable design education, research, and practice internationally. He sits on the board of several international organizations such as CUMULUS: the International Association of Universities and Colleges of Art, Design and Media, Alta Scuola Politecnica Italy, and DESIS, Design for Social Innovation and Sustainability. His latest book is *DESIGN Harvests: An Acupuncture Design Approach Towards Sustainability* (2011).

ACKNOWLEDGMENTS

Our sincere thanks go to all the authors who have dedicated their time and efforts to bringing this volume to fruition. We greatly appreciate their thoughtful and significant contributions to the continuing debate around design for sustainability, as well as for their patience and care in dealing with our editorial requests.

There are, of course, many researchers and authors contributing to design for sustainability whom we have not been able to include in this volume but who, nevertheless, have informed the ideas and concepts within it. Details of many of these authors' works can be found in the references that follow each chapter.

We are grateful, too, to all those people and organizations that have granted us permission to use their images, tables, and texts in this handbook.

Tristan Palmer, Simon Longman, and Simon Cowell at Berg have been supportive and encouraging throughout and have continued to offer advice and guidance.

Finally, and most importantly, we thank Helen L. Walker without whose organizational abilities, incisive scrutiny, and compilation of the entire manuscript this project would not have reached completion.

Stuart Walker and Jacques Giard

FOREWORD

JOHN THACKARA

A huge amount of creativity is emerging as citizens figure out new ways to meet their daily life needs—from clothing and food, to shelter, care, and learning. At a local level, these efforts are clustering in a wide variety of social micro-economies in which people share skills, time, and resources. There's an emphasis on collaboration and sharing; on person-to-person interactions; on the care and maintenance of existing assets. The main driver of this growing wave of social activity is necessity. Design for sustainability, it is turning out, is not about designers telling other people how to live. It's about the cocreation of tools and enabling platforms that make it easier for people to share resources—such as energy, matter, time, skills, software, space, or food. Developing grand visions for futuristic new systems is an important part of the mix—but so, too, is nurturing a continuous wave of small adjustments.

Design for sustainability is no longer a future prospect; it is already under way in thousands of projects around the world. These transformative actions are changing design itself. The notion, inherited from the industrial age, that design necessarily involves the production of something new is now a subset of a bigger panorama. We are learning that fundamental life qualities, such as health and wellbeing, are not something you deliver, like a pizza. This delivery metaphor—in which health is produced by one set of people (the professionals) for another (their customers)—is being replaced by an interest in ways to enhance the 95 percent of person-to-person care that already happens outside the biomedical system. Millions of people look after friends and loved ones who, for example, have dementia; if their time was billed at the minimum wage, the informal, unpaid care economy would be as big as a GDP.

Design and social innovation are discovering new roles, too, in the creation of local, living economies from the ground up. Designers are learning that cocreation, rather than individual authorship, is usually the most effective way to understand and meet social needs, and that their job is to design new tools and platforms more than finished artifacts as such.

The shift from hierarchy to horizontality, in society at large, suits designers well. As closed and rules-based organizations are replaced by networks and service ecologies, designers have an important contribution to make in helping a variety of different stakeholders to participate as coowners of the process. Design will be crucial as we figure out how to share valuable knowledge more effectively. Key issues, also, will be assessment and quality control. Learning today happens everywhere, not just in the classroom—but it is often difficult to get recognition for skills and achievements that occur outside school or college. The design of peer review platforms, such as Mozilla's Open Badges, is an important part of the institutional innovation that design for sustainability is now embracing. So, too, is the invention of new project models able to support relationships between small projects and big systems. Issues to do with scale, propagation, and the multiplication of successful models are also, now, design concerns. Support and coordination skills are becoming an important part of a designer's repertoire.

Today's design space is a complex landscape of services, relationships, and physical spaces. The biggest challenges we face—and the biggest opportunities—involve the creation of value without destroying natural and social assets. Think about the food systems of a city; the restoration of a river; the management of informal markets; the care of older people. Such challenges cannot successfully be addressed without the engagement of all the actors concerned. A variety of different stakeholders—formal and informal, big and small—need to work together. The process by which such different people and groups are enabled to work together is, itself, an important design priority.

The Handbook of Design for Sustainability is a timely arrival on this fast-changing scene. As a flurry of new challenges and issues command our attention, this collection helps us pause for a moment and reflect on the historical and theoretical perspectives without which our work can become formless and frantic. Here, too, is the latest thinking on the methods and approaches that designers in very different contexts have found to be effective. There are essays on how design for sustainability is working out in practice, again in a diversity of contexts. The volume concludes with a range of new perspectives on where design for sustainability is headed next.

This is a welcome and much needed book.

General Introduction: Design for Sustainability— A Reflection

STUART WALKER AND JACQUES GIARD

The term 'handbook' is commonly used to refer to a 'how to' manual. In academia it is also used to refer to a scholarly publication that consists of separately authored essays or articles on a specific subject. This latter interpretation is the one we have adopted here because our aim has been to develop a book that contains the latest thinking on design for sustainability from a wide variety of perspectives. Collectively these provide the reader with a reference to current and emerging ideas, approaches and concerns. Therefore, this volume is not a manual of how to do design for sustainability; such a project would not only have required the content to be far more prescriptive, it would also have been misguided. First, design for sustainability is a rapidly evolving field so prescriptive solutions would become quickly outmoded. Second, a cookbook approach to a fundamentally creative discipline would have been a self-defeating exercise. And third, design for sustainability has to be attuned to place and context (Van der Ryn and Cowan, 1996, p. 63); proposing universally applicable solutions is antithetical to a comprehensive understanding of design for sustainability.

Within an overall structure divided into four broad sections, authors have written about and reflected upon their own particular areas of research and knowledge. Readers are provided with leading expertise and latest thinking in the following areas:

I. Historical and Theoretical Perspectives
II. Methods and Approaches
III. Sustainability in Practice
IV. Emerging Directions and Sustainable Futures

With contributions from established as well as emerging researchers, this volume provides comprehensive, substantive, and foremost thought on the subject of design for sustainability for students, researchers, and practitioners.

There are essays and research findings from philosophers, theorists, and social commentators, and from specialists in architecture and urban design, design education, design history, fashion, jewellery, product design, marketing, design management, grass roots initiatives and community solutions, life-cycle practices, digital technologies, design activism and radical innovation, meta-design and design futures. Perspectives are brought together from all over the world—from Australia, Brazil, Canada, China, Finland, India, Italy, The Netherlands, New Zealand, the United Kingdom, and the United States. Taken together, these specialisms and the particular frame of reference that each author brings offer a panoramic vista of design for sustainability—its pedigree, its current state, the direction in which it is heading, the creative challenges it poses for the future of how we are to live, and insights into how we are to understand and imagine our place on this fragile, beautiful but bruised ball of clay we call home.

DESIGN FOR SUSTAINABILITY

Essentially, the term 'design for sustainability' is shorthand for a multifarious range of concerns, activities, approaches, and discussions that emerged during the last half of the twentieth century and which, in the twenty-first, are in a rapid state of advancement. Moreover, as design for sustainability is becoming more philosophically robust, its relevance is becoming ever more urgent. Design for sustainability, as well as sustainability more broadly, have become significant areas of contemporary debate, along with a plethora of associated topics such as green design, eco-design, eco-technology, eco-innovation, life-cycle design, slow design, design for resilience, social innovation, and product-service systems (PSS). To understand why this is so we have to step back from the details and significance of specific cases, broaden our horizons and consider design for sustainability in the context of the development of human ideas. Furthermore, we have to draw upon our capacity for imagining and attempt to see the world through different eyes because one of the recurring themes in contemporary discussions about sustainability is the narrowness and dangerous inadequacy of our predominant contemporary worldview; a worldview that, hopefully, will be capable of rapid and expansive change.

THE ORIGINS OF UNSUSTAINABILITY

For countless centuries humankind had lived in more or less balanced relationships with the natural environment. Ways of life were dependent on nature's cycles, and people lived and died according to its rhythms. Technologies were rudimentary and medical possibilities, based on traditional remedies, were minimal and often rooted in superstition. Securing the material requirements for survival depended on manual labour and any additional sources of power were few—the mule, the ox, the waterwheel and the windmill (Raymond, 1986, p. 155). Life was precarious and susceptible to the vagaries of nature, but for millennia, and through compulsion rather than choice, people lived according to the world's carrying capacity and the provision it afforded. However, physical hardships and corporeal vulnerabilities were endured within a context and a worldview that was quite different from that which is prevalent today. Within traditional or premodern worldviews, human meaning was not sought through notions of continual innovation and progress, material benefits or future potentialities. Continuity tended to be valued over change, and innovation was regarded with suspicion because it challenged approaches that had been tested and refined over centuries and which fitted with people and place. Meaning was found through observances of religion and ritual within the cycles and repetitions of sacred time, rather than the linear, past-forgetting, forward-facing interpretations of time we abide by today. Such ways of living, within communities of utilitarian and spiritual practices, provided supportive, meaningful ways of living, dying, and dealing with life's trials, and, being deeply located in place, the effects and impacts of human activities were immediately apparent, small scale, and continually adaptable.

Understandings and practices began to change around the sixteenth century, the effects of which can be seen as the root cause of today's anxieties about the future and the existential malaise that these are spawning. Investigations into the natural world through developments in science, and particularly the discoveries made by figures such as Copernicus and Galileo, began to change our understandings of humanity's place and role in the universe. Archaic, mythological interpretations that placed humankind at the centre of God's plan and the centre of the cosmos became undermined not simply by the discoveries of science but also by an increasing emphasis on the instrumental rationality that science favours. As a result, highly complex, layered mythic stories that had for centuries played a vital role in humanity's search for meaning began to be interpreted in simplistic, literalist ways, and the relevance and standing of sacred ceremonies, practices and rites declined. Accordingly, their profound anagogical meanings became progressively obscured and the knowledge they imparted, which is fundamentally practice-based and tacit (Armstrong, 2009, p. 4), became eschewed and marginalized. Consequently, over time, scientific explanations of the world came to be seen as more credible alternatives to religious interpretations—a state of affairs that is akin to dismissing the truth encapsulated in the story of the race between the tortoise and the hare because we have no physical evidence of the starting gun. The philosophy of materialism that developed assumes that physical matter is the whole of existence and reality, and does not recognize inner principles, attributes, or deeper meanings (Mathews, 2006, p. 86). Such an assertion, however, is not derived from or verifiable by science; rather, it is an ideology that is considerably narrower than the worldview it came to supplant.

The modern period emerged over several centuries from around the 1500s, with major developments in science, technology, and philosophy. The Industrial Revolution, from the mid-eighteenth until the end of the nineteenth century, characterized the period as one in which central priorities were industrialization, scientific endeavour, and technological advancement. This period was accompanied by a change from the traditional to the modern worldview, a worldview that was shallower and flatter than its predecessor (Taylor, 1991, p. 4). Traditional avenues of meaning-seeking were replaced by progress and the notion that the future could be, and through human endeavour would be, better than the present. However, such blinkered, entirely worldly optimism was, from the first, accompanied by doubts and the feeling that something profound was being lost (Taylor, 2007, p. 717).

The capitalist economic system that emerged used the profits of production to reinvest in expansion of production. This depended on ever enlarging markets to ensure continual economic growth. Colonialism and empire provided such markets for a time. Later, new technologies and advancements in transportation offered additional outlets. As markets became saturated, market share was sought through novelty and innovation and later by cynical strategies of built-in obsolescence. This whole economic system was based on consumption. New products became paramount and their production, in turn, depended on the extraction and processing of the energy resources and materials that the earth could provide. Consumption of goods and services became constantly encouraged through advertising and marketing strategies that employed evermore elaborate psychological mechanisms to entice and seduce people into buying things. Within this model of consumerism, people themselves became instrumentalized, being regarded not as whole persons but merely as units of spending power—that is, consumers, an increasingly distasteful term that is fundamentally linked to destructive, unsustainable lifestyles but which, nevertheless, remains prevalent today.

The twentieth century witnessed rapid advancements in science and technology, used for human benefit and also, in two world wars, for human destruction, which raised profound ethical questions about the role and application of science and technology. Following the Second World War, weapons factories were transformed into facilities for the production of consumer goods, and consumerism ramped up to hitherto unimagined heights. In the 1950s, an abundance of new products, cars, and plastic novelties became available, particularly in the United States and Europe. During this period, the campaign for nuclear disarmament grew amidst uncertainties created by the so-called Cold War. In the early 1960s, the effects on the natural environment of widespread pesticide use became apparent (Carson, 1962). Throughout the 1950s and1960s, civil unrest, the civil rights movement, human rights campaigns, feminism, a revived interest in religion, especially Eastern traditions, and the beginnings of an awareness of the environmental impacts of human activities collectively heralded a changing worldview. The certainties of modernity were no longer so certain. People sought representation, voice, and freedom from oppression as well as sources of meaning that had been progressively eradicated from the modern worldview. The values and priorities associated with modernity were no longer working, and so emerged a period that has been termed postmodernity. Although still dominated by the values and priorities of modernity, the most prominent features of postmodernity (or late modernity as it is sometimes referred to) are its recognition of social considerations in the form of human rights and concerns about social equity (Smith, 2001, p. 12; Wilkinson and Pickett, 2009) and an increasing recognition of the environmental consequences of human actions. These social and environmental concerns are two of the main pillars of sustainability and major factors in any comprehensive understanding of design for sustainability. Economic issues are usually identified as the third pillar, but this is seen by some as a potential inhibitor to effective change; de-linking economic considerations from our understandings and advancements of sustainability and design for sustainability may be a necessary, if radical, step in reimagining what we do and how we do it (Walker, 2011, p. 28). An additional factor, which is becoming increasingly important to our understandings of sustainability, is the notion of personal meaning—which encapsulates spiritual issues as well as associated ethical considerations of conscience and integrity that help direct human actions in the world (e.g., Buchanan, 1995, p. 55; Orr, 2002). This factor is essential to the development of deeper understandings of sustainability and design for sustainability. First, it implies responses and approaches that go beyond the essentially utilitarian, worldly methods represented by a triple bottom line of economic, social, and environmental issues (Elkington, 1997, p. 2). Such methods have done little to challenge the materialistic philosophy underlying the modern worldview, which is so closely connected to debilitating notions of progress, growth, and consumption. Second, this additional factor has a relevancy for each individual and is core to the development of a worldview that overcomes the loss of meaning associated with modernity (Frankl, 2000, p. 139). It is a vital ingredient of sustainability because it is fundamental to the development of post-materialist, postconsumerist ways of encountering the world.

THE EVOLVING CHALLENGE OF DESIGN FOR SUSTAINABILITY

Within this context, design for sustainability can be understood as an endeavour that calls upon human creativity to imagine, conceptualize, visualize, and effectively communicate alternative pathways for living meaningful lives while consuming far less in terms of energy and materials. Some estimate that those living in the wealthy nations will have to reduce per capita climate-changing emissions by up to 97 percent over the next few decades (Harrison, 2012) if dangerous increases in global temperatures are to be avoided. The sheer scale of such reductions signifies a massive change in lifestyles—in the types of food we eat, the clothes we wear, the products we use, our modes of transportation, our frequency and extent of travel, our recreational activities and so on. If we maintain our present expectations and priorities and our current worldview, such changes will be seen solely as unwelcome deprivations. Consequently, they will be resisted at every turn and we will progress further and further down a hazardous road. Alternatively, we can begin to adapt and change our expectations and see such change as a positive development that holds the potential for us to reconnect with things that really matter, with

- practical needs for living, which are dependent on but should be sympathetic to the natural environment;
- social needs, relationships, and fostering a sense of community, which are all vital to notions of human wellbeing; and
- personal needs encompassing spiritual and ethical concerns, which are less about having and more about being, less concerned with external things and more concerned with the inner search for meaning that is a characteristic of the human condition.

These three factors, the practical, the social and the personal, are, of course, intimately related and interdependent. Finding balance and harmony among them through appropriate actions and right judgments represents a continual human challenge and a critical human endeavour. In essence, it represents the age-old struggle to find meaning through our actions and encounters in the world. Today, this holds a new urgency because the path we have been treading for too long is one that has proved to be devastating to the natural environment, to the point where life supporting systems are becoming severely, perhaps irretrievably, impaired. It has also proved to be socially damaging and severely lacking in profound notions of personal meaning. A turn away from this destructive path, even if it means fewer gadgets, less travel and the disappearance from our supermarket shelves of fruits and flowers flown in daily from the other side of the world, could herald the return of a connection with people, place and deeper purpose.

CONTRIBUTIONS TO THE DEBATE

The essays in this volume address these various themes under four broad headings. In Part I: Historical and Theoretical Perspectives, the root causes of our present unsustainable ways of living are considered from several angles but are seen as being fundamentally connected to the practices and norms that have evolved during the period we call modernity—practices and norms that are now drastically outmoded and in need of rapid, systemic restructuring. The philosophical errors of modernity and materialism have brought us to our unsustainable present, and so this section includes an exploration of a post-materialist philosophy and its relationship to sustainable futures. Conventional understandings of the relationship between design and moral value rest on modernity's privileging of instrumental rationality, which misrepresents the nature of technology and posits a techno-optimistic, eco-efficiency route to sustainability; here, design for sustainability is presented as a practice of ontological inquiry that widens the field of possibility. In addition, the challenges of developing theory capable of supporting design for sustainability are considered in terms of a broad interdisciplinary approach, and different theory-building possibilities are explored; this includes a discussion of transition theory and the coevolution of systems. An overview of green and technocratic approaches to sustainable development and their inadequacies provides a basis for discussing a different direction entirely, one that aims for net positive change via open systems thinking. Part I closes with a reflection on the relationship of abundance to contemporary life, beginning with food and ending with a consideration of information abundance accessed via various forms of contemporary technology.

'Part II: Methods and Approaches' begins with an overview of the methods and practices being used to address design for sustainability along with case studies that illustrate practical applications. The preparation of new designers will be a vital ingredient in helping to ensure systemically different design futures, and so this section includes an examination of how sustainability is being integrated into design education within professional degree programs and the expectations of the various design professions. At the other end of the spectrum from design and product creation lie discarded detritus, waste, and overflowing landfill sites. The throwaway culture is both a dishonourable and an increasingly hazardous characteristic of mature industrialized economies, and it raises enormous challenges for countries undergoing rapidly economic development. It is argued here that new directions in public policy will be needed to incentivize lower consumption and less waste. In addition to public policy, this section also includes a consideration of sustainable consumption in relation to product design and argues that self-interest can play a role in voluntarily reducing levels of consumption. Marketing, too, has a role to play in this regard. The place of brands is discussed in facilitating more sustainable consumption through the use of design and the development of services, and by helping to normalize sustainable patterns of behaviour.

Small- and medium-sized enterprises (SMEs) represent the engines of the economy and are key creators of jobs. While they often lack the resources and therefore the capacity to innovate, they can be both agile and exceptionally creative, accommodating change in flexible, responsive ways that larger corporations cannot match. Therefore, if supported in their capacity to innovate, SMEs hold the potential to be key players in developing more sustainable ways forward. In this section, the argument is made that universities can play a vital role in working with small firms to raise their capacity for sustainable innovation. This is demonstrated through a design-led project that brings together an SME with university researchers in design for sustainability.

'Part III: Sustainability in Practice' includes a variety of projects and examples that demonstrate how sustainability is actually being manifested and implemented. These span a broad range of design disciplines and scales of intervention, from architectural forms, sustainable urban communities and projects in peri-urban areas to business innovation and sustainable fashion.

Architecture is considered as a soul-nourishing endeavour that occurs within natural systems. Materials, social considerations and spiritual factors interweave to create an embodiment of values and build spirit-of-place. Small footprint dwellings and higher densities are also considered, not only as more sustainable forms of architecture but also as a solution to the consequences of urban sprawl, and a community planned and built according to these principles is presented. Also in this section is a discussion of sustainable agriculture and food production created through social innovation. The development of a new ecology of communities in areas that occur between city and countryside helps to generate new local economies. While these are based around food production, they also reinforce tradition and culture, diversity and sense of place. The development of sustainable urban spaces and systems is also tackled by taking into consideration factors such as walkable communities, safety, wellbeing and transportation. Design decision-making is related to policy and governance, and the key role of visualization as a communication tool is underlined. Two essential aspects of sustainability are highlighted in an urban recycling project; firstly, social inequity and urban poverty, and secondly, environmental concerns. This project describes a survivalist economy in urban Brazil. Over a period of eight years, it has provided students with a basis for understanding dimensions of design that go far beyond its usual meaning in contemporary culture.

Product design and business considerations form the basis for constructing more accountable models that better serve our needs while generating lasting value for the environment, society, and economy. Part III is concluded with a discussion of sustainable fashion, which is seen as a powerful cultural lever that can influence and change today's consumption-based, mass-production economic model. Innovative practices in fashion design are considered such as Slow Fashion, non-plan fashion, and post-growth fashion.

'Part IV: Emerging Directions and Sustainable Futures' encompasses a range of themes that points in a common direction. A significant emphasis in this section is the requirement for a profound reappraisal of human values in today's society, a consideration of human meaning and the connection to locale, tradition, culture, and emotion, and a turn away from consumption-based, growth-based routes to wellbeing. Another major theme is critical inquiry as a key ingredient of practice-based approaches to design for sustainability. There is a recognition that design agendas are rapidly shifting, firstly, as a proactive rejection of design's destructive conventions, and secondly, as a reactive response to ensuing systems breakdown.

Part IV begins with a provocative reflection on the human need for cultural forms that are not necessarily ecologically sustainable. Indeed, modes of creation and consumption that are often encouraged by advocates of sustainability are challenged. This is followed by an examination of the meaning of design for sustainability in India within a context of rapid economic development and the widespread adoption of Western consumer-based lifestyles. The revival of small scale cottage industries is considered through the infusion of design for sustainability principles into the products they manufacture. This is put forward as an affordable, responsible and appropriate alternative that is both participatory and capable of improving standards of living. In China, consideration is given to the traditional *shè jì* system, which in recent years has become subsumed by Western style design approaches. The reevaluation of the role and importance of China's traditional design system in the context of contemporary sustainability affords an opportunity to develop new philosophies and approaches to Chinese design practice, education, and research. A chapter on emotionally sustaining design offers a refreshing alternative to eco-efficiency and techno-centric approaches as well as to large-scale macro agendas. This more intimate examination of our everyday accoutrements for living brings each of us closer to the core of the environmental problem. The subsequent chapter examines similar themes, making connections between sustainability and the essential characteristics and qualities of design as a discipline, including aesthetics, intuition, culture and socioeconomic contexts.

Design as a critical mode of inquiry and as a communicative medium is examined in the context of consumer culture and sustainability. It is argued that critical design offers a way of bringing to light and challenging the often unacknowledged values and assumptions that shape conventional practices. A startling reality check is incorporated within a chapter that highlights our embedded dependencies on massive and continuous flows of nonrenewable carbon-based energy resources. The transformation to renewable energy will necessarily herald a transformation in our systems of provision—of energy, water, food, transportation, and information. System considerations are also examined with the context of metadesign, described as a self-reflexive, comprehensive, and integrated framework for paradigm shift which employs a creative re-languaging as a strategy for invoking change.

Creative practice as an embedded element of design research is discussed in terms of its important contribution to knowledge development. Here, practice-based design within an academic research agenda is regarded as a way of generating questions-in-form rather than definitive solutions, thereby advancing inquiry and understandings of design for sustainability. Such approaches are a form of design activism, which is considered in a separate chapter. Design activism, which is manifested in a wide variety of forms across a range of design disciplines, aims at positive change by creating counter-narratives, raising awareness, and spurring behaviour change.

The relationship between sustainability and digital futures is examined under the rubric of cyber-sustainability, which is differentiated from more conventional green IT approaches by taking a more fundamental perspective that considers, in addition to environmental impacts, the psychological impacts of major technological trends and their relationship to emerging understandings of sustainability.

Signs of change and the limitations of our perceptual horizons are considered under the auspices of 'thinking in time', encompassing thinking and acting, and time as both measure and medium. This provides a basis for considering anthropocentrism, sustainment and the notion of the urmadic university.

These diverse themes and emphases clearly demonstrate that design for sustainability must depart radically from the instrumental conventions that so defined twentieth-century thinking and which persist, only too virulently, in the twenty-first century. It becomes necessary to embrace a more holistic notion of design that attends not only to economic requirements and user needs but also to environmental considerations, sociocultural concerns, and profound notions of personal meaning and spiritual nourishment. It is therefore appropriate that the final chapter steps away from design per se to offer a reflection on the human imagination, public language (and design can be regarded as a form of public language), and the relationship between literature and the environment. Foremost figures of the world's great imaginations—Anna Karenina, Madame Bovary, Captain Ahab—are considered as symbols of ourselves and our civilization. Our understandings of ourselves are inculcated into our language. This chapter argues that to invoke sustainable change we need to develop a different language.

DESIGN FOR SUSTAINABILITY IN CONTEXT

Collectively, the essays in this volume represent an understanding of design for sustainability in the first decades of the twenty-first century. However, we would be remiss if we were to close this general introduction without acknowledging the vital significance of earlier authors on whose work these current ideas rest. Today's understandings of design for sustainability are founded on decades of development and the groundbreaking contributions of such figures as Packard (1960), Carson (1962), Fuller (1968), Papanek (1971) and Schumacher (1973) who, among many others, realized the importance of contesting the conventions and assumptions of their times. Today, the need to question practices and perceptions remains and is evidently more pressing than ever. The authors represented in this handbook have risen to this challenge admirably. By testing and probing our understandings of history, the discipline of design, business norms, practices and purposes, these authors invite us to reflect on our ways of seeing the world and our own activities in order to steer design, and potentially society, in a more positive and fundamentally different direction.

REFERENCES

Armstrong, K. (2009), *The Case for God—What Religion Really Means*, Bodley Head: London.

Buchanan, R. (1995), 'Rhetoric, Humanism and Design', in Buchanan, R. and Margolin, V. (eds), *Discovering Design: Explorations in Design Studies*, University of Chicago Press: Chicago. pp. 23–66.

Carson, R. (1962), *Silent Spring*, Houghton Mifflin: Boston.

Elkington, J. (1997), *Cannibals with Forks: The Triple Bottom Line of 21st Century Business*, Capstone Publishing: Oxford.

Frankl, V. (2000/2011), *Man's Search for Ultimate Meaning*, Ebury Publishing: London.

Fuller, R. B. (1968/2008), *Operating Manual for Spaceship Earth*, Lars Müller Publishers: Zurich.

Harrison, K. (2012), *End of Growth & Liberal Democracy*, Lecture at the Australian Centre for Sustainable Catchments, University of Southern Queensland, http://vimeo.com/41056934, accessed 17 May 2012.

Mathews, F. (2006), 'Beyond Modernity and Tradition: A Third Way for Development', *Ethics & The Environment*, Indiana University Press: Bloomington, IN, vol. 1, no. 2: pp. 85–113.

Orr, D. W. (2002), 'Four Challenges of Sustainability', *Conservation Biology*, vol. 16, no. 6: pp. 1457–60, http://www.cereo.wsu.edu/docs/Orr2003_SustainabilityChallenges.pdf, accessed 30 August 2011.

Packard, V. (1960), *The Waste Makers*, Pocket Books: New York.

Papanek, V. (1971/1985), *Design for the Real World—Human Ecology and Social Change*, Thames and Hudson: London.

Raymond, R. (1986), *Out of the Fiery Furnace—the Impact of Metals on the History of Mankind*, Pennsylvania State University Press: University Park.

Schumacher, E. F. (1973), *Small is Beautiful—A Study of Economics as if People Mattered*, Abacus: London.

Smith, H. (2001), *Why Religions Matter: The Fate of the Human Spirit in an Age of Disbelief*, HarperCollins: New York.

Taylor, C. (1991), *The Malaise of Modernity*, House of Anansi Press: Concord, Ontario.

Taylor, C. (2007), *A Secular Age*, Belknap Press of Harvard University Press: Cambridge, MA.

Van der Ryn, S. and Cowan, S. (1996), *Ecological Design*, Island Press: Washington, D.C.

Walker, S. (2011), *The Spirit of Design: Objects, Environment and Meaning*, Earthscan-Routledge: London.

Wilkinson, R. and Pickett, K. (2009), *The Spirit Level—Why More Equal Societies Almost Always Do Better*, Allen Lane: London.

PART I

Historical and Theoretical Perspectives

Editorial Introduction

JACQUES GIARD AND STUART WALKER

No subject can be understood well without also understanding its context. Like two sides of a coin, subject and context are inseparable. Sustainability is no different. Indeed, the historical context leading up to our contemporary concerns about sustainability is especially important to understand and absorb. More than anything, it represents a particular world view or ideology—one that has not only proved to be too narrowly framed but also incredibly damaging. Moreover, it is a world view that remains pervasive and predominant. Emergence from this state of affairs, and therefore from the fundamental premises of unsustainability, will represent a major shift in understandings, priorities, values and lifestyles.

'Part I: Historical and Theoretical Perspectives' provides the reader with the requisite context for understanding contemporary design for sustainability and the variety of topics currently being addressed under this broad heading. It offers the perspectives of six authors, beginning with an overview of past decisions and actions of human society, followed by an appreciation of the moral position that supported these decisions and ending with reflections on and possible directions for a sustainable future.

It begins with 'The Roots of Unsustainability' by John R. Ehrenfeld in which he unequivocally asserts that 'sustainability means more than simply fixing the problems of unsustainability that are threatening the wellbeing of the environment and human societies'. In other words, doing less harm is no longer a viable option for society. More of the same technology in a world that has become machine-like—no matter how effective the technology may be—will not reverse our present unsustainable course. Yet, he believes that there is an answer amidst this morass. 'Design', he states, 'offers a pathway to change'.

It goes without saying that a great deal of the unsustainability referred to by Ehrenfeld is the result of the philosophy of materialism that has permeated societies of the developed world over the past few centuries. This being the case, it would appear that this same philosophical perspective is where the solution may reside. This is clearly the position taken by Freya Mathews. In her essay, 'Post-Materialism', she suggests that a case can be made for a more sustainable post-materialistic future if we attempt to better understand the philosophical imperatives of the past, those very imperatives that contributed to the materialistic but unsustainable present.

A philosophical approach is also taken by Aidan Davison in his 'Making Sustainability Up: Design beyond Possibility'. Davison posits the view that the moral values of the past—values underpinned by a 'determinist technological optimism', to use his words—are directly responsible for the unsustainable conditions of today. It is this same determinist approach in design that ultimately leads to a higher degree of unsustainability. He advocates for an alternative direction in design, one in which design becomes the 'ineradicable human knack of widening the field of possibility'.

Hence, Davison, Ehrenfeld and Mathews share the view that design offers an important, positive and practical way forward for realizing sustainability.

In 'Developing Theories for Sustainable Design', Dennis Doordan offers options for a possible next step. He does so by first examining theories that previously found favour with many disciplines, especially those theories grounded in the empirical world of the sciences. Predictably, this focus has resulted in the enhancement of one technical system or other but not always to the benefit of people. Doordan contends that there is an alternate approach, one based on a foundational critique of the status quo, that links sustainability to promoting human wellbeing rather than enhancing the efficiency of technical systems. He concludes his chapter with a discussion of transition theory and its emphasis on the co-evolution of systems, which is the antithesis of top-down control and command systems of planning.

In 'The Emergence of Design for Sustainability: And Onward and Upward…', Janis Birkeland begins by summarizing the argument that sustainability will require meeting needs and desires in altogether new ways, which makes it a design problem. She provides a capsule history of two competing paradigms in design for sustainable development: green and technocratic. Despite the fact that these two systems are merging, there is a need to reconsider any system based on a closed loop where the net result remains doing more good and less bad. As Birkeland says, 'We need to get out of the race entirely' and consider a transformation to Positive Development, which makes everyone better off, expands future options and increases ecological carrying capacity. She argues that such a direction is best guided by open systems thinking.

Abundance and sustainability and their relationship to contemporary life provide a closing chapter, one that reflects upon the role of design in the context of sustainability. Albert Borgmann leads the readers on this reflective journey in 'I Miss the Hungry Years: Coping with Abundance'. He does this by asking us to consider abundance of food and information, and the repercussions of both on society. While these ideas do not directly address the discipline of design, they are certainly pertinent to, and pose significant challenges for, design. Is it possible to ameliorate the downside of abundance—and if so, what is the role of design?

1

The Roots of Unsustainability

JOHN R. EHRENFELD

SITUATING SUSTAINABILITY

A distinguishing feature of being human, beyond the animals we are, is language. Language is one of the most important distinguishing features of our species. Language permits us to reflect on what we observe and to tell stories about the world we experience. Those stories are often explanations of actions and events we render to ourselves or to others. In particular, we have intentions (expressions of what we want the future to be) that guide our actions. The work of the German philosopher Alfred Schutz sought to understand action and its connection to consciousness and knowledge. One interpreter of Schutz put it this way:

> Action, then, can be conceived of as a dialectical relationship between the present and the future. While it is grounded and to a degree constrained by experience and the past, it is still open to alternative possibilities; there are still elements of choice of actions. Perhaps there is not the complete unrestrained freedom of the existentialist, but simultaneously there is not the complete determinism suggested by naturalistic social science. The major point is that the purpose of action is change: it is formulated to negate in some sense that which is existing. (Bolan, 1980, p. 267)

In addition to intentions, referring to the immediate present, humans also have aspirations—that is, visions of a desired, ideal future, for example, and one that produces security, wellbeing, wealth, or happiness. Sustainability, which is defined more specifically later in this chapter, refers to a state of the world in which one's aspirations are fulfilled over a long period of time. Sustainability is a general property of a (complex) system and, if it is to become a practical concern, must be further qualified by naming the aspirational end or ends being sought. Normally we act routinely in a world that we believe can produce the ends we picture, but occasionally we stop and reflect because we no longer believe that current conditions will allow our intentions to play out success-fully. If my wallet with my money and credit cards is stolen on the way to the market, my intention to buy tonight's food for my family will be thwarted, and I will have to find an alternative plan of action.

Now expand this scenario to a much larger world—the United States or the Euro-pean Union—and to a set of aspirations shared by all its citizens—for example, shar-ing the national dream, usually including freedom and wellbeing. As long as all share a sense that it is possible to realize this and other widely held social aspirations, life will go on routinely. If the actors begin to assess the condition of their world as inconsis-tent with the attainment of their dreams, they will express their concerns in some form. When that concern gathers enough weight to enter the public dialogue, it becomes la-beled and is sent to institutions that were created to solve the problems blocking the as-pirations and return the world to a state where they can be realized. In many cases, the problems can be narrowly defined and those institutions responsible for fixing the world are clear. The financial crises that began in 2008 are blamed on the failure to have ade-quate regulation, on the innovation of derivative packages, poor risk assessment mecha-nisms, greedy bankers, and more. The global financial system was incapable of creating sustainability in terms of those ends that had become associated with the economic sys-tem, but sustainability was not a word used to describe the crises and their future con-sequences. Proposals for action came from the U.S. Congress, Federal Reserve Bank, President Obama, and individual economists.

Sustainability, used without further qualification, has become a container for our highest aspirations, but, until we name those aspirations, has no practical meaning other than a very general sense of possibility and continuity. In other writings, I have given sustainability an explicit meaning through reference to a bundle of aspirations I lump together in the metaphor of flourishing (Ehrenfeld, 2008, p. 49). Flourishing gath-ers a bundle of qualities that have been at the center of human aspirations from time immemorial—the good life, health, solidarity, autonomy, freedom, dignity, and more. Flourishing incorporates any and all of these great ends of human societies and gives a name to the end-state that individual and collective actions are designed to produce, giving sustainability an explicit and practical sense. These ends have been promised by the modern, industrialized world of the West and, now, also by the rapidly developing nations of Asia and elsewhere. The need to name the explicit ends of action, now labeled as sustainable with no further elaboration, is frequently missed today. Sustainability is used by business, government, and other institutions in reference to such a widely vary-ing set of ends that it has lost its gathering power for spawning large-scale initiatives. In most cases, the intention implicit in the use of sustainability or sustainable is to slow down and reverse the deterioration of the conditions of the planet, a process I refer to as reducing unsustainability.

For many, many years, conditions of the world have been such that these univer-sal ends appear to be attainable and that problems standing in the way are amenable to solutions with the same set of beliefs and means that brought us such a long way toward achieving them. The modern era stretching back to its founders, Descartes, Bacon, Newton, and others, has been driven by a belief in progress—conceived as the continuing movement toward the perfection of human society. In recent times, however, according to the assessments of many citizens, the possibility of achieving the dream is fading; the world, they say, has become unsustainable and needs to be fixed. Climate change threatens to disrupt comfortable cultural patterns; the collapse of fisheries threatens the food supply; water scarcity will make regions inhospitable; poverty inhibits health; tyranny suppresses dignity and freedom. Actions are being taken to avert and prevent these changes from becoming so great that they would upset the Earth's generally hospitable environment and send our cultures into new, unknown, and unfriendly regimes. Almost all these sustainability remedies underway relate to some form of technological efficiency or technocratic innovations designed to run our economies, but with less damage to the world.

These technological frameworks for design and action have worked so well for so long that we take them for granted as the only way to run our modern societies. All are based on some manifestation of reductionism: cutting up the problem and its enveloping system into pieces, and parceling the job to fix things to experts working in the resultant associated, isolated areas. This very effective way of dealing with problems and unmet concerns has significant limits when the problem cannot be cleanly identified and placed in a well-defined bin of knowledge and expertise. Unsustainability, a general set of concerns that the future will not satisfy our aspirations, is just such a problem. We do not routinely identify and analyze its causes and, thus, cannot knowingly assign the tasks of remedy and repair. We are stuck in a circular pattern that does not fix these problems. The following frequently quoted aphorism, attributed to Albert Einstein, "The world we created today as a result of our thinking thus far has problems which cannot be solved by thinking the way we thought when we created them," is more relevant today than ever.

As long as efforts designed to create sustainability arise within the current way of thinking and action—the normal modern societal paradigm—the best we can hope for is some reduction in unsustainability. More efficient automobiles may slow down the rate of global warming, but the capability to reduce pollution will become questionable at some time in the future. Efficiency in general is only a temporary remedy. The lowered impacts it produces will eventually be overtaken by growth and any associated economic savings will be channeled into other consumptive ends, creating new or exacerbating old damaging patterns. We are so accustomed to this way of problem solving that we ignore a few important pathologies that arise when routine actions become so familiar that we are blind to outcomes other than those that were intended.

When the problems fail to respond to the solutions, we frequently intensify our efforts, producing unintended consequences showing up at other places and later in time. Further, we fail to stop and seek qualitatively different approaches that might work effectively. This pattern is the characteristic of addiction. An addict continues to apply the same ineffective solutions without regard to the underlying problem and without consciousness of other negative consequences that the unreflective repetition creates. Unsustainability is such an unintended consequence of normality within our modern ways of living. Applying this metaphor, our societies are addicted to the use of the beliefs, norms, tools, and institutions of modern, technological culture. If we are to turn the tide and begin to create sustainability and move toward our aspirations, we will have to look farther than the superficial reasons we attribute to the problems, and unearth the deepest roots of today's problems and address them directly, beyond the application of the temporary and short-lived fixes of technology and technological thinking. Reductionism, mentioned above, is one of the causes, but it is a consequence of an even more fundamental belief, the Cartesian notion of an objective, unchanging world that humans apprehend and inscribe in their minds.

Another cause that will be elaborated below is the omnipresence of technology in modern societies. Technological systems and institutions based on some form of technical rationality (technocracy) are called on to run the machinery of modern societies and to solve virtually every problem encountered in the normal course of events. The rational model for human action springing from Descartes's mind/world split and the view of the brain as a logical, optimizing machine is yet another root cause. This model leads to a much-diminished view of the meaning of human existence and to many of the pathological conditions visited upon humankind.

REALITY AND REDUCTIONISM

The origin and refractoriness of unsustainability can be attributed to many causes, but two stand out as critical: the Cartesian, scientific mindset of modern cultures and the hegemony of technological and technocratic solutions to all individual and collective problems. *Problem* in this sense is any perceived obstacle to the attainment of intentions or aspirations. Since the time of Descartes and even back to the Greek era, we have viewed the world as having existence out there separate from the mind, which stores and manipulates images of that external world. The basic existential model is a contemplative subject gazing on and thinking about an external, objective world. Our visions, images, reflections, and thoughts about this world form the foundation for what is frequently denoted as "objective reality." Objective refers to entities fixed in time and space, and also to the sense of pure or true representations of those things unfiltered by an observing subject's misperceptions. At the most general level, this view attempts to understand reality by separating the immediate perceived world into parts, each of which can be described by fixed rules of behavior, whether the object at hand is part of the inanimate world or is a living organism.

Our current practices are surprisingly close to those of Descartes, who proposed them in 1637 (1637/1998, p. 10). Descartes was "seeking the true method for arriving at the knowledge of everything of which my mind would be capable." One of his four methodological axioms is "to divide each of the difficulties I would examine into as many parts as possible and as was required in order better to resolve them." The consequences of adopting this reductionist way of discovering how the world works are profound. Out of Descartes's musings come many of the beliefs and norms that drive action in modern cultures. We can point to those particular characteristics that have an immediate and obvious connection to the present state of the world. The first is that the world is considered to be a mechanical system, composed of many interacting but separable parts. Further, we believe we can understand the whole system when we can describe and explain each of the pieces. The explanations can be expressed in mathematical terms or, if not so reducible, represented by rules.

The Cartesian model is predicated on an autonomous, thinking subject looking out at the world as an assemblage of objects. The scientific method that follows from this relationship places the observer apart from and outside of the system examined. Further, with roots going deep into history to Plato and the Eleatic school, the reality that is revealed by the method is timeless and universal; it exists outside of our mental processes and the place from which we observe. With this system in play, we eventually have come to see ourselves as disconnected from the natural world—as a separate and distinctive part of the planetary world. The absolute, unquestionable sense of this form of reality produces authoritarianism and domination, important contributors to the human dimensions of unsustainability. Humberto Maturana, a Chilean biologist and philosopher, has argued that our reductionist, Cartesian view of reality is the central question facing humanity today. He argues that in the system of objective reality, "a claim of knowledge is a demand for obedience" (1988, p. 29).

Complexity

The polar opposite to reductionism and the machine view of the world is the concept of complexity. Complex systems are formed when the connections among the parts become more important than the parts themselves. When parts are so multiply interconnected, it becomes impossible to predict how the system will behave when subjected to perturbations. These systems cannot be understood completely by aggregating knowledge about the parts. After remaining in a relatively narrow regime of behaviors, they may exhibit unpredictable behavior patterns, shifting from an apparently stable regime to a completely different one. Complexity is amenable to some analysis; for example, it is possible to understand the rules that bring order to a flock of birds or a school of fish but not to map the actual behavior. The errant behavior of a single member of the flock can turn the orderly movements back to chaos in a moment. The global financial system is an example of a complex system involving both technology and human beings. For a long time, the system ran smoothly, producing wealth and wellbeing, but in a moment it collapsed, creating a whole new regime. In the process of collapse, more than money and material wealth was lost. The system had also been creating immaterial properties like security, confidence, and trust, all of which emerged from coherent operations of the whole system. Flourishing or whatever quality is to be the measure of sustainability is such an emergent property.

The key to emergent phenomena is that they follow a set of rules but not necessary rules expressible in mathematical terms. We have such a set of rules that underlies economic institutions and economic behavior in modern developed countries. The rules have been known ever since Adam Smith pointed us to the "invisible hand." He connected the emergence of wealth and wellbeing to behavior driven by self-interest as then construed as the seeking of things that brought pleasure and the avoidance of pain. No one was directing the economic system. It ran all by itself, with the exception of government setting explicit rules to avoid the emergence of patterns that were not deemed good for society. Smith, himself, was concerned with inequality and monopolistic behavior.

This simple Smithian rule at the base of all modern market-oriented economies does not produce the right kind of emergence for sustainability. We do get more material output and more wealth measured by putting monetary values to all the stuff traded in the market, but we also get poverty, unfair distribution of wellbeing, and devastation of the natural system that supports life on Earth. And now we have much evidence that today's political economy even fails to produce pleasure and avoid pain for many, many people. As long as the economic system is designed on the basis of this fundamental rule, all the fixes that economists use cannot alter the emergent dynamics. They may mitigate a problem here and there but cannot change the basic patterns.

Complexity, itself, is not one of the root causes of unsustainability, but failure to recognize that social systems are complex is. When complex systems are thought to be like machines, the resulting ways in which we interact with them produce unexpected and unintended outcomes. The loss of fisheries is an example. Attempts to sustain fishery stocks through scientific management have failed. Using analytically derived positive knowledge to design the tools and management schemes for complex systems is risky. Complex behaviors expose our ignorance, revealing what we know we do not know and also what we do not know that we do not know. Fish schooling fits the first of the two classes above. If you understand complexity, you know that you do not know what the system is going to look like from one moment to the next. But if you mistake a complex system for a merely complicated machine, you do not know that you do not know how it works, with the possibility of finding it wildly out of control. It is important to distinguish between complex and complicated. A complicated system takes a form of a machine where the whole system can be broken down into its parts and the relationships between all the parts can be reduced to a closed set of analytic expressions.

If you know that you do not know, you can adopt a scheme of governance or control, including the artifacts that are designed for that purpose, which deliberately accommodates and expects adaptation, as understanding builds on observing and reflecting upon what is happening. Gardening is a classic case of operating in this fashion. The gardener plants in the spring and then watches very carefully as the plants sprout, employing understanding gleaned from experience with the garden. Good gardeners know that their plot is unique and that they cannot count on the rules used by the neighbor across the street. Everything they do is contingent. Their methods go into their bag of tricks if they seem to work, but become suspect when they fail the next time. The theories found in the textbooks at the local agricultural school may serve as starters, but more often than not have only short-lived utility. Good gardeners are pragmatists, not scientists.

This academic-like discussion is relevant to sustainability because the world we inhabit is the epitome of complexity. We are merely nodes in the web of life. Our scientific method has led us to believe that we exist outside of that system and can get to know it in the same way we design and fix automobiles, or at least the way we used to. Modern automobiles are becoming as complex as computers and attempt to control a very large number of interconnections. Toyota's recent troubles, related to product reliability and recall, in part sprang from the inability to understand how a car really works on the highway, as opposed to some engineer's computerized simulation model. Being outside, we think that someone else, a sustainability mechanic, is responsible for maintaining the system. Sustainability is the possibility of flourishing for all life on Earth. Until we accept that humans are an integral part of the complex system we call Earth, that possibility will be nil.

It seems to me that we have a new opportunity to recover our consciousness of the interconnected nature of the world and our place within (not outside) of it. Increasing interest in complexity keeps a fire burning under academic intellectual kettles. Natural and man-made catastrophes remind us that there is much we do not know we do not know. Understanding of the complexity of the Earth's environment is diffusing from the scientists' supercomputers to the everyday thoughts of many laypersons, but that is just the first step toward creating sustainability. We also have to recover the sense of the sacredness of the world, even of the cosmos, that envelops us. That's no easy task given the opposite thrust of modernity; as Max Weber wrote, "The fate of our times is characterized by rationalization and intellectualization and, above all, by the disenchantment of the world" (quoted in Gerth and Mills, 1946, p. 155). It takes humility, not hubris, and attention to Candide's rejection of the misplaced optimism of Dr. Pangloss. "Neither need you tell me," said Candide, "that we must take care of our garden" (Voltaire, 1918, p. 168). Maybe Voltaire was a gardener on the side and understood more about complexity than we might imagine.

Mistaken Identity

The Cartesian mind/body split, coupled with objective reality and its consequence, the machine metaphor for the world, has produced a model of human behavior that has harmed both the humans and the world. It has created the dominant economistic view of humans as a bundle of insatiable needs operating a maximization calculus on a computer in the mind. Economists gloss over the source of these needs and invoke a mysterious criterion—preference or utility. The notion of isolated economic agents whose values (utilities) are unchanged by the very transactional relationships they enter into can be traced back to Descartes's model of self: autonomous and acontextual (placeless, timeless, isolated). The reductionist scientific method is inadequate and imperfect when we try to understand ourselves. Mainstream economists have been criticized as suffering from the fallacy of misplaced concreteness (Whitehead, 1925/1967, p. 50). Closely related to reductionism, this fallacy involves the assumption that an abstraction derived from worldly observations is the same as the reality, leading thinkers to misplaced conclusions about the real world. The centrality of the fundamental abstraction, Homo economicus, of neoclassical economics, coupled with the hegemony of economics in the world of normative policy making, has produced a culture driven by consumption and largely unconscious of the critical role of nature as a life-support system (Daly and Cobb, 1994).

The idea of a utility-maximizing algorithm driving behavior results in expressing the value of everything in some sort of numerical terms, with money as by far the most common metric. Even the rich quality of flourishing has been transformed in measures of wellbeing largely expressed in monetary terms: more income and assets means a higher level on the wellbeing scale. In practice, the world does not work the way the models say it does. By people's own judgments, wellbeing increases for a while as income goes up to a point where basic subsistence needs are provided for, but then higher incomes become poorly correlated with assessments of happiness (Easterlin, 1974; Layard, 2005; Wilkinson and Pickett, 2009).

TECHNOLOGY

The ubiquitous presence of technology in modern societies is another of the root causes of unsustainability. The cause is not technology, per se, but its modern character and pervasiveness in our lives. I mentioned earlier that the use of technology has become addictive. We call on it to solve all of our problems. When we believe that a dangerous amount of greenhouse gases is being produced and emitted, the response is to invent more efficient engines or capture the dangerous components in the atmosphere and bury them deep in the earth. In another technological scenario, aerosols would be blown into the stratosphere to change the albedo—the reflective character of the atmosphere—so that less sunlight would strike the surface, reducing the potential heating effect.

Solutions like these allow us to take our eyes off the ball and avoid digging deeper into the structure of society that leads to the practices that caused the harmful effects. The functions that create unsustainability are, obviously, not intended by the innovators and practitioners of the technology, but arise because the knowledge upon which the technologies are based comes from reductionist methods that always leave something out. If the Earth and its inhabitants were part of a big machine, these unintended consequences might be avoided by deepening the scientific knowledge used in designing the systems and artifacts, and by employing ever more powerful computers. This, however, is not the case. The combination of complexity and reductionist design and management schemes is ripe for the fruiting of unintended consequences.

The Technological Mindset

The centrality of technology to our lives produces a mindset that attributes instrumentality to everything that shows up in the world to an observing human. This follows from the way we form and hold habits. When we have become so accustomed to particular patterns of action including the artifacts involved, consciousness fades. We act in an unreflected transparent manner. The things we use take on undifferentiated meaning; they are just devices to help us get long. When we encounter other things in the world that have yet to be thrown into the closet of familiar devices in our mind, we explain their presence metaphorically in reference to all these other useful things. These new things are just some as yet unfamiliar device or instrument for a future task. Natural objects, like trees and people, take on values linked to their potential use or to prices in an imaginary marketplace. The world becomes no more than standing reserve to be used in some way (Heidegger, 1977, p. 17).

Relationships become diminished. Social networks provide a good example of this thinning of what have been thick relationships. The richness of friendship becomes lost when friends are little more than an entry in Facebook. Numbers count more than quality. Not only interpersonal relationships are affected. Objects in the natural world lose their intrinsic existential being and our sense of connection to them. If they are only objects waiting to be exploited, there is no reason to take care of them. Some clever engineer will convert them to something I will want in the future. It is no wonder the natural world has fallen into such disrepair and we have become, as Weber said, "disenchanted." The important sense of interconnectedness that supports and nurtures care for ourselves, others, and the rest of the world vanishes. The eminent psychotherapist Erich Fromm argues that we have moved from an earlier way of Being, where we understood the essential nature of what being human means, into a Having mode of life (1976). In this latter mode, the meaning of life narrows to a measure of what we have. Qualities critical to flourishing, like dignity and autonomy, are lost in the addictive presence of technology. We literally have forgotten what it means to be human and cannot flourish without regaining that understanding.

Erosion of Personal Responsibility

Technological objects always stand between an actor and the world and affect the appearance of the world. In many cases, the disparities are inconsequential compared to the benefits the technology bestows. Spectacles change the perception of the world to a myope, but much to his or her satisfaction without any untoward effects. Unlike these simpler artifacts, many forms of modern technology separate the actor from the act in time and space. The separation increases the possibility of unintended consequences, as the actor cannot recognize outcomes beyond the horizon. The use of drones as a weapon places an operator/gunner in a trailer in the southwest of the United States and the target somewhere in Asia, removing the operator from experiencing the full impact that follows from pulling the trigger. The ethical consequences are profound. Acting responsibly, in the classic sense of not knowingly producing harm, becomes problematic. Knowing the consequences is impossible in many cases. Much of the damage to the world and to humans has been caused in this manner. The act of turning on a light switch creates pollution at a power plant many miles away. Household waste simply goes away when placed at the curb; few people ever thought that away was a real place where damages produced by the disposal practices contribute to unsustainability.

The development of the United States and nations that have emulated our history has roots in the philosophy of the Enlightenment and especially in the work of Thomas Hobbes, who saw that without a social contract based on ethical behavior, citizens would live in a "state of nature" characterized by "no arts; no letters; no society; and which is worst of all, continual fear and danger of violent death; and the life of man, solitary, poor, nasty, brutish, and short" (Hobbes, 1651/1929, p. 99). All modern democracies live under such a social contract, manifest in a constitution or other bodies of law. This dark side of technology interferes with the ethical context that is so essential to maintaining society in a state far from the Hobbesian state of nature.

Shifting-the-Burden

The unreflective use of technology contributes to unsustainability through a pattern of behavior that systems dynamicists call shifting-the-burden. When we individually or as a collective society automatically reach for some sort of technological solution without reflecting deeply on the roots of the problems, we are drawn away from means that might eliminate rather than simply fix the problem for a short time. Management scientist Russell Ackoff, writing about problem solving some years ago, noted that there were several ways of dealing with problems (1981). He defines a problem as a situation in which the actors have alternative courses of action available; the choice makes a difference, and the actors are not sure about what path to follow. He then notes that there are three types of action that can be taken. The first is to "resolve" the problem—that is, to select a course of action that is good enough to restore the action to the unproblematic state it was in before the problem cropped up. He writes, "To attempt to resolve a conflict [problem] is to accept the conditions that create it and to seek a compromise, a distribution of gains and/or losses that is acceptable to the participants" (Ackoff, 1978, p. 40). This approach, which he calls "clinical," often involves the qualitative judgments of the actors. In the long run, this action is not likely to satisfy the actors, as the problem is likely to recur since the underlying conditions still lurk in the background.

The second approach is to "solve" the problem through a course of action believed to lead to the best possible (optimal) outcome. This approach, which he calls "research," involves analysis and often the application of mathematical models. This way of treating problems tends to ignore parts of the problem system that cannot be fitted into the analytic framework, and is also unlikely to make the problem go away. Both fail to address and change the underlying structure that creates the problematic situations. This approach digs a little deeper into the underlying roots but still fails to expose the beliefs and norms that constrain the actors.

DESIGN AND SUSTAINABILITY

Ackoff offers a third way that is quite different: to "dissolve" the problem. Dissolvers idealize rather than optimize because the objective is to produce long-lasting satisfaction or at least get them back on track to attain their vision. Here the actors take a course that changes the context (that is, the underlying system creating the problem) such that the problem disappears. The change can be to the acting entity or to the environment impinging upon the entity or both. To distinguish the approach that must be taken for this path, Ackoff (1981, p. 21) calls it design. I add emphasis because I believe it is the only problem-addressing framework that can take on the challenge of producing sustainability. New problems can and do crop up because the world is always changing.

Design is a special word in the lexicon of sustainability. It is not the same as what fashion or product designers do. It is not the same as problem solving, except in Ackoff's notion of dissolving. In this new lexicon, design is a process in which new action-producing structures are deliberately created and substituted for old ones such that routine acts change from the old, ineffective patterns to new ones that produce the desired outcomes. Design is relevant in any domain where routines have stopped working effectively—that is, bringing forth the world that the actors envision. Design and learning are connected in this sense. Design is an activity that precedes learning. It provides new, alternate action-producing structures that change the mode of behavior from one that has been ineffective to a more effective regime.

Design, in this sense, is a conscious, deliberate effort to change the systemic presuppositions—beliefs and normal practices, including the use of technology—underlying action so that the desired end may be attained. If the design is successful and the consequent actions turn out as desired, this behavioral pattern corresponds to the double-loop learning process of organizational theorists (Argyris and Schön, 1978, p. 3) and to Ackoff's (1981, p. 21) dissolving. The designer or designers can choose to change any part of the context surrounding the unsatisfactory action, substituting new ways of viewing the world, new strategies, new forms of authority, or new technological resources for the old.

Design appears in several other common arenas, far from the conventional world of technology and mechanics, although we rarely, if ever, think of the processes there as design. Policy making is a form of design that tends to focus on changing the norms that govern social activities. It creates new institutions complete with sets of rights and wrongs: the values and norms we live by. Policy making also reorders authority and shifts power. Education is also a design process, with the student as the target. Education embeds new beliefs and normative strategies, and it enables one to expand competence to new areas. Education facilitates both problem solving and the ability to step into new domains arising from visions of the future.

Design is the only deliberate way out of the unsustainable, dominating, and addictive patterns of individual and social behaviors that have become the norms in the United States and in other affluent, consumerist societies. Exercising collective willpower is not effective. Studies of diet regimens to produce lasting weight loss show that willpower alone does not keep dieters from slipping into old patterns and gaining back what weight they had lost (Dansinger et al., 2005). Many doctors discourage quick fixes, such as stomach stapling, as they do not address the root problems; further, there is the argument that some form of designed intervention that changes the overall culture, in this case the public health context, is essential to cope with widespread addictive patterns of individual behavior. Sustainability poses a particularly daunting challenge to the world of design and designers. The methods must enable designers to operate at depths of understanding deeper than those that have been available for much of the modern era. The designers, themselves, must be willing and competent to think in new ways and be brave enough to break the proverbial mold. If not, we will continue to see marvelous new designs with unheard-of capacities for efficiency, intelligence, speed, and characteristics of which we are as yet unaware, but will also continue to see unsustainability grow at the same time.

REFERENCES

Ackoff, R. L. (1978), *The Art of Problem Solving,* John Wiley & Sons: New York.

Ackoff, R. L. (1981), "The Art and Science of Mess Management," *Interfaces,* vol. 11, no. 1: pp. 20–26.

Argyris, C. and Schön, D. (1978), *Organizational Learning: A Theory of Action Perspective,* Addison-Wesley: Reading, MA.

Bolan, R. S. (1980), "The Practitioner as Theorist: The Phenomenology of the Professional Episode," *APA Journal,* July: pp. 261–74.

Daly, H. E. and Cobb, J. B. (1994), *For the Common Good: Redirecting the Economy toward Community, the Environment, and a Sustainable Future,* Beacon Press: Boston.

Dansinger, M. L., Gleason, J. A., Griffith, J. L., Selker, H. P. and Schaefer, E. J. (2005), "Comparison of the Atkins, Ornish, Weight Watchers, and Zone Diets for Weight Loss and Heart Disease Risk Reduction," *JAMA,* vol. 293, no. 1: pp. 43–53.

Descartes, R. (1637/1998), *Discourse on Method,* Hackett Publishing: Indianapolis.

Easterlin, R. A. (1974), "Does Economic Growth Improve the Human Lot?," in P. A. David and M. W. Reder (eds.), *Nations and Households in Economic Growth: Essays in Honor of Moses Abramovitz,* Academic Press: New York, pp. 89–125.

Ehrenfeld, J. (2008), *Sustainability by Design: A Subversive Strategy for Transforming Our Consumer Culture,* Yale University Press: New Haven, CT.

Fromm, E. (1976), *To Have or To Be?* Harper & Row: New York.

Gerth, H. H. and Mills, C. W. (eds) (1946), *Max Weber: Essays in Sociology,* Oxford University Press: New York.

Heidegger, M. (1977), *The Question Concerning Technology and Other Essays,* Harper & Row: New York.

Hobbes, T. (1651/1929), *Leviathan,* Oxford University Press: Oxford.

Layard, R. (2005), *Happiness: Lessons from a New Science,* Penguin Press HC: London.

Maturana, H. R. (1988), "Reality: The Search for Objectivity, or the Quest for a Compelling Argument," *Irish Journal of Psychology,* vol. 9, no. 1: pp. 25–82.

Voltaire (1918), *Candide,* Boni & Liveright: New York.

Whitehead, A. N. (1925/1967), *Science and the Modern World,* Free Press: New York.

Wilkinson, R. and Pickett, K. (2009), *The Spirit Level: Why Greater Equality Makes Societies Stronger,* Bloomsbury Press: London.

2

Post-Materialism

FREYA MATHEWS

INTRODUCTION

One way of understanding the differences between societies, and the transformations those societies have undergone and may yet undergo, is in terms of the metaphysical premise on which each society rests. By the metaphysical premise of a society, I mean its foundational belief about the nature of the world. This foundational belief will determine, to a large extent, how the members of a society treat their world. How they treat their world will in turn constitute their basic *modality*, their way of comporting themselves in the world, where this modality will be discernible in everything they do—their entire culture will take its cue from it.

In the present discussion I would like to propose an interpretive schema consisting of three broad categories of metaphysical premise: pre-materialist, materialist and post-materialist. These categories give rise, I will argue, to three basic modalities of society: traditional, modern and prospective/future, respectively. This schema is not intended to be exhaustive; it offers a lens for comparing and contrasting certain ideal types of state societies. I specify state societies, meaning stratified societies with institutionalized systems of governance, because the schema does not include, in particular, indigenous societies of the hunter-gatherer variety: the distinction between pre-materialist (religious) and post-materialist (post-religious but not secular) metaphysics does not apply in any clear-cut way to them. The schema is, of course, like all schemas, highly simplified: real life will exceed its categories in numerous ways. But it does offer an initial way of organizing our thinking about the extraordinary fact that modern industrial societies are currently destroying the fabric of life in our world.

Since the pre-materialist/materialist/post-materialist schema revolves around the category of materialism, I will explain right away, at least in preliminary fashion, what I mean by this term. By materialism I mean the view that sees the physical manifold as in itself lacking any inner principle, any attribute analogous to mind—anything akin to subjectivity, spirit, sentience, intentionality or agency. Matter, from the materialist perspective, is sheer externality—there is nothing more to it than meets the eye (even if this eye is the eye of the microscope or telescope). Hence, in itself, it is devoid of the value-conferring attributes that accompany mind: meaning, purpose, intrinsic value and communicative capability. It is just stuff, brute and blind. Matter, moreover, or the larger manifold described by physics, is the sum total of reality. It is all there is. This is not to say that systems with mental attributes might not figure within a materialist frame of reference: organisms, for instance, might be admitted as physical systems that have evolved characteristics such as agency and intentionality. But such mental characteristics are always explainable, from a materialist perspective, in prior physical terms that themselves make no reference to mentality.

This materialist premise is highly conducive to an instrumental modality. If matter per se is brute and blind, devoid of meanings, ends, sentience, feelings or impulses of its own, then it possesses no moral significance in its own right. Since nothing matters to it, nothing that happens to it at our hands, in particular, can matter to it. We are therefore morally at liberty to act on it as we will. True, insofar as instances of mentality might emerge out of the intricacies of certain physical systems, those systems might make moral claims on us. But these are exceptions to the metaphysical norm of moral inconsiderability. The world understood in materialist terms is, in its larger outlines, a mere object for our agency and in that sense conducive to a fundamentally instrumentalist orientation in us.

With this brief introduction to the way the term 'materialism' is intended in the present context, let us begin to unpack the schema defined in terms of the metaphysical premises of society.

THREE TYPES OF SOCIETY

1. Pre-Materialist—Traditional

Pre-materialist societies are typically religious societies—that is, their metaphysical premises are encoded in religion. By religion here I mean a system of metaphysical beliefs or teachings that have been attained by extra-rational means (for example, by revelation) and recorded in scriptures or other sacred texts. Such texts are then mediated by religious authorities. The metaphysical premises of any such religious belief system are generally highly prescriptive—they entail truths about the nature of the good and the meanings and purposes of life. These prescriptive truths are interpreted by the relevant religious authorities—sometimes in ways that are life-giving but sometimes in ways that patently serve the interests of those authorities. They are sanctioned by the state and imposed on the populace, or the portions of the populace that fall under the moral jurisdiction of the religion in question. The religious authorities serve as the core source of authority for the religious state. Examples include the monarchies of Medieval Christendom, political systems based on caste in traditional India and certain recent regimes in the Islamic world—for example, Afghanistan under the Taliban. Generally speaking, the religious state is authoritarian. The populace is ruled—it may be benignly and paternalistically, or it may be oppressively and discriminatively—by a political class deriving its legitimacy from a religious metaphysics.

Although religion has been inextricable from the evolution of human culture, and has in this sense been an unavoidable aspect of society, there are many ways in which, historically, religion has contributed to the injustice, stasis and poverty that were a feature of many pre-materialist societies. Reliance on revealed religious truths stifled open-minded inquiry into the way the world actually worked. Natural phenomena were explained in terms of divine intentions and interventions rather than in terms of causal mechanisms. Reliance on religious authority as the source of knowledge thus blocked the development of science and the expansion of knowledge made possible by science. Ignorance of the actual mechanics of nature entailed a lack of technical control over the environment and consequently entailed susceptibility to poverty and disease, at least for a majority of the people. Lack of control over the natural world and people's consequent vulnerability to hardship and danger led to increased reliance on petitioning the supernatural/divine or the institutional representatives of the supernatural/divine on earth. This, in turn, strengthened the political grip of religious institutions on the state, with all the potential for the arbitrary exercise of power that flowed from this.

On the other hand, in pre-materialist societies there was a depth of meaning and a feeling for the profound mystery and poetry of human existence that tends to be lacking in materialist societies. Despite widespread disease, poverty and oppression, members of pre-materialist societies often evinced a certain confidence and largesse that came from a sense of being plugged directly into the sources of creation. Praise and gratitude animated their basic attitudes, resulting in everyday cultures of great beauty and grace. They enjoyed a state of effortless connectedness and belonging that is often painfully missing in members of modern societies.

The basic existential modality of pre-materialist state societies then—which is to say, the basic orientation of pre-materialist peoples to their world—was, on the one hand, gratitude and praise, but on the other hand, importunate dependence. Individuals and societies of course acquired a rudimentary knowledge of natural processes in order to secure their livelihoods, but at the same time they relied psychologically on assistance or succour from supernatural sources.

2. Materialist—Modern

There are innumerable analyses of modernity, but one of the classic analyses, deriving from Weber, characterizes modernity in terms of 'instrumental reason' (Weber, 1905/2002; Adorno and Horkheimer, 1947). To adopt an instrumental stance is to value things merely as means to our ends rather than as ends in themselves. Instrumental reason is the form of rationality that seeks to know the world only in order to utilize its resources for human purposes. This form of reason is usually equated with scientific method and described as scientific reason. The world it discloses is a world of mere objects, devoid of intrinsic meaning or value. To see the world this way is to empty it of moral and religious significance. Such a retreat from religious significance is seen by advocates of modernity as emancipation from false metaphysics; instrumental reason is accordingly valorized as the tool of this emancipation (Taylor, 1999).

However, it is clear that, despite its disavowal of religious metaphysics, modernity is itself by no means innocent of metaphysics. It takes its character from a metaphysical premise of its own—namely that of materialism. Indeed, the instrumental reason, which is often regarded as definitive of modernity, is instrumentalist only on account of this materialist premise. Reason in itself is neutral with respect to its outcomes; it is rendered instrumentalist only in the service of materialism. In the service of a different metaphysics, it would not necessarily be so. (In the context of animist-type metaphysics, for example, it would not be rational to treat the world in a purely instrumental manner; it would rather be rational to try to engage constructively with the agencies of the various forms of inspiritment that, according to the animist view, inhere in nature.) So although scientific reason has indeed assumed pre-eminence in modern societies, and although such reason is markedly instrumentalist in its orientation, both its exclusiveness and its instrumentalism rest on the assumption of materialism—the assumption that reality has no meanings of its own that can be imparted to us by extra-empirical means.

It does seem plausible then to identify modernity, for schematic and comparative purposes, in terms of its materialist premise. As we have seen, materialism qua metaphysics renders the world, in its larger outlines, a moral nullity—the materialist universe is indifferent to human concerns and has none of its own. Humanity has therefore to invent its own reasons for living—its own meanings and values. In the absence of religious revelation, and in the context of a reductive view of the mentality of living systems, human nature itself becomes the sole source of meaning and value: secular humanism replaces religious values, and human self-reliance replaces the importunate attitude, as well as the gratitude and grace, that prevailed in religious societies.

In those modern/materialist societies that developed along liberal (as opposed, for example, to socialist) lines, a distinction was drawn between public and private domains. Belief systems opposed to materialism, such as those offered by religion, were tolerated in the private but not in the public sphere. Decision-making in the public domain was (and still is) dictated by humanism: policy was addressed to people's material, as opposed to any supposed spiritual, needs. Public life, in other words, was post-religious— that is, secular—in tenor.

It was the materialist abandonment of religious revelation as a prime source of insight into the nature of the world that opened the way for the forms of empirical inquiry and causal explanation that characterize science. The strictly empiricist methods of science led to ever-increasing understanding of the mechanics of natural phenomena, where this in turn made possible ever-increasing technical control of the natural environment. Such control allowed for an expanding capacity to secure people's future and satisfy their material needs and desires. Moreover, since there was little in the way of moral constraint on the use that could be made of a natural environment under-stood in basically materialist terms, and since it was therefore morally permissible for society, with the help of science, to exploit nature to the limit, progress and development became hallmarks of modernity. That is to say, society was enabled and permitted to in-crease its standard of living indefinitely, at the expense of nature.

This new ethos of progress produced the distinctive profile of modernity: an imperi-ous and chronic dissatisfaction with the given, or with what currently exists, in favour of an imagined ideal. This dissatisfaction emanated in a characteristic regime of perpetual change which took the form of an unceasing quest to improve the world, to make it over in accordance with our own latest abstract conception of the good. Modernity is a rest-less condition, a condition of disconnection from the past. Unlike traditional societies, dedicated to maintaining continuity with the past, even at the risk of stasis and stagna-tion, modern civilization turns its face implacably towards the future, reaching beyond the given for new, more affluent and expansive styles of living.

The basic existential modality of materialist societies—their way of being in the world—is thus instrumentalist: such societies assume control of nature, progressively recalibrating it to serve human purposes.

The political implications of materialism are two-edged. On the one hand, its reli-ance on reason as opposed to religiosity is indeed emancipatory. The capacity for reason is intrinsic to human nature; rationality, unlike privileged religious or revelatory ways of knowing, is a faculty equally available to all human beings. No individual or caste can claim special access to rational truth; hence nor can one claim special authority over others. Societies premised on materialism thus tend towards liberalism and an implied egalitarianism in their politics: each individual, qua rational agent, is free to work out their own conception of the good in their own way, subject only to the requirement that their doing so does not compromise the right of others to do the same.

However, when instrumentalism becomes the basic attitude of society, there is a possibility of it resulting not only in the systematic appropriation of the natural world but in exploitative practices within the human realm as well: selected groups may become objectified and treated as means to the ends of more powerful others (Plumwood, 1993). In other words, when such an instrumental attitude takes hold, it may overwhelm the demystifying and hence liberal tendencies inherent in ma-terialism and lead instead to the rendering down of all potential, human and non-human alike, into a resource base for a state machine. At its limit, this instrumentalist tendency may result in totalitarianism. The most notable example of a regime that, though thoroughly materialist and hence modern in its basic attitude nevertheless eschewed liberalism, was the fascist regime of German National Socialism, which in-spired the original analysis of modernity in terms of instrumental reason (Adorno and Horkheimer, 1947/1972).

In addition to the conflicting social and political consequences of materialism, there are of course spiritual consequences. The most visible of these is the loss of a sense of deeper shared life-meanings in a materialist society. Materialism, as we have seen, is conducive to humanism: since the universe appoints no meanings and values for us, we are obliged to invent contingent meanings and deeper life-values for ourselves. This gives rise, at least in liberal variants of modern societies, to a benign tolerance of religious diversity in the private sphere: religious belief systems are recognized as vehicles for the life-meanings and values that individuals are obliged to invent for themselves. Thoughtful individuals, however, cannot help noticing that the enlightened relativism that liberalism seems to require is ultimately self-defeating: acquiescence in all life-meanings is actually endorsement of none. It is this withholding of endorsement that is the deeper truth of liberal-modern societies. The pluralism of liberal-modern societies does indeed then rest on an implied negation of the objective validity of any life-meanings; this negation of meaning may create a moral or spiritual abyss in society. The sense of vertigo occasioned by this abyss may cause doubt and unease even though those who feel it may have no yen to return to political systems based on religious authority.

The aesthetic consequences of a materialist outlook are also pronounced. Perceiving reality in materialist terms, as no more than an object for our agency, is conducive to a sense of entitlement in the face of creation, in contrast to the gratitude and grace of pre-materialist societies. While an aesthetics of everyday practice is a natural expression of the gratitude and grace—and sense of participation in larger meanings—of pre-materialism, the everyday practice of materialist societies is likely to reflect the bruteness and blindness, the functionality and utilitarianism, indeed the arrogance, of the materialist attitude. Aesthetics, no longer the response of human life in its entirety to a divine call, is relegated to the vestigial little sideshow of art, where it, like everything else in materialist societies, is duly subjected to the utilitarian logic of commodification.

Materialism then is complex in its effects: on the one hand, it is demystifying and emancipatory, conducive to expansion in knowledge and egalitarianism in politics. But on the other hand, it entrains a loss of shared values and meanings while fostering, as a basic attitude, an instrumentalism and utilitarianism that can lead to the conversion of all life, human and non-human alike, to resource. Of course, the conversion of all life to resource results not only in the hacking up and melting down of the living fabric of the biosphere but also in the displacement of meaning and aesthetics as the basic human response to existence.

In light of the mixed consequences of materialism, a process of popular inquiry and exploration born of disenchantment with the existential limitations of modernity is now under way in Western societies. This process takes the form of a restless interest in non-Western religions and meditational traditions, alternative therapies and remedies, new age theories and speculations, magic and pagan traditions. A more or less spiritual attitude to nature and a mystical emphasis on direct experience of the spiritual aspects of reality, even in the context of religions, are insistent features of this inquiry (Kohn, 2005; Tacey, 2003). When this is combined with the liberal legacy of pluralism with respect to questions of deeper life-meaning, we can see an anticipation of ineffability in spiritual matters already taking shape. At the same time, most of the new seekers in Western societies take the verities and amenities of science for granted; they are looking to supplement science with further meanings, not to supplant it. So it would seem that what I am about to describe as post-materialism is already an emerging, if minority, movement in at least some of the more established instances of modern society, notably those of the West.

3. Post-Materialist—Prospective/in the Future

By post-materialism I mean a view of reality that ascribes to it a more-than-material or mind-like dimension. This more-than-material dimension is not regarded as taking the supernatural form of immaterial entities—such as the gods or spirits of religion—that exist in addition to the material world; rather, it takes the form of an unseen and interior dimension of matter itself. This interior aspect of matter is understood not as the inner physical structure of things—their physical entrails, so to speak—but as a mind-like interior, unobservable to science in the same way that the mental life of a person is unobservable. Such interiority may be described by different theorists in different ways—as a kind of subjectivity, for instance, or agency or intentionality or inspiritment or conativity. My own preference is for the category of conativity. In the Spinozist tradition of metaphysics, dating from the seventeenth century, conativity is understood as the will or striving of things towards existence or self-increase (*conatus* being the Latin term for will, or striving). However the inner dimension of reality is theoretically construed, its expression in the world will be consistent with the findings of science though not exhausted by those findings. In other words, post-materialism does not reject science, nor the innumerable benefits for humanity that science has delivered. Rather, it looks beyond science, not by embracing the supernatural, but by seeking the interior realms of the natural.

Such an interior aspect of reality will undoubtedly have normative significance—that is to say, it will undoubtedly have directive meaning. Although this directiveness may be inferred from the appearances—from the way the world appears to us in perception—our apprehension of it will always remain open-ended and interpretive. It will never be codifiable in the manner of science because it lies outside the strictly empirical—and hence potentially universally shared—categories of science. Hence the normative implications of the inner aspects of reality cannot be congealed into any kind of common truth but will be revealed through personally and culturally specific experiences of communicative engagement. In prospective societies resting on the premise of post-materialism then, individuals will insist on staking out the terrain of this engagement for themselves. Bred to the expectation of their own epistemic autonomy through reason, they will not give up this autonomy to self-appointed external authorities, as members of pre-materialist societies, bred to dependence, generally did (though it must be said that minority traditions resistant to authorized interpretations of scripture or committed to direct mystical experience of the divine often also existed in pre-materialist societies). Individuals in post-materialist societies will discover for themselves eclectic frames of reference that reflect their own immediate experience of communicative engagement with the world.

For this reason then the post-materialist experience, occurring within an epistemic space prepared by science and still responsive to the requirements of reason, cannot be co-opted by religion: this experience is sensitive to personal and cultural context rather than susceptible of canonical exposition. Without the availability of canonical exposition or prescribed forms of worship, there is no possibility of institutional mediation, nor hence of religious authority, where such authority could lead to a resurgence of political authoritarianism. Individuals and groups in post-materialist societies are loath to delegate their spirituality; they prefer instead to discover their relationship with reality through communicative channels of their own devising, using the aesthetic resources of their own lives and cultures. Any metaphysical naming of the unobservable normative aspect of reality is understood to be provisional and open to negotiation. What is agreed upon, however, in the post-materialist situation, is the fact that the universe is no mere object but rather imbued with meanings and communicative capabilities of its own. Discovering for ourselves and responding to these meanings and communicative capabilities pulls our own lives into the coherence and eloquence to which as humans we arguably aspire.

Eschewing conventional religious terms, such as the sacred, let us select the term 'numinous' for a universe imbued with self-meaning and communicativity. (The term 'numinous' derives from the Latin *numen,* meaning a nodding or nod as an expression of a will, command or consent—usually of a god or other divine or spiritual presence [University of Notre Dame Latin Dictionary and Grammar Aid, n.d.]. This conveys the idea of a responsive potentiality or presence within objects, places or indeed worlds that guides the overt while itself remaining invisible.) We might then sum up our reflections on post-materialism as follows: acknowledging the numinosity of the universe, while not seeking to articulate in any definitive way the grounds of that numinosity, means that our response thereto cannot be prescribed or legislated. No set of rules for behaviour will follow from acknowledging it. Since we avow the normativity—the value-directedness—of this universe without definitively anticipating what its ultimate ends might be, we must simply try, moment by moment, to accommodate ourselves to the felt grain of its conativity. This means trying in every situation to detect the contours of its unfolding and accommodating our agency to these contours. Our task will be to develop modalities that enable us to pursue our legitimate ends while leaving the world free to continue its own unfolding. In post-materialist societies we will thus not be entitled simply to do as we please with the world—to treat it in the purely instrumental way that materialist societies do. We will be required rather to engage with it responsively, decoding its normativity afresh in every situation and adapting creatively to it.

Prospective post-materialist societies then are post-religious but not secular; that is, they are not post-spiritual. It is important to note that the scope of the post-material spiritual is not merely ecological but cosmological. It is not merely the biosphere that is conceived as having an inner dimension that makes a normative claim on us, but reality generally. In consequence, our thought and action in *every* context of life, not merely in the environmental context, must be consistent with this conativity, and must leave the world intact. In this sense, the ethos of post-materialism does not reduce to the ethos of ecology, though its consequences will be broadly consistent with ecological values, since they will be consistent with the conative grain of the larger cosmological systems within which ecosystems fall. In other words, if we adopt the post-materialist ethos in every department of life, we will not need any special department of environmentalism.

Parallel between Post-Materialism and Daoism

Although a fully post-materialist culture has not existed to date because post-materialism, in the present sense, is defined as having emerged in the context of science, certain indigenous traditions have nevertheless rested on metaphysical beliefs that strikingly anticipate the outlook of post-materialism. Noteworthy in this connection is the indigenous tradition of China, Daoism. Daoism revolves around the metaphysical notion of *Dao* or Way, a primordial principle that animates a universe conceived, like the post-materialist universe, as self-patterning and self-significant. Dao, like the psychoactive aspect of the numinous universe, can be intuited but not definitively named. In this sense, it is in no way comparable to the laws identified and specified by science. The unfolding of Dao is rather a continuity of self-patterning that occurs as a result of the inner cohering, the inner mutual attunement or sympathy, of all things. This inter-attunement of conativities ensures that the universe hangs together despite the fact that the things that constitute it are constantly changing. In other words, things hang together not because they are governed by arbitrary external laws of nature but because their own inner strivings pull them into seamless though endlessly dynamic and changing configurations.

Since Dao is the expression of these spontaneous inner strivings, rather than the result of conformity to an external law, Daoists are unable to predict (and hence control) the future course of events. Their universe is like Heraclitus's river, into which one can never step twice. It is not, however, the goal of Daoism to control events, as science does, but rather to adapt to present circumstances. The adaptive modality identified by Daoists is known as *wu wei* (Lafargue, 1992; Hall and Ames, 1998; Girardot et al., 2001). Wu wei literally means nonaction (*wu,* not; *wei,* action). It is a paradoxical notion that has been subject to many different interpretations (Loy, 1985), but most commentators agree that wu wei is not the same as quietism—it is not a matter simply of standing by and doing nothing. One interpretation, which I think makes sense of the appeal to wu wei in the present context, is that wu wei denotes a form of action that requires the least expenditure of effort on the part of the agent because it makes use of processes and energies that are already naturally unfolding in the world. The agent 'hitches a ride', so to speak, with these energies, these conativities in order to achieve his or her own ends. So wu wei is, on the one hand, a matter of letting things be, in the sense of leaving things to follow their own life-purposes or life-patterns, but it also, at the same time, involves harmlessly free-riding on these life-purposes or patterns in pursuit of one's own interests.

It is clear that wu wei is already implicit in much sustainability thinking, to the extent that sustainability involves taking what we need from nature without disrupting the integrity of natural structures and processes. Power, for instance, can be drawn from sources—such as solar, wind and methane—that tap existing energies without fracturing their pre-existing flow-patterns or cycles. Food can be gathered from productive ecosystems or grown in accordance with organic principles that rely on natural processes of fertilization, pollination, germination and pest control, thereby minimizing the human input required and preserving the ecological integrity of soils, waters and landscapes. Buildings can exemplify passive design, being sited and structured so as to trap natural light and energy while making best use of existing topography, rather than topography having to be reshaped to serve the requirements of buildings (Watts, 1975). Wu wei, in other words, enables us to dwell in the world without significantly disrupting it. Daoism takes it for granted that the universe is sacred, that it is indeed a spirit thing and that we should, accordingly, as far as possible allow the Ten Thousand Things to unfold towards their own ends; we should let them be, where this is consistent with satisfying human needs, provided we act in accordance with wu wei.

However, although wu wei is useful as a guide to the practice of post-materialism, its potential as a modality that could fully meet the needs of contemporary mass societies, with their vast human populations and advanced industrial organization, might still be doubted. For this reason, I think the modality of post-materialist societies needs to include not only a principle of letting-be but an element of proactivity—an element that allows us actively to change the course of events, without, however, compromising the world's integrity. One such mode of agency that might be proposed is *synergy*. (Whether or not synergy is already implied in the notion of wu wei depends upon which interpretation of wu wei one consults. Standard interpretations incline towards free-riding on ambient energies or processes; for an interpretation that is broadly compatible with the synergy reading, see Ames, 1989.)

Synergy

Synergy is here defined as a form of relationship between two or more parties who engage with each other in such a way that something new and larger than either of them, but true to the inner principle of each, is born. Synergy is a modality not so much of letting be as of engagement. In synergizing with the world, we are still in a sense following the path of least resistance but not merely by hitching a ride with existing energies or processes already unfolding according to their own nature or towards their own ends; rather, in synergy we engage the world in such a way that it spontaneously adapts or enlarges its ends in response to our encounter with it. This adaptation or enlargement occurs with the grain of its conativity and is, in that sense, a further elaboration of that conativity. Yet this new end is not one towards which the world would have moved had we not engaged with it. By way of synergy then we do change the course of events, yet we do so while still letting the world be, in the sense that we are still allowing it to follow its own inner principle: we are simply eliciting conative potentials that had hitherto not been manifest. Equally importantly, in any instance of synergy our ends as well as those of the other party to the engagement will be transformed. Synergy is a two-way street: it discovers in us potentialities we might not have known we had, just as it discovers such potentialities in the world.

The distinction between synergy and wu wei in its earlier sense can be illustrated by a return to the hitching a ride analogy. A hitchhiker in the wu wei mode hopes that the driver of some vehicle already on the road, travelling in the general direction of the hitchhiker's own destination, will offer him or her a ride. A hitchhiker in the synergistic mode, however, will flag down a vehicle and then engage with the driver in such a way that both the hitchhiker's plans and those of the driver might change. Their respective desires for their original, separate destinations might give way to a new, consensual desire for a destination they can share. Although their destination has changed as a result of their encounter, this new destination is as fully, if not more fully, in accordance with their desires than were their original separate destinations. Synergy is thus an essentially creative mode: it draws forth the new without contradicting the old, and hence without compromising the cohering of the world.

The ultimate template for synergy is the act of procreation: two parties join their essences to create a third entity, which taps into and makes manifest potentialities that pre-existed in each of the originals but could only become actualized when those parties joined with each other. As a basic modality then—an existential modality— synergy in fact recapitulates an underlying principle of creation itself, the principle of fertility. For in joining together two or more existing patterns of energy to create a new pattern, synergy allows for the emergence of new form in the world, but this is a new form which, like the offspring of two parents, carries within it the story of the old, the story of those from whom the new has arisen. The new that springs from synergistic interactions then is a new that in no way rests on a repudiation or destruction of the old. In this respect, we can contrast synergy with the modalities of both modernity and tradition. Modernity is dedicated to the new, but its new is an arbitrary new that rests on the wholesale erasure of the old; its effect is accordingly to shatter the integrity of the world. Tradition retains the old, but often at the expense of the new, and this can result in stagnation, the suppression of cultural creativity. Synergy, however, induces perpetual creative change whilst at the same time ensuring that the world continues to cohere.

Synergy then is an appropriate modality for denizens of a psychoactive (that is to say, a post-materialist) world. A psychoactive world—a world with its own conative meanings and inner directedness—is no mere object for our agency, but a locus of agency, of infinite agencies, in its own right. Through synergy we can interact with that world without impeding its unfolding; synergy, in other words, leaves the conative integrity of the world intact. A psychoactive world is moreover a world disposed to engage communicatively with us. Hence, it is capable of participating in the kind of inner-driven transformation that synergy envisages. In other words, a post-materialist world is both entitled to the respect that synergy, as a way of relating, ensures, and capable of the kind of inner-driven transactions that synergy entails.

The basic modality of a post-materialist society is thus, in the first instance, letting be (as exemplified in the Chinese notion of wu wei) and, by extension, synergy. Through synergy the inherent conativity of the world is preserved but hitherto hidden potentialities are activated: parties engaging in and open to synergistic encounter reroute each other's desires towards new goods that enlarge them both.

Like wu wei, synergy is a modality that can be adopted in any sphere of interactivity: we can revise all our interactions with one another and with the world along lines of synergy rather than imposition and control.

In the context of environmental design, synergy offers a key to a form of industrial and economic development that will not only be truly sustainable but also culturally and ecologically creative.

Synergy as a Key to Environmental Design

Achieving a form of development that is not merely sustainable but ecologically and culturally creative may not be a matter simply of reining in industry and construction in order to let nature be, nor of powering industry and construction by alternative energies, such as solar, wind and methane, in accordance with the principle of wu wei. From a post-materialist perspective, it might rather be a matter of synergy, of joining human conativity with ecological conativities to create new opportunities for both humans and living systems.

This synergistic principle is at work in new design philosophies currently going under the name of biomimicry or cradle-to-cradle design, in which products and the built environment are designed to create opportunities for nature whilst satisfying needs of ours (Benyus, 1997; Hawken, Lovins and Lovins, 1999; Braungart and McDonough, 2002). They do this by imitating nature in their functions. So, for instance, buildings are designed to generate more energy than they consume and release purer air and water into the environment than the air and water they took in. In the case of large structures, such as industrial plants, and large engineered systems, such as sewerage treatment plants, the water purification processes can provide a wetland habitat for birds and other wildlife. Likewise, manufactured products are designed so that their eventual disposal will not pollute but enrich the environment, as, for example, packaging that is designed to fertilize the soil when it is thrown away.

Architect William McDonough is an advocate of such a design philosophy. His aim is not to contradict the desires of consumers. Indeed, he is not uncomfortable with the capitalist ethos of consumerism, as the traditional environment movement, committed to restraint and frugality, is. Rather, McDonough seeks to turn the desires of consumers to ecological advantage: productive output should not be reduced, but products should be designed to give the environment what it wants while also satisfying the wants of consumers (Braungart and McDonough, 2002).

Many examples of products that satisfy consumer demand but at the same time nourish and support biological systems are cited by McDonough. The key to his design philosophy is the elimination of waste or the conversion of waste into resource. Products are designed so that they, and the by-products of the production process, can either be returned to the ecosystem as biological nutrient or recycled back into the industrial system as manufacturing nutrient: our products and our systems of production must be so designed that they support the conativity of natural systems.

McDonough emphasizes that products should be designed for return not only to the environment, in a generic sense, but to the particular local environments in which they will be used. So, for example, if a manufacturer is designing a hair gel, he or she should ask not only what does the consumer want from this hair gel?, nor only what does the environment want from this hair gel?, but what does the river into which this hair gel will eventually be discharged want from it? In other words, the designer should think about where the hair gel will eventually end up and how it can make a positive contribution to this site of disposal.

Clearly, this is a design scenario that, to a degree, anticipates the philosophy of synergy: instead of either restraining human desire for the sake of nature or sacrificing nature to human desire, McDonough seeks to make human desire serve the interests of nature, as well as vice versa. But in an important respect, the scenario that McDonough proposes falls short of synergy. For the parties to the interaction—consumer and environment—are not changed by their encounter. Prior to the encounter, the consumer wants hair gel, while the interest of the living system that is the river is in not being polluted. Each party may get what it wants, so to speak, but their respective desires have not been enlarged as a result of the exchange; nothing new has come into the world.

A living world cannot be sustained solely by such sterile transactions. To satisfy our desires in ways that do not actively harm the biosphere may be commendable, but the biosphere needs more than such restraint from its elements (Mathews, 2011). The biosphere is not a given from which we can endlessly take, even if by doing so we do no harm. The life system has to be continually recreated, not from some source outside the system but from inside it, from the very entities that draw their existence and sustenance from it. Sustaining the biosphere then means more than not harming it, more than merely ameliorating our impact on it; it means actively replenishing it, actively reconstituting the biosphere in everything we do. Ultimately this is a matter of wanting what the biosphere needs us to want. Our desires have to mesh with the needs of other elements in the sense that the effects of the actions we take to satisfy our desires must afford the very conditions needed by other elements of the system. This is how the biosphere works. Every being, in seeking its own good, is also serving the interests of others.

So, for example, the diminutive Australian honey possum, *Tarsipes Rostratus,* wants nectar, particularly the nectar of certain banksia blossoms. In obtaining this nectar the possum transports pollen from one banksia bush to another, thereby pollinating, and assuring the reproduction of, the species that sustains it (Wiens et al., 1979). A honey possum who decided it wanted sausages rather than nectar would not sustain its environment, and—if we add a few more species with aberrant desires to the equation—no amount of elaborate offsetting would compensate for the lack of ecological fit. The elements of ecosystems achieve this fit not because they make ad hoc arrangements to offset the ecological consequences of their desires but because their desires themselves are precisely referenced to those of one another and the larger system. Ecology is rooted in the specifics of desire, in the pared-back economies of intermeshing desires (Mathews, 2010).

Likewise, in post-materialist societies, human production will of course continue to serve human interests, but it will do so in ways that enact a conative economy intricately patterned to a larger jigsaw of desires. This economy, though by no means necessarily frugal, will nevertheless have to be exact: it will not countenance the phantasmagoria of trivial, fanciful and ecologically unreferenced commodities—such as hair gels—that are currently the stock in trade of modern—reconstructed or unreconstructed—consumerism. In other words, a thoroughgoing transvaluation of desires will be required, alongside McDonough-type design solutions, for a shift to sustainability in a post-materialist key (Mathews, 2010).

As a functional principle of design, synergy, with its built-in cycling of resources, ensures the kind of inter-coherence and economy of forms, permutation of themes and cross-referencing of styles that make for intrinsic elegance and fitness. An aesthetic of production is in this sense already assured by synergy, in contrast to the discordant effects of the materialist mode of production, which typically involves the reduction of living fabric to disparate, arbitrary and hence dissonant objects. Moreover, since every instance of synergistic praxis in a post-materialist society represents an occasion of engagement with a communicative reality, every detail of such a praxis can carry the imprint, the shared signature, of this communion. Such communion tends, as has been noted, to elude discursive definition but will, for the same reason, lend itself to aesthetic expression. The entire sphere of industry and economics, regarded as categorically removed from aesthetics in materialist societies, now becomes the principal locus for aesthetic expression. For if economics is defined in terms of deployment of energy required for the satisfaction of human needs, as Peter Kropotkin defined it more than a century ago, then it is through its economics that a society will enact its basic relation to the world (1913/1974, p. 14). In this sense, economics—and by implication, in a contemporary context, industry—becomes the premier vehicle of our engagement with ecological and cosmic conativity.

As the vehicle of this engagement, industry could take on the aspect, in a post-materialist society, of the great rituals of cosmic renewal performed in many pre-materialist societies. (Interestingly, the Daoist tradition offers one of the most impressive examples of this kind of ritual [Saso, 1990; Palmer, 1991].) In these rituals, human actors cast themselves as co-creators of the cosmos. They intuited that human conativity and cosmic conativity were not ultimately distinct but that human conativity could enhance and renew the life of the cosmos and vice versa. In effect, these rituals enacted a ceremonial synergy between humanity and cosmos. Traditionally, of course, they typically took place within the space of religion—a space of supernaturalism, or realm of entities such as gods and spirits additional and superordinate to the merely natural, even if also in communication with it. The challenge for post-materialist societies is to make the space of the natural itself, reconfigured as reanimated, the arena for cosmic renewal, for daily synergy with the universe, enlarging the scope and meaning of fertility and generating abundance for all life. As vehicles of cosmic renewal, post-materialist technologies and modes of production will be as deeply delineated by aesthetic values, arising from engagement with a communicative universe, as they will be by functional ones. In post-materialist industry the streamlined, adaptive functionality of synergy may blend seamlessly with a spontaneous aesthetics of synergistic encounter to produce technologies and systems of production consistent with twenty-first-century science and adequate to the requirements of mass societies yet as at home in the landscapes of mythopoetics as were the windmills and waterwheels of yesteryear.

NOTE

This chapter is an extensively updated and reworked version of 'Beyond Modernity and Tradition: A Third Way for Development?' which appeared in *Ethics and the Environment*, 2006, vol. 11, no. 2: pp. 85–114.

REFERENCES

Adorno, T. W. and Horkheimer, M. (1947/1972), *Dialectics of Enlightenment,* Cumming, J. (trans.), Herder and Herder: New York.

Ames, R. T. (1989), 'Putting the Te Back into Daoism', in Callicott, J. B. and Ames, R. T. (eds), *Nature in Asian Traditions of Thought,* SUNY Press: Albany, NY. pp. 113–44.

Benyus, J. M. (1997), *Biomimicry: Innovation Inspired by Nature,* William Morrow: New York.

Braungart, M. and McDonough, W. (2002), *Cradle to Cradle: Remaking the Way We Make Things,* North Point Press: New York.

Girardot, N. J., Miller, J. and Xiaogan, L. (eds) (2001), *Daoism and Ecology: Ways within a Cosmic Landscape,* Harvard Divinity School: Cambridge, MA.

Hall, D. L. and Ames, R. T. (1998), *Thinking from the Han: Self, Truth and Transcendence in Chinese and Western Culture,* SUNY Press: Albany, NY.

Hawken, P., Lovins, A. and Lovins, H. (1999), *Natural Capitalism,* Rocky Mountains Institute: Snowmass, CO.

Kohn, R. (2005), *The New Believers: Reimagining God,* HarperCollins: Sydney.

Kropotkin, P. (1913/1974), *Fields Factories and Workshops Tomorrow,* George Allen and Unwin: London.

Lafargue, M. (1992), *The Tao of the Tao Te Ching: A Translation and Commentary,* SUNY Press: Albany, NY.

Loy, D. (1985), 'Wei-Wu-Wei: Non-Dual Action', *Philosophy East and West,* vol. 35, no. 1: pp. 73–87.

Mathews, F. (2010), 'On Desiring Nature', *Indian Journal of Ecocriticism,* no. 3: pp. 1–9.

Mathews, F. (2011), 'Towards a Deeper Philosophy of Biomimicry', *Organization and Environment,* vol. 24, no. 4: pp. 364–87

Palmer, M. (1991), *The Elements of Taoism,* Element: Shaftesbury Dorset.

Plumwood, V. (1993), *Feminism and the Mastery of Nature,* Routledge: London, New York.

Saso, M. R. (1990), *Taoism and the Rite of Cosmic Renewal,* 2nd ed., Washington State University Press: Seattle.

Tacey, D. (2003), *The Spirituality Revolution: The Emergence of Contemporary Spirituality,* HarperCollins: Sydney.

Taylor, C. (1999), 'Two Theories of Modernity', *Public Culture,* no. 11: pp. 153–74.

University of Notre Dame Latin Dictionary and Grammar Aid (n.d.), <www.archives.nd.edu/cgi-bin/lookup.pl?stem=num&ending=en> accessed November 13, 2011.

Watts, Alan (1975), *The Watercourse Way,* Pantheon: New York.

Weber, M. (1905/2002), *The Protestant Ethic and the Spirit of Capitalism,* Baehr, P. and Wells, G. C. (trans.), Penguin (Twentieth Century Classics): New York.

Wiens, D., Renfree, M. and Wooller, R. O. (1979), 'Pollen Loads of Honey Possums (Tarsipes Spenserae) and Nonflying Mammal Pollination in Southwestern Australia', *Annals of the Missouri Botanical Garden,* vol. 66, no. 4: pp. 830–8.

3

Making Sustainability Up: Design beyond Possibility

AIDAN DAVISON

DESIGN IN DANGER

The 'environmental crisis' is not fundamentally the result of some error in reasoning…It is a slow (sometimes not so slow) downward spiral, a reduction in fact as well as in thought, in which our ideas are as much influenced by the state of the world as vice versa, and—crucially—each stage is impeccably rational.

(Weston, 2009, p. 59)

This chapter is premised on the claim that design is endangered in modern societies by the flood of technological novelty, which many take to be evidence that design thrives. In the context of this handbook, this claim is important because the present malaise and future prospects of design are central to the quest for sustainability. Evidence of unsustainability, in the form of ecological and social damage done by ill-designed technological systems, abounds. The solution to such bad design, and therefore the path to sustainability, seems self-evidently to be good design.

However, this framing of design as both problem and solution in the quest for sustainability too often leaves conventional understandings of design untouched. In particular, the reduction of technologies to abstract ideas, a core characteristic of modern epistemology, has led many to locate the source of unsustainable design in bad ideas. Mechanism, anthropocentrism and consumerism are among numerous concepts proposed as the font of unsustainability. Correspondingly, the ideal of sustainability has accumulated a large stockpile of good ideas—redemptive abstractions in the form of world views, principles and values—with which to redirect design towards ecologically robust and socially just futures (Davison, 2001). Framed this way, sustainable design appears to lie in wilful adoption of holistic cosmology, eco-centric ethics and post-materialist desire. Vergragt exemplifies this logic in suggesting that 'technology in itself is not the main problem; the problem lies in values, lifestyles, and economic growth, and present technology is just an expression of these values. The question then … [is] how to achieve changes in lifestyles and values' (2011). The answer is simple, according to the Earth Charter, a prominent statement of moral principle for sustainability: humanity must 'choose its future', 'decide to live with a sense of universal responsibility' and 'commit' to a 'change of mind and heart' (Tucker, 2003, pp. 141–2).

In this way, design is reconceived as a process by which technological efficiency is uncoupled from an unsustainable industrial order and harnessed to an ethic of sustainability, yielding a reality made objectively sustainable. Such effort to redirect design reflects genuine intent to address the destruction that has underwritten modern technological creation. Yet the assumption that design is the servant of conscious intention is at issue here. This assumption has led many to disregard ways in which the modern project of technological progress was also endowed with good intentions, including, arguably, the ideal if not the terminology of sustainability. Equally, this assumption has promoted uncritical optimism that the congenital disabilities of modernity—its iniquity, myopia and profligacy—can be designed out by a combination of ethical aspiration and techno-scientific ingenuity.

The assumption that design involves rational transcription of intent to things is a key element of the instrumentalist philosophy of technology that pervades much in contemporary modern societies (Kaplan, 2009). Asserting the political and moral neutrality of artefacts, this philosophy represents technology as the material outworking of pure, theoretical reason. Design is left open to political and moral question within this philosophy only to the extent that value-laden intentions are thought to set bearings for the impartial and universal process of applying technical knowledge to objective matter.

Instrumentalist philosophy of technology provides the rationale for the now dominant quest for sustainability in modern societies—that of sustainable development (Davison, 2001; Paredis, 2011). The 1987 manifesto for sustainable development, the Brundtland Commission's *Our Common Future,* envisioned a 'reorientation of technology' based on 'better' scientific knowledge of nature (WCED, 1987, p. 60). Examples of technology for sustainability offered by the Commission included the following:

> Information technology based chiefly on advances in micro-electronics and computer science…Coupled with rapidly advancing means of communication, it can help improve the productivity, energy and resource efficiency, and organizational structure of industry…The products of genetic engineering could dramatically improve human and animal health…Advances in space technology…also hold promise for the Third World. (WCED, 1987, pp. 217–18)

The subsequent 1992 United Nations Conference on Environment and Development, the Earth Summit, failed in its mission to initiate meaningful political reform in the name of sustainable development, other than at the municipal level. In particular, it failed to build common ground between the environmental agendas of wealthy nations, which aligned issues of unsustainability and population growth, and the social justice agendas of poor nations, which aligned issues of sustainability and resource consumption (Davison, 2001). The resulting political impasse increased emphasis during the 1990s on technological solutions to unsustainability. This shifted the focus of action from governments to producers and consumers and promoted what Gregg Easterbrook (1995) called the 'new environmental optimism', which displaced countercultural suspicion of technology with enthusiasm for eco-efficiency as a way to 'increase wealth while reducing resource use' (von Weizsacker et al., 1997). Similarly, earlier environmentalist interest in eco-design as the basis for the politics of alternative technology (Madge, 1993) was appropriated as a way to 'make efficient use of natural resources' (Philips Electronics in Sherwin, 2004, p. 22). The capitalist dimension of this appropriation of eco-design as means to the end of eco-efficiency is evident in Ken Yeang and Lillian Woo's *Dictionary of Eco-Design,* which defines eco-design as 'decisions at each phase of the design process that will reduce negative impacts on the environment and the health of the occupants, without compromising the bottom line' (2010, p. 79).

On entry to this century, sustainable development had been established as the hegemonic expression of sustainability in the form of a quest for eco-efficiency through eco-design that has enticed radical environmentalists (e.g., Hawken et al., 1999) and corporations (e.g., de Simone and Popoff, 1997) alike. In this quest, concepts of development, efficiency and design are inherited from earlier instrumentalist accounts of social progress, while adjectives and prefixes indicate a guiding normative commitment to sustainability. In keeping with this inheritance, the possibilities of design are reduced to those of efficiency and given over to engineering professions and economic incentives (Buchanan, 1985). As a result, issues of design for sustainable development have receded from public debate into insular technical jargon. What remains prominent in the public realm are 'repeated rhetorical assertions of unqualified faith in all possible forms of scientific and technological activity' (Stirling, 2007, p. 288).

The political force of the instrumentalist quest for sustainable development stems not from any explicit political contract but from the central role of design for efficiency in scientific and capitalist institutions. It is not accidental that the neologism eco-efficiency was coined by the (World) Business Council for Sustainable Development (WBCSD), in 1991. As the former head of this organization explains:

> We were looking for a single concept, perhaps a single word, to sum up the business end of sustainable development. Finding no concept on the lexicographer's shelf, we decided we would have to launch an expression. After a contest and much agonizing, we came up with eco-efficiency. (Schmidheiny in WBCSD, 2000)

While it is fitting for a capitalist initiative to emerge as the winner of a contest, it is curious that much agonizing was required, given the firm bond between capital accumulation and technological efficiency. Even the eco-design agenda of dematerialization—the attempt to invert proportional relations between resource consumption and capital accumulation—is hardly new, as the futurist R. Buckminster Fuller observed in the

1930s in his formula: 'Efficiency = doing more with less ∴ EFFICIENCY EPHEMER-
ALIZES' (1938/1973, p. 259).

Corporate advocates see in the pursuit of eco-efficiency through eco-design an opportunity to accommodate ecological knowledge in the sphere of instrumental reason.
Radical environmentalist advocates subscribe to this pursuit, as Langdon Winner predicted they would, hoping it to be a Trojan horse: a way of smuggling a transformative
ethic of sustainability into modern institutions in the guise of rational design (1986).
Daniel Christian Wahl and Seaton Baxter give voice to this hope: 'Designers can help
to change culturally dominant worldviews and value systems. In helping to shape the
intentionality behind material design, designers can effect changes in life-styles and resource use that will drive the sustainability transition' (2008, p. 83). The risk here is not
simply that this hope may not be realized but that in the project of eco-design it may
indeed be environmentalism that is in danger of being a Trojan horse, freighting instrumentalist logic inside ethical abstractions.

DESIGN IN QUESTION

> Readers of poetry see the factory-village, and the railway, and fancy that the poetry
> of the landscape is broken up by these; for these works of art are not yet conse-
> crated in their readings; but the poet sees them fall within the great Order not less
> than the bee-hive, or the spider's geometrical web.
>
> *(Emerson, 1844)*

In providing a thumbnail sketch of the convergence of instrumentalism, capitalism and
environmentalism in the quest for sustainable development through design, the previous section left out much detail. One detail that needs to be added here is that modern
modes of design, including eco-design, are not straightforward expressions of instrumental reason and capital accumulation, and exist in no straightforward opposition
to environmentalism. Design has, in fact, acted as a bridge between techno-scientific
projects of rational order and projects of aesthetic, emotive and moral expression (Buchanan, 1985). As Tony Fry puts it in *Design as Politics,* modern design has contributed
to an 'aesthetic of concealment' that facilitates 'elegant' modes of destruction, enabling
beauty to mask horror, sentimentality to co-evolve with brutality (2011). Recognition
of design as an experiential bridge between apparently distinct realms of technological objectivity and lived subjectivity helps to make sense of the ambivalence (Bauman,
1991) and resulting irony (Latour, 1993) evident in the dynamics of modern progress.
It helps to make sense of the fact that the blueprints of universal and categorical reason
on which modern reality has been built seem ever less reliable in explaining this reality.

That the ironical collapse of logical order in societies apparently devoted to logical
order has not led to the demise of the project of progress is due, in part, to the capacity
of design practices to hold together in modern experience antithetical expressions of reasoning and feeling. Awareness of the function of design in integrating incommensurable
phenomena in the fabric of everyday experience offers insight into the way in which

instrumentalism and romanticism have long been in lockstep. For, contrary to appearances, the modern history of yearning for reunion with nature is not so much a reaction against a technological project of controlling nature as it is a constituent of it. To the process of design has fallen the task of ensuring that alienation from *nature as resource for production* advances alongside expressions of aesthetic fascination for *nature as remote perfection*. Although instrumentalist discourse offers up technology as pure means, the task of modern design has been to harness aesthetics as means to the end of efficiency. The dexterity with which graphic designers grace corporate narratives of sustainability in annual reports with space race photographs of Earth—icons born of the prospect of nuclear Armageddon that first gave environmentalist narratives of sustainability existential force—offers an obvious example.

As I have argued elsewhere (Davison, 2009), a less obvious but important example of designed ambivalence can be found in the history of the modern suburb. Understood as a landscape and cultural ideal through which to simultaneously claim and reject modern order, the suburb was, from the beginnings of the Industrial Revolution, a design solution to untenable contradictions generated between the political dictate of impartial reason and the partialities of personal experience. This is not to say that this solution was preconceived or explicit, or even that it was the achievement of those usually designated as designers. Rather, the suburban ideal emerged first as a practical logic in everyday life for making modernity liveable, later becoming the focus of explicit design agendas, such as the garden city movement (Fishman, 1987). This is a design solution whose ultimate function was to help establish, in material form and moral awareness, public and private realms in modern society that appear to be at least partly autonomous and in which can apply incommensurable forms of behaviour and conscience.

A key function of design in modern societies, then, has been to give expression to disquiet and dissent generated in the experience of technological progress, while deactivating this ambivalence as a potential source of political resistance and transformation. The result, so clearly analysed by Herbert Marcuse, is that romanticism and other apparent negations of instrumental reason have been vital to its status and longevity as an organizing principle of modern societies (1964).

The appropriation of environmentalism within the instrumentalist project of eco-design thus has considerable precedent. First broadcast by Ian McHarg, the ideal of designing with nature has inspired many environmentalists in modern societies (1969). In relation to this ideal, the central task of design for sustainability is conceived to be mimicry of an inherently self-sustaining order in nature (Benyus, 1997). However, the apparently radical pursuit of subordinating technology to ecology more often inverts rather than rejects the modernist project of subordinating ecology to technology, perpetuating the modern heritage of many environmental movements, particularly in Western societies.

Despite being represented as holistic, and despite asserting humanity's birthright as part of nature, many expressions of design with nature do not question the foundational modern ontology that locates rational order and subjective experience in different domains of human existence. In this way, the messy political history of modern design can be left aside, as the rational prescriptions of technology are swapped for the rational prescriptions of nature. Rather than challenging the instrumentalist assumption that design stands with science and technology beyond politics, the project of eco-design relies on technical knowledge of nature's objective sustainability to direct social change. Daniel Vallero and Chris Brasier's textbook, *Sustainable Design,* for example, begins with the claim: It is only through scientific, particularly thermodynamic, 'understanding of the natural world that new strategies can emerge to replace the entrenched design mind-sets that have relied on traditional schemes steeped in an exploitation of nature' (2008, p. 1). As implied in this definition, it is also assumed that knowledge of objective nature is guided by respect for nature and that the project of eco-design can thus give expression to subjective desire for reunion with nature. As Bruno Latour observes in *Politics of Nature,* the apolitical nature studied by scientists flips easily to become the apolitical nature venerated by environmentalists as a sacred Other, and vice versa (2004, p. 4).

In appropriating environmentalism, the engineering project of eco-design has embraced scientific nature as an apolitical reference point for sustainability. In the process, this project has had its normative aspirations affirmed through association with environmentalist veneration of nature. This appropriation is evident in the decline of once resonant mechanistic metaphors of nature and the proliferation of organic metaphors of technology in conventional design practices. Industrial ecology, product life cycle, cradle-to-cradle management and ecological footprint are among such metaphors traded in eco-design discourse (Hawken et al., 1999; Sherwin, 2004; Yeang and Woo, 2010). These metaphors give expression to now widespread hope that technological progress is growing ever more natural: that 'life is the ultimate technology ... [and that] as we improve our machines they will become more organic, more biological, more like life' (Kelly, 1994, p. 212). On the surface, this hoped for union of what modern ontology has divided promises a radical break with modern history; an overcoming of humanity's alien status in the world around them. However, this vision of subsuming technology in nature as an objective principle of evolution continues to rest on an ontology that splits politics and ethics, and the question of ontology itself, from objective reality, and thus from matters of technology and nature (Davison, 2008).

In critiquing the project of eco-design, I am not claiming it is corrupt or Machiavellian. Nor do I deny that it may achieve crucial advances in the dematerialization, decarbonization and detoxification of modern technology. And, in the context of the terminological complexity of discussion about design for sustainability (Sherwin, 2004), nor do I use the term 'eco-design' descriptively to encompass everything gathered under this label. My use is analytical, intended to mark out instrumentalist modes of design for sustainability. My claim is that, like the project of progress to which it belongs, the project of eco-design is a thoroughly ambivalent phenomenon.

I now shift from critique to building the case that the possibility of sustainability requires nothing less than the redesign of design; that, in fact, sustainability is the designed impossibility of the present. As Clive Dilnot has put it, 'Sustainability is that which most cruelly exposes design. Nothing reveals more sharply both the necessity and inconsequentiality of design; its (absolute) necessity as a capacity and its (almost complete) irrelevance as a value or indeed as a profession' (2011). In the face of the determinist optimism that drives the project of sustainable development, the claim that sustainability is presently impossible appears only to invite pessimism, if not nihilism. In rejecting this polarity as a false choice, I argue in the next section that the essential role of design is precisely that of enacting the impossible, of opening up new possibilities in human encounter with reality. This ontological account of design confounds conventional representations of design in two ways. First, the sphere of design widens beyond design professions to encompass the practice of everyday life. Second, focus moves to the dialectics of material and non-material expressions of design. This is to pay attention to non-material artefacts—institutional logic, syntax and ethical narrative, say—and, more fundamentally, to the co-production of thinking and things.

DESIGN IN ESSENCE

'We,' as agents and actors, make ourselves in the world that makes us and in so doing, contribute to the making of a world that makes others.

(Fry, 2011)

It is curious that the term 'make-believe' refers to acts of pretence, to fictitious realities, for humans have always lived in a factual state of make-believe. Humans have always inhabited a fabricated reality. The very ability of humans to inhabit reality—to bring into being a world in which reality is rendered intelligible and accommodating—arises out of an ability to make things up. A world is a horizon of practical-conceptual possibility established in an unbounded field of potentiality. Within these horizons, the achievement of knowing reality is inseparable from the achievement of technological creation. Contrary to the modern habit of assuming acts of reason to be primary to those of technology, every world—including that of Descartes—is born out of the interplay of making and believing.

Making and believing are bound to each other as both cause and effect. It is true that reason shapes technology, but no less true that technology shapes reason. Desire shapes habit, but no more than habit shapes desire. Moral awareness shapes behaviour, but no more than behaviour shapes moral awareness. The point is that the whirling dynamics of making and believing begin, and inseparably entangle matter and awareness, long before reasoned analysis is possible. The poet Mary Oliver casts the point well: 'Time must grow thick and merry with incident before thought can begin' (1998, p. 25).

The dynamics that give rise to any and every world of human practice involve acts of conception that create matter in the reflection of ideas and meaning in the reflection of things. This is not to say that this conception is immaculate: such worlds are not created out of a vacuum, nor created by humans alone. Acts of technological and cognitive fabrication are collaborations with the Earth. Given that Earth itself participates in a cosmic collaboration of immense temporal and spatial scale, acts of human creation draw upon and invite fields of agency that overwhelm human comprehension.

In contrast to today's prevalent talk of society as an entity carved out of nature, and of culture as a realm of meaning distinct from society as a realm of structure, a world here refers to a coherent whole constituted by social, cultural and natural phenomena. This coherence is not conferred by any external, universal logic but exists as an internal state of human experience. Worlds of practice exist as coherent realities for those who make them, which is to say, for those who believe in them. While whole, then, no world has universal reach: all worlds are held within the temporal and spatial horizons of human possibility. Over time and through space many worlds have been created. Much variety exists today. These worlds encompass diverse sociocultural histories; diverse ecologies; diverse collections of beings, things, events, aspirations and attitudes. This diversity bears witness to the importance of a unique convergence of human and other-than-human agency in fashioning human possibility and intent in any time and place.

While the forgoing explanation of human ontology is brief and bare (for elaboration and accounting of debts, see Davison, 2001, pp. 115–58), I intend it to be sufficient to the task of articulating the essential meaning and function of design as ontological inquiry. For design is at the centre of the dynamics of make-believe. Encompassing a remarkable variety of material activities, conceptual endeavours and moral impulses, design is, at root, the act of intervening in the interplay of making and believing so as to open new possibilities in both. As Robert Grudin notes in his study, *Design and Truth:*

> There is something primal and essential about the act of designing, as though, more than any other act, it brings us in touch with or own nature. Design is so fundamentally human that our species has been called Homo faber (man the maker), implying that no historical influence will ever alienate us from the meticulous process of refitting our world. Design is a primary medium of human liberty, too; we must either design our own lives or subject ourselves to the designs of others. (2010, p. 7)

To say that design is fundamentally human is to say that human nature is inescapably contingent and plastic. Humans help to make themselves up in any time and place out of an excess of possibilities that also exceed human agency. Design is, in effect, the process of creating conditions of necessity, conferring coherence on a world of practice. In Cameron Tonkinwise's words, design transforms 'a merely desirable possible' into a 'natural' order, 'a new way of existing with all the force of the inevitable' (2011). Its capacity to sustain political order through material order, its capacity to circumscribe the field of social possibility enables design to serve the status quo. Whether expressed in the stature of a temple or in the banality of an electrical socket, design practices have the power to habituate a state of affairs and a state of mind, to align a world and a world view. Yet the process of creating the conditions of necessity by definition includes the potential to challenge existing conditions of necessity, throwing into question the coherence of a world of practice. In this sense, 'design makes material efforts to counter necessity. This is why design is the ontological opposite of evolution: design is the choosing of what to make necessary; it exists to refuse the status quo' (Tonkinwise, 2011).

Design, then, is a paradox inherent in a world of human practice. It describes an entrenched field of human possibility, in the form of entrenched patterns of construction and conceptualization that reproduce each other. At the same time, design describes the potential to reach beyond this field—to enact the impossible, to bring the automatic into question. Design aligns material form with belief about what is possible, but it does so in ways that leave open the prospect of new alignments of making and belief. Explained this way, design is not reducible to human agency. It is a material and conceptual property of a world of practice and thereby belongs to complex configurations of human and more-than-human agency. To say that design is fundamentally human is not to assert that it is hermetically human: design is, indeed, fundamental to humanity's immersion in a transcendent reality. Any and every human possibility is shot through with more-than-human possibilities. Every world is actively reproduced through existing design, yet holds the seeds of other worlds that await germination in acts of design.

While this discussion has moved a long way from the eminently practical quest for eco-efficiency through eco-design—and calls upon an ontological imagination only weakly cultivated in scholarship about sustainability—I contend it has moved closer to the nub of the contemporary relationship of design and sustainability. In the final section, in the context of worlds in which sustainability is *designed impossibility*, I locate the origins of design for sustainability in a recovery of design as an everyday practice of ontological inquiry into worldly ambivalence. Perceiving these origins to lie in sustained encounter with modern ignorance about sustainability, my account does not include prescriptions or illustrations with which to guide such design. Yet it is in no way offered as a substitute for the vital work of those tackling design questions of exactly what, how and why to build in the name of sustainability. Inspired by this practical work, I similarly hope to inspire, to encourage fresh air to flow into the quest for sustainability by affirming that to build is to have the possibility of resetting the terms of human possibility as well as of reality.

DESIGN IN THE IMPOSSIBILITY OF SUSTAINABILITY

Design is an activity that precedes learning.

(Ehrenfeld, 2009, p. 73)

The quest for sustainable development presupposes a need for urgent technological innovation and that design in the name of efficiency is best placed to guide it. Technological change is advocated in everything from the sources of electricity to the relationship of buildings to the sun, from the means of human movement to the means of human nutrition. And change is needed. The overwhelming evidence of unsustainability makes this point, if no other, unequivocally. Yet, of course, the call for novelty is the hallmark of modern societies. They are steadfastly devoted to change and to technological change above all. 'We know time to be a hurricane', de Botton reminds us in *The Pleasures and Sorrows of Work*: 'Our buildings, our sense of style, our ideas, all of these will soon enough be anachronisms, and the machines in which we now take inordinate pride will seem no less bathetic than Yorick's skull' (2009, p. 320).

Modern worlds are predisposed to the politics of locating human wellbeing in an instrumentalist quest for efficiency. That is the essence of their design. This reduction of human flourishing to technique—with the fiction of separate realms of qualitative ends and objective means it makes real—is the essence of their unsustainability. It is also, ironically, the basis for the emerging project of eco-design. Despite ritual avowals of justice, care and respect as the basis of sustainability, faith in eco-design—environmentalist as much as capitalist—reproduces existing political or ethical possibilities as a matter of course. In accepting as given a reality made of autonomous moral ends and neutral technological means, the quest for sustainability moves with the grain of modern worlds.

Am I therefore proposing that a politically transformative project of design for sustainability should form around the goal of resisting technological progress? That the project of eco-efficiency through eco-design should be dismissed in favour of a return to pre-modern craft? That capitalism and modern science should be denounced and hope found in local moral economies and the wisdom of direct experience? That consumerism should be confronted with an agenda of sacrifice, of doing without rather than doing with? No. Not really. No, but, in some ways, yes. I honestly do not have categorical answers these questions, and in this admission of ambivalence I think a proposal does lie.

While I aspire to ways of living that seem presently impossible, I do not think the challenge of design for sustainability can be met through any rejection of the modern worlds that gives rise to this challenge. It can be met only as a provocation to scrutinize the design of these worlds in great detail with an eye to opportunities for their transformation. Rather than offering false hope of a retreat from the unsustainable order of the present, design in the name of sustainability is best directed to interventions that promise more intimate contact with this order, and particularly with the strangeness that lies beneath its familiar surfaces. In this spirit, I have argued that despite the obsession with reason that gave rise to it, the modern project of progress is inherently illogical, fundamentally mixed up, and that modern modes of design have been dedicated to suppressing this ambivalence, or at least to making it coherent in practice if not in theory—to making it liveable. The grain of modern worlds does not run straight or true. This then raises the question of what might result if conceptual and technological effort in the name of design for sustainability was directed to resisting this suppression of ambivalence—if, even, such design aimed at amplifying contradictions and ambiguity embedded within modern worlds of practice.

What might happen if design for sustainability aspired to make modern worlds less liveable? What if discomfit was planned? What might happen if the interdependence of mutually exclusive phenomena in modern experience was exaggerated, and not masked, by premeditated intent? I have argued that designed transformation of the material world promises no linear, reliable transcription of intent to reality. I can offer, therefore, no predetermined answer to these questions, beyond the obvious conclusion that, given the dominant role of design in cultivating coherence in the project of progress, the strategic cultivation of ambivalence through designed intent can be expected to produce confusion. But, in worlds in which the quest for categorical knowledge reigns, and in which nothing seems more certain than the technological trajectory of self-destruction, confusion may well be extremely productive.

Unlike instrumentalist optimism in a linear, planned and panoptic transition to sustainability, designs that disturb the liveability of modern worlds in an effort to expose the contradiction that undergirds them promise lessons in the knack, the experiential know-how, of living with ambivalence. As John Ehrenfeld explains, this knack will be vital in the experience of this transition, which is likely to span many human generations and which of necessity entails an ability to live with dissonant realities:

> Sustainability lives in a world distinct from the present: one with a new vocabulary and cultural habits. As we reach toward that new world, we remain enmeshed in our modern milieu with the vocabulary and stories that have served us so well for centuries. Until the new story replaces the old, we will have to...hold on to two opposing models of reality and beliefs about ourselves while we use our intelligence to design the new tools and institutions that sustainability requires. (2009, p. 215)

Inquiry into ambivalence through designed intervention into modern worlds of practice promises not simply productive confusion about the designed impossibility of sustainability, it promises also to unsettle understanding about the presently pervasive possibility of unsustainability. For, as a structural characteristic of modern worlds, unsustainability is no less mixed up, no less ambiguous, than any other constituent of the project of progress. Developing in concert with the technological ontology of a shrinking planet, consequent on the latest—electronic—phase of globalization, narratives of unsustainability have done much to cultivate awareness of Earth as small, fragile and endangered by human action. These narratives so diminish earthly agencies and possibilities that humanity emerges not only as Earth's nemesis, but also as its only hope of salvation (Clark, 2011). As the body of scientific knowledge about a dawning Anthropocene grows, is it as if human encounters with transcendent agency wither. As awareness grows of an ongoing industrial accident that is remaking the atmosphere, the new unpredictability of Earth processes seems to tell only of human folly and not of the dynamic web of more-than-human agency that has been called into play by technological invitation. The fabric of modern worlds places humanity at the centre of things, generating desire for the face of the Other. But in worlds whose horizons are valorized for their impermeability, this desire remains largely unfulfilled, growing stronger all the while. Enfolded in modern worlds whose design projects human agency to the edges of the universe, the blaring irony of injunctions to humanity to save Earth by rejecting anthropocentrism is hard to hear. This diminishment of earthly agency is not objective fact. It is a fact of design. It is, in fact, a design problem: a problem with the lived fabric of modern worlds and one amenable to redesign.

Counter to the present quest for the certainty of sustainability through the techno-logical pursuit of ontological security—through the built myth of future-proofing—design strategies that enact sustainability in the absence of certainty promise genuine inquiry into the modern human condition. These strategies encompass material inter-ventions that unsettle thinking, without embodying any clear theory of sustainability, and conceptual interventions that unsettle habits of production, without offering any clear practice of sustainability. While not promising to secure sustainability, such intervention promises insight into the make-believe footings of unsustainability in modern worlds.

Such acts of design for sustainability in the absence of certainty promise to intervene in the co-production of the human condition and modern reality, widening the hori-zons of possibility at the expense of reducing predictability. They promise, perhaps, ex-periences that puncture modern confidence in human importance, momentarily stilling the hurricane of modern time, exposing the self-propelling strain of modern urgency. They promise, perhaps, technologies that refuse to recede into an underworld of insular expertise, that demand patient coaxing, exposing the blithe dissatisfactions in acts of ef-ficient consumption. They promise, perhaps, deliberate encounters with the Earth that run according to no script, exposing wildness as an ineradicable possibility in modern order. More than anything else, these interventions promise worldly declarations of ig-norance, embodiments of raw yearning for the mystery of sustainability rather than the technological pretence of its achievement.

REFERENCES

Bauman, Z. (1991), *Modernity and Ambivalence,* Cornell University Press: Ithaca, NY.

Benyus, J. M. (1997), *Biomicry: Innovation Inspired by Nature,* Perennial: New York.

Buchanan, R. (1985), 'Declaration by Design: Rhetoric, Argument, and Demonstration in Design Practice', *Design Issues,* vol. 2, no. 1: pp. 4–22.

Clark, N. (2011), *Inhuman Nature: Sociable Life on a Dynamic Planet,* Sage: London.

Davison, A. (2001), *Technology and the Contested Meanings of Sustainability,* SUNY Press: Albany, NY.

Davison, A. (2008), 'Ruling the Future? Heretical Reflections on Technology and Other Secu-lar Religions of Sustainability', *Worldviews: Global Religions, Culture, and Ecology,* vol. 12, no. 2–3: pp. 146–62.

Davison, A. (2009), 'Living between Nature and Technology: The Suburban Constitution of Australian Environmentalism', in White, D. and Wilbert, C. (eds), *Technonatures: Environ-ments, Technologies, Spaces and Places in the Twenty-First Century,* Wilfrid Laurier University Press: Waterloo, ON. pp. 171–93.

de Botton, A. (2009), *The Pleasures and Sorrows of Work,* Pantheon Books: New York.

de Simone, L. D. and Popoff, F. (1997), *Eco-Efficiency: The Business Link to Sustainable Develop-ment,* MIT Press: Cambridge, MA; London.

Dilnot, C. (2011), 'Sustainability as a Project of History', *Design Philosophy Papers,* 2011/2, <www.desphilosophy.com> accessed October 7, 2011.

Easterbrook, G. (1995), *A Moment on the Earth: The Coming Age of Environmental Optimism*, Viking: New York.

Ehrenfeld, J. A. (2009), *Sustainability by Design*, Yale University Press: New York.

Emerson, R. W. (1844), 'The Poet', in *Essays by Ralph Waldo Emerson*, University of Adelaide: Adelaide.

Fishman, R. (1987), *Bourgeois Utopias: The Rise and Fall of Suburbia*, Basic Books: New York.

Fry, T. (2011), *Design as Politics*, Berg: Oxford, New York.

Fuller, R. B. (1938/1973), *Nine Chains to the Moon*, Jonathan Cape: London.

Grudin, R. (2010), *Design and Truth*, Yale University Press: New Haven, CT.

Hawken, P., Lovins, A. B. and Lovins, L. H. (1999), *Natural Capitalism: The Next Industrial Revolution*, Earthscan: London.

Kaplan, D. (ed.) (2009), *Readings in the Philosophy of Technology*, 2nd ed., Rowman & Littlefield: Lanham, MD.

Kelly, K. (1994), *Out of Control: The New Biology of Machines*, Fourth Estate: London.

Latour, B. (1993), *We Have Never Been Modern*, Porter, C. (trans.), Harvard University Press: Cambridge, MA.

Latour, B. (2004), *Politics of Nature: How to Bring the Sciences into Democracy*, Porter, C. (trans.), Harvard University Press: Cambridge, MA; London.

Madge, P. (1993), 'Design, Ecology, Technology: A Historiographical Review', *Journal of Design History*, vol. 6, no. 3: pp. 149–66.

Marcuse, H. (1964), *One Dimensional Man: Studies in the Ideology of Advanced Industrial Society*, Abacus: London.

McHarg, I. L. (1969), *Design with Nature*, Doubleday/Natural History Press: New York.

Oliver, M. (1998), 'Home', *Aperture*, no. 150, winter: pp. 22, 25.

Paredis, E. (2011), 'Sustainability Transitions and the Nature of Technology', *Foundations of Science*, vol. 16: pp. 195–225.

Sherwin, C. (2004), 'Design and Sustainability: A Discussion Paper Based on Personal Experience and Observations', *The Journal of Sustainable Product Design*, vol. 4: pp. 21–31.

Stirling, A. (2007), 'Deliberate Futures: Precaution and Progress in Social Choice of Sustainable Technology', *Sustainable Development*, vol. 15: pp. 286–95.

Tonkinwise, C. (2011), 'I Love Sustainability', *Design Philosophy Papers*, 2011/2, <www.desphilosophy.com> accessed October 7, 2011.

Tucker, M. E. (2003), *Worldly Wonder: Religions Enter Their Ecological Phase*, Open Court Press: Chicago, La Salle, IL.

Vallero, D. and Brasier, C. (2008), *Sustainable Design: The Science of Sustainability and Green Engineering*, John Wiley & Sons: Hoboken, NJ.

Vergragt, P. J. (2011), 'Beyond Politicization of Technology and Sustainability: A Plea for Visioning', in *Foundations of Science*, ed. Aerts, D. Springer Publishers: New York, published online September 13, 2011.

von Weizsacker, E., Lovins, A. B. and Lovins, H. L. (1997), *Factor Four: Doubling Wealth-Halving Resource Use*, Allen & Unwin: Sydney.

Wahl, D. C. and Baxter, S. (2008), 'The Designer's Role in Facilitating Sustainable Solutions', *Design Issues*, vol. 24, no. 2: pp. 72–83.

Weston, A. (2009), *The Incompleat Eco-Philosopher: Essays from the Edges of Environmental Ethics*, SUNY Press: Albany, NY.

Winner, L. (1986), *The Whale and the Reactor: A Search for Limits in an Age of High Technology*, University of Chicago Press: Chicago.

WBCSD (World Business Council for Sustainable Development) (2000), *Eco-Efficiency: Creating More Value with Less Impact*, <www.wbcsd.org/web/publications/eco_efficiency_creating_more_value.pdf> accessed September 3, 2009.

WCED (1987), *Our Common Future. The Report of the World Commission on Environment and Development*, Oxford University Press: Oxford.

Yeang, K. and Woo, L. (2010), *Dictionary of Eco-Design: An Illustrated Reference*, Routledge: London.

4

Developing Theories for Sustainable Design

DENNIS P. DOORDAN

INTRODUCTION

Calculate, conserve, compensate; reduce, reuse, recycle; environment, economy, people: these are some of the now familiar mantras of sustainable design. They are the pithy distillations of efforts to rethink the terms of design practice in light of contemporary environmental concerns. The quest for design practices and products that satisfy needs and sustain culture is not new. In his first-century B.C.E. treatise *De Architettura,* the Roman architect Vitruvius advises architects to select sites for new towns that will ensure the healthfulness of the future city. He wrote, "I cannot too strongly insist upon the need to return to the method of old times" (1914, p. 20). He went on to argue that new towns should be sited near dependable supplies of fresh water and fertile land able to support the needs of the community. In the design of houses, Vitruvius maintained, architects should take into consideration location and climatic factors such as prevailing winds, solar orientation, and seasonal variations. In this, one of the earliest surviving articulations of what I will label the good-sense wisdom tradition in the planning of human settlements, the architect is an astute observer of locale and as knowledgeable about topography and climate as he is about geometry and proportion. Two thousand years later, in *Operating Manual for Space-ship Earth,* Buckminster Fuller offered a strikingly different description of the skill set required by a designer: "We will now tackle our present world problems with a family of powerful thought tools: topology, geodesics, synergetics, general systems theory, and the computer's operational *bitting*" (1969, p. 83). Today the challenge of developing a theory—or perhaps more usefully a constellation of theories—capable of stimulating and supporting sustainable design requires working across a spectrum that includes, on one hand, advice to heed the codified wisdom of past experience and, on the other, dramatic calls to reconceptualize the skill sets, knowledge bases, and professional identities of designers.

SUSTAINABILITY

The challenge begins with the naming of the goal: sustainability. The same word means different things to different people. Integrating concerns for environmental health, economic viability, and human wellbeing remains central to any attempt to identify what is implied in the concept of sustainability. It is enough to acknowledge this diversity as a way to prepare the reader for the different perspectives brought together in this chapter. Sustainability, as used here, is based on the definition offered in *Our Common Future,* the report of the World Commission on Environment and Development (WCED) published in 1987 and commonly referred to as the Brundtland Report (after the Commission's Chairperson Gro Brundtland): "Sustainable development is development that meets the needs of the present without compromising the ability of future generations to meet their needs" (WCED, 1987, p. 8). But for some commentators, this does not go far enough in suggesting the nature of the problem or the scope of the change in thought and practice required. It is no longer a matter of modifying production techniques, reducing consumption, and adopting less wasteful practices; the practices of production and consumption, along with the pattern of human settlement characteristic of the modern era, have irrevocably altered planetary conditions. "We simply can't live on the new earth as if it was the old earth—we've foreclosed that option," warns Bill McKibben (2010a, p. 61). From this perspective, the market-driven model of economic growth that fueled industrialization and urbanization since the late eighteenth century is bankrupt, and to the degree to which design thinking is embedded in such a model, it too is bankrupt. This critique of design for its complicity in despoiling the environment and promoting mindless consumption is not new; Victor Papanek (1971) took the design community to task for its role over forty years ago in *Design for the Real World.* In light of current environmental conditions, however, it has acquired a new sense of urgency.

Design is the process through which abstract ideas become concrete realities. If, as seems increasingly and unavoidably apparent, the status quo is no longer viable and a new more sustainable reality must be achieved, then what are the obstacles to promoting a pervasive and effective culture of sustainability? What must an authentic culture of sustainability address?

- Economic models that fail to account for environmental and societal costs of patterns of production and consumption and fail to adequately incentivize change.
- Knowledge bases that provide various constituencies—users, designers, educators, and so on—with the type of useful and usable information required to act in a purposeful and consistent manner.
- Political theories and policy guidelines that address questions regarding the degree of coercion acceptable in efforts to modify or replace existing patterns.

- A shared ethical framework for understanding the nature of humankind's obligations to the planet and to each other along with the implications of action and evaluating choices.
- A concept of wellbeing capable of informing philosophical and spiritual reflection on values and needs.

It is the nature of sustainability to escape easy definitions and definitive summations, and any list such as this could be extended. For our purpose here, it serves as a provocation and suggests the rudiments of a research agenda capable of stimulating work across a spectrum of issues and practices.

DESIGN THEORY

If naming the goal of sustainability is one challenge, arriving at an understanding of what is entailed in developing a theory of sustainable design is a second and equally weighty concern. What is theory? How does theory contribute to design? How does a theoretical framework or understanding connect knowledge (in its various forms) with action (in its various manifestations)? For the purposes of this essay, two different approaches to the task of theory building are employed. In one model, theory is the distillation of existing knowledge and experience in a particular subject area. "In its most basic form, a theory is a model. It is an illustration describing how something works by showing its elements in their dynamic relationship to one another" (Friedman, 2003, p. 512). Rooted in the natural and social sciences, theory-as-model seeks to construct sets of propositions that describe and predict performance or behavior. This concept of theory works well for design efforts intended to ameliorate the negative impacts of current practices and to develop new tools and strategies to facilitate desirable changes in existing systems. In the context of the discussion developed here regarding sustainability, this type of theoretical activity is increasingly focused on modeling the flow of energy and matter through various environmental systems.

If, however, the premise driving theory formation is that the existing systems are so thoroughly corrupted as to be constituent elements of the problem itself and thus beyond redemption through refinement, then a different model is required. An alternate approach conceptualizes theory as disciplined imagination that works through a process involving the development and evaluation of multiple possibilities simultaneously in an effort to make sense out of the observable world.

Theorists often write trivial theories because their process of theory construction is hemmed in by methodological strictures that favor validation rather than usefulness. These strictures weaken theorizing because they de-emphasize the contribution that imagination, representation, and selection make to the process, and they diminish the importance of alternative theorizing activities such as mapping, conceptual development, and speculative thought. (Weick, 1989, p. 516)

In this understanding, describing the status quo is linked to speculative exercises that explore ways to understand and align human values, environmental facts, and societal options, and thus promote sustainability. Effectively imagining a sustainable world (i.e., achieving sustainment) calls upon the skills of observation, transformation, and representation typically associated with design thinking. Imagination, what Richard Sennett describes as "the sense that what isn't yet could be" (2008, p. 209), will be a valuable part of theory building for sustainable design.

Theory as explanatory model and theory as disciplined imagination call for different forms of preparation and suggest different courses of action. Hence this discussion of design theory as it relates to a concern for realizing a robust comprehensive culture of sustainability will pursue multiple paths. One path takes as its point of departure the world as it is, focuses on the existing techno-sphere (i.e., the human-made world that coexists with and within the biosphere), and seeks to promote design interventions that enhance the performance of existing systems. A second path imagines a fundamentally different way of living on what McKibben calls this "new earth." It seeks to involve different stakeholders in concerted efforts to imagine an economically viable, culturally vibrant, and deeply satisfying culture not just capable of but committed to sustainable lifestyles.

SCIENCE AND THE MODEL OF PLANETARY BOUNDARIES

In her 1962 landmark study of the threat posed by the careless use of pesticides, *Silent Spring*, Rachel Carson warned, "There is still very limited awareness of the nature of the threat. This is an era of specialists, each of whom sees his own problem and is unaware of or intolerant of the larger frame into which it fits" (1962, p. 13). Much has changed since Carson published *Silent Spring*, and today environmental issues command the attention of policy makers, regulators, business people, educators, and concerned citizens groups around the globe. Whether the interest is motivated by a growing concern for adverse environmental impacts associated with climate change or by equally pressing geopolitical concerns regarding the sourcing and risks associated with different forms of energy, sustainable design practices are increasingly seen as critical for the better management of planetary (biological) and global (socioeconomic) systems.

Carson took specialists to task for their lack of interest in what she called "the larger frames" into which environmental issues fit. Today the science needed to support thinking about environmental conditions and sustainable design is far more robust, and scientists are able to provide the larger frameworks Carson advocated. Scientists are now able to identify, measure, and model the behavior of environmental systems with growing sophistication and to offer the results of their research in ways that can inform action in other, nonscientific arenas. One example is the important set of articles published in 2009 by a team of specialists led by Swedish environmental scientist Johan Rockström that introduced the concept of planetary boundaries. This framework identifies thresholds for nine critical biophysical subsystems or processes including climate change, rate of biodiversity loss, interference with the nitrogen and phosphorus cycles, ozone depletion, ocean acidification, freshwater and land use patterns, atmospheric aerosol loading, and chemical pollution (2009a; 2009b).

> The approach rests on three branches of scientific enquiry. The first addresses the scale of human action in relation to the capacity of Earth to sustain it...The second is the work on understanding essential Earth processes including human actions...The third field of enquiry is research into resilience and its links to complex dynamics and self-regulation of living systems, emphasizing thresholds and shifts between states. (Rockström, 2009b, pp. 474–5)

The concept of planetary boundaries and of the Earth as a series of biophysical sub-systems and processes inextricably linked is relevant for efforts to develop models of sustainable design. The proposed framework clarifies the nature of the problems to be addressed, identifies the most pressing causes for concern, and points to some of the most fruitful areas for design intervention. Of interest here are the implications of this kind of scientific understanding of the earth for what Buckminster Fuller labeled the "thought tools" available for designers. Or, to put it another way, if the goal of theorizing is to provide a model of how things work, then how can design be modeled to address the imperative of promoting sustainability?

LIFE CYCLE ANALYSIS

As one moves from the domain of science to that of design, the process known as Life Cycle Analysis (LCA) provides an important tool for designers. The term "life cycle" refers to the stages of an artifact's life span from its initial conceptualization through manufacture, use, maintenance, and eventual final disposal, including the raw material acquisition required to fabricate it (Chick and Micklethwaite, 2011, p. 108). LCA is a system for identifying, quantifying, and evaluating inputs (including both material and energy inputs) in a product's life span. It represents a cradle-to-grave approach, which begins with the acquisition of raw materials from the Earth and ends with the product's final disposal and the return of these materials to the Earth. LCA provides a provocative counter-model to the economic and legal understanding of designed artifacts as property. Rather than calculate cash flows and apportion legal responsibilities, LCA tracks the energy expended and mass consumed in products.

LCA and the premise that the laws of thermodynamics can be applied to economic analyses of production and consumption processes is not without its flaws. Critics point to problems with calculations based on faulty or inadequate data sets and the use of non-comparable units of measurement (Ayres, 2004). Measuring costs, benefits, and impacts remains the fundamental challenge in any approach to providing a *quantitative* basis for sustainable design efforts. In recent years, a number of alternative frameworks for modeling sustainability have emerged: Natural Capitalism, Social Return on Investment, the Natural Step, and the Sustainability Helix. In *Design is the Problem: The Future of Design*

Must Be Sustainable, Nathan Shedroff provides a useful review of such systems-level perspectives. But Shedroff warns his readers:

> The reality of most sustainability measuring is that there is no perfect score. At best, there are "better" and "worse"—and these aren't often clear. Complex systems, by definition, connect to many issues and often create surprising interactions and conclusions and even unintended consequences... So, as designer, if you are looking for a cookbook to tell you how or what to design, I'm sorry that there is none. (2009, p. 41)

DESIGN IN THE TECHNO-SPHERE

As happens so often in the literature on sustainability, what is a virtue in one system can be considered a vice in another. LCA tends to promote a more efficient use of materials, but efficiency is recognized and measured in terms of the larger systems of production and consumption to which it contributes. At the end of a cradle-to-grave analysis is still a grave, and, for many people, being more efficient—that is, less bad—is not good enough. In contrast to the cradle-to-grave approach, a cradle-to-cradle approach extends thinking about the true life cycle of a product beyond the grave. It is premised on the notion that side by side with the biosphere exists a techno-sphere that operates according to its own technical metabolism.

> There are two discrete metabolisms on the planet. The first is the biological metabolism, or biosphere—the cycles of nature. The second is the technical metabolism—the cycles of industry, including the harvesting of technical materials from natural places. With the right design, all of the products and materials manufactured by industry will safely feed these two metabolisms, providing nourishment for something new. (McDonough and Braungart, 2002, p. 104)

Treating designed artifacts as the nutrients of an industrial metabolism opens up new thought horizons. Designers now need to be "nutrient managers" (Daniels and Hamman, 2009, p. 13), seeking to configure products in ways that insure that the end of one life cycle leads to a new cycle and that whatever technical nutrients feed the first cycle either make the transition to a new cycle or exit the techno-sphere and return harmlessly to the biosphere. Recasting designers as nutrient managers contributing to the regulation of the planet's technical metabolism has broad implications for the way we need to think about other parts of the sustainable design puzzle.

What is a designed artifact—a chair, an appliance, a building—in the techno-sphere? Ultimately, it is always part of a system interacting with other features of the techno-sphere. In terms of sustainable design, understanding designed artifacts primarily in terms of their formal properties (shape, color, texture, etc.) and symbolic meanings is insufficient because it misses important dimensions of the way their existence ripples through the planetary systems that sustain life. Instead, promoting sustainability in the techno-sphere involves understanding artifacts "from the point of view of linked material and energy pathways" (Fernandez, 2006, p. 301). Designing with systems, flows, and pathways (and not just markets) in mind undermines the notion of an artifact as a discrete thing. Everything is part of something larger and modeling this something is central to efforts to develop sustainable design theory.

THE ORIGINAL GREEN

In 1926, Walter Gropius described the classrooms at the Bauhaus as "laboratories" (Conrads, 1971, p. 96), and the Bauhaus model proved enormously influential in the evolution of modern design theory. Experimentation and technological innovation replaced emulation of precedents and respect for local tradition as the values and working methods of progressive designers. The knowledge base required for design practice and the curricular models for design education were adjusted accordingly. Certainly in the industrialized world and increasingly across the entire globe, we inhabit the results of this adjustment. In recent years there has been a revival of interest in what was lost or abandoned along the way. The name coined to describe this new interest in old thinking is The Original Green.

> The Original Green is the sustainability all our ancestors knew by heart. Originally (before the Thermostat Age) they had no choice but to build green, otherwise people would not survive very long. The Original Green aggregates and distributes the wisdom of sustainability through the operating system of living traditions, because that which can reproduce and live sustainably is green; that which is incapable of doing so is not green. (Mouzon, 2010, p. 1)

In this view, wisdom derived from experience is increasingly important as a source of tried-and-true strategies for designing and maintaining sustainable lifestyles. Proponents of the good-sense approach draw upon two main sources for guidance. The first is a literary tradition that includes architectural treatises, builders' manuals, and craftsmen's handbooks. Knowledge here is explicit and accessible in the form of texts. As such, it transcends the circumstantial and local conditions out of which it emerged to form part of a general cultural patrimony accessible and applicable in diverse settings. The second is often tacit and exists in the form of vernacular typologies, local customs, and the craftsperson's knowledge of materials and techniques. This practical knowledge is often positioned within cultural belief systems that identify local practices as constituent elements in a shared mythos or cosmic order that sustains the society spiritually as well as materially. In more strictly rational rather than mythic terms, however, the tacit knowledge embedded in tools, techniques, and vernacular typologies is truly *local knowledge* subject to the limitations of local conditions. Knowing how to live in a hot, arid climate, for example, is of relatively little value to those who inhabit cooler, moist regions.

It is easy to romanticize the good sense of our ancestors, and there is ample evidence that past cultures used and abused their environments to the point of local collapse, as illustrated in the fate of the Mayan civilizations in pre-Columbian Mesoamerica (Yaeger and Hodell, 2009). Nonetheless, premodern wisdom constitutes a rich repository of know-how that can inform contemporary sustainable design practices if the tacit knowledge embedded in things can be extracted and expressed in ways that make it accessible to others. This is a big if, but theory construction demands a degree of explicitness that practice often does without. Traditional practices tend to be specific to a locale; they are seldom available in the kind of quantifiable values that allow abstracting and integrating with newer modes of thinking or scales of operations. And they often form part of cultural frameworks that conflate wisdom with prejudice, understanding with superstition, and fact with fable, thus deflating romanticized or nostalgic idealizations of premodern conditions. Recovering the good sense of traditional knowledge will involve more than simply reviving past practices. Potentially it requires that we reflect seriously on the relationship between the physical (practical knowledge) and the metaphysical.

SUSTAINABILITY IS A HUMAN PROBLEM

The willingness of the advocates for the good sense of traditional practices to look outside of the domains of modern science and economics for guidance opens up the issue of alternate ways to conceptualize the challenge of theorizing sustainable design. Driving efforts to imagine alternate approaches to sustainability is the conviction that refining existing practices in order to achieve greater efficiencies in managing the use of materials and energy will only extend the lifetime of technological systems and social patterns that are truly damaging to planetary wellbeing. In his book *Sustainability by Design,* John Ehrenfeld confronts this issue head on:

> Sustainability has been seen primarily as an environmental problem and only secondarily as a social problem. I believe that this is backward. Sustainability is first a human problem and then an environmental problem. If we fail to address the unsustainability of the modern human being, we will not be able to come to grips with other aspects of sustainability. (2008, p. 97)

Society, according to Ehrenfeld, is addicted to behaviors that are self-destructive. Too often the things we surround ourselves with, he argues, actually distract us from genuine self-realization. He believes design can promote an authentic and rich engagement with our surroundings and prompt us to be more mindful about our places, our actions, and our dreams.

Design shapes experience and Ehrenfeld uses the term "presencing" to identify the kind of experience he believes is needed. "Presencing is an experience in which an awareness of the worldly context of the action shows itself to the actor" (2008, p. 153).

In this way of thinking, unsustainability is the outcome of addictive behavior and mindless consumption; awareness, on the other hand, is the beginning of a process of questioning, reflecting, and (hopefully) acting responsibly. "Choice is the critical aspect of the [presencing] moment; by making a conscious, reflexive choice, the actor owns the world and all of its contextual elements: concerns, identity, place, and equipment. The action is authentic" (2008, p. 153).

It is important to note here that Ehrenfeld is not a design determinist. This line of reasoning does not lead to the idea that designers can imagine artifacts that will change the course of planetary history by magically weaning us of our bad habits. We may dream about such a scenario, but as Bill McKibben warns: "Get real. Most of us raised in the last fifty years are novelty junkies. A slower life, one not fixed on growth and change and speed but on a more plodding stability and security, will take a few generations to feel entirely comfortable" (2010b, p. 195). Ehrenfeld acknowledges that truly meaningful and authentic action is not inevitable and, despite the best of intentions, cannot be programmed through design. But he does outline a way to understand design and human behavior in terms of the decisions people make about consumption and to think about design strategies that at least open up genuine alternatives.

Presencing is one of a constellation of terms that have emerged in recent years—focal experience, caring, flourishing, and sustainment are others—to describe ways of conceptualizing a goal for design action that supports a broad movement toward sustainability. The term "wellbeing" is used here as an umbrella term for efforts to describe an informed and empowering sense of awareness recognizable at both a communal and a deeply personal level of consciousness. This is a vocabulary that explicitly resists the positivist approach characteristic of science and technology in the modern era. Whatever nuances different terms seek to capture, understood in broad strokes, planetary wellbeing is a fundamentally different, more philosophical goal than systems efficiency. Wellbeing cannot be modeled and measured (and thereby managed) in the same ways as the flow of matter and energy through the techno-sphere. But artifacts can be conceived in ways that promote wellbeing.

DESIGN AND SPIRITUALITY

Wellbeing and the kind of critical awareness Ehrenfeld calls for in his use of the term "presencing" posit a human condition of deep harmony with the natural world and a reconciliation of culture and nature. Whether one idealizes the premodern past as reflecting such a condition and seeks its return or works toward it as a future and novel state of being, its absence in the modern world is a given in discussions. The negative side of the modern experience is described not just in terms of degradation of biophysical systems that sustain life on the planet but also in terms of humankind's growing estrangement from nature. Our apparent ability to command the physical world grew while our appreciation for the metaphysical dimension of existence withered.

That there is a spiritual dimension to the problem of sustainability rooted in humankind's efforts to dominate the elements of nature rather than participate in its rhythms and cycles has long been a theme in the literature on this topic (Gore, 1993; White, 1967). Reviewing the contributions of philosophers and critics of technology including, among others, Martin Heidegger, Alfred North Whitehead, Jacques Ellul, and Carolyn Merchant, the environmentalist David Orr pointed out: "With varying emphases, all argue that modern science has fundamentally misconceived the world by fragmenting reality, separating observer from observed, portraying the world as a mechanism, and dismissing non-objective factors... The result is a radical miscarriage of human purposes and a distortion of reality under the guise of objectivity" (1992, p. 12). Orr's work has been widely read, and he has made a fundamental contribution to discussions of this theme.

As with so many other aspects of the discussion of environmentalism and sustainability, the question arises, what is the place of design within this discourse? In the modern era, it must be acknowledged that the theme of spirituality (as opposed, for example, to the definition of building typologies or efforts to optimize production practices) has occupied a marginal position with design discourse. This pattern is now changing and the exchange between philosophers and theologians on the one hand and designers on the other is enriching our understanding of how the environmental, social, and personal dimensions of existence are intertwined (Walker, 2011). Organized religions have turned consistently to architects, artists, and designers to satisfy ecclesiastical needs. But building a church or temple is not by itself necessarily a meritorious act or valuable contribution to the goal of achieving a rich culture of sustainability. A building that is poorly sited, badly constructed, and inefficient in its use of resources cannot be redeemed by the purest of intentions. Nor should the potential for design be limited to a narrowly prescribed set of liturgical design problems. In *Eco-Theology*, written from a specifically Christian perspective that speaks of a divinely generated creation, the eco-theologian Celia Deane-Drummond provides a useful overview of the field of religious environmentalism. In her postscript, "Towards a Theological Eco-Praxis," she calls for ways of living and structuring existence that would give the sacred a "special place in the stream of events" (2008, pp. 179–85). Such a transformative eco-praxis would, she writes, seek to

- acknowledge the spiritual dimension of life and the contribution of human sinfulness to the degradation of creation;
- move away from patterns of behavior that contribute to the loss of biodiversity and instead promote environmental health;
- celebrate the presence of divine in the midst of creation; and
- cultivate a profound sense of wonder and humility in light of the awe-inspiring complexity of the cosmos.

What, in the context of this essay, is striking about Deane-Drummond's call to know, to praise, and to live in certain ways is the opening it creates for design. These goals are laudable, but in order to be meaningful—that is, to realize an impact in the world—they must be *enacted*. Design is the vehicle through which abstract ideals become concrete realities. Design can reveal how things are what they are, develop alternatives to the way things are, and give form and scripts to rituals of celebration (both grand and humble, communal and personal).

DESIGN AND LANGUAGE

One of the salient features of contemporary thought is the importance attached to the critical analysis of language in efforts to understand the structure of belief systems and patterns of behavior. In this context, critical analysis reveals how language—and through language, discourse in any particular field—shapes and is shaped by cultural assumptions about the way the world is and value systems regarding how the world ought to be. Theorists have examined the role of language in establishing what passes for natural (and hence often unexamined) across a wide array of fields including feminism, colonial and postcolonial studies, and literary criticism. Design is no exception. If, as Ehrenfeld argues, sustainability is a social problem before it is an environmental one, then we must recognize language as a crucial factor in shaping discussions of the social dimension of sustainability. What do words like need or desire or freedom mean, and how do they shape our thinking about the way we live now and wish to in the future? What, for example does the word "freedom" identify? Does it describe a release from onerous restraints and the ability to pursue individual concerns? Or does freedom name the self-awareness that comes when we are freed from distractions that blind us to the truth of existence and accept our obligations to others and to caring for those things such as natural environments and human communities upon which we depend? Design theorist Tony Fry approaches the task of changing how we live by examining and then reimagining the words we use to speak about the world, beginning with the word "design." For Fry, design in the modern era is inextricably linked to the economic and technological worldviews that constitute the status quo and is incapable of doing anything beyond reproducing the situation of which it finds itself to be part. In a provocative move, he renames design "defuturing," a word that ignores the historical intent of the concept—that is, to project or prefigure a future—and instead, according to Fry, identifies its actual impact—that is, to eliminate a viable future through facilitating unsustainable practices that cast a toxic shadow over the future (2011). The examination of language is fertile territory for theory building as it pertains to sustainability.

TRANSITION

In this chapter, the initial effort to describe a theory of sustainable design began with a discussion of efforts to understand planetary systems and develop models to promote more efficient management of material and energy pathways through the environment. This approach is grounded in the rational empirical worldview and the sophisticated analytical tools of modern science and technology. This was followed by a discussion of foundational critiques of the status quo and efforts to reimagine the contribution design and designers could make to the nurturing of sustainable communities. It would be easy to see the progression in this discussion as a rejection of the techno-scientific approach. This would, however, be a misreading of my intention. The future will be a complex amalgam of multiple models and strategies, and what is too often insufficient or missing altogether in the foundational critique is attention to what can be labeled transition theory: how do we get from where we are now to where we need to be?

When it comes to design solutions to this question, there is no shortage of recommendations. Library bookshelves are sagging under the growing number of new titles reporting on exemplary design efforts or describing design strategies to achieve a more wholesome and sustainable future (Chick and Micklethwaite, 2011; Fuad-Luke, 2009; Shedroff, 2009; Williams, 2007). But it is easy to become discouraged or disoriented as one tries to come to terms with the sheer profusion of potential directions. The design of dense new eco-cities in Asia is, after all, a profoundly different enterprise than developing a supply network to support a locally sourced fresh food movement. And there are those who point out that efficiency in one area does not translate into improvements in others because sectorial advances often fail to address systemic problems. For example, efforts to reduce the carbon footprint of different transportation technologies can appear misguided when unintended consequences are taken into account. The benefits gained from improved automotive design and better fuel economy begin to lose some of their appeal when measured against the potential of such improvements to promote settlement patterns such as suburban sprawl that consume land and other resources at what are ultimately unsustainable rates of consumption (Christie, 2002, p. 1466). The emergence of sustainable transition theory in recent years holds the promise of providing a framework for understanding how—to cite an old adage of environmentalism—to think globally and act locally. Just as important for the purposes of this chapter, it suggests an important role for the design community in facilitating the transition.

Transition theory draws upon concepts and models of human behavior, social structures, and technological systems that span diverse disciplines and areas of study, including sociology, management, science, technology, social studies, and philosophy. It is rooted in a recognition of the significance of systems and an appreciation for the ability of systems thinking to conceptualize and model complex patterns of behavior. Systems thinking is not, however, simply the latest attempt by scientists to manage complex networks of biophysical interactions in the environment through a reductive process of quantification and ranking; it is not about optimization and control. Instead, as environmentalist and systems theorist Donella Meadows has argued, system thinking offers people ways to think about unpredictability and design.

> The future can't be predicted, but it can be envisioned and brought lovingly into being. Systems can't be controlled, but they can be designed and redesigned. We can't surge forward with certainty into a world of no surprises, but we can expect surprises and learn from them and even profit from them. We can't impose our will on a system. We can listen to what the system tells us, and discover how its properties and our values can work together to bring forth something much better than could ever be produced by our will alone. (2008, pp. 169–70)

In this way of thinking about systems, design still has an important role, but it is design now tempered by humility rather than driven by hubris.

Transition theory is informed by the principles and values central to the kind of systems thinking Meadows describes: listening attentively, accepting complexity, working cooperatively, envisioning desirable outcomes. Transition theory itself is based on four key concepts (Grin et al., 2010; Geels, 2005).

- Coevolution: the interaction between societal subsystems that influences individual subsystems in mutually reinforcing ways leading to irreversible change.
- Multilevel perspective: transition unfolds at three different levels of scale ranging from the local through the national to the global.

- Multiphase perspective: the temporal dimension of transition involves four phases: predevelopment, take-off, acceleration, and stabilization.
- Codesign and learning: the knowledge needed to drive sustainability is developed and shared through an interactive exchange among a range of stakeholders. Knowledge in this context is not just the knowledge of things and how they work but of people and how they understand reality.

Within this framework, change is conceptualized not as a simple linear sequence of cause and effect but as a more open-ended process in which different processes such as experimentation, mutual learning, community building, and structural change reinforce each other over time. In the case of the quest for greater fuel economy cited above, settlement patterns are not narrowly bound to automotive performance but driven by a diverse set of regulatory, economic, and social factors. Transportation systems and settlement patterns will coevolve although not necessarily in a simple or linear relationship. Therefore, designs to promote greater efficiency and address immediate problems associated with transgressing the planetary boundaries identified by science are not in-compatible with efforts to promote fundamental changes in how human and planetary wellbeing are understood.

Thinking about transition this way is appealing for several reasons. It recognizes the fallacy of the silver bullet—that is, the dream of a singular solution that can leverage complex systems. It offers a way to conceptualize socio-technical change that can accommodate multiple perspectives. It aims to be participatory and draw contributors from across the social spectrum and emphasizes the processes of knowledge creation and sharing. It values small-scale niche experiments while recognizing the need for major structural changes and suggests how one scale of effort relates to another (Olsthoorn and Wieczorek, 2006, p. 217). But thinking about transition this way is not without its critics. Mutual learning, codesign, coevolution as the way forward evokes the liberal ideal of social-democratic electoral politics and benign cultural pluralism. The nature of the crisis, according to some, demands action at a pace and cost incompatible with the existing ways of reasoning and acting. "Again we say: democracy cannot deliver Sustainment...Sustainment is an overarching political imperative—to which all other issues are subordinate (for without Sustainment we have nothing)—means that politics as we know and encounter it (including the politics and practices of sustainability) has to be superseded or totally transformed" (Fry, 2011, p. 131). Resolving the tensions between calls for action based on a sense of urgency and appeals to democratic and pluralist values is clearly one of the crucial challenges for achieving true sustainability in the coming decade. This is a challenge that transcends the boundaries of disciplines and professions and stands as a fundamental question confronting societies around the globe.

What are the implications of transition theory for the design community? Where or how do designers take their place in the ongoing processes outlined in the literature on transitioning? Ultimately it is not about the design of new greener products or services (although such traditional design activities are important) but about facilitating a culture of transformation. Transition theory's emphasis on the coevolution of systems, shared learning among diverse stakeholders in those systems, and participatory design efforts is the antithesis of top-down, control and command systems of planning. Transition theory opens up a conceptual space, based in great part on systems theory, in which it is possible to promote the alignment of values, different kinds of knowledge, resources, and people in ways and forms that advance the goal of sustainability.

> Clearly, this is not dependent solely on a solitary designer who skillfully puts together technical elements in a given design. It involves, in addition, a more diverse activity in which the design space is continuously cocreated through anticipations, theories, and imaginations of what can be or what is possible in our language, social order, and technological world. (Lyytinen, 2004, p. 224)

It is important to reiterate that in this new conceptual space, design theory is no longer focused on the development of strategies to achieve the optimal configuration of form and material to satisfy market conditions. Instead, designers bring a distinctive combination of skills and mental habits—that is, design thinking—to this space (Cross, 2011; Lawson, 2004). Abductive thinking, a tolerance for problem setting characterized by ambiguity, development based on multiple iterations and rapid prototyping, empathy with users, a diverse set of communication skills: these are increasingly recognized as the hallmarks of a design sensibility (Michlewski, 2008). Design thinking is embedded in key concepts of transition theory such as codesign and mutual learning, visioning exercises, niche experiments, and working at multiple scales (Sanders and Stappers, 2008).

CONCLUSION

A vital, viable theory of design for sustainability cannot just model ways of increasing systems performance and profoundly reimagine lifestyles. Certainly, theory building to these ends will overlap with related efforts in many other fields in the natural and social sciences, the arts, and politics. Given the systemic nature and complexity of the challenges we face in the early twenty-first century, this is to be expected. But design theorists are in position to make a distinctive contribution to the general challenge of simultaneously promoting environmental sustainability and social wellbeing. A truly provocative theory of sustainable design will identify how design instigates, informs, and sustains the multidimensional efforts of a global community to advance the goal of wellbeing. In this sense, sustainable design theory will be notable for the questions it poses to other disciplines and the way design thinking can be employed to interrogate as well as to suggest and support forms of human action. With this in mind, I offer two observations, one by the American conservationist and nature writer Aldo Leopold on the conservation and managements of natural environments and one by the Swiss architect Peter Zumthor speaking on the design of the built environment.

> A thing is right when it tends to preserve the integrity, stability and beauty of the biotic community. It is wrong when it tends otherwise. (Leopold, 1966, p. 262)

I carefully observe the concrete appearance of the world, and in my buildings I try to enhance what seems valuable, to correct what is disturbing, and to create anew what we feel is missing. (Zumthor, 1998, p. 24)

Both suggest a way to approach situations that begins with posing questions: what is beautiful and needs to be preserved? What is broken and needs to be fixed? These are the types of questions that initiate conversations among stakeholders, and in the end we are all stakeholders. Conversations will shape communities committed to action. Design will shape the application of values and resources to the opportunities such communities discover.

REFERENCES

Ayres, R. (2004), "On the Life Cycle Metaphor: Where Ecology and Economics Diverge," *Ecological Economics,* vol. 48, no. 4: pp. 425–38.

Carson, R. (1962), *Silent Spring,* Houghton Mifflin: Boston.

Chick, A. and Micklethwaite, P. (2011) *Design for Sustainable Change. How Design and Designers Can Drive the Sustainability Agenda,* AVA Publishing: Lausanne.

Christie, I. (2002), "Sustainability and Spiritual Renewal: The Challenge of Creating a Politics of Reverence," *Conservation Biology,* vol. 16, no. 6: pp. 1466–8.

Conrads, U. ed. (1971), *Programs and Manifestoes on 20th Century Architecture,* MIT Press: Cambridge, MA.

Cross, N. (2011) *Design Thinking,* Berg: Oxford.

Daniels, K. and Hamman, R. (2009), *Energy Design for Tomorrow,* Axel Menges: Felbach.

Deane-Drummond, C. (2008), *Eco-Theology,* Anselm Academic: Winona, MN.

Ehrenfeld, J. (2008), *Sustainability by Design. A Subversive Strategy for Transforming Our Consumer Culture,* Yale University Press: New Haven, CT.

Fernandez, J. (2006), *Material Architecture. Emergent Materials for Innovative Buildings and Ecological Construction,* Architectural Press: Boston.

Friedman, K. (2003), "Theory Construction in Design Research: Criteria, Approaches, and Methods," *Design Studies,* vol. 24, no. 6: pp. 507–22.

Fry, T. (2011), *Design as Politics,* Berg: Oxford.

Fuad-Luke, A. (2009), *Design Activism: Beautiful Strangeness for a Sustainable World,* Earthscan: London.

Fuller, R. B. (1969), *Operating Manual for Spaceship Earth,* Simon and Schuster: New York.

Geels, F. W. (2005), "Processes and Patterns in Transitions and Systems Innovations: Refining the Co-Evolutionary Multi-Level Perspective," *Technological Forecasting & Social Change,* vol. 72, no. 6: pp. 681–96.

Gore, A. (1993), *Earth in the Balance: Ecology and the Human Spirit,* Plume: New York.

Grin, J., Rotmans, J. and Schot, J. (2010), *Transitions to Sustainable Development: New Directions in the Study of Long Term Transformative Change,* Routledge: New York.

Lawson, B. (2004), *What Designers Know,* Architectural Press: Boston.

Leopold, A. (1966), *A Sand County Almanac with Essays on Conservation from Round River,* Ballantine Books: New York.

Lyytinen, K. (2004), "Designing of What? What is the Design Stuff Made of?" in Boland, J. and Collopy, F. (eds), *Managing as Designing,* Stanford University Press: Palo Alto, CA. pp. 221–6.

McDonough, W. and Braungart, M. (2002), *Cradle to Cradle. Remaking the Way We Make Things,* North Point Press: New York.

McKibben, B. (2010a), "Breaking the Growth Habit," *Scientific American,* vol. 302, no. 4: pp. 61–65.

McKibben, B. (2010b), *Earth. Making Life on a Tough New Planet,* Times Books: New York.

Meadows, D. (2008), *Thinking in Systems. A Primer,* Chelsea Green Publishing: White River Junction, VT.

Michlewski, K. (2008), "Uncovering Design Attitude: Inside the Culture of Designers," *Organization Studies,* vol. 29, no. 3: pp. 373–92.

Mouzon, S. (2010), *The Original Green. Unlocking the Mystery of True Sustainability,* Guild Foundation Press: Miami Beach.

Olsthoorn, X. and Wieczorek, A. (eds) (2006), *Understanding Industrial Transformation: Views from Different Disciplines,* Springer: Dordrecht.

Orr, D. (1992), *Ecological Literacy. Education and the Transition to a Postmodern World,* SUNY Press: Albany, NY.

Papanek, V. (1971), *Design for the Real World: Human Ecology and Social Change,* Pantheon Books: New York.

Rockström, J. (2009a), "Planetary Boundaries: Exploring the Safe Operating Space for Humanity," *Ecology and Society,* vol. 14, no. 2: pp. 1–33.

Rockström, J. (2009b), "A Safe Operating Space for Humanity," *Nature,* vol. 461, no. 24: pp. 471–5.

Sanders, E. and Stappers, P. J. (2008), "Co-Creation and the New Landscapes of Design," *CoDesign,* vol. 4, no. 1: pp. 5–18.

Sennett, R. (2008), *The Craftsman,* Allen Lane: London.

Shedroff, N. (2009), *Design is the Problem. The Future of Design Must Be Sustainable,* Rosenfeld Media: New York.

Vitruvius (1914), *The Ten Books on Architecture,* trans. by Morris Hicky Morgan, Harvard University Press: Cambridge, MA.

Walker, S. (2011), *The Spirit of Design: Objects, Environment and Meaning,* Routledge: London.

WCED (World Commission on Environment and Development) (1987), *Our Common Future,* Oxford University Press: New York.

Weick, K. (1989), "Theory Construction as Disciplined Imagination," *The Academy of Management Review,* vol. 14, no. 1: pp. 516–31.

White, L. (1967), "The Historical Roots of Our Ecological Crisis," *Science,* vol. 155, no. 3767: pp. 1203–7.

Williams, D. (2007), *Sustainable Design. Ecology, Architecture, and Planning,* John Wiley & Sons: Hoboken, NJ.

Yaeger, J., and Hodell, D. A. (2009), "Climate-Culture-Environment Interactions and the Collapse of Classic Maya Civilization," in Sandweiss, D. H. and Quilter, J. (eds), *El Nino, Catastrophism, and Culture Change in Ancient America,* Dumbarton Oaks: Washington, D.C. pp. 187–242.

Zumthor, P. (1998), *Thinking Architecture,* Lars Müller Publishers: Baden.

5

The Emergence of Design for Sustainability: And Onward and Upward…

JANIS BIRKELAND

INTRODUCTION

A few blades of grass can do more to dislodge concrete than a thousand marching feet.

(Anonymous)

One bright side of being older is to have watched the quiet revolution of sustainability for half a century. Like watching plants breaking through concrete, it takes many seasons to see real change. But the grassroots sustainability movement keeps springing back, ever hopeful. To be sure, it is still ignored, trodden upon, and sometimes sprayed with poison. Nonetheless, many ideas seeded in activist conferences, workshops and journals are sprouting up in the technocracy, as one-time activists have risen through the sedimentary layers of academia, government and the professions. The time lag is also in part due to that institutionalization process itself. When green theory and practice were grafted onto the trunks of various disciplines, the roots were left behind and vital energy was lost.

The potting of green ideas by scholars and practitioners has had both positive and negative outcomes. On the one hand, the adoption of sustainability values and vocabulary is occurring at a phenomenal rate. Every field has applied its tools to the sustainability imperative, even if the more transformative buds are pruned back. On the other hand, green growth in sustainability theory and practice are soon paved over with managerial bitumen. Technocratic frameworks, standards and metrics have tended to replace action with management, creativity with control, and imagination with templates and forms. Despite the enormous resources diverted into managerial processes in recent decades, things are less sustainable now. The road to sustainability was paved with the best intentions, but there is a total increase in energy and material flows, and an ever increasing disparity of wealth. These trends are not consistent with any grassroots conception of sustainability.

Meanwhile, a kind of race can be seen in most design fields between two competing sustainability paradigms: technocratic (lean and mean) and green (better than before). Those on the hard technocratic fast lane strive to make production more efficient, so more things can be produced. The soft green lane slows the rate of consumption to make energy and materials go further. Both lanes go in the same direction and are set in the same reductionist rock bed. But whether the human race goes faster or lasts a bit longer, it is still heading toward a dead end. In a race, one only has to try to go faster than those in the parallel lanes. Figuratively speaking, we are balancing wheels and tinkering with gears and pedals to increase performance. If there is only one direction, there is no point asking what road might lead to a truly sustainable environment.

It is time to question the racetrack itself. The dominant paradigm of sustainability was laid upon the foundations of industrialism: a linear conception of human progress that framed nature and progress in a zero-sum relationship (Capra, 1983; Merchant, 1980). Of course, the foundations of the paradigm are beginning to crumble. However, anything may emerge from the rubble of coevolutionary randomness or Darwinian markets. It is contended here that only by design can we change the underlying systems and relationships from negative to positive. This is because design thinking operates on an entirely different level from the dominant mechanistic and managerial decision-making frameworks. Generally, design means direct action to achieve intentional change (Beurer, 2001). Responsible or eco-logical design means generating syntheses, synergies, and symbioses that create new positive relationships with multiple positive spinoffs.

We will see that the technocratic and green lanes in built environment design are beginning to merge, as intellectual barriers are gradually transcended. Most sustainable development disciplines now accept that we must do more good and less bad through eco-efficiency and/or regeneration. Yet, while this is genuine progress, it is not nearly good enough. If the ecological base were somehow returned to its original state, it would not support the existing population for long—even assuming that population growth is radically curtailed. After a century of fossil fuel–based industrialization, environmental degradation, and genocide, any design or development that does not address the sustainability deficits created by past and current human systems cannot be considered sustainable.

Given the deficits, the ecological base needs not only to be restored and regenerated but also increased—beyond preindustrial conditions. This level of design requires questioning problem descriptions, assumptions, definitions, strategies and solutions to empower people to realize new possibilities. Positive Development would reframe the intellectual, institutional, and physical environment to create diverse environments that increase future options, the life support system, and life quality for everyone (see Birkeland, 2008). This is quite different from design and development that leaves the environment better than one found it. Eco-positive design would not only correct past systems design errors but would also increase natural capital, ecosystems, and ecosystem services beyond preindustrial conditions. Hence, a two storey building would need the equivalent of three floors of ecological space (using vertical landscapes, atriums, etc.) to become net positive. Otherwise it is still only less bad.

This chapter focuses on ecological sustainability, as myriad books explore the environmental, social, economic, spiritual, and other dimensions of sustainability. The fact that the term 'ecology' is used so often conceals the fact that sustainable development virtually ignores it. The chapter aims to progress this deconstruction and reframing process by looking at how

- the dominant technocratic paradigm of sustainable development fosters binary (either/or) thinking, which creates false choices and impedes positive change;
- despite gradually taking on board sustainable design concepts, managerial control mechanisms restrict design concepts with limited binary decision systems;
- the two lanes in sustainable development are now merging into closed-loop systems, but this can still impede genuinely net positive development; and
- sustainable design needs to at least include open systems thinking if the built environment is to become a sustainability solution.

THE LINEAR VIEW OF PROGRESS

Technocracies were necessary to wage high-tech warfare in the Second World War. Afterwards, military forms of management and technology were rapidly redeployed to the task of industrial progress and the race between East and West. The conversion of resources to development was almost a moral duty to some and a fatalistic prospect for others—expressed in the catch cry, 'You can't stop progress'. To distance politicians from conflict-laden decisions about dividing up natural resources, large resource agencies were installed. These authorities were delegated wide powers and made decisions with virtually no input from the public. The fossil-fuelled conveyor-belt from resources to waste was not questioned, even though the materials and energy used in these industrial systems exceeded outputs (Scheer, 2004). Inputs of fertilisers and pesticides to increase productivity or remineralize depleted farmland were already necessary in the 1940s.

Today, ten calories of fossil energy are required to produce one calorie of food, and one kilogram of corn costs two kilograms of topsoil (Pimental, 1980). In this linear production context, sustainability could only mean sustainable yield. Moreover, this industrial paradigm implanted the belief that environmental quality and world poverty could be achieved with wealth from large-scale industries through economies of scale. No one seemed to notice that impoverished communities around the world would never be able to afford industrial agriculture or centralized energy, sewage and water systems. Diseases and deaths in disadvantaged nations—that could be averted through available, low-tech design interventions—had to wait for unrealistic, centralized solutions that would never come.

THE DUALISTIC PARADIGM

Environmentalists began to trace the causes of unsustainability and its tenacity to various concepts deeply embedded in the dominant industrial paradigm (Ehrenfeld, 1978), which had eliminated earlier 'ethical and cognitive constraints' against the exploitation of nature (Shiva, 1988). Critiques of industrialism took a wide range of perspectives, so we will limit this discussion to one of these patterns of thought and language: hierarchical dualism. This is shorthand for the way reality was construed in Western cultures, as a projection of human power relationships (Warren, 1997; Salleh, 1997). Dualism refers to how the hard qualities associated with the conception of the masculine, such as strong and authoritative, were defined by opposition to their softer counterparts. Hierarchy refers to how the masculine or hard side of each duality was always deemed higher or more valuable in the great hierarchy of being. Modern industrial culture coevolved with this essentialist notion of male and female.

Despite rapid social change, hierarchical dualism is still reflected in all dimensions and fractals of society—but especially in the technocracy. Certain qualities (e.g., reductionist, positivist, rational, abstract, quantitative) are still deemed hard and thus higher than their opposites. In every discipline there has also been a minority critique deemed soft (e.g., subjective, representational, emotive, value-laden, intuitive, qualitative), which has often struggled for credibility. Sustainability is still often derided as soft and, ironically, not being in the real world. While the binocular view of reality is breaking down, it is still manifested on the personal level in either/or thinking. The polarization of views prevents the design of win-win solutions and thus preserves the status quo. For example, the demagoguery surrounding the climate debate is built upon this cultural lobotomy.

The marginalization of design by decision-making processes has also impeded design for sustainable development. Sustainable development has been seen as a matter of making choices: choosing to do the right thing as an individual or society, or choosing the best available technologies and practices as a firm. This means trade-offs: 'One of the most pervasive products of the ecological view is that every choice has a cost: for every realization precludes a hundred other' (Vickers, 1968/1970, p. 62). The role of the planner was deemed to make explicit the complex repercussions and value implications of alternative choices or actions (Webber, 1963). Thus, planning and design for uncertainty in a complex world was ironically more about predicting and choosing than design. Binary decision systems have meant dividing resources, which gradually close off future options—the opposite of sustainable design (Birkeland, 1993). Design, in contrast, can multiply layers of functions and increase options.

THE STARTING BLOCK

Before examining how dualistic (either/or) thinking obstructs positive systems change, we will review the origins of the race between the green and technocratic lanes of sustainable development. From the beginning, sustainability was framed as a change from linear to closed systems design (Boulding, 1966; Fuller, 1963). Although often based on the hard, closed system metaphor of Spaceship Earth, the budding sustainability movement was nonetheless demeaned as soft and utopian. Rachel Carson (1962), a hard scientist, was even given the Galileo treatment. The original intent of the grassroots sustainability movement was about improving everyone's life quality and increasing equity. However, given the closed system metaphor, it was believed that this could only be achieved by reducing production and consumption to conform to nature's capacity to recover and regenerate, called ecological carrying capacity.

Sustainable development first became widely known through the World Conservation Strategy: 'improving the quality of human life while living within the carrying capacity of supporting ecosystems' (IUCN/UNEP/WWF, 1980/1990). Since humans could not reproduce ecosystems, many environmentalists assumed that nature could, at best, be fenced off to slow down its inevitable demise. Consequently, it seemed that the impacts of physical development must be either negative or expensive. In fact, it was already too late for this modest nature conservation approach. By 1980, too much biodiversity (the food chain) had already been lost, and a major percentage of the accelerating human population was malnourished and/or overfed. Given this handicap, again, a truly sustainable development would need to be designed to do more than no harm and more than repair past damage.

Then came the influential United Nations Brundtland Report, which refocused sustainability on social and economic issues (WCED, 1987). It greatly increased global sustainability awareness by making it comprehensible to governments and technocracies. However, it redefined sustainable development within the dominant paradigm of government and economics. That is, it bypassed design. The economic system had been geared to incentivize industrial growth by allocating resources to development at below replacement cost. Certainly, sustainability requires the kind of systems change that only governments can bring about through economic reform. In government, however, sustainability was seen as a management problem: changing everyone else's behaviour—not changing governance itself. Sustainable development came to be growth management: an incremental balancing off of nature with each development approval. Meanwhile, enormous resources went into creating management systems to control problems that were caused by past management, on the theory that if something cannot be measured it doesn't count because it cannot be managed. The tolls taken by regulatory and/or management systems on the road to so-called smarter growth continues to rise.

DUALS OF THE DECADES FROM THE 1950s TO THE PRESENT

To paraphrase Einstein, a paradigm shift cannot occur within the paradigm that caused the problem. Green thinking was neither right nor left nor in the middle. It was outside the dominant industrial paradigm (Porritt, 1984). The dominant paradigm, however, has perpetuated itself by appropriating concepts from its critics and converting them back into the old framework. Thus, ironically, with each new generation, sustainability was rejected by many as being either about social or technological change, not new paradigm, so the wheels were reinvented. The techno-fix versus social sustainability dualism divided the movement and marginalized design in each decade.

Nonetheless, despite all the peaks and valleys, this journey shows that fundamental change is possible, as design concepts first rejected by the technocracy were adopted and adapted by it in subsequent decades. The following are a few snapshots of how sustainable design thinking has been stalled by dualisms. Yet they are grounds for optimism because the next logical step in each case requires design. This is not a history as such, as the categories and times overlap, especially in different classes and countries (see Table 5.1).

Top down or bottom up? After the Second World War, many in the design fields were still nostalgic for the (technocratic) Bauhaus movement, when designers were culture heroes (Rand, 1943). Yet some planning literature and practices, such as The Architects Collaborative (founded by Walter Gropius in 1945) and Arup (founded by Ove Arup in 1946) were built upon the idea of collaboration and cross-disciplinarity. Community participation in planning and design had a long history but was often used as a means of legitimizing policies, decisions, and designs. Stakeholders are now considered an integral part of the design process. The trend, while slow, is toward the citizenry becoming more than a mere stakeholder, a source of consumer information, or means of marketing in the design process.

Reactive or proactive? Aldo Leopold, although an environmental manager, was arguably one of the first sustainable design thinkers. Writing in the late 1940s, he proposed a form of adaptive management based on ecological processes and natural cycles. His *A Sand County Almanac* (1949) poetically expressed concepts like the intrinsic value of nature and the 'land ethic', challenging the dominant paradigm. His adaptive management continued to reemerge in various fields (Friedman, 1973), and today the term land ethic pops up everywhere. However, it is often focused on responding to threats. In time, adaptive management should proactively ensure natural security and safety, as opposed to risk-benefit analysis (developed in the 1970s), which sometimes supports gambling that low risks will not occur. The next step beyond that is design for reversibility.

Monetary or intrinsic values? Frank Lloyd Wright along with M. M. and W. B. Griffin were among the first public figures to present a vision of design *in* nature, if only for the sake of human amenity. However, nature protection was largely left to volunteer NGOs, such as the Audubon Society (incorporated 1905) and the Sierra Club (founded in 1892), that tried to inculcate nature appreciation. It was only when the benefits of nature could be measured in hard technical, economic, and medical terms that the technocracy began to value nature (Costanza et al., 1997). Today, many are trying to measure ecosystem functions and eco-services or natural systems that improve the air, water and soil, and produce clean energy, food, and so on (UNEP, 2005). Nonetheless,

TABLE 5.1   EVOLUTION IN SUSTAINABLE DEVELOPMENT

AN EVOLUTION IN SUSTAINABLE DEVELOPMENT APPROACHES IN BUILT ENVIRONMENT DESIGN

DECADE:	1960s ◄- - - - -				- - - ► 2020s
Sustainable development	Trading off ecology for social and/or economic gain seen as inevitable	Offsetting ecological losses by monetary compensation seen as acceptable	Reducing negative impacts of pollution on human health seen as adequate	Preventing offsite pollution through onsite treatment seen as optimal	Leaving the site "better than before" or zero net impact is seen as possible	Sustainability Standard will be "increasing the public and ecological values beyond pre-settlement conditions in relation to floor area"
View of nature in relation to development	Valuable assets (e.g., critical sites, cultural heritage, or nonrenewable resources) were often outweighed by imperative of economic growth	Critical ecosystems are seen as valuable assets (e.g., wetlands) and protected, but ecological losses not deemed "significant" are allowed despite limited assessment	Mitigation of impacts is all that is deemed possible, but development that has unusual ecological impacts could be stopped	Mitigation is based on quality of environmental media, but often not ecosystems; eco-restoration of brownfield sites is seen as profitable	The environment can be restored or improved by design; however, the ecology is usually left worse off overall due to "embodied waste"	Design comes to include providing the infrastructure to increase ecosystem functions in or on urban development to increase public space, access to the means of survival, social choice, and ecological space and resilience; urban areas become seed banks for the bioregion as well as future needs
Built environment design applications	Passive design concepts were associated with alternative lifestyles and not taken seriously in building industry	Energy reduction through passive homes briefly popular; buildings only reduced energy leaks and ventilation	Focus is on reduction of harm (e.g., energy, water, pollution, and materials) and occupant thermal comfort	Focus is still on human comfort and energy, not ecosystems; eco-services are noted but only measured in economic terms	Analogies in design to ecosystems and terms used like resilient and self-sufficient are common, but not actually eco-positive	Urban areas become seen as drivers of sustainability as they can increase future options and make everyone better off (not just owners); eco-cycling seen as possible through eco-retrofitting for eco-services and ecosystem functions as well as people
Concepts underlying assessment and approval	Impacts were not really assessed, as environmental costs were deemed collateral damage and resources were almost free	Developers needed to estimate impact in a cost-benefit framework that compared limited alternatives but not ecological gains	A project needed only be better than allowed by code or in comparison with typical buildings; cradle-to-grave costing is applied	Closed loop applications (in life cycle and material flows analyses) begins to be applied to development	Green point systems for development approvals include design concepts; many impacts are still not included	"Positive Development" processes, methods, and metrics are implemented to remove underlying conceptual biases; positive and negative impacts are put on the same scale and compared to preindustrial ecological conditions to expose net values

This typology of sustainable design draws upon a table by Knight-Lenihan (2011).

ecosystems will not be actively protected or expanded as long as decision-making is driven by economic frameworks (Heal, 2000). It is now necessary to design *for* nature as well as with or like nature.

Cities or nature? The terms 'ecology' (coined in 1866 by Ernst Haeckel) and 'ecosystem' (coined in 1942 by R. Lindeman) came into widespread use only in the 1960s. *Fundamentals of Ecology* (Odum and Odum, 1959) was perhaps the first systems analysis that explained humans and ecology as a vast set of interconnected ecosystems. Nevertheless, ecology developed as a hard science, so it focused on predicting impacts in nature, such as species extinction and thresholds. Ian McHarg's *Design with Nature* (1969) and Lewis Mumford's *The City in History* (1961) were groundbreaking contributions but did not really liberate nature from catchments, parks and backyards. Consequently, cities and ecology remained largely separate issues until the 1990s (Register, 1990). Today, people realize the design of cities is a cause of many problems in the hinterland, yet cities are still designed as what William Rees calls 'black holes' that suck up resources. In the future, cities should not just be likened to ecosystems but designed to support and replenish their bioregions.

Peace or environment? Appropriate technology came into vogue in the 1960s, as seen in the annals of the *Whole Earth Catalogue* (Brand, 1968). However, at that time, peace and environment were separate movements. Many in the peace and civil rights movements felt that softer issues, like environment and gender, could wait. As dualisms are used both ways, the environment movement was discredited by association with the peace movement, on the one hand, and by its presumed prioritization of nature over human welfare or social justice, on the other. Today, most people realize that environmental degradation perpetuates poverty, hunger, disease, inequity, injustice, and warfare. It must soon be realized that if nature is not increased by design then, ultimately, there can be no peace or justice.

Flows or nodal networks? Many books by visionaries and systems thinkers such as Jacobs (1961), Fuller (1963), Bookchin (1962), and Boulding (1966) appeared during the 1960s. These thinkers each took a fresh look at major *sectors* such as industry, society, cities, buildings, agriculture, and policy making. The relationship between urban development and environment was linked by analogy to human metabolism or separate organisms interacting with their environment (Wolman, 1965; Boyden et al., 1981). This was even expressed metaphorically in architecture in Japan in the 1950s, called the Metabolist Movement. Systems theories became popular in academia but were usually expressed as nodes and networks, which left out the site-specific needs of biota (McLoughlin, 1969; Emery, 1969). Humans, for example, are complex compositions of chemicals, elements, bacteria, and so on, not autonomous beings. Reductionist analyses that treat humans as independent, and nature as a source and sink, are increasingly seen as old paradigm.

Hard or soft systems? Systems analyses had been applied to human-nature relationships by the 1970s (Bateson, 1972; Commoner, 1971). Systems thinking was also soon applied to inter-human relationships. However, soft systems approaches still reflected a positivist (hard) view (Checkland, 1981/1999). Interactions were based on individualism and usually assumed negotiation and interest balancing rather than design. Many modelling tools now exist to help to provide design choices rather than to assist design. However, the behaviour of complex systems cannot be predicted or controlled—by definition. In the future, more priority should be given to fixing design problems over making better models of complexity.

Slum removal or renewal? Urban renewal was a euphemism for slum clearance in developed nations in the 1960s, as it is in some developing nations today. While culturally destructive urban redevelopment projects were being opposed one-by-one in urban areas, the industrial-government complex was globalizing third world cultures. Advocacy planning, funded in the United States in response to urban riots, took the view that community design could improve social conditions through what is now called 'place making'. Community design was soon disparaged as social determinism and defunded, although it is unclear if this was due to its success or failure. Today, however, Architecture for Humanity, Engineers without Borders, and many similar NGOs are now taking direct action to create low-cost, on-ground community improvements around the world. By enlisting benefactors and paid professionals, they avoid dependency on politics. In the future, their designs will not just ensure low-impact shelters but also ensure domestic access to means of survival, such as food and water.

Fossil or solar energy? Bernard Rudofsky's *Architecture without Architects* (1964) had shown the elegance of passive indigenous design and living in harmony with nature. By 1970, many youth were rejecting industrial, materialist society to build communities in nature such as Arcosanti in Arizona and Earthship in New Mexico. Schumacher's widely discussed *Small is Beautiful* (1974) challenged the modern industrial system. Shortly thereafter, however, the idea of living simply was ridiculed as either romanticism or communism. After OPEC and the oil spike of 1973, passive solar design was briefly endorsed by the U.S. government (HUD, 1976). However, the soft path was rejected in favour of access to global oil reserves (Lovins, 1977). Consequently, passive solar design was replaced by a hard, reductionist focus on energy and efficiency—which presupposed fossil fuels. Today, green buildings still rely largely on (reduced) fossil fuels and high-tech equipment. Soon, however, fossilized energy sources may be replaced with living systems, such as vertical algaetecture to produce fuel and clean air in urban areas (Henrikson, 2012).

Prediction or action? New computer modelling techniques emerged that could compare exponential growth in world population, industrialization, pollution, degraded soil, and resource depletion to the likelihood of technical solutions appearing (Meadows et al. 1972, 2004). Debates propagated over the methods and metrics ensured that no action would occur before the predictions were proven, when it would be too late. The rejection of hard scientific analyses showed that science could be characterized as soft when convenient. Today, the same arguments surround predictions concerning the climate debate, even though existing systems cost society billions each year (HM Treasury, 2006). The shift from prediction to the design and retrofit of urban environments in developed and developing areas could occur quickly however.

Population in third or first world? The public's attention was drawn to the 'population bomb' (Ehrlich, 1970) and the consequent zero-sum relationship between poor and rich nations. However, the advocates of population control were soon accused of blaming the third world, even though people in developed nations were using far more resources. Due in part to this false dualism, population is still a taboo subject, even though it has long been understood that with better health, more security, and empowerment for women, population growth reduces by itself. This year the UN warned that three billion people will slip into poverty unless the world can supply at least 50 percent more food, 45 percent more energy, and 30 percent more water by 2030 despite the changing climate. There are twenty million more undernourished people now than in 2000 (UN, 2012). The FAO estimates that 925 million people suffer from hunger and 178 million children under five years are stunted from undernutrition (FAO, 2010). Design must therefore increase future health options for people in both developed and developing nations.

Pollution: external or intrinsic? Pollution was attributed mainly to primary industries rather than the designs that created the demand for materials, products and energy in the first place. Economists called pollution an externality, instead of a problem intrinsic to the design of industrial systems. Making the polluter pay (in the form of royalties, taxes, licenses, fines, etc.) was meant to incentivize efficiencies, but it also assumed that money could somehow neutralize net losses in environmental quality. While taxes annoyed firms, the funds were used to support industrial development, such as roads and other fossil fuel subsidies, not ecological restoration. Fomenting conflict between industrialists and environmentalists avoided change. In the future, noncompliance with health standards should be dealt with by direct action by governments, with the costs recovered from the resource savings and returned to the public.

Efficiency versus innovation? With the rise of corporate power and the growing public access to government in the 1980s, the bureaucracy was no longer useful as a gatekeeper. Western leaders (e.g., Thatcher, Reagan) juxtaposed individual freedom against public responsibility. Consequently, environmentalists began trying to convince business directly that it was in their economic self-interest to avoid externalities (Hawken, 1993). Some community groups met directly with heads of companies and offered to help them design in efficiencies (Cohen and O'Connor, 1990). Governments later began providing loans to industry to avoid pollution by design. Design and innovation are now business terms, even though they usually appear in the context of creating new markets (WBCSD et al., 1997). Hopefully, priorities will one day be set according to the net public benefits of innovations, not profits.

Preferences or reason? Environmental decision frameworks were based on the same premises as in business. They assumed a rational decision-maker, even when described as 'muddling through' complex issues (Lindblom, 1973). Most people now accept the complexity of decision-makers' motives and emotions, as well as the complexity of sustainability issues. However, management is increasingly dependent upon automated and randomized consumer preferences tools—even though it is well-known that the way questions are framed influences the outcomes. Personal preferences replace substance, just as sound bites replace in-depth ethical debate. Whether debate or surveys are used, the public and politicians are asked to choose, not design. The design of decision-making systems should be tailored to the ethical nature of the issues at hand.

Markets or transparency? In the 1980s, deregulation was presented as the opposite of regulation and therefore more valid. This dualism is of course false because there is always regulation, whether primarily in the (theoretically) visible hands of government or the invisible hands of industry. Nonetheless, governments were canvassing market solutions (like emissions trading) for their potential to transfer responsibility to the supra-natural. After the 2008 global financial crisis, there were renewed calls for regulation and transparency. Paradoxically, greater surveillance has become a fact of life due to the rise of the Internet, but greater transparency in decision-making is still a challenge.

Design breakthroughs. Despite precedents for sustainable urbanism (Johnson, 1979) little progress occurred in this subject area until the 1990s, when new vehicles of sustainable design entered the race. For convenience, these can be grouped into four concepts: eco-innovation, biomimicry, cradle-to-cradle and regenerative design. These all call for participatory, integrated and cross-disciplinary design processes and are about making life better for people by working with nature (Papanek, 1995; Wann, 1996; Van der Ryn and Cowan, 1996; Mackenzie, 1991). However, they often differ in terms of their construction of nature and design:

- Eco-innovation: Amory Lovins once suggested that if the exhaust pipe of a car was fed back into the driver's seat, then innovation would soon be forthcoming. Greenpeace in Germany reputedly plugged a refinery pipe and the company managed to redesign the system—giving a whole new meaning to the term 'end-of-pipe solution'. Eco-innovation is about using the market to bypass market barriers to sustainability, such as the tendency of industry to purchase and shelve eco-design patents. For example, Lovins put his hypercar on the Internet so that car manufacturers could not say the technology did not exist. He and others showed that industry could be ten times more efficient. Today, the European Union and other governments are giving grants and awards for eco-innovations, to the extent that they are marketable.
- Biomimicry: Benyus's book on *Biomimicry* (1997) described nature as a source of innovation. Throughout history, many designers have drawn analogies between their own work and that of nature to inspire their designs and their clients (Downer, 2002). Today, due to the power of metaphor, design concepts that are mimicked off Internet sites are often declared 'inspired by nature'. Many biomimetic products, while amazing, are high-tech and geared toward

industrial manufacturing. In the built environment, however, patents are not necessary. Low-tech and passive design solutions already exist to replace mechanical equipment with the sun, wind, bacteria, fungi or algae and materials from agriculture waste.

- Cradle-to-cradle: architects have shown that homes and even inner city townhouses could be retrofitted for resource autonomy (Mobbs, 1998; Vale and Vale, 2000). McDonough and Braungart (2002) addressed embodied toxins in their cradle-to-cradle concept, which replaced the prior cradle-to-grave approach of life cycle assessment. Cradle-to-cradle design uses closed-loop systems to meet social, economic, and environmental goals, or even no-loop systems design where waste is designed out of a process almost entirely. For example, a green roof at a Ford plant in Michigan restored indigenous habitats, provided insulation, and also generated significant income in tourism, which exceeded the initial cost and maintenance of the roof.

- Regenerative: while Bill Mollison and David Holmgren developed the idea of productive and synergistic food landscapes by 1978 in *Permaculture One,* it was somewhat limited to gardening. 'Regenerative design,' a term used by John T. Lyle (1994), is where landscapes undo the past damage caused by industrial development and treat the water, air and soil. 'Living Machines', or microbial systems that produce clean water from waste in the built environment, were introduced by John and Nancy Jack Todd (1994). Regenerative systems not only purify environmental media but improve ecosystems and human health (Du Plessis, 2012). While buildings can become filters as well as healthy and productive habitats, regenerative design has only aimed to restore ecosystems. It is now necessary to increase the amount of natural ecosystems beyond preindustrial conditions; that is, to be net positive.

Despite the advances of the 1990s, dualisms continue to block change toward better systems design. These include the following:

Nature: real or social construction? One of the dualisms that obstructed these new design paradigms was postmodernism. It begins with the incontestable observation that our perceptions of reality are socially constructed. Yet, the idea of perceiving society as a part of nature was often disparaged as a social construction and therefore somehow less real. As several academics told me in the 1990s, 'Sustainability is passé, we are now into postmodernism'. In other words, the only reality is the postmodern one. By claiming to be beyond ideology, ironically, postmodernism rationalized capitalist values and reified consumer preferences (Orr, 2002). Logically, however, postmodernism should support a positive interpretation of nature. That is, if nature is socially constructed, why not perceive it in a way that makes society better off?

Climate: caused by humanity or nature? Debates about climate change were around by the 1980s (Gribbin, 1982). However, people are only beginning to see climatic events (storms, famines, floods, heat islands and fires) as outcomes of poor human-made systems, instead of acts of God or nature. Again, different technical forms of modelling and measuring led to different predictions, and this discrepancy was used to avoid any action. Given the status of Al Gore (1993) and Nicholas Stern (HM Treasury, 2006), derision and exclusion have begun to fail. But from a design (as opposed to a dualistic) perspective, it would not matter if climate change were real or not, man-made or not, predictable or not. The actions we would be taking to make everyone safer, healthier and happier are the same as those that would address climate change.

Densification or multiple functions? Sprawl was seen as a problem in the 1960s, but by the turn of the century, little was done to reduce greenfield development or retrofit the cities and suburbs. This was partly due to the debate between high and low density development (Newman and Kenworthy, 1999; Troy, 1996). Given this dualism, few noticed that neither choice was sustainable under current sustainable design norms and standards. It was perhaps assumed that the new (technocratic) rating tools would take care of design quality issues. However, much destructive development occurred in the name of sustainability by developers who were simply increasing urban density. While some new buildings will always be necessary, their embodied waste and energy is huge, whereas eco-retrofitting can pay for itself through subsequent savings (Romm, 1999). Nonetheless, to overcome institutional inertia, construction and development approval systems will need to incentivize eco-retrofitting.

Prediction or design? New tools proliferated that labelled buildings sustainable if they exceeded code requirements. These tools usually assess separate factors that are converted to a single unit in money, energy or carbon. Today, more kinds of factors are incorporated into complex modelling systems. But this reductionist approach can potentially continue to marginalize design, in part because the available data for these tools are mostly relevant to efficiency, not ecology. In other words, living things are still reduced to inanimate objects. Further, under the influence of earlier impact assessment frameworks, most tools only predict and assess negative (less bad) impacts and avoid their ethical implications. We must assess the lost opportunity for positive social and ecological gains due to poor design and the positive gains possible by good design.

Accountability or displacement activity? The trend toward accountability in government and industry was considered progress in itself, but it did not always change the tendency to avoid those policies or indicators that require action. Many professionals and academics are now held accountable for their manager's personal key performance indicators, instead of the public interest. No one has yet been accountable for the costs of the displacement activity that reporting has created. Moreover, the processes entail ever more complexity and transaction costs, and less design. Impact accounting activity is therefore increasingly outsourced to consultants, many of whom are not designers. The salience of accountancy tools over design is increasingly challenged, but it may be too late. When design is reduced to painting by numbers, designers learn to stay within the lines.

THE CROSSROADS

We have seen how dualistic thinking managed to obstruct the implementation of design solutions that benefit the general public. The technocratic and green approaches discussed above are often referred to as weak and strong, or deep and shallow, sustainability. But to the extent that they retain vestiges of the dominant negative paradigm, neither will lead to sustainable systems. The technocratic lane is now merging with what can be called closed-loop design with its origins in the green thinkers of the early 1960s (above). In such circular metabolisms, waste from one linear system becomes a resource for another (Tibbs, 1992; Girardet, 1992). Since there is always some waste in any industrial system, closing loops generally can only slow down environmental destruction. Moreover, this does not necessarily create positive ethical or ecological relationships. Even zero waste, or industrial or urban ecology strategies usually fail to expand ecosystem health, size and resilience in absolute terms.

Green and technocratic design paradigms still treat reductions in negatives as positive gains. While closed-loop analogies make very useful efficiency tools, closed system engineering approaches can restrict design. Cities are an intrinsic part of a complex open social and ecological system even if most of their physical components are manufactured. Yet, because they are conceived on the model of closed systems, most new eco-cities are essentially business parks and exclude the poor now living in old cities. That is, such designs may be very eco-efficient and modelled on nature but still violate basic social sustainability principles. Like roundabouts, closed-loop systems can change direction but not the nature of the industrial freeway itself.

The next section briefly outlines a third paradigm in sustainable design thinking based on open systems. In so doing, it is subject to the accusation that it is creating yet another competing dualism. However, it is not suggesting merely a new lane, new vehicle or even a change of direction; it suggests abandoning the drag race altogether. Of course, design draws on precedents from many schools of thought or models of nature. But it is not the shape of the system; it is whether the system is net positive or net negative that matters. After all, industrious earthworms are net positive linear systems that turn waste into resources—the opposite of human-designed linear systems. Open systems thinking helps designers to think outside the box. In particular, it can address what is perhaps the biggest barrier to sustainable design: the idea that we can only restore, rather than augment, nature.

POSITIVE DEVELOPMENT (PD)

PD aims for a whole systems paradigm shift from reducing negatives to creating positive synergies, using open (design) as well as closed (engineering) systems thinking. It rejects the idea that nature and development should be balanced in a closed system. When conceived as an open system, the designed environment could generate net positive impacts to expand nature, diversity, and future choice in cities and their bioregions, using urban structures as a platform. PD would seek opportunities to increase total ecological carrying capacity, instead of replacing nature with structures that function like ecosystems. PD is based on a positive conception of sustainability, nature, systems, built environments, design, methods, tools, standards, strategies and so on. As a partial summary, the following are some examples of how these basic concepts can be reframed in more positive terms:

- In PD, 'sustainability' means making everyone better off, including the wider community, and increasing positive future options, choice and opportunity through proactive design interventions (i.e., not just aiming for survival and health). PD would increase both the ecological base (natural resources, biodiversity, ecological carrying capacity, etc.), and the public estate (i.e., access to means of health, community, and survival)—relative to preindustrial conditions.

- In PD, nature is conceived as an abundant creative force, not a threat. After all, despite occasional catastrophes, the topsoil, biological diversity, and human culture had tended to increase until industrialization. Nature is not just a constraint or a metaphor for development. Designers can be positive catalysts that enable natural systems to provide healthier, more dynamic and interactive environments. Cities provide existing infrastructure that can be modified to support exosystems, biodiversity and (small) endangered flora and fauna in reciprocal and eco-productive ways.

- In PD, community participation would consider equity and ethical issues in the region that need to be corrected. Currently, planners seldom, if ever, provide the community with data enabling them to consider ethical implications, such as resource transfers in and out of the region, wealth distribution, resource security, open space allocation, and so on. Regardless of public engagement, however (which can be manipulated), basic sustainability principles would be nonnegotiable—such as reversibility, adaptability and expansion of ecological carrying capacity.

- In PD, the built environment is conceived of more like a reef or an open system, instead of a node in a network or separate organism dependent upon its environment. Because eco-retrofitting can pay for itself, the built environment could be proactively retrofitted to address its ongoing negative impacts and generate positive off-site impacts (appropriate to specific urban and regional deficits). Just as a reef spawns billions of living things that seed the ocean, urban areas can act as an artificial reef made from abandoned cars, or, even better, we can construct reefs to kick-start ecosystems (Jackson and Simpson, 2012, pp. 31–32).

- In PD, design and sustainability become almost synonymous, as sustainability is a design problem, not just a problem of behavioural or social change. Currently, sustainable design usually aims for self-sufficiency. It does not aim to correct inequalities caused by other developments in the region. Eco-positive design would aim to make everyone better off through net positive impacts and multifunctional services that increase future options as well as reduce trade-offs in space, time and resources.

- In PD, systems analyses are open, so instead of just reducing externalities, we would look for ways to amplify positive spillover effects and synergies by design for multiple, synergistic, net positive impacts. Eco-cycling is that which increases the ecological base and avoids the potential downsides of mere value-adding or up-cycling. Eco-cycling would increase human and ecosystem health but not total resource flows. A 'Hierarchy of Innovation' would determine development priorities by their net public benefits (see Birkeland, 2012).

- In PD, the benchmark is the preindustrial ecology of the site or bioregion. This sustainability standard means a project must go beyond zero negative ecological and social impacts. Regeneration is not yet used to mean an increase in preindustrial ecosystems, nor does it necessarily exceed the harm created by the intervention (Cole, 2012). Again, built environment design should expand the life support system. Aesthetics need not be affected, but one can imagine a time when buildings are judged by their degree of invisibility, rather than by current fashion.

- In PD, methods are designed around the relevant ethical and ecological issues at hand, instead of finding new problems for old methods. They are designed to overcome the biases of existing methods. For example, SMARTmode is a means to set planning priorities by using methods that make inequities and opportunities visible (e.g., the concentration of wealth, costs of inaction, and proportion of private and public spaces).

- In PD, design tools put positive and negative ecological impacts on the same spectrum, with positive impacts assessed in relation to land and floor area (as a green roof on a ten-storey building contributes far less than one on a single-storey building. Indicators are often used selectively and treat less bad as a gain. For example, health statistics sometimes estimate the reduction in people dying from, say, poor indoor air, separate from the percentage or the total. In a growing population, the total could be higher. An eco-positive design tool was devised to make positive and negative impacts and totals more transparent (see Birkeland 2012, p. 174).

- In PD, design for eco-services would be an integral part of urban development, not just landscapes. Buildings need to carry their own ecological weight and waste. There are myriad eco-innovations that could be integrated with buildings to provide environmental and building services and replace capital- and resource-intensive equipment with natural systems (for examples, see Birkeland, 2009). These can be integrated with prefabricated eco-retrofitting modules that adapt to different conditions.

- In PD, strategies focus on eco-retrofitting because the material flows, time, money, and toxins involved in replacing old cities with new ones are not sustainable. Eco-retrofitting is essential because cities now cause up to 75 percent of greenhouse emissions, and buildings alone are accountable for 40 percent of overall carbon dioxide emissions (WBCSD, 2009). Cities simply must be eco-retrofitted to increase adaptability and urban climate mitigation. Companies now exist that could retrofit an equal amount of floor area elsewhere on the developer's behalf, in the case of greenfield development.

THE FUTURE OF DESIGN FOR SUSTAINABILITY

Up-cycling and eco-cycling are beginning to occur at larger and larger scales to create constructive cross-pollinating cycles within and between existing agriculture, industry, construction, and transport. Soon, this cross-sectoral and cross-regional approach will be supported by multidimensional, geospatial, visualization technologies that can integrate heretofore missing data on ethics, ecosystems and resource transfers (Jackson and Simpson, 2012). Once eco-positive design and decision-making frameworks are in place, these virtual modelling technologies will put experts in diverse fields and lay citizens on the same page to facilitate public debate and envisage better futures.

Designers are only just beginning to think in open systems at the microscopic level. Microbial systems in industry and urban areas can replace fossil fuel–based systems with natural systems. For example, vertical landscapes, wetlands and algaetecture could consume carbon dioxide while producing biomass, oxygen and biofuels, without competing with land for food. We can of course eco-retrofit existing cities with passive systems to generate heating, cooling and other functions. However, we can also enlist the free services of fungi, bacteria, algae, plants and invertebrates like worms to provide eco-services such as clean air, soil and water. Bacteria already do jobs in the built environment like repairing and cleaning building facades and can produce light, oxygen, and serve as a means of generating and storing energy. Theoretically, sandstone buildings can even be constructed by bacteria (Larsson, 2008).

With the help of legions of little helpers, a rethink and redesign of sustainable development is possible. There is no scarcity of microbes and fungi because they multiply to meet the challenge, and they never go on strike (Stamets, 2005). Moreover, they simply disappear when their food source—material that is unwanted by humans—is consumed. Since enough different kinds of tiny workers exist for virtually any purpose, experimenting with genetic modification and nanotechnology, with their inherent risks, is not necessary. They grow by the billions, so the management class can remain gainfully employed counting them.

In summary, closed-systems thinking has led to major advances in theory and practice, but we are still on the same circuitous race track. Environmental policy, planning decision-making and assessment systems are binary, linear and reductionist. They have only served to reduce the collateral damage of development. Sustainability requires open-systems design that increases the life support system. The built environment can and must be retrofitted or redesigned to produce net positive increases in the life support system, not just zero waste. The transformation to PD—that which makes everyone better off, expands future options, and increases ecological carrying capacity and diversity, guided by open-systems thinking—is both fun and rewarding.

REFERENCES

Bateson, G. (1972), *Steps to an Ecology of Mind*, University of Chicago Press: Chicago.

Benyus, J. (1997), *Bimimicry: Innovation Inspired by Nature*, William Morrow and Co.: New York.

Beurer, B. (2001), 'The Transformation of Design', *Design Issues*, vol. 171, winter: p. 44.

Birkeland, J. (1993), 'Towards a New System of Environmental Governance', *The Environmentalist*, vol. 13, no. 1: pp. 19–32.

Birkeland, J. (2008), *Positive Development: From Vicious Circles to Virtuous Cycle through Built Environment Design*, Earthscan: London.

Birkeland, J. (2009), 'Design for Eco-Services. Part A—Environmental Services, Environment Design Guide 77, and Part B—Building Services', *Environmental Design Guide 78*, Canberra, Architects Institute of Australia, pp. 1–13, pp. 1–9.

Birkeland, J. (2012), 'Design Blindness in Sustainable Development: From Closed to Open Systems Design Thinking', *Journal of Urban Design*, vol. 17, no. 2: pp. 163–87.

Bookchin, M. (pseudonym Lewis Heber) (1962), *Our Synthetic Environment*, Knopf: New York.

Boulding, K. (1966), *Economics of the Coming Spaceship Earth*, Sixth Resources for the Future Forum on Environmental Quality in a Growing Economy, Resources for the Future: Washington, D.C.

Boyden, S. Millar, S. Newcombe, K. and O'Neill, B. (1981), *The Ecology of a City and its People: The Case of Hong Kong*, Australian National University Press: Canberra.

Brand, S. (1968), *Whole Earth Catalogue*, Self-Published.

Capra, F. (1983), *The Turning Point: Science, Society, and the Rise of Culture*, Simon and Schuster: New York.

Carson, R. (1962), *Silent Spring*, Houghton Mifflin: Boston.

Checkland, P. (1981/1999), *Systems Thinking, Systems Practice*, Wiley & Sons: New York.

Cohen, G. and O'Connor, J. (eds) (1990), *Fighting Toxics*, Island Press: Washington, D.C.

Cole, R. J. (2012), 'Transitioning from Green to Regenerative Design,' *Building Research and Information*, vol. 40, no. 1: pp. 39–53.

Commoner, B. (1971), *The Closing Circle: Nature, Man And Technology*, Knopf: New York.

Costanza, R., d'Arge, R., de Groot, R., Farber, DS., Grasso, M., Hannon, B., Limburg, K., Naeem, S., O'Neill, R. V., Paruelo, J., Raskin, R. G., Sutton, P., and van den Belt, M. (1997), 'The Value of the World's Ecosystem Services and Natural Capital', *Nature*, vol. 387: pp. 253–60.

Downer, J. (2002), *Weird Nature*, BBC Worldwide: London.

Du Plessis, C. (2012), 'Towards a Regenerative Paradigm for the Built Environment', *Building Research & Information*, vol. 40, no. 1: pp. 7–22.

Ehrenfeld, D. (1978), *The Arrogance of Humanism*, Oxford University Press: New York.

Ehrlich P. R. (1970), *The Population Bomb*, Sierra Club-Ballantine Books: New York.

Emery, F. E. (1969), *Systems Thinking*, Penguin: Harmondsworth, UK.

FAO (2010), 'The State of Food Insecurity in the World 2010', UN Food and Agriculture Organization Report, <http://www.fao.org/docrep/013/i1683e/i1683e.pdf> accessed April 2012.

Friedman, J. (1973), 'A Conceptual Model for the Analysis of Planning Behaviour', in Faludi, A. (ed.), *A Reader in Planning Theory, Urban and Regional Planning Series*, vol. 5, Pergamon Press: Oxford, pp. 345–370.

Fuller, B. (1963), *Operating Manual for Spaceship Earth*, E. P. Dutton: New York.

Girardet, H. (1992), *The Gaia Atlas of Cities: New Directions for Sustainable Urban Living*, Gaia Books: London.

Gore, A. (1993), *Earth in the Balance: Ecology and the Human Spirit*, Plume: New York.

Gribbin, J. R. (1982), *Future Weather: Carbon Dioxide, Climate and the Greenhouse Effect*, Penguin: Harmondsworth, UK.

Hawken, P. (1993), *The Ecology of Commerce: A Declaration of Sustainability,* HarperBusiness: New York.

Heal, G. (2000), *Nature and the Marketplace: Capturing the Value of Ecosystem Services,* Island Press: Washington, D.C.

Henrikson, R. (2012) 'Dream—Algae Landscape and Architecture Designs', *Algae Industry Magazine,* February 12, <http://www.algaeindustrymagazine.com/the-future-of-algae-pt-5/> accessed 24 February 2013.

HM Treasury (2006), 'Stern Review: The Economics of Climate Change', <www.hm-treasury.gov.uk/contact/contact_index.cfm> accessed 24 February 2013.

HUD (1976), *Solar Dwelling Design Concepts,* U.S. Department of Housing and Urban Development: Washington D.C.

IUCN/UNEP/WWF (World Conservation Union, United Nations Environment Programme, and WorldWide Fund for Nature) (1980/1990), *Caring for the Earth: A Strategy for Sustainable Living,* Earthscan: London.

Jackson, D. and Simpson, R. (eds) (2012), *D_City: Digital Earth, Virtual Nations, Data Cities,* DCity: Sydney.

Jacobs, J. (1961), *The Death and Life of Great American Cities,* Vintage Books: New York.

Johnson, R. (1979), *The Green City,* MacMillan: S. Melbourne.

Knight-Lenihan, S. (2011) *Sustaining Sustainable Transport in a Democracy,* University of Western Australia: Perth.

Larsson, M. (2008), 'Dune', Thesis at the Architectural Association, London, <news.bbc.co.uk/2/hi/technology/8166929.stmCached—Similar> accessed September 2011.

Leopold, A. (1949), *A Sand County Almanac,* Oxford University Press: Oxford.

Lindblom, C. E. (1973), 'The Science of "Muddling Through"', in Faludi, A (ed.), *A Reader in Planning Theory, Urban and Regional Planning Series,* vol. 5, Pergamon Press: Oxford.

Lovins, A. (1977), *Soft Energy Paths: Towards a Durable Peace,* Friends of the Earth International: San Francisco.

Lyle, J. T. (1994), *Regenerative Design for Sustainable Development,* Wiley & Sons: New York.

Mackenzie, D. (1991), *Green Design: Design for the Environment,* Lawrence King: London.

McDonough, W. and Braungart, M. (2002), *Cradle to Cradle: Remaking the Way we Make Things,* North Point Press: New York.

McHarg, I. (1969), *Design with Nature,* Natural History Press: New York.

McLoughlin, B. (1969), *Urban and Regional Planning: A Systems Approach,* Faber and Faber: London.

Meadows, D. H., Meadows, D. L., Randers, J., and Behrens, W. W. III. (1972), *The Limits to Growth: A Report for the Club of Rome,* Universe Books: New York.

Meadows, D. H., Randers, D. and Meadows, D. L. (2004), *Limits to Growth: The 30 Year Update,* Earthscan: London.

Merchant, C. (1980), *The Death of Nature: Women, Ecology, and the Scientific Revolution,* HarperCollins: New York.

Mobbs, M. (1998), *Sustainable House,* Choice Books: Sydney.

Mollison, B. and Holmgren, D. (1978), *Permaculture One,* Transworld Publishers: London.

Mumford, L. (1961), *The City in History,* Harcourt, Brace and World: New York.

Newman, P. and Kenworthy, J. (1999), *Sustainability and Cities: Overcoming Automobile Dependence,* Island Press: Washington, D.C.

Odum, E. P. and Odum, H. T. (1959), *Fundamentals of Ecology,* W. B. Saunders: Philadelphia.

Orr, D. (2002), *The Nature of Design: Ecology, Culture, and Human Intention,* Oxford University Press: Oxford.

Papanek, V. (1995), *The Green Imperative: Ecology and Ethics in Design and Architecture,* Thames and Hudson: London.

Pimental D. (1980), *Handbook of Energy Utilization in Agriculture,* CRC Press: Boca Raton, FL.

Porritt, J. (1984), *Seeing Green, the Politics of Ecology Explained,* Blackwell: Oxford.

Rand, A. (1943), *The Fountainhead,* Bobbs-Merrill: Indianapolis.

Register, R. (1990), First International Ecological City Conference, Urban Ecology, Berkeley, CA.

Romm, J. (1999), *Cool Companies: How the Best Businesses Boost Profits and Productivity by Cutting Greenhouse Emissions,* Island Press: Washington, D.C.

Rudofsky, B. (1964/1987), *Architecture without Architects,* University of New Mexico Press: Santa Fe.

Salleh, A. (1997), *Ecofeminism as Politics: Nature, Marx and the Postmodern,* Zed Books: London.

Scheer, H. (2004), *The Solar Economy,* Earthscan: London.

Schumacher, E. F. (1974), *Small is Beautiful,* Sphere-Abacus: London.

Shiva, V. (1988), *Staying Alive: Women, Ecology and Development,* Zed Books: London.

Stamets, P. (2005), *Mycelium Running: How Mushrooms Can Help Save the World,* Ten Speed Press: Berkeley, CA.

Tibbs, H. (1992), 'Industrial Ecology: An Agenda for Environmental Management', *Pollution Prevention Review,* spring: pp. 167–80.

Todd, N. J. and Todd, J. (1994), *From Eco-Cities to Living Machines,* Atlantic Books: Berkeley, CA.

Troy, P. (1996), *The Perils of Urban Consolidation,* Federation Press: NSW Australia.

UN (2012), 'Resilient People, Resilient Planet, A Future Worth Choosing: The UN Secretary General's High-Level Panel on Global Sustainability', <www.un.org/gsp/> accessed April 2012.

UNEP (2005), 'Millennium Ecosystem Assessment: Strengthening Capacity to Manage Ecosystems Sustainably for Human Wellbeing', <http://ma.caudillweb.com/en/about.overview.aspx> accessed June 2006.

Vale, R. and Vale, B. (2000), *The New Autonomous House,* Thames & Hudson: London.

Van der Ryn, S. and Cowan, S. (1996), *Ecological Design,* Island Press: Washington, D.C.

Vickers, G. (1968/1970), *Value Systems and Social Process,* Pelican Books: Middlesex.

Wann, D. (1996), *Deep Design: Pathways to a Liveable Future,* Island Press: Washington, D.C.

Warren, K. (1997), *Ecofeminism: Women, Culture, Nature,* Indiana University Press: Bloomington.

WBCSD (World Business Council for Sustainable Development) (2009), *Transforming the Market: Energy Efficiency in Buildings,* WBCSD Report, Geneva.

WBCSD (World Business Council for Sustainable Development), de Simone, L. and Popoff, F. (1997), *Eco-Efficiency: The Business Link to Sustainable Development,* MIT Press: Cambridge, MA.

WCED (World Commission on Environment and Development) (1987), *Our Common Future,* Oxford University Press: Oxford.

Webber, M. (1963), in Duhl, L. J. (ed.), *The Urban Condition,* Basic Books: New York.

Wolman, A. (1965), 'The Metabolism of Cities', *Scientific American,* vol. 213, no. 3: pp. 179–90.

6

I Miss the Hungry Years: Coping with Abundance

ALBERT BORGMANN

INTRODUCTION

Information technology is a marvel of ingenuity and engineering. It has been widely admired and used; it is being advanced by inventiveness and competition; and it is being promoted by politicians and education experts. But there has also been research and discussion of the liabilities of information technology. The abundance of information has not, as one might have expected, made people generally more attentive and knowledgeable. On the contrary, distraction and ignorance are spreading. That has to worry people in higher education.

I won't rehearse the evidence of widespread ignorance and distraction (see Bauerlein, 2008; Carr, 2010; Jackson, 2008; Jacoby, 2008; Sherman, 2008). Instead, I'll try to shed more light on the problem by calling attention to analogies between food and information. In particular, I'll suggest that what we are beginning to learn about how to cope with food we should apply to information.

Food, sex, and information must have been crucial to the evolution of humans. No doubt, some humans didn't care about food, were indifferent to sex, or were incurious. But the abstemious, frigid, or indolent presumably left fewer offspring and disappeared without a trace. We are the progeny of creatures who were always hungry for food, sex, and news, and so are we.

In premodern circumstances, however, human voraciousness was always met by relative scarcity, and thus overindulgence was for the most part impossible. But the culture of the advanced industrial countries gradually changed scarcity into abundance, first of food, then of information, and finally of sex. And now abundance has turned from a blessing into a curse.

My concern is with the abundance of information. I will set aside sex, and I will use food to illustrate a pathology and cure that are more evident in food and can help us to recognize problems with information that are more concealed if no less perilous. Food and information are large topics. But we can get a grip on what is crucial for information and education by paying attention to a pattern of development they share and that allows us to narrow our focus.

THE DEVELOPMENT OF ABUNDANCE

The trajectory of modern technology typically traces a path from the provision of basic and necessary commodities to the production of ever more refined and diverse consumption goods. That path is always traced by the conjoined processes of mechanization and commodification. An increasingly sophisticated and powerful machinery draws more and more goods and services out of the contexts of family and community and offers them at a price and in a variety that traditional producers cannot rival.

If we trace the mechanical path of agriculture, we see the improvement of plows, the invention of mechanical reapers, the introduction of steam power, the spread of tractors until we reach the contemporary food industry with its computers, GPS devices, and sophisticated biochemistry. The commodification trail leads from canned goods and mechanized bread baking to today's supermarket with its more than forty thousand different items.

The development of information technology led from the pony express to the railroad, from the man-powered printing press to the steam-powered rotary press, from the telegraph to the telephone, from radio to television, and, in the last quarter of the last century, to the computer revolution. Today the commodities of information are available on fine-grained and colored screens that are larger and smaller than ever.

The overall tendency, then, has been from scarcity by way of technological progress to an abundance of food and information. In our advanced industrial setting, people have a range of choices and a degree of control that amount to incredible power. You can summon most any food or information at any time and wherever you are. In fact, the rhetoric of empowerment has always driven and celebrated the growing availability of food and information.

THE DOWNSIDE OF ABUNDANCE

We have to be grateful for these developments, grateful to our ancestors who did incredibly hard and often crippling work to push the developments forward, grateful that we are spared the hunger, the illness, and the confinement that marked the lives of our forebears. But given the superlative successes of technology and the power it has lent us, we should expect more than the satisfaction of basic needs. We should see a powerful culture, a country of people who are physically vigorous and intellectually articulate, who are healthy and insightful.

Something went badly wrong, however. Instead of articulate vigor, we see physical and mental distension. We see shapeless bodies and distracted minds. We are also beginning to recognize what went wrong with food, and we should learn to apply what we have learned—from the fate of food to the future of information.

In the United States, two-thirds of the population are overweight or obese. Morbidity and mortality today are much more benign than they used to be. But what health and longevity we have is as much the result of medical scaffolding as it is of natural vigor. Many of the diseases that trouble our lives are self-inflicted through lack of exercise and bad nutrition. Bad nutrition? How can that be, given the variety and abundance of food? To understand what happened, we need to recognize the tendency of the machinery that has come between the fields and the mouth. Food has always been mediated through devices, at first through bow and arrow, through digging sticks and baskets, through fire and fermentation.

Until the middle of the nineteenth century, most of these tools were still under the direct control and within the direct experience of ordinary people. To produce the amount, the variety, and the attractiveness of today's mainstream food, a huge and sophisticated machinery is required. What comes out of the soil is distant raw material—distant in space, distant in shape and texture, and distant to our understanding of it all. But the final products are as close as they can be to our desires. They indulge the size of our appetites and our cravings for what is colorful, sweet, juicy, creamy, and salty.

Eating used to be the conclusion of an intricate and intelligible process, a lengthy sequence of steps we all had to take in greater or lesser part. It went from planting and raising to harvesting and slaughtering, to curing and storing, to preparing and cooking and then, finally, to eating. It is plausible to assume that the only thing that really matters in this process is the final stage: putting food in our mouths. If we could dispense with all the preceding tedium, so much the better, and if what we put in our mouths has to the highest degree those attractive features that make us want to chew and swallow it, so much better yet. Voilà, a Big Mac.

That is the tendency. It is not all there is to food. There are exceptions and countervailing forces. But the increase in the size and sophistication of the food industry, the progress in food engineering, the growth in the portions we eat, the effect that all this has had on average weight and health: all this amounts to an evident direction in which the development of food is moving. It has led to grave cultural losses. To start with, there is the loss of agriculture as a commendable form of culture, practices of raising plants and animals that are respectful of the environment, of the plants and animals, and of the workers. There is the impoverishment, if not the loss, of the common understanding where the food has been grown and how it has been treated. The opaqueness of food production is of course just the shell of the gigantic machinery that has displaced the communities of farmers, butchers, bakers, and grocers we once knew. In the domestic sphere, the culture of cooking and eating has declined, yielding to the constant and ubiquitous availability of food. Regular and common meals have been reduced to snacks that are scattered and bites that are grabbed whenever.

Food used to be a thing that was the disclosure and conclusion of a rich and intelligible context of engagements. It is one of the pivotal conceits of the technological culture that the conclusion is crucial and the context dispensable. The conceit becomes practicable when the burdens of the context can be given over to an industrial machinery, and it seems commendable when the concluding goods appear to be superior in variety and attractiveness to the things they displace. What gets overlooked is the fact that the loss of context amounts to a cultural impoverishment.

Here again we have to be careful. In many instances, the loss of richness is outweighed by a gain of health and leisure. Getting water from the well or the fountain is a rich experience, to be sure. But water so obtained can be contaminated or the well can dry up. To get enough water from springs and wells and meet sound sanitary standards is time consuming and a heavy burden for the household, which is still mostly run by women. Good judgment is needed to discern what should be left to the machinery of technology and what must be saved or retrieved for a life of excellence.

THE LESS VISIBLE PATHOLOGY OF THE INFORMATION CULTURE

Before I turn to the cures for the decline of the food culture, let me trace the more hidden pathology of the information culture. Information, like food, was once woven into the texture of everyday life; it was accessible and intelligible to all. Information came from nature, from the clouds that warned of rain, from the blossoms that foretold berries, from the tracks that pointed to game. It came from the stories of the elders, from the reports of those returning from gathering or hunting, and from the news conveyed by a member of the neighboring tribe.

Next came information that already required specialized instruction to be understood—notches on sticks, blazes on trees, cairns on hill tops. Then came writing and the expert knowledge of scribes, followed by literate communities that were vastly expanded through printing. Though reading and writing are demanding skills, they can be acquired by everyone and in the past gave everyone entry into a realm of information that was tangible in its ink-and-paper presence and intelligible to everyone in its form though not, of course, in all of its contents.

Beginning, roughly, with the telegraph, an information machinery began to develop that became ever less intelligible as it became more powerful. Few people understood how sound from distant places became audible in their radios; fewer still, how pictures could appear on their television tubes. And today, the machinery of computers and information links is incomprehensible to most users. As in the case of food, the growing size and sophistication of the machinery have greatly increased the quantity and variety of information. Advocates of this development have predicted a citizenry that is better informed and more insightful, leading to a richer cultural life. Supporters of social justice have been worried that the poor will be deprived of these blessings, and they have worked to level the digital divide. There cannot be any doubt about the power and convenience of information technology, nor is there a question of its value to the sciences and the conscientious citizen.

But again, as in the case of food, the transformation of the ends that comes with the transformation of the means has too often been overlooked. Does it make a difference to the information contained in a book whether it comes to me in a codex or on a Kindle?

The conveniences of a Kindle have been widely praised and appreciated. In a recent holiday season, Amazon sold more electronic books than paper books. To recognize the character of the electronic reading experience, we have to look ahead to the development of the device, the Kindle that makes the experience available. It is a sure bet that the austerity of the Kindle will yield to the richness of an iPhone. Not that the Kindle will replace the iPhone and its rivals. It's simply that users will expect additional conveniences, and competitors will oblige and even precede users. It will happen step by step. The Nook already has a color screen below the text display. Inexorably, color moves up to render pictures and graphs contained in books. And if books can be read on a Kindle, why not articles? And if articles can be read, why can't films be watched? And so on to iPhone capabilities.

Imagine now a student reading *Ulysses* or *The Man without Qualities*. He is a little tired and comes to a passage that strikes him as tedious. He needs a refreshing break. Why not check e-mail on the capable reading device? And then the preview of the Griz-Cat game? The NFL game that is in progress. The weather…When the student comes to, an hour has passed. It is obvious he won't get the reading done. But the tablet that has seduced him will help him out as well—or so it seems. There are summaries and race-gender-ethnicity critiques that will disburden him of the tedium of reading and thinking. When food is available abundantly, ubiquitously, and alluringly, people find themselves eating too much. They gain weight; their health suffers. When information is available abundantly, ubiquitously, and alluringly, people find themselves surfing too much. They become distracted; their knowledge suffers. A book presents information in an austere and secluded form that aids attentive and sustained reading. The book by itself won't restore thoughtful reading. Its preelectronic context was helpful, too—the greater resistance and distances that had to be overcome to get to distractions most especially. But the book can be a helpful focal point and starting point for better reading.

Information technology *can* be a powerful instrument. It has supported astounding and admirable work in the physical sciences and new and interesting work in the social sciences. It has been a great convenience in the humanities though it has not occasioned any kind of flowering that I'm aware of. In the culture at large, the abundance of information has been no more beneficial than the abundance of food. There has not been an overt catastrophe to be sure. Both food and information fulfill their basic task of keeping society going. Outrage would be misplaced. But sorrow about the enfeebling distensions of life is justified. What happened to food is happening to information. The refinements of information that the powerful machinery has made possible have obliged the stirrings of curiosity the way refined foods have answered the cravings of desire. Obesity and avoidable illness have their information analogues in distraction and avoidable ignorance.

COPING WITH THE ABUNDANCE OF FOOD

We now recognize that being overweight and obesity and the illnesses they bring with them are problems that require a public conversation and reasonable remedies. There are four measures that have received attention and may help us to cope with the abundance of food.

The first is lifting the hood of the food engine and beginning to understand how it works. One component of the engine is the corporate structures and policies that are pushing food. These include the employment of chemistry, the damage to the environment, and the devices of advertising and presentation. The necessary complement to corporate successes is the complicity of consumers, the chinks in our evolutionary armor of health, our vulnerability to the charms of availability, the more or less addictive cycle of craving, fulfillment, rising restlessness, more craving, and so on.

The second remedial measure is the recognition of partial alternatives to corporate machinery and consumer complicity. What's crucial here is the insight that preaching virtue is not enough and by itself can be worse than nothing. It leaves the preachers dispirited and the faithful defeated. What needs to be changed is the environment so that virtue has a chance to flourish. The production and availability of unhealthy food needs to be discouraged through public policy. Vice versa for healthy food.

Third and more concretely, we have to reweave the cultural context of food. The paths from the ground to the mouth need to be shortened and made evident as they are in the farm-to-college programs. The communal understanding of the origins and seasons of food has to be restored as it is in farmers' markets. And where possible, people should recover the skills and pleasures of gardening.

The fourth and perhaps least attended task is the rebuilding of the culture of the table, the common preparation of meals from basic and, whenever possible, local ingredients and the regular and pleasurable gatherings at the dinner table.

COPING WITH THE ABUNDANCE OF INFORMATION

We should take similar steps to cope with the surfeit of information. So the first task is to teach students what's under the platforms on which all the information is displayed. Youngsters are often praised for their computer savvy. But this is the kind of knowledge teenagers have of their city. They know all the cool places and how to get from one to the other. They know how to ride bikes, drive cars, and what to do about them if they crash. But they know little about the history of the city, its infrastructure, the zoning codes, city government, or mechanical engineering. Students should know some Boolean algebra, electronics, and programming. They should understand the structure of the Internet, the interplay of regulation and corporation. Here too, they should learn why and how evolution has made us curious, what piques our curiosity, what satisfies it fleetingly, and what enduringly.

Second, we have to understand that preaching against mindlessness and distraction is insufficient at best. We have to make classrooms places of concentration. Indiscriminate Wi-Fi availability is an invitation to distraction. Copious use of PowerPoint and slides scatters attention. Thoughtful speaking and listening are ancient human practices, less so than handling things and taking walks, but well-ingrained and rewarding as long as we don't let these talents atrophy the way we have let walking and handling wither away.

Third, information needs to be grounded in the actual and immediate world. Giving students a competent comprehension of the actual world is the task of general education. It is a task that is too often avoided by shaping general information after the pattern of the mechanization of information. Rather than teaching our students history and science, we teach them how to think like a historian, or we teach them the scientific method. Give them the means, and they will take care of the ends—that's the assumption. But the ends to which the powerful means of information technology are actually put in contemporary culture should tell us that the ends, the content and substance of knowledge, require instruction and appropriation.

General education teaches a student the crucial dimensions and features of the actual world. At a time when we allow media technology constantly to insert itself between humans and reality, immediate contact with the world needs to be reinvigorated as well. We have to insist that students do what social scientists have ruefully come to call "groundtruthing," checking on the ground what satellites and surveys are displaying on a screen. Students need to be taught and encouraged to observe, investigate, describe, report, and analyze what immediately surrounds them.

There is also the homely reality of pen and paper, the skills of laying down in unique and artful traces of ink what truly matters and will likely endure and even be treasured—letters, journals, essays. Writing in longhand is like taking a walk or cooking a meal, a little slow and laborious compared with keyboarding just as walking and cooking are compared with driving and stopping for burgers and fries, but more sustaining as well.

Finally, we should aim at the rebuilding of the culture of the word. The utility of information technology needs no justification or advocacy. It should remain a strand in the context of our lives. But within that context there has to be a central and secure place for reading and conversation, where electronic intrusions are kept at bay and our stages of discovery and pleasure—our books—surround us. We must make our students read *Hamlet* and *Lear*. But we should also encourage them to become lifelong readers of Shakespeare.

NOTE

This chapter was originally published in 2010 in *The Montana Professor*, University of Montana: Missoula, vol. 21, no. 1: pp. 4–7. It is reproduced here with kind permission of the author.

REFERENCES

Bauerlein, M. (2008), *The Dumbest Generation*, Tarcher: New York.

Carr, N. (2010). *The Shallows: What the Internet is Doing to Our Brains*, Norton: New York.

Jackson, M. (2008), *Distracted: The Erosion of Attention and the Coming Dark Age*, Prometheus: Amherst, NY.

Jacoby, S. (2008), *The Age of Unreason*, Pantheon: New York.

Sherman, R. (2008), *Just How Stupid are We?* Basic Books: New York.

Methods and Approaches

Editorial Introduction

STUART WALKER AND JACQUES GIARD

Part I gave an overview of the historical and theoretical contexts for design and sustainability. It looked at how we have arrived at our current state and the factors that underpinned this development, including our understandings of the world, our values and priorities and those things that, along the way, we set aside. And it considered the implications for design. A key feature that emerged during those discussions is the complexity of our current predicament and the daunting challenges that confront us as we move forward. 'Part II: Methods and Approaches' provides the reader with essential first steps as well as practical examples. The section includes discussions of methods and approaches that can be adopted by designers, manufacturers and marketing specialists, and by individuals in their everyday lives.

An overview of methods and practices is a logical starting point for this section, and this is provided by Tracy Bhamra and her colleagues Ricardo Hernandez and Richard Mawle. 'Sustainability: Methods and Practices' offers a wide-ranging survey of approaches and their application in design practice. The authors examine design for sustainability by focusing not only on incremental design that improves or redesigns existing products but also on radical innovation, which includes new concept development as well as system innovation. Their overview is supported by an analysis of the strengths and weaknesses of the various approaches and is supplemented by case studies that demonstrate the ways in which these methods have been applied in practice and the resulting products, services or systems. The chapter concludes with a consideration of the possible benefits and limitations that may arise from applying these approaches, the concentration on environmental issues and the relative lack of attention to social considerations, as well as emerging directions for research and their implications for the future of design.

Methods and practices in design for sustainability is also the theme for 'Integrating Sustainability in Design Education'. However, unlike the previous chapter with its focus on design practice, this discussion examines professional design education. It provides an overview of how our understandings of sustainability are being integrated into design education within professional programmes in the United States. Jacques Giard and Deborah Schneiderman compare and contrast different approaches, which include stand-alone courses on sustainability theory as well as practice-based studio projects that combine theory and practice. The chapter reflects on the context in which design education normally operates, especially the expectations of the various design professions and their respective accreditation agencies. It concludes with recommendations for integrating sustainability more effectively in design curricula, including the need to reconsider the tenets of design education in a post-industrial age.

Tim Cooper moves the discussion one more step forward by considering the sheer throughput of consumer goods, many of which still function when discarded. In 'Sustainability, Consumption and the Throwaway Culture', he expounds on the challenge that this situation poses not only to the existing economically developed countries but also to those countries that are in a rapid state of economic development, and that all too often tend to replicate the patterns of consumption found in the wealthier nations. In his view, and despite increased awareness of environmental threats by citizens and governments, product improvements alone will not bring about more sustainable forms of consumption or more sustainable ways of living. Too many people feel unable to make substantial changes to their lifestyles and, for their part, governments are locked into short-term, growth-dependent models of progress. Yet, Cooper is hopeful. 'A new direction in public policy is essential', he asserts, 'if the throwaway culture is to be transformed'.

The role that ordinary people can and should play in design and sustainability continues in Anne Marchand's chapter, 'Why Sustainable Consumers Don't Care Much about Green Products'. This chapter focuses on sustainable consumption in relation to product design but goes beyond the materiality of the product itself and suggests that equal concern be placed on how we relate to products as a way of contributing to a more viable, meaningful future. However, a challenge exists because of limits and uncertainties surrounding current forms of green or sustainable consumption, on the one hand, and the need to reduce our domestic consumption, on the other. In the face of this challenge, the question is raised as to what can possibly motivate people in their everyday lives to go beyond opting for greener product or solutions and to voluntarily curb their overall consumption. Marchand ends the chapter on a somewhat positive note by providing data showing that self-interest, though often perceived as being at the root of environmental problems, may actually play a constructive role in the shift from green to sustainable consumption.

Consumption patterns and their implications for sustainable consumption can also be facilitated by strategic marketing and branding. This is the position taken by Dorothy Mackenzie in 'Design, Sustainability and Marketing'. Brands have an important role to play in the normalization of consumption patterns. The same principles and practices that apply to regular consumption can have a similar impact on normalizing perceptions and behaviours in relation to issues of sustainability and the development of more sustainable behaviours. By employing such approaches, complex sustainability issues can be interpreted in ways that make them relevant to ordinary people. In this way, brands could act as advocates for more sustainable types of consumption behaviour, even to the extent of aligning themselves with reductions in absolute levels of consumption. Brands are increasingly seeking to develop deeper modes of engagement and collaboration with their audiences, and the goal of more sustainable consumption can be a powerful focus for this.

Part II concludes with a more detailed look at one of the important components in design and sustainability: micro-, small- and medium-sized enterprises or SMEs and their role in developing innovative solutions. In 'The Role of Design-Led Knowledge Exchange in Supporting Micro-, Small- and Medium-Sized Enterprises to Be Eco-Innovators in the United Kingdom', Anne Chick discusses how universities can participate in and contribute to the development of innovative approaches to sustainability within SMEs, thereby affecting and advancing our understandings of sustainability and innovation, both nationally and internationally. Her approach is supported by a case study, which she considers in relation to the competitiveness of SMEs in the United Kingdom. In this context, design becomes a crucial business interface between sustainability and innovation practices. This work demonstrates that a design-led approach can make a lasting impression on SMEs through deeper forms of engagement that lead to transformative learning. This is the kind of learning that can have a long-lasting impact on a firm's sustainability and innovation practices.

7

Sustainability: Methods and Practices

TRACY BHAMRA, RICARDO HERNANDEZ
AND RICHARD MAWLE

INTRODUCTION TO DESIGN FOR
SUSTAINABILITY APPROACHES

Design for sustainability is design with the intention to achieve sustainable outputs. It is design that considers the environmental and social impacts of a product, service or system at the same level that economic concerns are considered (Bhamra and Lofthouse, 2007). When implementing this within design projects, it must take a holistic perspective taking into account all the life cycle stages of the product, service or system, from extraction of raw materials, manufacturing, distribution and use to end-of-life scenarios to influence the outputs of the design process.

This systemic idea of design has made the public and private agendas on sustainability turn their attention towards design for sustainability as an engine of positive transformation: on one side, improving environmental performance of products, services and systems, increasing energy efficiency, encouraging the use of recycled materials, and/or reducing the use of toxic substances; on the other, achieving social benefits associated with issues such as usability, fair sourcing, design for human needs and socially responsible use of products and services. However, design for sustainability has also a great potential to change attitudes and behaviours. Within the radical dimension of innovation, design for sustainability can help to define a new direction, new lifestyles and new ways to identify and satisfy people's needs in environmentally efficient, socially equitable and profitable ways.

Design for sustainability can respond to the necessity to find a new direction for the way in which products and services are produced and consumed around the world. Designers should take this new direction to lead their projects and influence, through design, other dimensions in organizations, in communities, in private and public bodies. These changes and influences can be achieved by different routes. Design for sustainability can be described as a journey, broken down into different stages moving from incremental design to radical innovations (Brezet, 1997).

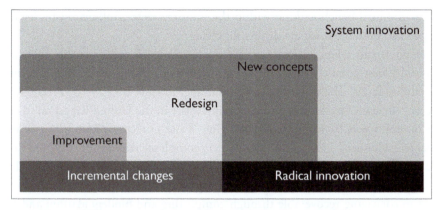

FIGURE 7.1   Different approaches to embark on design for sustainability.

In organizational terms, there is a need for structural changes rather than simply using new technologies to achieve more sustainable business. New scenarios of business with greater economic, social and environmental value are being explored rather than just reducing resource use (Rainey, 2006). Design has a major role in this organizational transformation towards sustainable businesses. It has been established, for example, that almost 80 per cent of the costs of product development, manufacture and use are determined in the design stage (Mascle and Zhao, 2008). So, the earlier environmental and social factors are considered in the design process, the greater the possible savings and positive performance of the product. This inclusion of environmental and social factors can be done through incremental innovations such as design for easy disassembly or packaging reduction, but it can also be executed in more radical ways such as designing new business concepts such as product service systems (PSS). This idea of the different routes to embark on design for sustainability is presented in Figure 7.1. This representation implies that the journey can start at any stage and that the more radical the approach the greater the number of less radical changes can also be included. For example, system innovation includes concepts, tools and principles from improvement, redesign and new concepts, but considered from a different point of view.

APPROACHES

The different approaches that can be used to embark on design for sustainability, outlined in Figure 7.1, are explored in this section. Their use is explained and examples of implementation given.

1. Improvement

Improvement is an incremental approach that can be used in design for sustainability. It is at the base of the possible routes that a designer can take to pursue sustainable products, services and systems. The idea is to make small modifications to the outputs of design by considering, as far as possible, both environmental and social aspects that result in products, services and systems that have better performance in the three dimensions: people, planet and profit. Usually these modifications are related to current legislation and to continual benchmarking within the industry sector, influenced by regulations and policies, both of which are drivers for change.

Designers can take advantage of the standards developed to enable their designs to consider best practice, for example, in the use of certain materials, packaging and recyclability levels. These standards, for example, include BS EN 13427:2004, which concerns the use of packaging and packaging waste in the United Kingdom to comply with the European Packaging and Packaging Waste Directive (94/62/EC) (European Parliament Council, 1994). This standard is complemented by BS EN 13430:2004, which is focused on the recyclability of packaging materials; BS EN 13431:2004, which deals with energy recovery of used packaging; BS EN 13432:2000, which relates to packaging recoverable through composting and biodegradation; and BS EN 13429:2004, which is oriented to packaging reuse. These types of standards give a framework that when combined with design for sustainability can help designers not only to comply with legislation but also produce innovative designs with greater environmental and social value.

In the case of electrical and electronic products, one of the main pieces of legislation introduced in Europe is the Directive 2002/96/EC on WEEE (Waste Electrical and Electronic Equipment) which requires producers to take responsibility for their products at the end of their products' life. This directive affects all producers of electric and electronic products who want to commercialize their products in Europe (Bhamra and Lofthouse, 2007). The final objective of this directive is to reduce the amount of e-waste by encouraging producers to take actions that lead to the reuse, recycling and recovery of their products. Designers have to be conscious of these regulatory frameworks in order to comply with the law but also because it can create an opportunity to modify designs and put products and services in a better strategic position.

In terms of energy consumption, the Ecodesign Directive (2009/125/EC) finalized in 2009 defines a framework for producers of energy-using products to improve the energy efficiency of their products (European Parliament Council, 2009). More specific standards, frameworks and directives related to environmental management can be found in other industries that affect the design of products and services, such as automotive, chemicals and printing. This complexity of legislation and standards makes improvement a challenging approach, even if it is implemented by the inclusion of small changes in the design process. Making design for sustainability part of the environmental management system (EMS) inside the organization could be one way to ensure that criteria such as energy efficiency, recyclability, waste and replacement of banned substances are taken into account from the outset of the product, service or system development. An EMS focusing on incremental improvements through constant evaluation of the system can be useful to ensure that these can be related to sustainable product, service or system design.

Finally, following this approach of incremental changes through improvement, designers should aim to gain an understanding of what design for sustainability means and reflect this through concrete actions in the design process. Some of these actions can be related, for example, to selecting low-impact materials by taking into account recycling rates, avoiding toxic substances according to the legislation or replacing non-renewable materials. In terms of energy efficiency, this can be achieved by identifying whereabouts in the life cycle the product, service or system consumes energy and encouraging low consumption. This can be done by active or passive means—for example, by displaying information to the user or embedding mechanisms to turn off the product, service or system when not in use (Brezet and Van Hemel, 1997). This can be accomplished, also, by considering waste and what the possible options are to dispose of the product or components of the system at the end of their life. The available options are shown as a waste hierarchy in Figure 7.2 (European Parliament Council, 2008).

Washing Machines, Panasonic Case: In general, the design of washing machines in terms of functionality and expected results is very similar today to what it was twenty years ago. However, the consumption of energy during use, which represents an important environmental impact, has been reduced considerably by a process of continual improvement in the design process to reach the targets established by law. Panasonic, for example, has been achieving environmental impact reduction in their washing machines by the incorporation of low washing temperature cycles, auto power-off functions, short washing cycles and, more recently, inverter control technologies (Panasonic, 2011).

In this example, it is possible to see a continual improvement approach whereby small modifications in the design of the final product are not only innovative but also improve sustainability performance. These modifications in the product design have not come all at once but are the result of years of development. However, even small modifications in design can have large implications in the interaction between customers and products. Low temperature cycles and short washing cycles, for example, could mean important changes in the behaviour of consumers. It is a risk for a company to

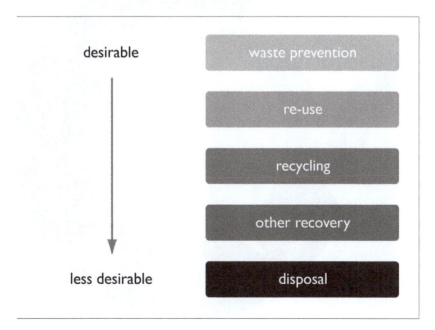

FIGURE 7.2   Waste hierarchy.

embark on an improvement approach, and for that reason it is also important to support the changes with mechanisms that consumers can understand and value. Panasonic certifies its machines with widely known eco-labels and with their own labels such as Energy Saving, Good Housekeeping Institute, Aquaprotection System and Ecoideas to fulfil this purpose, communicate its strategy and create value around environmental and social improvements (Panasonic, 2011).

2. Redesign

Though still an incremental change, redesign is a more proactive approach than improvement and considers the impact of a design over an entire life cycle. Whilst an overall design concept would remain unchanged, modifying the way in which design details are executed can lead to reductions in resource use, such as decreasing the amount of materials used and how much energy is consumed throughout a product's life.

In order to successfully redesign a product, service or system, it is important to have a clear understanding of the resources required for the creation of the current design. The initial step in this process is to examine the whole life cycle of the existing entity so that it can be assessed. As shown in Figure 7.3, the life cycle has several stages, starting

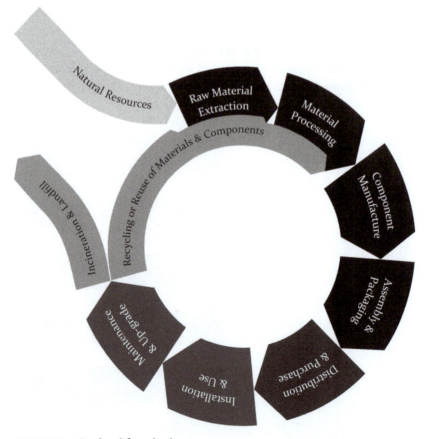

FIGURE 7.3   Product life-cycle phases.

with the extraction and processing of raw materials and followed by their conversion into components. These parts are then assembled, packaged and distributed. Once purchased by the consumer, there is a use phase, which ultimately leads to disposal followed by any reuse or recycling that may occur. All stages in the life cycle of a product, service or system consume natural resources, either directly as materials or indirectly as energy and in turn create an environmental impact in the form of emissions or waste (Fiksel, 2009).

To make an informed judgement on the best way to minimize any ecological impact, a proper evaluation of the full effect of the life cycle must be made, and this is generally done using a Life Cycle Assessment (LCA) technique. There are numerous LCA tools available, ranging in complexity, but in essence they all aim to quantify the inputs and outputs of the item being evaluated by breaking down the life cycle into manageable steps and calculating its environmental impact (ISO, 2006). A variety of different metrics can be used to achieve this, but embodied energy, carbon footprint and water usage are some of the most common. Having made this assessment, it is then possible to identify the appropriate areas for redesign, and it also enables improvements to be quantified and compared to the original.

Once an assessment of the existing product, service or system has been made, the points in the life cycle that have the greatest impact can be identified, and the most appropriate redesign strategies can be more easily identified. Table 7.1 shows redesign strategies as defined by Van Hemel (1998).

When considering the production and supply of materials or components, Strategies 1 and 2 are important because they focus on selecting materials with a low environmental impact as well as reducing the volume and number of materials. For the manufacture and assembly of components, Strategy 3 encourages the selection of clean production techniques, minimizing the energy used, and reducing the amount of material waste. The issues that arise in the distribution phase are covered by Strategies 2 and 4; the size and weight of packaging can have an important impact on the type of transport that can be used and how efficiently it can be organized. It is also important to take account of packaging and whether it can be reused or recycled. During the use phase, it is often the energy required in operation that has the biggest impact, though as Strategy 5 highlights, consumables may also be an issue worth examining. There are also situations where the energy invested prior to use is the most significant factor; in this case, Strategy 6 should be paramount, as it is concerned with maximizing longevity through initial reliability and ease of upgrade or repair. Finally, Strategy 7 is concerned with end-of-life and how this can be best optimized to minimize waste. Here there is a hierarchy (see Figure 7.2), with reuse being the preferred route; though if this is not feasible, recycling should be made as easy as possible and any remaining material should be disposed of safely.

The process of taking an existing design, looking at its life cycle, assessing where it has the largest repercussions, then applying a set of strategies to reduce these can help minimize its environmental impact. By taking this type of systematic approach to the redesign of products, services or systems, it is also possible to reduce costs because the

TABLE 7.1   DESIGN FOR ENVIRONMENT STRATEGIES (VAN HEMEL, 1998).

STRATEGY 1: Select low-impact materials

- Choose clean materials
- Choose renewable materials
- Choose materials with a low energy content
- Choose recycled materials

STRATEGY 2: Reduction of material usage

- Reduction of weight
- Reduction of (transport) volume

STRATEGY 3: Optimization of production techniques

- Choose alternative production techniques
- Fewer production steps
- Low/clean energy consumption
- Less production waste
- Few/clean production consumables

STRATEGY 4: Optimizing the distribution system

- Little/clean/reusable packaging
- Energy-efficient means of transport
- Energy-efficient logistics

STRATEGY 5: Reduction of the user impact

- Ensure low energy consumption
- Choose a clean energy source
- Reduce the amount of consumables required
- Choose clean consumables
- No waste of energy or consumables

STRATEGY 6: Optimization of initial lifetime

- Increase reliability and durability
- Ensure easy maintenance and repairs
- Ensure a modular, adaptable product structure
- Aim to achieve a classic design
- Ensure a strong product-user relation

STRATEGY 7: Optimization of the end-of-life system

- Stimulate reuse of the entire product
- Stimulate remanufacturing and refurbishing
- Stimulate material recycling
- Stimulate safe incineration with energy recovery
- Ensure the safe disposal of product scrap

Source: Van Hemel, 1998

efficient use of resources is both ecologically and commercially beneficial. However, there is a limit on what can be achieved without a more radical change and the creation of new design concepts.

Herman Miller, Mirra Chair: In essence, the design of office chairs has not altered greatly for many years, but Herman Miller has earned a reputation for creating iconic seating with enduring desirability. In addition, the company has managed to combine this aesthetic allure with enhanced ergonomics and improvements in environmental performance.

Herman Miller used the sustainable McDonough Braungart Design Chemistry (MBDC) Cradle to Cradle Design Protocol (MBDC, 2011) when producing the Mirra chair (Miller, 2011), with the main considerations at this level of design being material health, material reutilization and renewable energy use. These factors in turn led to the specification of more chemically safe materials; the maximization of recycled material content in production; the potential to disassemble the chair at the end of its useful life in order to facilitate reuse of parts; and the optimization of remaining parts that can be recycled. This resulted in a chair that is made from 33 per cent recycled material and that is 96 per cent recyclable at the end of its life. The Mirra chair also has improved longevity, facilitated by the specification of durable materials and the ability to easily remove and replace worn or broken parts. This improved performance is backed by a twelve-year warranty from Herman Miller. In addition to these direct design changes, the energy used in production comes from wind turbines and landfill off-gassing. When comparing these strategies to those shown in Table 7.1, it is clear the Mirra chair exhibits improvements in all the relevant areas discussed.

3. New Concepts

Developing new concepts is a more radical approach than using strategies to redesign an existing product, service or system. It requires designers to think about underlying needs and how they can be fulfilled, rather than focusing on methods of improving the current design. Considering innovative ways to achieve the same function or functions, such as replacing paper-based communication with email, can lead to more sustainable solutions.

The creation of new concepts requires designers to take a much more holistic view of what they are trying to achieve, with outcomes that may require multidisciplinary collaboration to realize. Although by its nature a new concept cannot be easily planned for, there are some guiding principles (Van Hemel, 1998) that can be useful in this kind of fundamental rethinking of existing solutions.

- Dematerialization: this is not the same as reducing material usage in a redesign but rather entirely replacing a physical object with an alternative means of providing the same service. An example of this could be substituting an answering machine with voicemail, or compact discs with downloadable digital audio files.

- Shared use of the product, packaging, service or visual communications: in this case, the use of a product or service may be divided between a number of people. This can be observed where functions are combined, such as using packaging as part of the final product.
- Integration of functions: by combining several functions into one item, the environmental impact can be significantly reduced. The emergence of the smartphone has clearly demonstrated the importance of multifunctionality, combining facilities such as email, satellite navigation and music player, along with the telephone, in one device.
- Functional optimization: new concept development starts with scrutiny of the function or functions that are trying to be provided. In the process of considering these functions, it may become clear that some aspects of the design are unnecessary or could be supplied in a more sustainable way. This overuse of materials can be seen in places such as the packaging of luxury goods or those marketed as gifts. However, in order to make any significant change in this area it may be necessary for a much wider organizational or cultural shift to take place before this type of packaging is seen as superfluous.

In order for this kind of approach to be successful, and for new concepts to be accepted, there may need to be a more meaningful change in the way users think about value and ownership. There is a complex and deep-seated desire amongst consumers to own the product or system they are using, and this requires changes to be made at a corporate and societal level in order to be undone. This change, along with the participation of a wide range of stakeholders, is necessary in order to innovate further and consider system innovation. However, despite the current situation limiting what can be achieved by designers alone and through creativity and ingenuity, designers can still influence more sustainable outcomes, and inspire others to do the same.

Knoend, lite2go: The lite2go (Knoend, 2007) is a light where the packaging is also used to create the lampshade. The main packaging is made from translucent polypropylene, with a paper label that contains the product information. Inside, there is a low-energy light bulb, power cable with fittings, a further roll of plastic and an instruction booklet. To assemble the lamp, the light fitting screws on to the folded packaging, the light bulb is attached, and then the additional plastic creates a sleeve that fits over the top of the original packaging. This is a very simple product that only leaves a small amount of paper and hemp twine to be disposed of once made. This type of approach, where there is a shared use of materials for different stages in a product's life, can improve resource use and enhance sustainability.

Solar Desalination Still, Watercone: The Watercone (MAGE, 2011) is a small device invented by Stephan Augustine for transforming saltwater into drinking water just using sunshine. Most desalination is currently done on an industrial scale either using distillation or separating out the salt using a semipermeable membrane. These methods are energy intensive and require an infrastructure to distribute the purified water. The Watercone, by contrast, is an individual device that uses sunlight to distil the water. It is a clear plastic cone with an eighty-centimetre diameter base that can either be floated directly on water, or placed on water that has been poured into the accompanying black pan. As the sun heats the water, it evaporates, rises and then condenses on the inside of the cone; it then trickles down the inner wall of the cone into a rim at the base. Up to one-and-a-half litres of water can be collected in twenty-four hours and poured out through a spout at the top of the cone. Rather than redesigning current desalination systems, the Watercone is a new concept that is portable and easy to use, and does not require any generated energy to use. Once distributed in areas of necessity, the Watercone not only has the potential to provide a reliable source of drinking water but also gives greater control over the supply to those who really need it.

4. System Innovation

To achieve higher levels of innovation, this approach adopts a more strategic view and involves the participation of many different stakeholders including communities, government, companies and customers. Here, designers are part of the development of new complete sustainable systems implying new lifestyles and ways to understand production and consumption of goods and services. This holistic approach not only responds to an evolution process but also aims to avoid the rebound effects often found as a result of partial improvements in products and services from less radical approaches (Roy, 2000).

Design for sustainability plays a very important role in this transformation of thinking; Manzini and Vezzoli (2003) highlighted the role in terms of 'the capacity to create new stakeholder configurations and develop an integrated system of products, services and communication that is coherent with the medium-long-term perspective of sustainability being, at the same time, economically feasible and socially appreciable today'. Designers have a wide field to innovate, to be creative and to participate in the design and development of these new configurations that may require changes in infrastructure, technologies, values and behaviours (Bhamra and Lofthouse, 2007).

One concept that has gained attention as part of this radical approach is the development of product service systems (PSS). Organizations embarking on the journey at this point should rethink how they identify the needs of their customers and what they really are, and then reimagine them in order to come up with innovative business offers based on combinations of products, services and systems. In general, PSS can help to dematerialize offers by replacing products with services; can increase life cycles and reduce the amount of waste by implementing reuse or sharing schemes; and can reduce materials flows and decrease energy consumption (Mont, 2002). These opportunities can also have positive implications in social and economic terms by creating new business opportunities, bringing producers closer to customers, creating collaborative networks between stakeholders and making basic services more accessible through communal infrastructure (Ness, 2007; Tukker and Tischner, 2004).

The range of PSS that has been developed during the last twenty years comes from a wide variety of industries and applications, from rent and sharing business models, especially in private transport, to complex medical systems. The range also includes flooring systems; communal services of lighting and clothes washing; printing platforms; digital music distribution; food production and distribution systems; as well as new furniture business models (Bhamra and Lofthouse, 2007).

However, PSS are not the only route to achieve system innovation; in general, a radical transformation of the business model, including changing values, behaviour, and infrastructure, is part of this approach. Design for sustainability could contribute to this transformation by being part of the creative process of design and giving a sustainable perspective from the beginning of the process. Some of the possible actions and considerations that should be taken into account include the following:

- creating a lasting attachment between product, service or system and the user;
- using industrial ecology;
- ensuring design ethics;
- encouraging the fostering of resilient communities; and
- designing to increase the quality of life for all.

Barclays Cycle Hire System: System innovation demands larger changes in how companies approach the design of products and services mainly to ensure consistency between products and services as part of the system. The main difference with the previous approaches is the idea of products and services creating value together around social, environmental and economic aspects as a system. One example that can illustrate this approach is the Barclays Cycle Hire System in London. The system is composed of docking stations, bikes, a payment platform and an information system that together create a transport system alternative in the city (Transport for London, 2011).

All the elements in this system have been designed to be part of the system and to create value together. For example, the bikes used in the system are modified designs that incorporate special features to perform as part of the system. They are tough in order to withstand public use by different kinds of customers in all extreme weather conditions. They have special locks and registration numbers to prevent thefts. They also have storage spaces, lights and a bungee cord to serve the needs of commuters who carry bags or briefcases in their daily routine. In terms of the docking stations, these are designed to safely store the bikes and allow the clients to make payments and collect and return the bikes. But they are also specially located around the city to provide the desired coverage as a transport system. Similarly, the information system provides a twenty-four-hour service with different commercial schemes as individual payments or as part of memberships (Transport for London, 2011).

In this brief example, it is possible to see the integration of products and services into a complex system that demands special design. If the objectives behind the system have a sustainable perspective, design has not only the responsibility to assure functionality and aesthetics but also sustainable performance of the system. In this sense,

Barclays Cycle Hire System has important benefits in environmental terms as a substitute for cars, providing a zero emissions means of transport. Socially, it contributes to a less congested city; for tourists, it is a useful opportunity to travel around the city; and for daily users, it is an alternative way to get to work quickly. In many cases, the Barclays system is a more comfortable way to travel and can also claim health benefits for its users.

Despite the benefits, there are also large changes in societal behaviour needed to make this kind of systems operable and profitable. In systems such as the Barclays Cycle Hire System, educational campaigns and other incentives are also needed in order to attract users and achieve real long-term results.

COMPARISON AND CRITICAL EVALUATION

The approaches to sustainable design have been described as existing on a continuum from incremental change to radical innovation. Whilst innovations in function or systems can achieve greater improvements in eco-efficiency, they are more complex and require significantly more time to implement than the lesser changes needed to improve or redesign a product, service or system. Figure 7.4 represents this correlation between innovation and the increased levels of sustainability that can be achieved. The size of the squares represents the relative level of commitment required to achieve these levels of change and the uncertainty that may be associated with this kind of transformation.

Legislation-led changes are likely to result in actions that ensure compliance rather than a wider change in thinking within an organization. Laws are generally made in reaction to events in the wider world, meaning they can be limited and slow to adapt to the realities of business. In addition, regulations and directives are created at a macro

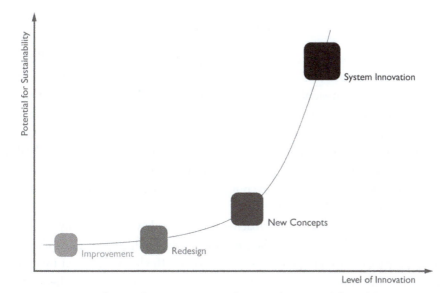

FIGURE 7.4   Influence that innovation can have on the sustainability of design.

level, often neglecting the significant variation that exists between the size of organizations leading to legislation and standards that can be too demanding for small and medium enterprises (SMEs). This is of particular concern because such a large proportion of design is carried out by SMEs. Redesign requires a more proactive approach but can deliver clear benefits in terms of resource efficiency and associated cost savings without radically changing design outcomes and their related markets. A full life cycle assessment does require time and expertise to produce useful results, which can be a barrier to change, particularly for smaller organizations. However, there are a number of tools and strategies available to help designers focus their attention on the appropriate aspects of their work, leading to some improvement in sustainability. These incremental changes can only produce a maximum of an 80 per cent improvement in eco-efficiency, whilst with more radical innovations the reductions in environmental impact could be up to 95 per cent (Van Hemel, 1998). Unfortunately, the ways of developing new concepts and creating system innovation are less well understood and much harder to make concrete. They both require the participation of a wide range of stakeholders, at the corporate level and in wider society, in order for changes to be successful. Embarking on this type of change carries a high level of risk because there are no established methods for conducting a transformation of this sort, and the associated costs are generally high due to the need for significant changes in technology and infrastructure. However, if successful, the potential rewards are far greater than with the more conservative changes because innovation at this level can create entirely new business opportunities and significantly differentiate the product, service or system from those of competitors. There are ecological improvements derived from all of the changes discussed, but ultimately the greatest environmental benefits come from the most radical innovations, and, despite the uncertainties, these in turn have the potential for providing the greatest financial reward.

DISCUSSION

The approaches for design for sustainability are proving to be useful and applicable to many industries. However, it is interesting to note that to date much of the focus has been purely on environmental issues rather than a more balanced approach that takes into account the social impact as well. The reasons for this are easy to understand as environmental issues are both easier to identify and measure, and they are more tangible and easy to recognize. This lack of focus on social impacts has resulted in less radical and innovative solutions within design for sustainability; this is something that needs to be addressed with some urgency if we are going to meet the challenging targets set for sustainable development in the future.

Another limitation of current approaches is that they have been mainly oriented to producers and little is known about the consumers' side. Design for sustainability could have great impact in changing consumers' behaviour. The lessons learned by industry during the last fifty years should be used to develop more systemic approaches and their scope should be widened to include the whole of society.

CONCLUSIONS

Design for sustainability is now becoming better established within industry and the design community. As a result, some interesting case studies are emerging. The current range of approaches outlined in this chapter provides a direction for designers and enables them to build skills, experience and confidence towards systems innovation. By enabling this transition to more innovation and sustainable solutions, it is possible for industry to begin to benefit from the new approaches and realize the success that innovation and sustainability can bring.

REFERENCES

Bhamra, T. and Lofthouse, V. (2007), *Design for Sustainability: A Practical Approach,* Cooper, R. (series ed.), Gower Publishing Limited: Farnham, UK.

Brezet, H. (1997), 'Dynamics in Ecodesign Practice', *Industry and Environment,* vol. 20: pp. 21–24.

Brezet, H. and Van Hemel, C. (1997), *Ecodesign: A Promising Approach to Sustainable Production and Consumption,* United Nations Environment Programme, Industry and Environment, Cleaner Production: Paris.

European Parliament Council (1994), European Parliament and Council Directive 94/62/EC of 20 December 20, 1994, on Packaging and Packaging Waste, <http://eur-lex.europa.eu/LexUriServ/LexUriServ.do?uri=CELEX:31994L0062:EN:NOT> accessed November 16, 2011.

European Parliament Council (2008), Directive 2008/98/EC of the European Parliament and of the Council of November 19, 2008, on Waste and Repealing Certain Directives, <http://eur-lex.europa.eu/LexUriServ/LexUriServ.do?uri=CELEX:32008L0098:EN:NOT> accessed November 16, 2011.

European Parliament Council (2009), Directive 2009/125/EC of the European Parliament and of the Council of October 21, 2009, Establishing a Framework for the Setting of Ecodesign Requirements for Energy-Related Products, <http://eur-lex.europa.eu/LexUriServ/LexUriServ.do?uri=CELEX:32009L0125:EN:NOT> accessed November 16, 2011.

Fiksel, J. R. (2009), *Design for Environment: A Guide to Sustainable Product Development,* McGraw-Hill: New York.

ISO (2006), *ISO 14040:2006 Environmental Management—Life Cycle Assessment—Principles and Framework,* Geneva.

Knoend (2007), lite2go, <http://www.knoend.com/productsF.htm> accessed July 5, 2007.

MAGE (2011), Watercone, <http://www.watercones.com/> accessed November 30, 2011.

Manzini, E. and Vezzoli, C. (2003), 'A Strategic Approach to Develop Sustainable Product Service Systems: Examples Taken from the "Environmentally Friendly Innovation" Italian Prize', *Journal of Cleaner Production,* vol. 11: pp. 851–7.

Mascle, C. and Zhao, H. P. (2008), 'Integrating Environmental Consciousness in Product/Process Development Based on Life Cycle Thinking', *International Journal of Production Economics,* vol. 112: pp. 5–17.

MBDC (2011), 'Cradle to Cradle Framework', *McDonough Braungart Design Chemistry, LLC,* <http://mbdc.com/detail.aspx?linkid = 1&sublink=6> accessed November 30, 2011.

Miller, H. (2011), 'Design for the Environment', *Herman Miller, Inc.,* <http://www.hermanmiller.com/About-Us/Environmental-Advocacy/Design-for-the-Environment> accessed November 30, 2011.

Mont, O. (2002), 'Clarifying the Concept of Product-Service System', *Journal of Cleaner Production,* vol. 10: pp. 237–45.

Ness, D. (2007), 'Sustainable Product Service Systems: Potential to Deliver Business and Social Benefits with Less Resource Use', *Greening the Business and Making Environment a Business Opportunity,* Bangkok, June 5–7.

Panasonic (2011), 'Intelligent Living Panasonic', *Panasonic UK,* <http://intelligent-living. panasonic.co.uk/washing-machines/our-technology.php> accessed November 28, 2011.

Rainey, D. L. (2006), *Sustainable Business Development: Inventing the Future through Strategy, Innovation, and Leadership,* Cambridge University Press: New York.

Roy, R. (2000), 'Sustainable Product-Service Systems', *Futures,* vol. 32: pp. 289–99.

Transport for London (2011), 'Barclays Cycle Hire', *Transport for London,* <http://www.tfl.gov. uk/roadusers/cycling/14808.aspx> accessed November 28, 2011.

Tukker, A. and Tischner, U. (2004), *New Business for Old Europe: Product-Service Development as a Means to Enhance Competitiveness and Eco-Efficiency.* Greenleaf Publishers: Sheffield, UK.

Van Hemel, C. (1998), *EcoDesign Empirically Explored: Design for Environment in Dutch Small and Medium Sized Enterprises,* Delft University of Technology: Delft, the Netherlands.

8

Integrating Sustainability in Design Education

JACQUES GIARD AND DEBORAH SCHNEIDERMAN

PREFACE

The integration of sustainability in design education is occurring worldwide. There is much evidence to support this claim, which could be drawn upon to provide an overview of best practices. As commendable as such an overview might be, it would necessarily be very broad and as such would be outside the scope of this chapter. Instead, the focus will be primarily on activities in the United States. Similarly, design is too broad and too diverse a domain to be treated as one sector. Therefore, the focus of the chapter will be primarily on architecture, graphic design, industrial design, and interior design.

That being the case, the reader should not infer that our decision is a deliberate omission of the excellent work that is being undertaken to integrate sustainability in design education in other parts of the world as well as in other design sectors.

INTRODUCTION

To reiterate, the focus of this chapter is the integration of design for sustainability in American design education, particularly in the areas of architecture, graphic design, industrial design, and interior design. While these four areas may be the focus, it is generally understood that design education relies on the integration of knowledge from allied disciplines such as the arts, the natural sciences, the social sciences, engineering, and business. It is also generally understood that this integration normally occurs in one of two ways. The student either learns the subject matter theoretically by enrolling in a course offered on the topic or learns it by incorporating the subject matter in a design project, thereby learning by doing.

There does not appear to be any evidence that clearly supports the superiority of one mode of integration over the other. Each approach has benefits and each has drawbacks.

To take an example, it is not unusual for design students to acquire some fundamental knowledge of psychology as part of a typical design curriculum. In such cases, design students enroll in and successfully complete a course in psychology. By doing so, they learn from experts in the field, which is clearly an advantage. Because design is not normally part of the learning experience in psychology, however, the design students are often left with little choice but to connect the dots between the theories of psychology and their applicability to design. The latter could be perceived as a missed opportunity, if not an outright disadvantage.

The alternative pedagogical direction is to integrate relevant aspects of psychology within a design course. One clear advantage of this approach is the elimination of the aforementioned need to connect the dots. However, there is at least one drawback with this approach: the design instructor not trained in psychology, leading to two possible consequences, neither of which is desirable. First, the information may not be current—designers teaching psychology may not be up-to-date with recent developments in the field; second, there is the possibility of misinformation because the knowledge being taught has little or no foundation, yet may have become part of popular design culture.[1]

The integration of sustainability in design education faces much the same pedagogical challenge. A great deal of the knowledge in sustainability neither originates with nor resides in design. Nevertheless, many design programs have addressed this challenge using one or both directions described above. The first direction offers knowledge of sustainability as a stand-alone learning experience, either within the design program by way of resident experts or via another academic unit that is specialized in sustainability. The second direction is the design studio model: it offers a more kinesthetic approach and integrates knowledge of sustainability directly into the design experience.

This chapter looks at the experience of dealing with sustainability in design education in several professional design programs. It begins by describing some of the contextual conditions under which this integration normally occurs. More specifically, it explores those external situations that impact design education such as government regulations, requirements from professional design associations, and accreditation standards. Quite logically, this context becomes the setting in which most American design schools operate in their quest to address sustainability in design education. Some of these directions will be described via examples in order to understand better the advantages and disadvantages of stand-alone sustainability courses (theory), studio projects on sustainability (practice), and a combination of both.

DESIGN IN CONTEXT

It is not possible to understand the place of sustainability in design education without first understanding design itself, especially as a profession. The professional practice of design is conditioned by and dependent on people, society, economics, and the environment. These conditioning factors exist for architecture, graphic design, industrial design, and interior design, albeit to different degrees of magnitude.

Setting aside the inevitable exceptions to the rule, design cannot claim to be successful without incorporating—explicitly or implicitly—the embedded values of people, society, economics, and the environment.[2] In practice, this is why it is not unusual to trace the failure of a design outcome to a missing link in one of these areas. In this context, it is perhaps apropos to introduce Herbert Simon's definition of design because of its more objective and less moralistic position: "Everyone designs who devises courses of actions aimed at changing existing situations into preferred ones" (Simon, 1996, p. 111). From this perspective, a design's success is directly connected to how well the design action meets the preferences of people in the context of society, economics, and the environment; people being the ultimate users of design.

In addition to the embedded values of people, society, economics, and the environment, design education in the United States has one more obligation: it must conform to the expectations of the design professions such as professional licensure for architecture and interior design. This particular relationship will be explored further below.

SOME HISTORICAL BACKGROUND

The inclusion of sustainability in design education is a relatively recent phenomenon (Leerberg et al., 2010, p. 311). This is understandable given the equally short time that sustainability, sustainable development, and the environment have become the concern of society, experts, and individuals alike. The scientific work and writing of Rachel Carson, especially *Silent Spring* (1962), is certainly considered by many as one of the first red flags about society's negative impact on the environment. Barry Commoner, an American scientist, was also an early pioneer in the environment movement, popularizing such concepts as ecology and sustainability in the 1970s, in part by way of his best seller, *The Closing Circle* (1971). For Commoner, ecology was the core system that had to be respected as the world was becoming more industrialized. There were others who followed and who voiced similar concerns, people such as E. F. Schumacher, Buckminster Fuller, and Victor Papanek. Each advocated for a greater understanding of and consideration for environmental issues especially as they pertained to the design of the built environment and its myriad artifacts. By 1983, there was a strong enough voice for the environment in general and sustainability in particular that the United Nations by way of the World Commission on Environment and Development (WCED), known as the Brundtland Commission, issued its findings. It defined sustainable development as "...development that meets the needs of the present without compromising the ability of future generations to meet their own needs" (WCED, 1987).

The United Nations has also been at the forefront of the sustainable education movement. At the UN Conference on Environment and Development in Rio de Janeiro in June 1992, it declared that formal and nonformal education was essential to altering students' attitudes and perceptions regarding sustainability: "To be effective, environment and development education should deal with the dynamics of both the physical/biological and socio-economic environment and human (which may include spiritual) development, should be integrated in all disciplines, and should employ formal and non-formal methods and effective means of communication" (United Nations, 1992).

Internationally, the development of documents centered on global sustainable education continued and now includes the following:

- UNESCO—Declaration and Integrated Framework of Action on Education for Peace;
- Human Rights and Democracy, Paris 1995;
- United Nations Millennium Declaration, 2000, Chapter: Values and principles;
- United Nations Decade of Education for Sustainable Development, 2005–2014; and
- Council of Europe White Paper on Intercultural Dialogue, June 2008 (Cabezudo et al., 2010, pp. 10–12).

Sustainability in Design and Design Education: Push or Pull?

With this generalized setting, the introduction of sustainability to design education began, albeit slowly. At present, design practice and design education in the United States seem to be reading from the same page. Both sectors perceive the necessity to incorporate sustainable practices into their professional agenda. However, their approaches in achieving this goal appear to be coming from opposite directions.

Generally speaking, there is awareness that sustainability should be included in design education (Yang and Giard, 2001). Many design educators also perceive the logic and the necessity of integrating sustainability in design practice. Their approach resembles what is often called innovation/push—that is, the body of scientific evidence that supports sustainability, which is new, must be convincingly integrated into design education as yet another tool in the designer's toolbox.

Design practice appears to be operating from a different position. To a large degree, the integration of sustainability is more often than not conditioned by external demands such as the economic forces of the marketplace or government regulations. This approach is reminiscent of the demand/pull scenario. In other words, conditions outside the design professions are pulling sustainability into the practice. The American automotive industry is a good example. The engineering design associated with fuel efficiency is driven in great part by standards set by the Environmental Protection Agency (EPA), an agency of the American federal government, and not by a corporate desire to be sustainable.

The resulting situation is somewhat perplexing and sends a mixed message. On one hand, design education is looking for proactive leadership from the design profession; on the other, the only leadership that appears to exist in the design professions is one that is reactive. A recent commentary by James P. Cramer, editor of *Design Intelligence,* is rather blunt on this note. In his opinion, and with reference to the American design professions, "The critical mass of [design] professionals is still behind the sustainability curve" (2011). This is not comforting news for design educators, who are doing their utmost to push sustainability in their curricula.

Sustainability, the Designed Environment, and Design Education

Addressing the sustainability of the designed environment and, with it, the education of designers is vital because so much of our time is spent in the built environment. Americans spend as much as 90 percent of their lives inside buildings. The many products and materials found within these buildings constitute a significant source of indoor pollution (U.S. Environmental Protection Agency, 2009a). These pollutants, which can have negative effects on human health, are present in many common building materials including (but not limited to) paints, adhesives, wall coverings, flooring, manufactured wood products, and furniture (U.S. Environmental Protection Agency, 2009b).

Given the obvious connection between sustainable practice in design and the impact of the built environment, design education can and should play a critical role in creating a sustainable future (Harmon-Vaughn, 2004, pp. 64–65). The interweaving of sustainability into coursework across the curriculum is essential to an integrated understanding of sustainable design practice (Shepard, 2007, pp. 88–90). At present, however, there appears to be a lack of appreciation by many design students of the interconnectivity that exists in the issues that underpin sustainability and design. It is therefore incumbent upon design educators to not only teach students to design for sustainability but also to educate students who, as professionals, will incorporate that knowledge robustly into all projects in their practice (Friend, 2004, pp. 72–73). In an ideal world, the integration of sustainability and education will become seamless, leading to a design education that will be implicitly in accord with the principles of sustainability.

To Lead or to Follow? That Is the Question for Design Education

If design education is to include sustainability in the most effective way, it will mean working collaboratively with its professional counterpart. Therefore, who should design educators look to for professional partners? Should it be industry? Or professional design associations? Perhaps government agencies? There does not appear to be one definitive answer.

Certain corporations have shown leadership in integrating sound sustainability practices into their operations. Herman Miller, the American manufacturer of office and business furniture, is a case in point. It has consistently developed, applied, and even shared best-practice approaches to design for sustainability. Interface, an American carpet manufacturer, is another example. It began instituting sustainable practice in 1994 with a multipronged approach (Weeks, 2006, p. 12). One of the company's key divisions, InterfaceFLOR, set a vision in 1994 that by 2020 it would be the first company to demonstrate the meaning of sustainability in all its dimensions. InterfaceFLOR incorporates social sustainability into product development, has introduced carpet recycling programs, and has streamlined its operations by reducing energy usage, water consumption, and waste (Neals, 2007, p. 10; Turner, 2007, pp. 190–91).

Similarly, some professional associations have provided leadership in raising the level of understanding in sustainable practice. The Industrial Designers Society of America (IDSA) has a committee called EcoDesign and has positioned good sustainable practice high on its agenda. It has also been a strong advocate and promoter of the Okala guide, which is used extensively by programs of industrial design in the United States (IDSA, 2011a; IDSA, 2011b).

For its part, the International Council of Graphic Design Associations (ICO-GRADA) passed a resolution at its general assembly in Beijing, 2009, in which it declared to "…embrace sustainability as a key component of professional practice in communication design…" (2009). This action comes at an appropriate time because "Within the graphic design curriculum, the conversation on sustainability is just beginning to gain momentum…" (Benson, 2007). Closer to home, the AIGA, the professional association for graphic designers in the United States, launched a sustainability initiative "…born out of the design profession's need for an aspirational and actionable framework for integrated sustainability" (AIGA, 2011).

The American Institute of Architects (AIA) supports an ongoing education in sustainability. In February 2007, the AIA Conference on Sustainability in Architecture and Higher Education, held in Pomona, California, convened educators and practitioners specifically to discuss sustainability in architecture and higher education. There was a consensus that it was essential to provide tangible and innovative solutions to environmental problems, which resulted in an accreditation recommendation that specifically called for schools to teach sustainability as a global issue (2007/2009). Additionally, starting in 2009, the AIA revised its continuing education to include four hours per year focused on sustainable design (Wendt, 2008). The AIA also supports sustainable initiatives with the Sustainability Resource Center website and the SustAIAnability 2030 Toolkit, a website launched to support the AIA goal of reducing the carbon emissions generated in the construction and operation of all new and renovated buildings, and for buildings to be carbon neutral by 2030 (2011a). In 2011, the AIA released Document D503, a construction document to support contractual considerations particular to sustainable design (2011b).

The International Interior Design Association (IIDA) has instituted two policy statements focused on Sustainability: I.3 Position Statement on Sustainability and 1.3A Position Statement on the Environment (2011a). The IIDA also supports the practice of sustainable interior design with The Sustainability Forum. The Forum "…was created to facilitate increased collaboration among existing IIDA Forums. IIDA is committed to enhancing the quality of life through excellence in interior design and advancing interior design through knowledge. To that end, issues of sustainability and green design are no exception" (2011b).

Accreditation agencies can also play a leadership role and most often do. The Interior Design Educators Council (IDEC) and the Council for Interior Design Accreditation (CIDA) regard sustainability as a critical component of interior design curricula. In 2006, an IDEC taskforce presented the *Preliminary Teaching Manual for Sustainable Design Education.* The teaching manual is a seventy-page open forum available to the public on the IDEC website (the manual does not include lecture modules but rather guidelines, sample syllabi from past courses, and sample reading lists). Also in 2006, CIDA revised their twelve educational standards to reflect environmental awareness. In

July 2009, the twelve standards were revised into sixteen standards. The revised standards integrate principles from various disciplines and take a holistic approach to the development and advancement of environmental awareness in interior design curricula (Schneiderman and Freihoefer, 2012; Council for Interior Design Accreditation, 2006, pp. II 9–II 11).

The National Architecture Accreditation Board (NAAB), which is responsible for assessing all programs in architecture for accreditation in the United States, first introduced a concern for sustainable education in 1998 with the inclusion of program assessment for social equity and human resource development (AIA, 2007/2009). Though some requirements existed for sustainable architectural education, more stringent criteria for accreditation were highly anticipated for the 2009 NAAB requirements. Though a number of groups pushed for a stronger requirement for environmental responsibility as a core element of architectural education, the general consensus was one of disappointment (Hubbert and Grondzik, 2010).

Not all American accreditation agencies have been proactive in promoting an agenda of sustainability in design education. The National Association for Schools of Art and Design (NASAD) is a case in point. It is the national accreditation body for both graphic and industrial design programs in the United States. Its accreditation guidelines make little if any direct reference to a minimum number of credit hours in the area of sustainability.[3]

Certain government agencies have provided some leadership to the professions, although the influence has varied. In some cases, intervention has come in the form of recommendations for voluntary compliance. At the other extreme, legislation has been created to force the hand of industry, such as the EPA standards for vehicular gas mileage mentioned earlier. International guidelines, such as the ISO standards, have also been established and have found acceptance among several industrial sectors.

If there is one program that has shown clear direction in the United States, it is the Leadership in Energy and Environmental Design Green Building Rating System, commonly known as LEED. According to the U.S. Green Building Council, which developed the LEED system, LEED "…encourages and accelerates global adoption of sustainable green building and development practices through the creation and implementation of universally understood and accepted tools and performance criteria" (LEED Steering Committee, 2006). LEED is considered a benchmark for the design construction and operation of high-performance green buildings in the United States and, increasingly, abroad. It gives architects, designers, engineers, building owners, and operators a tool kit for the measurement of the impacts of their buildings. The five key areas measured in the LEED criteria are human and environmental health, sustainable site development, water savings, energy efficiency, materials selection, and indoor environmental quality (LEED Steering Committee, 2006). LEED provides certifications and strategies for a diverse range of project types and includes specific certifications for the architecture and interior design of a building. However, LEED knowledge and certification cannot assume a true ecological appreciation for the limitation of the Earth's resources and, as understood by students, it often devolves to being merely a checklist for sustainable design strategy. Still, core environmental needs constitute a strong impetus for requiring that students both comprehend and apply the critical requirements within LEED standards.

Leading experts and writers in the area of sustainability have also had an impact on the integration of sustainability in design education, although in an indirect way rather than at a policy level. Most design educators and many design students are familiar with the writings of Victor Papanek, William McDonough, Paul Hawken, David Orr, Penny Bonda, Susan Winchip, and Bruce Mau, to name but a few.

TEACHING STRATEGIES FOR SUSTAINABLE DESIGN

The integration of sustainability in design education is occurring in a variety of ways. Three models, however, appear to be most common:

- stand-alone schools or programs of sustainability that offer courses in sustainability made available to the institution at large including students in design;
- notions of sustainability integrated into the studio experience common in design education; and
- courses in sustainability offered in schools or programs of design.

It should be noted that models that combine parts of each of these three models in a unique combination also exist.

Stand-Alone Programs of Sustainability

Most higher education programs of sustainability are part of larger units, usually in the natural sciences. However, some institutions, especially research-intensive universities, have stand-alone schools or programs of sustainability.

The School of Sustainability at Arizona State University (ASU) is one such stand-alone program. It was launched in 2007 and is part of a larger initiative called the Global Institute of Sustainability. As described on its website, the school is "... engaged in collaborative relationships with colleges and programs across the University and with institutions and corporations worldwide—with the aim of creating a community of experts to address complex environmental and social challenges" (School of Sustainability, 2011). Moreover, the school projects itself as transdisciplinary; consequently, it perceives its role in a holistic way by dealing with broad issues such as social, environmental, and economic challenges. More specifically, its curriculum provides a strong focus on global issues such as "... energy, materials, and technology; water quality and scarcity; international development; ecosystems; social transformations; food and food systems; and policy and governance" (School of Sustainability, 2011).

Students were first admitted in 2008 and can select among three academic programs: a bachelor's, master's, or doctoral degree in sustainability. The school also offers concentrations in sustainability for students in three other degree programs: business, engineering, and law. At present, there is no concentration in either architecture or design. Nevertheless, in recent years a small percentage (ca. 5 percent) of students from architecture and design have enrolled in courses at the School of Sustainability.

Similar stand-alone programs exist at Colorado State University, the University of South Florida, and Chatham University. Chatham University has a stand-alone program in sustainability and programs of study in design in interior architecture and landscape architecture. The School of Sustainability and the Environment at Chatham University was founded in 2009 "... as a transdisciplinary academic institution that recognizes the three foundations of sustainability—economic development, social wellbeing, and a robust environment" (Chatham University, 2011a). The school now houses the Rachel Carson Institute (named for Chatham alumna and author of *Silent Spring*), founded in 1989, which focuses on community outreach. The school only accepted its first class in fall 2010, with a master's in food studies. A Master of Sustainability enrolled its first class in fall 2012. At present there is no program in sustainable design, though the first class in the Master of Sustainability program will have the opportunity to help design a new campus for the school (Chatham University, 2011b).

Embedding Sustainability into the Studio Experience

Embedding knowledge of sustainability into the studio experience is perhaps the more logical and practical approach for design education. It permits the students to grasp the interdependency of sustainability to the design process, and connects more effectively what appear to be two disparate elements: sustainability and design.

InnovationSpace at ASU is a program that follows this approach. It has created a design experience imbued not only with sustainability but also within an interdisciplinary agenda. From its perspective, the integration of sustainability in design education has moved beyond a silo approach and embraces the reality of product development in which engineering and business are also involved. As a result, undergraduate students work in interdisciplinary teams (from industrial design, graphic design, engineering, and business) with industrial partners on projects in which sustainability underpins the learning experience (Shin et al., 2008).

The embedded approach exemplified in the InnovationSpace projects integrates sustainability in a constant and consistent way throughout the duration of the designing process, a form of slow ingestion as opposed to binging, which often typifies the knowledge acquisition of a stand-alone course. For the InnovationSpace students, two important principles become a recurring theme in their learning experience. The first is an understanding of the triple-bottom line. If nothing else, placing the resulting product in this broad context demonstrates the true and potentially overwhelming impact that design can have. The second principle is life cycle assessment (LCA), which obliges the students to move beyond the more traditional, albeit necessary, considerations of shape, form, and color. The learning experience is equally relevant for the business and engineering students on the team. They too begin to consider the broader impact of their actions in light of the triple-bottom line and LCA. According to professor Prasad Boradkar, one of the leaders of this course, the students are able to understand these principles much better because they learn them early in the semester and because they have to apply them to design problems. And, as a consequence, the solutions devised by the teams were significantly more thorough (Giard, 2011).

Similar to InnovationSpace, Pratt Institute has also moved beyond a silo approach and connects disciplines through The Center for Sustainable Design Studies and Research (CSDS):

> Pratt's new Center for Sustainable Design Studies and Research (CSDS) has been established as a catalyst to focus the talent and energy of the Pratt community by providing a gathering place, resources and funding to support faculty and students in realizing large and small scale projects, course development and partnerships in the areas of clean-tech energy, environmental issues and the "greening of our built and manufactured environment." (Pratt, 2011a)

The center also houses a comprehensive case studies and materials library and provides access to LCA tools. CSDS's mission to support interdisciplinary collaboration and encourage the use of the Pratt campus as a living lab for innovation is exemplified in the 2009 Living Lab Project. Students and professors in the interior design and the industrial design programs, through CSDS, worked collaboratively to develop a plan for the sustainable renovation of a dorm room on the Pratt campus. A year later, in 2010, the institute agreed to build the test dorm room, a new venture in the relationship between academics and facilities on the Pratt campus. The project was later exhibited at the Storefront for Art and Architecture (Pratt, 2011b).

The interior design program at Pratt, as evidenced in the aforementioned project, approaches sustainability predominantly through integration into existing curriculum and studio projects. It is an example of a hybrid approach to design for sustainability education as it also offers a specific course in sustainable design. The goal for the sustainable design course is for it to be a place of investigative exploration on advanced issues, and/or it disappears entirely as sustainable thinking becomes so integrated into the curriculum and our design process that there is no need to offer a stand-alone course.

Courses in Sustainability Offered in Schools or Programs of Design

Some design schools address sustainability in their existing design programs by way of stand-alone courses in their programs. This direction is different from the stand-alone courses offered by another academic unit as described above because the sustainability expertise resides in the design school. There are several reasons for such a direction. The design school may be situated at an institution, often a small one, where expertise on sustainability does not exist elsewhere in the institution. Consequently, that expertise must be developed from within. Or the expertise on sustainability may reside elsewhere in the institution but connections with the school of design are for one reason or another not possible. Or, better still, the school of design has decided that it must be proactive in integrating sustainability into design education and has therefore targeted a faculty position for that purpose. Such an approach exists in several schools of architecture and design.

Some design schools have also created new graduate degrees specifically in sustainable design, including Harvard, University of Texas at Austin, Boston Architectural College, New York School of Interior Design, and Philadelphia University. In 2007, Philadelphia University introduced the master of science in sustainable design (MSSD) and graduated its first class in 2009. It was the recipient of a 2009 Excellence in Green Building Education Recognition Award from the United States Green Building Council (USBGC). The MSSD degree program exists within the School of Architecture, which also houses programs in architecture, interior design, landscape architecture, and construction management. The post-professional degree program serves multiple disciplines including architecture, interior design, landscape architecture, construction, and engineering. The MSSD has six core tenets: "... trans-disciplinary learning; integrated design education, which uses an 'open source' sustainable design charrette process; design/quantify/build methodology that recognizes the need for a balance between aesthetics and performance; activism and leadership to prepare graduates to be leaders; enterprise and entrepreneurship; and equity and diversity" (USGBC, 2009). Courses have been developed specifically for the MSSD rather than repurposed from an existing curriculum. The core skills taught in the program include LCA and carbon footprint calculation; daylight analysis for LEED; energy modeling; integrated design facilitation; and collaborative and multidisciplinary design (Philadelphia University, 2011).

A POSSIBLE NEXT STEP

It appears that design education has two directions when considering the inclusion of sustainability into its curricular agenda. The first direction—and the more obvious one—is to add sustainability, especially courses and studio projects, to the current curricula. Many design school have done just that and the examples cited above shed light on three distinct patterns.

Implicit in this direction is the recognition that there is an issue that needs addressing. According to the USGBC, for example, buildings in the United States are "... responsible for 39 percent of CO_2 emissions, 40 percent of energy consumption, 13 percent water consumption ..." (USGBC, 2012). Clearly, acknowledging that there is a problem is the first step towards its resolution. The examples provided in this chapter are an indication of this recognition, which is especially important because of the significant impact design has on the environment.

Second, design education needs to be part of the solution and not part of the problem. At least this is one conclusion that can be drawn if we are to perceive the addition of courses and design projects in sustainability at so many institutions. In some design schools, students now have the opportunity of graduating with LEED certification. Ultimately and with more design programs onboard, few design students will graduate without coming into contact with issues of sustainability.

These different steps taken by design institutions are commendable. The end result will be graduate designers who will practice with a greater understanding of both the theory and practice that underpin sustainable design. But as commendable as these steps may be, they may be misplaced because of a fundamental flaw. Most contemporary design activities in architecture, graphic design, industrial design, and interior design are still conditioned by the precepts of industrialization. At its heart, this system is based on growth, materiality, and a fixation on an artifact—values that are generally contrary to the underpinning principles of sustainability. This being the case, is there an alternative direction when considering the integration of sustainability in design education? We believe that there is.

A Scenario from the Past

The challenge of integrating sustainability in design education has a tinge of déjà vu about it. Design—both practice and education—faced a similar challenge 100 years ago. The time was the turn of the twentieth century, when the Beaux-Arts ethos was the direction of choice in architecture and design—the comfort zone for design, so to speak. Lurking everywhere, however, were the first signs of the machine age. Industrialization was beginning to transform all aspects of quotidian life—people, society, economics, and the environment. For its part, design would not be left untouched. Every aspect of design—from existing standards and the making of artifacts to how architects and artisans were trained—would have to be reconsidered if industrialization was to be integrated into the design process. Things could not remain the same.

To be effective, changes in design practice and design education had to be as significant as the changes implicit in industrialization itself. Incremental changes would not be sufficient. This is exactly what the Bauhaus proposed; that is, a complete reconsideration of how architecture and design were to be taught.

With this reconsideration came what would become one of the defining legacies of the Bauhaus: less is more. That is, design should reflect the ethos of industrialization and shed, among other things, the unnecessary ornamentation that had become the trademark of the Beaux-Arts period. Moreover, the less-is-more approach had to permeate the new design pedagogy at every level and not merely be an addition to or tinkering of the old educational model.

MOVING BEYOND INDUSTRIALIZATION

In the context of sustainability, contemporary design education is at a watershed similar to the early days of industrialization. Minor modifications to an existing educational model may not be sufficient to meet the challenges implicit in the integration of sustainability to design education. Starting with a clean slate may be the only option. Therefore, where do we begin?

One option is to consider issues of sustainability as nothing less than a prime and fundamental factor in design education much like less-is-more became a prime factor at the Bauhaus. In such a scenario, sustainability will need to be integrated throughout the design curriculum and embedded at every level. This direction goes well beyond what we have seen in the examples described above; in other words, the integration of sustainability via a few courses and design projects will not be enough. Much like the Bauhaus integrated the ethos of industrialization in all aspects of design education, nothing less will effectively address the issues of sustainability.

That said, total integration of sustainability in a design curriculum underpinned by a context of industrialization may still not meet the environmental challenges facing us. We may be beyond a so-called point of no return. To borrow a well-worn reflection, embedding the ethos of sustainability throughout the design curriculum may be nothing more than rearranging the deck chairs on the *Titanic*. The challenge is no longer what subject matter is being taught or to what degree it is being taught. The challenge is contextual; that is to say, we now find ourselves in a context that was not only created because of industrialization but that has moved beyond industrialization.

Given this contextual shift, a case could be made that design education needs to radically alter its course of studies if it is to effectively integrate sustainability. As we know, the concept of growth is at the core of industrialization, which caused the displacement of an artisanal workforce by machines because of mass production. Industrialization also forever changed the role of design in industry. Beginning with the Bauhaus, design programs the world over made the logical choice of connecting the context of industrialization to the curricula in architecture, graphic design, industrial design, and interior design. The same sense of logic now needs to be applied because the context has changed. The premise of most professional design programs, which is based on industrialization, will have to be replaced with a premise based more on realities emanating from a postindustrial world.

In this vein, Walker and Nielsen have proposed a pedagogical model that, in theory, attempts to address the lacunae that have appeared in efforts to fit an educational model predicated on industrialization into a postindustrial world (1998, p. 16). Their proposal addresses four fundamental facets of the dilemma: moving from product-oriented design to design that is more issues-oriented; creating harmony between the seemingly opposing forces of technological innovation, on the one hand, and sustainable development, on the other; moving from product orientation toward service orientation as dematerialization becomes a reality; and placing a greater attention to the phenomenon of community-based enterprises (1998, pp. 16–17). This is but the first step in a journey that will force design educators to seriously evaluate their educational agenda if they are to situate sustainability in its proper context.

CONCLUSIONS

Most contemporary design education models in schools of architecture, graphic design, industrial design, and interior design reflect values derived from industrialization. The ethos of the artisan designer, such as we witnessed with people like William Morris, gave way to the designs of the machine age as we discovered with leaders such as Walter Gropius and Le Corbusier. The impact of industrialization was perhaps more obvious with industrial design and graphic design, but it was nevertheless present in architecture and interior design. After all, it was Le Corbusier who referred to the house as a machine for living.

The industrial or machine ethos changed the design process to the point that it no longer resembled the fundamental premise of Beaux-Arts, the process that preceded it. Given that issues of sustainability are as significant to design today as industrialization was a century ago, it is only fair to assume that sustainability will have a similar if not greater impact in the reconsideration of the designing process and, with it, design education.

This being the case, it is inevitable that design imperatives will need to be developed in order to seamlessly integrate sustainability into professional design education. These can be summarized as follows:

- Sustainability is a foundation block for the future of the planet. It is not a fad, a fashion, or a trend, but a fundamental condition for survival.
- Sustainability imposes a significant change to the existing operational model in design, one that is based on industrialization.
- Consequently, the integration of sustainability in design education must reflect the nature of a postindustrialization model.
- For design education, the challenges implicit in the integration of sustainability may be too broad to be met by mere adjustments to a design curriculum underpinned by operational principles derived from industrialization. Therefore, curricular changes will have to be commensurate with the significance implicit in sustainability.
- Design educators will also need to become proactive in the research aspect of sustainability theory and its applicability to design. Reacting to the research of others is insufficient if sustainability is to be relevant to design education.
- In the end, sustainability in design education will have to be integrated in a way that is seamless and transparent, and implemented in such a way that it would be totally unimaginable to teach design as we have done in the past.

NOTES

1.   Fonts such as Helvetica or Times New Roman are ubiquitous. Their everyday use makes them known to most everyone, resulting in a kind of comfort zone for the reader as well as for designers. Therefore, selecting such a font as a means of enhancing learning would seem to be a logical decision. It appears, however, that such is not the case. Research has shown that because of its unfamiliarity a less well-known font forces the reader to read with more attention thereby leading to an improved learning experience (Carey, 2011).

2.   Success is, of course, relative. For some individuals, it is strictly quantitative, such as sales volume. For others, it is more qualitative, such as a design selected for the permanent collection of a museum. Given the polarity of the issue, the discourse for the meaning of success in design will be left for another time.

3.   It should be noted that the AIGA and IDSA, the professional associations for graphic and industrial design in the United States, were both instrumental in establishing the NASAD accreditation standards for graphic and industrial design.

REFERENCES

AIA (American Institute of Architects) (2007/2009), *AIA Draft White Paper for the NAAB Accreditation Review Conference,* http://blog.aia.org/whitepaper/2007/09/, accessed June 10, 2011.

AIA (American Institute of Architects) (2011a), *Toolkit SustAIAnability 2030,* http://info.aia.org/toolkit2030/index.html, accessed July 8, 2011.

AIA (American Institute of Architects) (2011b), *AIA Document D503™—2011: Guide for Sustainable Projects, including Agreement Amendments and Supplementary Conditions,* Washington, DC.

AIGA (2011), *The Living Principles for Design,* www.aiga.org/the-living-principles-for-design/, accessed July 7, 2011.

Benson, E. (2007), *FLUX: Design Education in a Changing World,* DEFSA International Design Education Conference, Cape Town.

Cabezudo, A., Christidis, C., Carvalho da Silva, M., Demetriadou-Saltet, V., Halbartschlager, F. and Mihai, G. (2010), *Global Education Guidelines: Concepts and Methodologies on Global Education for Educators and Policy Makers,* North-South Centre of the Council of Europe: Lisbon.

Carey, B. (2011), "Come On, I Thought I Knew That!" *New York Times,* April 19, p. D5.

Carson, R. (1962), *Silent Spring,* Houghton Mifflin: Boston.

Chatham University (2011a), "The School of Sustainability and the Environment," http://www.chatham.edu/sse/dean.cfm, accessed August 18, 2011.

Chatham University (2011b), "About the School of Sustainability and the Environment," http://www.chatham.edu/sse/about.cfm, accessed July 13, 2011.

Commoner, B. (1971), *The Closing Circle: Nature, Man and Technology,* Random House: New York.

Council for Interior Design Accreditation (CIDA), (2006), "Professional Standards," www.accredit-id.org/profstandards.php, accessed June 15, 2011.

Cramer, J. P. (2011), "Newsletter," *Design Intelligence Update,* July 12.

Friend, S. (2004), "Embracing Cradle-to-Cradle," *Interiors and Sources,* vol. 11, no. 6: pp. 72–73.

Giard, J., (2011), Personal conversation and communication with professor Prasad Boradkar, September 18–October 10, 2011.

Harmon-Vaughan, B. (2004), "Sustainable Design + Students," *Interiors and Sources,* vol. 11, no. 8: pp. 64–65.

Hubbert, K. T. and Grondzik, W. T. (2010), "Perceptions of Environmental Responsibility," *Architectural Education,* www.ases.org/papers/177.pdf accessed September 19, 2011.

ICOGRADA (2009), "Resolution 10.5–Icograda General Assembly 23, Beijing, China Sustainable Communication Design," www.icograda.org/smallbox4/file.php?sb4af0cbbd309ec, accessed September 18, 2011.

IDSA (Industrial Design Society of America) (2011a), *Okala Ecodesign Guide,* http://www.idsa.org/okala-ecodesign-guide, accessed September 22, 2011.

IDSA (Industrial Design Society of America) (2011b), "Ecodesign," http://www.idsa.org/WHATSNEW/SECTIONS/ECOSECTION/okala.html, accessed June 6, 2011.

IIDA (International Interior Design Association) (2011a), "IIDA Policy Statements," http://www.iida.org/content.cfm/iida-policy-statements, accessed July 8, 2011.

IIDA (International Interior Design Association) (2011b), "Sustainability Forum," http://www.iida.org/content.cfm/sustainable-design, accessed July 8, 2011.

LEED Steering Committee (2006), *LEED Policy Manual,* United States Green Building Council (USGBC): Washington, DC.

Leerberg, M., Riisberg, V. and Boutrup, J. (2010), "Design Responsibility and Sustainable Design as Reflective Practice: An Educational Challenge," in *Sustainable Development,*

Wiley Online Library, http://onlinelibrary.wiley.com/doi/10.1002/sd.481/abstract, accessed February 24, 2013.

Neals, S. (2007), "Beyond the Price Tag: the Costs and Benefits of Going Green," *Ecos,* vol. 139: p. 10.

Philadelphia University (2011), "M.S. in Sustainable Design," http://www.philau.edu/green/, accessed July 15, 2011.

Pratt Institute (2011a), "Center for Sustainable Design Studies," http://csds.pratt.edu/csds_about.html, accessed August 18, 2011.

Pratt Institute (2011b), *Center for Sustainable Design Studies—Living Lab,* http://csds.pratt.edu/green_dorms.html, accessed August 18, 2011.

Schneiderman, D. and Freihoefer, K. (2012), "A Pre- and Post-Evaluation of Integrating Sustainability Curriculum by Inserting Okala Modules Into an Interior Design Materials and Methods Course," *International Journal of Sustainability in Higher Education,* vol 13, no. 4: pp. 408–423.

School of Sustainability (2011), Arizona State University, http://schoolofsustainability.asu.edu/about/school/directors-message.php, accessed September 18, 2011.

Shepard, K. (2007), "Higher Education for Sustainability; Seeking Affective Learning Outcomes," *International Journal of Sustainability in Higher Education,* vol. 9, no. 1: pp. 87–98.

Shin, D., Boradkar, P. and Fischer, A. (2008), "A Green Dream Team," *Design Management Review,* vol. 19, no. 4: pp. 49–55.

Simon, H. (1996), *The Sciences of the Artificial,* MIT Press: Cambridge, MA.

Turner, M. (2007), *Driving Sustainable Innovation: InterfaceFLOR,* Sustainable Innovation 07, 12th International Conference: Surrey, UK.

United Nations (1992), "Promoting Education, Public Awareness and Training," chapter 36, agenda 21, paragraph 1, http://www.un.org.ezproxy1.lib.asu.edu/esa/sustdev/documents/agenda21/english/agenda21chapter36.htm, accessed July 10, 2011.

U.S. Environmental Protection Agency (2009a), "An Introduction to Indoor Air Quality: Organic Gases (Volatile Organic Compounds—VOCs)," http://www.epa.gov/iaq/voc.html, accessed June 12, 2011.

U.S. Environmental Protection Agency (2009b), "The Inside Story: A Guide to Indoor Air Quality," http://www.epa.gov/iaq/pubs/insidest.html, accessed June 12, 2011.

USGBC (United States Green Building Council) (2009), *Excellence in Green Building Education Recognition Awards and Incentive Grants,* Washington, DC.

USGBC (United States Green Building Council) (2012), "Green Building Facts," http://new.usgbc.org/articles/green-building-facts, accessed February 24, 2013.

Walker, S. and Nielsen, R. (1998), "Systematic Shift: Sustainable Development and Industrial Design Pedagogy," *The Journal of Sustainable Product Design,* vol. 4, January: pp. 7–16.

WCED (World Commission on Environment and Development) (1987) *Our Common Future, Report of the Brundtland Commission,* Oxford University Press: Oxford.

Weeks, J. (2006), "TAKE THIS PRODUCT BACK AND RECYCLE IT!" *Business,* vol. 28, no. 6: p. 12.

Wendt, A. (2008), "AIA Requires Sustainability in Continuing Education," *Greensource: The Magazine of Sustainable Design,* http://greensource.construction.com/news/080602aiaconted.asp, accessed June 15, 2011.

Yang, Y. and Giard, J. (2001), *Industrial Design Education for Sustainability: Structural Elements and Pedagogical Solutions,* Industrial Designers Society of America National Educators Conference: Boston.

9

Sustainability, Consumption and the Throwaway Culture

TIM COOPER

THE PROBLEM OF OVERCONSUMPTION

A primary symptom of the failure of people in the industrialized world to adopt sustainable lifestyles is an excessive throughput of resources. Each year, on average, an individual in such countries is responsible for the use of around sixteen tons (14.5 tonnes) of minerals, ores, fossil fuels and biomass (United Nations Environment Programme, 2011). This rate of consumption is evidently unsustainable. According to the World Wide Fund for Nature (WWF), the total impact of human activity on the Earth, our ecological footprint, exceeds its biocapacity, the area available to produce renewable resources and absorb carbon dioxide emissions, by around 50 per cent: thus, 'people used the equivalent of 1.5 planets in 2007 to support their activities' (WWF, 2010a, p. 34). If everyone throughout the world consumed at the same level as the average consumer living in the relative affluence of Britain, the equivalent of 2.75 planets would be required to meet their demands (WWF, 2010b).

The future presents an even greater challenge. Rapidly rising consumption in newly industrialized countries such as China, India and Brazil is putting further stress upon the global environment. The global predicament that this poses is that people in affluent countries are unwilling to give up, while in newly industrialized and other poorer countries people are unwilling to do without (Robins, 1999). Yet if it is accepted that greater equity in consumption should be sought and this will involve many people in poorer countries consuming more in order to gain an appropriate quality of life, people in more affluent nations are faced with the major challenge of reducing their consumption.

The Speed of Resource Consumption

A primary characteristic of today's affluent industrialized economies is the speed at which consumption takes place. The logic of the market, applying the principles of traditional neoclassical economics, is that rational consumers will act on an assumption that more is better. Accordingly, there are no limits to people's aspiration for greater wealth; no concept of enough. As a consequence, people often feel under pressure to strive to consume and yet are constrained by their incomes. Companies respond by producing goods of varying levels of quality. Many are manufactured relatively cheaply in order to meet predetermined price points for the mass market, and this has implications for product lifetimes. A recent study suggested that people's expectations of these lifetimes, at least for some types of product, are in decline (Defra, 2011a). In addition, many functional items are replaced before they have developed a fault or worn out because people are continually striving to upgrade their acquisitions to newer items or ones of higher quality. They are encouraged to do so by manufacturers who, in the face of competitive pressure, regularly update their product ranges, and high street retail chains whose business model is dependent upon high-volume sales.

The outcome is an ever-faster throughput of resources in the global economy. During the twentieth century the extraction of construction materials grew by a factor of thirty-four; ores and minerals, by a factor of twenty-seven; fossil fuels, by a factor of twelve; and biomass, by a factor of four. By the start of the twenty-first century, the rate at which total primary resources were being harvested, forty-seven to fifty-nine billion tons annually, was around three times that of 1960 (United Nations Environment Programme, 2011). The speed of this throughout was lessened only slightly by greater resource productivity as manufacturing processes used energy more efficiently and created less waste, electronic goods were miniaturized, appliances made more efficient, and more products were recycled.

These trends and technological trajectories, once combined, imply a resource throughput that is clearly unsustainable. The International Energy Agency (2010) does not expect global production of conventional crude oil to return to its peak level of 2006, while the United States has long been dependent on imports: its production peaked in 1970, since when its proven reserves have halved (Energy Information Administration, 2011). Yet global energy demand is set to rise by more than one-third over the next twenty-five years, not least due to an anticipated 75 per cent growth in demand from China (International Energy Agency, 2010).

The supply of metals and minerals is similarly finite, and a threat of inadequate access to important raw materials as a consequence of rising demand has raised widespread concern. A paper for the Academy of Sciences in the United States highlights the problem: 'Providing today's developed-country level of services for copper worldwide (as well as for zinc and, perhaps, platinum) would appear to require conversion of essentially all of the ore in the lithosphere to stock-in-use plus near-complete recycling of the metals from that point forward' (Gordon et al., 2006, p. 1209). Absolute scarcity is not in prospect. The threats are rising economic and environmental costs of extraction and political challenges arising from insecurity of supply. As the more accessible oil supplies become depleted, oil companies are seeking to use controversial extraction methods such as hydraulic fracturing and sources such as bituminous sands. Similarly, as the more accessible reserves of metals such as copper and gold become depleted, greater amounts of energy and freshwater are required for extraction. A recent study contrasted the copper ore mined at the beginning of the twentieth century, which contained around 3 per cent copper, with the current typical ore grade of around 0.3 per cent and concluded: 'Although, in theory, metals will always be available and no one can predict the extent of technological innovation in exploration and mining, it seems likely that, as reserves dwindle in future, these resources will come at increasing cost' (Green Alliance, 2011, p. 11).

Awareness that the process of resource extraction normally uses fossil fuels has meant that long-overdue attention is now being directed in the climate change debate to the embedded carbon in goods. Hitherto, Western countries have benefited in international negotiations from the protocol by which carbon emissions are attributed to the country of manufacture rather than that of consumption. Thus, 'the carbon footprint of the British is much higher than reported under Kyoto-based carbon production measures' (Helm, 2011, p. 242). In other words, claims by successive governments that Britain's carbon emissions have declined convey a false impression: official statistics indicate that emissions fell by 15 per cent between 1990 and 2005, whereas on a consumption basis they went up by around 19 per cent (Helm et al., 2007). This reflects the long-established trend of goods consumed in Britain being manufactured overseas.

At the other end of the product life cycle is the volume of waste generated, which remains unduly high in most industrialized countries although it is generally managed better than in the past. The speed of resource throughput is, again, highly relevant: the amount of waste arising from discarded household products is determined by longevity and whether households buy replacement products or, perhaps, make additional acquisitions, retaining but downgrading the old items (Strandbakken, 2009; Oguchi et al., 2010).

The United Nations Environment Programme and European Commission have responded to this excessive resource throughput by considering the potential for decoupling economic and environmental activity, defined as 'using less resources per unit of economic output and reducing the environmental impact of any resources that are used or economic activities that are undertaken' (United Nations Environment Programme [UNEP], 2011, p. xiii). It is relatively easy for countries to achieve relative decoupling, whereby resource consumption does not increase as fast as economic growth, but this is unlikely to result in the necessary reduction in overall resource use at a global level (Jackson, 2009). Instead, absolute decoupling is required, whereby 'the growth rate of resource productivity is faster than the growth rate of the economy' (UNEP, 2011, p. 5), which represents a profound challenge.

The Limitations to Circularity

In the face of these concerns about resource use and waste, a few governments, notably those of Japan and China, have promoted the concept of a circular economy (Ellen Macarthur Foundation, 2011). This contrasts with a traditional, linear model of the economy, in which unrestrained access to raw materials and waste disposal facilities is assumed. Japan passed a Fundamental Law for Establishing a Sound Material Cycle Society in 2000 and introduced its first Fundamental Plan three years later, and a second in 2008. China adopted the concept in its 11th Five Year Plan and passed a Circular Economy Promotion Law in 2008. The concept is advocated by many environmental researchers and campaigners, although in Britain, at least, it has failed to attract the crucial support necessary from treasury ministers.

The circular economy model draws upon the cradle-to-cradle principle, which proposes that all inputs into the industrial system should, ultimately, be recycled (Braungart and McDonough, 2009). A change in this direction is certainly crucial but, leaving aside some technical and logistical obstacles, closed-loop recycling may well not be sufficient for sustainability. While recycling is generally preferable to other waste management options, it nonetheless has some negative environmental impacts (Cooper, 1994): for example, energy—most of which is not derived from renewable sources—is used for transporting discarded products, reprocessing secondary materials and manufacturing and distributing new products. Thus, while shifting from a linear to a circular economic model is an imperative, it is also important to slow down the throughput of resources (Cooper, 2005). This implies confrontation with the growth-orientated nature of traditional economics, which is indeed already under way in the form of growing critiques of growth as an indicator of progress or wellbeing (e.g., Layard, 2006; Jackson, 2009). The circular economic model may also lead to limitations from a creative perspective, at least in the foreseeable term, in that designing products to be 100 per cent recyclable is liable to restrict choice of form and materials.

How might this slower rate of consumption come about? Individuals who choose frugal or low-carbon lifestyles (Goodall, 2010) periodically attract attention in the media and from academics (Galvagno, 2011), although a deliberate strategy to reduce the flow of consumer goods would normally be derided as politically unfeasible for government and commercially suicidal for industry. Most politicians argue that a healthy economy requires sustained economic growth and evidently assume that people are essentially materialistic and will vote accordingly. Most manufacturers and retailers are comfortable with resource efficiency as a means of reducing unnecessary costs, but their business models are predicated on the desirability of ever-increasing sales volumes. Yet there is evidence to suggest that many people would prefer less consumerism: a survey in Britain indicated that around one-quarter of the population had taken voluntary steps to change their lifestyles in a way that reduced their earnings (and, by implication, their consumption) at some point during the previous decade (Hamilton, 2003).

One means of reducing consumption without raising the threat of households owning fewer possessions would be for consumer products to last longer (Cooper, 2010). Such a strategy is now attracting attention from public authorities.

European Union member states are required by the Waste Framework Directive to develop national waste reduction programmes and 'the reuse of products or the extension of the life span of products' is suggested as an example of waste prevention (European Union, 2008), while the Ecodesign Directive provides a framework within which compulsory design requirements for energy-using products may be set, with parameters that include 'extension of lifetime as expressed through: minimum guaranteed lifetime, minimum time for availability of spare parts, modularity, upgradeability, reparability' (European Union, 2005).

In Britain, the government has published research that concluded that longer product lifetimes would normally offer environmental benefits, largely through lower manufacturing volumes, and any negative effect on the economy would be offset by positive developments in repair, refurbishment, maintenance and second-hand markets (ERM, 2011). In a review of waste policy, the government indicated that it favoured an economy in which materials would be used sustainability 'through design for longer life, upgrading, reuse or repair' and that it was looking for businesses to 'design and manufacture goods that are more efficient, durable, repairable and recyclable' (Defra, 2011b, pp. 23, 27). Meanwhile the publicly funded Waste & Resources Action Programme (WRAP) has been undertaking a substantial programme of research on reuse as a means of product life extension, having concluded that it is one of the best resource efficiency strategies for reducing greenhouse gas emissions (WRAP, 2009).

Obsolescence and Design

In order to assess the likelihood of the British government's proposed approach being adopted, it is necessary to consider some recent trends in design and their implications for product longevity. Influences upon product lifetimes have been described in depth elsewhere (Cooper, 2010) and are only summarized briefly below.

Manufacturers have long been accused of deliberately curtailing product lifespans through planned obsolescence (Packard, 1963; Slade, 2006). Concern at an apparent decline in product quality and shortening of lifetimes grew within the business community in the United States in the 1950s (Mayer, 1959; Stewart, 1959), but it was primarily the influence of *The Waste Makers* by Vance Packard (1963) that raised public concern and popularized the term 'planned obsolescence'. Packard categorized planned obsolescence as obsolescence of function, quality and desirability. He associated obsolescence of function with improved technical performance and considered it acceptable; his criticism focused on a perceived decline in the quality of products and periodic changes in style that made products already in use appear less desirable (a form he also termed 'psychological obsolescence'). Consider each in turn.

Societal progress is often understood to be dependent upon advances in science and technology that lead to functional improvements in products over time. In the case of electronic products, for example, the case for longer lifespans is sometimes questioned on the basis that most consumers aspire to own the latest models and, once affordable, would not want to retain their existing products. Such logic has led governments to sympathize with the argument that planned obsolescence may be regarded positively as a 'vehicle of technological progress' (Fishman et al., 1993). Indeed, the most significant example of government intervention relating to product lifetimes in recent years did not concern an increase in longevity but a decrease: across much of North America and Europe the introduction of car scrappage schemes in response to the global economic recession that began in 2008 offered consumers financial incentives to replace older, less fuel-efficient vehicles, although the environmental case for such schemes has been subject to dispute (van Wee et al., 2011).

There is inadequate evidence to make definitive claims about trends in quality and the decline in product lifetimes perceived by Packard and subsequent critics. It is clear, however, that advances in product performance relating to sustainability have addressed energy efficiency and recyclability rather than longevity. Governments and consumers have a shared interest in energy efficiency (i.e., lower carbon emissions and cheaper running costs) and public policy has focused on recycling, not waste prevention. Stahel (2010) has argued that any shortening of product lifetimes would be a logical outcome of the present industrial system because in saturated markets it is the only way to increase sales volumes. Market forces can certainly exert an influence upon product lifetimes. For example, when companies in industrialized nations relocate manufacturing to low-wage countries in order to reduce costs, replacement tends to become economically attractive relative to repair because repair is a labour-intensive activity normally undertaken in the (high wage) industrialized country and thus relatively expensive.

The periodic changes in style criticized by Packard have been underpinned by a culture of mass consumption that has sought to legitimize 'expendability' (Whiteley, 1987). New styles that may initially be developed by companies to gain competitive advantage gradually become the industry norm if they prove popular. Yet this results in many people feeling compelled to replace outdated goods, even if they're functional. Fashion is an important means of expressing human creativity, but the discarding of products because of outmoded appearance, as distinct from faults, is properly criticized in the context of environmental sustainability by people who see benefits in design that prioritizes functionality and avoids colours and forms that are susceptible to transience in popularity.

The initial response from designers to the debate on planned obsolescence in the 1960s and early 1970s reflected prevailing cultural norms in industry. Only a few, most notably Victor Papanek (1972), argued that the design community should assume a greater degree of social and environmental responsibility. Another twenty years were to pass before such thinking entered the mainstream.

One of the first signs of change in the United Kingdom came in 1986, when the Design Council held its exhibition *The Green Designer.* The following year saw the publication of *Our Common Future,* the report by the World Commission on Environment and Development (1987) that popularized the term 'sustainable development' and proposed a meeting of world leaders. This meeting duly took place in 1992 in Rio de Janeiro and became popularly known as the Earth Summit, its formal title being the United Nations Conference on Environment and Development. In the meantime, eco-design, alternatively termed green design (Burall, 1991; Mackenzie, 1991) or design for environment (Fiksel, 1996), began to attract interest. Initially a response to specific environmental concerns such as energy efficiency and recyclability, the concept was gradually refined through the incorporation of economic and social perspectives and adoption of life cycle thinking, and is now more commonly known as sustainable design.

Over the same period, interest in product lifetimes was being promoted by the Dutch design network Eternally Yours (Van Hinte, 1997, 2004) and UK-based Network on Product Life-Spans (Cooper, 2010), and design principles relating to product longevity were developed (Vezzoli and Manzini, 2008). New research was undertaken exploring the potential for optimizing product lifetimes and preventing premature replacement (Chalkley et al., 2003; Van Nes and Cramer, 2005, 2006), products and associated behaviour that defied obsolescence (Park, 2003, 2010) and the relationship between users and products (Chapman, 2005; Mugge et al., 2005).

GREENING CONSUMERISM?

The foregoing discussion has established that present consumption patterns are unsustainable, asserted that decoupling and circularity offer only partial solutions and proposed that increased product longevity is essential. Having suggested that there has been a growth of interest in and awareness of sustainable design, does the answer to the throwaway culture simply lie in the design of longer-lasting products? If so, would they prove attractive to consumers and be used appropriately?

Products designed to have a reduced environmental impact became notably more visible from the late 1980s onwards. The first Green Consumer Week, in 1988, saw high street chains promoting products designed to have fewer negative environmental impacts and the publication of resources designed to help consumers identify such products, notably *The Green Consumer Guide* (Elkington and Hailes, 1988). Many leading companies accelerated efforts to understand and reduce the environmental impact of their products. The limitations of a single-issue approach, focusing solely on, say, recycling or energy efficiency, were increasingly understood, and tools such as life cycle analysis were developed to enable companies to evaluate overall product performance. Governments, too, took a growing interest in the environmental impact of consumption. Environmental labelling schemes were established in many countries, and in the European Union an energy labelling scheme was established in 1992 and mandatory energy efficiency standards for refrigeration equipment applied from 1996.

Over the past twenty years, then, considerable progress has been made in designing products for a reduced environmental impact. Examples abound of best practices in sustainable design (Fuad-Luke, 2009; Proctor, 2009). Car engines and household appliances have become more energy efficient. Washing machines and dishwashers use less water and improved detergents enable clothes to be washed at lower temperatures. Electronic products have been miniaturized. Niche markets have emerged, such as sustainable fashion. More products are designed for recyclability. The management of discarded products has improved, too, enabling greater exploitation of their potential for reuse or recycling.

Yet there is a distinct lack of firm evidence that product improvement alone will be sufficient to steer the economy onto an environmentally sustainable course. Despite improvements in product performance, the environmental impact of consumption in Britain, if measured by greenhouse gas emissions, has continued to increase: based on consumption, emissions rose by almost 20 per cent between 1990 and 2008 (Defra 2011c).

The Role of Consumers

'Consumer sovereignty' is a term often used to convey a belief that societal welfare is maximized when consumers are given the greatest freedom to choose products (Cooper, 2008). Whether used in a positive (descriptive) or normative (prescriptive) sense, the assumption is that consumers can be powerful. In an environmental context, governments have acted on an assumption that making information available to consumers (through, for example, environmental labelling) will result in more appropriate choices, and this will lead to a restructuring of the market and a shift towards more sustainable products. In a few cases, such an approach has already proved successful: energy labels, for example, have been highly influential in increasing sales of the most energy-efficient appliances. Do consumers have the power to transform the throwaway culture, and, if encouraged to do so through, say, better information on product lifespans, would they want to utilize this power? Put another way, to what extent are consumers complicit in our throwaway culture?

Various factors affect the ability and willingness of consumers to purchase products designed for longevity and then to maintain them carefully and retain them throughout their intended lifespans. One of the most obvious is knowledge: consumers need an ability to differentiate between products according to their design life at the point of purchase. At present, it is relatively rare for products to be supplied with relevant information. Items of kitchen hardware are sometimes guaranteed for life—a premium brand of household appliances markets its products as designed for twenty years and light bulbs are increasingly labelled with the number of hours of anticipated use alongside energy data, but these are exceptions rather than the norm. The length of guarantee may signify a manufacturer's confidence in a product's reliability: televisions, for example, are sometimes sold with a five-year guarantee. Often, however, consumers have to resort to brand reputation, point-of-sale information, word of mouth or physical inspection to predict longevity, methods which may be unreliable. For example, consumer organizations have concluded that brands sometimes have good reliability for some types of product but not others (Cooper and Christer, 2010).

If consumer sovereignty is to be applied in practice, not just in theory, more information must be provided on the design life of products. The form of such information would need to be tailored to the type of product: in the case of many household appliances, anticipated number of uses might be more relevant than number of years. However, a strategy of providing more environmental information has certain limitations. For example, there may be trade-offs between conflicting environmental goals, as when the use of composite materials improves durability but hinders recycling. Product testing is not only expensive but may be imperfect and reliable information on outsourced components may be unavailable. Whether manufacturers would provide such information voluntarily is doubtful. Even aside from the cost involved (e.g., for testing products), the risks of revealing it, such as the possibility of increased consumer claims in the event of faults arising, are likely to be considered greater than the possible benefit of competitive advantage. It is also obvious that purchasing decisions are influenced by many factors other than information provision: social norms, peer pressure, habits, routines and situational context, to name but a few.

Perhaps a greater obstacle to the purchase of longer-lasting products than lack of information, however, is that they are liable to be relatively expensive, being of higher quality, and consumers will be unable or unwilling to purchase them. One reason why the throwaway culture persists is that consumers have grown accustomed to products becoming relatively cheap while, as noted earlier, too, appearing to have lowered their expectations of product lifetimes (Defra, 2011a). Some consumers might be able to purchase products designed for longevity but prefer not to do so because they would need to reduce their expenditure on other goods and services and devote more time on maintaining their possessions; in other words, they would need to accept a rather different lifestyle.

There are many possible explanations. Consumers may have values and attitudes that predispose them to accept relatively short-lived products: for example, they may associate cheapness with good value, enjoy the convenience of disposable products or gain pleasure from new purchases (Campbell, 1992). They may not be persuaded by claims of excessive waste (Lomberg, 2001). Some overcome guilt about waste by seeking to make it beneficial to others. Thus, those who discard functional goods salve their consciences with the thought of it helping others: discarded electrical products being shipped to Africa or Asia, unwanted furniture given to social businesses to pass onto poorer households, clothing given to charity stores, and, if unsold, sent overseas.

The significance of maintenance was noted in the aforementioned government report on longer product lifetimes, which warned that 'extending product lifetimes does not only mean designing products to last longer—it also requires consumers to use products until the end of their lives' (ERM, 2011, p. 2). There is evidence to suggest that, having purchased their possessions, consumers vary in the degree of effort that they make to maintain and retain them (Evans and Cooper, 2010). Managing one's possessions (or, to put it another way, taking caring of them) takes time, and the effort required to get a faulty product repaired may appear excessive, particularly when the economic benefit is uncertain and replacement easier (McCollough, 2012). Throughout much of the twentieth century, many people were capable of repairing products and undertook the necessary work themselves: men would tend to tinker with cars and household appliances, while women would repair worn or damaged clothes. In recent times, however, cars have become less easy to repair without specialist equipment and training, and user repair of household appliances is deterred by warnings of the warranty being void if equipment is opened and designs that prevent easy access to faulty components. Meanwhile, the relative cheapness of new clothing and a decline in skills once widely taught through home economics has resulted in fewer people repairing their clothes.

In summary, the term 'throwaway society' may convey an impression that in general consumers are wasteful, a view reinforced by evidence that appliances, furniture and clothing are often still functional when discarded (Defra, 2009; Curran, 2010), and yet other studies reveal that many people take considerable effort to find alternative users for products that they no longer want (Gregson et al., 2007). Consumer interest in product lifetimes has been described as 'sporadic and idiosyncratic' (Defra, 2011a, p.7), and certainly people's behaviour in this regard appears inconsistent. Evans and Cooper (2010) found substantial variation in behaviour at different phases in product life: people who sought durability when purchasing products did not necessarily maintain them well and sometimes discarded them prematurely. Similarly, their behaviour was inconsistent between types of product, as people who tried to maximize the lifespan of some products did not necessarily do likewise for others.

DESIGNING SYSTEMS OF LONGEVITY

If consumers are liable to accept only a limited role in overcoming the throwaway culture, what of the potential contribution of designers?

Some designers have an interest in product longevity as an element of sustainable design, while others simply want their designs to be valued over a prolonged period. In addressing product lifespans, there are a range of variables to consider that include, depending on the type of product, choice of raw materials or components, quality of manufacture and assembly, reliability, adaptability, ease of maintenance and potential for repair, upgrade, reuse or remanufacture (Vezzoli and Manzini, 2008).

The starting point may be for the designer to define an optimal lifespan (Chalkley et al., 2003; Van Nes and Cramer, 2006; Kim et al., 2003, 2006). From an environmental perspective, this normally equates to maximum, although there may exceptionally be a case for replacing the most inefficient energy-using products (Lenski et al., 2010; van Wee et al., 2011).

Concerns relating to intrinsic durability are rarely insurmountable as long as design allows for repair in response to wear and tear or material failure arising from atmospheric conditions (such as dampness). More problematic is how to address technological advance, style and fashion, people's circumstances and market conditions.

The obvious means of addressing the technological obsolescence so pervasive in electronic goods is to design for upgradeability, a strategy long recognized in theory if not widely adopted in practice, at least in the consumer goods sector (Bayley, 1995; Umeda et al., 2005). Upgrading typically requires modularity and appropriate fixtures and fittings to allow outmoded parts to be readily exchanged. An obvious example is the personal computer, although even in this case more could be done to support users who lack the necessary confidence or technical knowledge to undertake upgrade work. Upgrading may also involve appropriate software design, as in the case of mobile phones on which new applications can be uploaded. The prospect of more widespread upgradeability remains uncertain, however, given that prices of many new electronic products have continued to fall, and items that are technologically obsolete may also have an outmoded visual appearance.

Trends in style are similarly problematic for designers who want products to last. Park (2010) has noted how certain styles become described as classic when they have proven attractive over a prolonged period; they thereby defy obsolescence. As examples, he suggests the Morris Mini, Ant chair and Tizio table lamp. Clothing lifespans are susceptible to the cycles of fashion, although in recent years there has been far greater acceptance of a range of different styles, including items that are deliberately marketed as being of a different era, as in the case of vintage clothing. In a recent study, designers pointed to the importance of using a neutral style and durable aesthetics when asked about their approach to product longevity: 'One spoke of the risk of adopting an "out-spoken design" that would end up as a niche product with a short life cycle. Another pointed to the risk of design being "too aggressive"' (Cooper, 2012).

Products also become obsolete when people or their circumstances change. An obvious example is children, for whom physical growth often makes products obsolete relatively quickly. Design for adaptability has been one response, notably in the furniture sector, where examples include the Stokke Tripp Trapp chair and Leo cot bed. In the event of changes in circumstances, such as new family situations arising from marriage, separation or death, the ownership of products may change, in which case the potential for them to be transferred between individuals or passed on to other people is an important consideration. In such situations, the idea of customization, often regarded positively as a means of increasing people's attachment to their products, may instead become a problem.

Many designers feel that they have only a limited ability to influence product lifespans because they are working to briefs with restrictive cost parameters for clients who feel that they themselves have little power to influence the market (Cooper, 2012). As with other aspects of sustainability, product longevity is influenced by the system in which products are made, acquired, used and, finally, discarded (Tukker et al., 2008; Vezzoli and Manzini, 2008). If designers are to play a more significant part in transforming the throwaway culture, they need to look beyond products and turn their attention to this system, its processes and associated business models and public policy.

Recent debate on product longevity has addressed the need for companies to find alternative business models that do not depend on an ever-increasing throughput of goods (Stahel, 2010). In product-service systems such as leasing, for example, the service required by consumers is sold, as distinct from the product, enabling suppliers to gain a profit stream without depending on regular product replacement (Mont et al., 2006). The potential need for this systemic change has been recognized by the British government, which has established a Waste Prevention Loan Fund intended 'to enable organizations to introduce business models and processes which make more efficient use of material resources'; the examples given include 'product reuse, repair and upgrading services (e.g., through leasing)' (WRAP, 2012).

Designing a system that will facilitate product longevity requires each phase in the product's life to be addressed within its situational context. Thus at the acquisition stage, the way in which the owner obtains a product may affect its ultimate lifespan: was the product planned or an impulse purchase, bought for personal use or as a gift, accompanied by adequate information and marketed appropriately? Such factors will help to determine whether or not a product is appropriate for the user and affect the owner's expectations of its lifespan and emotional attachment to it. Designers may not always be able to influence all relevant factors but need to be mindful of them during the creative process.

The use phase is, of course, critical. An obvious way in which design can influence the likely lifespan of products is by paying attention to ease of repair and maintenance. If a product contains components liable to fail, such as elements in kettles and toasters, replacement of faulty parts should be made possible. Products are less likely to be repaired if designed in a way that does not enable quick access to faulty parts or if they have snap fittings, which are liable to break, rather than screws. When an item is normally displayed, as with furniture, or when hygiene is a concern, as in the case of kitchen items or children's toys, its lifespan is likely to be influenced by whether it is easy to keep clean. Again, designers may not always have influence: they can strive to avoid oversights, but flawed designs may be the outcome of cost considerations.

Systems innovation in retailing is especially relevant with regard to acquisition and use. The retail infrastructure currently tends to be based on the dominant business model of chain stores, generally in prime locations, aiming to sell high volumes of new items, which is not in keeping with the goal of longer product lifetimes with supporting after-sales services. Some rethinking of this model is required, perhaps involving planners and interior designers alongside product designers, to make service options such as repair, reuse and hire or lease as accessible and attractive to consumers as sales of new items. Such service options need to become more visible. One significant development is a collaboration between the UK high street retailer Marks & Spencer (M&S) and the charity Oxfam through which M&S customers are offered discount vouchers in exchange for returning used clothes, which are then resold in Oxfam stores.

Lastly, designers increasingly need to consider the end-of-life phase of products, not least in response to increasingly stringent waste-related legislation. Regulation should not, however, be the only motivator. While some products are purchased, used until they wear out and then discarded, many follow a rather more complicated journey: they are stored, traded, swapped, shared or passed on to other people either once or, perhaps, many times. Nonetheless, despite growing awareness of the environmental benefits of reuse (WRAP, 2011), many functional products end up as waste. Designers can play a role in preventing such waste by considering principles such as adaptability and ease of disassembly in order to facilitate reuse and repurposing. Designers can also contribute creative thinking to systems of reuse: once limited to jumble sales and classified advertisements, these now include car boot sales, online auction sites such as eBay and, most recently, the various sharing, lending and swapping initiatives collectively described as collaborative consumption (Botsman and Rogers, 2011).

Engaging Governments

Many consumers and designers are aware that they have a role to play in transforming the throwaway culture. In Britain, for example, ethical consumption and many forms of reuse are thriving. Even so, consumption-based carbon emissions are rising and waste volumes remain excessive because many consumers favour replacement over repair and are unable or unwilling to pay for products designed for longevity. Meanwhile, designers have become better informed about the principles of sustainable design and are well aware of the means by which products could be made to last. Yet they are often unable to put design-for-longevity principles into practice because they are working according to restrictive briefs.

The unsustainable nature of the status quo and systemic nature of the problems outlined above suggest a need for governments to assume a stronger role in facilitating a transformation of the present throwaway culture. In doing so, they will need to consider which policy approach is likely to be most effective in increasing product lifespans. Which type of instrument (regulatory, market-based or voluntary) will be most appropriate, and what might be the effect of the policy upon companies and consumers? If new business models are needed, how might they be encouraged? If consumers need more information to make appropriate choices, should the requirement be voluntary or mandatory? The wide range of options available (Cooper, 2010) can only be summarized here.

Regulation is sometimes favoured on the basis that when rules apply to all companies, regardless of size or origin, a level playing field is created that enables change with the benefit of certainty and less risk. Governments could, for example, require minimum performance standards relating to longevity for certain products. Jackson has argued that 'product standards could make vital differences between durability and obsolescence, between efficiency and waste, between recyclability and landfill' (2005, pp. 129). Such standards might be based on design for disassembly; they could, for example, require products such as toasters and kettles to be fitted with replaceable elements.

A more radical approach would be to adopt minimum durability criteria as a 'legally binding prerequisite' for certain types of product, as proposed in a recent report on waste reduction (Eunomia et al., 2007, p. 339). This implies some form of lengthy guarantee, a key policy proposal in a rare international study published some thirty years ago (Organisation for Economic Co-operation and Development, 1982). A requirement to provide a long guarantee would bring the business model closer to that of a product-service system.

Preventing products deemed inappropriate from being placed on the market (in the present context, those unduly short-lived) has a precedent in European Union directives setting minimum efficiency standards for refrigeration equipment and boilers, as well as in product safety legislation. As noted earlier, the Ecodesign Directive has raised the possibility, in the case of energy-using products, of minimum guaranteed lifetimes and rules relating to spare parts, modularity, upgradeability and reparability.

Another possible policy mechanism, again mentioned earlier, is lifespan labelling. This is not as straightforward as energy labelling because product lifetimes may be dependent upon user behaviour, particularly the frequency or intensity with which consumers use the product. This aspect may make manufacturers reluctant to support the introduction of such labelling, as it may be seen as providing a guarantee against which consumers could make claims. Notwithstanding such complications, Cooper and Christer (2010) concluded that much more could be done to inform consumers about the intended lifespan of products. For example, variation in the length of manufacturers' guarantees to reflect different levels of quality, which is common for kitchen furniture, could be encouraged in other markets, such as electrical goods.

Finally, at a more systemic level, a market-based approach could be taken in the form of ecological tax reform, shifting taxation from labour to resources (Ekins and Speck, 2011). A range of fiscal measures to encourage longer product lifespans are possible. Taxes could be reduced on after-sales activities such as repair and reuse, which tend to be labour-intensive. For example, value-added tax (VAT) could be removed from such activities. In Britain, reduced VAT for repair work was proposed in a report by the House of Lords Science and Technology Committee on waste reduction (2008). Already, the European Union has allowed member states to charge a lower rate of VAT on labour-intensive services such as minor repairs, including mending and alteration, to bicycles, shoes and leather goods, clothing and household linen on an experimental basis (European Union, 1999, 2009). Other fiscal options are available, including changes to company taxation, and indeed in an initial evaluation of its VAT experiment, the European Commission (2003) concluded that reduced labour charges might be more effective.

CONCLUSIONS

As industrialized nations have become more affluent, expectations of economic growth and the business model of maximizing sales volumes have underpinned a throwaway culture that has led to an unsustainable throughput of resources. As newly industrialized countries seek to imitate this pattern of development, environmental threats appear set to worsen.

The need to decouple economic and environmental activity is widely accepted by international authorities, and the potential for a shift towards a circular economic model, in which recycling becomes the norm, has attracted considerable interest. Such an approach has limitations, however, and this chapter has argued that it needs to be complemented by a strategy of increasing product longevity in order to slow the rate of resource throughput adequately. Signs are beginning to emerge that interest in product lifetimes, previously evident in concerns voiced about planned obsolescence, is reviving.

In order to achieve a shift towards longer-lasting products, the roles of consumers and designers need to be understood. Products could be designed to last longer, just as other sustainability criteria are increasingly taken into account, but there is also a need for consumers to be willing and able to purchase them. This would not only require improved information but for consumers to demand products that, being of higher quality, are likely to be more expensive. Together with the repairing and maintaining of products rather than frequent replacement, this implies some not insignificant changes in lifestyle.

Designers are generally aware of the different factors that influence the lifespan of products and the means by which products could be made more durable. These factors include technical choices relating to raw materials and methods of assembly together with strategies to address technological advance, trends in style and changes in individual circumstances. The ability of designers to instigate change is limited, however, because most normally work to clients' briefs, with strict cost parameters that are determined by market conditions. It is necessary, then, to consider the context within which products are situated and how designers might contribute creative thinking to an evident need for systemic change.

The scale and urgency of the change required is such that a new direction in public policy appears essential if our throwaway culture is to be transformed. In recent years, a range of policy proposals has been developed, including product standards, information provision and fiscal reform. Governments now need to consider which of these are most appropriate and plan for their implementation.

REFERENCES

Bayley, N. (1995), *Making the Most of Life: Upgradeability,* UK Centre for Economic and Environmental Development: Cambridge.

Botsman, R. and Rogers, R. (2011), *What's Mine Is Yours: How Collaborative Consumption Is Changing the Way We Live,* Collins: London.

Braungart, M. and McDonough, W. (2009), *Cradle to Cradle: Remaking the Way We Make Things,* Vintage Books: London.

Burall, P. (1991), *Green Design,* Design Council: London.

Campbell, C. (1992), 'The Desire for the New', in Silverstone, R. and Hirsch, E. (eds), *Consuming Technologies,* Routledge: London. pp. 48–64.

Chalkley, A. M., Billett, E., Harrison, D. and Simpson, G. (2003), 'Development of a Method for Calculating the Environmentally Optimum Lifespan of Electrical Household Products', *Proceedings of the Institution of Mechanical Engineers, Part B. Journal of Engineering Manufacture,* vol. 217, no. 11: pp. 1521–31.

Chapman, J. (2005), *Emotionally Durable Design,* Earthscan: London.

Cooper, T. (1994), *Beyond Recycling: The Longer Life Option,* New Economics Foundation: London.

Cooper, T. (2005), 'Slower Consumption: Reflections on Product Life Cycles and the "Throwaway Society"', *Journal of Industrial Ecology,* vol. 9, nos. 1–2: pp. 51–67.

Cooper, T. (2008), 'No Need to Edit? Is Faith in Consumer Sovereignty Justified?' in *Rethinking Consumer Behaviour for the Wellbeing of All: Reflections on Individual Consumer Responsibility,* Council of Europe: Paris. pp. 33–39.

Cooper, T. (ed.) (2010), *Longer Lasting Products: Alternatives to the Throwaway Society,* Gower: Farnham, UK.

Cooper, T. (2012), 'Design for Longevity: Obstacles and Opportunities Posed by New Public Policy Developments', Design Research Society Conference, July 1–4, Bangkok.

Cooper, T. and Christer, K. (2010), 'Marketing Durability', in Cooper, T. (ed.), *Longer Lasting Products: Alternatives to the Throwaway Society,* Gower: Farnham, UK. pp. 273–96.

Curran, T. (2010), 'Extending Product Life-Spans: Household Furniture and Appliance Reuse in the UK', in Cooper, T. (ed.), *Longer Lasting Products: Alternatives to the Throwaway Society,* Gower: Farnham, UK. pp. 393–415.

Defra (2009), 'Maximising the Reuse and Recycling of UK Clothing and Textiles', <http://randd.defra.gov.uk/Document.aspx?Document = EV0421_8745_FRP.pdf> accessed March 23, 2012.

Defra (2011a), 'Public Understanding of Product Lifetimes and Durability (1)', Final Report to the Department for Environment Food and Rural Affairs by Brook Lyndhurst, July, <http://randd.defra.gov.uk/Document.aspx?Document=Publicunderstandingproductlifetimes1_Finalpublishedreport.pdf> accessed January 1, 2012.

Defra (2011b), 'Government Review of Waste Policy in England 2011', <http://www.defra.gov.uk/publications/files/pb13540-waste-policy-review110614.pdf> accessed March 22, 2012.

Defra (2011c), 'Greenhouse Gas Emissions Relating to UK Consumption', <http://www.defra.gov.uk/statistics/environment/green-economy/scptb01-ems/> accessed January 1, 2012.

Ekins, P. and Speck, S. (eds) (2011), *Ecological Tax Reform: A Strategy for Green Growth,* Oxford University Press: Oxford.

Elkington, J. and Hailes, J. (1988), *The Green Consumer Guide,* Gollancz: London.

Ellen Macarthur Foundation (2011), 'The Circular Economy', <http://www.ellenmacarthurfoundation.org/about/circular-economy> accessed January 1, 2012.

Energy Information Administration (EIA) (2011), 'U.S. Crude Oil Proved Reserves', <http://www.eia.gov/dnav/pet/hist/LeafHandler.ashx?n=PET&s=RCRR01NUS_1&f=A> accessed January 1, 2012.

ERM (Environmental Resources Management) (2011), 'Longer Product Lifetimes', Final Report for Defra, February, <http://randd.defra.gov.uk/> accessed January 1, 2012.

Eunomia Research & Consulting, The Environment Council, Öko-Institut, TNO and Atlantic Consulting (2007), 'Household Waste Prevention—Policy Side Research Programme', Final Report for Defra, National Resource and Waste Forum Collaborative Project, Eunomia Research & Consulting: Bristol.

European Commission (2003), 'Experimental Application of a Reduced Rate of VAT to Certain Labour-Intensive Services', COM(2003) 309 final, <http://eur-lex.europa.eu/LexUriServ/LexUriServ.do?uri=COM:2003:0309:FIN:EN:PDF> accessed February 24, 2013.

European Union (1999), Council Directive 1999/85/EC of 22 October 1999 Amending Directive 77/388/EEC as Regards the Possibility of Applying on an Experiment Basis a Reduced VAT Rate on Labour-Intensive Services, <http://eur-lex.europa.eu/LexUriServ/LexUriServ.do?uri=OJ:L:1999:277:0034:0036:en:PDF> accessed July 11, 2012.

European Union (2005), Directive 2005/32/EC of the European Parliament and of the Council of 6 July 2005 Establishing a Framework for the Setting of Ecodesign Requirements for Energy-Using Products, <http://eur-lex.europa.eu/LexUriServ/LexUriServ.do?uri=OJ:L:2005:191:0029:0029:EN:PDF> accessed July 11, 2012.

European Union (2008), Directive 2008/98/EC of the European Parliament and of the Council of 19 November 2008 on Waste and Repealing Certain Directives, <http://eur-lex.europa.eu/LexUriServ/LexUriServ.do?uri=OJ:L:2008:312:0003:0030:EN:PDF> accessed July 11, 2012.

European Union (2009), Council Directive 2009/47/EC of 5 May 2009 Amending Directive 2006/112/EC as Regards Reduced Rates of Value Added Tax, <http://eur-lex.europa.eu/LexUriServ/LexUriServ.do?uri=OJ:L:2009:116:0018:0020:EN:PDF> accessed July 11, 2012.

Evans, S. and Cooper, T. (2010), 'Consumer Influences on Product Life Spans', in Cooper, T. (ed.), *Longer Lasting Products: Alternatives to the Throwaway Society,* Gower: Farnham, UK. pp. 319–50.

Fiksel, J. (1996), *Design for Environment*, McGraw Hill: New York.

Fishman, A., Gandal, N. and Shy, O. (1993), 'Planned Obsolescence as an Engine of Techno-logical Progress', *Journal of Industrial Economics*, vol. XLI: pp. 361–70.

Fuad-Luke, A. (2009), *The Eco-Design Handbook*, 3rd ed., Thames and Hudson: London.

Galvagno, M. (2011), 'The Intellectual Structure of the Anti-Consumption and Consumer Re-sistance Field: An Author Co-Citation Analysis', *European Journal of Marketing*, vol. 45, nos. 11/12: pp. 1688–701.

Goodall, C. (2010), *How to Live a Low-Carbon Life*, Earthscan: London.

Gordon, R. B., Bertram, M. and Graedel, T. E. (2006), 'Metal Stocks and Sustainability', *Pro-ceedings of the National Academy of Sciences of the USA*, vol. 103, no. 5: pp. 1209–1214.

Green Alliance (2011), *Reinventing the Wheel: A Circular Economy for Resource Security*, Green Alliance: London.

Gregson, N., Metcalfe, A. and Crewe, L. (2007), 'Identity, Mobility and the Throwaway Society', *Environment and Planning D*, vol. 25: pp. 682–700.

Hamilton, C. (2003), 'Downshifting in Britain: A Sea-Change in the Pursuit of Happiness', Aus-tralia Institute Discussion Paper No. 58, <https://www.tai.org.au/documents/dp_fulltext/DP58.pdf> accessed January 1, 2012.

Helm, D. (2011), 'Sustainable Consumption, Climate Change and Future Generations', *Royal Institute of Philosophy Supplements*, vol. 69, no. 1: pp. 235–52.

Helm, D. R., Smale, R. and Phillips, J. (2007), 'Too Good to Be True? The UK's Climate Change Record', <http://www.dieterhelm.co.uk/sites/default/files/Carbon_record_2007.pdf> accessed January 1, 2012.

House of Lords Science and Technology Committee (2008), 'Waste Reduction', 6th Report of Session 2007/08, HL Paper 163.

International Energy Agency (IEA) (2010), 'World Energy Outlook 2010', <http://www.worldenergyoutlook.org/docs/weo2010/weo2010_es_english.pdf> accessed April 20, 2012.

Jackson, T. (2005), 'Motivating Sustainable Consumption: A Review of Evidence on Consumer Behaviour and Behavioural Change', Report to the Sustainable Development Research Net-work, Centre for Environmental Strategy, Surrey University.

Jackson, T. (2009), *Prosperity without Growth: Economics for a Finite Planet*, Earthscan: London.

Kim, H. C., Keoleian, G. A., Grande, D. E. and Bean, J. C. (2003), 'Life Cycle Optimization of Automobile Replacement: Model and Application', *Environmental Science & Technology*, vol. 37, no. 23: pp. 5407–13.

Kim, H. C., Keoleian, G. A. and Horie, Y. A. (2006), 'Optimal Household Refrigerator Replace-ment Policy for Life Cycle Energy, Greenhouse Gas Emissions, and Cost', *Energy Policy*, vol. 34, no. 15: pp. 2310–23.

Layard, R. (2006), *Happiness*, Penguin: London.

Lenski, S. M., Keoleian, G. A. and Bolon, K. M. (2010), 'The Impact of "Cash for Clunkers" on Greenhouse Gas Emissions: A Life Cycle Perspective', *Environmental Research Letters*, vol. 5, no. 4, <http://iopscience.iop.org/1748-9326/5/4/044003> accessed February 13, 2013.

Lomberg, B. (2001), *The Skeptical Environmentalist*, Cambridge University Press: Cambridge.

Mackenzie, D. (1991), *Green Design: Design for the Environment*, Laurence King: London.

Mayer, M. (1959), 'Planned Obsolescence: Rx for Tired Markets?' *Dun's Review and Modern In-dustry*, vol. 73, February: pp. 40–80 passim.

McCollough, J. (2012), 'Determinants of a Throwaway Society: A Sustainable Consumption Issue', *Journal of Socio-Economics*, vol. 41, no. 1: pp. 110–17.

Mont, O., Dalhammar, C. and Jacobsson, N. (2006), 'A New Business Model for Baby Prams Based on Leasing and Product Remanufacturing', *Journal of Cleaner Production*, vol. 14, no. 17: pp. 1509–18.

Mugge, R., Schoormans, J.P.L. and Schifferstein, H.N.J. (2005), 'Design Strategies to Postpone Consumers' Product Replacement', *Design Journal*, vol. 8, no. 2: pp. 38–48.

Oguchi, M., Tasaki, T. and Moriguchi, Y. (2010), 'Decomposition Analysis of Waste Generation from Stocks in a Dynamic System: Factors in the Generation of Waste Consumer Durables', *Journal of Industrial Ecology*, vol. 14, no. 4: pp. 627–40.

Organisation for Economic Co-Operation and Development (OECD) (1982), *Product Durability and Product-Life Extension: Their Contribution to Solid Waste Management*, OECD: Paris.

Packard, V. (1963), *The Waste Makers*, Penguin: Harmondsworth.

Papanek, V. (1972), *Design for the Real World*, Thames and Hudson: London.

Park, M. (2003), 'Product Examples of Design Features and Behavioural/Consumption Factors that Contribute to Product Longevity', Seminar Proceedings: Product Life and the Throwaway Society, Sheffield Hallam University, May 21, <http://www.ntu.ac.uk/research/document_uploads/108814.pdf> accessed January 1, 2012.

Park, M. (2010), 'Defying Obsolescence', in Cooper, T. (ed.) (2010), *Longer Lasting Products: Alternatives to the Throwaway Society*, Gower: Farnham, UK. pp. 77–106.

Proctor, R. (2009), *1000 New Eco Designs and Where to Find Them*, Laurence King: London.

Robins, N. (1999), 'Making Sustainability Bite: Transforming Global Consumption Patterns', *Journal of Sustainable Product Design*, vol. 10: pp. 7–16.

Slade, G. (2006), *Made to Break: Technology and Obsolescence in America*, Harvard University Press: Cambridge, MA.

Stahel, W. (2010), 'Durability, Function and Performance', in Cooper, T. (ed.), *Longer Lasting Products: Alternatives to the Throwaway Society*, Gower: Farnham, UK. pp. 157–77.

Stewart, J. B. (1959), 'Planned Obsolescence', *Harvard Business Review*, vol. 37, no 5: pp. 14–174 passim.

Strandbakken, P. (2009), 'Sociology Fools the Technician? Product Durability and Social Constraints to Eco-Efficiency for Refrigerators and Freezers', *International Journal of Consumer Studies*, vol. 33: pp. 146–50.

Tukker, A., Charter, M., Vezzoli, C., Stø, E. and Munch Andersen, M. (eds) (2008), *System Innovation for Sustainability 1: Perspectives on Radical Changes to Sustainable Consumption and Production*, Greenleaf: Sheffield, UK.

Umeda, Y., Kondoh, S., Shimomura, Y. and Tomiyama, T. (2005), 'Development of Design Methodology for Upgradable Products Based on Function–Behavior–State Modelling', *Artificial Intelligence for Engineering Design, Analysis and Manufacturing*, vol. 19: pp. 161–82.

United Nations Environment Programme (UNEP) (2011), 'Decoupling Natural Resource Use and Environmental Impacts from Economic Growth', Report of the Working Group on Decoupling to the International Resource Panel, <http://www.unep.org/resourcepanel/decoupling/files/pdf/decoupling_report_english.pdf> accessed January 1, 2012.

Van Hinte, E. (ed.) (1997), *Eternally Yours: Visions on Product Endurance*, 010 Publishers: Rotterdam.

Van Hinte, E. (ed.) (2004), *Eternally Yours: Time in Design. Product Value Sustenance*, 010 Publishers: Rotterdam.

Van Nes, N. and Cramer, J. (2005), 'Influencing Product Lifetime through Product Design', *Business Strategy and the Environment*, vol. 14: pp. 286–99.

Van Nes, N. and Cramer, J. (2006), 'Product Lifetime Optimization: A Challenging Strategy towards More Sustainable Consumption Patterns', *Journal of Cleaner Production,* vol. 14, nos. 15–16: pp. 1307–18.

van Wee, B., De Jong, G. and Nijland, H. (2011), 'Accelerating Car Scrappage: A Review of Research into the Environmental Impacts', *Transport Reviews,* vol. 31, no. 5: pp. 549–69 (DOI: 10.1080/01441647.2011.564331).

Vezzoli, C. and Manzini, E. (2008), *Design for Environmental Sustainability,* Springer: London.

Whiteley, N. (1987), 'Toward a Throw-Away Culture. Consumerism, "Style Obsolescence" and Cultural Theory in the 1950s and 1960s', *Oxford Art Journal,* vol. 10, no. 2: pp. 3–27.

World Commission on Environment and Development (1987), *Our Common Future,* Oxford University Press: Oxford.

WRAP (Waste & Resources Action Programme) (2009), *Meeting the UK Climate Challenge: The Contribution of Resource Efficiency,* <http://www.wrap.org.uk/downloads/Final_Report_EVA128_SEI_1_JB_SC_JB3.3304a279.8038.pdf> accessed March 23, 2012.

WRAP (Waste & Resources Action Programme) (2011), *A Methodology for Quantifying the Environmental and Economic Impacts of Reuse,* <http://www.wrap.org.uk/downloads/Final_Reuse_Method.1657704e.11443.pdf> accessed March 23, 2012.

WRAP (Waste & Resources Action Programme) (2012), *Waste Prevention Loan Fund,* <http://www.wrap.org.uk/retail_supply_chain/home_electrical/wplf.html> accessed March 29, 2012.

WWF (World Wide Fund for Nature) (2010a), *Living Planet Report 2010,* <http://wwf.panda.org/about_our_earth/all_publications/living_planet_report/> accessed January 1, 2012.

WWF (World Wide Fund for Nature) (2010b), 'Ecological Overshoot Rockets whilst Tropics Suffer Catastrophic Declines in Biodiversity', WWF-UK Living Planet Report Press Release, October 13, 2010, <http://www.wwf.org.uk/what_we_do/press_centre/?unewsid=4291> accessed January 1, 2012.

10

Why Sustainable Consumers Don't Care Much about Green Products

ANNE MARCHAND

INTRODUCTION

As citizens and in order to contribute positively to the project of sustainability, we are invited to consider, among other things, the impact of our consumption choices. Fundamentally, these choices are informed by one's understanding and perceived quality of life, pursuit of meaning and identity formation. They are also driven and influenced by a number of factors and forces such as infrastructures, regulations, products and services, norms and institutions, economic frameworks and technology (Mont, 2007, p. 22).

While it is becoming clearer that people in developed economies need to consume less, few of us venture beyond opting for green products to questioning the quantity of goods we buy or to reevaluating the significance such objects hold in our lives. This leads to an important question: what can possibly motivate someone to not only opt for products or product-service systems that are greener but also to voluntarily renounce the pleasure accompanying the acquisition of new objects (a nice pen, a new kitchen in which to welcome friends and family, a trendy handbag) despite having the purchasing power to acquire them?

This chapter explores this question and suggests that current initiatives and manifestations of sustainable consumption in civil society hold lessons for our understanding of the conditions that might lead to more sustainable material cultures. First, it offers an overview of questions that animate the debate in the field of sustainable consumption. Second, it reflects on how the product design profession is concerned with and can be mobilized by this issue. Third, the limits and uncertainties surrounding the current forms of green or sustainable consumption are discussed. Finally, based on two empirical studies conducted among consumers, including voluntary simplifiers, this chapter concludes with the idea that self-interest can play a significant role in supporting the transition from green consumption to sustainable consumption.

THE MALAISE WITH RESPECT
TO SUSTAINABLE CONSUMPTION

There is a growing critique in academic circles to the effect that the debate about sustainable consumption has for too long been confined to technological eco-efficiency measures and green products. A rich body of literature now calls for more inclusive ways to frame the issue in order to capture levels and patterns of consumption and, more fundamentally, lifestyles and infrastructures (Schrader and Thøgersen, 2011, p. 4).

Sustainable consumption, a necessary requirement alongside sustainable production for sustainable development, was discussed seriously for the first time at the World Summit in Rio de Janeiro in 1992. Three years later, in 1995, the United Nations Commission for Sustainable Development officially adopted a working definition of the concept, which is still in use today: 'The use of services and related products which respond to basic needs and bring a better quality of life while minimizing the use of natural resources and toxic materials as well as the emission of waste and pollutants over the life cycle so as not to jeopardize the needs of future generations' (United Nations Environment Programme, 2002, p. 10).

Sustainable development is described by Parson as an 'objective with uncertain boundaries' (2001, p. 344), and thus the conception of sustainable consumption varies. According to Robins and Roberts, confusion often arises as to whether sustainable consumption is, in the first place, dealing with the consumption of natural resources (an environmentalist interpretation) or the consumption of goods and services (an economist interpretation). As the authors point out, both are linked: 'natural resources are consumed throughout the economy in the production as well as consumption stage.' They further suggest that 'the special focus of sustainable consumption is on the economic activity of choosing, using and disposing of goods and services and how this can be changed to bring social and environmental benefits' (1998, p. 15).

Klasinc underlines that sustainable consumption is now often understood and discussed in the following terms: it calls for individuals to think about their personal consumption patterns and to become aware of the environmental and social impact of their consumption choices; governments are needed to provide an appropriate framework of economic, social and environmental policies; current economic models must be revised; and the abundance in consumer goods comes at a price, in the destruction of the environment, the exploitation of developing countries, and the further increases in the gap between rich and poor (2010, p. 32).

For Fuchs and Lorek, moving towards sustainable consumption requires two distinct but interrelated developments. First, it involves an increase in efficiency of consumption. As stated by the authors, this can be reached through technological improvements, which implies, for example, 'a reduction in resource consumption per consumption unit due to improvements in production processes or an efficiency friendly design' (2005, p. 262). Second, it necessitates changes in consumption patterns and in consumption levels. They specify that 'this sufficient condition requires changes in infrastructures and choices as well as a questioning of the levels and drivers of consumption' (2005, p. 262). However, a study conducted by the same authors showed that international governmental organizations have given attention to the former but failed to address the latter. Political and economic agendas in industrialized countries seek to increase, rather than decrease, levels of consumption in order to maintain economic growth.

Nevertheless, there is a rising sense of consensus in political and academic spheres about the need to reduce levels of domestic consumption if we are to move towards more viable, sustainable societies. Even though this is starting to be acknowledged, a general malaise remains palpable when the issue is raised because, at present, material consumption in developed economies is still inextricably linked to economic wellbeing. The associated difficulty of conceiving and implementing an alternative model that challenges the role and place of consumption in the economy and in our lives has tended to limit the scope of sustainable consumption and weaken its potential contribution.

Lorek distinguishes two types of sustainable consumption: *weak* and *strong*. Weak sustainable consumption focuses on products and services, and consumers are encouraged to take responsibility by buying green or more sustainable products. It relies primarily on the eco-efficiency of goods and production processes. Strong sustainable consumption has a broader scope, covering both product eco-efficiency and consumption sufficiency (2010, p. 23). This latter factor includes levels and patterns of consumption; the social embeddedness of purchase and lifestyles decisions; wellbeing as a condition that is independent of material commodities; and social innovations. As described by Reisch and Scherhorn, 'While *efficiency* largely depends on technical innovations as well as on an eco-design of products; *sufficiency* relies on individual behavioural changes as well as on social innovation' (1999, p. 678). According to these authors, '*Sufficiency* means adapting one's personal lifestyle to a "sustainable" level and structure, which might, for example, include a change in patterns of work and leisure, an increase in subsistence production and informal work' (1999, p. 678).

DESIGN FOR SUSTAINABILITY: CREATIVE PROBLEM DEFINING

Situated where production meets consumption, product design is well positioned to bring together eco-efficiency issues, related to production, and sufficiency issues, linked to consumption. The need for sustainable production and consumption actually reinforces the relevance of product design, since the profession concerns itself with the nature of objects and the relationships we pursue with the material world. Innovation is required in technological and social realms, and design can contribute to the greatest challenge of our time with its capacity to imagine, materialize and communicate sustainable alternatives to current products and practices.

Product designers are now, more than ever, invited to be creative, to understand the forces driving change in our societies and to identify opportunities for positive transformation. Examples include the foreseen increase in oil prices (Sorrell et al., 2010; Ruben, 2009) and the associated prospect of greater localization in the production and consumption of goods. Such transformations have cultural, social, economic and environmental implications, and represent an opportunity for engaging in new ways of designing and thinking about things, for exploring new material and visual cultures, and for questioning the conceptual nature of objects.

Design thinking, with its capacity for creative problem solving and, more importantly, creative problem defining, can contribute positively to a more viable and meaningful future. Sustainable consumption requires designers to be able to propose design solutions where existing products are made more resource efficient, where the outcome of a traditional product is delivered in a different and more sustainable way, and/or where the need fulfilled by the object and how it is achieved is questioned in order to propose alternatives (Fletcher et al., 2001). As Cooper has written, sustainable consumption involves rethinking how needs are met and products are conceived. According to Cooper, product development in the context of sustainable consumption 'will involve finding a mix of products and services through which consumers will be able to buy less, use less, and dispose of less without suffering a loss of wellbeing' (2000, p. 50). He further suggests that 'as a consequence, designers and other actors involved in the product development process will, increasingly, need to be skilled in understanding consumer psychology and the forces which drive consumerism as much as the commercial pressure to improve the technical efficiency of products' (2000, p. 50).

The next section considers the consumer's perspective and reflects on whether there is such a thing as a sustainable consumer or whether we are merely witnessing various shades of green consumerism.

IS THERE SUCH A THING AS A SUSTAINABLE CONSUMER?

The motivational drivers underpinning the act of consumption represent a way of being, of interacting with the world. Consumption is far from a straightforward concept, and, if anything, the question should be, When aren't we consuming? (Chapman, 2005, p. 36).

While some of us may opt for greener products or solutions, fewer people are inclined to reduce their overall level of consumption for the sake of the environment. Even though there is no evidence that, beyond a certain level of consumption, wellbeing continues to increase with consumption (Scott, 2009), and although consumer societies have failed on their own terms to deliver on their promise of full happiness (Kasser, 2002), the prospect of having less and consuming less is not very appealing to most of us.

In fact, the prospect of advancing from green consumption to sustainable consumption is highly uncertain. As explained above, the former relies on the efficiency principle and amounts only to weak sustainable consumption. It is rather convenient for consumers because it doesn't require significant lifestyle changes. It is also comfortable for governments and corporations because economic growth can continue in its conventional form; eco-efficiency can even increase profits due to its more efficient use of materials and energy, and reduced waste production. The latter implies a more significant transition, from products to product-service systems, and an overall reduction in consumption levels. By integrating efficiency and sufficiency, we can make the transition from weak to strong sustainable consumption, as discussed earlier.

The contribution of the green consumer to sustainability is not clear. A study found that even if 40 percent of consumers report being willing to buy green products, only 4 percent actually do so (United Nations Environment Programme, 2005). Similar attitude-behaviour gaps are found in the organic food sector (Hughner et al., 2007). There are significant differences between consumers' intentions to consume environmentally and ethically and their actions (Jackson, 2005; Carrington et al., 2010; Bray et al., 2011). Also, green and/or ethical attributes of products can be a decisive factor for consumers in choosing between two similar products with similar prices, but the extent of their willingness to pay a premium for more sustainable products has not yet been clearly established (Young et al., 2010). Current research on this topic yields inconsistent findings.

One can also wonder to what extent green consumption is actually green. Green consumers may switch from traditional consumerism to eco-consumerism and construct a new identity with specialized ecological products, all the while getting trapped in the Diderot effect, just as they would with traditional consumerism. The Diderot effect is defined by McCracken as 'a force that encourages the individual to maintain a cultural consistency in his/her complement of consumer goods' (1988, p. 257). It is a phenomenon through which we seek an internal consistency in what we own based on lifestyle and renew it in function of our new desired self. This leads to a spiralling consumption through search for products that hold together—a sort of 'consumption constellation' (Solomon and Assael, 1987). Gentrification of the green lifestyle, where new aesthetic conventions are linked with eco-luxury products and experiences, can also stimulate further consumption (Brooks, 2003).

The rebound effect that can accompany green consumption also adds uncertainty to its reach and scope. Porritt notes that more efficient resource use usually reduces costs in a way that makes it naturally attractive to companies but elicits a different response from consumers, in that any personal savings they incur may stimulate further consumption (2005). For example, buying an efficient car may lead to an increase in the use of the car or in savings that will eventually be spent elsewhere, resulting in no overall environmental benefit. Greater efficiency of a given product or process may eventually increase consumers' desire to use more of that product, service or resource due to its lower price. It may also increase the amount of disposable income spent on other products and services, such as holidays (Sorrell and Dimitropoulos, 2007). Hence, achievements resulting from efficiency alone are very often offset by increases in consumption volume (Greening et al., 2000).

On its own, green consumption appears severely limited in its capacity to contribute to a sustainable future. It does not represent a reduction in consumption levels, and indeed it could even increase them. In that sense, the consequences of green consumption may not be as green as one would expect. This raises an important question: What can motivate someone to not only opt for greener products or product-service systems but also scale back the acquisition of goods (and, by extension, resources) and limit the plea-surable experiences that often accompany the acquisition and ownership of things? The following sections explore this question by reporting motives that lead some citizens, who fall into the broad category of voluntary simplifiers, to reduce their consumption levels.

VOLUNTARY SIMPLICITY: A PATH TOWARDS SUSTAINABLE CONSUMPTION

The voluntary simplicity movement, if indeed we can speak of it as a movement, is rela-tively prominent among citizen-based initiatives that focus on sustainable consumption. Voluntary simplicity (VS) can be understood as an attempt to achieve a better quality of life by minimizing the detrimental impact of our way of living on both the human and natural environments. Based on the writings of American social philosopher Richard Gregg (1936), the publication of *Voluntary Simplicity* by Duane Elgin in 1981 marked the beginning of this social movement, also known as simple living in the United States. The movement has since spread to several Western countries, including Belgium, Can-ada, England, France and Spain. A second important publication, *Your Money or Your Life* by Joe Dominguez and Vicki Robin, published in 1992, further encouraged the movement in the 1990s. With significant media coverage in recent years, and with the help of the Internet, this philosophy of life has become a more popular phenom-enon connecting people who, to different degrees, identify themselves with its tenets—including those who adhere to the principles but dislike the label.

For Etzioni, 'Voluntary simplicity refers to the choice out of free will...to limit ex-penditures on consumer goods and services, and to cultivate nonmaterialistic sources of satisfaction and meaning' (2003, p. 7). In this regard, VS can be criticized, to some ex-tent, for 'being the prerogative of those free to choose their standard of living rather than the sordid poverty of those on the lower socioeconomic rungs of the hierarchy' (Japp and Japp, 2002, p. 84).

Burch (2003) broadly expresses the characteristics of voluntary simplicity as follows:

- a rejection of a culture of consumption;
- a search for autonomy based on a social conscience;
- a revision of consumption choices and a preference for more ecologically sound lifestyles;
- adoption of a reflective approach to life as opposed to impulsive or unques-tioned behaviours;
- applying principles that reflect a global vision of health;
- attention to the spiritual self; and
- nonviolent, empathic relationships with others and nature.

Shaw and Newholm propose a distinction between 'downshifters' and 'ethical sim-plifiers' (2002). The former are those who work and/or consume less to improve their quality of life; the latter are primarily concerned about the environment and others. As the authors write, these categories are nonexclusive. In fact, for many voluntary simplifiers, both aspects are integrated into a coherent discourse even though one of these dimensions may be predominant.

Even if voluntary simplicity openly promotes sustainable consumption, not all self-identified simplifiers both favour eco-friendly goods and curb consumption. Some may opt for eco-products while not consuming significantly less. Simplifiers can also practice conspicuous simplicity, where old possessions are replaced—possibly at great expense—with items that symbolize their new simplified lifestyle (Ballantine and Creery, 2010). This profile can be linked with the phenomenon of gentrification of the green lifestyle that was mentioned earlier.

According to many authors, the ethical, social, and environmental values promoted by voluntary simplicity represent a path toward sustainable consumption patterns and lifestyles (McDonald et al., 2006; Etzioni, 2003; Maniates, 2002; Shaw and Newholm, 2002). Therefore, its adherents can provide key information regarding the conditions underlying sustainable domestic consumption, which in turn can inform design thinking for sustainability.

SELF-INTEREST MOTIVES FOR CURBING CONSUMPTION

Researching voluntary simplifiers who have already adopted sustainable consumption lifestyles may provide an initial answer to the question raised earlier: What can possibly motivate someone to not only opt for greener products or product-service systems but also to reduce the acquisition of goods and limit the experience of pleasure that goes with acquiring and owning new things? Actually, a qualitative study aimed at examining the perceptions and preferences of identified responsible sustainable consumers showed that self-interest can play an important role in the adoption of more sustainable consumption patterns (Marchand et al., 2010). While the study indicated that opting for environmentally and socially sound goods among voluntary simplifiers is often directly related to eco- and socio-altruistic motives, it also revealed that reducing consumption levels was closely related to self-interest motives, notably in reaction to the negative effects of what Princen calls 'misconsumption'. As Princen states, humans misconsume when, for example, they fall into the advertiser's trap of 'perpetual dissatisfaction'; when they purchase an item that provides only fleeting satisfaction, resulting in yet another purchase; when they overwork to meet this consumption pattern and, in turn, with more income but less time, attempt to compensate for overworking by using the additional income to consume more (2005, p. 33).

With regard to self-interest or perceived individual benefits, a study of voluntary simplifiers who practice sustainable consumption revealed the following elements as central factors for voluntarily reducing consumption:

- having more time;
- reducing stress; and
- having a healthier, balanced lifestyle.

In relation to the world of goods, this took the form of a reduced level of consumption and a preference for products or product-service systems that allowed them to invest less time, money, and care in replacement, maintenance or repair.

Participants in the study explained their motives for reducing consumption and questioning the need for a product in terms not only of ecological consciousness but also of perceived personal benefits, which included the following:

- being less dependent on work and credit; unencumbering their life and mind by giving away objects;
- spending less energy and time in caring for and caring about possessions; practicing do-it-yourself activities; and opting for secondhand goods to reduce expenses and, thus, enjoying a more fulfilling life by avoiding the work-and-spend cycle; and
- opting for product-service systems that require investment of less energy, money, and time in a product's maintenance cycle as compared with owning a product.

Self-interest is traditionally seen as a major contributor to environmental and social problems, but more recent research suggests that personal benefits derived from environmentally responsible behaviours can be part of the solution and can complement altruistic motives (Kaplan, 2000; De Young, 2000; Soper, 2007). However, appealing exclusively to self-interest, without regard for the environment and the quality of life of others, when promoting pro-environmental behaviours could lead to a rebound effect, as discussed earlier (Power and Mont, 2010). On the other hand, the idea of sacrifice solely for the sake of the environment is also subject to critique (Schor, 2011). The social sphere of sustainability is about the wellbeing of societies as well as their members. This is something that is often neglected in the dominant sacrifice-oriented discourse that surrounds the promotion of more sustainable lifestyles. In such discourse, the vested interests of individuals, their family and their close community are seen as negligible, if not contrary to, virtue.

The next section deals with an ongoing study that further explores motives and conditions of sustainable consumption in relation to products and services, and generally to lifestyle and wellbeing.

INSIGHTS FROM GREEN AND SUSTAINABLE CONSUMERS

To further explore motives and conditions for domestic sustainable consumption in relation to products and services, my research focuses on green consumers and sustainable consumers. The research program aims to understand people's expectations, experiences, and perceptions with regard to products in relation to their commitment to sustainable consumption. Results from a recent study reveal specific characteristics of green and sustainable consumer profiles.

The insights presented below are the result of the qualitative study involving in-depth individual interviews with a total of twenty-seven consumers. Based on the evaluation of their commitment to sustainable consumption, eleven consumers belonged to the 'low to medium' (L-M) profile, and sixteen to the 'medium to strong' (M-S). L-M corresponds to green consumption and to a weak form of sustainable consumption, and M-S, to sustainable consumption and to a strong form. A multiple-choice questionnaire that participants were invited to complete prior to the in-depth interviews enabled an evaluation as to whether their reported actions and attitudes corresponded to a 'low to medium' or a 'medium to strong' form of sustainable consumption. The questions have been developed around the following criteria of sustainable consumption (based on Hansen and Schrader, 1997, and Cooper, 2000):

- refraining from consumption or, in some cases, consuming less;
- regarding consumption that exceeds one's basic needs as rather negative;
- choosing products on the basis of their broad-based ecological qualities; and
- identifying substitutes to traditional consumption (e.g., switching from product to service; borrowing instead of buying).

The individual interviews, ranging from one to two hours each, looked at the experiences of the respondents in relation to products and consumption in the context of sustainable consumption. The content was transcribed, coded and analysed quantitatively. Results that relate to the ideas discussed earlier are discussed below.

Understandings and expectations as to what constitutes a green product differ between the two profiles. For the L-M profile, a green product is mainly perceived as a new product produced by a medium-to-large enterprise, presenting eco-certifications as well as a visual language that refers somehow to the idea of nature. This corresponds to what might be termed a 'traditional' or 'common' green product. Among the M-S profile, a green product is understood as a secondhand object, a craft product and/or a locally produced product. The M-S participants reported that they prefer to opt for secondhand goods, DIY solutions or borrowed goods before opting for new, albeit green, products. Although the L-M participants do not significantly reduce their consumption levels, the desire and/or the pressure to do their part were present in their discourse. Their green purchases were justified on an altruistic basis—they report doing it for the planet and for future generations. In addition to altruistic motives, perceived self-interest was also a significant factor in the narrative of the M-S participants. Questioning the need for a given product and identifying substitutes to traditional consumption, such as reusing, repairing, making products, and buying secondhand objects, were linked with both a perceived increase in quality of life and a positive contribution to others and the environment. Through the adoption of such consumption habits, M-S participants perceive economic benefits that support a healthier and more meaningful lifestyle that is disconnected from the work-and-spend cycle and its detrimental effects on people and the planet.

Interestingly, sustainable consumers—that is, participants exhibiting the M-S profile—are not particularly receptive to traditional green products, which resonate with the L-M profile. First, for the M-S profile, the local, craft, or secondhand character of a product constitutes the main criterion for its being in accord with the principles of sustainability. Second, those of the M-S profile report looking for alternatives before opting for traditional green products. The research begins to suggest that sustainable consumers appear not to care very much about green products. Rather, priority is given to lifestyle and consumption alternatives that are supported by altruistic and personal motives.

For both profiles, opting for green and/or ethical products is mainly supported by altruistic motives. While sustainable consumers report personally benefiting from sustainable patterns of consumption, green consumers, who do not have a vested interest in sustainable consumption, are not inclined to significantly reduce their consumption level, nor to modify their lifestyles. These insights confirm and add scope to the earlier research findings, which indicated that self-interest motives or vested interests can play an important role in the transition to more holistic approaches to sustainable consumption.

CONCLUSIONS

As Friedman wrote, 'Consumption is a material realization, or attempted realization, of the image of the good life' (1994, p. 169). This discussion has provided theoretical and empirical indications that the shift from green consumption to sustainable consumption is a matter of one's understanding and experience of the good life. It starts to show that sustainable consumers, in contrast to green consumers, are motivated by personal interest and by an alternative conception of the good life that supports a holistic approach to sustainable consumption. It suggests that the idea of sacrifice for the sake of the environment alone, and because we have to, may encourage the consumption of green products but, so far at least, has proved to be an insufficient challenge to the dominant unsustainable social and aesthetical norms and conventions of product consumption.

According to Tonkinwise, designers 'can be part of an intentional transformation of what is initially considered normal' (2011, p. 3) in seeking and materializing preferred futures rooted in desire (I want this) and not only in the rhetoric of necessity (I need to do this) currently surrounding sustainability discourses. Product design has always responded to and contributed in forging our conceptions of the good life. Designed objects are tangible manifestations of these conceptions. Today's designers, theoreticians, and practitioners are presented with the particular challenge of helping to define preferred sustainable futures and of designing the paths toward them.

REFERENCES

Ballantine, P. and Creery, S. (2010), 'The Consumption and Disposition Behaviour of Voluntary Simplifiers', *Journal of Consumer Behaviour,* vol. 9, no. 1: pp. 45–56.

Bray, J., Johns, N. and Kilburn, D. (2011), 'An Exploratory Study into the Factors Impeding Ethical Consumption', *Journal of Business Ethics,* vol. 98, no. 4: pp. 597–608.

Brooks, D. (2003), 'Conspicuous Simplicity', in Doherty, D. and Etzioni, A. (eds), *Voluntary Simplicity: Responding to Consumer Culture,* Rowman & Littlefield Publishers: Lanham, MD. pp. 175–82.

Burch, M. A. (2003), *Stepping Lightly: Simplicity for People and the Planet,* New Society Publishers: Gabriola Island.

Carrington, J., Neville, B. A. and Whitwell, G. J. (2010), 'Why Ethical Consumers Don't Walk Their Talk: Towards a Framework for Understanding the Gap Between the Ethical Purchase Intentions and Actual Buying Behaviour of Ethically Minded Consumers', *Journal of Business Ethics,* vol. 97, no. 1: pp. 139–58.

Chapman, J. (2005). *Emotionally Durable Design: Objects, Experiences and Empathy*, EarthScan: London.

Cooper, T. (2000), 'Product Development Implications of Sustainable Consumption', *The Design Journal*, vol. 3, no. 3: pp. 46–57.

De Young, R. (2000), 'Expanding and Evaluating Motives for Environmentally Responsible Behavior', *Journal of Social Issues*, vol. 56, no. 3: pp. 509–26.

Dominguez, J. and Robin, V. (1992), *Your Money of Your Life*, Penguin: New York.

Elgin, D. (1981), *Voluntary Simplicity*, Bantam Books: New York.

Etzioni, A. (2003). 'Voluntary Simplicity: Psychological Implications, Societal Consequences', in Doherty, D. and Etzioni, A. (eds), *Voluntary Simplicity: Responding to Consumer Culture*, Rowman and Littlefield Publishers: Lanham, MD. pp. 1–25.

Fletcher, K., Dewberry, E. and Goggin, P. (2001), 'Sustainable Consumption by Design', in Cohen, M. and Murphy, J. (eds), *Exploring Sustainable Consumption: Environmental Policy and the Social Sciences*, Pergamon, Elsevier Science: Oxford. pp. 213–24.

Friedman, J. (1994), 'The Political Economy of Elegance', in J. Friedman (ed.), *Consumption and Identity*, Harwood Academic Publisher: Chur, Switzerland. pp. 167–87.

Fuchs, D. and Lorek, S. (2005), 'Sustainable Consumption Governance: A History of Promises and Failures', *Journal of Consumer Policy*, vol. 28: pp. 261–88.

Greening, L. A., Green, D. L. and Difiglio, C. (2000). 'Energy Efficiency and Consumption: The Rebound Effect—A Survey', *Energy Policy*, vol. 28, nos. 6–7: pp. 389–401.

Gregg, R. (1936). *The Value of Voluntary Simplicity*, Pendle Hill: Wallingford, PA.

Hansen, U. and Schrader, U. (1997), 'A Modern Model of Consumption for a Sustainable Society', *Journal of Consumer Policy*, no. 20: pp. 443–88.

Hughner, R. S., McDonagh, P., Prothero, A., Shultz, C. J. and Stanton, J. (2007), 'Who Are Organic Food Consumers? A Compilation and Review of Why People Purchase Organic Food', *Journal of Consumer Behaviour*, vol. 6, nos. 2–3: pp. 94–110.

Jackson, T (2005). *Motivating Sustainable Consumption: A Review of the Evidence on Consumer Behaviour and Behavioural Change*, A Report to the Sustainable Development Research Network, Policy Studies Institute: London.

Japp, P. M. and Japp, D.K. (2002), 'Purification Through Simplification: Nature, The Good Life and Consumer Culture', in Meister, M. and Japp, P. M. (eds), *Enviropop: Studies in Environmental Rhetoric and Popular Culture*, Greenwood Publishing Group: Westport, CT. pp. 81–94.

Kaplan, S. (2000), 'Human Nature and Environmentally Responsible Behavior', *Journal of Social Issues*, vol. 56, no. 3: pp. 491–508.

Kasser, T. (2002), *The High Price of Materialism*, MIT Press: Cambridge, MA.

Klasinc, K. (2010), *Sustainable Consumption in a Globalised World*, VDM Verlag Dr. Muller Aktiengesellschaft & Co. KG: Saarbrücken, Germany.

Lorek, S. (2010), *Towards Strong Sustainable Consumption Governance*, Lambert Academic Publishing: Saarbrücken, Germany.

Maniates, M. (2002), 'Confronting Consumption', in Princen, T. Maniates, M. and Conca, K. (eds), *Confronting Consumption*, MIT Press: Cambridge, MA.

Marchand, A., Walker, S. and Cooper, T. (2010), 'Beyond Abundance: Self-interest Motives for Sustainable Consumption in Relation to Product Perception and Preferences', *Sustainability*, vol. 2, no. 5: pp. 1431–47.

McCracken, G. (1988), *Culture and Consumption*, Indiana University Press: Bloomington.

McDonald, S., Oates, C. J., Young, C. W. and Hwang, K. (2006), 'Toward Sustainable Consumption: Researching Voluntary Simplifiers', *Psychology and Marketing*, vol. 23, no. 6: pp. 515–34.

Mont, O. (2007), 'Consumption and Ecological Economics: Towards Sustainability', in Pertsova, C. C. (ed.), *Ecological Economics Research Trends*, Nova Sciences Publishers: Hauppauge, NY. pp. 13–44.

Parson, E.A. (2001), 'Défis Constants, Innovations Incertaines: Une Synthèse', in Parson, E. A. (ed.), *Gérer l'Environnement: Défis Constants, Solutions Incertaines*, Les Presses de l'Université de Montréal: Montreal. pp. 343–78.

Porritt, J. (2005), *Capitalism: As If the World Matters*, Earthscan: London.

Power, K. and Mont, O. (2010), *Dispelling the Myths about Consumption Behaviour*, ERSCP-EMSU Conference, Delft, The Netherlands, October 25–29.

Princen, T. (2005), *The Logic of Sufficiency*, MIT Press: Cambridge, MA.

Reisch, L. A. and Scherhorn, G. (1999), 'Sustainable Consumption', in Dahiya, S. B. (ed.), *The Current State of Economic Science*, vol. 2: pp. 657–90.

Robins, N. and Roberts, S. (1998), 'Consumption in a Sustainable World', in Roberts, S. (ed.), *Report of the Kabelvåg Workshop*, International Institute for Environment and Development, Norway, June 2–4.

Ruben, J. (2009), *Why Your World Is About to Get a Whole Lot Smaller*, Random House Canada: Mississauga.

Schor, J. B. (2011), *True Wealth*, Penguin Books: New York.

Schrader, U. and Thøgersen, J. (2011), 'Putting Sustainable Consumption into Practice', *Journal of Consumer Policy*, vol. 34, no. 1: pp. 3–8.

Scott, K. (2009), *A Literature Review on Sustainable Lifestyles and Recommendations for Further Research*, Stockholm Environment Institute: Stockholm.

Shaw, D. and Newholm, T. (2002), 'Voluntary Simplicity and the Ethics of Consumption', *Psychology and Marketing*, vol. 19, no. 2: pp. 167–85.

Solomon, M. R. and Assael, H. (1987), 'The Forest or the Trees? A Gestalt Approach to Symbolic Consumption', in Umiker-Sebeok, J. (ed.), *Marketing and Semiotics: New Directions in the Study of Signs for Sale*, Mouton de Gruyer: Berlin, pp. 189–218.

Soper, K. (2007), 'Re-Thinking the 'Good Life': The Citizenship Dimension of Consumer Disaffection with Consumerism', *Journal of Consumer Culture*, vol. 7, no. 2: pp. 205–29.

Sorrell, S., Brandt, A., Speirs, J., Miller, R. and Bentley, R. (2010), 'Global Oil Depletion: A review of the Evidence,' *Energy Policy*, vol. 38, no. 9: pp. 5290–5.

Sorrell, S. and Dimitropolous, J. (2007), 'The Rebound Effect: Microeconomic Definitions, Limitations and Extensions', *Ecological Economics*, vol. 65, no. 3: pp. 636–49.

Tonkinwise, C. (2011), 'I love Sustainability (Because Necessity No Longer Has Agency)', *Design Philosophy Papers*, vol. 2. <www.desphilosophy.com>, accessed February 24, 2013.

United Nations Environment Programme (2002), *Tracking Progress: Implementing Sustainable Consumption Policies*, United Nations Publications: New York.

United Nations Environment Programme (2005), *Talk the Walk: Advancing Sustainable Lifestyles Through Marketing and Communications*, United Nations Publications: New York.

Young, C. W., Hwang, K., McDonald, S. and Oates, C. (2010), 'Sustainable Consumption: Green Consumer Behaviour when Purchasing Products', *Sustainable Development*, vol. 18: pp.18–31.

11

Design, Sustainability and Marketing

DOROTHY MACKENZIE

INTRODUCTION

Marketing and brands are important tools of the consumer society and are complicit in contributing to the unsustainable consumption patterns we now have to address. But the expertise and influence they represent can be directed towards promoting more sustainable behaviours. In most countries, the products and services we consume contribute a huge proportion of the country's total environmental footprint, and as more and more developing economies become consumer societies the problems associated with consumption will increase. For UK citizens, the Department for Environment, Food and Rural Affairs (Defra) has calculated that 75 per cent of carbon emissions are from the products we buy and use (Defra, 2011, p. 5). Defra's Sustainable Lifestyles Framework sets out key behaviours that constitute a sustainable lifestyle, such as wasting less food, reducing energy use and choosing sustainably sourced foods. Many of these individual behaviours are things that companies, through their brands and marketing activities, can influence either positively or negatively. More and more companies are beginning to explore how they can influence not just the direct impacts caused by the consumption of their products but also broader patterns of behaviour. For many companies that manufacture consumer goods, most of their impact comes not from their own sourcing and production but from what happens when the products go into the hands of the consumer, so addressing sustainable business will increasingly entail addressing consumption impacts.

Changing behaviour tends to be difficult, as behaviour is influenced by so many different factors, many of them systemic and cultural, but there is a growing realization that brands and marketing have a significant role to play and that a marketing-inspired approach, supported by a good understanding of behavioural economics, may be a better starting point for influencing consumer behaviour than information provision and exhortation.

The products we consume play an important part in our lives, far beyond their functional value; as Tim Jackson has explained, 'Material goods are important to us, not just for their functional uses, but because they play vital symbolic roles in our lives. This symbolic role of consumer goods facilitates a range of complex, deeply engrained "social conversations" about status, identity, social cohesion, group norms and the pursuit of personal and cultural meaning' (2005, p. v).

Brands are an important part of this. They embody meaning, carry significant stores of trust, are highly visible and have easy access to people, which gives them the opportunity and permission to influence what people do and think.

This chapter explores how organizations can, through their marketing expertise and activities, play a role in encouraging more sustainable patterns of consumption by individuals and by society in general. It covers two areas: how this can be done through the marketing of more sustainable products and services and, more broadly, how marketing and brands can be used to promote more sustainable behaviour in general.

HOW CAN MARKETING AND BRANDS PROMOTE MORE SUSTAINABLE PRODUCTS AND SERVICES?

It is the job of the engineers, designers, the R&D team and supply-chain experts to work out how to lower a product's direct impacts. However, there is no point developing a more sustainable product if people do not buy it—because they do not believe it works, do not understand it or believe that it is simply 'not for me'. To achieve anything like the scale of improvements required to move towards more sustainable consumption will mean that everybody, not just a small proportion of people who are particularly committed, will have to use more sustainable products and services. And this can be a challenge because people, while they may be broadly concerned about sustainability issues, do not always have this concern in their minds when they make everyday purchases.

This gap between concern and purchasing behaviour has been noted in a wide variety of reports. The 2011 ImagePower Green Brands Survey by Penn Schoen Berland found that 73 per cent of Americans say they would like to buy from green companies, but their actions do not always reflect these good intentions (Penn Schoen Berland 2011).

Marketing has at least three specific roles to play here:

- to use deep understanding of people and their needs and aspirations to provide insights into how to motivate people towards more sustainable consumption;
- to use brands to normalize more sustainable products and services, by embedding sustainability within what brands stand for and how they deliver their benefits; and
- to communicate effectively to make more sustainable products and services appealing.

Marketing Delivers Insights and Understanding into What Motivates Consumption Behaviours

The starting point for marketing is people and their needs, rather than products. It is the role of the marketing person to understand what is important to people, what drives their desires and aspirations, what concerns them—and then to provide something that addresses this. In the context of what is important to people about everyday products, such as tea, coffee or washing powder, people tend to focus on the main reasons they use these, and prioritize benefits such as good taste or cleaning effectiveness. Aspects such as sustainable sourcing or reduced environmental impact are not the main reasons people buy, and therefore sustainability attributes need to be framed in a way that shows how they contribute to the overall benefit of the product. For example, if tea or coffee is sustainably sourced, it is likely to be produced carefully in a way that enhances product quality and therefore the taste. A cleaning product that creates reduced environmental impact needs to be presented as an effective way of cleaning clothes first and foremost. People tend to be motivated by 'what's in it for me' more than by altruism or responsibility, which is why when Kraft launched their Kenco coffee Eco Refill pouch pack, they provided consumers not only with 97 per cent less packaging but also an attractive price saving over glass jars. People do want more sustainable products, but they need to have them presented in a way that makes the products relevant to the main functions they deliver and the main benefits they offer.

Insights into consumer behaviour gained through ethnographic studies can reveal opportunities for more sustainable products. A Unilever example is described in *Influencing Consumer Behaviour—A Guide for Sustainable Marketing*:

> In Turkey, research for the Omo brand showed that Turkish consumers prewashed their clothes much more regularly than other EU consumers, using unnecessary water at a time of water shortage. Saving water was therefore a key consumer priority, which Unilever had the opportunity to influence by using technology to eliminate the need for prewashing. Its Omo detergent was re-launched in a more powerful, compacted form that also reduced chemicals and packaging. (Business in the Community, 2011)

However, consumers had to be reassured that the new format was effective, and Unilever's insights into consumer thinking led to the development of the message that Omo was now 'so powerful that you don't need to prewash', but consumers also perceived the brand as caring and responsible. The result was an increase in market share.

While it is important when marketing more sustainable products to be realistic about consumer priorities and to look for ways in which sustainability attributes can support the product's primary benefits, it is also important to seek ways in which more sustainable offers can address important consumer needs and concerns. Brand marketers want to address deeper needs, such as the need to belong, the need to express oneself and the need to protect one's family, as these are very powerful motivations and therefore the most effective way of engaging people emotionally. Frameworks of thinking such as Maslow's hierarchy of needs or Jung's archetypal needs are used extensively in marketing to help understand the deep-rooted needs and concerns that lie behind much of our consumption activity. A criticism of much green marketing over the last few years has been that it has not offered consumers benefits they find relevant or motivating, and it has been uninspired, too rationally based and too focused on offering environmental benefits as premium priced add-ons. Joel Makower, writing in GreenBiz in 2011 declared,

> Companies' marketing efforts have been largely half-hearted, humorless and uninspired. Green products themselves have been variously underwhelming, overpriced, inconvenient, ineffective or unavailable. Too often, green marketers have attempted to prod consumers to act by relying on guilt or by encouraging people to 'save the Earth,' neither of which has turned out to be particularly aspirational or appealing. And consumers have made it crystal clear: They don't want to change, at least in the name of Mother Earth or the greater good.

More sustainable products and services could be offered in ways that more obviously address some of the very powerful and universally important lower level needs, such as security, health, family, friendship, peer comparison. Marketing is continually developing better ways of gathering insights into what really matters to people and therefore what is likely to motivate their behaviour. Tools based on psychology or ethnography will be increasingly important in understanding how to align more sustainable products and behaviours with deep, universal motivations.

Brands Have an Important Role to Play in Normalizing More Sustainable Products and Services

If the task is to move all consumer behaviour to be more sustainable, then major brands bought by mainstream consumers have a vital role to play. While it could be useful that more sustainable is seen as an aspirational benefit, it is arguably more important that more sustainable simply becomes normal and expected as part of basic product performance. This is increasingly the view from the mainstream marketing and communications world, based on consumer research, as reflected in the Mainstream Green study from Ogilvy & Mather:

> Our research shows us the path to closing the Green Gap is through popularizing and normalizing the desired behavior. Normal is sustainable. Abnormal or exceptional beliefs and behaviors will remain abnormal and exceptional and not successfully cross over to mass adoption. (Bennett and Williams, 2011)

Many major brands have been slow to take even quite basic steps towards improving their social and environmental impact, and have instead offered small green alternatives, or one green line within a wide range of products. Sometimes this approach has been justified by technical or supply-chain challenges of moving large businesses quickly, but offering consumers greener choices can simply emphasize that more sustainable is not yet normal and runs the risk of consumer demand becoming the deciding factor in the pace at which the overall offer is made more sustainable. It is much better to take a brand-led approach, simply moving towards a more sustainable offer overall, and then telling people what this is and why it works for them. The decision by leading UK DIY retailer, B&Q, to stop stocking electric patio heaters was an effective way of stating that this device is no longer normal. They have edited the range of choices they are prepared to offer consumers, thereby framing consumers' perception of the options they have and influencing their behaviour.

What other people are doing is highly important in normalization. The Ogilvy Mainstream Green study cites the example of OPOWER in the United States, which adds to people's utility bills a chart showing how their consumption compares with that of their neighbours. The provision of this information resulted in much higher levels of participation in energy saving programs than usual, as people want to do what they believe many other people are already doing.

Normalization can be accelerated by properly integrating sustainability within the brand and by providing helpful and relevant information to build understanding and knowledge. UK retailer Asda, part of Walmart, believes that sustainable behaviour is already normal for their customers—at least in certain areas—with people making links between minimizing waste and saving money, between sourcing local products and maintaining local communities. To quote Paul Kelly, external affairs director, at Asda stores 'green isn't new, it's just the norm. And our customers are living it every day' (Asda Stores 2011).

When it comes to integrating sustainability within the brand, this cannot be regarded as a one season, optional, promotional idea; it is a never-ending journey for all companies and brands. Unilever's Brand Imprint tool helps brand teams identify opportunities for improvement, and sustainability attributes may be embedded into the brand model—the enduring framework that defines what the brand offers and stands for. This ensures that the brand makes a long-term commitment by hard-wiring sustainability attributes into the brand's DNA. This enduring commitment to making sustainability aspects part of what the brand is all about is an important part of normalization. Sustainability attributes become part of how consumers see the brand, contributing to their perceptions of brand values and building valuable brand equity. Procter & Gamble (P&G) refers to this as 'benefit led sustainability'—ensuring that an environmentally improved product works at least as well as it did before, and has a reduced impact, making it easy for consumers to adopt.

Each incremental sustainability aspect will be visible for a while but will then simply become expected. It now feels completely expected that Starbucks provides fair trade coffee—it is part of the core offer and experience of the brand. Brands such as Patagonia and Stoneyfield Farm, where a commitment to sustainability was from the start a fundamental part of the brand story, can provide inspiration for brands for whom this is something new. Timberland, a brand well known for effective action and campaigning on a wide range of sustainability issues, is increasingly demonstrating its commitment through its approach to the design and manufacture of the products it sells. One example of this is the company's Earthkeeper shoes, which are made with linings made from recycled plastic bottles and with Green Rubber outsoles, made from recycled waste tyres. IBM's Smarter Planet platform, which embraces sustainable living and working at its core, has become the corporate platform for the whole organization rather than a separate initiative.

In addition to simply incorporating sustainability attributes, brands can also help to raise awareness and build knowledge through providing the right information in the right way. Brands are vehicles to bring messages to large numbers of people. In areas such as health, people increasingly expect food brands to provide clear, understandable information about nutrition. Brands can help to make people aware of sustainability issues and ensure that sustainability attributes become part of normal purchasing decisions by incorporating accessible information in their labelling or communications. We know that information alone, in particular if it is too technical, too confusing or lacking in credibility will not significantly influence purchase. However, provided that the information is made understandable and helpful, it will not only contribute towards greater understanding, it will also support the brand's aim of being transparent, useful and empathetic. On the packaging, Timberland's Green Index provides the full details of the environmental footprint of the product in a style familiar to consumers from nutritional labelling. The incorporation of recognized eco-labels by major brands can also contribute to the process of normalization. Of course, it is essential that the greater visibility of information around sustainable attributes should not be undermined by bad practices and green-washing (Ottman, 2011, pp. 107–30).

It can be useful for brands to be able to present succinct, relevant claims, although there are some claims that should be avoided due to the risk of confusion (Futerra Sustainability Communications, 2010, p. 17).

Communicating Effectively and Persuasively

The effective promotion of more sustainable products and services is obviously essential if they are to succeed in the market and contribute to more sustainable behaviours. In the early days of green marketing, a common mistake made by some brands was to adopt a clearly identifiable—often somewhat sanctimonious—tone and style of communication that was very different from their usual approach, to signal that they were now talking green. Packaging and advertising took on a brown and green tinge, and wit, humour or appealing aesthetics was absent. This was not only usually unappealing but also felt inauthentic, as though the brand was trying to be something it was not. This contributed to the idea that green offers were niche, not for everyone, rather than green being normal and expected. Nowadays, we recognize that effective, appealing presentation and communication is an essential part of ensuring that more people want to buy more sustainable products and services, and the increasing visibility and quality contributes to the normalization process. ZipCar is building demand for more flexible ways of accessing car services, and therefore more sustainable car usage, through positioning itself as modern, highly convenient and user friendly. Their distinctive brand identity and tone of voice is very different from most car imagery and promotion, and supports it as the aspirational choice for in-the-know people in towns. The sustainability benefits are support points rather than the main focus, as they recognize that people are more likely to be motivated by convenience, cost and flexibility than they are by environmental considerations. However, as people become used to the new behaviour that the ZipCar enables, they are likely to appreciate that they are doing something that may have environmental benefits, too.

Cleaning brand Method's beautifully designed packaging plays an important role in stimulating purchase, positioning the brand as aspirational and aesthetic rather than environmentally responsible. From this platform, the company can encourage people to use refill packs, to use less product and to learn more about the benefits of plant-based ingredients, without having to lecture or appear too worthy.

Communicating in a way that is appropriate to the brand and appealing to the consumer makes an important contribution to normalization. In the United Kingdom, P&G's Ariel brand produced typically hard hitting, clear and persuasive advertising to support its 'Turn to 30' campaign encouraging people to wash at lower temperatures. The approach was entirely credible and appropriate, executed in a way that reinforced to consumers that this is the new normal. In the United States, Timberland's 'Nature Needs Heroes' campaign to support the Earthkeeper boots used a humorous approach to appeal to its young male target group, whether these males saw themselves as eco-conscious or not. As Ogilvy & Mather note in its Mainstream Green report, 'Communication should embrace the fact that sustainability is a deal-maker, not a deal-breaker, for the mainstream consumer' (Bennett and Williams, 2011).

A communications campaign for SCA's Velvet toilet paper in the United Kingdom offered 'Luxury for you, trees for the planet', as a way of communicating a sustainable sourcing policy that would be relevant and appealing to the mainstream consumer. Understanding people, and trying to meet their most important needs in a way they understand and appreciate, should be a good basis for communicating more sustainable products and services effectively to inspire more people to switch to these.

However, marketing and brands can do, and should do, more than simply improve their own products and services and encourage people to use these. Brands are tools of influence and engagement and have a broader responsibility.

HOW CAN MARKETING DIRECTLY PROMOTE MORE SUSTAINABLE FORMS OF BEHAVIOUR?

There are a variety of ways in which brands can actively promote new, more sustainable forms of behaviour, beyond simply producing more sustainable products and services and encouraging people to buy them. For example, marketing has always involved interpreting and framing technological developments, social trends and social issues, making these accessible and acceptable to people, from introducing new technologies that offer greater convenience in the home to challenging social attitudes about race and gender. This role as interpreter of trends and influencer of social norms will be important in making more sustainable behaviours more acceptable.

Brands can of course create very explicit campaigns advocating new behaviours—and more and more brands are beginning to do this. In addition, brands have the motivation and the methods to reach out to people and engage them in interesting and important conversations and collaborations in pursuit of outcomes that are individually and socially beneficial.

Brands as Interpreters of Trends and Complex Issues

The scope of marketing includes not just in-depth understanding of people's motivations and needs but also a broad understanding of the context in which people operate. It is essential, if brands are to stay relevant, for them to study and interpret trends, whether these are hard trends based on demography or economy or soft trends based on developments in social attitudes, political aspirations or the emergence of new cultural themes. The behaviour of major brands can indicate when there are turning points in society's attitudes—for example towards racial integration, the role of women, the acceptability of smoking. Because of their reach and influence, brands, through their marketing and communications activities, can affect our view on what is a normal or aspirational lifestyle. One of the eco-pioneers, Dave Kimbell, chief marketing officer of Seventh Generation, advocates behaviour placement as an effective way to express the brand's values and create a dialogue with consumers. By portraying people in advertising cycling or taking public transport, drinking tap water, recycling or using energy-efficient appliances, these behaviours become more acceptable and less conspicuous, as most of us tend to want to do what we feel everyone else is doing. Promoting green behaviours and green product placement in films is another development. Climate change charity Global Cool is working with the British Independent Film Awards to encourage this, citing the use of BMW's i8 plug-in hybrid in the 'Mission Impossible' film *Ghost Protocol* as a way of normalizing lower carbon transport, and thereby encouraging people to reduce their carbon emissions—without requiring them even to be interested in climate change.

Marketing very often has the challenge of taking complex issues and making them more understandable, by finding the right language and by making them seem relevant to people. Politicians, scientists and even campaigners can find this very challenging, and important issues can seem remote to many people, resulting in them being dismissed as too hard and therefore unlikely to influence behaviour. This is an area where marketing and brands could potentially make an important contribution. Many issues around sustainability are so complex and huge that a rational response is simply to say, 'What can I do about this?' Biodiversity is certainly one of these issues and of course needs to be addressed by companies and governments working together rather than left to consumer choice. However, some brands have been trying to engage consumers in the issue by focusing on very specific sub-issues that people can relate to and believe they can contribute to. In the United Kingdom, Jordans is encouraging people to turn 10 per cent of their garden into a home for wildlife, mirroring the company's work with farmers over many years to promote biodiversity in the countryside. In the United States, Häagen-Dazs has been explaining, through their 'Honey Bees' campaign, the role that bees play in pollinating one-third of foods. Other brands have been taking major, complex sustainability challenges and presenting these to consumers with suggestions of what these might mean for them and what courses of action could be taken both by corporations and by citizens. GE and Philips are exploring the impact of cities, while others such as Coca Cola are considering the implications of a water-poor world.

Brands Are Increasingly Trying Directly to Influence and Facilitate New Patterns of More Sustainable Behaviour

Companies clearly have to take responsibility for reducing the negative direct impacts of their products and services, but an increasing number of companies are beginning to address the issues of the impacts that arise from how consumers use their products and services. In many cases, the environmental and social impact of product use is significantly greater than the impacts from product sourcing or manufacture. In their 2011 Sustainable Living Plan, Unilever PLC published the results from a study on the greenhouse gas (GHG) emissions across the lifecycle of over 1,600 representative products, covering 70 per cent of their sales volume. Raw material cultivation contributed 26 per cent of total GHG emissions, with consumer use at 68 per cent. Manufacture and transport together contributed only 5 per cent of total estimated emissions. This analysis showed that the product categories that accounted for the largest proportion of the GHG footprint are showering, hair washing and laundry, where the consumer uses heated water. This is providing a focus for efforts to influence consumer behaviour, such as the 'Turn-Off-the-Tap' campaign from the company's shower brand Suave in the United States. This encourages users to pledge to reduce the length of their shower by two minutes and to turn off the tap when shampooing and conditioning their hair, to save water and energy:

> We aim to reach and persuade 400 million consumers to change their shower habits by 2020, using the power of our brands to reach into households across the world, and our influence to help prevent the rise of greenhouse gases in the atmosphere. (Unilever PLC, 2011)

Method actually suggests shower-sharing as a way of saving significant quantities of water. Dong, the major energy provider in Denmark, has run an advertising campaign promoting the benefits of air-drying clothes. Levi's advocates a clothes care regime involving cold washing, line-drying and then giving away unwanted clothes to others to prolong product life and reduce waste. Levi's is concerned to educate people without lecturing them and so has presented the advice through the 'Care Tag for our Planet'—knowing that the care tag is one place that most people will look for information about the product.

UK retailer Sainsbury supported the government's desire to reduce the burden of excessive food waste through its 'Love your Leftovers' initiatives, providing imaginative recipe ideas to help people use up leftover food.

From a marketing perspective, initiatives promoting responsible behaviour may iron-ically perhaps have a positive effect not simply on consumer attitudes and behaviour and brand reputation but also on product sales. Marks & Spencer's (M&S) link with Oxfam to encourage people to take unwanted M&S clothes to the charity shop in exchange for a voucher redeemable against future purchases of M&S clothing certainly results in an influx of clothing for Oxfam to resell, but also could be encouraging people to simply replace old clothing with new clothing.

A more radical approach has been launched by Patagonia and eBay. The 'Common Thread' initiative is much more overt in its advocacy of lower overall consumption levels. Patagonia suggests that people buy fewer, better quality clothes, then resell the clothes they are finished with through eBay, with whom it has established a long-term partnership. Patagonia asks people to 'Reduce, Repair, Reuse, Recycle' and then finally 'Reimagine—a world where we take only what nature can replace'. The striking press advertisement proclaiming 'Don't Buy This Jacket' featured as *Adweek*'s ad of the day in November 2011, setting a new tone for the apparel industry and raising questions about the appropriateness of minimal consumption as a potential theme for other sectors.

Will these types of behaviour-influencing initiatives have any traction with consum-ers? A strong case is put forward in 'I'll Have What She's Having' (Bentley et al., 2011), supporting the idea that if enough other people do something, then everyone ends up doing it. Ideas and behaviours spread because we have a fundamental urge to do what other people do. Despite individual choice being the focus of so much marketing atten-tion, we are in fact influenced to a large degree by social influence and social learning. Mark Earls is quoted at a Guardian Sustainable Business seminar in 2011 as suggesting,

> The best initiatives are not one-to-one conversations between brands and individ-ual consumers, but between brands and groups of people whose interests they nur-ture. Outdoor company Patagonia and sportswear brand Howies for example both encourage their customer's passion for outdoor activities such as hiking and BMX-ing, and link this to caring for the natural world. (Rowley, 2011)

Brands Are Using Innovative Communication and Engagement Methods to Advance Behaviour Change

While traditional forms of marketing such as advertising campaigns, promotional of-fers and product communication have a role in promoting desirable new behaviours, brands are also exploring new territories to find different ways of engaging people in the challenges involved. The explosion of social media and the increasing resistance of consumers to traditional marketing techniques are prompting new thinking generally in marketing about how to build relationships and better connect with consumers. Sustainability may well provide a rich and emotionally engaging platform that prompts the desire to interact with brands far more strongly than other platforms can do. Brands wish to have conversations with people, to draw them more deeply into their innovation processes, to find ways of involving them in the brand experience far beyond the simple consumption of the product or service. This is based on the premise that a more involved and engaged consumer is likely to have a more positive attitude towards the brand and therefore over time will choose it and advocate it to others. This desire to connect and interact with consumers aligns with the need to influence their behaviour in more sustainable directions. Eric Lowitt, in *The Future of Value,* describes GE's 'Smart Grid Challenge' campaign, through which the company proposed the need for a smart grid and then engaged the general public and customers in generating ideas that could bring it to life. He says, 'The company's commitment to and follow-up on its crowd-sourcing campaign enhances the perception that GE is a transparent (and hence trustworthy) company' (2011, pp. 151–3).

One of the tools being used increasingly by brands to engage consumers is gamification—using game thinking and processes to make connecting with brands fun. This builds on the popularity of the mechanics and processes used in computer games, particularly among the generation that has grown up with computer games as a primary form of entertainment. Some brands are exploring the potential of game mechanics to incentivize different, more sustainable behaviours in their customers, drawing on people's competitiveness and desire to improve their performance. Several car brands, including the Ford Fusion hybrid and the Nissan Leaf electric car, are using dashboard feedback to help people drive more ecologically. For example, using a green virtual plant that grows on the dashboard the more ecologically you drive. You can also compare your driving against your friend or against your previous performance.

Recyclebank is a company established to reward people for making environmentally conscious purchasing and behaviour decisions through winning redeemable points or cash rebates. Recyclebank believes that digital media will be key to motivating mass behaviour change and is using games to engage, educate and inspire people not just to recycle but to reduce energy and water use, use public transport and support their local community. The company uses partnerships with well-known brands to extend its impact and reach, such as working with Brita, the water filter company, to help consumers reduce the number of water bottles they use each day. With Transport for London, Recyclebank developed a mobile app that rewards people for cycling and walking in London.

WHAT IS THE WAY FORWARD FOR MARKETING TO CONTRIBUTE TO BEHAVIOUR CHANGE?

The understanding, skills and techniques that marketing has fine-tuned can be used to address behaviour change challenges, and there are many examples of this happening already. Skills of insight into human needs and motivations, the ability to make complex, remote issues accessible and interesting, the sophistication with which traditional and emerging communication channels can be used to educate and inspire: these are valuable abilities and methods that can serve a move towards more responsible consumption. There is an interesting intersection between the trajectory on which mainstream brand thinking is travelling already and the evolving thinking about behaviour change, which could lead to brands emerging as enthusiastic standard-bearers for large-scale action to promote behaviour change.

Brands are eager to develop conversations and collaborations with consumers—in their role as consumers but also in their role as citizens—in order to foster strong relationships and gather deeper understanding of their needs and aspirations. These conversations may well be more compelling and rewarding if they are based around significant issues related to sustainability and responsible behaviour. The future of marketing may lie in brands with a purpose that extends to social purpose, a concept referred to as Social Equity Brands in *Brand Valued* (Champniss and Rodés Vilà, 2011).

Brands often wish to move away from being defined by the products or services they have traditionally been associated with, and prefer to be seen as entities that address needs, offer benefits and solutions and deliver outcomes. This is very consistent with the huge effort and innovation that will be needed if we are to uncouple consumption from resource use, as companies such as Unilever have committed to doing. Part of this may involve ideas such as swapping and sharing—and increasingly brands are viewing these activities as revenue-generating, positive ways of deepening and extending their consumer relationships rather than as unwelcome restrictions on product sales.

As consumption patterns in developing countries change, it is important to consider the challenge of transnational behaviour change. In her submission to the House of Lords Science and Technology Select Committee call for evidence on behaviour change, Dr. Elizabeth Shove made the interesting point that unsustainable consumption is promoted by the export of Western/Northern European views of what constitutes normal behaviour. The development of a new normal of embedded sustainable behaviour within mainstream marketing and brand activities is perhaps therefore more urgent and important than ever. The UK is an influential centre of leading thinking and high-level execution in marketing and the creative industries, and must therefore take responsibility for leading the way in the integration of sustainability into marketing and branding best practices. Dr. Shove comments, 'Discussions of transnational behavior change have yet to get underway—this is a field where more research is required. Such research would do well to pay specific attention to the part that the UK plays, perhaps unwittingly, in producing and circulating unsustainable interpretations of wellbeing and normal behavior' (Shove, 2010, p. 91).

Of course, marketing cannot take the primary responsibility for promoting behaviour change. Huge systemic changes will be required, together with changes in regulation, tax systems and pricing signals, if mass responsible consumption is to be achieved. But those responsible for marketing will increasingly have to understand and address the sustainability impacts of their products and services, leading to the emergence of a new type of marketing professional, working within organizations where sustainability is embedded into the organization. Speaking before the annual conference of the UK's Marketing Society in November 2011, Keith Weed, Unilever's chief marketing and communications officer, said,

> My key responsibilities cover Marketing, Communications and Sustainability. The need for more sustainable consumption requires more sustainable approaches to business and products. Marketing needs to engage with this agenda to innovate more sustainable solutions and to help change consumer behaviour. With a predicted 9 billion people on the planet by 2050, it's easy to see why we have put Sustainable Living at the heart of everything we do. (Lewis, 2011)

Unilever continues to be at the forefront of thinking about the role of marketing in addressing sustainable behaviour, but it is very probable that it represents the vanguard of a significant change of focus in marketing, requiring new priorities, new methodologies and new performance metrics.

REFERENCES

Asda Stores (2011), 'Green Is Normal', <http://your.asda.com/system/dragonfly/production/2011/12/15/16_13_37_444_Green_is_Normal_ASDA_SustainabilityStudy.pdf> accessed March 17, 2012.

Bennett, G. and Williams, F. (2011), 'Mainstream Green: Moving Sustainability from Niche to Normal', <http://www.ogilvyearth.com/wp-content/uploads/2011/05/OgilvyEarth_Mainstream_Green.pdf> accessed June 19, 2012.

Bentley, A., Earls, M. and O'Brien, M. J. (2011), *I'll Have What She's Having*, MIT Press: Cambridge, MA.

Business in the Community (2011), 'Influencing Consumer Behaviour—A Guide for Sustainable Marketing', <http://www.bitc.org.uk/resources/publications/influencing_consumer.html> accessed November 16, 2011.

Champniss, G. and Rodés Vilà, F. (2011), *Brand Valued*, John Wiley & Sons: Chichester, UK.

Defra (2011), *The Sustainable Lifestyles Framework*, Department for Environment, Food and Rural Affairs (Defra), <http://archive.defra.gov.uk/environment/economy/documents/sustainable-life-framework.pdf> accessed February 24, 2013.

Futerra Sustainability Communications (2010), 'The Greenwash Guide', <http://www.futerra.co.uk/story#go=the-greenwash-guide-3-3822> accessed February 10, 2012.

Jackson, T. (2005), 'Motivating Sustainable Consumption: A Review of Evidence on Consumer Behavior and Behavioral Change', Report to the Sustainable Development Research Network, Centre for Environmental Strategy, University of Surrey, <www.surrey.ac.uk/eng/data/staff/rp/JacksonSDRN-review.pdf> accessed November 20, 2011.

Lewis, E. (2011), 'Keith Weed, Unilever's Chief Marketing and Communications Officer', <http://blog.marketing-soc.org.uk/2011/11/keith-weed-unilever-cmo/> accessed November 20, 2011.

Lowitt, E. (2011), *The Future of Value*, Jossey-Bass: San Francisco.

Makower, J. (2011), 'Green Marketing Is Over. Let's Move On', <http://www.greenbiz.com/blog/2011/05/16/green-marketing-over-lets-move> accessed February 10, 2012.

Ottman, J. (2011), *The New Rules of Green Marketing*, Berrett-Koehler Publishers: San Francisco.

Penn Schoen Berland (2011), 'ImagePower Green Brands Survey', <http://www.psbresearch.com/files/PSBGreen2011.pdf> accessed March 17, 2012.

Rowley, S. (2011), 'Can Brands Make Consumers See Sustainable Behavior as Desirable?' <www.guardian.co.uk/sustainable-business> accessed November 16, 2011.

Shove, E. (2010), 'Submission to the House of Lords Science and Technology Select Committee Call for Evidence on Behaviour Change', <www.parliament.uk/documents/lords-committees/science-technology/behaviourchange> accessed November 10, 2011.

Unilever PLC (2011), 'Sustainable Living Plan', <http://www.sustainable-living.unilever.com> accessed February 10, 2012.

12

The Role of Design-Led Knowledge Exchange in Supporting Micro-, Small- and Medium-Sized Enterprises to Be Eco-Innovators in the United Kingdom

ANNE CHICK

INTRODUCTION

Micro-, small- and medium-sized enterprises (SMEs) require knowledge, perspectives and resources from various external actors, including higher education institutions (HEIs), as they often lack the capacity to innovate and address various sustainability challenges on their own (Sarkis et al., 2010; Lehmann et al., 2010). Design can be an effective mechanism in supporting eco-entrepreneurs to innovate (Chick and Micklethwaite, 2004a, 2004b; Micklethwaite and Chick, 2005). The role of HEIs in the United Kingdom within innovation for sustainability knowledge exchange is still in its infancy (Sarkis et al., 2010, p. 7), but over the past decade British design academia has begun to explore and deliver such support for SMEs (O'Rafferty and O'Connor, 2007, 2010).

Sustainability today, in a business context, means increasing attention is being given to the triple bottom line—an integrated set of business practices that aims to contribute to restoring ecological systems, fostering social equity and community wellbeing as well as assuring financial prosperity (Elkington, 1997; Hawken, 2007; McDonough and Braungart, 2002; Rainey, 2006). Triple bottom line practices are generally contextualized within the eco-modernist paradigm and so is this chapter, due to the Remarkable

Limited case study. The author is advocating the main principles of sustainability and eco-innovation that harnesses design-led processes. Such initiatives can be applied within the eco-modernist and radical-ecological paradigms. The latter is calling for environmentally minded development with zero economic growth, without big-scale consumption or production, with less urbanized areas and self-sufficient communities including outside of the eco-modernist discourse (Pepper, 1984).

SMEs are socially, economically and environmentally important since they represent over 90 per cent of all businesses in the European Union. Of these enterprises, over 90 per cent are micro-businesses (European Commission, 2011a; Wymenga et al., 2011). Ninety-nine per cent of businesses in the UK are SMEs, with most active in the services sector (European Commission, 2011c). Globally there are various definitions for what denotes an SME. For the purposes of this discussion, the EU's updated definition of an SME will be used (European Commission, 2009b). There are three broad parameters that define an SME:

1. Micro-enterprises are firms with up to ten employees.
2. Small enterprises employ up to fifty workers.
3. Medium-sized enterprises contain up to 250 employees.

An objective of the European Union is to stimulate business development that addresses sustainability challenges resulting in competitive SMEs (European Commission, 2009a). This strategy is divided into two themes:

1. Environmentally sound products, services, and systems as competitive advantage.
2. Continuous improvement of operational developments.

UK HEIs through their research and third mission agendas have been responding to these two EU strategy themes including the design-specific aspects. HEIs are increasingly recognized as important actors in local, regional, national and international sustainability and innovation systems and have a key role in raising the competitiveness of enterprises, especially SMEs (Edquist, 2005; Mowery and Sampat, 2005).

INNOVATING TOWARDS SUSTAINABILITY:
THE ROLE OF DESIGN

Policy-makers, academics and organizations note that enterprises can benefit in their pursuit of addressing various sustainability agendas from intelligent innovation processes, but the conceptual muddle over sustainability can hamper such attempts (Steketee, 2010, p. 139; European Commission, 2009a, p. 5). By its nature, innovation is interactive, involving a variety of actors both within and external to an organization. The diversity amongst ways of looking represents a key element of innovation—the ability to view new connections (Kelly and Littman, 2001). It needs to be recognized that sustainability, innovation and design are flexible terms and that they can be interpreted in different ways, leading to possible misunderstanding and misappropriation of the terms. The European Commission defines innovation as

> the implementation of a new or significantly improved product (goods or services), or process, a new marketing method, or a new organisational method in business practices, workplace organisation or external relations. The minimum requirement for an innovation is that the product, process, marketing method, or organisational method must be new (or significantly improved) to the firm. (Technopolis, 2006, p. 591)

Sarkis et al. (2010, p. 2) point out that 'sustainability is about equilibrium and permanence, innovation is about changing the way things are done'.

Eco-innovation is viewed by the European Union and academics as having a crucial role to play in putting Europe on the path to a resource- and energy-efficient economy and significantly reducing the environmental impacts in important identified areas such as housing, mobility and food and drink (European Commission, 2010; Bleischwitz et al., 2009). This requires the engagement of many different actors in society and strategies implemented from many different sides. Engaging industry as well as society in developing eco-innovations for sustainable ways of living is essential (Jackson, 2009). Reid and Miedzinski's (2008, p. 2) definition of eco-innovation is viewed as comprehensive, and this definition will also be used for the purpose of this chapter. The definition states that eco-innovation is

> the creation of novel and competitively priced goods, processes, systems, services, and procedures designed to satisfy human needs and provide a better quality of life for everyone with a whole-life-cycle minimal use of natural resources (materials including energy and surface area) per unit output, and a minimal release of toxic substances.

The Wuppertal Institute and Stockholm Environment Institute (Bleischwitz et al., 2009, pp. 63–64) have identified six 'strategy areas' where industry could 'eco-innovate':

1. creating and satisfying demand for green and fair products;
2. communicating for low-impact product use;
3. innovative after sales services;
4. product and service innovations;
5. service-oriented business models; and
6. leadership for social change and socially responsible business.

Many micro- and small enterprises across Europe understand process improvements, but performing research and development, understanding regulatory requirements and standards in global markets, understanding new customer sensing, designing products and services for new markets and developing effective marketing communications are new challenges for them within the sustainability context (Gerstenfeld and Roberts, 2000; Christensen and Raynor, 2006; SEE, 2009). Most innovation barriers seem to exist with regard to market and customer relations as users are often only getting involved when an eco-innovation is ready to enter the market (Hofman and de Bruijn, 2010, p. 131).

Design is a holistic approach that takes user needs, aspirations and abilities as well as markets as its starting point and focus (European Commission, 2009a; SEE, 2009, p. 6). Therefore, design could support SMEs to address the above innovation barriers. The Sharing Experience Europe Project (SEE) defines design as 'a tool for the realisation of innovation. It is the activity of conceiving and developing a plan for a new or significantly improved product, service or system that ensures the best interface with user needs, aspirations and abilities' (SEE, 2009, p. 6). Design is increasingly acknowledged, by policy-makers, knowledge organizations and enterprises as a crucial business interface between sustainability and innovation practices and as an effective aid to innovating through to marketing (Dröll, 2011; European Commission, 2009a, 2011b). The policy landscape for design across Europe has recently evolved, resulting in the launch of the European Design Innovation Initiative in early 2011 (European Commission, 2011b). Innovation is interactive by its nature, involving a variety of actors both within and external to an enterprise. A key element of innovation is gaining diverse perspectives on a situation—the ability to view new connections (Kelly and Littman, 2001). An intelligent design process has an understanding of multi-stakeholder contexts, including the sustainability agendas, and can create an integrated approach to innovation. Unfortunately, SMEs still seem unaware of design as a strategic resource and lack an appreciation of the benefits design can bring or the experience of commissioning design (Acklin, 2011; HM Treasury, 2005). An exception is Remarkable Limited, which is an example of a small UK firm that has become a design-led company and thereby reaped the commercial and environmental benefits (Blewitt, 2008, pp. 211–12; Micklethwaite and Chick, 2005).

Third Mission: Knowledge Exchange between SMEs and UK HEIs

SMEs in the United Kingdom, including eco-entrepreneurs, lack the capacity to innovate and address given sustainability challenges on their own. They require the knowledge, perspectives and resources from various external actors, such as HEIs, to determine the successfulness of an innovation (Hofman and de Bruijn, 2010, p. 115; Sarkis et al., 2010; Lehmann et al., 2010; Chick, 2008). HEIs in the United Kingdom through their third mission strategies have proliferated programmes to support SMEs over the last decade (Lambert, 2003; Benneworth, 2007). The third mission is concerned with the generation, use, application and exploitation of knowledge outside academic environments.

Since the 1990s, knowledge exchange (also referred to as knowledge transfer) has become a major activity for HEIs in the European Union. Higher education is regarded as having an important role in raising the productivity of enterprises, especially SMEs, and has been incentivized by authorities to strengthen links via funding (Williams et al., 2008, p. 31). 'Knowledge exchange' is used throughout this chapter because it is the ideal situation and describes the exchange of knowledge between an HEI(s) and others, such as local and regional government and enterprises, rather than a straight transferring of knowledge from the HEI to an external organization.

The Triple Helix Model (THM) of university-industry-government relations has gained significance, during the last decade, and emphasized the role HEIs play in the so-called knowledge economy (Etzkowitz and Leydesdorff, 1997). The National Institute for Triple Helix Innovation (2012, p. 1) states,

> Combined, triple helix innovation is a process by which academia, government, and industry collaborate (i.e., engage in a process of mutually beneficial leveraging of resources) to create or discover new knowledge, technology, or products and services that are transmitted to intended final users in fulfillment of a social need. Final users then consume the knowledge, technology, or products and services or they use them to produce new goods and services that are ultimately sold or consumed. In addition, serendipitous benefits of the new knowledge, technology, or products and services accrue to unintended final users.

Etzkowitz and Zhou (2006, p. 81) state that the triple helix 'holds that the university and its role in society is enhanced by engaging in the translation of knowledge into use, with feedback into theorising and the opening up of new research questions as a positive consequence of such engagement'. The success of this model has influenced local, regional, national and international policy-making and the design of programmes aimed at improving the framework conditions supporting innovative activities, including those targeted towards addressing the main principles of sustainability (Etzkowitz and Leydesdorff, 2000; Etzkowitz and Zhou, 2006).

UK HEIs, generally through their research and enterprise strategies, have developed infrastructure, programmes and practices to support SMEs in response to such policy initiatives (Lambert, 2003; Benneworth, 2007). In addition, entrepreneurial potential within HEIs through entrepreneurial academics, students and graduates has been released (NESTA et al., 2008). Consequently, knowledge exchange has been a growth activity within UK HEIs. Knowledge exchange itself is not prescriptive and there is no single model, and approaches will vary depending on the funding objectives, needs of the target enterprises, the THM relations, the mission of the HEI and the focus of the local or regional economy (Lambert, 2003, p. 50; Smith, 2010, p. 10). Knowledge exchange between HEIs and SMEs in the UK can often take the form of

- training and conference events: enterprises learn from and network with one another;
- disseminating best practices to SMEs;
- providing products and services that can help the enterprise increase its competitiveness; and
- new knowledge development and exchange through specific schemes.

The role of UK HEIs within innovation for sustainability knowledge exchange is still in its infancy (Sarkis et al., 2010, p. 7). Over the past decade design academia in the United Kingdom has begun to explore and deliver such support for SMEs.

These support activities are often anchored to a region due to authorities' funding criteria (O'Rafferty and O'Connor, 2007, 2010). The technology and production-specific aspects of SMEs have, to date, seemed to be the dominant knowledge exchange support from HEIs in the United Kingdom and Europe (Van Hemel and Cromer, 2002; Tukker et al., 2000; Woolman and Veshagh, 2006). The delivery of incremental improvements through eco-design and cleaner production has been the main approach. There is a gap in knowledge provision for deeper design interventions that provides knowledge that improves product, service and process innovation, especially with regard to the marketing and visual communications aspects (Woolman and Veshagh, 2006; Blewitt, 2008, pp. 211–12). The European Commission has recently acknowledged the need for a move towards support for SMEs focusing upon eco-innovation and finding new customers and new markets (Ezell and Atkinson, 2011). This should provide an impetus for a broader perspective and comprehensive approach to design-led knowledge exchange activities from HEIs that also contributes to an SME's business strategy, marketing and sales.

REMARKABLE LIMITED KNOWLEDGE EXCHANGE CASE STUDY

Remarkable Limited (Remarkable) is a small UK manufacturer of stationery products that are made from recycled materials. It was incorporated as a company in 1996. Ed Douglas Miller, the founder and eco-entrepreneurial owner-manager, set up the business with the sole aim to recycle UK waste materials back into useful products to be manufactured in the United Kingdom (Chick and Micklethwaite, 2004b). Remarkable, like other small enterprises developing and commercializing eco-innovative products and services, faces several constraints in accessing specialist resources, information and knowledge from private, public and HEI actors (Chick and Micklethwaite, 2004b; Micklethwaite and Chick, 2005; Chick, 2008). This is particularly the case for more radical innovations that divert more substantially from existing patterns of production and consumption, as this requires various changes that go beyond the capabilities of the enterprise (Chick, 2008; Hofman and de Bruijn, 2010, p. 118). So it was for Remarkable as well as other eco-entrepreneurs attempting to incorporate recycled materials into their product innovations (Chick and Micklethwaite, 2004b; Micklethwaite and Chick, 2005; Chick; 2008). Remarkable's resulting products, such as pencils, pens and mouse mats, positioned them initially with the green niche customers who wanted to buy environmentally considered products, including those manufactured from recycled materials (Micklethwaite and Chick, 2005) (see Figure 12.1).

As a result of the author's research into raising awareness and understanding of recycled products and materials among UK designers and architects (Chick and Micklethwaite, 2004a) and her case study research into small UK recycled product manufacturers (Chick and Micklethwaite, 2004b), she founded the WestFocus Sustainability in Practice (SiP) Network and Inspired Recycling, a knowledge exchange initiative (WestFocus, 2006; Chick, 2008).

FIGURE 12.1 Remarkable's first graphic designs strongly emphasize the recycled content of the products with the use of a 'Recycled' banner. Photo with permission of Remarkable (Pencils) Ltd., Worcester, UK.

WestFocus was a knowledge exchange consortium of six universities in the south-east of England; Inspired Recycling was a programme funded by WestFocus and London Remade, which enabled regional SMEs to access recycled materials, WestFocus academics and private and public funding (Westfocus, 2006). These initiatives aimed to provide eco-innovation business support through involving actors from the private and public sectors as well as WestFocus universities, a form of triple helix innovation.

The value network Remarkable had generally been operating in had not included an HEI or the design community (Micklethwaite and Chick, 2004, 2005). It was difficult to sell knowledge from design academics to Remarkable and be confident about how to make actual use of it. The author began to build a relationship with the senior management at Remarkable due to her funded case studies research into small UK recycled product manufacturers. In addition, senior staff from Remarkable attended WestFocus training and networking events. The initial discussions with Remarkable were dominated by offers of eco-design and clean production projects due to Inspired Recycling being limited in the types of support it could supply due to funding restrictions. Other UK and European schemes had similar support funding constraints (Woolman and Veshagh, 2006, p. 285). Remarkable wished to improve the environmental performance of its operations but the priority was to focus on the market and customer-specific aspects of its business with the aim of attracting extensive new customer groups and creating new markets. Developing a market strategy, followed by a new brand image and the resulting visual communications including a logo, was financially critical for

Remarkable (Micklethwaite and Chick, 2005). Because of the author's access to re-sources and funding, Remarkable was able to receive the support it required, which Gerstenfeld and Roberts suggest is the most effective approach for supporting SMEs: 'flexible, accessible, inexpensive, cooperative, locally based and unique' (2000, p. 122).

The author concurred with Acklin that 'starting to use design as a strategic resource involves a learning process on the side of SMEs on how to tackle and to manage this new knowledge or strategic resource' (2011, p. 3). The knowledge exchange arrangements were negotiated and facilitated by the author and the owner-manager, Miller. Furthermore, the project goals and tasks for each actor flowed from the design-led project including the research plan. This research highlighted the need to work closely with and receive total commitment to the proj-ect from the owner-manager, including his personal engagement, to aid his knowledge. The leadership of the owner-manager has a significant impact on the performance of an SME (Smith, 2010). It was unclear at the start of the project what knowledge exchange mechanism to adopt, and at the time it seemed irrelevant to the actors at Remarkable. What was impor-tant to them was the development of a flexible, collaborative problem-solving approach that enhanced and expanded all the key actors' knowledge and competencies. 'We [the Remark-able senior managers] had to make the most of the opportunity we had been given to develop our brand but it had to work around running the business. It was such a busy time for us…I couldn't waste time on some academic whim' (Miller, 2011).

Remarkable had an ambitious business plan. Notwithstanding, research under-taken by Dr. Paul Micklethwaite and the author meant that it had to break out of its comfortable niche market position. The core actors soon realized they needed to address Remarkable's marketing communications, particularly the development of the brand. Following dialogue with the key supermarket chains and retailers, it transpired that they were concerned about consumers' negative perceptions of the quality of products made from recycled materials and the marginality of green products (Micklethwaite and Chick, 2005). Remarkable had to address such perceptions if its products were to be stocked by the major supermarket chains. The answer was, in part, for Remarkable to establish a brand identity that would be acceptable to mainstream consumers (Micklethwaite and Chick, 2005; Blewitt, 2008, pp. 211–12; Chick and Micklethwaite, 2004b).

The core actors throughout the project needed to understand how Remarkable could effectively move its communications away from green niche and into the consumer mainstream but still communicate its sustainability values. To make new knowledge effective in innovative processes, it is essential to generate concerted action (Christensen and Raynor, 2006), and this can occur if a design-led project approach is adopted. The author and the owner-manager negotiated a project that focused on satisfying the needs of both Remarkable and the Inspired Recycling academic team, resulting in a 'collab-orative research mode' of knowledge exchange (Library House, 2008, p. 13). Action re-search, or, as Swann (2002) refers to this approach, 'research for design', where research informed the design decisions and other knowledge exchange activities, seemed the most appropriate methodology.

To succeed and achieve the objectives of Remarkable and the academics, the core actors needed to generate common understanding, mutual trust and tolerance for a project that combined business, knowledge exchange and research goals (Karlsson et al., 2010, p. 35). Through developing a cooperative design-led approach accompanied with hands-on design-led exercises, Remarkable actors learned to trust and value this inter-active approach (Miller, 2011). Lundvall (1992) stresses the importance of interactive learning and focusing on elements such as trust and the mechanisms of exchanging tacit knowledge (based on skills, experience and routines) in innovation processes (Lund-vall et al., 2002). This interactive, problem-based approach generally provides quality results, particularly in the transferring of tacit knowledge and scenarios where instruc-tions for the development of certain processes cannot be transferred through step-by-step information (Raulik et al., 2006). The motivation for concerted action is dependent on the social capital. 'The term social capital captures the idea that social bonds and norms are critical for sustainability. Where social capital is high in formalized groups, people have the confidence to invest in collective activities, knowing that others will do so too' (Pretty, 2003, p. 1912). It has been argued that knowledge exchange is facilitated through social capital that adheres in collaborative situations (Inkpen and Tsang, 2005).

The academics and external brand agency used design thinking tools; they compiled existing corporate and product branding examples to demonstrate how enterprises were promoting various corporate responsibility and sustainability values in their marketing, brand and visual communications, including the written copy. These examples were se-lected also to demonstrate the value of design and how other enterprises communicated their corporate values. Visual designs and corporate storytelling styles were used and dis-cussed throughout the project. This is an approach used successfully by other design or-ganizations such as the Design Council, with its Designing Demand mentoring service for SMEs in the United Kingdom, to inform the 'analysis for action' (Design Council, 2008, p. 39). It is an approach also recommended by Topalian (2002), who suggests that actors can learn more and will be more interested in subjects with which they can estab-lish tangible links to their own activities. Using familiar problems and project circum-stances to that of an external SME is likely to provide more powerful lessons for them than addressing problems unrelated to those of pressing concern (Raulik et al., 2006). The resulting products, which illustrate the product branding, are shown in Figure 12.2 and Figure 12.3.

Transformative Learning Required

Miller, owner-manager of Remarkable, had 'used the experiences gained continu-ally to guide Remarkable's communications, branding and design decisions. It [the knowledge exchange project detailed above] has had a lasting impression on me and has helped me in ways I'm not sure I have fully grasped' (Miller, 2011). This is evident in Remarkable still abiding by the original branding strategy formulated during this collaboration, even though in 2010 the company commissioned a new logo and vi-sual communications (Remarkable, 2011). Remarkable's marketing materials continue to communicate design-led innovation and the passionate nature of the company's en-vironmental mission. A key recommendation from the original collaboration was that

FIGURE 12.2   The Lava Sky range: the resulting Remarkable brand from the knowledge exchange and research project undertaken in April 2003. Photo with permission of Remarkable (Pencils) Ltd., Worcester, UK.

FIGURE 12.3   The Lava Sky range: Remarkable Limited pen made from recycled computer printer components. Photo with permission of Remarkable (Pencils) Ltd., Worcester, UK.

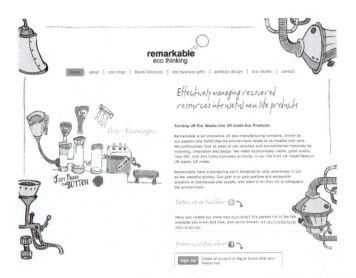

FIGURE 12.4   Latest Remarkable redesign. Image with permission of Remarkable (Pencils) Ltd., Worcester, UK.

design had to be a core selling point. A page from Remarkable's web page, illustrating their marketing materials, is shown in Figure 12.4.

In written evidence to the British Parliament's Science and Technology Committee, the Design Council described Remarkable as a design-driven enterprise and how design is an important part of its eco-innovation process:

> Remarkable collaborated with a specialist university research unit and also with external design agencies to come up with a brand identity that communicated the essence of the company's values. Since its launch Remarkable has sold more than 100m pencils and has achieved listings with numerous high profile retailers. Douglas Miller said: 'Design was integral to the whole thing'. (Design Council, 2011)

Miller (2011) and the present Remarkable visual communications indicate transformative learning may have occurred for Miller during and after the project (see Figure 12.5).

Working towards a clear set of goals increases the likelihood that the actors involved in a knowledge exchange activity will indeed become more deeply engaged and experience transformative learning (Wilson and Parrish, 2010). The sustainability discourse entails a need for change and transformative learning (Bergeà et al., 2006, p. 1441). Transformative learning is a process that 'involves helping the recipients adapt and apply those practices to new situations, to create new "knowledge" and put into action' (O'Dell and Grayson, 1998, p. 7). One encompassing definition for knowledge is

> a fluid mix of framed experience, values, contextual information, and expert insight that provides a framework for evaluating and incorporating new experiences and information. It originates and is applied in the minds of knowers. In organizations, it

FIGURE 12.5   The Punk Metal range: The resulting Remarkable brand from the knowledge exchange and research project undertaken in April 2003. Photo with permission of Remarkable (Pencils) Ltd., Worcester, UK.

often becomes embedded not only in documents and repositories but also in organizational routines, processes, practices and forms. (Davenport and Prusak, 1998, p. 5)

In a business context, this transformative learning can be referred to as the enterprise's 'absorptive capacity'. This is the ability of an enterprise to recognize the value of new information, assimilate it and apply it to commercial ends. It has been said that in order to be innovative, a firm should develop its absorptive capacity (Cohen and Leventhal, 1990). Knowledge has to be absorbed; otherwise it has not been transferred. Moreover, it is important to highlight that transmission and absorption together have no useful value if the new knowledge does not lead to some change in behaviour or the development of some new idea that leads to new behaviour. From their research, Raulik et al. (2006, p. 11) identified a number of methods that improve design knowledge transfer with SMEs: demonstration, observation, practical applications, experience and implementation, networking, joint problem-solving, visual communication, sharing similar situations, use of a shared language. The design-led approach assists the relationships and interactions between the core actors serving as the carriers of knowledge, and the interactions as the process by which new knowledge is produced and learned (Lehmann et al., 2010, p. 44). This reflects the assumption that neither SMEs nor people innovate alone. Knowledge exchange framed as a practical cooperative design-led project can benefit the SME actors as they are engaged in the knowledge creation process. The actors have to take into account multiple inputs (generally a wide set of unstructured data and information) to perform difficult tasks and make complex decisions (including environmental sustainability decisions) amongst multiple ways of doing the work, each one implying different levels of risk and possible benefits (Still, 2007, p. 106).

The design process, more simply described, transforms certain inputs into desired outputs. Based on the knowledge view, these inputs and outputs are considered to be knowledge. The actors involved in this project were therefore involved in knowledge processes; more specifically, the Remarkable team was learning design tacit knowledge from the academics and branding agencies' actors when rooted in the context of the branding and design assignments. This was enhanced through the practical design workshops and learning in action project approach. Tacit knowledge has been described as personal, nonarticulated, silent, hidden experience-based and skill type bodily knowledge—and 'what we know but cannot articulate' (Nonaka and Takeuchi, 1995, p. 284). Tacit knowledge in design can provide new insights and hence value to the innovation process and the learning of the small enterprise. It can bring the fresh perspectives and insights needed for developing innovations that address pressing sustainability challenges. The design-led and team approach also helped the owner-manager to step out of his prevailing view of his company, including its core values, and review his business from other perspectives.

The pace of the project was fast, which was imposed by the owner-manager due to the urgent need to address the identified market problem, and the author felt it decreased the reflective time necessary for learning for all the actors. The author attempted to create time and space for the Remarkable team to learn at the individual and group level. This usually occurred in an informal and unorganized manner during a social situation, such as over lunch. The insightful questioning and reflective approach of the academic team was additionally useful to the owner-manager (Miller, 2011) in encouraging significant learning.

CONCLUSION

How design and design management capability is built in SMEs with little or no prior design experience has been insufficiently investigated to date (Acklin, 2011). Remarkable was such an enterprise, and the project was therefore partly about learning how to use design as an effective knowledge exchange tool as well as how to deploy design knowledge effectively. Following the completion of this project, Remarkable employed an in-house designer with eco-design experience to implement and manage the new brand, and to build upon the enterprise's newly acquired design and design management capabilities. This has helped the owner-manager have a deeper understanding of designerly ways of knowing and doing things. Their new-found design knowledge capabilities continue to aid the enterprise's specific business, marketing and innovation contexts and challenges (Miller, 2011). Research shows that design-driven enterprises are more innovative than others (European Commission, 2009a, p. 14). This design knowledge seems to have been to Remarkable's financial benefit (Brewitt, 2008, pp. 211–12;

Remarkable, 2011). Remarkable moved in 2005 to much larger manufacturing premises and grew to employ over seventy people in 2009 (Miller, 2011).

This collaborative project demonstrates the importance of considering an applied design-led project approach as a valid knowledge exchange mechanism for supporting SMEs to innovate while addressing sustainability challenges. This Remarkable project has highlighted it can be more effective if it is

- undertaken in direct conjunction with a small enterprise;
- specific to the enterprise's needs;
- critical to business performance; and
- interpersonal in its approach rather than formal when involving SMEs with academia.

Also, SME owners and senior managers are advised that it is an important skill to develop relationships with academics to enhance opportunities to initiate collaborative projects and support. This approach through a design-led project can aid and lead to the development of new ideas and concepts as well as encourage the gathering of multiple perspectives on complex problems, such as the sustainability agendas.

Generic instructional methods and standards of knowledge exchange are effective, but if its activities are to make a lasting impression on individual SMEs there is a need for deeper kinds of learning engagement that have a demonstrable long-lasting impact on practices, and this is particularly relevant for the acquiring of design knowledge. In addition, design is a creative process for identifying challenges and inefficiencies and implementing solutions, and the Remarkable project demonstrates a design-led focus can also became an effective vehicle for transformative learning, especially within a project team. The actors can detect and observe different perspectives and viewpoints, which can be beneficial for complex contexts such as addressing the sustainability agenda.

REFERENCES

Acklin, C. (2011), 'Design Management Absorption Model—A Framework to Describe the Absorption Process of Design Knowledge by SMEs with Little or No Prior Design Experience', 1st Cambridge Academic Design Management Conference, September 7–8, Cambridge University, Cambridge.

Benneworth, P. (2007), 'Research Report—Leading Innovation: Building Effective Coalitions for Innovations', NESTA: London, <http://www.gencat.cat/economia/ur/doc/doc_13675813_1.pdf> accessed October 10, 2011.

Bergeà, O., Karlsson, R., Hedlund-Åström, A., Jacobsson, P. and Luttropp, C. (2006), 'Education for Sustainability as a Transformative Learning Process: A Pedagogical Experience in Ecodesign Doctoral Education', special issue 'Ecodesign—What's Happening?' *Journal of Cleaner Production*, vol. 15: pp. 1421–42.

Bleischwitz, R., Bahn-Walkowiak, B., Black, A., Bohunovski, L., Eggl-Forseo, B., Giljum, S., Hawkins, E., Hinterberger, F., Irrek, W., Kuhndt, M., Lutter, S., Pratt, N., Schepelmann, P., Schmidt-Bleek, F. and van der Veen, G. (2009), 'Eco-Innovation—Putting the EU on the Path to a Resource and Energy Efficient Economy', European Parliament, Brussels, <http://mpra.ub.uni-muenchen.de/19939/1/MPRA_paper_19939.pdf> accessed October 20, 2011.

Blewitt, J. (2008), *Understanding Sustainable Development*, Earthscan: London.

Chick, A. (2008), 'Green Entrepreneurship: A Sustainable Development Challenge', in Mellor, R. (ed.), *Entrepreneurship for Everyone*, Sage: London. pp. 139–50.

Chick, A. and Micklethwaite, P. (2004a), 'Specifying Recycled: Understanding UK Architects' and Designers' Practices and Experience', *Design Studies*, vol. 25, no. 3: pp. 251–73.

Chick, A. and Micklethwaite, P. (2004b), 'Closing the Loop—The Role of Design in the Success of Six Small UK Recycled Product Manufacturers', in Bhamra, T. and Hon, B. (eds), *Design and Manufacture for Sustainable Development*, Professional Engineering Publishing: Bury St Edmunds. pp. 249–62.

Christensen, C. M. and Raynor, M. E. (2006), *The Innovator's Solution: Creating and Sustaining Successful Growth*, HarperCollins: New York.

Cohen, W. and Leventhal, D. (1990), 'Absorptive Capacity: A New Perspective on Learning and Innovation', *Administrative Science Quarterly*, vol. 35, no. 1: pp. 128–52.

Davenport, T. H., and Prusak, L. (1998), *Working Knowledge: How Organizations Manage What They Know*, Harvard Business School Press: Cambridge, MA.

Design Council (2008), *Designing Demand Review*, <http://www.designcouncil.org.uk/ Documents/Documents/Publications/Designing_Demand_Review_Design_Council.pdf> accessed October 30, 2011.

Design Council (2011), '(SIM 19): Designing to Recycle and Remanufacture: 6.3. Strategically Important Metals—Science and Technology Committee', <http://www.publications.parliament. uk/pa/cm201012/cmselect/cmsctech/726/726we12.htm> accessed October 30, 2011.

Dröll, P. (2011), 'SEE Project Final Conference—Policy, Innovation & Design', Speech, Flemish Parliament, Brussels, March 29.

Edquist, C. (2005), 'Systems of Innovation: Perspectives and Challenges', in Fagerberg, J., Mowery, D. C. and Nelson, R. R. (eds), *The Oxford Handbook of Innovation*, Oxford University Press: New York. pp. 181–208.

Elkington, J. (1997), *Cannibals with Forks: The Triple Bottom Line of 21st Century Business*, Capstone Publishing: Oxford.

Etzkowitz, H. and Leydesdorff, L. (eds) (1997), *Universities and the Global Knowledge Economy: A Triple Helix of University-Industry-Government Relations*, Pinter: London.

Etzkowitz, H. and Leydesdorff, L. (2000), 'The Dynamics of Innovation: From National Systems and "Mode 2" to a Triple Helix of University-Industry-Government Relations', *Research Policy*, vol. 29: pp. 109–23.

Etzkowitz, H. and Zhou, C. (2006), 'Triple Helix Twins: Innovation and Sustainability', *Science and Public Policy*, vol. 33, no. 1: pp. 77–83.

European Commission (2009a), 'SEC(2009)501 Commission Staff Working Document— Design as a Driver of User-Centred Innovation of 7 April 2009', <http://ec.europa.eu/ enterprise/newsroom/cf/_getdocument.cfm?doc_id=2784> accessed October 20, 2011.

European Commission (2009b), 'SEC(2009)1350 Final—Commission Staff Working—Document on the Implementation of Commission Recommendation of 6 May 2003 Concerning the Definition of Micro, Small and Medium-Sized Enterprises', <http://ec.europa.eu/enterprise/ policies/sme/facts-figures-analysis/sme-definition/index_en.htm> accessed October 20, 2011.

European Commission (2010), 'COM(2010)546 Communication from the Commission to the European Parliament, the Council, the European Economic and Social Committee of the Regions of the 6 October 2010: Europe 2020 Flagship Initiative—Innovation Union SEC(2010) 1161', <http://ec.europa.eu/research/innovation-union/pdf/innovation-union-communication_en.pdf> accessed October 11, 2011.

European Commission (2011a), 'European Commission Directorate-General for Enterprise and Industry: Industrial Innovation—Innovation in Services', <http://ec.europa.eu/enterprise/policies/innovation/policy/innovation-services/index en.htm> accessed October 11, 2011.

European Commission (2011b), 'Industrial Innovation: European Design Innovation Initiative', <http://ec.europa.eu/enterprise/policies/innovation/policy/design-creativity/edii_en.htm> accessed October 11, 2011.

European Commission (2011c), 'SBA Fact Sheet: United Kingdom 2010/11', <http://ec.europa.eu/enterprise/policies/sme/facts-figures-analysis/performance-review/pdf/2010_2011/uk_en.pdf> accessed October 11, 2011.

Ezell, S. J. and Atkinson, R. D. (2011), 'International Benchmarking of Countries' Policies and Programs Supporting SME Manufacturers', Information Technology & Innovation Foundation, <http://www.itif.org/files/2011-sme-manufacturing-tech-programss-new.pdf> accessed October 20, 2011.

Gerstenfeld, A. and Roberts, H. (2000), 'Size Matters: Barriers and Prospects for Environmental Management in Small and Medium-Sized Enterprises', in Hillary, R. (ed.), *Small and Medium-Sized Enterprises and the Environment: Business Imperatives,* Greenleaf Publishing: Sheffield. pp. 106–27.

Hawken, P. (2007), *Blessed Unrest: How the Largest Movement Came into Being and Why No One Saw It Coming,* Viking/Penguin Group: New York.

Hofman, P. S and de Bruijn, T. (2010), 'Chapter 7: The Emergence of Sustainable Innovations: Key Factors and Regional Support Structures', in Sarkis, J., Cordeiro, J. J. and Vazquez Brust, D. (eds), *Facilitating Sustainable Innovation through Collaboration.* Springer: London. pp. 115–33.

HM Treasury (2005), *Cox Review of Creativity in Business: Building on the UK's Strengths,* HM Treasury: London.

Inkpen, A. and Tsang, E. (2005), 'Social Capital, Networks and Knowledge Transfer', *Academy of Management Review,* vol. 30, no. 1: pp. 146–65.

Jackson, T. (2009), *Prosperity without Growth: Economics for a Finite Planet,* Earthscan: London.

Karlsson, R., Backman, M. and Djupenstrom, A. (2010), 'Chapter 2: Sustainability Considerations and Triple-Helix Collaboration in Regional Innovation Systems', in Sarkis, J., Cordeiro, J. J. and Vazquez Brust, D. (eds), *Facilitating Sustainable Innovation through Collaboration,* Springer: London. pp. 17–40.

Kelly, T., and Littman, J. (2001), *The Art of Innovation: Lessons in Creativity from IDEO, America's Leading Design Firm,* Doubleday Publishing: New York.

Lambert, R. (2003), 'Lambert Review of Business—University Collaboration: Final Report', HM Treasury: London, <http://www.hm-treasury.gov.uk> accessed October 10, 2011.

Lehmann, M., Christensen, P, and Johnson, B. (2010), 'Chapter 3: Partnerships and Sustainable Regional Innovation Systems: Special Roles for Universities?', in Sarkis, J., Cordeiro, J. J. and Vazquez Brust, D. (eds), *Facilitating Sustainable Innovation through Collaboration,* Springer: London. pp. 41–58.

Library House (2008), *Metrics for the Evaluation of Knowledge Transfer Activities at Universities,* Library House: Cambridge.

Lundvall, B. A. (1992), *National Systems of Innovation, Towards a Theory of Innovation and Inter-active Learning,* Pinter: London.

Lundvall, B. A., Johnson, B., Anderson, E. S. and Dalum, B. (2002), 'National Systems of Production, Innovation and Competence Building', *Research Policy,* vol. 31: pp. 213–31.

McDonough, W. and Braungart, M. (2002), *Cradle to Cradle: Remaking the Way We Make Things,* North Point Press: New York.

Micklethwaite, P. and Chick, A. (2004), 'Remarkable Pencils Ltd: Developing a "Recycled" Brand', International Conference on Innovation by Brand and Design, Seoul, November 11–12.

Micklethwaite, P. and Chick, A. (2005), 'Remarkable Pencils Ltd: Breaking Out of the Green Niche', *Design Management Review,* vol. 16, no. 3: pp. 23–28.

Miller, E. D. (2011), Personal communication, October 21.

Mowery, D. and Sampat, B. N. (2005), 'Universities in National Innovation Systems', in Fagerberg, J., Mowery, D. C. and Nelson, R. R. (eds), *The Oxford Handbook of Innovation,* Oxford University Press: New York. pp. 209–39.

National Institute for Triple Helix Innovation (2012), 'Taxonomy of Triple Helix', <http://www.triplehelixinstitute.org> accessed June 16, 2012.

NESTA, NCGE and CIHE (2008), 'Developing Entrepreneurial Graduates Putting Entrepreneurship at the Centre of Higher Education', NESTA: London, <http://www.ncee.org.uk/publication/developing_entrepreneurial_graduates.1.pdf> accessed October 10, 2011.

Nonaka, I. and Takeuchi, H. (1995), *The Knowledge Creating Company: How Japanese Companies Create the Dynamics of Innovation,* Oxford University Press: New York.

O'Dell, C. and Grayson, C. J. (1998), *If We Only Knew What We Know: The Transfer of Internal Knowledge and Best Practice,* Free Press: New York.

O'Rafferty, S. and O'Connor, F. (2007), 'Case Study of Good Design Support Practice: UK—Creating the Ecodesign Centre Wales', <www.seedesign.org> accessed October 10, 2011.

O'Rafferty, S. and O'Connor, F. (2010), 'Regional Perspectives on Capacity Building for Ecodesign—Insights from Wales', in Sarkis, J., Cordeiro, J. J. and Vazquez Brust, D. (eds), *Facilitating Sustainable Innovation through Collaboration,* Springer: London. pp. 159–83.

Pepper, D. (1984), *The Roots of Modern Environmentalism,* Croom Helm: London.

Pretty, J. (2003), 'Social Capital and the Collective Management of Resources', *Science,* vol. 302: pp. 1912–14.

Rainey, D. L. (2006), *Sustainable Business Development: Inventing the Future through Strategy, Innovation and Leadership,* Cambridge University Press: Cambridge.

Raulik, G. C., Larsen, P. and Cawood, G. (2006), 'Paper 0114: Design Support and the Transfer of Knowledge to SMEs', 2006 Design Research Society International Conference, Lisbon, IADE, <http://www.iade.pt/drs2006/wonderground/proceedings/fullpapers.html> accessed October 21, 2011.

Reid, A. and Miedzinski, M. (2008), *Eco-Innovation: Final Report for Sectoral Innovation Watch,* Technopolis Group: Brighton.

Remarkable (2011), *History of Remarkable,* <http://www.remarkable.co.uk/about-us/history-of-remarkable/> accessed October 30, 2011.

Sarkis, J, Cordeiro, J. J. and Vazquez Brust, D. A. (2010), 'Chapter 1: Facilitating Sustainable Innovation through Collaboration', in Sarkis, J., Cordeiro, J. J. and Vazquez Brust, D. (eds), *Facilitating Sustainable Innovation through Collaboration,* Springer: London. pp. 1–16.

SEE, Whicher, A., Raulik-Murphy, G. and Cawood, G. (eds) (2009), 'SEE Policy Booklet: 01—Integrating Design Into Regional Innovation Policy, SEE Project', <www.seeproject.org> accessed October 10, 2011.

Smith, S. (2010), 'Innovation in Teaching and Learning: Knowledge Exchange in Dialogue with SMEs, Government and Higher Education', <http://www.leydesdorff.net/th9/Sue%20Smith%20Triple%20Helix%20paper%20sub%20theme%203.4.pdf> accessed October 10, 2011.

Steketee, D. M. (2010), 'Chapter 8: Disruption or Sustenance? An Institutional Analysis of the Sustainable Business Network in West Michigan', in Sarkis, J., Cordeiro, J. J. and Vazquez Brust, D. (eds), *Facilitating Sustainable Innovation through Collaboration,* Springer: London. pp. 135–57.

Still, K. (2007), 'Exploring Knowledge Processes in User-Centred Design', *The Electronic Journal of Knowledge Management,* vol. 5, no. 1: pp. 105–14.

Swann, C. (2002), 'Action Research and the Practice of Design', *Design Issues,* vol. 18, no. 2: pp. 49–61.

Technopolis (2006), 'Strategic Evaluation on Innovation and the Knowledge Based Economy in Relation to the Structural and Cohesion Funds, for the Programming Period 2007–2013. A Report To: The European Commission Directorate-General Regional Policy Evaluation and Additionality: Synthesis Report', <http://ec.europa.eu/regional_policy/sources/docgener/evaluation/pdf/strategic_innov.pdf> accessed October 30, 2011.

Topalian, A. (2002), 'Promoting Design Leadership through Skills Development Programs', *Design Management Journal,* vol. 13, no. 3: pp. 10–18.

Tukker, A., Ellen, G. J. and Eder, P. (2000), *Eco-Design: Strategies for Dissemination to SMEs. Part I: Overall Analysis and Conclusions—An ESTO Project Report,* European Commission: Brussels.

Van Hemel, C. and Cromer, J. (2002), 'Barriers and Stimuli for Ecodesign in SMEs', *Journal of Cleaner Production,* vol. 10, no. 5: pp. 439–53.

WestFocus (2006), 'Case Study: Inspired Recycling Greener Practices for London's Manufacturing', <http://fada.kingston.ac.uk/includes/docs/research/sdr/partnerships/11_Inspired_Recycling_CaseStudy.pdf> accessed October 30, 2011.

Williams, L., Turner, N. and Jones, A. (2008), *Embedding Universities in Knowledge Cities: An Ideopolis and Knowledge Economy Programme Paper,* Work Foundation: London.

Wilson, B. G. and Parrish, P. E. (2010), 'Transformative Learning Experience: Aim Higher, Gain More', *Educational Technology,* vol. 51, May: pp. 1–9.

Woolman, T. and Veshagh, A. (2006), 'Designing Support for Manufacturing SMEs Approaching Ecodesign and Cleaner Production—Learning from UK Survey Results', 13th CIRP International Conference on Life Cycle Engineering, Katholieke Universiteit, Leuven, Belgium, pp. 281–6.

Wymenga, P., Spanikova, V., Derbyshire, J. and Barker, A. (2011), 'Are EU SMEs Recovering from the Crisis? Annual Report on EU Small and Medium Sized Enterprises 2010/2011', <http://ec.europa.eu/enterprise/policies/sme/facts-figures-analysis/performance-review/pdf/2010_2011/are_the_eus_smes_recovering.pdf> accessed October 10, 2011.

PART III

Sustainability in Practice

Editorial Introduction

JACQUES GIARD AND STUART WALKER

Design for sustainability is not limited to theories and methods, past or present; there is also a need to embed sustainability into design practice. There is now ample evidence that this is occurring, even if it is not yet mainstream. 'Part III: Sustainability in Practice' offers seven unique approaches in which the scope of activities as well as the scale aptly demonstrates the effectiveness of design for sustainability.

Christopher Day sets the tone by situating our quest for a more sustainable built environment within a greater appreciation of place and the life-enhancing benefits that can be derived from place. In 'Architecture: Building for Sustainability or Spirit Nurture?' Day is explicit about the role that each one of us plays in making choices and how these choices are, in part, influenced by our surroundings. As he states so insightfully, 'People make community, but design facilitates it'. It is the implications of these choices, however, that need to be understood, such as the selection of natural materials and natural systems over industrial ones. From Day's perspective, the former are not only more sustainable but also soul nourishing.

Choices also pervade the types of habitation we build for ourselves. In a society increasingly aware of the human toll on the natural environment, common notions of housing and development practices are being re-examined to lessen their long-term impacts. In 'Principles of Sustainable Dwellings and Community Design', Avi Friedman discusses a narrow row house design called the Grow Home, which was built initially as a demonstration project at McGill University but later adopted by private sector builders. This row house design is underpinned by two interconnected principles: the planning of communities and the design and construction of sustainable dwellings. From a contemporary perspective, dwellings with smaller footprints can play an important part in reducing some of the environmental consequences of urban sprawl. Factors such as higher densities, reduced use of resources and lower energy usage all contribute to the development of more sustainable forms of urban living.

The theme of community continues with 'Design for Territorial Ecology and a New Relationship between City and Countryside: The Experience of the Feeding Milano Project'. In this chapter, Ezio Manzini and Anna Meroni foresee the need for a profound change in agriculture and its relationships to cities. It is their view that 'there will be no sustainable agriculture and no sustainable cities without a redefinition of their mutual interactions; that is, without a new ecology of communities and places'. With the Feeding Milano Project, Manzini and Meroni show that a mix of bottom-up initiatives as well as design-led initiatives can make a difference. This example, as well as similar ones from around the world, represent an innovative design process (planning by projects or 'acupuncture' planning) capable of promoting and sustaining a new territorial ecology.

'Sustainable Urban Futures' continues on the general theme of sustainable communities, but with a focus on the decision-making process implicit in community planning. Here, Rachel Cooper and Christopher T. Boyko look at the design of sustainable urban spaces and systems that are in accord with sustainability—walkable communities, safety, health and wellbeing and transport. A direct connection is made between policy and governance, and how creative design and visualization can enhance communication among stakeholders, leading to an urban decision-making process that is more effective and more sustainable.

Community planning in the context of design and sustainability does not occur only as a formalized process. There are circumstances where the process is informal and unstructured. We can learn a great deal from such examples. The Recyclable Materials Collectors National Movement in Brazil is described by Maria Cecilia Loschiavo dos Santos in her chapter, 'Educational Experience in Design for Sustainability: Enhancing a Critical Perspective among Undergraduate Students'. She begins by informing the reader of two important issues in contemporary Brazilian life: urban poverty and environmental concerns. In this context, homeless people have created a survivalist economy, one that is based on the reuse of trash found in Brazilian cities. However, Loschiavo dos Santos goes one step further. She shows how the phenomenon of organized trash collection has become an integral part of design education at the University of Sao Paulo and how, over eight years, this education experience has helped develop a critical perspective among students by offering an understanding of design that goes beyond its mundane meaning in contemporary culture.

In 'Sustainable Fashion', Kate Fletcher provides a positive yet unexpected picture of an industry whose practices are synonymous with design but not always with sustainability. She explains that fashion is a powerful influence within the consumption-based, mass production economic model we have today. She also shows that it is this very model that has come to dominate and restrict our experiences of fashion and that has associated the fashion sector with ethically problematic practices. However, she goes on to describe some emerging areas where fashion is acting as a positive force to develop and drive practices in more responsible, more sustainable directions. She describes innovative and affirming design approaches and reviews key themes of research and practice including Slow Fashion, non-plan design and post-growth fashion. She contextualizes these activities within a broader perspective of sustainability work in the fashion sector, tracing its development over the last twenty years.

In the final chapter in this practice-oriented section, JohnPaul Kusz makes an argument for a broader and deeper design ethic; one that reaches beyond mere products to include processes that are more comprehensive and accountable. In 'A New Design Ethic for a New Reality', Kusz's argument is predicated on our consciousness about the current situation, one in which what we design and how we design reflect our reality. If change towards a more sustainable state of affairs is to occur, design must move beyond products as its main focal point; it must incorporate the businesses from which products are born as well as the systems in which they operate. Kusz holds the view that we can design and construct models that better serve our needs whilst generating lasting value in our environment, our society and our economy.

13

Architecture: Building for Sustainability or Spirit Nurture?

CHRISTOPHER DAY

INTRODUCTION: TECHNOLOGY OR ENVIRONMENTAL NOURISHMENT?

It is widely agreed that the built environment accounts for some half of all climate damage, pollution and energy (Energy Saving Trust, 2009). With the transport it depends on included, the total is three-quarters. In this context, has anyone any right to be concerned with mere aesthetics? Surely human survival is the issue. For survival, we need to address technical issues unfettered by artistic complications. This is a widespread view, fully justified by the facts as so presented. As usual, however, reality is more complicated than simple statistics suggest.

First of all, climate damage is broadly related to the amount of things made and power used: a consumption issue. Technology, although indispensable, can never sufficiently reduce humanity's environmental impact on its own, or in time. A five-fold efficiency improvement in three decades is unlikely. True, we can make new buildings nine times more thermally efficient than old ones. Twenty per cent of new Austrian homes meet Passivhaus standards, requiring hardly any heating (Siddall, 2009, p. 19). Most buildings, however, are already built. Neither economically nor ecologically is premature replacement affordable. Furthermore, despite the many ethically motivated individuals involved, technical development is funded by sales. Sales mean more, albeit better, products. Additionally, improved insulation doesn't necessarily reduce energy consumption. Historically, it has more commonly just made homes warmer, sometimes even increasing energy consumption, as thermal comfort is, at long last, attainable. Computers have not brought about the much-vaunted paperless revolution either: they have actually increased paper use by 40 per cent (Vale and Vale, 2009, p. 330) and also, more significantly, electricity demand and dependency. Moreover, they have made us dependent on possessing them—yet more things, more energy and more vulnerability to system collapse and power supply failure.

Anyway, technology on its own does not deliver reduced energy consumption. It is how we use it that does. Even zero-carbon buildings typically fall short of their potentially achievable targets—even in BedZed, where most residents are eco-committed, by 12 per cent (BioRegional, 2010; Energy Saving Trust, 2009), but sometimes by 50 per cent elsewhere (Roaf, 2010, p. 7). More significantly, our individual environmental impacts divide roughly into quarters: heating and cooling buildings, travel and transport, what we buy and things outside our control (Riddlestone, 2008, p. 24). Three-quarters of these environmental impacts are related to buildings. But a largely overlapping three-quarters are about lifestyle: personal choices. These choices are greatly influenced by how much our surroundings nourish or alienate us. If they are not soul-nourishing, we buy things to improve them and get away whenever we can: perhaps by weekend-break flights. This can easily quadruple environmental impact: particularly carbon dioxide—hence climate damage (Desai, 2010, pp. 43–55).

ENVIRONMENTAL NOURISHMENT

Environmental nourishment is place-based. Buildings' external appearances coalesce image, but life takes place in spaces, indoor and outdoor, private and public. We may feel proud to be associated with the Eiffel Tower or Nelson's Column, but it is rare to want to live in them. If not in iconic landmarks, where do we want to live? Homes are much more than roofs to keep off the rain. They provide safety, identity anchorage and, especially, homeliness: spirit of home. That is why we will pay a thousand times more for them than for tents. Moreover, environmental quality affects the human soul and spirit. Beauty is deeply nourishing. Without it, we are only half-alive. Unfortunately, however, it is out of fashion. From the 1930s, architectural theorists considered it too romantically wishy-washy, not objectively measurable. Indeed, in the 1960s, anti-beauty (Brutalism) came into fashion. In various forms, this current remains.

Soul-nourishment intertwines material factors (e.g., comfort) with social (e.g., security) and spiritual (e.g., homeliness). Similarly, space (a material description) does not become place (an identifiable individuality) until it has its own life, soul-mood and spirit. Just as homes are not homely if they fail to keep off the rain, mood and spirit have material starting points. For places to be liveable, they must offer an acceptable thermal environment. Indoors, this is about heating and cooling, but outdoors, it is about microclimate. Microclimate determines whether places are enjoyable, how they are used and consequently their financial success. Pavement cafés that are wind-scoured and in permanent shade do not stay long in business. Microclimate is linked to sensory delight. Contrast typical twentieth-century downtowns (dense, hard-edged building shadows; gusty downdrafts, updrafts and street-funnelled winds; exhaust-laden air; hard, echo-magnified acoustics, harsh light, glare and mirror-reflected heat) with park-scape (dappled, dancing leaf shade; fresh, aromatic, gentle air; grass-absorbed muted sounds and softened light). This is not about the contrast between the built and the grown. Buildings, even city centres, can be infused with nature-based, life-enhancing qualities. In our Californian city centre development, we relied on leaf shade (vine pergolas over pedestrian streets), water-cooled air (streamlets, cascades on building façades and Flow-forms) and temperature differences between water-cooled air and sun-warmed roofs and south walls to induce air movement. In fact, the heating and cooling needs of buildings depend on the microclimate immediately around them (e.g., temperature, wind speed and humidity). Consequently, in cool regions, windbreaks can reduce heating bills by 20 per cent (U.S. Department of Energy, 1988, p. 1) (see Figure 13.1). Similarly, vine-covered walls reduce heating by 5 to 20 per cent (Dodd, 1989) and, in California, cooling up to 95 per cent (Sandifer and Givoni, 2000). Indoors, mechanical systems provide for the body, but the more natural systems are, the better they fulfil soul needs. (Forced-air heating and cooling, for instance, do not feel the same as radiant heating and fresh air through windows.) This is about life imprint.

All life depends on nature. Life survives only because our global ecosystem can re-balance. Spiritually as well as physically, nature is our life support. Archetypically, humanity has spent most of its life in verdant natural surroundings. We crave contact with nature (Roszak, 2002). This can prevent low-level stress accumulating to crisis levels (Kay-Williams, 2007, p. 72). Public greenery improves physical health (Ellaway et al., 2005, p. 331). Five minutes of exercise in green surroundings markedly improves psychological health (BBC, 2010). Public greenery reduces crime (Kuo, 1998, pp. 823–51; Kuo and Sullivan, 2001, pp. 343–67; Monbiot, 2010), strengthens community (Coley et al., 1997, pp. 468–92; DePooter, 1997; Monbiot, 2010; Desai, 2010, pp. 117–18)

FIGURE 13.1   Nant-y-Cwm Steiner Kindergarten, Wales: sheltered from wind by trees, but sun can enter at use times (arrival and outdoor play periods). Courtesy of Christopher Day.

and increases property values (Anderson and Cordell, 1988). Even mere views of nature strengthen health (Ulrich, 1994) and improve productivity (Kellert et al., 2008). Many consider that disconnection from nature accounts for high levels of neurosis—allegedly 90 per cent of the population of some cities (Boldina, 2010, p. 10). It certainly makes the environment easier to abuse. Child psychologist Anita Olds (2001, p. 411) considers nature contact essential for children's emotional development. Nature is all about life, and nature nurtures life.

Wilderness appreciation in Europe, however, is a relatively modern phenomenon, dating from the Romantic era reaction to industrial despoliation. In medieval times, life was bound by nature, and wilderness was terrifying. Even only a century ago, sailing round Cape Horn was common: hardly stress free. Unlike human society, which ranges from supportive to stressful, the limited doses of nature that we encounter in modern life are stress free. Moreover, 90 per cent of life nowadays is in or amongst buildings— which means being in generally lifeless forms and urban- and indoor-polluted air. Used air and lifeless surroundings sap energy. Fresh air regenerates body and soul. It is cleaned and reoxygenated by vegetation. Globally, rainforests and ocean algae do most of this reoxygenation, but locally, every leaf helps. The greener cities are (with vegetation on walls, roofs and ground as well as trees), the cleaner, fresher and more temperature-moderated their air. Fully greened cities can mitigate summer heat by 11 degrees Celsius (Welsh School of Architecture 2007). The capacity for fresh air to reinvigorate us is rein-forced by the sensory experience: green views, leaf rustle, lapping wavelets and suchlike.

Design for soul-nourishment, therefore, isn't only about how places look. Indeed, it is about how they are, not simply how they appear. Different senses tell us about dif-ferent aspects. Together they build a whole picture (Aeppli, 1955; Steiner, 1916/1975, pp. 8–13; Davy, 1975, pp. 43–49; Bittleston, 1975, p. 4). Sight tells us what the out-sides of things look like, but only their outsides. On its own, therefore, it offers emo-tionally detached observer consciousness (Pallasmaa, 2005). Furthermore, for children's mental development, sensitizing the senses is vital (Davy, 1975, pp. 40–43; Olds, 2001, p. 16). They learn little about this in school but much from their everyday surroundings (Day, 2007). In contrast to mono-sensory visual appearances, multisensory experiences tell us what things are. Ambient place-mood affects how we feel. It is multisensory.

Where sensory information conflicts (e.g., visual tranquillity beside motorway noise and fumes), the negatives tend to overwhelm the positives. Where different senses rein-force each other, place-mood is clear. Cosiness, for instance, is largely thermal, but also involves space, tactility, aroma, acoustic absorbency and visual character. Environmen-tal quality is all about this sensory complementarity. Sometimes non-visual senses shape design. Aroma, for instance, can be so powerfully inviting that restaurants can gain by locating kitchens to be street-facing, and bakeries, by having their vents outlet there. Mountain cabins, being refuges from cold, feel (tactilely and chromatically) warmer if made of wood rather than steel, concrete or stone. As the nature of materials affects con-struction, this influences their shape.

Related to this, living forms and spaces and undemandingly subtle sensory stimu-lation enlivens us (Fiske and Maddi, 1961, p. 10). In contrast, we feel half-dead if we are all day in lifeless, sensorially unchanging spaces (Nute, 2006). Whereas buildings of manufactured materials are unvaryingly even, those of natural materials exhibit slight irregularities, unevenness. This offers (subtle) multisensory stimulation. These materials are the product of time, so record constant variation in the environment (for timber, half to several centuries; for slate, compression over 500 million years). Unlike manufactured materials (which are at their best at point of sale), natural materials are continually matured by the workings of time: what Ruskin (1849/1961, p. 177) called 'the golden stain of time... the real light, and colour... of architecture'. Moreover, natural materials connect us to source: the less processed, the stronger our connection.

Local, natural materials not only reduce transport and processing energy but also connect us to place. Indeed, place-image is often bound to building materials: we associate New Mexico with adobe, Norway with wood, the Netherlands with brick. Local materials and their resultant building forms root us in time and place—hence in ecological context—helping confirm where we are and who we are. This involves locally traditional constructional materials (and hence form, scale and design-detail implications) (see Figure 13.2). This, of course, reduces pollution embodied in buildings and guarantees suitability to local climate. Fundamentally, however, it is all about honesty and meaning: integrity.

In the early twentieth century, reaction to meaningless stylism produced the Functionalist architecture movement. Its philosophy was based on honesty (of materials,

FIGURE 13.2   Workshop from local materials (many from within a mile) roots this building into place. Photo with permission of Green Building Press, Llandysul, Wales.

structure and space matched to functional needs) encapsulated by slogans such as 'orna-ment is a crime', 'truth to materials', and 'form follows function'. It symbolized a new world, totally freed from the old outlooks, which had led to the carnage of the 1914–18 Great War. Stylistically, however, it was based on the pure solids (cube, sphere and cyl-inder) espoused by the Bauhaus movement. These are easy forms for machines to make but are hardly functional. Humans (for whom architecture is meant) are not rectangu-loid, nor are our movements. Even le Corbusier's (1923/2008) immortalized description of homes as 'machines for living' is a misnomer. Very few machine parts are rectangu-loid, nor are many machine movements. Rectanguloids are good for easy storage, as-sembly, dimensional description and, especially, manufacture. They are economically practical but hardly functional for anything to do with life. Life just does not fit into boxes—or into box shapes.

Nature's forms are supremely functional—mostly multifunctional. But none are rectangular. Not surprisingly, nonrectangular and, especially, curvilinear spaces are more alive than rectangular ones. Most alive are those shaped by life energy, not (simple) geometry. Catenary arches are force-formed: semicircular arches, shaped by abstract thought; flat lintels, by laziness (no need for thought); those with (visually) unsupported brick courses, by disregard for honesty. Force-formed and function-formed curves have meaning (see Figure 13.3). Purely stylistic ones do not. Meaningful things, we can rely on. Meaningless things disorientate us. The more levels of meaning in forms and places, the greater their integrity. Personally, I am not satisfied unless my designs fulfil practical, social, microclimatic, ecological and (visually obvious) structural functions, and provide space-moods matched to the needs of the activities within them. These functions, physi-cal and spiritual, produce the form: appearance follows need. Multilayered functional-ism means we need fewer things. Moreover, it gives multilayered meaningfulness: things are what they say they are at many (hopefully all) levels. Just like being amongst honest, unpretentious people, surroundings that manifest honesty and unpretentiousness make us feel trusting, secure and at ease. This is about design as servant, not self-advertiser.

As well as integrity, multilayer meaning and subliminally recognized forces, the material shape of space also affects soul-mood, hence our state of being. Being life-related, curves tend to be invigorating. Not coincidentally, dead straight lines tend to feel dead. Curvilinear space is formed by life; orthogonal space, by thought (Day, 2002, p. 121). Curves are about energy; rectangles, about proportion. To be surrounded solely by curvilinear forms is relaxing to the point of dreaminess; by unrelieved rectanguloids, arid. Balanced, everyday life is neither dreamy nor arid. We need both life vigour and encouragement to think, but in varying proportions according to circumstance. Our surroundings, therefore, need to manifest both the straight and the curved. To unify life vigour and thought, it is most effective if the straight is within the curved (as in facet-ted arches) and the curved within the straight (as in subtly off-straight lines). Mixing straight and curved lines, shapes and forms often merely emphasizes their contrasting qualities (Day, 2006, p. 92).

Spatial gestures affect us similarly to human gestures, but more subliminally. Like open arms, obtuse angles embracingly welcome us. Like cattle-pen funnels, acute

FIGURE 13.3   Gridshell Roof. We subconsciously perceive the structural forces in forms. If a form (or the space it produces) is structurally economical, we recognize its gracefulness. Photo with permission of Green Building Press, Llandysul, Wales.

internal angles cramp us. Whereas sharp, external corners arrow at us, gentle curves ease us round. (We feel this clearly if we walk, gesture or draw these shapes.) Both physically and psychologically, planes met head on confront us. Hence obliquely entered spaces are more welcoming and relaxingly informal than frontally entered ones. Similarly, clashing

FIGURE 13.4   Ffald-y-Brenin, Pembrokeshire, Wales. Gently harmonious plane-meetings en-gentle buildings so they are less dramatic, hence less ostentatious, and fit more harmoniously into place. Courtesy of Christopher Day.

shapes or colours fight; those that absorb and listen to each other's energy, converse. This is about harmony induction (Day, 2006, pp. 84–90) (see Figure 13.4). Apart from architectural elements, there is a whole range of secondary ones (e.g., screens, curtains, furniture, colouring, lighting) that can intercede to transform conflict-laden plane-meetings into harmonious ones. (This, of course, parallels nature's model: ground-air interface, intertidal zones, woodland-edge shrubs and so on.) This is no mere matter of personal aesthetic preference. The shape of space resounds in us.

This is about how spatial qualities affect, nourish or assault the soul. But it is the imprint of human effort that ensouls places. Everything built is human-made, took human effort. Without machinery, pollution is infinitesimally low, but drudgery exhaustingly high. (I know! For twenty-five years, I tried this.) Machines relieve this, but, although bringing many advantages, they distance products from the hands that formed them. There are no straight lines in hands. To make these, we need tools. The straighter the lines, the more they are tool- or machine-formed, the less hand-formed. Hand is irrevocably bound to heart. We cannot make things without feeling involved with them. (We can, of course, also hate what we're doing. This imprinted resentment also always shows.) Traditionally, emotional commitment gave rise to pride-in-work traditions. It makes the maker's life meaningful. It always shows. Consequently, the more handmade buildings, or even their components, are (e.g., handmade bricks, split shakes or natural slates), the greater their soul content. Industrially made buildings, of industrial materials, can look impressive, even graceful, but always lack soul. Making things takes time, takes part of the maker's life. Machinery saves time, hence cost, but also reduces this life imprint. It substitutes mechanical (often pollution rich) energy for nature-given life. Handmade means low embodied energy; machine-made usually means high embodied energy. Cost-wise, however, it is the reverse: handmade is relatively expensive; machine-made, relatively inexpensive. The issue, therefore, is not hand *or* machine work, but where is each appropriate? Machines are made to repeat things, so tend towards producing perfectly uniform products. In our contract-bound age, soul-rich variation is too hard to objectively quantify, so uniformity is often taken as a criterion for perfection. Perfection (meaning uniformity) is very expensive by hand. Furthermore, humans vary from person to person and are fallible. They're best suited to make individually (albeit only slightly) varied things. Indeed, this (subtle) imperfection imparts life to repeated elements (e.g., brickwork). So what level of imperfection is acceptable, where? Imperfection is certainly not welcome in plumbing or electrical work, but in surface finishes (as in floor tiling) is sometimes preferable. Low skill (as is typical of DIY and volunteer building) tends to produce imperfect workmanship. In appropriate places, this can increase charm. It often also requires oversize elements, hence encourages the use of reused materials. Low skill also reduces labour expense and oil-fuelled power. Reused materials reduce embodied energy. Both increase life-imprinted charm and soul. Under normal contract-based construction, however, neither is affordable. Both reused materials and handwork take too much (expensive) time. But for many, contract-based construction is anyway too expensive. For these, a combination of contractor work and self-finishing can make buildings affordable.

Traditional cities were built by hand, hence manifest slight (or sometimes great) irregularities and sensory variation. As manifested by city-break tourism and holiday postcards, everybody feels this hand imprint. Tourists do not visit soulless cities (Moe, 1996, p. 1). But for building, the economics have changed. So long as oil is cheap, handwork is (relatively) prohibitively expensive. Consequently, the less handwork, the less expense, but also the less heart. The connection we feel to places, therefore, declines. Although oil will not remain cheap for long, this cost balance shapes current thinking. So how can new (affordable) cities, buildings, homes and rooms be (at least) as soul-nourishing as old ones? Should we repeat traditional design? Copying surrounding forms or style, however, does not make new buildings feel as if they belong in the place, time and social and cultural context. Only respect for spirit-of-place and the human spirit, coupled with forms generated by the ecological, social, socioeconomic and climatic continuum do.

A key soul-nourishment factor is ambience. For homes, room-mood is crucial. In the outdoors, place experience is more important than the appearance of the buildings. This requires buildings to be non-assertive, reticent. Whereas iconic buildings are normally served by space (rarely place), nowadays, traditional buildings have condensed from, hence serve, place-mood. Traditionally, things happened in places and people flowed along routes between these. Wherever obstructions checked flow, activities occurred and new places formed. In due course, the activities were roofed, then enclosed by buildings.

But as places came first, building façades merely confirmed their edges. Similarly, the qualities of buildings, including their appearance, suited, and thereby enhanced, the mood-character of places.

Can we do this today? Streets, plot-boundaries and the built context are already fixed. Nonetheless, it is still the interaction of life with environment that generates place. Place still can (and should) generate buildings. The mood qualities of the activities that buildings house still can (and should) determine their placing, form, entrances (doors) and eyes (windows). This gives everything meaningfulness and integrity. It grows and strengthens spirit-of-place.

This is a process. Unlike paper (or computer) design, which is about a fixed product, traditional cities progressively grew into form: they happened in response to evolving circumstance. Artists (albeit stylistically retro) can make happenings. Developers cannot. No master plan means no planning consent: no business plan, no funding. Nonetheless, we can still condense form out of the synthesis of place, community and circumstance.

PROCESS AND FORM INTEGRITY

The Consensus Design process condenses form from spirit-of-project, to ally this new spirit, to pre-existing spirit-of-place (Day, 2003, pp. 67–75). It starts not with the future project (easy to disagree about) but the present place. This is an established fact—hence easy to agree about. It first, therefore, studies the place's physical characteristics: measurable and indisputable. Then comes place biography (and/or experience-sequence, if appropriate to the project). Place biography is visible (through many clues) from distant past to present, but it does not stop now. It will continue unbroken into the future. From what we know of the past, therefore, we try to extrapolate this journey into the future. Next, we study place-moods and draw mood maps. Now, we can ask what the place says, what is its spirit-of-place. The design phase reverses this process. It slowly condenses form from spirit, stepwise through mirrored levels: spirit to mood, to life-related sequence (development and experience sequence), to place gestures, hence form, materials and detailed design. It is surprisingly easy to find consensus because no matter how contentious each step might be on its own, as part of this sequence, it serves previous decisions. Place-mood serves spirit-of-project; spatial gestures serve place-mood; building form serves place gestures; construction materials serve form quality. This is about listening to place (hence its ecology) and people's needs (hence their interaction with this). It is the absolute opposite of idea-shaped design, where ideas (which originate in individual people—hence have off-site roots) are imposed on places and communities.

The core of this method is concern for what places say. This is crucial. Places' subliminal messages affect everybody: they are soul-nourishing or soul-wounding. Image contributes to this, but only superficially. Office dress codes alter our behaviour but hardly change who we are. Similarly, architectural image changes how we like to be thought of but not what buildings and places say to us. This is about embodied values. No amount of dressing up appearance can conceal these. Places that seek to profit from us are un-mistakably different from those that earn their profit by benefiting us. We immediately recognize exploitation or service.

Consensus design is only one amongst many design participation techniques. In-volving residents and users means designs are much more likely to work as planned. Outsiders—even experienced designers—are unable see how places work beneath the surface and can only assume what people need. Residents, however, know how places function through direct experience (Day, 2003) or 'from the inside out, from the street, not from the drawing board' (Gratz, 1994, p. 160). Moreover, they have invested part of themselves in the design. The place (new or transformed) that results is now theirs. Occupants of air-conditioned offices will only tolerate 1 degree of deviation from 21 de-grees, but those able to open windows to control ventilation/cooling, a 6-degree temper-ature increase (Willis et al., 1995, p. 7). Similarly, participants in place design are more likely to do things to overcome problems than to just resent and vandalize. Newcastle's Byker Estate demonstrates this. Although over forty years old, upkeep is good and there is little vandalism (Hatherley, 2011). Meaningful (not just tokenistic) participation in-duces a high level of care for public places, even those with no clear ownership.

Community Supportive Place

Participatory design is only one, albeit essential, step towards de-egoizing design. This is essential, as the people who live in—and hence are daily influenced by—places are rarely those who become famous by designing them. Fundamentally, to make soul-nourishing places, which both serve and reflect community needs, we have to shift attitude from competitive individualism to cooperative communalism. Personal life is inevitably (and healthily) individualistic, but communal life needs to be communal: we depend on each other. Society—and human life—cannot exist without this mutual interdependence (Dalai Lama, 1999, pp. 37–39). This is about another key aspect of ensouled places: so-cial imprint. Conviviality does not just happen. It depends on whether, how and in what circumstances and place-moods people meet. In public spaces, there must be enough people and things going on (Whyte, 1988, p. 55, p. 108): urban vitality (or lifelessness) is self-reinforcing (Gehl, 2006). With one person per 150 square feet (13 sq m), public spaces are vibrant; less than one per 500 square feet (45 sq m), dead (Alexander et al., 1977, p. 597). Just as people facing each other feel more a group than those turning backs to each other, buildings facing each other support a feeling of community, and their entrances focus pedestrian flows into communal public space, not private behind-building parking lots. As empty premises are a death knell for towns, street-level com-mercial premises should be suitable for a variety of uses—twelve-foot (4 m) height and twenty-seven-foot (9 m) depth suits a wide range of retail, office and workshop uses (*DpdINFO Newsletter,* 2007). Radial layouts—typical of medieval towns—focalize ac-tivity in town centres, unifying community. Uniting periphery and centre, this maxi-mizes population diversity and activity variety (Hillier in Bentley and McGlynn, 2000, pp. 2–13). Whereas dormitory suburbs and mono-use districts are depopulated outside

use hours, mixed use extends activity hours (Hood and Sakal, 2008, p. 13). It also reduces traffic (hence carbon dioxide) and road space and parking demand—hence lower
development costs and a less hostile environment (Desai, 2010, p. 126). Nowadays, we
spend most of our time indoors, so cloaking boring building types (e.g., multistorey
parking, offices, banks, superstores) with life (e.g., micro-retail) makes streets more interesting to be in. (Generally, as we rarely look up, this can be limited to ground level.)
To maximize street life, the use times of different activities need to overlap and linkages
between them be made via ground-level public space, as only here does public life happen. Routes at different levels (as in London's Thames South Bank) just flow over each
other (*Building Design,* 1997, p. 14). As local businesses strengthen local identity, hence
attractiveness to shoppers (Gruen, 1999, pp. 4–6), this has implications for the size and
letting policy of retail units. Smaller (hence more numerous) premises and stratified uses
(hence tenants) encourage diversity. Dividing façades into bays maximizes perceived
diversity.

Conviviality depends on linger-ability. Lingering needs social and climatic protection, so takes place around the edges of spaces. This makes edge-design critical: shops
and cafés to go to, places to sit, stand and linger with views of life going on. A hostile microclimate discourages lingering. Arcades, colonnades, façade indentations, internal corners, sun traps (in cool climates) and shade pools (in hot) increase appeal. So do seating
and leaning opportunities facing activity. Empty benches make places look abandoned
(so feel unsafe), but informal seats (e.g., walls, steps, ledges) do not (Whyte, 1988,
pp. 112–16). Similarly, bollards, columns, pilasters or trees provide things to lean on.
Public life is about urban vitality, but community life is about strengthening community bonds (Brill, 2001). These overlap but are subtly different, so town and neighbourhood centres have similar needs but with a different emphasis. On a neighbourhood
scale, shops focalize community but need sufficient customers to keep them in business.
With residential densities below fifteen homes per acre (thirty-five homes per hectare),
they are rarely viable. Symbiotic activities reinforce each other, so triangulated activities
strengthen viability (Gehl and Sim, 2007, p. 170). Besides noise and pollution, traffic
sunders community (Desai, 2010, p. 115).

Driving does not encourage us to become friends with strangers we bump into.
Walking does. Community formation, therefore, depends on walkability. As few people have the time or energy to walk longer than five minutes (a third of a mile, or
400–500 m) from home to community centre, this limits community size to one that
takes ten minutes (half a mile, or 800–1,000 m) to walk across. Perceived distance,
however, depends on the quality of the walking experience, making multisensory attractiveness, human scale and interest-stimulating variety crucial: 500 yards (500 m)
of superstore-lined arterial road is long; of riverside footpath, short. Walkability, supported by safe cycleways and convenient public transport, allows 40 per cent of Vauban households to be car free (Vauban District, 2013).

Our social identity is multilayered: nationality, region, town, neighbourhood, street,
family (Gehl, 2006). At a sub-neighbourhood scale, the clearer spaces shared by groups
of homes are, the more cohesive is small-group identity. This applies equally to front

spaces (e.g., street, home zones, courtyard) and back spaces (e.g., child-safe green play areas, vegetable plots). Social magnets (e.g., grouped parking, recycling points and communal greenhouses) increase neighbour contact. Front-of house activities, including keeping an eye on children playing in home zone streets, encourage sociability. Anything that prolongs time in the semi-public realm (e.g., low-fenced front gardens) further supports this (Gehl, 2006). At all scales, people make community, but design facilitates it.

ENVIRONMENTAL IMPACT

Community makes places feel good to live in. Conviviality makes them friendly. Sensory attractiveness makes them appealing. Soul-nourishment depends on these qualities. But what does soul-nourishing design have to do with environmental impact?

Soul-nourishing places are more valued, so better cared for, than soul-impoverishing ones. Valued public places are safer and more community-fostering (Newman, 1972, pp. 53–61; Whyte, 1988, p. 55; ODPM, 2004). Moreover, unless technical systems offer sensory delight (as woodstoves and solar heat do), we do not fully connect to them, so they often are not properly cared for or used. This commonly halves their efficiency (Roaf, 2010, p. 7; Desai, 2010, pp. 60–61). We must also consider what we buy: do we invest in consumption or conservation? Solar water heating, for instance, saves money and carbon dioxide but doesn't feel of anything. Fitted kitchens cost two to five times as much but feel nice to be in. Not surprisingly, they are more popular (Vale and Vale, 2009, pp. 13–14). Moreover, TV house improvement programmes rarely mention energy conservation.

It is widely thought, however, that the pressures of sustainability restrict creativity to a limited range of technically led options, marginalizing concern for how places feel. But, as Haggard and Cooper (2006, pp. 18–21) observe, the issue is less a matter of how much (minimization) than it is of how (appropriateness). Nature, for instance, uses vast amounts of energy and produces vast amounts of carbon dioxide, but her energy import-export balance remains constant and all carbon dioxide remains within the system. Concern for 'how' is much more creativity-demanding than for 'how much'. Indeed, building for sustainability is not about choosing between technology and soul- and spirit-nurture. It is about how they intertwine to reinforce each other. It is, after all, our awakened sense of responsibility that motivates eco-technology, and soul-nourishment that ensures its uptake.

Additionally, soul-nourishing design tends to have lower environmental impacts. For instance, even in 1996, Sick Building Syndrome cost $75 billion a year in the United States: $15 billion for medical care and $60 billion in indirect costs (Wilson and Malin, 1996, p. 1). Whereas air conditioning is a major cause, and is expensive—35 to 45 percent of construction budgets, and it needs to be replaced every fifteen years (Ford, 1998)—natural cooling and ventilation reduces carbon dioxide five-fold, feels better, is healthier and is free. Solar heating is likewise free and zero-carbon. Natural, minimally processed construction materials also feel, smell and look better than industrial

FIGURE 13.5 Ffald-y-Brenin Interior. Much furnishing is short-lived, so has disproportionately embodied energy. Many modern rooms are not 'soul habitable' without furniture and ornaments. Even unfurnished, this room needs none. Courtesy of Christopher Day.

products. Generally, they are healthier to live with (no toxic vapours), are not compromised by the wear-and-tear of life and are easier to recycle into living systems. Their environmental costs are minimal and are mainly due to transportation. As every area has building traditions based on local materials, transportation costs can be easily minimized. In short, natural systems, materials and the lifestyle choices they encourage tend to be sustainable: economically, socially and ecologically.

In contrast, industrially produced things, power and imported design are, by nature, newcomers. Some fit; some do not. Without new breath, life stagnates. But the inappropriate, imposed new disrupts the continuities that keep ecological, economic, social and cultural systems unified and functioning. New ideas and people (and their cultural outlooks) enrich our sensory life and thinking. Imported materials (e.g., synthetics), power (e.g., oil) and design (e.g., parachuted-in International Style), however, make us dependent on things we have no connection to, no control over, no responsibility for and soul-investment in. They can easily disrupt the continuity that anchors our identity, our society's economy and our environment's ecology. Not surprisingly, they often feel alien and soul-impoverishing.

More subtly, but even more significantly, environment influences behaviour: lifestyle and consumption, awareness and responsibility. Although it cannot determine how we act, environment greatly influences what we want. If we do not have to buy things or experiences to compensate for soul-poor surroundings, consumption falls. The less we buy, the lower our impact; the greater our awareness, the stronger our sense of responsibility. With three-quarters of our environmental impact being due to lifestyle choices (much more if we choose an energy-indulgent lifestyle), soul-nourishing environments can make a huge contribution (see Figure 13.5).

REFERENCES

Aeppli, W. (1955), *The Care and Development of the Human Senses*, Steiner Schools Fellowship of Great Britain: Forest Row.

Alexander, C., Ishikawa, S. and Silverstein, M. (1977), *A Pattern Language*, Oxford University Press: New York.

Anderson, L. and Cordell, H. (1988), 'Influence of Trees on Residential Property Values in Athens, Georgia', *Landscape and Urban Planning*, vol. 15: pp. 153–64.

BBC (2010), *Today Programme*, Radio 4, interview with Jules Pretty, researcher from the University of Essex, May 1.

Bentley, I. and McGlynn, S. (2000), 'Re-Making the Mall: Working towards New Centres for Post-Industrial Urbanism', in Roaf, S., Sala, M. and Bairstow, A. (eds), *TIA Conference Proceedings 2000*, TIA on behalf of the European Commission Directorate General XVII for Energy and Transport: Oxford.

BioRegional (2010), 'Sustainable Solutions at Every Scale: 2010–2011 Review', <http://www.bioregional.com/files/publications/BioRegionalAnnualReview1011.pdf> accessed July 10, 2012.

Bittleston, A. (1975), *The Golden Blade*, Rudolf Steiner Press: London.

Boldina, E. (2010), 'A Place to Practice Freedom', *Anthroposophy Worldwide*, vol. 4: p. 10.

Brill, M. (2001), 'Problems with Mistaking Community Life for Public Life', *Places,* fall, <http://www.traditional-building.com/Previous-Issues-08/OctoberFeature08.html> accessed July 10, 2012.

Building Design (1997), 'Space Syntax', May 2: p. 14.

Coley, R. L., Kuo, F. E. and Sullivan, W. C. (1997), 'Where Does Community Grow? The Social Context Created by Nature in Urban Public Housing', *Environment and Behaviour,* vol. 29: pp. 468–92.

Dalai Lama (1999), *Ancient Wisdom, Modern World,* Abacus: London.

Davy, J. (1975), 'On Coming to Our Senses', *The Golden Blade,* Rudolf Steiner Press: London. pp. 39–52.

Day, C. (2002), *Spirit & Place,* Architectural Press: Oxford.

Day, C. (2003), *Consensus Design,* Architectural Press: Oxford.

Day, C. (2006), *Places of the Soul: Architecture and Environmental Design as a Healing Art,* 2nd ed., Architectural Press: Oxford.

Day, C. (2007), *Environment and Children,* Architectural Press: Oxford.

DePooter, S. (1997), 'Nature and Neighbors: Green Spaces and Social Interactions in the Inner City', master's thesis, University of Illinois, Urbana-Champaign.

Desai, P. (2010), *One Planet Communities,* John Wiley & Sons: Chichester.

Dodd, J. (1989), 'Greenscape: 2. Climate and Form', *Architects Journal,* vol. 16, no. 189: pp. 81–85.

DpdINFO Newsletter (2007), Department of Planning and Development, City of Seattle Government, February.

Ellaway, A., McIntyre, S. and Bonnefoy, X. (2005), 'Graffiti, Greenery and Obesity in Adults', *British Medical Journal Online,* <http://www.bmj.com/highwire/filestream/399920/field_highwire_article_pdf/0/bmj.38575.664549.F7.full.pdf> accessed February 14, 2013.

Energy Saving Trust (2009), 'BedZED: The UK's Biggest Eco-Community', <http://www.energysavingsecrets.co.uk/bedzed-the-uks-biggest-eco-community.html> accessed July 10 2012.

Fiske, D. and Maddi, S. (eds), (1961), "Functions of Varied Experience," Dorsey Press: Homewood, IL, p. 10.

Ford, B. (1998), *Sustainable Urban Development through Design,* RIBA CPD lecture at Cambridge University, February 12.

Gehl, J. (2006), *Life between Buildings,* Arkitektens Forlag: Copenhagen.

Gehl, J. and Sim, D. (2007), 'Life between Buildings: Foundations for a Successful Community', in Sterling, P., *Calderwood Master Plan,* Stirling Developments: Edinburgh: pp. 169-170.

Gratz, R. B. (1994), *The Living City,* Preservation Press: Washington, DC.

Gruen, N. (1999), 'What Makes a Successful Downtown', *California Downtown Association Newsletter,* vol. 9, no. 4, November: pp. 4–6.

Haggard, K. and Cooper, P. (2006), *Fractal Architecture,* BookSurge Publishing: Charleston, NC.

Hatherley, O. (2011), 'Yes, Minister, We Need More Bykers', *Building Design,* April 8, <http://www.bdonline.co.uk/comment/columnists/yes-minister-we-need-more-bykers/5016418.article> accessed February 24, 2013.

Hood, S., and Sakal, R. (2008), 'One Lot at a Time', *Traditional Building,* <http://www.traditional-building.com/Previous-Issues-08/OctoberFeature08.html> accessed July 10, 2012.

Kay-Williams, S. (2007), 'Don't Forget—The Garden', *Green Building,* vol. 17, no. 1, summer: p. 72.

Kellert, S. R., Heerwagen, J. H. and Mador, M. L. (2008), *Biophilic Design: The Theory, Science and Practice of Bringing Buildings to Life,* John Wiley & Sons: Chichester, UK.

Kuo, F. (1998), 'Fertile Ground for Community: Inner-City Neighborhood Common Spaces', *American Journal of Community Psychology,* vol. 26, no. 6: pp. 823–51.

Kuo, F. E. and Sullivan, W. C. (2001), 'Environment and Crime in the Inner City: Does Vegetation Reduce Crime?' *Environment and Behaviour,* vol. 33, no. 3: pp. 343–67.

le Corbusier (1923/2008), *Vers une Architecture,* Frances Lincoln: Exeter.

Moe, R. (1996), 'Growing Smarter: Fighting Sprawl and Restoring Community in America', lecture, Fresno, California, November 20, National Trust for Historic Preservation, San Francisco.

Monbiot, G., (2010), 'Turning Estates into Villages', <www.monbiot.com> accessed August 9, 2010.

Newman, O. (1972), *Defensible Space,* Macmillan: New York.

Nute, K. (2006), *The Architecture of Here and Now: Natural Change in Built Spaces,* proposal for Architectural Press: Oxford.

ODPM (2004), *Safer Places—The Planning System & Crime Prevention,* Office of the Deputy Prime Minister, London and Home Office, February, <http://www.communities.gov.uk/documents/planningandbuilding/pdf/147627.pdf> accessed July 10, 2012.

Olds, A. R. (2001), *Child Care Design Guide,* McGraw Hill: New York.

Pallasmaa, J. (2005), *The Eyes of the Skin,* John Wiley & Sons: Chichester, UK.

Riddlestone, S. (2008), 'What Makes an Eco-Town?' *Green Building,* vol. 18, no. 3, winter: p. 24.

Roaf, S. (2010), 'Oh Behave, If You Want Real Low Carbon Buildings!' *Green Building,* vol. 20, no. 2, autumn: p. 7.

Roszak, Theodore (2002), *Ecopsychology: Eight Principles,* <http://ecopsychology.athabascau.ca/Final/intro.htm> accessed July 10, 2012.

Ruskin, J. (1849/1961), *The Seven Lamps of Architecture,* Noonday Press: New York.

Sandifer, S. and Givoni, B. (2000), 'Thermal Effects of Vines on Wall Surfaces', in Roaf, S., Sala, M. and Bairstow, A. (eds), *TIA Conference Proceedings 2000,* TIA on behalf of the European Commission Directorate General XVII for Energy and Transport: Oxford, <http://www.sbse.org/awards/docs/Sandifer.pdf> accessed February 24, 2013.

Siddall, M. (2009), 'Preparing the UK for Passivhaus', *Green Building,* vol. 18, no. 4, spring: p. 19.

Steiner, R. (1916/1975), 'The Twelve Senses and the Seven Life Processes in Man', in *The Golden Blade,* vol. 27: pp. 7–21.

Ulrich, R. (1994), in McKahan, D. C. (ed.), *Ensouling Healthcare Facilities,* Lennon Associates: Del Mar, CA.

U.S. Department of Energy (1988), *Landscaping for Energy Efficient Homes,* April, p. 1.

Vale, R. and Vale, B. (2009), *Time to Eat the Dog?* Thames & Hudson: London.

Vauban District (2013), Freiburg, Germany, <www.vauban.de/info/abstract.html> accessed January 5, 2013.

Welsh School of Architecture (2007), <http://www.cardiff.ac.uk/archi/> accessed October 29, 2007.

Whyte, W. H. (1988), *City,* Doubleday: New York.

Willis, S., Fordham, M. and Bordass, B., (1995), *Report 31: Avoiding or Minimising the Use of Air-Conditioning,* Building Research Energy Conservation Support Unit, Building Research Establishment: Garston, Watford, UK.

Wilson, A. and Malin, N. (1996), 'The IAQ Challenge: Protecting the Indoor Environment', *Environmental Building News,* vol. 5, no. 3, May/June, <http://www.buildinggreen.com/auth/article.cfm/1996/5/1/The-IAQ-Challenge-Protecting-the-Indoor-Environment/> accessed February 14, 2013.

14

Principles of Sustainable Dwellings and Community Design

AVI FRIEDMAN

ENVIRONMENTALLY FRIENDLY DWELLINGS

In recent years, governments and construction associations around the world have begun to establish standards for sustainable building practices. These standards go beyond national building codes, set stricter efficiency level criteria, and act as accreditation systems. Builders and projects are qualified and distinguished according to the scope of their environmental pursuits. In North America, the U.S. Green Building Council (USGBC) established the Leadership in Energy and Environmental Design (LEED) (U.S. Green Building Council, 2007). The standard in the UK is known as Building Research Establishment Environmental Assessment Method (BREEAM). These methods have become a way of developing new building strategies, and their thrust can be summarized in the following principles.

The path of least negative impact focuses on limiting both short- and long-term adverse effects on environmental, economic, societal, and cultural facets of a project. For example, smaller homes lessen the initial impact of construction through reduced amounts of building materials. The long-term performance of a project can be planned to be a self-sustaining process of resources and activities, such as lessening energy requirements by including photovoltaic panels. As certain systems become more independent, others can also work in a supporting relationship. While this approach requires an expanded understanding and heightened sensitivity, building smaller houses to reduce urban sprawl and infrastructure costs is a well documented approach. Also, life cycle considerations take into account the project's evolution in terms of its continuity as a system throughout all the phases of its use—aiming for the least negative impact (Friedman, 2007). It is commonly assumed that many environmental problems are unsolvable in the absolute sense. They can perhaps be minimized, but they cannot be eliminated.

Design of small-footprint dwellings within the context of sustainable development requires a minimization of the toll on natural resources. This implies that the following strategies will be adhered to:

Minimize the environmental impacts of building materials: this can be done through a judicious selection process to reduce embodied energy and resource depletion and its effect on ecosystems while maximizing durability. The basic design of a unit can be modified to provide a more economic and environmentally responsible product without compromising the occupants' living comfort and health.

Improve the energy efficiency of the building envelope: the consumption of nonrenewable energy resources can be minimized through proper design, materials selection, and choice of technologies for heating and cooling. Strategies to minimize energy losses include energy-efficient building practices, the use of energy efficient mechanical systems and windows, airtight construction, and introduction of passive solar design strategies.

Improve the efficiency of use of renewable resources: the rate of use of renewable resources can be minimized by implementing systems that require the least amount of resource consumption to accomplish a given task. Common strategies include the minimization of water consumption through application of technologies such as low-flow toilets, showerheads, and faucets. In addition, significant savings can be achieved, for example, through xeriscaping, a landscaping technique that minimizes irrigation requirements through use of naturalized gardens, native plants, and drought-resistant species. Such xeriscapes also require less maintenance and fertilizers, thereby reducing the impact of nonrenewable energy and mineral resources.

Minimize waste generated: the efficient use of nonrenewable resources and minimization of the negative environmental impacts associated with waste disposal requires that nonrenewable resources be recycled. Homes can be designed to maximize inclusion of recycled materials or those that originate from recycled sources. In addition, the design of communities and units can be made consistent with waste minimization through efficient recycling and composting programs. These principles have been embedded in the design of dwellings by the author, primarily in the Grow Home, which is described below.

THE GROW HOME

Narrow housing represents a tangible response to the demand for more affordable dwellings as well as upholds the general principles of sustainable development noted above.

The Grow Home was first built on the campus of McGill University in Montreal as a demonstration project. It was a townhouse with a footprint of fourteen by thirty-six feet(4.3 m by 11.0 m). Several objectives underlined the principles of this design. The first and foremost was to demonstrate that affordability and resource efficiency can be achieved by reducing unit size, while maintaining high-quality construction and materials. A second objective was to demonstrate that socioeconomic changes in North America have created a demand for different house forms that better address the spatial needs and lifestyle concerns of clients that, in the past, were considered marginal. This second objective addressed the social dimension of sustainability. The Grow Home has been modified by builders to meet these demands and, as a result, has been successful in the marketplace with over ten thousand units built in the approximately ten years since its introduction in 1990. The prototype has also since continued to be desirable to builders and homeowners. The design of the Grow Home was based on several principles that contributed to its sustainability; these are outlined below (Friedman, 2001).

Narrow Row House

The house that shares its side walls with its neighbours is known variously as a row house, townhouse, or terraced house and is a traditional urban solution that dates back at least to medieval times. During the Industrial Revolution, the row house became the main form of housing in cities, both in Britain and America. Its chief advantages were that it could be built on a fairly narrow plot, typically between twenty- and twenty-four-feet (6.1 m and 7.3 m) wide, that allowed relatively high densities but that also incorporated most of the advantages of the individual, single-family home: a private entrance, easy access to the ground, and a clear definition of a public, street side, and a private, rear garden.

The inclusion of narrow homes in a project has important implications on land-use. A single story detached dwelling on a 60-by-100-foot (18.3 m by 30.5 m) lot results in a gross density of about five homes per acre (twelve homes per hectare); a two-story, fourteen-foot-wide row house on a 14-by-100-foot (3.4 m by 30.5 m) lot gives a gross density of twenty-four homes per acre (fifty-nine homes per hectare). Put another way, an acre (0.4 hectares) of land can accommodate about twenty persons living in bungalows. The same amount of land, and the same amount of roads, sewers, waterlines, and storm drains can accommodate more than four times as many people living in narrow row houses. Hence, such housing makes a considerable contribution to reducing sprawl because it is about four times more land-efficient. The effect on the environment of denser neighbourhoods is considerable: less automobile travel, fewer roadways with less rainwater runoff, and less energy invested in constructing community infrastructure.

Plan Simplification

One of the simplest ways of reducing material use and heat loss is by simplifying the unit's configuration. A more complex building form requires more corners and a greater perimeter, which in turn requires more 'skin'. This results in higher construction costs and increased heat loss. Generally, the ratio of floor area to perimeter should be maximized. A simple plan costs less to build since there are fewer corners and, most likely, fewer windows. Envelope costs, from the basement to the roof, are reduced while simple configurations generally require less cutting and fitting of building materials. Consequently, the amount of material wasted is reduced, and the management task is simplified.

Modular Design/Dimensioning and Efficient Framing Practices

Another simple and effective way of reducing waste is through careful dimensioning of the building to accommodate the modular configuration of materials. At the most basic level, designing within standard dimensions for structural wood framing members such as studs, joists, and plywood could result in substantial savings. It has been estimated that in a typical detached home, using sixteen-inch module (405 mm) stud spacing, placing and dimensioning windows accordingly, and locating partitions to line up with the structural studs may altogether save a ton of lumber in an average home. Designing for four-foot (2.2 m) modules and twenty-four-inch (610 mm) stud spacing alone can reduce lumber use by 8 per cent. Providing for efficient details at corners and intersections of exterior walls and interior partitions doubles these savings (Carpenter, 2009).

With more careful planning and material selection, the same principle could be implemented to accommodate interior finishes such as drywall and floor tiles. Cost savings are achieved not only through efficient use of materials but also through reduced labour requirement, since less cutting and fitting is needed.

Area Distribution/Floor Stacking

While the vertical distribution of a unit's floor area will have the greatest impact on land use efficiency and housing density, it can also have substantial effects on the use of building materials and, to some extent, energy efficiency. Vertical designs make the most efficient use of space, since more stacking results in the need for less construction material. The cost of a two-story square house, for instance, is lower than a one story with equivalent area, since it has half the foundation and roof area. Floor-to-floor heights, which are affected by floor thickness and the presence of suspended ceilings, will also have an impact on the amount of raw materials that go into construction, especially in the building envelope.

Grouping/Joining Units

One of the most effective ways of reducing energy consumption is by joining units into semidetached or row house configurations, since heat loss is limited to two walls (or three, for a semidetached unit) and a smaller roof area. Grouping units is also an effective way of improving construction efficiency. The repetition of design in a set of row houses usually results in a shorter construction period per unit. The reduction in perimeter area can significantly affect the delivery time, since construction of the envelope is a labour-intensive operation.

The joining of units into groups of two or more can also provide important savings in both construction and energy. Joining four detached units into semidetached units, for instance, reduces the exposed wall area by 36 per cent. Grouping four units as row houses provides an additional 50 per cent savings. Heat-loss reductions of approximately 21 per cent can be achieved when two dwellings are attached, and a further 26 per cent savings is achieved for the middle unit when three or more dwellings are joined as row houses.

Size Reduction and Efficient Planning

Efficient planning of the unit's interior layout can be instrumental in reducing both construction costs and energy consumption. By increasing the ratio of usable to gross floor area, the quantity of construction materials is reduced, as are the space-heating requirements. The design objective would be to trim the fat and provide a smaller house with the same usable floor area so as not to disrupt the occupants' living comfort. This can be achieved in several ways.

One possibility is to reclaim the attic, especially for small houses. Most types of prefabricated trusses can be wasteful where small spans are involved, particularly since they render the attic space unusable for living purposes. Using knee-type trusses or stick-build framing methods in the roof can increase the floor space without necessarily increasing construction costs. For a fourteen-by-thirty-six-foot (4.3 by 11 m) area, for instance, an eight-foot (2.4 m) clearance could be achieved with a roof slope of 6:12. Assuming that forty per cent of this space is usable for occupancy, an additional 200 square feet (19 sq m) of floor space could be added to this home.

Eliminating the basement could also be beneficial where there is sufficient living space on the main and upper floors, or where accessible dwellings are desired. Slabs on grade, crawl spaces and pier foundations use less concrete, are less expensive to build, and use less energy to heat. Where a basement is deemed necessary, the use of preserved wood foundations, particularly in the form of prefabricated panels, can provide dry, energy-efficient basements that are relatively easy to finish. The use of wood rather than concrete reduces the amount of embodied energy by about 30 per cent.

As far as the internal layout and space division are concerned, there are several factors that should be considered. The open interior plan, for instance, is the most flexible and energy efficient, and uses fewer materials. Local heat gains and losses are more easily equalized, and energy demand for mechanical ventilation is reduced, since there are no obstructions to the air flow. Circulation paths and hallways, which receive marginal use, should be reduced to a minimum. Design for concentric or circular movement patterns are generally most efficient. Planning and resource efficiency can also be increased by grouping spaces with similar functions and environmental control needs. Pipe, duct, and conduit runs can be minimized by planning for close bathroom, kitchen, and laundry areas, preferably with back-to-back sinks.

Unpartitioned Space

The contemporary market is characterized by an unprecedented heterogeneity. The nuclear family of the 1950s still exists, of course, but it now represents a minority of all households (Statistics Canada, 2006). First-time homebuyers may also be a childless couple, single parents with children, two unrelated adults pooling their money to share the cost of a home, empty nesters, single adults, or parents with returned grown children. These groups have different space needs, resources, and priorities. For example people who work at home need offices; people with small children need nurseries; people with elderly parents need a guest room; and childless couples may prefer large, open spaces.

Different priorities have added significance in a small, inexpensive house since they lead to very different trade-offs. One way to accommodate these trade-offs is to leave part of the house unpartitioned—in effect, creating a loft space. Provision can be left for service hookup for a future bathroom. The homeowner could choose to use the loft as a single open space or build (or have built) partitions as required. Leaving the second floor unpartitioned not only helps to reduce the initial construction cost of the house, it also provides an adaptable home that can be completed according to the wishes, needs, and financial resources of the user (Friedman, 2002).

Do-It-Yourself Components

It has long been the European custom to provide homes without built-in closets; these components are provided later by the homeowner. This strategy has several advantages. First, the quality of these elements—which can vary considerably—is left up to the discretion of the occupants. They can choose a minimum amount of cabinetry and complete it when additional funds are available. Conversely, handy people might decide to do the carpentry themselves. There is an additional advantage to leaving the exact location of clothes closets to the homeowner, since it makes it possible to use space more efficiently by placing storage elements only where required.

Finally, there is an economic advantage to removing the cost of such finished carpentry from the construction cost of the home, and hence from the mortgage. Every dollar included in the house mortgage means two or three dollars expended by the mortgage holder. Home improvements made out of personal savings avoid this penalty. These cost considerations contribute to the economic aspect of the triple bottom line of sustainability.

Sustainable Materials

The building materials industry offers a wide range of sustainable choices to the home designer. Careful research is required to identify and select materials and components that are environmentally sound, energy-efficient, and perform efficiently over the life of the building. Using poor-quality windows or reducing insulation values, for example, is, in the long run, a poor strategy for saving, since the cost of future upgrading will be high.

Finishing materials account for a large percentage of the construction cost, and here one could take a different approach. It is possible to achieve significant savings through the use of less-expensive materials in cases where these can be easily and practically replaced with better-quality ones in the future. Vinyl tile, for example, is the least-expensive flooring and can be recycled and replaced with other products. The same applies to hollow-core doors, light fixtures, and interior paint (Meisel, 2010).

SUSTAINABLE COMMUNITY PLANNING

The design challenge for narrow row house developments is to make these communities, with squeezed space, pleasant and liveable environments for all inhabitants. The economic stigma attached to this type of low-cost housing, especially in established communities where the single-family detached home predominates, may be overcome if the denser configurations are designed with care and attention to factors that have been identified as important in achieving pleasant environments: parking and vehicular circulation, private and public open spaces, and unit and community identity (Kats, 2010). The author has developed patterns for planning and designing row house communities that address these three crucial factors.

Parking and Vehicular Circulation

New communities are almost always located on or beyond the urban fringe: the potential benefits of such developments are lower home prices due to reduced land costs and the relocation of the labour force closer to employment centres that have been moved out of the city cores. The disadvantages, however, include urban sprawl, higher transportation costs resulting from increased commuting distances to local amenities or downtowns, and a greater dependence on the car which aggravates the associated problems of automobile emissions, traffic congestion, and parking (Owen, 2009). Whether in an urban or suburban setting, the car is an inescapable reality in communities. Parking in a project of eighteen to twenty-four units per acre (forty-five to sixty units per hectare) can account for nearly 50 per cent of the total site area. The higher the density of a development, the greater will be the need for parking and vehicular circulation. It is, therefore, of utmost importance in high-density developments to deal with parking in an efficient and unobtrusive manner (Condon, 2010).

The visual effect of very wide roads, expanses of asphalt in large parking lots, and long series of repetitive garage doors can be reduced when parking is integrated into the landscaping to diminish its presence. Several smaller, screened parking areas, rather than one large lot, can be introduced and relegated to the rear of the units. When sites for sustainable communities are marginally located, parking areas can be used to separate the housing from unattractive adjacent elements. Paving lots with textured blocks instead of asphalt not only enhances their visual effect but also allows storm water to be more readily absorbed, thereby reducing the infrastructure required for storm runoff. Centralization of parking in an underground area to reduce paved surfaces with their inherent construction costs and storm drainage can enhance the pedestrian quality of the neighbourhood by discouraging the use of the car within the development.

Vehicular circulation in high-density communities often creates conflicts with pedestrian circulation and play areas for children. Narrowing street width and establishing a clear hierarchy of priorities reduces costs and also improves safety by slowing automobile speeds. Designing parking areas on the periphery of the developments leaves the core of the site vehicle-free (Cooper Marcus and Sarkissian, 1986). The use of speed bumps, cobblestone segments, and highly textured driving surfaces—such as stamped concrete—and the emphasis of entryways by the placement of gateways are useful strategies for controlling vehicular speed.

Private and Public Open Spaces

When personal space is diminished in a row house community, communal space takes on an added significance. In order to achieve successful public spaces and accommodate a variety of activities, it is essential to establish various levels of privacy by having a clear demarcation of boundaries through landscaping and hardscaping. Clear distinction between private and communal open areas is of the utmost importance. Lynch (1990) maintains, 'Careful manipulation of the edge and the access system is the key to design.' Cooper Marcus and Sarkissian (1986) stress that the delimitation of the private from the public in high-density developments, emphasizing the differentiation, is 'especially necessary where private open spaces abut onto a communal landscaped area.'

The front yard in the row house community provides both a transition zone between the private and public realms of the house and a link with the social fabric of the neighbourhood. A clear definition of front-yard ownership combined with its status as a location where residents can socially interact with their neighbours embodies this transition zone and link. Even when the building is pushed forward to create a larger backyard space, the identity of the front yard can be maintained with defining landscaping and/or fencing. The demarcation provided by the front entrance of the home can be achieved with a step, porch, or other carefully selected detailing. Where private open space in the front of the property is highly limited, balconies affixed to staggered units provide valuable outdoor areas. In the backyard, the importance of visual privacy is achieved with hedges, fences, screens, and trellises, which offer a sense of enclosure for personal activities and domestic chores. Where patios or decks are available, sliding glass doors provide a direct link to and extension of the kitchen or living room. The backyards themselves, although small, are enhanced by the variety obtained through creative landscaping and covered patio space, integrated with an available facility for the storage of outdoor equipment. Microclimate is another consideration in the design of backyards: shelter from the wind and snow and a careful balance of sun and shade provide orientations that extend seasonal use.

Any reduction in private open space can be compensated by large public open areas. Shared spaces such as neighbourhood greens, squares, and community gardens provide social gathering points and contribute to community identity (Van der Ryn and Calthorpe, 1986). The proximity of public open space to the row house units is important. 'Access is a matter of psychological, as well as physical, connection. An open space must seem to be close and easily reached, which is very much a matter of design' (Lynch, 1990).

Unit and Community Identity

The high degree of repetition required for economy to be maintained at the level of the individual unit can be alleviated by ensuring that a fixed number of variable elements can be combined in interesting ways to create the impression of diversity and personalization. Even though the designer may be restricted for reasons of economy to a limited number of exterior components, the rearrangement and combination of these features in a creative manner can lead to novel variations in the appearance of the individual units. At the unit level, a traditional approach is well suited to the design of modest, comfortable row houses. Tradition as a central concept in the community design is essential to the neotraditionalists Duany and Plater-Zyberk. Their philosophy involves the reuse, revitalization, and improvement of existing planning forms (Krieger, 1991).

Community identity is eventually established through evolution and a slow process of accretion, but the conditions for such a process to occur can be provided in the initial design. Cooper Marcus and Sarkissian (1986) maintain that the general exterior impression of the community 'significantly affects how residents feel about their homes, sometimes even how they feel about their own worthiness as human beings.' Their approach allocates a considerable proportion of the design budget to landscaping and site amenities, even at the expense of limiting the budget on interior finishes, in order to provide 'a quality milieu'. The planting of trees and variation in communal outdoor areas are vital considerations, while the sequencing of views creates interest at the scale of the overall site by punctuating the design to avoid dullness.

To further illustrate the above principles and the implementation of the Grow Home, a project is described below.

A SUSTAINABLE NEIGHBOURHOOD

The design of Quartier Jardin began when a development firm, which owned 102 acres (forty-one hectares) of land, wanted to build a community and approached the author. Located six miles (ten kilometres) northeast of Montreal on the edge of a small town, called L'Assomption, with a population of sixteen thousand, the proposed project offered an opportunity to consider a neighbourhood based on sustainable principles. Several programmatic attributes were combined to pose both a planning challenge and an opportunity. The developer foresaw that the majority of the clients would be young, first-time homebuyers from L'Assomption and other neighbouring towns. A significant segment of buyers were also expected to be made up of seniors who might trade a large, costly-to-maintain home. Both buyer groups, it was assumed, were likely to opt for a smaller, energy-efficient dwelling, which in turn can lead to the design of a denser community.

The project's size ran the risk of launching the town onto a sprawl path. Therefore, it became clear that appropriate strategy and better practice must be followed early on to avoid such an outcome. Another imposing issue was the site's location and natural conditions. The town served as a hub and provided services to the neighbouring farming communities. In fact, the property was a former farm. The flat terrain had hardly any flora left, and soil tests demonstrated that it was suitable for building low-rise residential structures. The southeast side of the site was bordered by the L'Assomption River, which was regarded by the developer as an important marketing feature and a draw. Also, the town's land-use planning prohibited building near the river and a strip of land along the bank had to remain as a park.

Site Planning

Planning a walkable community was a central design feature of the project. It began by including built features that would encourage walking and reduce reliance on cars. The location of the school in the neighbourhood's centre, an easy walking distance from each home, was meant to instil in young people the habit of biking or walking. The school was also designed to be used after hours and house a library and community centre. Introduction of commercial spaces on both the edge and at the heart of Quartier Jardin offered residents access to basic amenities. During the design phase, it was assumed that when the community matured, it would likely be the location of a convenience store or a café. To make walking safe, narrower streets were proposed as a car-slowing measure. The homes were clustered around loop roads, which further slow speeds. Whenever possible, pedestrian paths were introduced. It was also decided that the main avenues, those that cross the community in the east-west direction, would have clearly marked bicycle paths. One needs, however, to bear in mind that the harsh Canadian winter often restricts walking and biking activities for a significant part of the year. Therefore, orienting the street away from the prevailing wind and creating windbreaks was an important consideration if encouraging walking throughout the year was to be achieved.

Once the general objectives had been established, their integration in the planning began. Roads of different widths reflected anticipated traffic loads. Linking the new neighbourhood to the existing part was done through an entry boulevard and a square on the eastern end and an access from the west. To make efficient use of costly infrastructure, most of the streets have homes on both sides. Yet, in order not to create a wind tunnel effect, green open spaces have been placed at many of the street ends or intersections. Also, to enhance a better sense of human scale, taller buildings frame wider roads. Due to the high density, parking was judged to be a challenge. Several alternatives were used. Lower-cost homes had common parking lots placed behind them. To alleviate the negative impact of massive parking lots, smaller areas were placed on the northern edge in between groups of homes. For other dwellings, covered or enclosed parking was offered.

When the design of outdoor spaces began, it became abundantly clear, given the site's natural conditions and lack of vegetation or other topographic features, that green areas would have to be created. Here, too, the design process started by examining and deciding what kinds of open spaces would be offered and what their scale should be. It is common to see regional parks serve several new developments. Such an approach discourages physical activity among residents—primarily the young, as they need to drive or be driven to a relatively faraway place. The open space strategy in Quartier Jardin was to integrate the linear park along the L'Assomption riverbank into the community.

FIGURE 14.1   Site plan of Quartier Jardin showing a variety of housing types.

This approach also stood to draw residents of the older part of town into the new. The proposed school's open space, it was expected, would also be open for use by all citizens. Another phase of the public open space design was to place homes at the site's north end, in front of a narrow landscaped area, which provided a play space for toddlers and young children under the watch of parents (Figure 14.1).

Dwellings Design

The motivation of the design of homes in Quartier Jardin was a regard for societal, economic, and environmental issues. The choice and integration of the homes was seen as part of the overall approach to community planning. The need to mix unit types led to the consideration of both apartments and single-family homes totalling 889 units, with the majority being single-family attached homes. It was anticipated that seniors might be more inclined to reside in the lower floors of these units. To achieve a range of price tags, single-family detached, semidetached, and row housing were proposed. Flexibility was a prime objective in designing the units' interiors. A wide range of options, therefore, was offered, with a variety of kitchens and bathrooms. A built model of four different homes was constructed, and buyers could see and purchase only the items they needed and could afford.

The evolving needs of the household were also considered. The basement was left unfinished for residents who lacked the means at the time of occupancy to complete later. The space above the garage was also left for the homebuyers to arrange as per their space needs and lifestyle. Some residents, it was envisioned, would turn it into a home office, while others might house an older member of the family in that space. Therefore, the units were designed to be a single-family home or to serve two households. An extended family member could, for example, reside in an independent dwelling on the ground floor or in a room of their own in the combined space. By regarding a single structure

FIGURE 14.2   The Grow Home was used as the housing types in Quartier Jardin.

and, in fact, the entire community in a flexible, open-ended manner, a mix of ages, incomes, and uses was established.

Designers of high-density residential environments run the risk of diminishing the level of individual identity as expressed through the home. Creating diversity within overall harmony, therefore, was the strategy adopted in Quartier Jardin. Each cluster of homes was given its own identity with unique landscaping, architectural style, and brick colour. Yet, all the clusters conform to the same overall guiding principles. Also, in the design of each home, areas were left for personal intervention through a choice of roof tile colours, shade of door frame, door style, and landscaping (Figure 14.2).

The design of Quartier Jardin was a balancing act between a program set by a developer, the needs of the town, and the community's future residents. The effect of decisions made on sustainable developments is reflected upon below.

CONSIDERING SUSTAINABILITY ASPECTS

The Quartier Jardin site did not pose an environmental challenge. Built on former farmland, the developer's intention was to initiate a community with a higher density, which led to the integration of principles that contributed to the project's sustainability.

Nonetheless, the decision to build a compact community also had a significant and positive environmental effect. It lessened impact by avoiding construction of long service roads, hence reducing commuting time and decreasing pollution. Avoiding the building of vast common parking lots by tucking parking spaces between and behind homes left fewer areas that would visually stigmatize the neighbourhood, thereby fostering greater pride among its residents, especially with regard to the curb appeal of their community. A decree by the town's administration to prohibit construction along the riverbank was another step in ensuring that the much-needed forested area would contribute to the social and environmental integrity of the community. A common tendency is to offer such prime locations to builders of luxury estates or tall apartment buildings, which may block the view. This tendency was avoided here and so benefited the entire neighbourhood.

In addition, construction of smaller row housing helped save valuable natural resources. The amount of materials consumed in the construction of these homes was far less than conventional houses with similar usable floor space. The strategy of letting buyers select and pay for those components that they needed and could afford not only benefited the occupants monetarily but also reduced consumption of unnecessary goods. Placing the school at the heart of the community can also be regarded as contributing to a least negative impact effect as students do not have to be driven daily to and from school. Locating stores within the community can similarly reduce commuting.

Other design decisions contributed to the view of the project as a self-sustaining entity. The construction of taller homes and their attachment led to energy savings. Since hot air rises, lower floors keep upper ones warm. Also, heat loss in one dwelling is likely to find its way to adjacent units rather than escaping into the atmosphere. Orienting as many homes as possible to a southern exposure contributes to passive solar gain that stands to benefit the homes' energy management. Offering the option to buyers to have a home-based business helps with the home's purchase, as expenses associated with running an office can be deducted from income tax; additionally, working from home eliminates commuting. Having one parent work at home also helps families with toddlers and reduces the need for commuting to and from daycare. The building of smaller, affordable homes for young, first-time buyers and the elderly also contributes to the self-sustaining nature of the community. Rather than lose a segment of its young population and care for its elderly, the new project helps the city of L'Assomption house both. It is likely that older residents and their married children will reside in the project, thereby fostering supportive relations.

Locating public open spaces near homes also helps bond the community together. As 10 per cent of the development area was required to be allocated to green space, a decision not to concentrate this into a single area but to place small patches near clusters of homes encourages encounters among residents and physical activities by children and adults. Also, by allocating special pedestrian and cycle paths, reliance on cars is reduced and contribution to a healthy society achieved. The decision to have a higher-density development not only drew buyers to the project but also provides economic justification to the construction of commercial nodes. Walking to a corner store also helps reduce driving. In initial discussions about the school design, it was recognized that the building would also house the local library and community centre. Investment in a pub-lic building, therefore, would have additional benefits.

Many of the planning decisions were affected by a long-term view of the project and the needs of its occupants. The designs of the homes were perhaps the best manifestation of such an approach. Regarding the dwellings and, in fact, the entire community as a con-tinuously changing entity contributed to its sustainability. Occupants can complete and modify their homes as needs arise rather than relocate. The design of narrow roads also benefits the community in the long run. Not only were funds saved initially but savings on repair and maintenance throughout the project's life will also be made. Less land allocated to streets also reduced sprawl and saved on pollution caused by extensive commuting.

The tendency is often to assume that the mark of a sustainable development is its em-phasis on environmental components. Quartier Jardin demonstrates that by considering society, economy, and environment as an interrelated system, contributions can be made to each of these elements while benefiting the whole.

REFERENCES

Carpenter, W. (2009), *Modern Sustainable Residential Design: A Guide for Design Professionals,* Wiley: Hoboken, NJ.

Condon, P. (2010), *Seven Rules for Sustainable Communities: Design Strategies for the Post-Carbon World,* Island Press: Washington, D.C.

Cooper Marcus, C. and Sarkissian, W. (1986), *Housing as if People Mattered: Site Design Guide-lines for Medium-Density Family Housing,* University of California Press: Berkeley.

Friedman, A. (2001), *The Grow Home,* McGill-Queen's University Press: Montreal.

Friedman, A. (2002), *The Adaptable House: Designing for Choice and Change,* McGraw-Hill: New York.

Friedman, A. (2007), *Sustainable Residential Developments: Design Principles for Green Communi-ties,* McGraw-Hill: New York.

Kats, G. (2010), *Greening Our Built Environment: Costs, Benefits, and Strategies,* Island Press: Washington, D.C.

Krieger, A. (1991), 'Since (and Before) Seaside', in Krieger, A. and Lennertz, W. (eds), *Andres Duany and Elizabeth Plater-Zyberk: Towns and Town-Making Principles,* Harvard University Graduate School of Design, Rizzoli: New York, pp. 9–16.

Lynch, K. (1990), 'The Openness of Open Space', in Banerjee, T. and Southworth, M. (eds), *City Sense and City Design: Writings and Projects of Kevin Lynch,* MIT Press: Cambridge, MA, pp. 396–412.

Meisel, A. (2010), *LEED Materials: a Resource Guide to Green Building,* Princeton Architectural Press: New York.

Owen, D. (2009), *Green Metropolis: Why Living Smaller, Living Closer, and Driving Less Are the Keys to Sustainability,* Penguin: New York.

Statistics Canada (2006), 'CYB Overview 2006: Population and Demography', <http://www41.statcan.ca/2007/3867/ceb3867_000_e.htm> accessed August 11, 2009.

U.S. Green Building Council (USGBC) (2007), 'An Introduction to LEED', <www.usgbc.org/Display Page.aspx?CategoryID = 19> accessed August 11, 2009.

Van der Ryn, S. and Calthorpe, P. (1986), *Sustainable Communities,* Sierra Club: San Francisco.

15

Design for Territorial Ecology and a New Relationship between City and Countryside: The Experience of the Feeding Milano Project

EZIO MANZINI AND ANNA MERONI

This collaborative research is presented in two parts, 'Territorial Design' by Ezio Manzini and 'Feeding Milano' by Anna Meroni.

TERRITORIAL DESIGN

Skills and Abilities

The topic of this chapter is social community building (Magnaghi, 2000) and what design does, and could do, to collaborate in this vast, complex co-evolutionary process. Before we go into the merits of this process, however, it is useful to reflect briefly on what we mean by design in this context and especially on its passage from being the most delocalized of design disciplines to its current, increasingly frequent presentation as a mix of more specialized skills and abilities that are applicable to the particular localized requirements of territorial designing.

So let us go back a step. Design was born as a mix of skills and abilities directed towards the conception and development of industrial products, meaning those products that were thought up for mass production according to the production models dominant in the last century, with no particular consideration for the place where they were conceived and produced, their use and consumption, or their end transformation into waste (or new resources). If that were still the normal procedure, design would have no role to play in the territorial processes we wish to talk about here. However, that is no longer how things are. Over the past two or three decades, the theory and practice of design have changed radically. Following evolutions in technology, economy and society as a whole, design is breaking away from the twentieth-century industrial production model, albeit not without some difficulty. So what we are talking about here is a mix of skills and abilities that can be applied to all fields of activity where human industrious-ness may find a voice and lead to feasible results (see the definition proffered by ICSID [International Council of Societies of Industrial Design], which states, 'The adjective *in-dustrial* put to design must be related to the term industry or in its meaning of sector of production or in its ancient meaning of *industrious activity*' [n.d.]). It follows therefore that design today is an activity where the object of design is more and more frequently not a product, but a service, a kind of social organization or, more generally, a process. This means that it is a system of people, things and places with a specific consistency and duration in time. It is a complex entity (because it includes human actors), and it is necessarily localized (in the sense that we cannot consider it independently of the place where it is set up).

This transfer of focus from product to process is a transformation largely brought about by design but to which design has also had to adapt, calling into question the very basis of its ethos and practice (Thackara, 2005; Manzini, 2009; Meroni and Sangiorgi, 2011), and in so doing, it has come up against territorial issues (Verwijnen and Karkku, 2004; Meroni, 2008a).

Projects and Processes

Everything that has traditionally represented the most stable and long-lasting dimension of territory is today entangled in a mesh of flows and dynamic artefacts. The traditional density and inertia of places seems to dissolve in a much more fluid socio-technical system (Castells, 1996; Bauman, 1998; Appadurai, 1990, 2001). In this fluid world, the quality and identity of places emerge as a result of design activities that impact on the place, generating processes that, by transforming the social, economic and cultural context, produce territory.

These processes are widely differing dynamic systems, but they are endowed with certain common traits: they have a clear sociocultural collocation (in other words, they are activities that take place in the true sense of the word); they have a time (the time of the interactions between the actors involved and between them and the things and the places of reference for that process). In addition, they are strategic activities where case by case the actors are defined according to the nature of the process itself and, above all, according to its ability to attract the partners required and get them to work together.

Up to now, the dominant outcome of this designing activity has been to trivialize and standardize places by turning them into products, into something that can be conceived, created, sold and consumed as a commodity (Augé, 1995; Bryman, 2004). The diffusion of shopping centres, gated communities, theme parks and tourist villages is the result of territory-building projects and processes that are leading to the destruction of the territory itself by erasing its history, identity and wealth in terms of social resources and common goods. However, the same logic in territory-building projects and processes can also lead us in a totally different direction, towards a new territorial ecology, where the design projects we are talking about may lead to multifarious processes capable of dialoguing and working together.

Design and Processes

Design has certainly played an important role in the conception and development of destructive territorial projects, which we have called 'transformation of places into products'. This role is clear and obvious in the planning and furnishing of spaces. However, it is also and above all apparent in the planning of services, communication and the creation and promotion strategies on which such destructive processes are based.

This role of design as a destructive agent, actively promoting the transformation of places into products, is not the only tale to be told today. In the complexity of territorial experience over the past few years, we can also recognize cases where the role of design has been completely the opposite—cases where design has operated positively in the regeneration of places or, to use our terminology, in the production of a new territorial ecology.

In many experiences that we have undergone so far, we can see that territory building through projects and the resulting territorial ecology can be advanced by using the skills and tools proper to design. Very often this has happened without these skills and abilities being acknowledged as design as such (we can refer to this as implicit design). In a growing number of cases, however, the presence of design is explicitly recognized (and appreciated). One example is the Feeding Milano (Nutrire Milano) project promoted by Slow Food Italia, the INDACO Department of the Politecnico di Milano and the Università di Scienze Gastronomiche.[1] This is a framework project aiming to redefine and enliven the relationship between city (Milano) and countryside (the Parco Sud di Milano) through an open series of projects and processes, three of which are setting up a farmers' market in Milano; rebuilding the bread chain on a local basis; and reorganizing agricultural and distributional activities to supply zero-kilometre fresh vegetables (Meroni et al., 2009).

Projects like this, operating with a similar approach to the theme of new relationships between city and countryside, can be found in many other places at an international level. For example, a project is under way on an island near Shanghai: the Chong Ming Eco-Community Project (Chong Ming Eco-Community Project, 2009). The general aim and procedure of this project, promoted by the Tektao studio and the Tongji University of Shanghai, are similar to those of the Feeding Milano project.

A similar arrangement, addressing the social and economic dynamization of regions in difficulty, has been adopted by the British Design Council in two inspiring territorial projects: Design of the Time 2007 or Dott07 (Dott07, 2007) and Design of the Time Cornwall (Dott Cornwall, 2010), where the general aim is being pursued through a series of projects emerging from careful attention to local demand. The local projects in Dott07 are diverse and tackle areas such as urban agriculture, energy saving, health and prevention and services for the elderly.

Another example addressing urban dynamization is a project in New York by the DESIS (Design for Social Innovation and Sustainability) Lab Parsons, the New School for Design, funded by the Rockefeller Foundation. The name of the project is significant: Amplify: Creative and Sustainable Lifestyles in the Lower East Side (Amplify Creative Communities, 2012). The project is located in a neighbourhood in Manhattan (the Lower East Side), and its method is to start with existing cases of social creativity and use various strategic and communication design tools to make them more visible, thus turning them into catalyzers for other more widespread territorial initiatives (Staszowski, 2010).

Still on the theme of urban dynamization, another example is the Living Lab promoted by the University of Malmo in Sweden (MEDEA 2012). In this case, the general theme is addressed through local projects orientated towards the social integration of the immigrant population, proposed as an extensive and creative application of the principles of participatory design (Bjorgvinsson et al., 2010).

In view of these examples and others, the common trait that emerges is a design approach that has various levels. At one level, there is the framework project with oversight of a series of local projects, which are developed in relative autonomy. The framework project oversight allows the creation of a synergy between the individual local projects within a general vision. This approach generates a flexible, adaptable, large-scale project that over time blossoms in a multiplicity of small-scale projects: social micro-experiments each with their own local and social specificity. Clearly this is totally coherent with the new territorial ecology perspective we have been talking about (Landry, 2000; Jegou and Manzini, 2008; Meroni, 2008a; Bjorgvinsson et al., 2010).

This way of designing, design for territorial ecology, breaks down into a series of activities, the most important of which are fostering convergence of actors around a shared vision (scenario design); organizing this shared vision into different workable initiatives (strategic design) and design the requires service interfaces (service design); and publicizing and setting up effective communication for the entire process (communication design). At the same time, activation of the required skills and abilities in the general framework of territorial ecology projects also requires a radical change in the position and role of designers in the designing process. Indeed, in all these projects designers must work with a variety of other social actors who, though not design professionals, are all designers in their own way (Cottam and Leadbeater, 2004; von Hippel, 2004; Leadbeater, 2008; Brown and Wyatt, 2010). In other words, design for territorial ecology requires designers to realize that what they are seeking to encourage is a complex, collaborative design process and that their role is to use their special design capabilities to enable a much wider group of social actors to develop their own design capabilities.

Application Fields

To place all this into a wider perspective, it may be useful to outline some of the fields of activity in which design for territorial ecology could best show its potential, along with other disciplines (Manzini, 2010).

Environmental Technology

These are activities on the rise throughout the world. Their positive, concrete application requires the activation of adequate territorial projects (Pauli, 1996, 2010; Pehnt et al., 2006; Hopkins, 2009). These environmental technologies are, by definition, bound up with the nature of places and their resources. This puts them in a relationship with the local that may be either negative or positive depending on the peculiarities of their various applications. On this ground, and on the proposals that may be put forward, design may and should have much to say and do in utilizing its full range of disciplines: from product design to service and strategic design.

The Diffusion of Networks

This is an over-discussed dynamic reality. However, its impacts on society and territory are, for the most part, yet to be discovered (Bauwens, 2007; Tapscott and Williams, 2007). The fact is that, while its dominant role is one of deterritorializing and dematerializing, there is another dynamic emerging in the opposite direction: that of networks and digital services as catalysts and organizers, in the physical world, of scattered social resources (Rheingold, 2002; Leadbeater, 2008; Baek, 2010). Of course, this tendency towards using networks to valorize local resources does not automatically lead to our immediate focus of interest, and it presents several contradictions. However, it also has great potential, and it can offer much to design (especially to the design of services, interaction and communication).

Distributed Systems

This is another growing phenomenon, with great potential for the purposes of developing a new territorial economy. The adjective 'distributed' here indicates the nature of a system in which different parts carry out activities autonomously, on a local level, while they are at the same time connected together. Consequently, they are able collectively to create vast flexible, adaptable systems that are able to impact enormously on the general situation. Internationally successful cases such as the Internet and distributed computing are distributed systems, as are promising solutions such as smart grid and distributed power generation (a multiplicity of interlinked small energy-producing systems). There are also great technical possibilities, and concrete financial interests, in developing a distributed manufacturing that could offer lighter, more recommendable solutions than those offered by the stupidity of contemporary globalized production

(Fiksel, 2003; Johansson et al., 2005; Biggs et al., 2010). In this framework, the idea, now accepted worldwide, of the workability of food networks based on short chains and zero-mile food is another, and in this case undoubtedly very positive, example of a distributed system with the economic and technological, as well as political and cultural, prospects that such systems open up (Petrini, 2007). As far as design is concerned, it is obvious that distributed systems call for a vast design programme: an entire world of products, services and infrastructure must be thought up and relocalized in the light of this new possibility.

Social Economy

This is perhaps the least observed and least discussed of the trends referred to here, yet it may be the most significant. There is no widely accepted definition of social economy, but its meaning is familiar to anyone who deals with territory, community and sustainability. Apart from any formal definition, it is used to indicate an economy characterized by an ecology of different economies according to the actors in question (market, state, foundations, active citizens and so on) (Mulgan, 2006; DEMOS, 2007; Meroni, 2007; Murray, 2009; Murray et al., 2010). Nowadays, all over the world, it is this complex economy that enables the activation of most projects of social and environmental interest, and it is in this economic framework that we find all the bottom-up activities that we often refer to when talking about local social innovation. We must also add that this trend, which is so important for a new territorial ecology, requires a complexity of projects to be articulated in a system. In addition, as far as design is concerned, it calls for the special awareness and sensitivity, skills and abilities of design for social innovation (DESIS, 2010).

FEEDING MILANO—A DESIGN FOR TERRITORIAL ECOLOGY PROJECT

A Project with and for the Community

The project, Feeding Milano: Energy for Change (Nutrire Milano. Energie per il cambiamento), mentioned above, is an example of territorial ecology design. Though making no pretences to generalize the model, which is, by definition, locally specific, it very effectively encapsulates a series of methodological and context conditions that enable us to reflect on this way of interpreting and undertaking design today.

Feeding Milano: Energy for Change is an action research project funded by local institutions (Fondazione Cariplo, a bank foundation with the Comune di Milano and Provincia di Milano) and developed by a partnership, as earlier mentioned, between Slow Food Italia, the Politecnico di Milano and the Università di Scienze Gastronomiche. On the design side, it is led by a research group of service, communication and strategic designers from the INDACO Department of the Politecnico di Milano.

The project investigates how design for social innovation can contribute to sustainable place development by creating a local foodshed that serves to connect local food production in peri-urban areas (and in particularly in the huge agricultural park bordering the south of the town, the Agricultural Park South) with its consumers in the towns (Simeone and Cantù, 2011), giving rise to a local food community (Irving et al., 2007, p. 21).

With a planned duration of several years, the project's ambition is to conclude with the building of a service network for the production and distribution of zero-mile agro-food products throughout the peri-urban countryside and the city of Milan (Meroni et al., 2009). Its objective is to build a sustainable agro-food model also coherent with the intentions of World Expo 2015 to be held in Milan and dedicated to sustainable food. By its very nature, it is difficult to define a formal conclusion, and it may be better to describe it as the start-up of a systemic process, rather than the designing of a desirable state. Or, more clearly stated, it is the design of a continuous and in-progress sequence of desirable states evolving towards a scenario. It therefore conforms to the characteristic of working on a process rather than a product and consequently opens the difficult question of planning an exit strategy for the initiative. In other words, if by project we mean an activity where some designers apply their research and innovation capabilities to a determined issue to identify and develop solutions, then this activity requires Feeding Milano to have a totally immersive and participatory approach. This means the full and continuous presence of designers in the large community involved in the project: producers, associations, institutions and citizens. This presence must not only be professional, but it must also be motivational to the same degree; that is, it must be comparable to that of an activist capable of leading the community and supporting it with technical and professional skills. This is the substance of what we call Community Centred Design (Meroni, 2011): an approach that must provide for the presence of designers in the community for long enough to activate the particular initiative or initiatives and enable the designers to pursue their path of innovation and implement the project, visualizing it as a common, shared aim; that is, adopting a strategic design perspective (Meroni, 2008b).

This way of operating opens the question of continuity-discontinuity in the contribution and presence of designers in the local communities and social enterprises, which are the main interlocutors in these initiatives but are usually not equipped to receive such professionalism in a structural way. However, we can interpret the diffusion and the most recent evolutions of Living Labs and agencies specialized in participation as an answer to these changed conditions and an attempt to support these relatively unstructured, scattered social actors, with professional skills (Bjorgvinsson et al., 2010).

Let us take a more detailed look at the Feeding Milano project to spur and deepen the reflections we have started.

The Scenario

Shortening the food chain by demediated services, fostering multifunctionality in the systems, and implementing collaborative practices is the key concept of the project,

which aims at generating tangible shifts and perceivable changes in the way farmers and citizens relate. More specifically, it intends to lead producers towards more
sustainable production systems, offering a greater guarantee of profitability due to a
wider, more solid and more organized demand via direct sales to a diversified consumer
base. The project also aims to encourage new purchasing habits that are more advanta-
geous from a quality/price-point of view, more attentive towards health and the environment, richer on a relational level, but undoubtedly different from the usual trip to the
supermarket. Together, these actions imply the use of seasonal food requiring preparation in the home.

The main actions of the project are as follows:

- supporting existing best practices and resources in the agricultural field;
- activating resources that are as yet unvalued or are no longer used; and
- creating new services.

These actions lead to a general framework of initiatives that forms the reference
scenario of Feeding Milano. This scenario includes a collection of services that work
in synergy (i.e., economies of scale and scope as well as complementarities) and that
are mainly carried out on a collaborative basis. They link the contributions of different subjects into a system, partially integrating already existing initiatives and
activating new resources. Conviviality is the underlying principle of this scenario.
Conviviality is not just about eating together, but it is actually about creating pleasurable and collaborative relationships in every activity of life. Food, in Latin cultures,
means conviviality, pleasure, taking care of others, loving and being loved. Slow food
is actually not so much about cooking and eating slower as about connecting people
so as to regain the meaning of rituals related to food in everyday life. And it is about
sustainability.

We can see food as the most powerful and natural tool for conviviality, since by conviviality we mean a condition of sociability open to the contribution of all kinds of individuals: autonomous, creative, cheerful intercourse among people.

The project plays on the fact that conviviality may convince various actors to reconsider their own choices towards industrial production and sales systems, favouring
elements of relational value and trust. This emerges clearly from the description of the
various services that constitute the scenario and that encapsulate the meaning of the
planning approach to projects.

Finally, Feeding Milano seeks to become a scenario of city-supported agriculture,
an advanced system of community-supported agriculture that aims to involve a wider
array of subjects, proposing services with fewer access barriers and commitment conditions for participants, whether they are producers or consumers—as compared to the
virtuous models of promising practices existing in cities today. To this purpose, the rationalization of certain practices—the standardization and simplification of variables of
the offering, synergy and sharing of technical and communicative infrastructure—are

seen here as paths towards making the activities more fluid and optimizing them in terms of organization and logistics, while the quality of products and interactions, relational richness, the social and aesthetic value of contexts are considered as indispensable to the intrinsic and convivial value of the scenario. Multifunctionality in the production and distribution systems is the strategy pursued to achieve these objectives, since it transmits that natural richness and diversity of practice (agricultural, on one hand, and supply, on the other) that creates synergy, enriching the quality of work and experience.

The Service Network

The general scenario for Feeding Milano can be seen locally through a network of services conceived to bring about synergy and reach various targets. It forms a platform of interconnections between services and context.

The Earth Market

Launched in December 2009, this is a farmers' market for local producers, organized according to the principles of Slow Food, where products are 'good, clean and fair' (Petrini, 2007). The participants, together with some guests who offer special products in rotation (Slow Presidia, ethnic communities, regional specialties), come from within a radius of twenty-five miles. As well as direct sales, there are didactic workshops and taste laboratories offering cultural information and practical knowledge about food issues. Street kitchens and convivial tables enable visitors to stay and eat together. At present, it takes place every month on Saturday mornings and in an urban public park, but the intention is for it to become weekly soon (moving from neighbourhood to neighbourhood) as a continuous service with a greater impact on the Milanese context.

A series of unique characteristics distinguishes the Earth Market from similar initiatives: it is a multifunctional service—that is, it diversifies its offerings, which enables it to optimize certain logistic and promotional activities, on the one hand, and offer visitors a rich and convivial experience, on the other (Illich, 1973) (see Figure 15.1).

This translates into the pleasure of indulging in the activities, socializing and enjoying the market, which triggers radically different behaviour from that at the supermarket or conventional markets, where speed and efficiency are the rule. The difference in the mood of the participants can be clearly felt; in this way, the Earth Market is a place where one can rediscover the deeper value of food and gastronomic culture, where they become a talking point in a typically Italian way of behaving. Food meanings and rituals associated with eating together and conviviality come out in a big way in a place that becomes dense with significance for the richness of the stories that intermingle there.

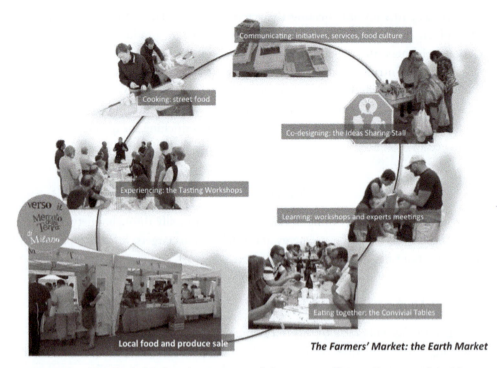

FIGURE 15.1 The Earth Market: An overview of the service offering. Courtesy of A. Meroni, Politecnico di Milano.

Ideas Sharing Stall

A distinctive feature of the Earth Market is its *Ideas Sharing Stall,* a stand where the designers of Feeding Milano discuss emerging ideas for new services with visitors and participants, asking for comments and inviting creative contributions spurred by ad hoc conversation topics. These are semi-finished ideas that help stimulate design thinking with the community in accordance with the participatory model, and that enable the structure and organization of new services to be roughed out or refined as we go along.

The stand is really the first step that the design community takes from theory to practice, by starting up activities through the drafting of pre-prototypes with potential users. This is the trigger or starter of what we call 'design experiments' and it is, effectively, a visible design bureau in the Feeding Milano community for enabling participatory design. It provides a tangible presence for design and is one of the immersive situations in which the community-centred design approach takes shape. At present, it constitutes one of the more visible manifestations of design in the project (see Figure 15.2).

The Ideas Sharing Stall is thus the methodological junction for a work approach that is based on the rapid passage from design to implementation, geared to make things happen quickly in order to become effective and credible within a vast community of actors (Simeone and Corubolo, 2011). It enables designers to activate a community of intents and actions where their professional, human presence is as necessary as that of the

FIGURE 15.2 The Earth Market: The Ideas Sharing Stall. Courtesy of A. Meroni, Politecnico di Milano.

service providers, the producers, Slow Food and the other participants in the project. Through this stand pass all the other services that Feeding Milano designs.

The Farmer's Food Box

This is a weekly delivery service of local vegetables and fruit. It was first prototyped in June 2011. The box is delivered to users at a collection point convenient to them, which acts as a local order collection platform. This may be a neighbourhood shop, a bar, a cultural centre, a school, an office or some other habitual transit point. The service is organized in this way both to optimize costs and logistics and to trigger virtuous dynamics at the collection point. It is therefore based on a relational principle that calls for direct, personal contact between those involved, and, unlike other similar home-delivery services, it is conceived as a neighbourhood service.

The back-office of the service—that's to say, all the operations needed to provide the service to the user that take place out of view—works on a similar logic: producers deliver the produce to country hubs where it is sorted and placed into the boxes. This forms a system where relatively few hubs gather produce from various farmers and supply different collection points, determining a heterogeneous assortment of boxes, each depending on the peculiarities of the producers supplying one hub. While this kind of organization is undoubtedly positive because it implies the creation of a collaborative producer network, it also reveals the difficulty of maintaining a service standard. Such a standard is essential to guarantee the reliability and quality of the service. To solve this difficulty, the service design element of the project is now evolving towards creating a peer-to-peer mutual learning network.

Pick-Your-Own-Produce

This is a do-it-yourself service where consumers pick their own fruit (we plan to add vegetables in future) on the farms. Already at the experimental stage on some farms, the project aims to raise the quality and effectiveness of this practice and to create the technical conditions for it to spread in other farms. It does so by introducing ad hoc cultivation (where the layout of cultivation is carefully vetted to facilitate safe harvesting) and programmed visits.

The Collaborative Supermarket: SuperCo-Op

This is a supermarket based on a cooperative principle to distribute high quality, fresh, local, organic produce at prices that are good value, thanks to work carried out mainly by customer/members. The customers, who periodically lend a hand in various roles, basically run the supermarket. The project uses the Park Slope Food Co-op in Brooklyn (Park Slope Food Co-op, 2012) and the People's Supermarket in London as models (People's Supermarket, 2012). Known as SuperCo-Op, it is now being considered as part of the Feeding Milano project after an initial exploration by a Service Design Studio at the Design School of the Politecnico. The complexity of the activities involved requires a far more detailed explanation than is possible here; however, it is useful to mention two aspects. The first is the need to identify an appropriate business model, based on collaborative principles that are workable both by business people (producers and managers) and private citizens. The second is the desire to create a situation that is attractive and welcoming in the Milanese context, that is capable of uniting functional activities (shopping) with relational, recreational activities (eating and spending time together) in a neighbourhood context. From a producer's point of view, the organization of the SuperCo-Op could benefit from numerous synergies with the Earth Market and the Farmer's Food Box, and would address a partially different target depending on time of year and purchasing habits.

The Local Bread Chain

Since December 2010, there has been a pilot production of local grain for bread alongside the aforementioned services. More recently, with a view to renovating an antique mill to grind the flour, bread-making has begun, again as a pilot project. The service provides an opportunity to rethink the way in which bread is offered and consumed in the Milanese context. From a staple food, bread has become a complementary addition, which requires new forms and circumstances to find its place and importance in diet and shopping habits.

Zero-Mile Tourism

Together with services directly geared to the production and sale of food products, the Feeding Milano project is working on the capability of farms to offer hospitality and accommodation to proximity tourists and more. Essentially, it is a question of reinforcing the multifunctional nature of the farms, thus building value for them through complementary or supplementary production cycles (e.g., agritourism and catering, on one hand, and the opportunity for city dwellers to enjoy the local countryside and its products, on the other). Once again, the logic is one of conviviality and the enrichment of relational experiences. The organization is basically entrusted to the visitor on a do-it-yourself principle. The project's aim is to create platforms that enable city dwellers to self-manage various initiatives ranging from picnics to cycling, with the support of infrastructure and activities provided by the farms but without overloading the farmers with extra work. An initial series of activities has been designed and prototyped as a pilot project by students in the design laboratories of the Master of Product Service System Design programme and the Alta Scuola Politecnica at the Politecnico di Milano.

A digital web platform (www.nutriremilano.it) has also been developed to facilitate the realization of these services, to enable direct contact with users, to bring together supply and demand and to gather opinions and reactions. Under continual development, the web platform was created with the intention of supporting activities both on the front end and backstage, in a way that is simple and transparent. In particular, the idea is to make technology disappear. The digital platform, together with traditional emails and telephone calls, is actually just one component of a larger human platform that encourages the last mile (the touch-point between the individuals) to be a human mile and, therefore, relationships to happen according to the philosophy of the project.

A Modus Operandi

The Feeding Milano project can be seen as an attempt by one community to develop a form of territorial ecology by creating a sustainable foodshed. In this sense, it is an experimental platform for a variety of activity models and modus operandi. Built on a network of trust and sympathy among producers, consumers and designers, it is a tool for practicing our capacity, as a society, to design change and to exercise a culture of continuous transformation and self-critique that involves citizens, farmers, academics and students.

As a whole, the project assumes and potentially exemplifies the possibilities of local distributed systems, which must find efficiency and effectiveness in collaborative strategies. In doing so, it proposes an unprecedented mix of organizational and economic models—public and private, profit and non-profit, professional and amateur—and requires a profound rethinking of the organization and structuring of services.

Finally, since Feeding Milano is a relational platform, it calls for the support of a digital network designed according to the philosophy of the project—that is, a system mainly based on personal, human relationships as the ultimate contact.

We like the idea of this human platform having a malleable quality that makes reciprocal understanding and respect possible, while increasing the user's autonomy. Referring to Illich, we can thus consider the capacity to promote autonomy in itself to be a fundamental characteristic of convivial tools (1973). As Tim Brown has suggested, this is a shift from designing for the community to designing with the community, and finally to letting communities design 'by themselves' (2009, p. 59).

In Feeding Milano, we can see how the concept of conviviality also informs the practice of designing. Emphasis is on the values of being there, spending time within the community and participating in the first-person in the process of change. Empathy, sympathy and collaboration are therefore the key words in design practice today. They call for skills that result from the combination of service design and social intelligence. Community-centred design requires two kinds of competences: one relating to the capacity to gain knowledge about the community and the habitat where it lives; the other relating to the capacity to creatively collaborate with non-designers. The former results in field immersion, so as to pursue a direct experience of the contexts and develop empathy with the community. The latter requires applying designer creativity in a slightly different way. Feeding Milano offers the chance to apply both.

Deep diving into a creative community has the purpose of gaining insights, of understanding behaviours, and the crucial network of values and relationships that influences the structure of the community so as to orient any subsequent design actions to make these values emerge or become more tangible. This way of looking at communities has much to do with what Buchanan (2001) defined as human-centred design, meaning respect for the quality of human culture and dignity that can be expressed through products, services and solutions. Moreover, immersion allows designers to gain insights into innovative behaviours, opportunities and unexpressed needs that can bring about truly radical innovation. Finally, immersion is the most effective way to develop an empathic relation with people: empathic design is an approach where designers move into real contexts, so that projects benefit from the emotions of both users and designers (Leonard and Rayport, 1997). Feeding Milano is teaching us that immersion must be followed and complemented by proactivism, which implies a very deep integration into groups and contexts. This means helping collaborative design practices to happen by fostering conversations around systemic changes exemplified at the level of everyday experiences as well as materializing shifts in tangible lifestyles and business opportunities (Meroni and Sangiorgi, 2011). Most of all, it means being good at motivating the community. In our direct experience, empathy is not only a welcome condition that can enrich the project, but it is the only possible precondition to deeply understand a community and to learn something about how to activate people, to spur them to take action and collaborate in doing things.

CONCLUSIONS

We are discovering that, contrary to what was thought in the past, the joint phenomena of globalization and networking have given rise once again to the local dimension.

A local that is now something very removed is meant—as opposed to what was understood in the past—and that combines the specific features of places and their communities with the new phenomena generated and supported worldwide by globalization and by cultural, socio-economic interconnection. Today, these phenomena are often characterized by extremely negative tendencies that, on the one hand, swing between traditionalist stances, supporting local interests, and reactionary positions and, on the other hand, that are inclined towards turning what remains of traditions and landscapes into a show for tourist purposes (a kind of tourist-oriented Disneyization of the local, which is just another side of the standardizing aspect of globalization, from which there is the desire to break away).

Fortunately, a closer look provides more interesting and promising cases. Local communities that invent unprecedented cultural activities, forms of organization and economic models represent an interesting perspective. For example, they provide ways of being and doing that are characterized by the balance between being rooted (rooted in a place and in the community related to that place) and being open (open to global flows of ideas, information, people, things and money). This balance is quite delicate and is the territorial ecology we have referred to here; that is, a territorial ecology that generates a new sense of place and culture—a place and local community that are no longer (almost) isolated entities but junctions of a network, points of connection among short networks. This territorial ecology generates and regenerates the local social and production fabric, as well as large networks, that connect that place and that community with the rest of the world.

This new territorial ecology is already appearing at the interfaces between cities and countryside (in peri-urban areas), driven by a wave of social innovation that has been touching both urban spaces and countryside. This is generating unprecedented food communities where multifunctional farming, demediated food chains and new urban communities merge. In this chapter, the Feeding Milano project has been presented as a good example of this emerging trend. This example, along with other similar ones in the world, can be considered as the application of an innovative design process: a planning-by-projects approach capable of promoting and sustaining a new territorial ecology.

All topics discussed above require a large and articulated research programme, which need not be developed by designers only. Nevertheless, designers have an important role to play. And relevant design knowledge has to be produced—specific scenarios, solutions, and tools—in order to facilitate new designing networks and their co-design processes.

In practical terms, who could drive this programme? Quite obviously, the whole design community and all the other design-oriented actors should play their part. And, among them, design schools could provide a major contribution (intended here as all the design-oriented universities and colleges). Thanks to the students' enthusiasm and the teachers' experiences, design schools are—or at least, could be—active laboratories where complex problems could be tackled, new visions generated and new tools defined and tested. In other words, these schools, or part of them, could become active and produce meaningful contributions in an open and free way.

REFERENCES

Amplify Creative Communities (2012), <http://www.amplifyingcreativecommunities.net> accessed April 7, 2012.

Appadurai, A. (1990), 'Disjuncture and Difference in the Global Cultural Economy', <http://www.intcul.tohoku.ac.jp> accessed February 10, 2012.

Appadurai, A. (ed.) (2001), *Globalization,* Duke University Press: Durham, NC.

Augé, M. (1995), *Non-Places: Introduction to an Anthropology of Supermodernity,* Varso: London.

Baek, J. S. (2010), 'A Socio-Technical Framework for Collaborative Services', PhD thesis, Politecnico di Milano, Milano.

Bauman, Z. (1998), *Globalization,* Sage Publications: London.

Bauwens, M. (2007), 'Peer to Peer and Human Evolution', <p2pfoundation.net> accessed February 10, 2012.

Biggs, C., Ryan, C. and Wisman, J. (2010), *Distributed Systems. A Design Model for Sustainable and Resilient Infrastructure,* VEIL Distributed Systems Briefing Paper N3, University of Melbourne, Melbourne.

Bjorgvinsson, E., Ehn, P. and Hillgren, P. A. (2010), 'Participatory Design and Democratizing Innovation', *PDC Participatory Design Conference 2010,* November 29–December 3: pp. 41–50.

Brown, T. (2009), *Change by Design,* Harper Collins: New York.

Brown, T. and Wyatt, J., (2010), 'Design Thinking for Social Innovation', *Stanford Social Innovation Review,* winter: pp. 29–37.

Bryman, A. E. (2004), *The Disneyization of Society,* Sage Publications: London.

Buchanan, R. (2001), 'Human Dignity and Human Rights: Thoughts on the Principles of Human-Centered Design', *Design Issues,* vol. 17, no. 3, summer: pp. 35–39.

Castells M. (1996), *The Rise of the Network Society. The Information Age: Economy, Society and Culture,* vol. 1, Blackwell: Oxford.

Chong Ming Eco-Community Project (2009), <http://chongmingtao.blogspot.com> accessed April 7, 2012.

Cottam, H. and Leadbeater, C. (2004), *Health: Co-Creating Services,* Design Council—RED unit: London.

Dott Cornwall (2010), <http://www.dottcornwall.com> accessed April 7, 2012.

Dott07 (2007), <http://www.designcouncil.org.uk/our-work/challenges/Communities/Dott-07/What-was-Dott-07/> accessed April 7, 2012.

DEMOS (2007), 'The Collaborative State. London: DEMOS', <http://www.demos.co.uk/publications/collaborativestatecollection> accessed February 10, 2012.

DESIS Design for Social Innovation and Sustainability Network (2010), <http://www.desis-network.org> accessed February 10, 2012.

Fiksel, J. (2003), 'Designing Resilient, Sustainable Systems', *Environmental Science and Technology,* vol. 37: pp. 5330–9.

Hopkins, R. (2009), *The Transition Handbook: From Oil Dependency to Local Resilience,* Green-Books: Totnes, UK.

ICSID (n.d.), 'Definition of Design', <http://www.icsid.org/about/about/articles31.htm> accessed February 10, 2012.

Illich, I. (1973), *Tools for Conviviality,* Harper and Rowe: New York.

Irving, J., Milano S., Minerdo, B. and Novellini, G. (2007), *Terra Madre: 1,600 Food Communities,* Slow Food Editore: Bra, Italy.

Jegou, F. and Manzini, E., (2008), *Collaborative Services, Social Innovation and Design for Sustainability,* Polidesign: Milano.

Johansson, A., Kish, P. and Mirata, M. (2005), 'Distributed Economies: A New Engine for Innovation', *The Journal of Cleaner Production,* vol. 13: pp. 971–9.

Landry, C. (2000), *The Creative City,* Earthscan Publication: London.

Leadbeater, C. (2008), *We-Think,* Profile Books: London.

Leonard, D. and Rayport, J. (1997), 'Spark Innovation through Empathic Design', *Harvard Business Review,* November–December: pp. 102–13.

Magnaghi, A. (2000), *Il progetto locale,* Bollati Boringhieri: Torino.

Manzini, E. (2009), 'New Design Knowledge', *Design Studies,* vol. 30, no. 1: pp. 4–12.

Manzini, E. (2010), 'Small, Local, Open and Connected: Design Research Topics in the Age of Networks and Sustainability', *Journal of Design Strategies,* vol. 4, no. 1, spring: pp. 8–11.

MEDEA (2012), 'Living Lab Malmoe', <http://medea.mah.se/taggar/living-lab-malmo> accessed April 7, 2012.

Meroni A. (2007), *Creative Communities. People Inventing Sustainable Ways of Living,* Polidesign: Milano.

Meroni, A. (2008a), *Strategic Design to Take Care of the Territory: Networking Creative Communities to Link People and Places in a Scenario of Sustainable Development,* Paper presented at the P&D Design, Brazil Design Research and Development Conference, São Paulo, October 8–11.

Meroni, A. (2008b), 'Strategic Design: Where Are We Now? Reflection around the Foundations of a Recent Discipline', *Strategic Design Research Journal,* vol. 1, no. 1, <http://www.unisinos.br/sdrj> accessed February 10, 2012.

Meroni, A. (2011), 'Design for Services and Place Development. Interactions and Relations as Ways of Thinking about Places: The Case of Periurban Areas', in Lou, Y. and Zhu, X. (eds), *Cumulus Proceedings: Shanghai Young Creators for Better City & Better Life,* Aalto University, Helsinki, Finland. pp. 234–40.

Meroni, A. and Sangiorgi, D. (2011), *Design for Services,* Gower: Farnham, UK.

Meroni, A., Simeone, G., Trapani P. (2009), 'Servizi per le reti agroalimentari. Il Design dei Servizi come contributo alla progettazione delle aree agricole periurbane', in Ferraresi, G. (ed.), *Produrre e scambiare valore territoriale: dalla città diffusa allo scenario di forma urbis et agri,* Alinea Editrice: Firenze. pp. 161–200.

Mulgan, J. (2006), *Social Innovation. What It Is, Why It Matters, How It Can Be Accelerated,* Basingstoke Press: London.

Murray, R. (2009), *Danger and Opportunity: Crisis and the Social Economy,* NESTA Provocation 09: London.

Murray, R., Caulier-Grice, J. and Mulgan, G. (2010), *The Open Book of Social Innovation,* NESTA Innovating Public Services: London.

Nutrire Milano (2012), Energie per il cambiamento, <http://www.nutriremilano.it/> accessed March 6, 2012.

Park Slope Food Coop (2012), <http://foodcoop.com/> accessed April 7, 2012.

Pauli, G. (1996), *Breakthroughs: What Business Can Do for Society,* Epsilon Press: Dallas.

Pauli, G. (2010), *The Blue Economy,* Report to the Club of Rome: Rome.

Pehnt, M., Carnes, M., Fischer, C., Praetorius, B., Schneider, L., Schumacher, K. and Voss, J.-P. (2006), *Micro Cogeneration. Towards Decentralized Energy Systems,* Springer: Berlin.

People's Supermarket (2012), <http://www.thepeoplessupermarket.org> accessed April 7, 2012.

Petrini, C. (2007), *Slow Food Nation: Why Our Food Should Be Good, Clean and Fair,* Rizzoli: Milano.

Rheingold, H. (2002), *Smart Mobs: The Next Social Revolution,* Basic Books: New York.

Simeone, G. and Cantù, D. (2011), 'Feeding Milano. Energies for Change. A Framework Project for Sustainable Regional Development Based on Food Demediation and Multifunctionality as Design Strategies', in Lou, Y. and Zhu, X. (eds), *Cumulus Proceedings: Shanghai Young Creators for Better City & Better Life,* Aalto University, Helsinki, Finland. pp. 458–64.

Simeone, G. and Corubolo, M. (2011), 'Co-Design Tools in "Place". Development Projects. An Ongoing Research Case', DPPI: Designing Pleasurable Products and Interfaces Conference, Milano, June 21–23.

Staszowski, E. (2010), 'Amplifying Creative Communities in NYC: A Middle-Up-Down Approach to Social Innovation', SEE Workshop, Florence.

Tapscott, D. and Williams, A. D. (2007), *Wikinomics: How Mass Collaborations Changes Everything,* Portfolio: New York.

Thackara, J. (2005), *In The Bubble: Designing in a Complex World,* MIT Press: London.

Verwijnen, J. and Karkku, H. (eds) (2004), *Spark! Design and Locality,* University of Arts and Design: Helsinki.

von Hippel, E. (2004), *The Democratization of Innovation,* MIT Press: Cambridge, MA.

16

Sustainable Urban Futures

RACHEL COOPER AND CHRISTOPHER T. BOYKO

INTRODUCTION

Urban environments are messy, complex, constantly evolving places. At times dense, vibrant, innovative and pluralistic, they also can be sprawling, vacant, resource-intensive and autocratic. New influxes of people, changes in government and global shocks to the system all play a role in how these environments are shaped and will continue to be shaped in the future. Without effective leadership and informed decision-makers, however, some cities may lose their competitive edge and their ability to host new people, products, services and ideas.

For cities to thrive, decision-makers have to make some sense of the messiness and the complexity of urban environments. Not only must they be fluent in policy and politics (with a big *and* a small 'p'), they also need to be able to engage in practice. This requires effectively translating lofty goals into tangible outcomes that citizens can see, feel and experience. It involves actively listening to and co-designing where possible with the diversity of communities that live, work and recreate within urban environments. In addition, consideration must be given to how decisions will impact the city and region socially, environmentally and economically as well as across the temporal spectrum, from short to long term.

To help make sense of urban environments and make more informed, sustainable design decisions for the future, decision-makers need to understand how their city works and how it has evolved from a design perspective. One strategy for doing this is to explore the process for how developments, neighbourhoods and wider areas come to be. That is, decision-makers must look at when design decisions are being made, who is making those decisions, what tools or resources are being used to make decisions and how—if at all—sustainability is being considered in urban decision-making. From this information, processes can be improved so that sustainable design thinking is woven into each process stage, thereby creating an outcome that will be more resilient, no matter what the future holds.

The chapter begins with a discussion about sustainability, and, in particular, urban sustainability, to give the reader an idea of the particular challenges facing the design of cities. The subsequent section describes the need for a clear urban design decision-making process that incorporates sustainability throughout as well as innovative tools and resources for making sustainable decisions. To that end, aspects of two research projects undertaken by the authors, VivaCity2020 and Urban Futures, are highlighted. The chapter concludes with a discussion of the future of cities and questions whether or not a sustainable city will ever exist.

SUSTAINABILITY

In its various guises, the concept of sustainability has existed for millennia. Quammen (1996, pp. 538–9), for example, writes about Ashoka, the first Buddhist king of India (304–232 B.C.), who declared in his 'Pillar Edicts' that natural resources must not be exploited beyond sustainable means. Concern for the way that humans were treating the environment in which they lived became more pronounced in the nineteenth century, when writers, poets and scholars such as Dickens, Blake and Engels vividly depicted towns and cities in the midst of the Industrial Revolution. Other writers and poets of the time, including Thoreau, Keats and Shelley, contrasted the beauty of the countryside with the deplorable conditions of industrial society (Wheeler and Beatley, 2009, p. 8).

Over the next 150 years or so, different people took up the mantle of sustainability, though not calling it by that name necessarily. For example, Ebenezer Howard (1902) transformed the way that urban planners and designers considered people's relationships with nature with his concept of garden cities. Lewis Mumford brought the issue of urban overcrowding and urban sprawl to our attention in his 1961 book, *The City in History.* Rachel Carson (1962) warned us about the dangers of using pesticides and herbicides, as they can irreparably harm the Earth. And Garrett Hardin's (1968) essay about the tragedy of the commons argued that people are quickly consuming global resources for personal gain and in the process are fouling the planet for everyone.

It was not until the early 1970s that sustainability and sustainable development started to become concepts in their own right (Byrne and Glover, 2002; Holmberg, 1992). In *The Limits to Growth,* Meadows et al. (1972) predicted a global collapse due to a toxic mixture of growing populations and worsening environmental conditions, using the term 'sustainable development' for the first time (Wheeler and Beatley, 2009, pp. 48–49). Also in 1972, Stockholm hosted the United Nations Conference on the Human Environment, bringing sustainability to a global and political audience. By 1987, the World Commission on Environment and Development published *Our Common Future,* which gave us the Brundtland definition of sustainability, focusing on meeting needs, both now and in the future (p. 26). Since this time, writers and scholars have been eagerly exploring and debating the dimensions of sustainability.

The Dimensions of Sustainability

Since the Rio World Summit in 1992, sustainability has been discussed along three dimensions or pillars: environmental, economic and social. The dimensions are seen as both separate and interconnecting, and various scholars have produced schematics to represent their thoughts on how the dimensions/pillars fit—or do not fit—together (e.g., Barbier, 1987, pp. 104–7; CIDA, 1997, Chapter 2; Findeli, 2008; Kearns and Turok, 2004; Lehtonen, 2004; Lozano, 2008; Mebratu, 1998; Rassafi et al., 2006, pp. 64–65; see also Knowles, Walker and Blair, this volume). New dimensions also have been added (e.g., cultural, political, personal meaning; see Gibson, 2006a, pp. 172–3; Hawkes, 2001; Walker, 2011), and new dimensional configurations abound. Nonetheless, the three conventional pillars are often seen as a starting point in helping to further describe sustainability.

Due to the prevalence of the environmental movements of the 1960s and 1970s, sustainability is often viewed as nurturing a strong, ecological focus (Marcuse, 1998, p. 104). Emphasis on the environmental dimension of sustainability concerns issues such as the protection of ecology, habitats, biodiversity and wilderness; improving air and water quality by reducing pollution; the conservation of resources, both renewable and nonrenewable (Paehlke, 2005, p. 38); and considerations of carrying capacity. Underpinning these issues is an ideology about the environment that is founded on weak or strong sustainability (Turner, 1993). The former, weak sustainability, states that humans see the environment or nature as separate from them and as a resource to be exploited (O'Riordan, 1996). Should the need arise for replenishment of resources, science and technology will provide the solutions (Williams and Millington, 2004). In contrast, the latter approach of strong sustainability suggests that humans are part of nature (Dickens, 2004; Lovelock, 1979) and need to limit growth to within the carrying capacity of the earth. In this view, technology should be used to increase efficiency, not development (Daly, 1991; van den Bergh and Nijkamp, 1991).

The economic dimension of sustainability highlights the idea that sustainable development should be cost-effective, should not reduce productivity (i.e., growth) and, concomitantly, should not be detrimental to the environment (Tolba, 1987). However, the notion of economic growth and maintaining a healthy environment may be at odds with one another (Ayres, 1995, 1996), as profit-seeking from businesses and consumerism often comes at the expense of environmental degradation. Economic systems therefore need to be better managed so that today's citizens can live off the interest earned by conserving the capital stock of natural resources as well as maintaining and even improving that stock for future generations (Pearce, 1988; 1993, pp. 31–34; Pearce et al., 1989, pp. 37–44; Repetto, 1986, pp. 14–22; Victor, 1991, pp. 210–11; Wackernagel and Rees, 1996, pp. 41–44). Furthermore, more attention needs to be paid to the fairer and more efficient distribution of resources (i.e., intragenerational equity, Gibson, 2006b, p. 270; Gibson et al., 2005, pp. 101–3) and issues of cradle-to-cradle design and manufacturing (McDonough and Braungart, 2002).

Finally, the social dimension of sustainability is concerned with development that is compatible with civil society and that supports cultural and social diversity while simultaneously encouraging integration and an enhanced quality of life (Polèse and Stren, 2000, pp. 15–16). Additional issues include meeting basic needs, fostering social responsibility, regard for current and future generations, empowering people in decision-making, the equitable distribution of opportunities (Sinner et al., 2004, pp. 15–16), capacity-building, wellbeing, social justice (Colantonio, 2011, p. 40) and the sustainability of community (Dempsey et al., 2011, pp. 293–4; see also Coleman, 1988). Inherent to this dimension is the notion that societies cannot be studied, sustained and/or improved without an understanding of the spaces they inhabit (McKenzie, 2004, p. 17). Here, we are concerned with urban spaces and how to improve their sustainability.

Urban Sustainability

While definitions and descriptions of sustainability abound, a dearth of definitions exist for urban sustainability (Alberti and Susskind, 1996, pp. 220–1). From a scan of the literature, three are notable. Yiftachel and Hedgcock (1993, pp. 139–41) see urban sustainability as a composite of social (subdivided into equity, community and urbanity), environmental and economic components included within urban planning and policy. For urban sustainability to be realized, the authors believe that strong policy and the ability, vision and leadership to enact that policy is required. Satterthwaite (1997, p. 1682) prioritizes environmental performance, suggesting that cities need to improve environmental quality within their boundaries and not transfer environmental costs to other people or ecosystems or into the future. While useful, not enough information about how people minimize costs (e.g., socially, economically) is provided, thus leaving room for further expansion. A third definition, offered by Camagni et al. (2001), emphasizes the interconnectedness between the traditional dimensions of sustainability while set within the urban environment,

> a process of synergetic interaction and co-evolution among the basic sub-systems that constitute the city—namely, the economic, the social, the natural and built environment—which guarantees a non-decreasing welfare level to the local population in the long run without jeopardising the development options of the surrounding territories, and which contributes to the reduction of the negative effects on the biosphere. (p. 133)

This definition is the most comprehensive of the three, allowing for multiple interpretations of how best to create the conditions for a synergetic process. However, Maclaren (2007) warns that,

> there is no single 'best' definition of urban sustainability, since different communities are likely to develop slightly, or even significantly different conceptualizations of

urban sustainability, depending on their current economic, environmental, and social circumstances and on community value judgments. (p. 186)

Haughton (1999), via Keirstead and Leach (2008, p. 331), suggests exploring principles of sustainability that resonate with the urban context—for example, intragenerational and intergenerational equity, treating people fairly, and the importance of biodiversity—as a way to understand urban sustainability. Maclaren (2007) also believes that developing indicators, which are used by the public and private sectors to gauge conditions or problems, is a good strategy for obtaining both a top-down and bottom-up understanding of the key facets of urban sustainability. Issues that have inspired indicator development in urban environments include transportation and traffic (Brown, 2006; Cervero, 1998; Mazza and Rydin, 1997; Newman and Kenworthy, 1999); land use, architecture and urban design (Calthorpe, 1993; Jenks et al., 1996; McDonough, 1993; Wheeler, 2002); ecology (Beatley, 1994); food and water (Brown, 2006); energy (Giradet, 1999); environmental justice and social equity (Perlman and O'Meara Sheehan, 2007); health and wellbeing (Cooper et al., 2011; Government Office for Science, 2008); and economic development (Hawken, 1997; Pearce and Barbier, 2000; Shuman, 2000). Each of these issues is challenging: for example, within land use, architecture and urban design, how do decision-makers create safe, walkable communities when city councils are forced to reduce their budgets for lighting urban areas and sidewalk maintenance?

Regardless of the issue, decision-makers need to be able to make informed decisions that will positively (or at least neutrally) impact the sustainability of their urban environments. This means possessing information about issues and how they relate to other issues, breaking out of professional and disciplinary silos in an attempt to work with a broad range of stakeholders and knowing what tools and resources to use to make decisions and when to use them. The next section describes how one process, for urban design, can be made more sustainable through effective decision-making.

DESIGN DECISION-MAKING IN URBAN ENVIRONMENTS

Urban design refers to the art and process of creating, making and managing spaces and places for people (Boyko et al., 2005, p. 119; DETR/CABE, 2000, p. 8; Rowley, 1994, pp. 181–2, pp. 188–9, p. 195). The scale at which such design occurs may be at the street, neighbourhood or wider city level. Policy has attempted to incorporate urban design principles into various guidelines and statements, including those involving sustainability (e.g., CLG, 2012; ODPM, 2004, 2005a, 2005b). While these policies outline how leaders envision the design of their cities, the practice of successfully implementing urban design in a sustainable manner is a different story. Myriad decision-makers and stakeholders, each with their own issues and ways of working, and the dizzying array of tasks involved in undertaking urban design development projects mean that the process is rarely as smooth as it could be. When the goal of sustainability is added to the mix, things become even more complex.

As part of the UK Engineering and Physical Sciences Research Council–funded project VivaCity2020,[1] the authors were charged with mapping the process for urban design. This involved creating a map of what is known about the urban design process from the academic and professional literature; what is undertaken in urban design practice; and what an improved map that featured sustainability would look like.

The Urban Design Decision-Making Process from the Literature

In terms of the first map, a review of the urban design literature revealed that an explicit urban design decision-making process did not exist. Thus, one would need to be mapped from an amalgamation of processes and ideas found within relevant professions and disciplines. These included architecture (RIBA, 1999); urban/town planning (Bressi, 1995; Nelessen, 1994; Okubo, 2000; Roberts, 2003; Wates, 1996, 1998); urban design (Biddulph, 1997; CIP, 2000; Rowland, 1995); construction, manufacturing and engineering (Austin et al., 2001; Cooper et al., 2005; Woodhead, 2000); business (Smith and Jackson, 2000); and non-governmental organizations (English Partnerships, 2000; Heritage Lottery Fund, 2000) (see also Macmillan et al., 2002). Looking across the processes, similarities existed between many of the stages and activities such that a literature-based process map could be created (see Figure 16.1).

This first process map consists of four stages and four feedback, or transition, stages. Stage 1 involves creating teams, appraising the situation and forming goals.

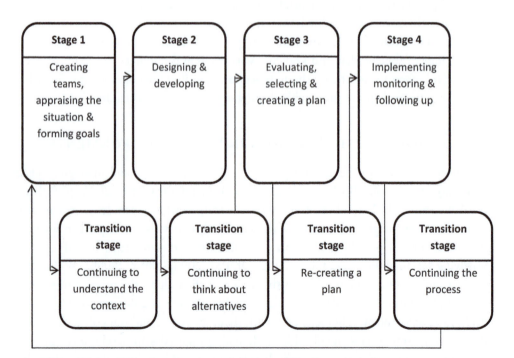

FIGURE 16.1   The urban design decision-making process from the literature.
Source: A simplified version of Boyko et al. (2005, p. 121). Image with permission of ICE Publishing, London.

Here is when decision-makers prepare for an urban design project by gathering together members of the team in which they want to work. The team surveys the context in which the project is situated using a variety of tools and resources. In addition, projects goals or objectives are written, funding is sought, and timescales are outlined.

In Stage 2, design options for the project are undertaken, based on material gathered from Stage 1. The team's design brief helps guide activities within this stage. Initial testing and evaluating of design options—which includes eliciting feedback—is paramount before more detailed testing can be done.

In Stage 3, design options are formally tested and evaluated with an eye towards the team's objectives and the design brief. Once a design has been selected and, where possible, stakeholder feedback is given on the chosen design, a plan for construction can be drawn up. Part of the construction plan will include a timescale and costs.

The final stage, Stage 4, sees the chosen design option realized. This means that the team will build the design, and, once completed, it will be monitored for a fixed period of time, often by a management company. Any outstanding costs will be settled.

The transition stages that exist in between each of the four stages above act as 'soft gates', allowing the team to reconsider past actions and plan ahead to future stages (Cooper et al., 2005, pp. 12–15, 75). Having the transition stages means that the process is iterative and continues as part of a larger urban design cycle of pre-design and design (where the four stages above sit); use, management and maintenance; and decline, demolition and/or regeneration (Cooper et al., 2009, p. 12).

The Urban Design Decision-Making Processes from Practice

Once this map was complete, the authors set about creating a process map—or set of maps—based on urban design practice. For this, the researchers undertook case studies in three UK cities—London, Manchester and Sheffield—and chose three urban design projects (for more details of the specifics of the case studies, see Boyko et al., 2012). For each case study, the researchers uncovered the process for urban design decision-making, who was making decisions, what they were using to make decisions and whether or not sustainability was considered.

Findings revealed that no one followed an explicit urban design process; instead, an ad hoc and implicit approach was taken, shaped by past experiences, knowledge, policy, the needs of the private sector and public sector planning regulations. In each case study, a different process was mapped, showing local variation and vulnerability to outside shocks (in one project, the crash of the dot.com boom halted development). Most of the decisions were made by city council planners, as they had the definitive voice in deciding whether or not a planning application would be successful. Private sector developers and architects also made within-development-team decisions but often consulted with landowners, clients, financiers and insurance brokers. Local businesspeople and residents did not make urban design decisions but may have influenced city council planners when consulted at the planning application stage.

The tools used to make decisions were various. National, regional and local government guidance; specific planning documents; academic journals and trade magazines; interpersonal skills; oral and written communication skills; leadership traits; having the 'right' team; knowing the local context (including have prior experience in the area); and holding pre-planning application meetings were all named as frequent tools and resources used by decision-makers. Computer-based tools were rarely mentioned. Finally, sustainability was considered throughout the three mapped processes, but it was not considered by everyone all the time. Rather, sustainability decisions were mostly made during design and planning brief presentations by city council planners, while designing and developing by city council planners and private sector developers and architects, and when evaluating and selecting a design for planning approval by city council planners. In one of the case studies, sustainability had been written into planning briefs, guidance and policy but was not fully enforced, a fact that the private sector architect could exploit when designing. In the other two case studies, sustainability was mentioned but not officially (e.g., a green park should be created for families as an urban oasis), or not mentioned at all.

The Improved Urban Design Decision-Making Process

Based on the information gleaned from the processes-in-practice, as well as the process from the literature, the authors created an improved process—one that includes sustainability at each stage. Moreover, because of the wide variety of decision-makers that come and go throughout an urban design project, two decision-maker teams were created which allowed for flexibility as to who and how many people were involved at any one time. The Development Team reflects those people who wanted to develop something, whereas the Project Sustainability Group comprises those who respond to and help to co-design the development, and have a strong interest in making the development as sustainable as possible. The latter team can consist of city council planners, residents, local businesses and even members of the Development Team. Finally, the improved process provides some of the many tools and resources that may be used in decision-making, including those developed as part of the VivaCity2020 project (see Figure 16.2).

Figure 16.2 consists of three orange-coloured bands interlaced by interconnected loops. The top band outlines the decision-making stages and is mostly consistent with the stages as found in the literature-based map. The first two stages—Need/Opportunity Identification and Exploration—were originally part of one stage, but the processes-in-practice indicated that they should be separated, allowing for different decision-makers and additional discussion of sustainability to emerge. The last three stages are identical to the stages found in the literature-based map, although the names are changed slightly to better align with existing architecture, and design and construction, processes (e.g., Cooper et al., 2005; RIBA, 1999).

The middle band consists of four different sustainability tasks that decision-makers need to undertake as part of the urban design project. The sustainability tasks occur in between each of the top band stages, and, along with the sustainability reviews, act

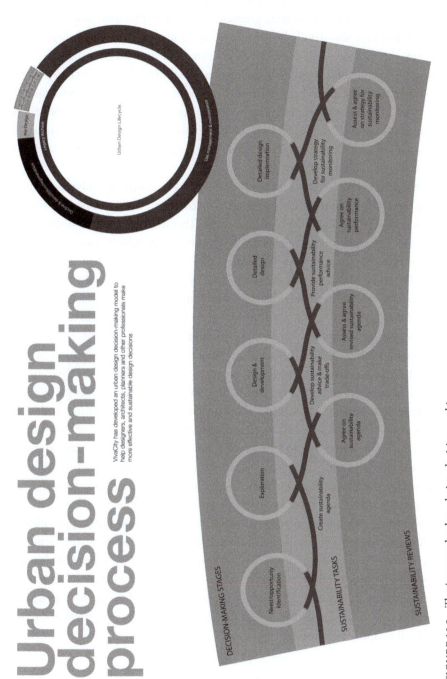

Urban design decision-making process

VivaCity has developed an urban design decision-making model to help designers, architects, planners and other professionals make more effective and sustainable design decisions

Urban Design Lifecycle

Pre-Design
Legacy Archive
Use, management & maintenance
Decline & demolition/redevelopment

DECISION-MAKING STAGES

Need/opportunity identification

Exploration

Design & development

Detailed design

Detailed design implementation

SUSTAINABILITY TASKS

Create sustainability agenda

Agree on sustainability agenda

Develop sustainability advice & make trade-offs

Assess & agree revised sustainability agenda

Provide sustainability performance advice

Agree on sustainability performance

Develop strategy for sustainability monitoring

Assess & agree on strategy for sustainability monitoring

SUSTAINABILITY REVIEWS

FIGURE 16.2 The improved urban design decision-making process.

Source: Boyko, C. and Cooper, R. (2009), 'The Urban Design Decision-Making Process: A New Approach', in Cooper, R., Evans, G. and Boyko, C. (eds), *Designing Sustainable Cities*, Wiley-Blackwell: London. pp. 43–50.

somewhat like the transition stages from the literature-based map. The first task—Create a Sustainability Agenda—is carried out mainly by the Project Sustainability Group and involves people creating a ranked list of sustainability issues that they believe are important (information about local context, gleaned from the Exploration stage, is helpful here). Part of this task also details how both groups understand sustainability and the chosen sustainability issues, and their significance to the urban design project.

The second sustainability task—Develop Sustainability Advice—occurs at pre-planning application meetings between the two groups. Here, information about the project is shared, advice is given and sought about sustainability, and trade-off discussions occur in relation to the ranked list of sustainability issues in the Sustainability Agenda. As a result of the trade-off discussions, new sustainability issues may need to be ranked, as could old issues be removed.

The third sustainability task—Provide Sustainability Performance Advice—also occurs during pre-planning application meetings. Advice is shared about how the proposed designs aim to perform if implemented in context. This leads to the final sustainability task—Develop Strategy for Sustainability Monitoring—in which management and maintenance plans are drawn up for the project and surrounding area in the short and long term. The strategy should include a timeline, budget and a list of decision-makers and stakeholders who will take over management and maintenance duties.

The third band in Figure 16.2 encompasses sustainability reviews. Each of these reviews—Agree on Sustainability Agenda, Assess and Agree on Revised Sustainability Agenda, Agree on Sustainability Performance Advice and Assess and Agree on Strategy for Sustainability Monitoring—gives both groups a final opportunity to agree on the sustainability issue rankings they believe to be important for the urban design project as well as to have final trade-off discussions about sustainability before moving to the next stage (as shown by the interconnected loops in Figure 16.2, the rankings and trade-off discussions may continue somewhat so long as the main points have been debated and some form of agreed-upon consensus has been reached). In addition, the second sustainability review allows for the Project Sustainability Group to agree on the Development Team's preliminary designs, and agreement between the groups at the third review gives the Development Team the green light to proceed with submission of a planning application.

In addition to the tripartite process, a number of tools and resources were generated by the entire research team of the VivaCity2020 project that could be used by decision-makers from both groups at different stages. Table 16.1 lists the tools and indicates when they may be used in the process. These tools are just a sample of many that can be used during the process; thus, the urban design decision-making process provides a framework in which to apply such tools.

Additional Decision-Making Tools and Resources

Further tools are always being developed. For instance, another EPSRC-funded project called Urban Futures[2] is developing an Urban Futures methodology. This tool allows decision-making teams to make informed, reasonable predictions as to whether sustainability

TABLE 16.1   DECISION-MAKING TOOLS AND RESOURCES AND WHEN IN THE PROCESS TO USE THEM

WHEN IN THE PROCESS TO USE THE TOOL OR RESOURCES	DECISION-MAKING TOOL OR RESOURCE
Between Stages 0 and 2	Bibliographic review of mixed-use, organized by theme
	Environmental quality case studies: includes innovative, mixed-methods approaches for gathering environmental quality data[a]
	Housing case studies: includes typologies of UK housing from 1820 to the present day
	Liveability postal survey: captures residential satisfaction in an area, divided into four themes: upkeep and management of public spaces and buildings; road traffic and transportation-related issues; abandonment or non-residential use of domestic property; and antisocial behaviour
	Night-time economy and crime case studies
	Retail and crime case studies
	Space Syntax analysis: shows relationships between street layout and residential property value as well as the value and formation of urban centres
	Toilet user personas: creation of 'archetypal users' who seek toilet provision in downtowns
	Toilet user surveys: used to indicate people's feelings about how provision meets local communities' needs
	Creative arts interpretations of researcher data: gives alternative insights into sustainability and the urban experience of city users
Between Stages 2 and 3	Environmental quality case studies (see above)
	Inclusive toilet hierarchy: identifies a hierarchy of away-from-home toilet provision in cities and is used to inform debates about the number and types of accessible toilets in any context
	I-VALUUL: a presentation that explores residential burglary and street robbery and the value of personal and property security
	New Urbanist case study: assesses whether the case study area has become a safer, more sustainable place in which to live
Between Stages 2 and 3	Open Space Strategy: quantitative dataset for thirty housing schemes detailing figure-ground ratios of buildings and open spaces, local street hierarchy, and the type, height, transparency and permeability of building façades and secondary boundaries
	Spatial data analysis: used to map economic, social and land-use diversity using GIS. Can be used with Space Syntax to identify street and pedestrian routes, and with on-street surveys to identify pedestrian movement
	Toilet user personas (see above)
	Toilet user surveys (see above)
Between Stages 3 and 4	Toilet design templates: used to help design accessible and inclusive toilets
After and including Stage 4	Urban design process case studies
	Spatial data analysis (see above)

[a] All case studies were completed in London, Manchester or Sheffield in the United Kingdom.
Source: Cooper and Boyko (2010, pp. 265–70).

solutions (i.e., decisions, methods, techniques, instruments, designs, policies, guidance, etc. implemented today in the name of sustainability, Boyko et al., 2012, p. 2; Lombardi et al., 2012, p. viii) will be resilient by using future scenarios. The scenarios, adapted from work undertaken by the Global Scenarios Group (Gallopin et al., 1997; Raskin et al., 1998, 2002) and applied to the UK urban context, are used to tell a story in both words and numbers to show how the future might unfold (Raskin et al., 2005, p. 36).

With four scenarios to-hand—two conventional (Market Forces and Policy Reform) and two less conventional (Fortress World and New Sustainability Paradigm), yet plausible, scenarios for the year 2050—decision-makers would test whether or not the sustainability solution would be robust for reasonable estimates of what the future could hold. Testing involves reading through the scenario descriptions and making judgements about whether or not a particular future could support the sustainability solution. Using rainwater harvesting as an example of a sustainability solution, the decision-making team would first consider all the necessary conditions needed to support the solution (e.g., adequate rainfall, low air pollution, pitched roofs, systems maintained, clean roof surface). The team would then look for clues in the descriptions of the scenarios to uncover whether or not the solution's necessary conditions are resilient to the future. For example, in a conventional Market Forces scenario, the futures literature implies that rainwater harvesting may not work in poorer parts of the city because localized air pollution may be higher, as wealthier citizens make concerted efforts not to pollute their neighbourhoods. In a conventional Policy Reform scenario, rainwater harvesting may be mandated for all new developments, but developers may not want to pay more to construct pitched roofs, nor may residents want them. Upon analysing the necessary conditions across all the scenarios, decision-makers then could see that, in this instance, rainwater harvesting would not be robust to different futures. The decision-making team could reconsider the sustainability solution or suggest a new one to test.

Tools and measurement against sustainable objectives are indeed prevalent and used by a variety of decision-makers. Yet really understanding the nature of a place or space and how liveable, viable and generally sustainable it is a challenging task. Once initial ideas are articulated, they can be visualized, which helps decision-makers to more easily understand the physical form of the idea and its relationship to people, resource use and fitness for purpose. Architects and urban designers have always used two-dimensional design drawings and models to help the client, developer, planner and politician understand what could exist. They also may use artistic licence, along with demonstrative rhetoric (Buchanan, 1985), to promote a particular solution or aesthetic. However, the complexity of urban design and decision-making, and the need to understand more transparently the implications of proposals and designs at aesthetic, technical, economic and social levels, have given rise to the use computer-aided design, virtual reality, models and prototypes.

Modelling-based systems exist for almost every aspect of the city, including climate, hydrology and water, energy, biodiversity, population density and traffic. However, computer scientists and professionals in this field have created a multilayered digital archive that stores all these urban aspects and more (Bassanino et al., 2010; Fernando et al., 2009, pp. 244–51). Architecture has moved towards this through Building Information Modelling (BIM), which not only includes three-dimensional computer models of a building but also introduces a fourth dimension, time sequencing of a building construction program, and even a fifth dimension of quantity and cost of materials. BIM is aimed at both an efficient design and construction process. However, it remains to be seen whether the complexities of dynamic urban environments can be modelled in a manner that can be understood and appreciated by the professional urban design decision-maker, let alone the urban resident. There are other visualization techniques that enable us to empathize and understand the nature of places and, thus, our reactions to living in them—the ultimate test. These techniques may be found in the creative industries, such as gaming or film, which enable us to imagine places and spaces. Pervasive digital technologies, such as displays and sensors in urban environments, also may help us to understand our impact on a place or space. These technologies are emerging and eventually will enable the urban citizen to connect to the place, to the decision-makers—and perhaps have a real-time effect on how we use our cities and how we design them in the future.

CONCLUSIONS

The design of the urban environment is one of the biggest challenges that faces us today. For cities to continue growing in a healthy way, decision-makers need to be able to make more informed decisions that are based on the tenets of sustainability. This chapter has given an example of an urban design decision-making process that reminds decision-makers when and how to make sustainable decisions. Also, it has illustrated some of the many tools and techniques to support this process. It is critical to remember, though, that professional urban designers and architects are just a small cog in creating urban places and spaces. It is citizens that create the atmosphere, the culture, the economy and the life of a city. For us to achieve the goal of more sustainable cities that support a good quality of life, we must find new means of designing cities that include everyone in the process. At the same time, it is imperative that everyone, especially politicians, planners, developers and investors, understand the implications of decisions on the design, function and ambience of places.

For professional designers, there are new processes, tools, techniques and technology that will enable them to share visions of the future and co-create the city with others. However, their profession does not exist in a vacuum: a city already has an established infrastructure that forms a kind of urban skeleton and citizens who create the soul of a place. At the intersection of both lies sustainability. Because of the dynamic relationship between infrastructure and people, it is probably not possible to achieve a sustainable city. Nonetheless, with the help of informed and democratic designers, co-design and co-creation of urban environments may enable us to get closer to that goal and establish a more sustainable urban future.

NOTES

1. For more information about the VivaCity2020 project, please see www.vivacity2020-eu.
2. For more information about the Urban Futures project, please see www.urban-futures.org.

REFERENCES

Alberti, M. and Susskind, L. (1996), 'Managing Urban Sustainability: An Introduction to the Special Issue', *Environmental Impact Assessment Review,* no. 16: pp. 213–21.

Austin, S., Steele, J., Macmillan, S., Kirby, P. and Spence, R. (2001), 'Mapping the Conceptual Design Activity of Interdisciplinary Teams', *Design Studies,* vol. 22, no. 3: pp. 211–32.

Ayres, R. U. (1995), 'Economic Growth: Politically Necessary but Not Environmentally Friendly', *Ecological Economics,* vol. 15, no. 2: pp. 97–99.

Ayres, R. U. (1996), 'Statistical Measures of Unsustainability', *Ecological Economics,* vol. 16, no. 3: pp. 239–55.

Barbier, E. (1987), 'The Concept of Sustainable Economic Development', *Environmental Conservation,* vol. 14, no. 2: pp. 101–10.

Bassanino, M., Wu, K., Khosrowshahi, F., Fernando, T. and Skjaerbaek, J. (2010), 'The Impact of Immersive Virtual Reality on Visualisation for a Design Review in Construction', in *14th International Conference on Information Visualisation,* IEEE Computer Society: London. pp. 585–9.

Beatley, T. (1994), *Habitat Conservation Planning: Endangered Species and Urban Growth,* University of Texas Press: Austin.

Biddulph, M. (1997), 'An Urban Design Process for Large Development Sites', *Town and Country Planning,* vol. 66, nos. 7–8: pp. 202–4.

Boyko, C. and Cooper, R. (2009), 'The Urban Design Decision-Making Process: A New Approach', in Cooper, R., Evans, G. and Boyko, C. (eds), *Designing Sustainable Cities,* Wiley-Blackwell: London. pp. 43–50.

Boyko, C. T., Cooper, R. and Davey, C. (2005), 'Sustainability and the Urban Design Process', *Engineering Sustainability,* vol. 153, no. ES3: pp. 119–25.

Boyko, C. T., Gaterell, M. R., Barber, A.R.G., Brown. J., Bryson, J. R., Butler, D., Caputo, S., Caserio, M., Coles, R., Cooper, R., Davies, G., Farmani, R., Hale, J., Hales, A. C., Hewitt, C. N., Hunt, D.V.L., Jankovic, L., Jefferson, I., Leach, J. M., Lombardi, D. R., MacKenzie, A. R., Memon, F. A., Pugh, T.A.M., Sadler, J. P., Weingaertner, C., Whyatt, J. D. and Rogers, C.D.F. (2012), 'Benchmarking Sustainability in Cities: The Role of Indicators and Future Scenarios', *Global Environmental Change,* vol. 22, no. 1: pp. 245–54.

Bressi, T. (1995), 'The Real Thing? We're Getting There', *Planning,* vol. 61, no. 7: pp. 16–21.

Brown, L. R. (2006), *Plan B 2.0 Rescuing a Planet under Stress and a Civilization under Trouble,* W. W. Norton: New York.

Buchanan, R. (1985), 'Declaration by Design: Rhetoric, Argument, and Demonstration in Design Practice', *Design Issues,* vol. 2, no. 1: pp. 4–22.

Byrne, J. and Glover, L. (2002), 'A Common Future or Towards a Future Commons: Globalization and Sustainable Development since UNCED', *International Review for Environmental Strategies,* vol. 3, no. 1: pp. 5–25.

Calthorpe, P. (1993), *The Next American Metropolis: Ecology, Community and the American Dream,* Princeton Architectural Press: New York.

Camagni, R., Capello, R. and Nijkmap, P. (2001), 'Managing Sustainable Urban Environments', in Paddison, R. (ed.), *Handbook of Urban Studies,* Sage: London. pp. 124–39.

Carson, R. (1962), *Silent Spring*, Houghton Mifflin: Boston.

Cervero, R. (1998), *The Transit Metropolis: A Global Inquiry*, Island Press: Washington, DC.

CIDA (Canadian International Development Agency) (1997), *Our Commitment to Sustainable Development*, CIDA: Ottawa/Hull.

CIP (Canadian Institute of Planners) (2000), 'The Urban Design Process', <http://www.cip-icu.ca/English/aboutplan/ud_proce.htm> accessed June 24, 2004.

CLG (Communities and Local Government) (2012), *National Planning Policy Framework*, CLG: London.

Colantonio, A. (2011), 'Social Sustainability: Exploring the Linkages between Research, Policy and Practice', in Jaeger, C. C., Tàbara, J. D. and Jaeger, J. (eds), *European Research on Sustainable Development, vol. 1: Transformative Science Approaches for Sustainability*, Springer: Berlin. pp. 35–58.

Coleman, J. S. (1988), 'Social Capital in the Creation of Human Capital', *American Journal of Sociology*, vol. 94: pp. S95–S120.

Cooper, R., Aouad, G., Lee, A., Wu, S., Fleming, A. and Kagioglou, M. (2005), *Process Management in Design and Construction*, Blackwell: Oxford.

Cooper, R. and Boyko, C. (2010), 'How to Design a City in Five Easy Steps: Exploring VivaCity2020's Process and Tools for Urban Design Decision Making', *Journal of Urbanism*, vol. 3, no. 3: pp. 253–73.

Cooper, R., Boyko, C. T. and Cooper, C. (2011), 'Design for Health: The Relationship between Design and Noncommunicable Diseases', *Journal of Health Communication*, vol. 16: pp. 134–57.

Cooper, R., Boyko, C., Pemberton-Billing, I. and Cadman, D. (2009), 'The Urban Design Decision-Making Process: Definitions and Issues', in Cooper, R., Evans, G. and Boyko, C. (eds), *Designing Sustainable Cities*, Wiley-Blackwell: London. pp. 4–16.

Daly, H. E. (1991), 'Elements of Environmental Macroeconomics', in Constanza, R. (ed.), *Ecological Economics: The Science & Management of Sustainability*, Columbia University Press: New York. pp. 32–46.

Dempsey, N., Bramley, G., Power, S. and Brown, C. (2011), 'The Social Dimension of Sustainable Development: Defining Urban Social Sustainability', *Sustainable Development*, vol. 19: pp. 289–300.

DETR (Department of the Environment, Transport and the Regions)/CABE (Commission for Architecture and the Built Environment) (2000), *By Design: Urban Design in the Planning System*, DETR: Rotherham.

Dickens, P. (2004), *Society and Nature*, Polity Press: Cambridge.

English Partnerships (2000), *Urban Design Compendium*, English Partnerships: London.

Fernando, T., Aouad, G., Fu, C. and Yao, J. (2009) 'IT Infrastructure for Supporting Multidisciplinary Urban Planning', in Cooper, R., Evans, G. and Boyko, C. (eds.), *Designing Sustainable Cities*, Wiley-Blackwell: London. pp. 242–62.

Findeli, A. (2008), 'Sustainable Design: A Critique of the Current Tripolar Model', *Design Journal*, vol. 11, no. 3: pp. 301–22.

Gallopin, G., Hammond, A., Raskin, P. and Swart, R. (1997) *Branch Points: Global Scenarios and Human Choice*, Stockholm Environment Institute: Stockholm.

Gibson, R. B. (2006a), 'Sustainability Assessment: Basic Concepts of a Practical Approach', *Impact Assessment and Project Appraisal*, vol. 24, no. 3: pp. 170–82.

Gibson, R. (2006b), 'Beyond the Pillars: Sustainability Assessment as a Framework for Effective Integration of Social, Economic and Ecological Considerations in Significant Decision-Making', *Journal of Environmental Assessment Policy and Management*, vol. 8, no. 3: pp. 259–80.

Gibson, R., Hassan, S., Holtz, S., Tansey, J. and Whitelaw, G. (2005), *Sustainability Assessment: Criteria and Processes*, Earthscan: London.

Girardet, H. (1999), *Creating Sustainable Cities*, Green Books: Devon.

Government Office for Science (2008), *Foresight Mental Capital and Wellbeing Project*, Government Office for Science: London.

Hardin, G. (1968), 'The Tragedy of the Commons', *Science*, vol. 162, no. 3859: pp. 1243–8.

Haughton, G. (1999), 'Environmental Justice and the Sustainable City', *Journal of Planning Education and Research*, vol. 18, no. 3: pp. 233–43.

Hawkes, J. (2001), *The Fourth Pillar of Sustainability: Culture's Essential Role in Public Planning*, Common Ground: Altona, Australia.

Hawken, P. (1997), 'Natural Capitalism', *Mother Jones*, March/April: pp. 40–53.

Heritage Lottery Fund (2000), *Building Projects: Your Role in Achieving Quality and Value*, Heritage Lottery Fund: London.

Holmberg, J. (ed.) (1992), *Making Development Sustainable*, Island Press: Washington, DC.

Howard, E. (1902), *Garden Cities of Tomorrow*, S. Sonnenschein: London.

Jenks, M., Burton, E. and Williams, K. (eds) (1996), *The Compact City: A Sustainable Urban Form?* E&FN Spon: London.

Kearns, A. and Turok, I. (2004), *Sustainable Communities: Dimensions and Challenges*, ESRC/ Office of the Deputy Prime Minister Postgraduate Research Programme, Working Paper 1, Office of the Deputy Prime Minister: London.

Keirstead, J. and Leach, M. (2008), 'Bridging the Gaps between Theory and Practice: A Service Niche Approach to Urban Sustainability Indicators', *Sustainable Development*, vol. 16: pp. 329–40.

Lehtonen, M. (2004), 'The Environmental-Social Interface of Sustainable Development: Capabilities, Social Capital and Institutions', *Ecological Economics*, vol. 49, no. 2: pp. 199–214.

Lombardi, D. R., Leach, J. M., Rogers, C.D.F. Barber, A., Boyko, C. T., Brown. J., Bryson, J., Butler, D., Caputo, S., Caserio, M., Coles, R., Cooper, R., Farmani, R., Gaterell, M., Hale, J., Hales, C., Hewitt, C. N., Hunt, D.V.L., Jankovic, L., Jefferson, I., MacKenzie, A. R., Memon, F. A., Phenix-Walker, R., Pugh, T.A.M., Sadler, J. P., Weingaertner, C. and Whyatt, J. D. (2012), *Designing Resilient Cities: A Guide to Good Practice*, IHS BRE Press: Bracknell, UK.

Lovelock, J. E. (1979), *Gaia: A New Look at Life on Earth*, Oxford University Press: Oxford.

Lozano, R. (2008), 'Envisioning Sustainability Three-Dimensionally', *Journal of Cleaner Production*, vol. 16, no. 17: pp. 1838–46.

Maclaren, V. W. (2007), 'Urban Sustainability Reporting', *Journal of the American Planning Association*, vol. 62, no. 2: pp. 184–202.

Macmillan, S., Steele, J., Kirby, P., Spence, R. and Austin, S. (2002), 'Mapping the Design Process during the Conceptual Phase of Building Projects', *Engineering, Construction and Architectural Management*, vol. 9, no. 3: pp. 174–80.

Marcuse, P. (1998). 'Sustainability Is Not Enough', *Environment & Urbanization*, vol. 10, no. 2: pp. 103–11.

Mazza, L. and Rydin, Y. (1997), 'Urban Sustainability: Discourses, Networks and Policy Tools', *Progress in Planning*, vol. 47, no. 1: pp. 1–74.

McDonough, W. (1993), *Design, Ecology, Ethics and the Making of Things: Centennial Sermon on the 100th Anniversary of the Cathedral of St. John the Divine*, New York City, February 7.

McDonough, W. and Braungart, M. (2002), 'Design for the Triple Top Line: New Tools for Sustainable Commerce', *Corporate Environmental Strategy*, vol. 9, no. 3: pp. 251–8.

McKenzie, S. (2004), 'Social Sustainability: Towards Some Definitions', in *Hawke Research Institute Working Paper Series (No. 52)*, University of South Australia: Magill.

Meadows, D. H., Meadows, D. L., Randers, J. and Behrens, W. W. (1972), *The Limits to Growth*, Universe: New York.

Mebratu, D. (1998), 'Sustainability and Sustainable Development: Historical and Conceptual Review', *Environmental Impact Assessment Review*, vol. 18: pp. 493–520.

Mumford, L. (1961), *The City in History*, Harcourt: San Diego.

Nelessen, A. C. (1994), *Visions for a New American Dream: Process, Principles, and an Ordinance to Plan and Design Small Communities*, 2nd ed., Planners Press: Chicago.

Newman, P. and Kenworthy, J. (1999), *Sustainability and Cities: Overcoming Automobile Dependence*, Island Press: Washington, DC.

ODPM (Office of the Deputy Prime Minister) (2004), *The Planning and Compulsory Purchase Act*, ODPM: London.

ODPM (Office of the Deputy Prime Minister) (2005a), *Planning Policy Statement 1: Delivering Sustainable Development*, ODPM: London.

ODPM (Office of the Deputy Prime Minister) (2005b), *Sustainable Communities: People, Places and Prosperity*, ODPM: London.

Okubo, D. (2000), *The Community Visioning and Strategic Planning Handbook*, National Civic League Press: Denver.

O'Riordan, T. (1996), 'Environmentalism on the Move', in Douglas, I., Hugget, R. and Robinson, M. (eds), *Companion Encyclopedia of Geography*, Routledge: London. pp. 449–76.

Paehlke, R. (2005), 'Sustainability as a Bridging Concept', *Conservation Biology*, vol. 19, no. 1: pp. 36–38.

Pearce, D. (1988), 'Economics, Equity and Sustainable Development', *Futures*, vol. 20, no. 6: pp. 598–605.

Pearce, D. (1993), *Blueprint 3: Measuring Sustainable Development*, Earthscan: London.

Pearce, D. and Barbier, E. (2000), *Blueprint for a Sustainable Economy*, Earthscan: London.

Pearce, D., Markandya, A. and Barbier, E. (1989), *Blueprint for a Green Economy*, Earthscan: London.

Perlman, J. E. and O'Meara Sheehan, M. (2007), 'Fighting Poverty and Environmental Justice in Cities', in Worldwatch Institute (ed.), *State of the World 2007: Our Urban Future*, Worldwatch Institute: Washington, DC, pp. 172–239.

Polèse, M. and Stren, R. E. (eds) (2000), *The Social Sustainability of Cities: Diversity and the Management of Change*, University of Toronto Press: Toronto.

Quammen, D. (1996), *The Song of the Dodo: Island Biogeography in an Age of Extinctions*, Pimlico: London.

Raskin, P., Banuri, T., Gallopin, G., Gutman, P., Hammond, A., Kates, R. and Swart, R. (2002), *Great Transitions: The Promise and Lure of the Times Ahead*, Stockholm Environment Institute: Stockholm.

Raskin, P., Gallopin, G., Gutman, P., Hammond, A. and Swart, R. (1998), *Bending the Curve: Toward Global Sustainability*, Stockholm Environment Institute: Stockholm.

Raskin, P., Monks, F., Ribeiro, T., van Vuuren, D. and Zurek, M. (2005), *Global Scenarios in Historical Perspective*, in Carpenter, S. R., Pingali, P. L., Bennett, E. M. and Zurek, M. (eds), *Scenarios (for the Millennium Ecosystem Assessment). Ecosystems and Human Wellbeing*, vol. 2, Island Press: Washington, DC. pp. 35–44.

Rassafi, A. A., Poorzahedy, H. and Vaziri, M. (2006) 'An Alternative Definition of Sustainable Development Using Stability and Chaos Theories', *Sustainable Development*, vol. 14, no. 1: pp. 62–71.

Repetto, R. (1986), *World Enough and Time: Successful Strategies for Resource Management,* Yale University Press: New Haven, CT.

RIBA (Royal Institute of British Architects) (1999), *RIBA Plan of Work,* RIBA: London.

Roberts, M. B. (2003), 'Making the Vision Concrete: Implementation of Downtown Redevelopment Plans Created through Visioning Process', PhD thesis proposal, University of California, Irvine.

Rowland, J. (1995), 'The Urban Design Process', *Urban Design Quarterly,* vol. October, no. 56, <http://www.udg.org.uk/> accessed July 14, 2004.

Rowley, A. (1994), 'Definitions of Urban Design: The Nature and Concerns of Urban Design', *Planning Practice and Research,* vol. 9, no. 3: pp. 179–98.

Satterthwaite, D. (1997), 'Sustainable Cities or Cities That Contribute to Sustainable Development?' *Urban Studies,* vol. 34, no. 10: pp. 1667–91.

Shuman, M. (2000), *Going Local: Creating Self-Reliant Communities in a Global Age,* Routledge: New York.

Sinner, J., Baines, J., Crengle, H., Salmon, G., Fenemor, A. and Tipa, G. (2004), 'Sustainable Development: A Summary of Key Concepts', *Ecologic Foundation: Nelson, New Zealand,* no. 2.

Smith, J. and Jackson, N. (2000), 'Strategic Needs Analysis: Its Role in Brief Development', *Facilities,* vol. 18, nos. 13/14: pp. 502–12.

Tolba, M. (1987), *Sustainable Development: Constraints and Opportunities,* Butterworth-Heinemann: London.

Turner, R. K. (ed.) (1993), 'Sustainability: Principles and Practice', in *Sustainable Environmental Economics and Management: Principles and Practice,* Belhaven Press: London. pp. 4–36.

van den Bergh, J.C.J.M. and Nijkamp, P. (1991), 'Operationalizing Sustainable Development: Dynamic Ecological Economic Models', *Ecological Economics,* vol. 4, no. 1: pp. 11–33.

Victor, P. A. (1991), 'Indicators of Sustainable Development: Some Lessons from Capital Theory', *Ecological Economics,* vol. 4, no. 3: pp. 191–213.

Wackernagel, M. and Rees, W. (1996), 'Urban Ecological Footprints: Why Cities Cannot Be Sustainable and Why They Are a Key to Sustainability', *Environment Impact Assessment Review,* vol. 16, no. 4–6: pp. 223–48.

Walker, S. (2011), *The Spirit of Design: Objects, Environments and Meaning,* Earthscan/Routledge: London.

Wates, N. (1996), 'A Community Process', *Urban Design Quarterly,* no. 58, April, <http://www.udg.org.uk/> accessed July 14, 2004.

Wates, N. (1998), 'Process Planning Session. Special Report: Methods', *Urban Design Quarterly,* no. 67, July, <http://www.udg.org.uk/> accessed July 14, 2004.

Wheeler, S. M. (2002), 'The New Regionalism: Key Characteristics of an Emerging Movement', *Journal of the American Planning Association,* vol. 68, no. 3: pp. 267–78.

Wheeler, S. M. and Beatley, T. (eds) (2009), *The Sustainable Urban Development Reader,* 2nd ed., Routledge: Abingdon, UK.

Williams, C. C. and Millington, A. (2004), 'The Diverse and Contested Meanings of Sustainability', *Geographical Journal,* vol. 170, no. 2: pp. 99–104.

Woodhead, R. M. (2000). 'Investigation of the Early Stages of Project Formulation', *Facilities,* vol. 18, nos. 13/14: pp. 524–34.

World Commission on Environment and Development (1987), *Our Common Future,* Oxford University Press: Oxford.

Yiftachel, O. and Hedgcock, D. (1993), 'Urban Social Sustainability: The Planning of an Australian City', *Cities,* vol. 10, no. 2: pp. 139–57.

17

Educational Experience in Design for Sustainability: Enhancing a Critical Perspective among Undergraduate Students

MARIA CECILIA LOSCHIAVO DOS SANTOS

INTRODUCTION

The word *design* has become very popular over the last decade. Its use has been inflated and trivialized; consequently, its meaning has been weakened (Maldonado, 2000; Bonsiepe, 2007).

> The truth of the matter is that the word design is no longer trustworthy. Although it is used and has certainly been abused almost everywhere, this word is so vague that it has become increasingly irritating. Since it is applied to respond to the programmatic (and promotional) needs of all kinds of activity—that of architects, engineers, designers, fashion designers, scientists, philosophers, managers, politicians, programmers, administrators—the word has lost its specific meaning. (Maldonado, 2000)

This trend has serious consequences for the entire field of design education.

As well as this trivialization of the word design, it is equally important to recall Victor Papanek's statement (1974, p. 235) pointing out that 'the main trouble with design schools seems to be that they teach too much design and not enough about the social, economic, and political environment in which design takes place'. As a result, designers generally do not tackle the real problems and needs that exist.

In this context, it is relevant to rethink design philosophy and education in order to discuss epistemological issues and knowledge production in design as a means of enhancing a critical perspective among students, thus stimulating them to confront the real world. In contrast to the dominant approach of design conditioned by self-indulgent, self-expressive attitudes as well as the mundane meaning of design in our contemporary culture, this chapter presents an educational experience that looks at design from the perspective of people on the edge. In Brazil, the crisis that has developed in the material culture of our cities, mainly due to increasing rates of urban poverty, raises a host of issues that is impossible to avoid.

This level of poverty means that millions of people living in cities do so in unbearable conditions—in high risk areas such as the banks of rivers, in *favelas,* shanty towns, and slums—while there are thousands of abandoned street children and an unacceptably low level of public health provision and basic education. In addition, there is a high level of violence against landless peasants and the urban homeless.

During the past decade, the debate on the role of design and its contribution to problematic social contexts has increased worldwide, constituting a highly important field of inquiry in the development of design knowledge. For example, contemporary poverty has become worse with the alarming increase of urban populations; such issues can potentially benefit from a creative design perspective. Education is a fundamental facet of design culture; it pervades the realms of both professional and experimental practices. It is a powerful medium for the dissemination of ideas in a broad range of contexts. From this perspective, recyclable material collection and urban poverty are emergent issues for design education and research. Examining the challenges presented by these issues through the lens of design requires a reconceptualization of design, one that stresses design's epistemological roots.

Design can be categorized in relation to physical paradigms as well as paradigms in the social sciences. Thus, design has a double rationality: the mathematical paradigm to explain physical phenomena and the paradigm to understand social phenomena. The first kind of rationality is the mathematical paradigm for the explanation of physical phenomena; it is a structure based on causality; in other words, the occurrence of entity B depends on the occurrence of entity A. The explanation involves technical rationality, and specialized skills and competencies.

The second kind of rationality is the paradigm located within society itself. It is a structure based on intentionality, which is the property of being about something else, which follows the theory of this happened, therefore this will happen. Understanding has to do with the problematization of social phenomena in order to intervene. Intentionality points to the future and has to do with establishing criteria and priorities for action. This is highly relevant in the construction of design education and agendas in design research.

Understanding both rationalities—physical and social—of epistemological design is crucial in understanding the possibilities for design as an agent of intervention in the challenges presented by current urban conditions. These challenges are immense and include the urban environment, urban poverty, homelessness, displacement, and collection of recyclable material as well as many others.

According to Harland and Santos (2009), 'Design education that is orientated toward the satisfaction of the few meeting the needs of relatively wealthy individuals or institutions, is sustained by privileged economic circumstances, and is symptomatic of design for greed.' The educational experience analyzed in this chapter provided under-graduate design students with the opportunity to critically examine the transformation of 'design for greed' into design for need. This experience was provided to students and faculty as a way of integrating intention/intentionality in order to respond to broader demands and expectations of contemporary societies. The unsustainability of excess demands because of the humanitarian needs of millions of people is a matter of urgency.

Intentionality and intention are grounded in ideas of value, and reference to values presupposes an appreciation of values. This kind of appreciation enables us to evaluate how design education feeds a system of greed rather than a system of need. What are the values present in these two types of design education orientation? The reference to value, for example, in the context of housing in the developing countries as discussed above forces us to evaluate the role of design education in the enhancement of human life, including dwelling and conditions for survival. In this case, it asks the question, how can design education address the gap between people in need and people in wealthy conditions, and how can design provide tools in design education that will enhance human life and human rights?

Returning to Papanek's statement on how designers are educated, problems arise because of the lack of connection to the real world. Papanek called for design to be more focused on real problems—the kind of problems that exist outside of the luxury of the technological, moneyed, and cultural elite of every nation. In designing for the real world, there is no room for the fulfillment of individual creativity; the main focus is on a better understanding of otherness.

THE RECYCLABLE MATERIALS COLLECTORS NATIONAL MOVEMENT: PROCESS, STRUGGLE, AND ACHIEVEMENTS

The activity of recyclable collectors on Brazilian city streets has been around for several decades, but it was only at the beginning of the 1980s that the first initiatives arose to organize them through associations or cooperatives. In the city of São Paulo, at the beginning of the 1980s, a group of church workers assisted homeless people who found subsistence in the waste that was discarded by homes, industries, and trade in the downtown area. They began to hold meetings at the Community Center of the Street Sufferers in the Glicério neighborhood, which became the meeting point for these collectors. The original idea for collecting began with one purpose: raising money to hold a religious party during Easter.

The history of organizing the collectors and homeless is filled with violent confrontations and evictions. In 1985, in a political conflict with the municipal administration of São Paulo, the collectors marched through the main streets demanding the right to circulate with their carts in the downtown area. This march was a way of manifesting their political voice. Four years later, in 1989, COOPAMARE, the Cooperativa de Catadores Autônomos de Papel, Papelão, Aparas e Materiais Reaproveitáveis (Cooperative of Autonomous Paper, Cardboard, Scraps, and Reusable Materials Collectors) was founded, initially with twenty collectors. This was the first cooperative of recyclable collectors in

Brazil. In 1990, ASMARE, the Associação dos Catadores de Papel, Papelão e Matérias Recicláveis (the Association of Collectors of Paper, Cardboard, and Recyclable Materials) was created in Belo Horizonte[1] based on socio-pedagogical work developed by the Street Pastoral of the Belo Horizonte Archdiocese. In 1993, the Belo Horizonte Project of Selective Collection was implemented in partnership with ASMARE by the Superintendency of Urban Cleaning (SLU), helping give a semipublic status to the work of the collectors' cooperative (Dias, 2007). The organization of the work of these collectors gradually began to provide income, and throughout the 1990s, cooperative work in several Brazilian cities developed and expanded (Santos, 1999).

The collectors, who are part of a type of economic organization and are now formally organized in work- and income-generating cooperatives, established the National Movement of Recyclable Materials Collectors (MNCR) in September 1999 at a meeting held in the city of Belo Horizonte in the state of Minas Gerais, which brought together NGOs, the government, and the private sector. At this event, the collectors of recyclable materials, in partnership with organizations that worked with the adult population in a street situation, created the basis for a national forum.

In June 2001, the First National Conference of Paper and Recyclable Materials Collectors took place on the campus of the National University of Brasília (UNB), and there the National Movement of Recyclable Materials Collectors (MNCR) was officially created. I was fortunate to be at the conference as an invited speaker and to witness this historical achievement. Collectors from all over Brazil came to the sunny capital of the country, arriving in crowded buses. This was the major event for the collectors' political expression—and it led to the writing of a political agenda to advocate their rights. It also led to the establishment of partnerships with different sectors of civil society.

During the conference, the Letter of Brasilia was written and entitled, 'For the End of Trash Dumps: Recycling by Collectors: at Once!'; it was a document that summarized the main guidelines and demands of the MNCR including proposals for MNCR actions to be taken concerning the executive branch of government, the productive chain of recycling,[2] and the citizenship of the homeless.

The collectors demanded of the executive branch of government that it guarantee that collectors would receive funds and subsidies with a view to their social inclusion through work. They also demanded qualification for their work, proposing the inclusion of their militants in the federal government's National Plan of Professional Qualification, and the adoption of policies and measures that would enable their technological improvement as well as the eradication of trash dumps in the country.

As for the productive chain of recycling, the requirement was to create institutional devices that would ensure that recycling be performed as a priority by social companies of collectors of recyclables. With regard to the citizenship of the homeless population, one of the main points was that the recognition of the homeless by including them in the national demographic census performed by the Brazilian Institute of Geography and Statistics (IBGE).

In 2003, in Caxias do Sul, Rio Grande do Sul, the First Latin American Congress of Collectors took place. Collectors from Uruguay and Argentina participated, thus demonstrating the strength of the organization among the movements in South America. During this event, the statement known as the Letter of Caxias do Sul was written, spelling out, by means of a historical consciousness reported in the text, who collectors are in the throwaway society:

> This struggle is not new. It is the result of a long history of women and men who, working as collectors, ensured survival from what society discards and throws away. It is a history in which we discover the value and significance of our work: collecting and recycling disposable materials, we are environmental agents and we help clean the cities. The organization of associations and cooperatives created the possibility of work and income for the more excluded sectors of society... recycling life itself. (MNCR, Caxias do Sul, 2003, p. 1)

Besides spelling out the social identity of this collective, the letter contained claims and guidelines for collaboration between government, cities, and collectives. One of its commitments was 'to work for a greater integration of the communities of our cities with the collectors' organizations, through policies and programs of environmental education, ensuring cooperation for separating and delivering recyclables, for controlling the actions of government, for valuing the work of Collectors, for participating in public policy Management Forums' (MNCR, Caxias do Sul, 2003, p. 1).

In the opening session of this event, Dona Geralda Marçal, who has been a collector since the age of eight, stated, 'Collectors do not need cesta básica (basic food); we want to have our own factory for recycling materials' (MNCR, Caxias do Sul, 2003). This dream came true with the inauguration of the Plastics Factory, which is owned and managed by the collectors, in the greater metropolitan area of Belo Horizonte in 2005.

With regards to government initiatives at the federal level, the Inter-Ministerial Committee of Social Inclusion of Recyclable Materials Collectors was instituted in 2003 by presidential decree. The purpose of this committee is to implement the interministerial project 'Trash and Citizenship: Fighting Hunger Associated with the Inclusion of Collectors and the Eradication of Trash Dumps', with MNCR representing the collectors.

Also in 2003, the federal programs began the transfer of funds to municipalities for the eradication of dumps and the elaboration of Integrated Management Plans for Integrated Management of Urban Solid Waste, with a component including collectors. Among the planned requirements is support for the organization of collectors and the establishment of selective collection partnerships.

In 2006, the federal government instituted the rule that recyclable waste discarded by agencies and entities of direct and indirect federal public administration must be donated to collectors' associations and cooperatives. A great achievement of the collectors was the creation in 2007 of the National Policy of Basic Sanitation, which rules on contracts and bidding. The modification involves the authorization to employ, without the need for bidding, recyclable collectors associations or cooperatives to carry out collection and associated activities related to recyclable solid waste. It should be highlighted that the collectors worked very actively to be included in the national policy.

Changes instituted in 2008 put into place certain principles such as polluter pays and reverse logistics. These principles apply specifically to industries manufacturing agricultural pesticides, batteries, fluorescent lamps, tires, and electric and electronic products. They also make it mandatory for municipalities to implement management plans for waste that are integrated to those of basic sanitation. In addition, fiscal incentives are foreseen, including credit lines with lower interest for activities that generate less waste and recycle or implement selective collection systems.

Since the beginning, the dynamics and characteristics of expansion of the recyclable-production sectors in Brazil have depended on the labor force of thousands of collectors working under precarious conditions. Nevertheless, collectors are turning their fragile situation into a relevant economic and social asset. Through their efforts, *catadores* have moved from extreme vulnerability in garbage dumps to becoming socially secure, economically viable, and environmentally conscious citizens. In August 2010, the government signed the national Law of Solid Waste, Law 12.305/2010, which has had a significant impact on the work of collectors. In general terms, this law regulates the solid waste sector and provides new challenges and responsibilities to society as a whole, with the social inclusion of the collectors.

DESIGN OF URBAN ARTIFACTS: A PEDAGOGICAL PRACTICE

This section looks at the educational experience of design for social responsibility within the context described above as conducted at the University of São Paulo from 2003 to the present. Considering the relevance and the potential of the recycling work performed by collectors to improve environmental conditions in the São Paulo metropolitan area and working as an activist with COOPAMARE, I proposed a course on Design for Sustainability (Santos, 2000, 2004).

The Cooperative: COOPAMARE

The increasing joblessness and homelessness in Brazil over the last twenty years has led to the development of a new strategy of income generation: to overcome poverty. Some urban residents have even started recycling activities as their major means of subsistence. They mainly collect discarded mass-produced objects and all kinds of recyclable materials. COOPAMARE is located in the western part of São Paulo under the Paulo VI viaduct. Permission to use the land under the viaduct was a concession made by the city; however, working conditions in these areas are precarious.

Gradually the collectors have improved the situation; they now have electricity, running water, and restrooms. Collectors are engaged in the development of an environmentally friendly economy as they clean the city. The materials they find are sorted and reintegrated into the productive cycle. Although collectors play an important role in urban waste management, they receive no healthcare, housing, social security, or education benefits. Despite high significant progress over the decades, they are still looked upon as dirty people—even delinquents—rather than productive members of our society.

The Dynamics of the Course: Teaching and Learning for Change

The student experience is a central component in the course dynamics. Initially, the students attended some preparatory lectures in order to discuss issues of gender, class domination, privileges, social equality, and how design historically conveyed these aspects and values.

The diverse ways in which student experiences were produced and organized were very important to understand a new paradigm for the production of design knowledge and practice. Aside from the traditional ways of knowledge production, there was another major feature: the direct contact between the students and the collectors and, at different levels, the contact between the students and the neighborhood and municipality. The contact with the collectors at the cooperative was a very rich and productive experience, and the students soon realized and evaluated the complexity of the problem. They were also encouraged to ask to what extent the design of urban artifacts acknowledges the complexity of multiple scales between artifacts, processes, social need, and urban context.

From the point of view of the collectors, this design course gave them the opportunity to convey their extensive knowledge on practical aspects of discarded materials, including their knowledge of both the selection and the collection processes. During the meetings with the students, the collectors provided important information, such as the durability of cardboard and its resistance to the weather; where in the city collectors can salvage certain types of material; and how the condition of the materials can hamper the collectors' working process. A specific discussion pertained to Tetra Pak milk and juice packaging and the frequent presence of residual contents, which cause fermentation, deterioration, and an unpleasant smell, as recounted by Anderson, one of the collectors. According to Manoel, another collector, 'We can teach our practice to the students and the students can teach us the theory; no one knows everything.'

The course also enabled the sharing and comparison of the students' and collectors' knowledge and how the transformation of both their actions required rethinking the knowing process. This was further explained by Paulo Freire's methodology and critical education concepts:

Knowing, whatever its level, is not the act by which a Subject transformed into an object docilely and passively accepts the contents others give or impose on him or her. Knowledge, on the contrary, necessitates the curious presence of subjects confronted with the world. It requires their transforming action on reality. It demands a constant searching. It implies invention and re-invention. In the learning process the only person who really learns is s/he who appropriates what is learned, who apprehends and thereby re-invents that learning; s/he who is able to apply the appropriate learning to concrete existential situations. On the other hand, the person who is filled by another with 'contents' whose meaning s/he is not aware of, which contradicts his or her way of being in the world, cannot learn because s/he is not challenged. (2002, pp. 100–1)

Another aspect worth stressing is the improvement of students' observational and analytical skills in reading the urban environment for which they have designed artifacts, communication systems, and so on. They have begun to pay more attention to certain parts of the city that are usually taken for granted or even segregated, such as the area used by the cooperative under the viaduct, which is the central part of the conflict area between the neighborhood and the collectors.

Students' work has also provided an opportunity to consider alternatives to the main paradigm of market-oriented product design education that dominates design schools. This is especially important because at present we can observe an explosive increase in the number of design schools around the world.

At the University of São Paulo, students enrolled in the design course were highly interested in the inclusion of particular forms of knowledge that have been ignored by the traditional design curricula, and they were enthusiastically committed to a critical practice of design, thus enhancing their interpretations of the social and material world. The various meetings with the collectors brought out the issue of voices and sources of knowledge about design, raising the following questions: whose design of history are we addressing? Whose history are we talking about? For whom are we designing? These questions raised another crucial aspect: how does the interaction with diverse cultural identities impact the methods and objectives for which design students are designing?

These questions reinforce the need to support and implement educational programs on social design in developing countries in order to shift the educational paradigms of design education from one that serves only the needs of market-oriented suppliers and affluent consumers to the needs of local populations.

THE MAIN FINDINGS

Students created meaningful proposals and had important experiential learning opportunities around the theme of design and its relationship to urban conflict, social justice, human rights, communication, and community development. They also worked with a wide variety of materials and strategies.

During the design course, there were discussions on how critical design practices based on a collaborative and participatory process are important when dealing with conflict. The course has also stressed the importance of the collectors' input and participation, either by their generous conversation or by their open dialogue with the students. It is important to note that the dialogue between them was the key point of a successful pedagogical experience because dialogue requires an equal participation, which involves the recognition and legitimization of the collectors as knowledgeable agents. In this process, even the traditional teacher position as repository of knowledge was reshaped, and we had an extraordinary opportunity to experience what Freire considered the main feature of a successful educator—that is, his or her ability to engage in dialogue that educates in a basis of reciprocity (1998). This pedagogical experience provided us with a reflective and effective design learning process. It indicated that limits give us the impetus to make imaginative use of the limited resources available and bring new solutions into the design experience.

During the design course, each group made its presentation. The rest of the class, together with the collectors, actively participated by asking questions and making suggestions. Afterward, the students and collectors realized that they had developed a real comprehension of design alternatives by reusing salvaged materials and products from the city.

Moreover, it is important to convey our feelings in words. We are tremendously thankful to the COOPAMARE collectors' community, who have welcomed us in their working spaces and who have provided invaluable information and friendship to all of us.

FINAL COMMENTS

Teaching this design course gave me an opportunity to rethink the comment by Paulo Freire and Ira Shor:

> The official pedagogy constructs them [students] as passive/aggressive characters. After years in dull transfer-of-knowledge classes, in boring courses filled with sedating teacher-talk, many have become non-participants, waiting for the teacher to set the rules and start narrating what to memorize. These students are silent because they no longer expect education to include the joy of learning, moments of passion or inspiration or comedy, or even that education will speak to the real conditions of their lives. (1987, p. 122)

Teaching this design course gave to all participants the possibility of understanding the psychological, social, economic, and environmental struggles of the vibrant catadores.

NOTES

1. The productive chain of recycling includes the process of managing solid wastes from the moment they are discarded, put through triage, packed in bales, sold as material, transported, and processed by industry, to when the market for the product they become has been developed (Gonçalves-Dias, 2009).
2. Meeting at COOPAMARE, November 10, 2004.

REFERENCES

Bonsiepe, G. (2007), 'The Uneasy Relationship between Design and Design Research', in Michel, R. (ed.), *Design Research Now*, Birkháuser Verlag: Berlin, pp. 25–40.

Dias, S. (2007), *Do lixo à cidadania-catadores: de problema social à questão socioambiental. In Seminário Nacional Movimentos Sociais, Participação e Democracia, 2, 2007Florianópolis,* UFSC/NPMS: Florianópolis.

Freire, P. (1973/2002), *Education for Critical Consciousness,* Continuum: New York.

Freire, P. (1998), *Pedagogy of Freedom. Ethics, Democracy and Civic Courage,* Rowman & Littlefield: New York.

Freire, P. and Shor, I. (1987), *A Pedagogy for Liberation: Dialogues on Transforming Education,*
Bergin and Garvey: South Hadley, MA.

Harland, R. G. and Santos, M. C. Loschiavo dos (2009), 'From Greed to Need: Notes on
Human-Centred Design', Interrogations: Creative Interdisciplinarity in Art and Design
Research, AHRC Postgraduate Conference, pp. 141–58.

Maldonado, T. (2000), Design Plus Research Conference, opening lecture, Milan.

MNCR, Caxias do Sul (2003), 'Letter of Caxias do Sul I Latin American Congress of
Collectors', <http://www.mncr.org.br/box_1/principios-e-objetivos/carta-de-caxias-do-sul/>
accessed July 19, 2012.

Papanek, V. (1974), *Design for the Real World. Human Ecology and Social Change,* Paladin Books:
London.

Santos, M. C. Loschiavo dos (1999), 'Castoff/Outcast. Living on the Street', in Correll, T. and
Polk, P. (eds), *The Cast-Off Recast: Recycling and the Creative Transformation of Mass-Produced
Objects,* UCLA Fowler Museum of Cultural History: Los Angeles, pp. 111–40.

Santos, M. C. Loschiavo dos (2000), 'Spontaneous Design, Informal Recycling and Everyday
Life in Postindustrial Metropolis', in Pizzocaro, S., Arruda, A., de Moraes, D. (eds), *Design
plus Research Conference,* Politecnico di Milano: Milano, pp. 459–66.

Santos, M. C. Loschiavo dos (2004), 'Re-Shaping Design. A Teaching Experience at COOPAMARE:
Listen to the Recyclable Collectors Voice', Presented at Cumulus Conference, Utrecht,
<http://www.cumulusassociation.org/component/content/1002-cumulus-working-
papers-utrecht-1304/185>, accessed February 24, 2013.

18

Sustainable Fashion

KATE FLETCHER

INTRODUCTION

A few years ago, a small gallery in central Istanbul presented an exhibition called *Fashion for Sustainability* (Garanti Galeri, 2008). The show was modest but progressive, exploring six themes that reflected some of the diversity of thinking that was emerging around social and ecological activity in the fashion sector and showcasing directional practice. At the end of the opening week, the exhibition provoked a column in the Turkish daily newspaper, *Radikal.* The columnist was both animated and incredulous—not about the content of the show (he never saw it) but rather the exhibition's underlying premise that fashion and sustainability could ever share a common platform. How, he wondered out loud, could fashion—something defined by transience and image—ever endure into the future? For are they not two opposing ideas? It was, he concluded, impossible; a contradiction in terms. And the notion of fashion as a supporter of sustainability? Nothing more than a business-boosting marketing stunt.

This is not an isolated view. For fashion has come to represent much of that which is destructive and morally unconscionable about modern, globalized mass production and consumption. Its omnipresence and position at the heart of consumerist, materialistic culture has seen it branded—often for good reason—as an individual, social and industrial practice in need of greater material restraint, connectedness, ethics and values. Fashion is condemned for its commerciality, for the trivial temporariness of perpetually changing styles or trends as a way to influence consumer spending and a consumer habit of mind attuned to understanding fashion only as the new, to looking or watching (rather than, say, actively making) and instant gratification through consumption. These practices, symbolized by our experience of commercialized mass-market fashion, are now so pervasive and routine that we almost accept them as a sort of natural order. Yet these are not practices of the fashion industry per se. They suffuse all parts and products of consumerist societies. They need to be understood within a broader framework of economic imperatives, business practices and culture—to be engaged with for what they are: business models, marketing tools and social behaviours tied to a specific set of economic priorities. It is certainly the case that these models, tools and associated behaviours have become synonymous with the fashion sector, but the source of our unease with them is found at a deeper, more systemic level than an industry designing and manufacturing garments. It lies within the larger systems of economics, culture and society and the commercial agendas, political priorities and technical mechanisms of our world. What is more, these mechanisms through which fashion manifests itself are at odds not just with the sustainability imperative but also with the aspirations of fashion itself, which seeks to communicate between society and the self, to foster belonging and identity and link us in time and space.

Thus, design engagement to address issues of sustainability in fashion has taken place against a backdrop where fashion is seen as a sector dominated by commerce, notions of change, consumption, superficiality and appearance. As in other sectors and design disciplines, this engagement is widely variable in approach, intent and rigour. Also, like in other disciplines, much of this work is preoccupied with managing resource flows and with overcoming technical and organizational challenges of production. In this present discussion, the debate has focused on managing the lower end of the waste hierarchy, in particular recycling, and questions of materials selection, sourcing and manufacture. This is important work, for the physical resource implications of fashion production and consumption are substantial. For instance, the amount of water alone that is required to grow and process enough cotton for a single T-shirt is around 600 litres (Turley et al., 2009, p. 22). And yet these same water resources are embodied in a T-shirt that is often barely used: people in industrialized countries are buying more than ever, regardless of need (Allwood et al., 2006, p. 2).

Yet while attention has been focused on the practical, technical issues of fibre and fabric selection and processing and supply chain management—greening the garment's materiality—the design of the fashion system has been largely neglected. Also overlooked have been the values, perceptions, habits and thought processes of an industry and set of consumers that drive the system of fashion consumption and production. This is slowly changing and a growing body of critical and broad-based work is now taking place within a new paradigm or framework of analysis and understanding of the larger economic realities, social structures, thought processes, power relations and consuming traditions that shape the fashion industry. This chapter reviews some of this work and identifies key themes of research and practice including Slow Fashion, non-plan design and post-growth fashion. It also seeks to contextualize this activity within a bigger picture of sustainability work in the fashion sector, tracing its development over the last twenty years.

DEFINING FASHION AND SUSTAINABILITY

The origins of the word 'fashion' can be traced back to the Latin *facere* (to make), and early experiences of fashion were as a practice of making clothing, often in groups.

An aesthetic sense was an important part of these experiences, evolving with the understanding about how to make and use tools (such as needle, thread and scissors) and undertake cooperative projects.

In the ateliers of Paris in the 1850s, courtesy of industrial innovation around reproduction of garment designs, the practice of cutting and sewing garments was transformed from artisan dressmaking to a commercial artistic practice. This led the making activity to become eclipsed by the product of this making process, and more particularly the garment's potential as a social signifier of status, identity, belonging and difference (Simmel, 1971, p. 301). Fashion became understood as an item of clothing that communicates between the self and society.

Today, much of this communication is shaped by the logic of commerce and the stylistic variations or trends—known as 'fashion'—that render an existing garment psychologically obsolete and drive a fresh round of consumption and production of functionally and imaginatively similar products. Yet outside of the commerce-led shopping and magazine format, fashion is part of wider material, individual and social processes reflecting the way people express themselves and connect with others and with time and place through clothing. Cultural theorist Joanne Finkelstein describes fashion as 'a hybrid phenomenon, located at the interstices between economics and art, psychology and commerce, creativity and banality...as a social, economic and aesthetic force and more often than not, all three at the same time' (1996, pp. 5–6). Adding a more personal element to the analysis, sociologist Juliet Schor characterizes the practice of dressing and adorning as 'being at the center of how human beings interact' and thus 'a vital part of the human experience' (2002, p. 53); that is, a practice that is central to our social and cultural lives. Framed in this way—as part of the process of life—fashion becomes dynamically interconnected with sustainability (another life process) and a key part of the relationship between human culture and ecological flourishing.

The language used to describe this relationship in the fashion sector reflects some of the complexities of bringing it into practice—and reflects the development of terminology in design for sustainability more generally. While terms such as 'green fashion', 'ethical fashion', 'eco-fashion' and 'sustainable fashion' are often used interchangeably, there are subtle differences in meaning that mark an evolution in both theory and practice. 'Green fashion', for instance, was preferred in the early years of work in this area and on occasion still by industry. It has an explicitly environmental agenda and often has as single (ecological) product or processing issue as its focus as exemplified in *Green Designed Fashion* (Bierhals, 2008). 'Ethical fashion' is sometimes used as shorthand to refer to generic sustainability-related work in fashion, though often it describes specific activity relating to human and animal ethics particularly associated with labour conditions in manufacture and materials selection (e.g., fibres cultivated/processed with non-harming methods). 'Eco fashion' largely denotes the design of products that maximize resource efficiency and minimize waste, largely through an ethos of making refinements to the current system. Examples of these activities can be found in a number of texts on fashion and environmental and ethical issues; see, for example, *Eco Fashion* (Brown, 2010) and *Eco Chic* (Black, 2008). By contrast 'sustainable fashion' or

'fashion for sustainability' suggests awareness of systemic influences and complex interconnections between material, social and cultural contexts in fashion across the long
term as demonstrated by *Fashion and Sustainability* (Fletcher and Grose, 2012), *Shaping
Sustainable Fashion* (Gwilt and Risannen, 2011a) and *Sustainable Fashion and Textiles*
(Fletcher, 2008).

FASHION AND SUSTAINABILITY: EVOLUTION
OF THINKING AND PRACTICE

As the development of terminology suggests, the relationship between fashion and
the sustainability and resource consumption agenda has evolved through a number
of stages. Up until the late 1980s, the physical environment was viewed as largely
irrelevant by the majority of the sector. When the sector did seek to respond to
environmental concerns, such as those around climate change highlighted by the
United Nations Earth Summit in Rio de Janeiro in 1992, it was in order to minimize disruption to its operations rather than to positively contribute to a burgeoning
sustainability agenda. One of the most noteworthy early exceptions to this general
rule was the work of the San Francisco–based fashion brand Esprit, which designed
and produced a collection (E-collection) that reduced the impact of production
in material selection, manufacturing and specification of product hardware (e.g.,
buttons, zips) among other issues (Grose, 1994, pp. 77–81). Esprit's initiative was
perhaps the first evidence that good environmental performance could lead to competitive advantage for a fashion brand. Even more noteworthy was the fact that this
environmental and commercial win-win was led by designers employing creative
thinking to tackle, in a coordinated way, ecological concerns arising at a variety of
different points in the supply chain.

E-collection was distinctive for being grounded in data and environmental knowledge, which was in marked contrast to much environmental activity in fashion marketing and journalism at the time. More typically, fashion marketing and journalism
responded to key themes only superficially and with the same thinking and approaches
they had always used (as demonstrated, for example, in *Textile View*, 1993, p. 17). Typically in the early 1990s, the environment was treated not as a challenge to the production
and consumption priorities of the sector as a whole but as a source of design inspiration for forthcoming collections. The look became natural: natural fibres like cotton
and wool were favoured. The colour palette was oatmeal, drained of synthetic-appearing
shades. Photo shoots took place in pristine mountains, forests and shorelines. Garments
and the imagery around them were manufactured by an unscrutinized process (which
was also often environmentally damaging) of design and production to imitate popular
views of an environmentally friendly aesthetic. In effect, clothing was made to resemble
an imaginary idea of what nature-philic garments must surely look like—garments that
have grown out of the Earth herself fully rendered, ready to wear. The environment became absorbed into existing structures and practices of the industry. It was assimilated
as a trend used to differentiate products and increase sales. It was business as usual but

in natural fibres dyed muted brown and green. Thus, it was understood as a new way to differentiate products and stimulate consumption.

There have been many repercussions of the treatment of environmental concerns by the fashion industry in early 1990s; not least, the enduring legacy of a clichéd idea about what constitutes a sustainability aesthetic in fashion. Still today, two decades on, natural colours, plant and animal fibres and nature-based imagery are frequently assumed to convey ecological credibility to a public with low sustainability awareness, irrespective of the design and production process. Further, levels of knowledge about sustainability in the sector—while improving—are still low and often based on popular understanding and reportage of key themes rather than on grounded assessment. This is caused by, and continues to perpetuate, the flippant way in which fashion is commonly viewed both from outside and inside the profession: 'an immoral, self-indulgent industry…that lacks gravitas and a strong conceptual framework' (Tham, 2008, p. 194). This perceived shallowness is further augmented by an ongoing gender bias that associates fashion with femininity (Vinken cited in Tham, 2008, p. 193) and a favouring of the feminine skills of intuition, personal creativity and craft over the masculine intellectual enquiry that is seen as an essential part of sustainability. This being said, a number of educational projects focused on fashion design students and tutors, such as the Labour Behind the Label project Fashioning an Ethical Industry (FEI, 2011), have been working to improve knowledge and skills around sustainability in general and, in the case of FEI, workers' rights in particular.

For the best part of a decade following the early 1990s, the fashion industry's overt interest in environmental and social concerns waned as the recession reinstated economic considerations and the short-term business cycle as key influences over design and production. Yet during this time, development was under way of the foundations of a life cycle approach in the sector. This began with a life cycle assessment (LCA) study of a women's polyester blouse by consultants Franklin Associates, published in 1993. This study, funded by the American Fiber Manufacturers Association (AFMA), the trade association for American companies that manufacture synthetic and cellulosic fibres, found unequivocally that the majority of the environmental impact in the life cycle of a blouse arises not from the production phase but from the consumer laundering of the blouse. It concluded that as much as 82 per cent of energy use, 66 per cent of solid waste, over half of the emissions to air (for carbon dioxide, specifically, the figure is 83 per cent) and large quantities of waterborne effluents (96 per cent if measured by Biological Oxygen Demand alone) are amassed during washing and drying of the blouse rather than its production.

Doubtless, this LCA was, like many others, commissioned to defend key products and producers against environmental requirements (Heiskanen, 2002, p. 429). For its conclusions categorically turn the spotlight away from the synthetic fibre manufacturers and onto consumers, their homes and their washing practices. Yet irrespective of its political currency, this study and those that followed were central in seeding a new approach that has since had a major influence on the dynamics of the fashion and sustainability debate. They provided data-driven information that helped identify high-impact life cycle stages and target where environmental measures may be most effective. Organizationally, they helped reimagine the industrial supply chain as a circular flow of resources, rather than a sequence of isolated processing steps. And philosophically, they were based on holism—that is, on practices that gain their purpose and meaningfulness from the view that environmental issues are systems extending beyond the boundaries of individual companies. In the case of the polyester blouse, for example, if this ethos is used to galvanize action and whole system improvement, then fashion designers, textile producers and white goods manufacturers together with electricity providers and consumers would be encouraged to work together to bring about change. If this translated into better laundry practices, for example, where a garment is washed on cold temperatures and dried on a line instead of in a tumble dryer, then total life cycle energy consumption could be reduced by a factor of four, according to data for polyester garments (Franklin Associates, 1993, pp. 3–4), and a factor of two for cotton items (Allwood et al, 2006, p. 40).

Given added succour by LCAs, life cycle thinking in fashion, as in other product areas, has widely permeated sustainability approaches initiated in both design and manufacturing and is now the common rationale for both research and commercial work in this area. Retailer Marks and Spencer (M&S)—which accounts for around 10 per cent of the UK's clothing market—combines strands of work that tackle environmental resource impacts in both the use and disposal phases of the life cycle. In addition, the retailer conducts work in more familiar territory for retailers in areas such as materials selection, processing and garment manufacture. In its 'Think Climate—Wash at 30°C' initiative (M&S, 2007), for example, the company has attempted to reach into consumers' homes and influence domestic laundry practices (and energy consumption) by modifying care labels in its garments to recommend lower wash temperatures. Further, through 'Clothes Exchange' (M&S, 2008), a collaboration with the aid and development charity Oxfam, M&S has sought to foster pro-environmental behaviour around clothes recycling. Here shoppers are rewarded for donating unwanted M&S clothing to Oxfam with a money-off voucher to spend at M&S stores. According to the retailer, over half-a-million shoppers are now recycling their clothes in this scheme, which has raised around £2 million for Oxfam.

Such initiatives demonstrate that much of the power to affect change towards sustainability in fashion has now begun to coalesce around large corporations eager to protect and augment the reputation of their brands. This has had the effect of emphasizing particular research questions, which span industrial, academic and political agendas. In the United Kingdom, for example, a recent government-funded initiative in the fashion sector, the Sustainable Clothing Action Plan, commissioned research into the long-favoured questions around resource stocks and flows (e.g., new and emerging fibres [Turley et al., 2009], recycling [Morley et al., 2009] and supply chain and dyehouse efficiency in India [DEFRA, 2010]). Beyond the shores of the United Kingdom, these recurrent research themes also dominate. They include the following:

- The development of agricultural initiatives to improve the resource efficiency of established fibre crops, such as cotton for mass-market consumption, by supporting farmers to adopt practices, seeds and approaches that best suit local soil conditions and climate (bettercotton, 2011).

- The introduction of novel fibres such as those based on cornstarch (Farrington et al., 2005) and soybean (Brooks, 2005).
- New-generation dye and process chemicals and associated methods of application being brought to market that now reduce both resource inputs and pollution outputs in the processing of fibre to fabric to garment (see, for example, *Ecotextile News,* 2010).
- Work to influence the information flows that impact the sustainability of the sector, such as through technologies like *String* which enable the gathering and sharing of supply chain information by global retailers, who now track and trace orders as they flow through the long and complicated textile manufacturing chain (historicfutures, 2011).
- Cross-brand initiatives such as the 'Sustainable Apparel Coalition' to develop a pre-competitive, common approach for measuring and evaluating fibre and fabric efficiency and improve supply chain performance industry-wide (apparelcoalition, 2011).

The speed and breadth of change to the technical and organizational structures of the fashion sector in favour of sustainability is both welcome and impressive. Yet irrespective of the variety, these improvements are alike philosophically and reflect the operationalizing of a techno-centric position on sustainability (Pepper, 1996, p. 37). Here a technological- and science-led revision of existing ways of doing business leads to modified practices and minimized harm, and shapes a debate and research agenda that focuses around production aspects of an unscrutinized industrial paradigm. Yet even though this production-focused approach is the most popular form of response to sustainability in the fashion sector, it is relatively ineffective at securing substantive change to the way in which societies and economies are structured—a point that has been recognized by design for sustainability scholars for many years (e.g., Manzini, 1994; Margolin, 1998; Walker and Nielsen, 1998). For the existing model's values, perceptions and habits of mind are themselves the root cause of the problem of unsustainability (Ehrenfeld, 2008). Without changing how fashion is thought about, both as a sector and as a set of individual and social practices, the very issues that cause unsustainability will prove resilient.

EMERGING RESEARCH AREAS

Recognition of the need to invoke new thinking around fashion and sustainability and to create narratives that show and tell stories of different possibilities is becoming more widespread. Perhaps some of the most obvious signals of changing habits around fashion can be found in a clutch of unconnected anti-consumption initiatives. Examples include the Little Brown Dress (Gwilt and Risannen, 2011b, pp. 122–5) and Uniform (theuniformproject, 2011) projects, where protagonists wear the same dress every day for a year and document this process online to demonstrate alternative ways to enjoy fashion and the creative possibilities of styling. Also, Free Fashion Challenge (freefashionchallenge, 2011) provides a place for people to exchange experiences and stories after agreeing to abstain from buying clothes for a year. Each of these projects is perhaps more a protest against the underlying consumerism of the existing fashion industry than the evolution of new habits of mind around fashion. Nevertheless, they do provide evidence of a growing interest, by designers and consumers, in the ideas and practices that drive the system of fashion consumption and production.

In order to engage with the system of fashion consumption and production, research questions are beginning to be focused on the industrial system as a whole and the thought patterns or paradigms of that system. Mostly these questions have emerged out of a desire to foster understanding about the behaviour of that system—about what is happening and why—and about how to leverage change towards sustainability. A system, like the fashion (industrial) system, is 'a set of things interconnected in such a way that they produce their own pattern of behavior over time' (Meadows, 2009, p. 2). I have argued elsewhere (Fletcher, 2008, pp. 60–73) that insight gained from systems thinking can aid the process of transformation towards sustainability in the fashion sector. It involves moving from a reductionist approach to sustainability issues (i.e., looking at individual sources of pollution, problematic materials, inefficient processes) to a whole industry-as-system approach. Systems thinking can, for example, help explain why certain types of change or design approaches are preferred—most commonly, those that produce benefits quickly, that are felt directly by the innovator and that are already within its sphere of influence. The result is that decisions made in short-term best interests can produce cumulative results that no one likes or wants. In addition, it shows how, somewhat counterintuitively, this most common approach to driving improvements brings the smallest promise of change.

Systems thinking has also been used as part of design for sustainability work in fashion to build understanding about how to deliver big change—most often leveraged by influencing system goals and behaviour. By changing a system's overall objectives, the perceptions, habits and thinking of the fashion sector alters, with far-reaching implications. Modelling the fashion sector as a complex system offers an overarching framework for understanding the potential effectiveness of an array of different design approaches with a range of different scales, targets and time frames. It also provides a platform from where design for sustainability work with a changed epistemology can develop and thrive, such as the emerging body of work around Slow Fashion.

SLOW FASHION

In the fashion sector, low-cost, homogeneous, quantity dressing has seen the UK's budget clothing market grow by 45 per cent in the last five years, twice the rate of the normal clothing market (Shah, 2008, pp. 10–11). A combination of low price and a commercial fashion business model based on growth has overseen a change in purchasing and wearing habits where garments are often bought in multiples and discarded quickly, for they have little perceived value. Against a backdrop of growth-obsessed industrial activity, a movement promoting slow culture and values in fashion has emerged, albeit with less coherence than in the sector that is its inspiration: food.

The Slow Fashion movement is built from recognition of a systemic need to discontinue the practices of today's sector; that is, to break from the values and goals of fast (growth-based) fashion (Fletcher, 2010, pp. 259–66). It has a vocabulary of small-scale production, traditional craft techniques, local materials and markets. It challenges growth fashion's obsession with mass production and globalized style and becomes a guardian of diversity, and proponents of it can be seen around the world. It questions growth fashion's emphasis on image and watching rather than making (Clark, 2008, pp. 427–46). It offers a changed set of power relations between fashion creators and consumers compared with growth fashion, based on the forging of relationships and trust that is possible at smaller scales. It professes a heightened state of awareness of the design process and its impacts on resource flows, workers, communities and ecosystems. It prices garments higher than in the growth model to reflect true ecological and social costs, and as a production model it offers a radical alternative to high-volume, standardized fashion, making profit by selling fewer higher-priced items. Slow culture (even with associated high prices) is also seen to promote the democratization of fashion not by offering more people access to clothes by lowering prices (a claim often made in support of fast, growth fashion) but by offering these same people more control over institutions and technologies that affect their lives. A range of practitioners are working with some of these ideas, including the small knitwear brand Keep and Share (keepandshare, 2011)—which produces garments designed to be shared and through such experience to foster emotional durability—and the London-based studio and shop Here Today Here Tomorrow (heretoday-heretomorrow, 2011) that, through its workshop and training courses, erodes the distance between the making and using of fashion.

Yet, perhaps unsurprisingly, for a sector like fashion, which is dominated by the commercial potential of change and surface, slow fashion has been superficially mediated and adopted particularly by the fashion media as a literal descriptor of speed (see, for example, Britten, 2008). Here 'slow' is understood and equated with, say, durable products, traditional production techniques or design concepts that are seasonless. The term 'slow fashion' is used to segment and differentiate garments produced in the growth fashion model in a fresh way, to offer a new marketing angle on products and brands that happen to have a long heritage, durable pieces or classic design. Slow Fashion— largely because it is the lexicographical opponent of fast fashion—is wheeled in to offer apparent legitimacy to existing products and business models, conferring upon them a sense of ethics and resourcefulness because the normal cycle of trend-induced change and consumption is eschewed.

Yet despite its years of superficial misappropriation, Slow Fashion is beginning to emerge as a social movement of systemic change in fashion. Essential to it is a deep questioning of the role of economic growth, underlying values and world views in fashion. For Slow Fashion necessitates the framing of the fashion sector as a subsystem of the larger system of economics, society and planetary ecosystems. It recognizes that in order to change fashion, economic and social practices that shape, limit and give meaning to the sector have to be part of the fashion debate. The question is not, Can we produce more fashion? (we know that this is possible) but, What sort of fashion system would best serve our overall needs?

CO-DESIGN AND DESIGNING NON-PLAN

Considering the question of overall needs in the fashion context, a growing number of researchers, cultural activists, and design practitioners are now exploring themes related to co-design (i.e., designing with others) to promote sustainability through transformation of fashion power structures and consumer passivity. In co-design, the design and production model is shaped fundamentally by the goal of collaboratively designing products with the people who will use them. Its principles of inclusiveness, cooperative processes and participative action work to disrupt hierarchical power relations (as exemplified in most fashion brands) and offer users of clothes more control over their garments' design and production. Not dissimilar to ideas underpinning Slow Fashion, co-design contests the economic growth-driven logic of most fashion activities today. It sits at the fringes of fashion activity, offering a small-scale, human and skill-centred response to conventional fashion practice. One example of a co-design fashion practice is Antiform Industries (antiformindustries, 2011), which works within the Hyde Park community in Leeds to cooperatively create fashion. Tapping into pre-existing sewing, repair, craft and embellishment skills, and offering training where skills are in short supply, Antiform has facilitated the creation of an eight-piece collection with sixty-four local people (beaders, knitters, artists, seamstresses and volunteers); the collection is sold through outlets in the Leeds area.

In co-design practices, the designer begins to inhabit roles outside of the traditional private and product-based routes and contribute instead to the public, social and ecological good—as facilitator, intensifier and educator. These ideas build on the ethos of 'non-plan' developed by Paul Barker in the 1960s: 'Non-plan was essentially a very humble idea: that it is very difficult to decide what is best for *other* people' (Barker cited in Dunlop, 2010, p. 40). Here design activity focuses on the establishing of 'frameworks for decision' (Barker et al. cited in Dunlop, 2010, p. 40), a direction explored in the pioneering fashion design activism work of researcher Otto von Busch, who has worked with techniques including hacking (to 'open up' the cultural fashion system and influence it from within [2008]) and skills-building, such as through his 'recyclopaedias', which support users to rework old clothes into new fashion pieces (von Busch 2011).

LOCAL WISDOM AND POST-GROWTH FASHION

Other strands of fashion and sustainability research are looking to explore the social context of garments and use this knowledge to design and redesign systems of production and consumption. The Local Wisdom research project (localwisdom, 2011) draws on ethnographic methods and photography to explore the material, individual and social practices associated with using garments—described as the 'craft of use'; that is, to uncover the ingenuity and skilled practices that accompany garments after the point of purchase. These are not necessarily done within the rubric of intellectualized concerns or commercial opportunities for sustainability but instead emerge from the culturally embedded wisdoms of thrift such as domestic provisioning, care of community, freedom of creative expression and connectedness to nature. This explicit emphasis on the wide-spread practices of use, rather than the challenges of production, as a starting point for change towards sustainability signals a departure from what has gone before. It privileges sensitivity to people's lived experience rather than industrial or commercial ideas about what sustainability is or should be. The craft of use is a process of cultivating sustained attentiveness to tending and using garments and not just creating them—and to feed this into designing new forms of fashion practice (Fletcher, 2011) (see Figures 18.1 and 18.2).

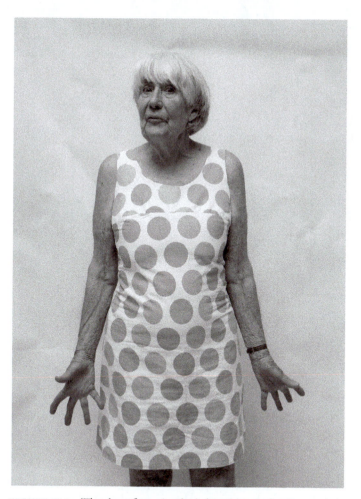

FIGURE 18.1 'The dress from Antibes' shared by six family members from the Local Wisdom project. Image courtesy of Local Wisdom. Photo credit: Sean Michael.

FIGURE 18.2 'Fell into my path' sweater found on the floor and still the favourite from the Local Wisdom project. Image courtesy of Local Wisdom. Photo credit: Paige Green.

Critically, the myriad practices that make up the craft of use typically involve few materials and little money but act to enhance people's fashion experiences within the limits of clothing they already own. As such, the deep inner space of the wardrobe offers up potential inspiration to a sustainability-oriented design process concerned with qualitative improvement rather than quantitative growth in material throughput. Such work contributes to the radical post-growth sustainability agenda that critiques the central importance of growth to notions of prosperity and attempts to define and describe economic activity by biophysical limits. This was developed over thirty years ago by Herman Daly (1992), among others. Here an alternative to the predominant economic model (which is structurally reliant on economic growth tied to increasing resource use) involves a transformed economic logic that works within planetary limits and looks for ways to add value, meet needs and provide employment without constantly expanding material throughput. Framed in this way the craft of use offers tentative starting points for understanding opportunities for how fashion in a post-growth economy may develop, and Local Wisdom looks to amplify these practices and increase their uptake.

'PHYSICAL' VIEW OF FASHION

Design for sustainability research themes, such as those concerned with the craft of use, move from a relatively abstract or imaginary vision of fashion derived by economics towards a more physical view informed by biophysical systems. They shift from a view of fashion as residing in an imaginary and emotional 'world of ideas' that is 'essentially groundless' (Farrell, 2008) to a world in which the Earth, while abundant, has limits. This grounding emphasizes the value of the material, product, place and person (farmer, seamstress, user) within sustainability and has been called 'true materialism', which contrasts sharply with the kind of materialism prevalent today. Juliet Schor (2002, p. 55) cites the cultural critic Raymond Williams when she says, 'We are not truly materialist because we fail to invest deep or sacred meanings in material goods. Instead our materialism connotes an unbounded desire to acquire, followed by a throwaway mentality.' A number of researcher-practitioners are exploring different ways to deeply value the material component of fashion; among them is Timo Risannen (2008), who is exploring ways to value more highly the material resource of fashion products through experimental techniques in pattern-cutting. His work, along with others such as Holly McQuillan (2011), is leading to changed garment silhouettes because the various fabric pieces or pattern blocks that make up a garment are modified in shape to reduce waste in the cutting process. This work is grounded in ideas of resourcefulness and brings a contemporary critique to the fashion sector based on historically important practices of creating garments without waste. It also speaks of a changed relationship between the fashion sector and the materials it uses, inspiring longer-term ideas that place great value on maintenance and endurance—that is, 'Clothes that are never finished' (Risannen, 2011, p. 136).

CONCLUSIONS

Design for sustainability research and practice in fashion is beginning to dive deeply into the thought processes, values, habits and social and cultural practices surrounding garments—offering a growing body of work that stands alongside the production-focused commercial activity of the large brands and retailers. Much of this research and practice is slow to enact—not fitting within existing frameworks and practices and falling outside of (mass) commerce—and hence, fashion as we have come to know it. Yet it is starting to influence the intellectual scope of the sustainability challenge for the sector as well as the responses to this challenge. It is giving rise to the development of fashion products that are no longer only optimized around the goals and rules of consumerism but that find a new resilience, beauty and value in sustainability. It moves sustainability in fashion from a responsive mode to one based on ingenuity.

REFERENCES

Allwood, J. M., Laursen, S. E., Malvido de Rodriguez, C. and Bocken, N.M.P. (2006), *Well Dressed?* University of Cambridge Institute of Manufacturing: Cambridge.

antiformindustries (2011), <http://www.antiformindustries.com/> accessed November 2, 2011.

apparelcoalition (2011), <http://www.apparelcoalition.org/> accessed November 2, 2011.

bettercotton (2011), <http://www.bettercotton.org/> accessed November 2, 2011.

Bierhals, C. A. (2008), *Green Designed Fashion,* Avedition: Ludwigsburg.

Black, S. (2008), *Eco Chic the Fashion Paradox,* Black Dog: London.

Britten, F. (2008), 'Future Proof Your Look', *Sunday Times,* August 24, <http://women.timesonline. co.uk/tol/life_and_style/women/fashion/article4542542.ece> accessed September 26, 2011.

Brooks, M. M. (2005), 'Soya Bean Protein Fibres: Past, Present and Future', in Blackburn, R. S. (ed.), *Biodegradable and Sustainable Fibres,* Woodhead: Abingdon. pp. 398–435.

Brown, S. (2010), *Eco Fashion,* Laurence King: London.

Clark, H. (2008), 'SLOW + FASHION—an Oxymoron—or a Promise for the Future...?' *Fashion Theory,* vol. 12, no. 4: pp. 427–46.

Daly, H. (1992), *Steady-State Economics,* 2nd ed., Earthscan: London.

DEFRA (2010), 'Baseline Evidence: Mapping of the Sustainability Impacts and Interventions of Clothing', <http://archive.defra.gov.uk/environment/business/products/roadmaps/ clothing/evidence.htm> accessed September 26, 2011.

Dunlop, P. (2010), 'Unravelling Design: Fashion: Dressmaking, Ethos', PhD thesis, Queensland University of Technology, Brisbane.

Ecotextile News (2010), 'Water Saving Dyes Make a Big Splash', vol. 39: pp. 20–23.

Ehrenfeld, J. A. (2008), *Sustainability by Design,* Yale University Press: New Haven, CT.

Farrell, R. (2008), 'Fashion and Presence', *Nomenus Quarterly,* vol. 3: unpaginated.

Farrington, D. W., Lunt, J. and Blackburn, R. (2005), 'Soya Bean Protein Fibres: Past, Present and Future', in Blackburn, R. S. (ed.), *Biodegradable and Sustainable Fibres,* Woodhead: Abingdon. pp. 191–220.

FEI (2011), 'Fashioning an Ethical Industry', <http://www.fashioninganethicalindustry.org/ home/> accessed January 7, 2011.

Finkelstein, J. (1996), *After a Fashion,* Melbourne University Press: Melbourne.

Fletcher, K. (2008), *Sustainable Fashion and Textiles: Design Journeys,* Earthscan: London.

Fletcher, K. (2010), 'Slow Fashion: An Invitation for Systems Change', *Journal of Fashion Practice,* vol. 2, no. 2: pp. 259–66.

Fletcher, K. (2011) 'Post Growth Fashion and the Craft of Users', in Gwilt, A. and Rissannen, T. (eds), *Shaping Sustainable Fashion,* Earthscan: London. pp. 165–75.

Fletcher, K. and Grose (2012), *Fashion and Sustainability: Design for Change,* Laurence King: London.

Franklin Associates (1993), *Resource and Environmental Profile Analysis of a Manufactured Apparel Product: Woman's Knit Polyester Blouse,* American Fibre Manufacturers Association: Washington, DC.

freefashionchallenge (2011), <http://freefashionchallenge.com/> accessed November 2, 2011.

Garanti Galeri, (2008), *Fashion for Sustainability,* exhibition catalogue, Garanti Galeri: Istanbul.

Grose, L. (1994), 'Incorporating Environmental Objectives through the Design Process and through Business', in *World Conference Proceedings,* Textile Institute: Manchester. pp. 77–81.

Gwilt, A. and Rissannen, T. (eds) (2011a), *Shaping Sustainable Fashion,* Earthscan: London.

Gwilt, A. and Rissannen, T. (2011b), 'Personalizing Fashion', in Gwilt, A. and Rissannen, T. (eds), *Shaping Sustainable Fashion,* Earthscan: London. pp. 122–25.

Heiskanen, E. (2002), 'The Institutional Logic of Life Cycle Thinking', *Journal of Cleaner Production,* vol. 10: pp. 427–37.

heretoday-heretomorrow (2011), <http://heretoday-heretomorrow.com/> accessed November 2, 2011.

historicfutures (2011), <http://www.historicfutures.com/> accessed November 2, 2011.

keepandshare (2011), <http://www.keepandshare.co.uk/> accessed November 2, 2011.

localwisdom (2011), <http://www.localwisdom.info> accessed November 2, 2011.

M&S (2007), 'M&S Helps Customers to "Think Climate" by Relabelling Clothing', <http://corporate.marksandspencer.com/media/press_releases/product/Menswear/23042007_MSHelpsCustomersToThinkClimateByRelabellingClothing> accessed June 23, 2009.

M&S (2008), 'M&S and Oxfam to Launch "M&S and Oxfam Clothes Exchange"—UK's Biggest Clothing Recycling Campaign', <http://corporate.marksandspencer.com/investors/press_releases/company/15012008_MSandOxfamtolaunchMSandOxfamClothesExchange UKsbiggestclothingrecyclingcampaign> accessed March 18, 2010.

Manzini, E. (1994), 'Design, Environment and Social Quality: From "Existenzminimum" to "Quality Maximum"', *Design Issues,* vol. 10, no. 1: pp. 37–43.

Margolin, V. (1998), 'Design for a Sustainable World', *Design Issues,* vol. 14, no. 2: pp. 83–92.

McQuillan, H. (2011), 'Zero-Waste Design Practice', in Gwilt, A. and Rissannen, T. (eds), *Shaping Sustainable Fashion,* Earthscan: London. pp. 83–97.

Meadows, D. H. (2009), *Thinking in Systems: A Primer,* Earthscan: London.

Morley, N. J., Bartlett, C. and McGill, I. (2009), *Maximising Reuse and Recycling of UK Clothing and Textiles: A Report to the Department for Environment, Food and Rural Affairs,* Oakdene Hollins: Aylesbury.

Pepper, D. (1996), *Modern Environmentalism: An Introduction,* Routledge: London.

Rissannen, T. (2008), 'Creating Fashion without the Creation of Fabric Waste', in Hethorn, J. and Ulasewicz, C. (eds), *Sustainable Fashion: Why Now,* Fairchild: New York. pp. 184–206.

Rissannen, T. (2011), 'Designing Endurance', in Gwilt, A. and Rissannen, T. (eds), *Shaping Sustainable Fashion,* Earthscan: London. pp. 127–38.

Schor, J. B. (2002), 'Cleaning the Closet: Towards a New Fashion Ethic', in Schor, J. B. and Taylor, B. (eds), *Sustainable Planet: Solutions for the Twenty-First Century,* Beacon Press: Boston. pp. 45–59.

Shah, D. (2008), 'View', *Textile View Magazine,* vol. 82: pp. 10–11.

Simmel, G. (1971), *On Individuality and Social Forms,* University of Chicago Press: Chicago, London.

Textile View (1993), 'Trends', no. 22: p. 17.

Tham, M. (2008), 'Lucky People Forecast: A Systemic Futures Perspective on Fashion and Sustainability', PhD thesis, Goldsmiths, University of London, London.

theuniformproject (2011), <http://www.theuniformproject.com/> accessed November 2, 2011.

Turley, D. B., Copeland, J. E., Horne, M., Blackburn, R. S., Stott E., Laybourn, S. R., Harwood, J. and Hughes, J. K. (2009), *The Role and Business Case for Existing and Emerging Fibres in Sustainable Clothing*, Defra: London.

von Busch, O. (2008), 'FASHION-Able: Hactivism and Engaged Fashion Design', PhD thesis, Art Monitor, Gothenburg.

von Busch, O. (2011) 'Recyclopaedias', <http://www.kulturservern.se/wronsov/selfpassage/disCook/disCook.htm> accessed September 26, 2011.

Walker, S. and Nielsen, R. (1998), 'Systemic Shift: Sustainable Development and Industrial Design Methodology', *Journal of Sustainable Product Design*, no. 4: pp. 7–17.

19

A New Design Ethic for a New Reality

JOHNPAUL KUSZ

INTRODUCTION

Throughout history, design has evolved along with changes in technology and society. Designers have been a part of the change process, serving industry and markets. As we move toward the center of the twenty-first century, we will face unprecedented challenges, many of which are born of the very technologies we have created.

If we are to create a more sustainable world, then it is likely that we will need to change the very nature of design and designing. We might well start by making a commitment to ourselves that is much like the one that R. Buckminster Fuller made in 1927, dedicating himself to "a world that works for 100% of humanity, in the shortest possible time, through spontaneous cooperation, without ecological offense or disadvantage to anyone" (quoted in Zung, 2001, p. xix).

UP AGAINST A WELL-DESIGNED WALL

In the summer of 1992, the Industrial Designers Society of America (IDSA) under the auspices of its educational foundation Worldesign and the International Council of Societies of Industrial Design (ICSID) organized a one-week program at San Jose State University in California to explore the potential of design to address the ecological and social issues that were emerging. With funding from the U.S. Environmental Protection Agency (EPA) and the National Endowment for the Arts—the first time these two agencies had cosponsored anything—students from industrial design programs in eight countries were brought together to learn, to think, and then share their ideas about how designers might use their skills in addressing the challenges of a postindustrial society. These challenges included energy use, urbanization, new housing paradigms, transportation, poverty, and waste. The program was entitled Ecologically Affirmative Design.

Those fortunate students who participated heard from Victor Papanek, who had written *Design for the Real World* some twenty years earlier, in one of his last speaking engagements; Paul Hawken, prior to the publication of *The Ecology of Commerce;* Hunter Lovins before she and Amory Lovins collaborated with Paul Hawken to write *Natural Capitalism;* David Wann, author of *Biologic,* a precursor to the idea of biomimicry; and Mary Ann Curran, who was leading the U.S. EPA's life cycle assessment initiative and later authored a definitive book on the subject, *Environmental Life-Cycle Assessment.*

As an organizer and contributor to this program, I saw firsthand how students from around the world explored the issues that they would be confronting while they listened and learned from progressive designers and nondesigners about how they might work together to create a better world.

The results of this workshop were showcased in a simple and minimalist exhibit that was replicated for each of the participating schools in order to spread the thinking and the consciousness back to the communities of the participants.

Ecologically Affirmative Design was a worthwhile experience, yet I wonder how much of the experience was internalized by those students and other participants and how it might have been incorporated into their thinking and their work as designers and members of the world community. The exhibit's title panel was very telling. Simply labeled Up Against a Well-Designed Wall, it portrayed the palm of a hand as if pressing on a pane of glass that was invisible until encountered and seemingly immovable. It illustrated the frustration that its creators were experiencing when they began to seriously explore the issues and confront the challenges; challenges that are in large part a product of the world we have designed.

It has been over twenty years since that program and the writing of this chapter. The students who participated in it are likely practicing designers today. Some are carrying the experience and its influence with them into their consciousness and work, shaping a reality with a new and emerging design ethic. But the progress is slow and there is always resistance.

In the time since that experience, even more challenges to our environment, our society, and our economy have surfaced. Twenty years later, it has become apparent that much more needs to happen if we are to successfully redesign and reshape a world that has any semblance of viable sustainability. It seems we are still up against a well-designed wall.

CONSUMER CAPITALISM

We design in the now, the current reality, based upon our experience and our interpretation of what we have learned and observed. Since design is the commingling of art and science, like art and science it is a part of the zeitgeist, the expression of our collective consciousness. Through the process of design in the now, we connect the past to the present, while we project into the future our expectations for a next reality. We put change into motion, a design trajectory that includes not only the benefits we have planned but frequently consequences that had not been anticipated. With our designs, we shape the future, and in doing so we inescapably bear responsibility for it.

After the Second World War, when talking about the rebuilding of London, Winston Churchill said, "We shape our buildings, and thereafter they shape us." Churchill was alluding to the dialogue between people and place. It is a dialogue of change that moves us through time. But it is more than buildings that we shape. Through the process of design, we shape products and services, and the systems that produce and support them. Like buildings, our products, the business models that bring them into being, and the systems in which they operate shape us as well. But even more so and because products are fluid, they can be quickly replicated and therefore become pervasive. Today, products, business models, and the systems in which they operate come into being at a speed, a scale, and with a scope that creates impacts that can dwarf the impacts associated with even the largest single edifice.

Looking back at the twentieth century and the emergence of the consumer society, we have an opportunity to see the many benefits of the products we have created and made available to an ever-growing community of users as well as the financial returns those products have generated for their producers. The concept of mutual benefit is the underpinning of the market-based system of enterprise that we have come to know as capitalism through the early musings of Adam Smith (1776/1994). Our ability to anticipate needs, generate solutions, and produce the goods and services that meet those needs has been remarkable. With hindsight, however, we can examine the cultural and political dynamics of this period and how we created a legacy of unintentional consequences—both good and bad—that we are encountering in the present.

In the middle of the twentieth century, a world that had survived the calamity of the Second World War was reinventing itself by utilizing and expanding the machinery and the capacity that had been built to win a war. The products created, the business models that generated those products, and the political and organizational systems that supported them were built on the same linear-throughput/military-industrial-complex paradigm that had proven itself in winning a war. In that moment in time, growing economies based on converting resources to materials and then into durable and consumable goods was a seemingly logical and achievable road back to prosperity.

The idea was institutionalized in the words of the often quoted retailing analyst Victor Lebow:

> Our enormously productive economy demands that we make consumption our way of life, that we convert the buying and use of goods into rituals, that we seek our spiritual satisfactions, our ego satisfactions, in consumption. The measure of social status, of social acceptance, of prestige, is now to be found in our consumptive patterns. The very meaning and significance of our lives today expressed in consumptive terms. The greater the pressures upon the individual to conform to safe and accepted social standards, the more does he tend to express his aspirations and his individuality in terms of what he wears, drives, eats—his home, his car, his pattern of food serving, his hobbies. These commodities and services must be offered to the consumer with a special

urgency. We require not only "forced draft" consumption, but "expensive" consumption as well. We need things consumed, burned up, worn out, replaced, and discarded at an ever increasing pace. We need to have people eat, drink, dress, ride, live, with ever more complicated and, therefore, constantly more expensive consumption. The home power tools and the whole "do-it-yourself" movement are excellent examples of "expensive" consumption. (1955, p. 7)

During the Eisenhower administration, the chairman of the President's Council of Economic Advisers stated, "The American economy's ultimate purpose is to produce more consumers goods" (Suzuki, 2003).

Capitalism had been effectively morphed into consumer capitalism—a theoretical economic and political condition in which consumer demand is manipulated in a deliberate and coordinated way, and on a very large scale through managed marketing techniques to the advantage of sellers.

Within twenty years of the Second World War, Germany and Japan, two of the most devastated countries on the planet in 1945, had embraced the consumer capitalism model and had recovered and grown both economically and politically. They continued to grow at rates that appeared to justify this decision relative to alternative economic models, namely models of nonconsumer capitalism. Within forty years, countries that had embraced other models were also turning to consumerism. The trend was clear. Growth through consumption was the fastest way to increase wealth. Consumption of material-based goods had become the underpinning of the economy and the largest share of what we measure to define our wealth, the comparative metric now known as the gross domestic product (GDP). The GDP soon became a driver of economic activity, not an indicator of it. With economic growth as a central goal, decisions about investment in enterprise were directed toward those activities that generated the highest revenue and returns, not necessarily toward those that best met a given need.

Today many emerging markets are going through their own reinvention based on industrialization and consumer capitalism. India and China are experiencing industrial transitions that are around ten times faster, and, together, 200 times larger than the British Industrial Revolution. Over the next two decades, the world will witness the emergence of an additional three billion middle-class consumers. We can only imagine what those consumers will want and how meeting those wants will influence the world's natural resource landscape. Demand for resources in the twenty-first century will continue to surge. We will continue to see a confluence of geopolitical strategies and business strategies aimed at identifying and securing natural resource supplies (Dobbs et al., 2011).

When the generation of wealth became linked to the consumption of products, a new dynamic or system model emerged. It set in motion activities that supported and reinforced the wealth it created. Like all system models, this model had within it a number of reinforcing feedback loops. As the system matures, it gets stronger and creates more momentum. It is self-serving and self-preserving. Since the middle of the last century, adoption of the model as well as the adaptation to the model resulted in the design and redesign of many products, business models, and system models. Design became part of the system. Design became complicit.

There are numerous examples in many sectors that clearly illustrate the impact of linking the generation of wealth to consumption. As a designer working in the medical instruments sector early in my career, I was often tasked with the challenge of converting medical instruments from enduring products that were repeatedly used in surgery after autoclave sterilization into one-time use, disposable products that were delivered to the surgical suite presterilized with ethylene oxide gas and disposed of through incineration after surgery. The changes that occurred at the level of the business model and the system models associated with these disposable products were very significant. The amount of energy and resources used expanded exponentially. The materials themselves shifted from durable and repairable materials to nondurable disposable materials: in many cases from stainless steel to high-grade plastics. The business model migrated from a sales-and-service model with highly knowledgeable salespeople to a sales model that relied more on numbers (quantity) than on knowledge (quality). The reliance on equipment free of contamination by the surgical suite was outsourced to the supplier whose quality control was based on statistical methods, not upon the personal responsibility of those who were charged with the efficacy of the surgical suite.

As businesses adopt linear models and equate consumption with wealth generation, growth becomes essential to drive efficiencies of scale in production. This is because scale reduces fixed costs with more profitability per unit. The resulting momentum creates a paradox from which it is difficult for an enterprise to escape. We have constructed complex, linear, and vertically integrated systems of manufacture that produce products as they consume resources. Simply put, we have designed a monster that demands to be fed. The bigger it gets, the more it needs; the more it needs, the bigger it gets. To keep the system going and growing, we must continually grow consumer demand.

But eventually the market becomes saturated. It is at this point that the enterprise needs to find new outlets for its output. The monster is hungry. The situation can be exacerbated by continued investment in capacity that often exceeds demand. This causes falling returns and contraction leading to lost opportunity for the capital that has been spent building the excess capacity.

To avert this, an enterprise will often reduce margins in the areas over which it has some control, such as labor costs, and begin commoditizing the product in order to penetrate untapped markets that are more cost sensitive. But this can begin a "race to the bottom" between enterprises in terms of cost management, which can result in the externalization of any costs that can be pushed into the social sphere, such as waste management and pollution control, health and safety, and labor costs and benefits. The externalizing of the costs by private, for-profit enterprises is, in effect, a form of welfare support for corporations and a false discount to the consumer. As this system generates sales volumes, and savings to those few who benefit from the product, the externalized costs are borne by the entire society. Externalized costs are marginalized, minimized, and not accounted for within the operating profile, making them difficult to ascertain and make visible. This opacity is a consequence of the system model in which our current enterprise models operate.

Alternatively, enterprise can also use design to generate incremental improvements that entice the consumer to purchase a next generation of the product in question, to continue the feeding frenzy. This strategy is known as planned obsolescence. It is a strategy that was born of the design community and has inexorably connected industrial design to a wasteful consumer society. The term "planned obsolescence" was first coined in 1932. It was introduced as a strategy to restart spending during the Great Depression (London, 1932). Its popularity as a business strategy is credited to Brooks Stevens, an American industrial designer, who in 1954 used it and described it as a design and business strategy. To quote Stevens, it is the role of designers to "instill in the buyer the desire to own something a little newer, a little better, a little sooner than is necessary" (Stevens, 1954).

The support of consumer capitalism was well-entrenched by the late 1960s. The consumer capitalism system model grew and became dominant due to many factors that converged in the 1950s, generating momentum and an almost intoxicated exuberance about growth. The inertia that resulted once the system was institutionalized as the model of choice made any subsequent change to this system, and even the suggestion of change, daunting and risky. Alternatives were tied to alternative political models and demonized because of that association. The path forward was consumption, the alignment of the players complete and formidable, and design an important part of the system. Indeed, persons who challenged the system found themselves up against a very well-designed wall. Then something happened.

CONSCIOUSNESS AND AN EMERGING NEW REALITY

In the mid-to-late 1960s, social and political turmoil moved through the United States and other parts of the world. A few designers observed the changing landscape and began to share their observations with the world. Designers such as R. Buckminster Fuller and Victor Papanek began to publicly challenge the complicity of design in consumerism and suggested a new path forward for the profession. What they saw was a troubling reality, obliging them to confront the current worldview.

Fuller wrote *Operating Manual for Spaceship Earth,* in 1969. Papanek's *Design for the Real World* was published in 1971. Their efforts and their views of the situation were largely ignored or rebuffed as counterproductive or even blasphemous. Nonetheless, they were a part of a small but growing group of professionals—scientists, sociologists, engineers, and other disciplines—who were challenging the status quo. The group included critical thinking biologist Garret Hardin, whose seminal piece, "The Tragedy of the Commons," appeared in the journal *Science* in 1968. This paper revisited and expanded upon a pamphlet written by William Forster Lloyd in England in 1833, entitled *Two Lectures on the Checks to Population* that examined the issue of unbridled exploitation of resources (Lloyd, 1833).

These authors were beginning to see that if the flawed world being shaped by design continued on its trajectory, it would lead us down an untenable path. They were talking about challenges of sustainability before sustainability became a word in common usage. They were talking about social equity, a flawed economic model, and the consequences of resource depletion and environmental damage associated with population growth.

Their consciousness was a result of the kind of observation, analysis, and synthesis that is germane to good design thinking—the cross-fertilization of disciplines and the reframing of the challenges they saw facing humanity. Like many others, Fuller and Papanek were influenced by events of the day, not the least of which occurred in 1968, when Apollo 8 astronaut Bill Anders, looking from his capsule at the earth, said, "We came all this way to explore the moon, and the most important thing is that we discovered the earth." That image burned in the consciousness of many the reality that we live on a finite planet, and we are dependent on its resources for our survival. Subsequent images of the planet and feedback from space allowed us, as a species, to see and study our impacts on the planet.

The realization that we have been witnessing a new and dangerous epoch in the history of the world has become undeniable. The Anthropocene, a new geologic era characterized by humans as a force in shaping nature, had begun. Studies by ecologist Erle Ellis at the University of Maryland have shown that the vast majority of ecosystems on the planet now reflect the presence of people. There are more trees on farms than in wild forests and anthropogenic biomes are spread about the planet in ways that the ecological arrangements of the prehuman world were not. We have changed the balance of basic elements in the environment, from the intentional manufacture of nitrogen to fertilize our crops to the unintentional release of carbon dioxide in the generation of energy from fossil fuels (*The Economist*, 2011).

With our overwhelming impact on the planet, we have unwittingly made ourselves its caretakers. If we as a species are to survive, and hopefully thrive, in the future, we will need to take full responsibility for our actions and their consequences; fix what is broken if we can; mitigate damage; and adapt to the unfamiliar conditions of a planet that author Bill McKibben calls *Eaarth* (2010). In positing the name *Eaarth*, McKibben is indicating that this new, fundamentally changed planet, while still recognizable, is also very different. Like it or not, we have crossed the Rubicon; we cannot return. We will be stewards designing our course forward with intention and greater precaution, or we will gamble our own future on the unintended consequences of our actions.

A COPERNICAN MOMENT

We are in a Copernican Moment, one of those moments when we, individually or as a society, begin to see reality differently. These are times when the rules change. Some, like Copernicus, see these changes sooner and are criticized, even persecuted. If what they see is real, inevitably but slowly, society then moves from denial to acceptance, grieving the disappearance of comfortable and familiar constructs as we would any personal loss. Elizabeth Kubler-Ross, the author of *On Death and Dying*, suggested that there are the five stages of grieving a loss: denial, anger, bargaining, depression, and acceptance (1969). It is not surprising that old ideas and constructs would die slowly, as the beliefs and the institutions that were built upon them resist change, whether they are represented by a world of conspicuous consumption and cheap energy, or a world of privileged access to protected and plentiful natural landscapes. As with any loss, some are in denial, some are angry, some are bargaining, many are depressed, and more and more are accepting this new reality or, as some have come to call it, the new normal. Our reactions vary, and during the period of transition we express them differently, until finally the change has been accepted by the vast majority.

The work of Copernicus forever changed our view of humanity's place in the cosmos. No longer could we legitimately think of our world as being at the center of the universe. Today, we are coming to realize through an emerging collective consciousness that our relationship to our world is not what we might have once thought it to be. We can no longer deny the truth of the convergence of population explosion, energy and resource depletion, climate change, toxic overload, and the inevitable consequences of economic insecurity and decline. In truth, we depend on the planet and its abundance. It does not depend on us. Our choice is to preserve and steward it in this Anthropocene era or to continue exploiting it.

The sobering reality is clear: we are entering a period of convergence and contraction. The worst-case scenario is what James Lovelock, author of *Gaia* and more recently *The Revenge of Gaia*, calls a "sustainable retreat" (2007), a reduction of the world's population to a number that can be sustained by the ever-diminishing carrying capacity of the planet. Not a very appealing future.

A better approach might be to create a new normal to replace the current anomaly with a relationship to the world that is defined by what has come to be called a steady-state economy, an ecological economy in which a society learns to live on its current income, the income from natural and human capital, without compromising its health and preferably enhancing the health of both over time.

This is a challenge that is nothing less than existential. What we must change is our relationship to the source of our wealth—natural capital. This demands not only a change in thinking but also a change in being. Now that is a design problem!

RETHINKING THE PRODUCT/BUSINESS/SYSTEM MODEL

The change in being starts with reframing the current model of consumption at every level. It is about making sure that our product and business models fit into a system model that is sustainable by design. Arguably, it seems that what we have been doing to date is trying to fit so-called sustainable ideas and concepts into our sacred business models without realizing that the business model is transient and exists at the pleasure of the planet's system model, which is here to stay.

A framework of management that is based on the ideals of sustainable development can shape contemporary thinking on the management strategies we apply to the capital we need. New ideas, based on ideals, might effectively operate on enterprise in ways that are not linear and hierarchically structured (a military model) but self-organizing and aligned to a mission or purpose creating a beneficial path forward toward a sustainable future (a system or natural model). Interest in self-organizing models based on systems thinking continues to grow, with work by early system dynamics pioneers like Forrester, Meadows, and Meadows, and, more recently by Senge, author of *The Fifth Discipline* (1990).

The objective of an alignment based on the ideals of sustainable development would be to drive decisions toward the highest order of economic viability, environmental integrity, and social equity, resulting in new and innovative products and business models. In their book *Natural Capitalism,* Hawken, Lovins, and Lovins discuss the three other forms of capital (natural capital, human capital, and physical capital) in addition to conventional financial capital (2000). They explore the concept of natural capital with some discussion of the value of human capital, viewing it as a source of labor, knowledge, and innovation. The view builds on Adam Smith's assertion that labor and the commodities it produces, rather than silver and gold, are fundamental to value (1776/1994).

In addition to being viewed as a measurable unit of labor, human capital's greatest value might be embodied in its potential, a subject much discussed by management experts like Drucker (1989) and Rajan and Zingales (2003), who see the rise of the "knowledge worker" as a form of capital. This new reality is also reflected through shifts occurring within many organizations. It can be seen in adjustments in the semantics that relate to human activity, such as changing a department name from Labor Relations to Human Resources, and then to Human Capital or Human Assets. When the lexicon changes, it often reflects and affects our perceptions, our expectations, and ultimately our performance and the associated outcomes.

Human capital works in the gap between natural and physical capital, bridging the two by translating and filtering information and converting resources with human activity into energy and material. It is at this nexus that opportunities for rethinking and redesigning the processes of industry occur. The combination of systems (flows of materials and energy) and networks (the people and organizational models that manage the systems) are the replicate of ecology in an industrial context—industrial ecology. Modeling industrial ecology to be as effective and efficient as the natural ecology is a key challenge of the new century. Although the practice of industrial ecology is continually evolving, it is a primary ingredient in the transition to a sustainable future, both in the redress and the realignment of existing enterprise, and in the innovations that might define enterprise in the future. One of its key concepts is the notion of working with only the current income of our natural capital. Perhaps one of the best overviews on the subject and its potential was written by Tibbs, an industrial designer. Tibbs pointed to the phenomena of self-organizing communities, such as Kalundborg in Denmark, as a first stage in the development of industrial ecology and the eventual emergence of an "Eco-industrial Infrastructure," a critical component in attaining sustainability (1993).

Perceiving the parts of and contributors to the enterprise model as being composed of capital may implicitly suggest that they be treated in a fashion quite different from when they were called, and thence regarded as, labor or resources. Attitudes of exploitation and depletion of people and place might shift to maintenance and mitigation, and then to enhancement and restoration. Based on a more equitable and balanced view of these forms of capital, their characteristics, and what they contribute to, this enterprise model might include the following:

- natural capital, including materials, their designs, the systems that support them, and the unknown potential of natural capital;
- human capital, in the form of labor, skills, knowledge, networks, organizational structure (operating models), and potential;
- physical capital, not only plant and equipment, but the product born of them in the form of durables, consumables, and service components; and
- financial capital, conventionally the primary metric and the surrogate for the real forms of capital: natural, human, and physical.

There is an order here that suggests one form of capital emanates from the other. Natural capital begets human capital, which together beget physical capital, all of which are the basis for a human construct—a metric and transaction surrogate—called financial capital. The objectives of a sustainable enterprise would include a balanced allocation of returns to each of the forms of capital, insuring the health and enhancement of each form. We know the metrics of reinvesting financial capital into physical capital. It is a function of the firm. But the metrics of reinvestment in human and natural capital need further development and institutionalization.

Human capital cannot exist for long without a healthy base of natural capital for subsistence and further development. Physical capital cannot exist without the interaction of human capital on natural capital. Lastly, financial capital is a construct devised to value physical capital, and to some extent human capital and natural capital. Attempts to value anything but physical capital with the associated property rights, and responsibilities, have been anything but successful. How do we value the potential of natural and human capital?

WASTE, RESOURCE, OR ASSET?

How we manage all these forms of capital affects the way we think about the role of enterprise, how our enterprise relates to its markets (customers), and the value proposition that we offer to those markets. We can choose to manage these as wastes, resources, or assets.

The cost of waste management was once considered external. Now that it has been internalized through mandate and regulation as well as a new consciousness (both ethical and economic in its origins), waste has been targeted as a cost worth avoiding. As a result, the creative forces that operate very well in private enterprise have begun to eliminate real waste (valueless output). There are countless examples such as the U.S. federally mandated Toxic Reduction Inventory and 3M Corporation's Pollution Prevention Pays initiative, both of which have turned waste into resources and in the process have saved or made billions of dollars.

Creative enterprise may either eliminate waste or look upon it as a resource to be re-directed; it then becomes a source of potential wealth. A good example is the Interface Carpet story. Interface offsets the need for purchasing external resources by utilizing internally produced waste, or it brings financial capital into the enterprise when waste product that cannot be used within the company is sold on to an external user. In this way, once-valueless output is reduced or eliminated and a higher order of return on the resource is achieved. Waste management begets resource management. As more of the resources are managed within the enterprise, the notion of their presence as a linear throughput may be reassessed and changed to a fixed resource or an asset.

At the present, the move from a resource management strategy to an asset management strategy seems to be more a function of innovation in business design and technology, but that reality would not preclude the conscious effort to design for transitioning resources to assets as a business management strategy and applying it to all the forms of capital that contribute to the enterprise.

The concept of an asset has been traditionally linked to its ability to generate wealth continually, over time. This is markedly different from the one-time benefit that is generated by converting a resource into a product and profiting from whatever margin the market might bear. The former is designed to be, more or less, permanent whereas the latter is transient.

If this trend can be set into motion for all forms of capital that are used by the enterprise, the inevitable outcome is potentially very exciting. It would demonstrate an economic link between environmental management (waste and resources) and economic or enterprise management (assets). The objective of the enterprise as it relates to the capital that comprises it would be to move wastes to resources and then to assets, with the ideal being an expanded Total Asset Management (eTAM) model of the entire enterprise that includes all the forms of capital.

The enterprise that continually strives to move the management strategies associated with all the forms of capital to ones of asset management becomes more efficient, more effective, and more competitive. Reinvestment in assets is an acceptable business practice with precedent. As the asset is enhanced, its value to the firm is increased, in terms of both the market value of the firm and the current/future income potential of the asset. That is a very powerful economic reason for doing it!

Efficiency happens internally as wastes are eliminated, resources are managed, and assets are created and enhanced. We can move the effectiveness of this strategy outside the enterprise if we shape our products into assets. If we can transform products (durable and consumable products) and services (human and product components) into forms of physical capital and human/physical capital, the value associated with them can be managed as an annuity or return on an asset as opposed to a cost and margin on a linear transaction.

If products and services are considered a form of capital and are managed as assets, then the stage is set for external initiatives in the community (market), such as product stewardship or a consensus-based integrated product policy that can also serve the economic interests of the enterprise.

The benefits of products and services being managed as assets have been explored with total asset management concepts such as leasing aircraft systems like the Beachcraft

Starship and franchises like the efforts at ServiceMaster US. At ServiceMaster, physical capital and the human capital are joined to create service benefits—the value proposition to the customer—producing an array of services to households and industry. Corporate research and a mandate that was created by this self-regulating mechanism that stewards the three real forms of capital is focused on minimizing impacts of the enterprise on all the capital forms, including the surrogate/metric, financial capital (risk reduction). The model supports the assets and serves to drive up their real value.

Initiatives like Producer Responsibility and Product Responsibility build relationships that associate the enterprise as a brand that has aligned its economic interests with those of the community it serves. The feedback loops that emerge as a result of nested interfaces are implicit in the relationships associated with the application of asset management strategies to products and services. A stage has been set for both continual improvement and innovation through mutually beneficial collaboration—also known as codesign. The drive to assets creates a dynamic environment where opportunities can be explored in transitioning products, services, and the entire business model.

Raising the strategies of capital management to the asset management level can promote the attributes that are the basis of sustainability: economic viability, environmental integrity, and societal equity.

Working together with all the stakeholders while focusing on their needs, an enterprise can move toward achieving a sustainable, healthy economy as it attends to the needs of individuals who live in a community, the businesses that provide vital economic activity, and the natural attributes such as clean air, water, and the open spaces that define both the environment and the quality of life. Designers working with enterprises that evolve to this point need to be able to work collaboratively with multiple disciplines with varying interests and agendas while facilitating an optimal outcome for all the stakeholders, including beneficial returns to all the forms of capital that are directly and indirectly affected by the solution.

If everything that enters the enterprise system is viewed and managed as an asset, the resulting model of wealth creation is circular and contained rather than linear. The continuous dividends generated by the asset management model lead to an effectiveness that defines the next level of competitiveness in the business model and the nature of wealth (health) in the community model. A process focused on the real return on our investment to all the forms of capital can further our understanding of our ecology (the logic embedded in the patterns and structures of our habitat—our place) and our economy (the calculus and the principles of managing ourselves in our place), resulting in a better environment, a healthier society, and a more resilient economy as its product.

A new reality can be shaped by a new design ethic that expands the role of design, linking the products on which we have historically focused with the business and system models that are an intrinsic part of the fulfillment of the needs of the community of users. Our efforts can result in solutions that work for 100 percent of humanity, in the shortest possible time, through spontaneous cooperation, without ecological offense or disadvantage to anyone.

REFERENCES

Anders, B. (1968), " 'The First Earthrise' Apollo 8 Astronaut Bill Anders Recalls the First Mission to the Moon," http://www.museumofflight.org/press/first-earthrise-apollo-8-astronaut-bill-anders-recalls-first-mission-moon, accessed July 23, 2012.

Dobbs, R., Brinkman, M., Oppenheim, J., Thompson, F. and Zornes, M. (2011), "Resource Revolution: Meeting the World's Food Energy and Materials, Foods and Water Needs," McKinsey Global Institute, McKinsey Sustainability and Resource Productivity Practice, November.

Drucker, P. (1989), *The New Realities,* Harper and Row: New York.

Hardin, G. (1968), "The Tragedy of the Commons," *Science,* vol. 162: pp. 1243–8.

Hawken, P., Lovins, A. and Lovins, H. (2000), *Natural Capitalism,* Little Brown: Boston.

Kubler-Ross, E. (1969), *On Death & Dying,* Simon & Schuster/Touchstone: New York.

Lebow, V. (1955), "Price Competition in 1955," *Journal of Retailing,* vol. 31, no. 1, spring: pp. 5–10, 42, 44.

Lloyd, W. F. (1833), *Two Lectures on the Checks to Population,* Oxford University Press: Oxford.

London, B. (1932), *Ending the Depression through Planned Obsolescence,* University of Wisconsin: Madison.

Lovelock, J. (2007), *The Revenge of Gaia: Earth's Climate Crisis and the Fate of Humanity,* Basic Books: New York.

McKibben, B. (2010), *Eaarth, Making a Life on a Tough New Planet,* Times Books, Henry Holt: New York.

Rajan, R. and Zingales, L. (2003), *Saving Capitalism from the Capitalists,* Crown Business: New York.

Senge, P. (1990), *The Fifth Discipline,* Doubleday: New York.

Smith, A. (1776/1994), *An Inquiry into the Nature and Causes of the Wealth of Nations,* Modern Library Edition: New York.

Stevens, B. (1954), *Brooks Stevens,* Wisconsin Historical Society, http://www.wisconsinhistory.org/topics/stevens/, accessed July 23, 2012.

Suzuki, D. (2003), "Consumer Culture Is No Accident," *Science Matters,* March 18.

The Economist, (2011) "The Anthropocene, A Man-Made World, Science Is Recognizing Humans as a Geological Force to Be Reckoned With," May 26, 2011, http://www.economist.com/node/18741749, accessed February 14, 2013.

Tibbs, H. (1993), *Industrial Ecology, An Environmental Agenda for Industry,* Global Business Network: Emeryville, CA.

Zung, T. (2001), *Buckminster Fuller, Anthology for the New Millennium,* St. Martin's Press: New York.

PART IV

Emerging Directions and Sustainable Futures

Editorial Introduction

STUART WALKER AND JACQUES GIARD

At this point in the handbook, the reader will be aware of the causes of our present situation, the challenges facing society and some of the measures needed to tackle these challenges. Several authors have been unequivocal in their view that society cannot continue on its present path of growth if it also wishes to be sustainable, and several have argued convincingly that technology alone cannot provide the requisite solutions. Others have discussed examples of design for sustainability that constructively demonstrate alternative forms of human enterprise. Building on these themes, the final section considers 'Emerging Directions and Sustainable Futures', which further explores the nature and place of human intervention in relation to sustainability and the particular role and responsibility of design.

Part IV begins with a contemplation of the human condition and the modes of creation that derive from it. In 'Sustainability and the Condition of Being Human', Alexander Manu asserts that culture in its various forms is not a sustainable activity in the ecological sense, yet, without these forms of knowledge and cultural transmission, humanity is not sustainable as a species. He finds a moral dissonance between, on the one hand, the condition of being human and, on the other, the modes of creation and consumption that are proposed by some advocates of sustainability. Sustaining human life on Earth is, he says, too complex a task to achieve without first understanding what it means to be human. He suggests that, short of purposefully changing the context and meaning of what it is to be human, the rhetoric against current forms of consumption is challenging the nature of being human. This controversial view is one that we should consider in developing our understandings of sustainability so that they provide not just for ecological sustainability, vital as that is, but also for sustaining meaningful notions of being human.

In the two chapters that follow, the nature of the human condition is examined within the context of specific societies and cultures. In 'Sustainability: Context and

Design', Shashank Mehta explores the potential for sustainable design within the small-scale cottage industries of India. Through such enterprises, employment opportunities have been created, people's standards of living have improved, and efforts by cooperative organizations have generated opportunities of self-employment in rural areas. More-over, products and services have become more affordable to that stratum of Indian so-ciety situated in the lower half of the development pyramid. By infusing the concept of sustainability into these industries, not only have important facets of Indian cultural life been recognized, but their significance has also been acknowledged. Evidence shows that design in the Indian context has succeeded in creating a harmonious integration between sustainability and the needs of Indian society.

In 'Shè Jì—Change for Sustainable Futures', Lou Yongqi looks at traditional prac-tices of China's past and considers their relevance for today's understandings of design for sustainability. The chapter presents the reader with an overview of China's shè jì (design) system, which was once part of the Chinese tradition of making but which has more or less been displaced by design disciplines and practices imported from Western societies. This consideration of shè jì and the advantages it offers present a culturally sig-nificant, contextually appropriate and timely opportunity to reflect, rethink, re-evaluate and redesign at a time when China is considering a more sustainable future. With the use of short case studies, Lou contends that the reinitiation of the shè jì approach could provide new philosophies and methodologies for Chinese design, design education and design research, which would position design as a key agent for sustainable social and economic changes in China.

In 'Emotionally Sustaining Design', Jonathan Chapman argues that the macro-concerns that underpin sustainability—climate change, degradation of the natural envi-ronment, threats to biodiversity and social disintegration—serve to cripple the creative mind-set, rather than inspire and motivate it. This becomes evident when we recog-nize that we live in a world in which products are desired, acquired, briefly used and promptly discarded, with devastating ecological consequences. This chapter aims to bring us closer to one of the roots of our ecological crisis whilst signposting new and critical directions for design.

In a direction that parallels the one proposed by Chapman, Gijs Bakker and Lou-ise Schouwenberg ask us to consider the provocative notion that anyone who isolates sustainability from the bigger picture and who makes it the main objective for design is essentially obstructing the necessary freedom that the creative mind demands. Their chapter, 'I Am a User, Not a Consumer', goes further by declaring that sustainability should not be a stand-alone subject for design because knowledge of any kind—including knowledge of sustainability—should be part of every designer's toolkit. More essential for that toolkit are elements such as idealism, intuition, a sense of aesthetics and an awareness of the ever-changing social, cultural, economic and political contexts in which products are born and function. Each of these elements is relevant in varying degrees, yet they are inextricably linked.

Design, as a means to a greater end, infuses several of the chapters that follow, be-ginning with 'Design Sleepwalking: Critical Inquiry in Design' by Craig Badke and

Stuart Walker. This chapter explores the capacities and attributes design offers as a critical mode of inquiry. As explicated by Badke and Walker, critical inquiry in design offers unique opportunities for research in sustainability, especially in understanding the role artefacts play in our lives and the contexts that shape their creation. Also included in the discourse is the place of social sustainability and how we conceive, produce, use and relate to each other through artefacts. Critical design inquiry offers a means of illuminating and questioning these often unseen or unacknowledged contexts and the values and assumptions that shape current practices in the production and consumption of material culture. The premise of design as critical inquiry is supported with examples of work of designers and the possibilities that they offer in steering our culture in more sustainable, humane and meaningful directions.

Design and critical inquiry are also the themes of 'Critical Agendas: Designing for Sustainability from Products to Systems'. For Chris Ryan, however, the field for inquiry and the potential for design go well beyond the world of artefacts per se. As he points out, our constructed world of products, buildings, services and systems of resource provision has for too long had an embedded dependence on large continuous flows of carbonaceous energy, but that embedded dependency has to come to an end. Two centuries of development based on the exploitation of fossil fuels has left us with legacies we must rapidly transcend. Ryan is of the view that 'design for sustainability will assume a critical role'. But in order to do so, both design and designers must change. The next era of designers will have to deliver goods and services based on renewable energy resulting in the transformation of systems of provision of energy, water, food, transport and information. In the face of changing climatic conditions and extreme weather events the design focus will shift more and more to post-carbon pathways and resilience.

Paradigm shifts of such significance cannot occur without an equally significant shift in human behaviour. Discussion of such a shift begins with a reflection from John Wood. He considers the apparent disconnect in our present situation—that, despite all good intentions, design for sustainability has not saved us because specialist designers are not trained to change behavioural paradigms. This conundrum is examined in 'Meta-Designing Paradigm Change: An Ecomimetic, Language-Centered Approach'. In essence, the heart of the issue is the fact that while catalysing behavioural change may resemble a design task, human habits cannot be designed like discrete products or services. And this is where the disconnect resides: in employing design methods meant for products and services to change human behaviour. Instead, Wood proposes an approach he calls meta-design, which is a self-reflexive, comprehensive and integrated framework for changing paradigms. It is a combinatorial process that synchronizes sets of strategic changes in parallel, and that combines existing resources to create novel synergies. As new paradigms usually seem counter-intuitive from within the old ones, a creative 're-languaging' strategy is an important feature. This helps teams of meta-designers to transcend fixed hierarchies, leaders, pretexts or rules, and to work, collectively and intuitively, towards a 'synergy-of-synergies'.

A shift need not necessarily begin with everything new, with everything old tossed aside. Building on past practices but with a discerning eye to new conditions also affords novel possibilities for emerging directions in a sustainable future. This is exactly what Stuart Walker proposes in 'Imagination's Promise: Practice-Based Design Research for Sustainability'. This chapter considers the role of creative practice in design research and its contribution to knowledge in product design for sustainability. It describes how the creative activity of designing, as a component of the research method, can be a powerful way of developing and illustrating ideas and advancing an ethos of sustainability. The discussion looks at how the inherently unpredictable design process can synthesize disparate, often diverging, priorities into a unified whole. This creative facet of design research is discussed in terms of its relationship to an understanding of design for sustainability that embraces not only social and environmental considerations but also deeper notions of human meaning and purpose. This position is complemented by a series of object examples, developed by the author, which demonstrate the potential of propositional design to advance knowledge. Importantly, within such a practice-based approach, such objects are regarded *not* as solutions but as questions in form.

Innovative and critical design practices and research-through-designing for sustainable futures can be seen as fruitful elements that fall under a general banner of design activism. Collectively, these activities begin to demonstrate alternative directions for design and designers. This is the theme of Alastair Fuad-Luke's 'Design Activism: Challenging the Paradigm by Dissensus, Consensus, and Transitional Practices'. Design activism has a strong historical lineage and is, once again, a resurgent and divergent phenomenon that is critically addressing our eco-social condition and consciousness. The term 'design activism' embraces diverse design disciplines but finds common ground in aiming for positive change by creating counter-narratives/dialogue, raising awareness and inculcating actions to change behaviour, while simultaneously challenging design practice and knowledge. Design activism firmly addresses the political, as distinct from politics, and invokes responses by dissensus, consensus and transitional practices. These practices impact on human, social and cultural capital in a variety of social spaces, from the private to the public, from the real 'space of places' to the technological 'space of flows' and conceptual spaces of design research. In doing so, design activism offers a reorientation of the personal, the private and the collective, while simultaneously challenging the activity and directionality of designing.

In most chapters up to this point, the world of artefacts has been assumed to be mostly products and services. These are the things that we overproduce, oversell and eventually discard. This assumption, however, ignores another world of artefacts. This is the digital world, a world of mostly intangible and non-physical artefacts. Bran Richards, Stuart Walker and Lynne Blair take a look at this world in 'Design for Cyber-Sustainability: Toward a Sustainable Digital Future'. Although a number of researchers are looking at the potential for green IT, this chapter takes a broader and arguably more fundamental perspective. Cyber-sustainability describes necessary considerations for the future of the digital economy, including the environmental and psychological impacts of major technological trends. Drawing from a range of literature related to psychology, sociology, sustainability, computing and design, the authors discuss radical alternatives for Web development and attempt to redefine 'progress' in the digital age in a way that is conducive to both human and planetary wellbeing.

The last two chapters impart a more future-oriented and self-reflective view of ourselves as we tread knowingly but with trepidation towards a world that is more sustainable. Tony Fry's 'Emerging Directions' seeks out and reads signs of change but also attempts to think ahead. We face a dilemma, however, because our perceptual horizons are limited. Beyond reading the tea leaves of the blindingly obvious, we are generally not very good at futural insight. Our dilemma is exacerbated further because our future is dependent on two factors: gaining a far more effective ability to identify what is directing our future and what we need and can (re)directively do. To move beyond this dilemma, Fry believes that society must become better at 'thinking in time'. The term implies thinking before it is too late, and therefore acting in time, but equally it suggests thinking in the medium of time.

If there is one inevitable conclusion from the preceding chapters it is that, ultimately, a sustainable world is totally dependent on humanity's imagination and capacity for change. John Ralston Saul champions this position in his chapter, 'Literature and the Environment'. In it, he reasons that, to address the environmental degradation the world is facing, the human imagination, expressed through literature and other forms of public language—and design can be regarded as a form of public language—is probably much more important and relevant than science. Despite this, we have yet to find the right words. With the Canadian Arctic as its backdrop, this discussion challenges embedded assumptions about evidence-based research, 'proof' and utilitarian concerns, as well as the short-term interests of commerce and politics. Tragic figures from the world's greatest imaginations—Anna Karenina, Madame Bovary, Captain Ahab—become symbols of ourselves and our civilization as we move inexorably towards self-destruction. Our understanding of ourselves is inculcated into our language; to invoke change we need a different language, and in developing such a language we can learn much from other cultures—aboriginal languages, oral cultures—that stand outside the Western tradition.

20

Sustainability and the Condition of Being Human

ALEXANDER MANU

INTRODUCTION

We love, and love consumes. We are passionate about things, and passion consumes. We are curious about us and about things, and curiosity consumes. We play, and play consumes. We create, and creation consumes. We memorialize our dear ones and ourselves, and this consumes.

But can we survive and sustain our human spirit without love, without passion, without art, without play, without ways to preserve our memories, without creating marks of our existence on Earth? I do not think so. And here is where I find a moral dissonance in the current discourse about sustainable practices (see Figure 20.1).

The dissonance comes in the conflict between the condition of being human—what I call here the human behaviour space—and the modes of creation and consumption that are proposed by advocates of sustainability. Reduce. Reuse. Recycle and all. This is a dissonance between meaning and the means we create as humans. Short of purposefully changing the context and meaning of what it means to be human—that will involve re-designing humanity, which is a neat project, but not a doable one by designers—the rhetoric against current forms of consumption is a rhetoric challenging the nature of being human, without proposing viable alternatives to sustaining this condition. Reduction is not an alternative to consuming art—and by consumption and reduction, I mean consumption of the substantive means described in this chapter as giving meaning to human life, and not trivial products and services. I propose that for us to move forward in this discourse, we must include in any approach that seeks to change our means of being human, a reasoned and balanced understanding of the meaning of humanity.

Sustaining human life on Earth is too complex a task to embark on before understanding what being human is in the first place. I have the view that art is not sustainable for the planet in the ecological perspective. Culture in the forms of music, design,

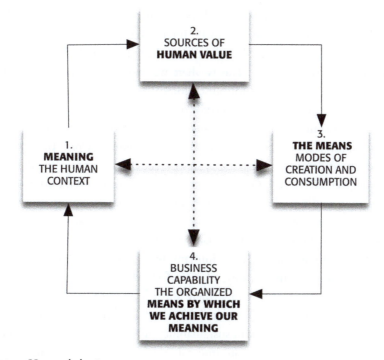

FIGURE 20.1   Human behaviour space.

painting, movies, sculpture, printed literature and so on are not sustainable; yet humans without these forms of knowledge and culture transmission are not sustainable as a species. We need to formulate future scenarios about humans as they really are; just like every other animal, we seek places of comfort and pleasure. It just happens that beavers find comfort in a dam, and humans find comfort in the Taj Mahal.

This is why I think the place to start change and transformation is in retooling the individual—our desires, motivations, behaviours, greed and expectations—as a first step, rather than retooling the products and services we create by design. These thoughts may not fit in the current discourse, unless we are open to a real dialogue and not to technocratic solutions, which politicians can opportunistically legislate.

With these warnings, and with the request that you keep an open mind while reading this chapter, here are a few points of departure I consider necessary in any discussion about the challenge and beauty of being human.

THE CHALLENGE AND BEAUTY OF BEING HUMAN

Of all animals, we are the animal that knows about our limited time on Earth; we all learn very early in life that we will die. As a result, our life becomes a series of plans for achieving, in any way possible, continuity on Earth. A continuity in the form of the objects we create, which in turn create our ways of life, manifestations of our transcendence from our animal nature. It is in the plans we make to ensure our life has meaning that we can find the seeds of change and transformation. Until we look at the actions of being alive, we will just continue to be intellectually dishonest about change and sustainability. As humans, we think and act from the gut, through the heart and into the brain. This is where we live from. This is where we have created masterpieces from, the monuments that we leave behind for our children, as proof that we have existed. It is in the gut of this humanity that change needs to first take place.

The current discourse around sustainable models of living seems to ignore the main actor in the transformation at hand, and that is the human actor. The discourse feels constructed on academic coordinates, around a thesis based on selected sets of data. We are being given life prescriptions—'an inconvenient truth'—with little or no interest in allowing us to think, to discover the *why* and the *what*. I see great danger in this, as these are prescriptions for thinking; they create belief systems that render many individuals intellectually atrophied. The discourse is not about ideas, but about facts, numbers and tools. It is not about who we are as humans, but a means by which we can run away from talking about our human reality, what we feel, what we desire and how did we get here in the first place. I want to know where and what I need to change in me, instead of being given prescriptions to attenuate the withdrawal from a life of consumption. Design that is concerned only about sustainability limits our wider human potential. As designers, working from purely environmental briefs, we find ourselves limited in philosophical and practical terms, our creative potential constrained to a single dimension. To be clear, our environment must be protected, and fiercely, with careful consideration of each material and process used. But we can and must do more. After all, design is nothing more, and nothing less, than carving, for a moment in time, the best circumstances for the way we experience life. It is these circumstances that form the human behaviour space and the richness and variety of the human experience of life.

In the next few pages, I will explore the drive humans have toward becoming more than they are, which is the drive to be human, the drive to leave a mark and the drive to participate. It is only when we are ready to examine our desires and motives for creating, by design, the tools that surround us and the ecosystems that support them that we will be ready to engage with sincerity in the sustainable enterprise of life on planet Earth.

I have structured my contribution in four sections in an attempt to illustrate the current state of dissonance. The four sections (Figure 20.1) look at the human context; sources of human value; the means of humanity: modes of creation and consumption; and business capability: the organized means by which we achieve meaning.

THE HUMAN CONTEXT: MEANING AND HUMAN LIFE

We humans are either the proof that nature is not perfect—our ways not being in tune with the ways of most other species—or we are an example of transcending our nature as species. Is it possible that at one point human beings decided that nature is not enough, that we are not just a species anymore? We need culture to survive, and grow, and culture is by practice and definition not sustainable. Culture demands and consumes red pigment for the sake of red as a colour, and not for the sake of red as a signal for danger.

Red as a colour speaks about our human conditioning to communicate through symbols and archetypes: red is symbolic of love, passion, life.

Human life is not only about efficiency. Human life is about storytelling, literature, music, all of which are not sustainable. Human life is about meaning, and meaning that is well beyond the efficiency of survival. So let us recap the essentials so we do not fool ourselves:

- We read books, and that is not sustainable. We like to live from stories, to learn from them, to pass them along to others like us. Literature is not sustainable—it consumes in production, manufacture, marketing, transportation, purchase of books and the act of reading.
- We like going to movies, and that is not sustainable. The totality of the entertainment industry—second largest on the planet—is not sustainable as it consumes voraciously everything from film, tape, equipment and so on.
- We like listening to music, and that is totally unsustainable. Music consumes energy without returning anything back to the ecosystem. It consumes at every single level—creation, duplication, production marketing, purchasing and listening. Add to this the making and distribution of musical instruments and the construction of concert halls and you have the picture of an entire ecosystem dedicated to the production of pleasant sounds.
- We like looking at paintings and sculptures because we feel that art is a means for transcending our nature as a mere species. Art is totally unsustainable. We not only enjoy looking at art and producing art, but we teach art, an activity that is completely unsustainable, as it compounds the original unsustainable nature of art itself.
- We like sports, both as an activity to perform and an activity to look at as spectators. Participating in sports consumes without returning anything back to the system. Is there anything more unsustainable than sports? Probably only art, music, painting, sculpture, movies and literature combined.
- We pursue knowledge. Can anyone imagine any activity that consumes as much energy in the pursuing act itself, and results in the consumption of more energy, in all the discoveries we make by this pursuit? Totally, completely, utterly unsustainable. And with no limits: there is no limit of knowing; there is no moment when humans will declare, 'I now know enough!'

Read again. This is a short introduction to your life and to some of the reasons you live it. This is your human condition.

Hannah Arendt (1965, p. 10) outlined the human condition as being the artefacts that define our life as humans on this Earth at any given moment. At any given moment, things—the objects, services, or ideas we use—condition us. We are equally conditioned by the Internet, as we are conditioned by cooking our meats on the kitchen stove, ironing our shirts, brushing our teeth, reading and writing ideas on paper. Our purpose—what conditions us—is the desire to leave a mark and to participate. Leaving a mark and participating is what we do right now on YouTube, on Facebook, on Flickr and on Wikipedia. We participate. Keep this idea in mind while you consider the Zulu concept of *Ubuntu,* which means 'me through Your eyes'. In other words, 'I exist because you see me.' Therefore, I will do whatever it takes to exist in a way in which you will see me as the best possible me at this time. I will wash, wipe, smell good, look good, know more and want more. Be more, become better. In your eyes. Better. I will do whatever it takes to exist at a new level every time you see me.

SOURCES OF HUMAN VALUE

> Humans are conditioned beings because everything they come in contact with turns immediately into a condition of their existence.
>
> *(Arendt, 1965, p. 29)*

Arendt introduced the concept of *vita activa,* which helps in understanding the nature of the questions we pose when coming in contact with any event that has influence on our life activities. Vita activa is the human behaviour space. It is the why and what of why humans do what they do.

> With the term vita activa, I propose to designate three fundamental human activities: labour, work, and action. They are fundamental because each corresponds to one of the basic conditions under which life on earth has been given to human beings. (Arendt, 1965, p. 27)

Labour, work and action are the activities for which we design, the activities for which we have built and created the world of tools, the world of education and the world of laws, as well as all the constructed spaces we now call civilization. This is the world we refer to by the generic term of 'technology'.

Arendt defines labour as 'the activity which corresponds to the biological process of the human body, whose spontaneous growth, metabolism and eventual decay are bound to the vital necessities produced and fed into the life process by labour. The human condition of labour is life itself' (1965, p. 27).

In this condition, the question asked is in the realm of the tactical: the question is, how? How do I survive? How do I find food? How do I build shelter? This is a condition related to the having side of the human being, a side interested in the quantity of things, their performance, durability, appropriateness for the task, numbers and the sequence of action. A condition concerned with the tactics of life.

Perfecting the performance of tools is also a how question, suitable to what Eric Fromm has termed the 'having mode', a mode dominated by our interest in acquiring things that are fixed and describable. According to Fromm, 'Most of us know more about the mode of having than we do about the mode of being, because having is by far the more frequently experienced mode in our culture... Being refers to experience, and human experience is in principle not describable' (1976). Fromm points to a quality unique to humans: the quality of being, of becoming through experiences and learning. This is the quality that completes us and gives meaning and reason to why we need to always move forward, searching for more ways to experience life, for why we need to learn, to explore in order to have more worth and merit. The quality that allows us to become. To leave a mark through our work and deeds. To have mattered, for others. To be seen through their eyes.

For Arendt, work is the activity 'which corresponds to the unnaturalness of human existence…Work provides an "artificial" world of things, distinctly different from all natural surroundings…The human condition of work is worldliness' (1965, p. 27). In other words, the creation of worth, using our tools, answers the question, why?

The Role of Desire: What Do We Find of Value in Human Life

It becomes necessary to discuss the role desire plays in creating the ethos for designing products, services, and the ways of life these create in return. The reality is that in product design, we, humans, are the product, as we redesign ourselves every time we create new tools for our survival and betterment. We are redesigned by these tools, and we redesign with them our human behaviour space.

Aristotle said, 'Desire is the ultimate source of action' (Lawson-Tancred, 1986). The desire to survive, the desire to achieve a different level of existence: these are the ultimate sources of action. The question for you right now is, What do you desire? How open are you to understanding what you desire and to believing that this desire can transform the way you look at everything else? Understanding the nature of your desire can create a path for a new journey of life.

What is it that we desire? The media that both define where we are and where we want to go in life. We humans exist not because we are here, now, but because we want to become. Because we strive for more. Readiness to exist starts in the moment you define yourself as more than the trees, the flowers and the butterflies, all of which do not have a choice. This is where the human animal is different: striving for more, wanting to become, are foundations for the architecture of existence.

The question, Who are we? is in good measure a statement about who we have become through our desire. Everything we ask is a desire, so what is it that you desire? To leave a mark, to participate, to know, to understand, to maintain, to enhance, to actualize and to propagate? We propagate by leaving a mark, by participating. The Taj Mahal would have never been built if we did not want to leave a mark. Most of the monuments that you know are about us, making sure that we are being seen through other people's eyes. Somebody needed to be seen, and that's how the Eiffel Tower was built. Every human artefact that is of value to us must answer this singular question: how is this media for me? How can this allow me to satisfy, to actualize, to propagate, to participate? How does this allow me to leave a mark? How does this allow me to reach my next destination?

What Is Your Destination?

If change is needed, then this will be a good place to start: by redefining your destination. It may not be easy to change the destination, but it may be worth pursuing. What we need to analyze more deeply is where the idea of that destination originates. We need to create a new vision of the everyday self, a new way to see the future and, more importantly, a new perspective from which we see the future. We are in constant need of media because we need a constant tool for our new direction in life. Every tool that we create is an expression of our current understanding of the destination, and these tools always modify our destination.

Humans are always in multiple states of being: who we were yesterday, who we are today and who we will be tomorrow. We are in constant need for tools as new platforms for possibility, and through them, new destinations for becoming.

Wanting to become means both recognizing and desiring new conditions. Beneath this desire is a value judgment—an implicit personal assigning of meaning to change—an embracing and ranking of different states of existence. Against what criteria do we make these judgments? Is it our hope for purpose that drives the urge to pursue one destination more than another? Or is it merely the belief in the destination that ensures that the journey will continue? Wanting is the pursuit of possibility and implicitly assigns meaning to change. Perhaps because we mortal beings can imagine ourselves as different from what we currently are, we feel a responsibility: to become something more, to connect in order to understand ourselves through others, to pursue a destination.

Throughout history we have shaped stories to share and validate our wants, and our hindsight generates new questions. What do we ultimately want? As noted earlier in this chapter, we need to analyze where the idea of that destination originates. The destination is in us.

A Few Words about Becoming, Desire and Life Ethos

Our actions are instigated by the desire for, and in pursuit of, something. It follows that human behaviour is a goal directed by human desires:

- Ultimate desires for the nourishment of the mind: knowledge, understanding, hope.
- Motivating desires for the growth of the individual: to participate, to leave a mark, to maintain, to enhance, to actualize, to propagate.
- Basic desires for the nourishment of the body: smooth, soft, shiny, sweet, fragrant, intoxicating, beautiful and pleasant.

These are the compelling motivators for human action. We frame our life around strategies designed to experience manifestations of all of these desires, through the products we consume, the services we use and the actions we undertake toward our contribution to society. We permanently seek higher and higher media for the manifest satisfaction of these goals. Each moment of experience leads to another goal: there is no benchmark for how smooth 'smooth' can be, or for how sweet 'sweet' can be, or for what is knowledge. If we accept the premise that desire is the driver of the economic system, we also have to accept that desire is also the driver of the design outcomes that engage behaviour and create business opportunities. Where would Google be without our desire for knowing and understanding? Where will Facebook be without our desire to participate in the plurality of people? And YouTube without our desire to leave a mark? Finally, where would all the companies of the Dow Jones Industrial Index be without our desire for, and pursuit of, something?

Where do we need to start in changing our nature as beings? The starting point will define both the process and the nature of the outcome. But no matter where we start, we must be clear about the meaning of the compelling motivators, and the reasons we seek them. So here is the short list of what humans find compelling:

- Smooth: we desire smooth surfaces to the point of creating a huge industry for the provision of smooth. And why do we want to make things smooth? It is all about pleasure, safety and hope. It is pleasurable to run your hand on a smooth countertop or a smooth piece of sculpted marble. It is safer to walk on a smooth, clear, wooden floor, than on a rough, cluttered surface. Smoothness is the hope for health and perennial youth. We desire smooth and manufacture it. It is a choice we make as humans. Smoothness is not a rational choice, as it cannot be benchmarked; smoothness is an emotional choice. A human choice.
- Soft: soft is pleasure and comfort, and it comes in plenty of forms: the petals of a flower and the material properties of cotton and silk, or the manufactured properties of foam rubber. And why do we like soft? Because it is pleasurable, just like coffee, just like giving flowers to the ones we love, just like liking smooth. Because we are human. To make things soft, we need to use oil, electricity, fire. Soft is the manifestation of our desire to transcend the condition in which we, humans, were just a few thousand years ago, in ages of hardship, danger and death. Softness is a concept before it is a percept: the measure by which we define ourselves as different from other animals, as we have mastered manufacturing it at will. A soft pillow is the distinction between pleasure and hardship, between the life before, and life after we discovered ourselves as humans conditioned through pleasure.
- Shiny: shiny means new. Shiny means healthy. Shiny reflects. Shiny is light. Mirrors are shiny. So are windows, and we live surrounded by windows; we seek to have the environment we live in reflected in our homes. We also want to see ourselves in the shine of water. And we create tools to make things shiny because shiny is the pleasure of something intrinsically good. By choice, we have made shiny one of the conditioning factors in our lives. It may be as simple as this: happiness is light that shines on you and all you care about.
- Sweet: the human animal consciously and purposefully manufactures sweet for the purpose of consumption. How much of the industry of the civilized world is involved in the manufacture of sweet? How many pieces of equipment, how many transportation devices, how much effort? What is your guess? Sweet is one of the basic taste sensations alongside bitter, sour and salty. These are the cornerstones of our gastronomic preferences. In contrast with the others, sweet is pleasurable. And a daily measure of our life as humans. A life with chocolate.

- Fragrant: perfume is the pursuit of pleasure in the form of scent. It is also the pursuit of memory; we recall scents faster than we recall flavours or images. Scent can unlock memories of long-forgotten moments or people. Smells are embedded in us, identifiable and yet hardly describable. Smells are about the pursuit of memory. And the pursuit of memory is a badge that humans wear with distinction among the other animals.
- Pleasure: how much time do we dedicate in our lives to the acquisition of things that give us pleasure—be that in physical or intellectual things? Why are you reading this book? You are reading in the hope of becoming better. That is connected somehow to pleasure. The cushion on the chair you are sitting on is connected to pleasure; the picture on your wall and the flower you gave to a loved one recently are connected to pleasure. We search for media that will bring about the state, or feeling, of being pleased. And in turn, we create media for the satisfaction of this temporary and subjective state of mind. Pleasure is value positive. (Santayana, 1955). The opposite of pleasure is pain.
- Beauty: we seek beauty because, as George Santayana (1955) brilliantly defined it, 'Beauty is pleasure objectified.' Beauty is a unique state of mind. Unique to humans who seek a state of pleasure, one moment at a time.
- Hope: hope is a longing for a new possibility, a belief that personal actions will positively affect outcomes in our life. Hope unlocks our latencies and makes our subconscious goals manifest. In some measure, hope is what we buy in all products and services; it is what we are all about. Hope is how we are different from other animals. Hope is about the possibility of our life.

THE MEANS OF HUMANITY: MODES OF CREATION AND CONSUMPTION

Let us review the human value map, which shows the stimuli we need to experience in order to exist as humans. The list is very long, so for this discussion I will restrict it to just a few headlines.

Retrieval and Preservation of Memory as Human Condition

The need for remembrance is intrinsic to the human condition of worldliness, of transcending just being and wanting to become more for others, to leave a mark. We expend incalculable resources in order to be remembered and to remember others. Remembering is part of our human narrative and part of sustaining civilization; as seen in other examples early in this chapter, sustaining civilization is not a sustainable enterprise from the presently limited ecological perspective. The pursuit of memory might be—in all its extrovert manifestations discussed later in this chapter—the most unsustainable action in which humans engage. It takes the following shapes.

Consider the Photographic Camera

Why do you think people take pictures? Images of memory. What is a camera all about? It is about the retrieval of a life's experience. We seek the full recovery of ourselves in one specific moment in time. This is not about the high definition of the image; it is about the moment being captured in any way, shape, or form. The moment is about what you perceived in a particular place, at a particular time. About what you felt. About what you sensed. About what you experienced. And most of all, about what you want others to share of this moment. You will want to keep that moment and share it with the group that defines your plurality as a human. Memory is about retaining, recalling, and most of all, about sharing information that defines who you are for you, and for others.

Our purpose as human beings is to create something that attests to our presence on Earth. We need to survive for sure, but after that, we are involved in a quest for meaning, a quest for worth as measured by others. Nothing to do with survival, but everything to do with being human. We need to create and let others know we have created. This fulfils our human condition of plurality. To be with others, to make sure others know we exist. We did not build the Eiffel Tower because we want shelter and are trying to survive. We built the Eiffel Tower because we are trying to tell something about ourselves, to ourselves in the present and the future. We need to leave a mark; it is the condition of our humanity.

Consider mausoleums: a mausoleum is a gigantic construction serving a single purpose—to memorialize the existence of someone important to someone else. That is human, but it may not be sustainable. It takes thousands of man-hours and many tons of material to build the expansive structure holding King Mausolus's tomb. But life without this memorial will be less human for Artemisia, the broken-hearted queen he left upon his death—and for us, who a few thousand years after this all took place, are still visiting this monument by the millions. After all, we say to ourselves, it is one of the seven wonders of the ancient world. We write books about it, take pictures, tell our children about it and people dedicate their lives to studying it. This is our story. This is our accomplishment.

Consider the Taj Mahal

In 1631, Shah Jahan's wife Mumtaz dies during childbirth. The powerful shah is grief stricken, and what better way to memorialize his love for his dear one than by erecting the structure we now call the Taj Mahal. This was 380 years ago. Understanding why a husband built a gigantic building to commemorate his wife is one thing. Understanding why two to four million people visit this structure annually is another dimension of our human context.

Consider the 9/11 Memorial

The desire to memorialize is not restricted to historic times; it is a modern preoccupation, which substantiates our humanity as different and more complex than the life of other animals on our planet. Memorializing is also a concept; it is not a trivial pursuit. It is not about the self but about the importance of the others to the self. To all of us as a community of people. The majority of us did not lose relatives or friends in the twin towers collapse of 9/11. But we all understand the need to memorialize the lives lost that day. We may complain at times about the means and the cost but not about the meaning of the enterprise of commemorating the lives lost during the terror attacks. And the cost? Measured only in money, the cost is rumoured to pass the $1 billion mark. Too much? Too little? Necessary?

There is no logic here, just emotion. Humans operate from emotion and from the need to manifest it at all costs. Everything else is timely but unsubstantiated rhetoric.

Consider Museums and the Industry of Cultural Heritage

As described earlier, we exhaust resources by creating and by admiring art, but it does not stop there: we build special holding places for this work. These are buildings one can find in almost every city on the planet, with specialized staff and specialized equipment for the protection and proper display of these works. Vast civic works that serve no other purpose but to remind us of who we are and where we came from and who was here before us. The pyramids, MOMA and the Louvre. Are these colossal expenditures of our planet's resources a necessary condition for maintaining and enhancing human life on earth? Before you answer this question, take a look at a few of the works that MOMA holds on permanent display, and ask yourself if in the current sustainability discourse, storing them, displaying them, protecting them and restoring them is a sustainable activity.

Do you want MOMA to stop showing *Broadway Boogie Woogie* by Piet Mondrian; *Les Demoiselles d'Avignon* by Pablo Picasso; *Love Song* by Giorgio De Chirico; *Number 31, 1950* by Jackson Pollock; *The Dream* by Henri Rousseau; *The Persistence of Memory* by Salvador Dalí; *The Sleeping Gypsy* by Henri Rousseau; *The Starry Night* by Vincent van Gogh; *Water Lilies* by Claude Monet?

BUSINESS CAPABILITY: THE ORGANIZED MEANS
BY WHICH WE ACHIEVE MEANING

What now that we know all this? What is the business model that will deliver the values we hold as primal to our being, while at the same time minimizing consumption of the limited resources of our planet? But more importantly, what is the mindset leading to the business model that will ensure that the means by which we achieve our meaning maintains a balance between our humanity and what we can reasonably expect to expend of the resources of the Earth?

It is all a question of how one defines business. I define the role of any business as 'the organized capability of creating and delivering media for the manifestation of human behaviour'. The tools we use, the staples we consume every day to maintain who we are and to become more than what we are. Knowing that we are dealing with ever-diminishing natural resources, are we ready to lower our expectations of ourselves? Is it the role of business to determine what we shall consume or should we, the consumers, start playing a substantial role in redefining the media that is created for our consumption? I believe in the latter.

It is not the place here to debate the pros and cons of sustainability as an ideology or as a tool for convenient legislation. It is, however, imperative that we look at sustainable proposals as meaningful signals of change, as long as they signal even the slightest inclination that the place to start change and transformation is in retooling the individual—our desires and expectations—as a first step, rather than retooling the products and services we create by design.

A Little Exercise in Mirroring Your Life

Think of your automobile. Once accepted by our behaviour and therefore by choice, the automobile creates its own ecology of dependencies, its own ecosystem. What does the automobile create? What tools are created, and what further behaviours are created in turn? On analysis, we will find a number of positive and negative attributes (negative now in retrospect). We created ways to improve our lives through the transportation of goods; we have reshaped the food chain and increased our standards and our quality of life. We have created means to distribute culture in a physical sense in unprecedented ways. Do the costs balance the benefits? If looking at the quality of life of most people in the industrialized world, the answer is unquestionably yes.

Would the urban ecology be any less complex if we had the Smart Car from the beginning? The answer is no. Posing these questions shows that issues are not as simple as they look. We cannot solve problems by mitigating two or three of the unpleasant consequences of using the automobile; the automobile is us, a whole and not just a component. Technical solutions are not the answer to the complexity of the ecology created by the invention of the automobile. Can the electric cars fix this? Fixing is a mitigation of the problem, not a solution to the problem. The solution is reimagining. Having the empowerment to reimagine your own life, not to fix it. If the tool is broken, we fix it. If the tool is emitting dangerous levels of carbon dioxide, we fix that; we put a filter on it, and we legislate others to do the same. But in order to change behaviour, we need to change motivation, and for that, we need to reimagine. We need to reimagine our way of life, we need to reimagine our values and we need to move them to a new level. So what is that you want to do? Imagine or fix? Figure 20.2 will help: it is the framework that we need to balance.

Change starts with ideas, and ideas depend on imagination. This is why it is hard for us to move forward, because we are trying to fix and mitigate our way out of problems that require reimagining. Change also starts with understanding who and what we are: products of desire. From the moment you can point, you desire. Desire shapes values, and values shape our tools. This has been so for thousands of years and people sometimes divert themselves from this reality because we learn very little history in schools, and we do not deal with business in cultural terms. The desire to survive, the desire to procreate, the desire to achieve a different level of existence: these are the ultimate sources of action.

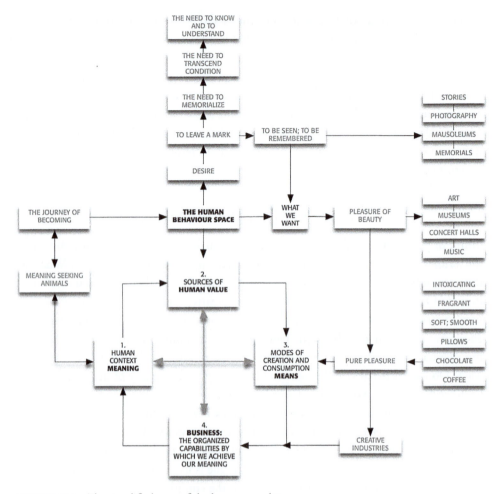

FIGURE 20.2   The simplified map of the human condition.

A Few Takeaways for Balancing the Framework of Sustainable Human Life

- The goal of becoming—rather than just simply being—may be unique to the human animal, and it is at the root of our behaviour of engaging in new experiences of learning, of exploration, of a permanent search for more. More understanding, more worth. Our goals are closely tied to our purpose—that of creating artefacts that will transcend our mortality and will attest to our presence on Earth.

- Plurality: a condition of being human; you cannot be human without being plural. Being human means not being alone; it also means sharing what and who you are. From the moment we are born to the moment we die, we strive not to be alone and we will do whatever necessary not to be alone. *Ubuntu*. It is the condition in which I do not exist without you.

- Our worth is measured in what we are worth for others, in their eyes. It is our condition of plurality. Human survival is more than just being alive; it is the quality of being alive that matters to most of us. This is why we go to school, this is why we participate in society and this is why we build careers. We are leaving a mark for others. We are telling them what our destination was. We are asking them to continue our journey. For all of us, in the community. These are the choices we make as humans, choices that define not only the journey, but also likely, the destination.

In a first reaction to these ideas, you may feel they have nothing to do with business, with markets, with design, or with the financial and economic system. Think inside yourself. You will discover you want something, and you will discover that you are ready to make the choice of engaging in an exchange to get it. This is business. And the choices we make on the journey to transform ourselves are the economic system.

So, where do you want to go from here? This is the question, and every question we ask is a desire. So what is it that you desire? Are you, the reader of these words, ready to recognize the nature of your desire as an individual, as an organization? If you are ready, the answers you give will provide your map.

And the Earth will be the honest mirror of your progress.

REFERENCES

Arendt, H. (1965), *The Human Condition,* University of Chicago Press: London.

Fromm, E. (1976), *To Have or To Be,* Harper & Row Publishers: New York.

Lawson-Tancred, H. (trans.) (1986), *Aristotle: De Anima,* Penguin Books: London.

Santayana, G. (1955), *The Sense of Beauty,* Dover Publications: New York.

21

Sustainability: Context and Design

SHASHANK MEHTA

INTRODUCTION

With a population of more than 1.2 billion (India's Population, 2011), India can aptly be called a land of people. India is also one of the fastest growing economies in the world. From a 4.9 per cent growth in the GDP in 1990, the Indian economy has witnessed an increased growth rate in 2010–2011 (Economic Overview, 2006–2007). The process of liberalization that began almost two decades ago has brought about a phenomenal change in the Indian economy. By 2020, it is expected to be the third largest economy in the world after the United States and China. More than 50 per cent of India's current population is below the age of twenty-five, and over 65 per cent of the population is below the age of thirty-five (India's Population, 2011). Thus, in the present scenario, India comprises a major section of people in the working-age population.

Enriched with culture and tradition drawn from a civilization that is more than five thousand years old, India possesses an infinite treasure of indigenous knowledge and practised wisdom, both of which are being constantly used and practised in daily life. 'Creativity, in each of the culturally cohesive Indian societies was recognized as a quality that was as essential and as ordinary as the act of breathing', observed noted historian Kapila Vatsyayan during her convocation address at the National Institute of Design (NID), Ahmedabad (1989, p. 120).

Today, over 70 per cent of India's population lives in more than 630,000 villages spread across thirty-five states of the country; therefore, villages are the backbone of the nation in more ways than one. Agriculture and crafts are the main sources of income for people in the villages. Moreover, the majority of Indian industries comprise micro-, small- and medium-scale enterprises (SMEs). Consequently, indigenous innovation is an essential aspect of daily life here. By nature, Indians are highly enterprising, and they find ingenious and amazing ways to earn a living by making the most of the resources and skills at their disposal. Design is the way of life in India. The Indian economy is primarily a service- or process-oriented economy, rather than a material- or product-oriented one, as is prevalent in some countries. Collaboration, sharing, cooperation, community life and peaceful coexistence are the distinguishing characteristics of Indian culture. Socialization is also part of Indian culture, and it happens at various levels within the multilayered Indian society. Every layer or segment is large enough to form its own community, while at the same time, it is also closely linked to other layers of society. The modern and traditional, rich and poor, new and old—all such opposite aspects coexist in India. The diversity in culture, traditions, ethnicity and economic dimensions offers a variety of opportunities and challenges for designers to develop creative solutions.

The opening up of the Indian economy, however, has also resulted in increased consumption, reduced shelf life of products, mass production, fierce competition and saturated markets. All this has led to rapid industrialization and urbanization in Indian society. The speedy proliferation of capital-intensive and automated and centralized industries has resulted in reduced employment opportunities and has induced mass migration of the labour class from the rural areas to the cities. This migration has not only distanced people from their traditions and their roots but has also resulted in excessively saturated cities. Haphazard development of cities is another outcome of this migration. Thus, the country's rapid economic growth has also been accompanied by rapid urbanization, high unemployment, inequality, illiteracy and poverty.

The Indian economy requires different solutions—solutions that are 'people centric', where people are seen not merely as consumers but as human beings. It requires solutions that generate new employment opportunities utilizing the existing skills of people and improving their standard of living, while preserving the values of traditional society. This necessitates the development of a product design methodology that addresses this unique need to make use of the abundant ingenious and indigenous resources available in the country, apart from encouraging sustainability in all its forms, and also focusing on improving the quality of the life of people involved.

GANDHI'S VISION FOR SUSTAINABLE ECONOMIC DEVELOPMENT OF INDIA

A popular saying, commonly attributed as a Native American proverb, goes, 'We do not inherit the earth from our ancestors; we borrow it from our children'. If we are to heed these words, we must strive to allow for a more equitable distribution so that everyone has what they need to suffice their needs (but not necessarily their wants). In this context, Mahatma Gandhi said, 'I would prize every invention of Science made for the benefit for all' (Mashelkar, 2011; Platt, 2010). Gandhi inspired us to get 'more from less for more and more people of the world' (Mashelkar, 2011). He gave the world new thoughts on non-violence and sustainable living. Gandhi believed that the 'earth provides enough to satisfy every man's need but not every man's greed' (Mashelkar, 2010). Curbing greed, according to Gandhi, is the major challenge. Realizing the importance of the body and mind, he emphasized the approach of simple living and high thinking (Rajvanshi, 2004). Mental happiness and simple living, according to him, could form the basis of sustainability. His insistence on use of our own labour for fulfilling the majority of our needs was legendary. According to him, education must aim at educating an individual in totality, instead of concentrating on one aspect of the person. Gandhi believed that sustainable economic growth can only be achieved through development of the entire human personality and by maintaining the relationship between people and nature. He therefore emphasized the need for educating students in schools and colleges about sustainability, thus instilling in them a love for nature (Rajvanshi, 2010). True education, according to him, is an all-around development of the faculties, which is best attained through action.

Gandhi also taught us that economic activities cannot be isolated from human life. A country's economy can attain sustainable growth only through a balanced development of all its regions. He believed that optimum utilization of human resources was essential for a country such as India. Production by the masses rather than mass production, therefore, would be more appropriate for India. Gandhi therefore encouraged decentralization and regional self-reliance through small-scale and cottage industries. These industries would be able to create employment opportunities for the rural population by utilizing the locally available resources and skills. Opportunities for self-employment would empower all individuals and instil confidence, self-respect and entrepreneurial spirit in them. Gandhi propagated the concept of self-sustainability for the community, one that is less dependent on external support and government organizations. With this bottom-up approach towards development, a community can generate its own income and sufficient resources to gain self-reliance in ways that cater to its unique needs (willourworld, 2012). A strong supporter of equality, ethics, non-violence, non-exploitation of workers and social welfare, Gandhi was a strong advocate of the development of the village economy, an economy that focuses on the vast rural population of India. Such an approach could empower almost 80 per cent of the country's population. Significantly, it would help bring equality in society because the income generated gets distributed more equitably among the working people in the rural areas.

SUSTAINABILITY AND THE INDIAN CONTEXT

For the labour-intensive society of India, generating new entrepreneurial and employment opportunities becomes an important criterion in determining the sustainability of the product. Production by the masses and for the masses, coupled with a global outlook in terms of its quality and performance, will therefore be more relevant than a model that fosters centralization of industry and massive urbanization. Utilizing existing skills and resources, these opportunities should be created at the doorsteps of the people. The opportunities should offer creative, constructive and positive engagement in a collaborative and cooperative environment. These will help create that much-needed confidence among the people and equality in the society, while arresting migration from the villages. Sustainable design in the context of India needs to give greater emphasis on the wellbeing of human life, both to those engaged in the making of the product and to the users of this product.

Globally, various efforts are being directed towards reducing, reusing and recycling materials and towards greener and more environmentally friendly methods of production. However, it has been observed that many of these incremental improvements are being aimed at existing products. However, if these products cannot be comfortably accommodated into the Indian perspective, such approaches will have inherent limitations in the particular context of sustainability in India (Mehta, 2003a, p. 7).

In their buying habits, the rural middle-income population tends to be very sensitive to cost and is conscious of change. Determining factors surrounding the products they buy include considerations such as longevity of use and life cycle, reusability, serviceability/reparability, adaptability to a variety of tasks, affordability, resale value and recyclability. All these factors inform the demands of consumers. Criteria such as product performance, quality and cost of production have a direct bearing on the design of the products and the industries in which such products get manufactured.

Traditionally, local needs were served through crafts that were practised by utilizing available skills and resources. The products thus manufactured evolved over generations. Consequently, these traditional products have been refined and perfected to suit the functional demands of the community. The crafts have succeeded in maintaining their aesthetic appeal, and the craftspeople share a sense of belongingness with the community they are a part of. Through such means, the crafts sector provides employment for up to thirty million people, thus making it the second largest employment-generating sector in the country. The vast majority of the products in India, almost 94 per cent, are manufactured by its SMEs. These SMEs are spread all over the country and mainly operate on a regional basis; they understand the needs and aspirations of the users. Being small, they are quickly able to adapt to changes and provide customized solutions and services. Fierce competition among these twenty-six million SMEs and auxiliary units in India help bring about constant refinement and upgrading of products. These industries employ more than sixty-one million people and constitute around 45 per cent products and services exported from the country.

Indian society is based on a service economy, with a major focus on agriculture, which comprises the largest middle-income and rural segment. Thus, the agricultural sector, the rural crafts sector and the SMEs as the main industrial sector all encourage development of countrywide, indigenous and ingenious ways earning a livelihood.

As mentioned above, this rich resource of indigenous knowledge evolved over generations and has been constantly used and practised in efforts towards survival and progress. As might be expected, therefore, one comes across amazing innovations that have been developed to meet the specific needs and requirements of a person or a region. By the very nature of their development, these innovations will have inbuilt considerations related to ecological and sustainability aspects. There is, therefore, great scope for developing these ideas by drawing on the traditional knowledge that underpins them and creating contemporary solutions for local applications. This could benefit a large number of people living in the rural regions and would also generate employment opportunities. Such indigenous innovation and knowledge could thus form a significant resource that could be developed into marketable products and thereby help create business successes at the local and small-scale level. In turn, this would encourage decentralization and regional self-reliance. Indigenous design and development capabilities are the keys to gaining a competitive edge and represent a vital direction for a country like India in making the transition into an innovation-driven economy (Mehta and Mokashi-Punekar, 2005).

Due to limited resources and skills and a paucity of job opportunities, it becomes difficult for the majority of the people to find a secure job that ensures them a regular income. Therefore, people turn towards self-employment from a very early age. For developing countries such as India, services offer great opportunities for employment right at the doorstep of the people, while utilizing existing skills, resources and time. Generally, services are low on investment and help reduce capital and infrastructural investments. Services encourage customized and localized solutions. Typically, one finds a variety of services employing individuals and groups. These may be offered in an organized manner (for example, through community-based cooperatives) or in an unorganized manner, through the vast number of ad hoc, specialized enterprises. Either way, services have a great scope of encouraging societal interaction. They can meet the user's needs directly by reducing or eliminating the need for products or other tangible solutions. Services help distribute the income to a large segment of the society, and they improve the rural economy thereby helping to arrest migration from the villages.

DESIGN: THE INDIAN CONTEXT

Design in the Indian context focuses on people, their environment and various socio-cultural issues. Participatory and inclusive approaches that centre around the primary objective of improving the quality of life of all involved is the most appropriate approach for design interventions in India. Such interventions preserve the values of traditional Indian society and can generate new employment opportunities. They also hone existing skills and foster cooperative practices, which bolster the social fabric of community life as well as financial empowerment.

Design here means developing solutions together as a team. The design profession brings in the much-needed empathetic understanding and holistic vision to connect and integrate various efforts towards a positive outcome. The designer works both as a coordinator and team member and has the responsibility of creating contextual and appropriate solutions, systems, services or products. A sensitive designer, with wide exposure and experience and an ability to take a holistic view, can easily connect with the users' needs. Hence, the designer can act as a catalyst to help bring in changes and a new vision for the team he or she works with, for society or for industry. Thus, in the Indian context, design can encourage social innovation and sustainability in all its various forms. Therefore, the designer's role and responsibilities can be of great significance in the Indian context (Mehta, 2003b).

Shri Mahila Gruh Udhyog Lijjat Papad (www.lijjat.com) is a successful cooperative organization. It provides opportunities to thousands of women, many of whom are illiterate and come from the economically backward strata of society, to earn a living in their homes with their limited skills. Every day, more than 42,000 of these women roll out nineteen million *papads*. A staple Indian food, papads are thin pancakes made of lentils, pepper and salt, and can be roasted or fried. Women get the dough from the organization every morning and make the papads in the afternoon, immediately after completing their daily household chores and all other family members have gone out to work. The organization also provides them the platform to come together and discuss various issues related to their life. A similar success story is that of the White Revolution that was initiated by Amul (www.amul.com). It is jointly owned by some 2.8 million milk producers, most of whom come from the rural areas. The organization collects milk from the villages and processes it in its state-of-the-art plant. Thereafter, it markets the milk and milk products all over India as well as in other parts of the world.

Both examples, through their innovative cooperative networks, have helped people at the grass-roots level gain economic viability, greater independence and a sense of dignity and self-respect, while keeping their social and cultural structure intact. These employment opportunities created at mass scale in the villages themselves have thus helped arrest migration to cities. Hence, these organizations have succeeded in striking an appropriate balance between traditional Indian society at the grass-roots level and quality-conscious and demanding buyers and users.

The *dabbawalas* of Mumbai (www.mydabbawala.com) form another such story but, in this case, within the urban setting. An estimated five thousand dabbawalas collect every day around two hundred thousand lunch boxes from individual homes and take them to their respective owners in their places of work with the utmost punctuality.

Design here must address the needs and demands of the large strata of the society that is in the lower half of the development pyramid. To this end, the concept of 'Gandhian engineering' proposed by R. A. Mashelkar (2011), and based on the philosophy of 'getting more (performance) from less (resources) for more (people) and not just for more profit', could be an appropriate approach for the Indian context. Gandhian engineering, according to this view, advocates developing low-cost products and services that the poor of the world can afford, thus raising their standard of living and quality of life. This helps create an equitable and sustainable society. This approach will help India and could also help China and other emerging nations to join the global economy as equals but in a manner that not only retains rural communities, indigenous knowledge and traditional skills but also helps prevent rapid urbanization, along with the accompanying social problems. These low-cost products and services will be high on performance and quality. While creating a profit for companies, they will help democratize technology by reaching out to the world's poorest citizens.

There are many inspiring examples of low-cost solutions being developed and widely used in India and elsewhere:

- A hepatitis B vaccine, developed by Varaprasada Reddy of Shantha Biotech, is one-fortieth the cost of traditional vaccines and meets UNICEF's quality requirements. The vaccine is today used for about 50 per cent of immunization programs worldwide (Platt, 2010; Chakma et al., 2011, p. 9).

- Aravind Eye Care's cataract surgeries are one-one hundreth of the cost of similar treatments in other countries and also meet global quality standards. These cataract surgeries are performed on three hundred thousand patients annually (Aravind Eye Clinics, 2011).
- Ram Chandra Sharma from Jaipur developed an inexpensive prosthetic limb, the Jaipur Foot, which costs $28 (Platt, 2010), thereby making it affordable for people in the lower economic strata of the society (Jaipurfoot, 2007).
- Faqir Chand Kohli, former chair of the Indian software company TCS, created a computer-based literacy program at the cost of $2. A person can learn to read in just six to eight weeks using this program (Tata Solution, 2005).
- The Tata Nano is the cheapest car in the world, costing about $2,200 (Mashelkar, 2010), thereby making it affordable for families and most importantly making travel safer for those who could otherwise only afford two-wheeled transport.

These and many others are examples of Gandhian engineering and an approach of inclusive innovation. Design here complements craft to connect its skills to contemporary markets while offsetting its limitations in terms of resources. In this way, design helps create new employment opportunities for artisans.

An exchange student from Germany, as a part of his design project at NID, worked with a crafts community from Gujarat that is traditionally involved in making kitchen knives. These knives were sold at fairly low prices and mostly as single pieces. The student-designer developed a set of knives, each of which could be used for different requirements in the kitchen. By utilizing the community's existing skills and resources, the student succeeded in creating a new set of knives that have ergonomically comfortable handles. The motif used on the handle was inspired by the camel, because the artisans were natives of Kutch, a desert region in Gujarat, where camels are an integral part of the lives of the local people. This motif has given the knife a unique identity. This substantial value addition has helped revitalize the craft. Such design projects have helped various crafts, social sectors and SMEs in the country to connect with contemporary markets and demands. They have enabled these sectors to sustain themselves, even in the face of limited capital investment and resources.

Design, by humanizing technology, helps connect products and systems to the masses. Emphasis is placed on improving people's standard of living by generating new opportunities. Hence, a designer in the Indian context has to design products and solutions that encourage sustainability in its varied forms. These designs are developed locally so as to succeed in satisfying the needs of the region in which they are produced. While converting constraints of resources into unique opportunities encompassing aspects such as their reusability, recyclability, reparability and increased life cycle, design in India can improve the working conditions of the people and enhance the technological prowess of the industries. Many of these design solutions are low on capital investment but technologically intensive. Product servicing, rather than replacement, also increases employment opportunities.

The majority of the industrial units in India operate on a small scale, employing people from a wide variety of backgrounds. Thousands of people can be involved in one product or product segment. It becomes important for the designer to fully under-stand and be sensitive to this context before embarking upon any design intervention. Design intervention for these industries goes beyond product design solutions, which is the conventional approach of industrial design. Design here also provides much-needed hand-holding to create the linkages with customer needs, markets and so on. Through value addition at every stage of product development and production, design helps im-prove the quality of life of the people involved. Such interventions also have a strong impact on the sustainable development of the Indian economy.

For the various indigenous innovations developed locally, design interventions help bring in a much-needed user perspective, thereby utilizing the skills and resources avail-able at the local context to more effectively target user needs. Product refinements in function, aesthetics, production, packaging, transportation, maintenance and service all help to ensure marketable and sustainable products. The designer's ability to view the problems from different perspectives with a particular focus on quality helps bring about a holistic understanding of the problem. In addition, the designer's ability to create and evaluate multiple alternatives while helping to communicate with various stakeholders, each with different backgrounds and expertise, helps reduce the number of iterations, thereby saving time and resources (Mehta, 2003a).

DESIGN METHODOLOGIES

Charles and Ray Eames, the iconic designer duo, who were commissioned by the government of India in 1958 to present their recommendations for the setting up of a design institute in the country, suggested a 'sober investigation into those val-ues and those qualities that Indians hold important to a good life... that there be a close scrutiny of those elements that go to make up a "Standard of Living"'. With a major emphasis on improving the quality of life, they further recommended that this search should begin at the village level. Based on the Eames's report, now fa-mously called *The India Report* (Eames and Eames, 1958), the first design institute in India, the National Institute of Design (NID), was established in 1960 with its mandate to impart design education, research, training and design awareness in the country.

Since its establishment, NID and its alumni have worked extensively with the coun-try's varied industrial and social sectors, and government and non-government orga-nizations. In doing so, the institute has gained valuable experience in solving typical problems that arise in India's labour-intensive society at the grass-roots levels, and also in the country's large SMEs and crafts sectors. Design here means developing solutions in a cooperative manner with the client, who may be a self-made entrepreneur or craftsper-son, and with the workers on the shop floor, and in consultation with the vendors and users. Five decades of active and enduring involvement with various industrial sectors in India have helped designers develop an empathy and concern for all the stakeholders involved. These experiences have led to unique design intervention methodologies that are most appropriate to these sectors.

These design methodologies differ from those prevalent elsewhere, particularly in the Western world, where greater emphasis is laid upon economic issues and the profitability of the industry. In India, design intervention methodologies, largely based on participatory approaches, centre around the primary objective of improving the quality of life for all the stakeholders involved. As such, these experiences and design intervention methodologies would also seem appropriate for other developing and densely populated countries.

The Indian model of production by the masses means that there may be thousands of families whose survival depends upon one product segment. Therefore, the designer has to be extremely sensitive and cautious in offering any modifications and changes. Before embarking upon any design intervention, it becomes important to gain a holistic understanding of the context, need, strengths and weaknesses in terms of resources and levels of skills, training and experience available, sociocultural issues involved and market demands. A detailed design need assessment survey or feasibility study is carried out to develop a comprehensive road map and future direction for interventions in terms of infrastructure, skills and resource requirements and appropriate training schemes. Such measures also help to determine the scope and direction for design interventions. Upgrading of skills, training programs and design awareness seminars help sensitize the participants and the industries to new design requirements while also informing them about contemporary market demands. In addition, design intervention projects provide opportunities for designers to become involved over an extended period, thereby enabling the enterprises to conduct extensive explorations of new materials, techniques, designs, markets and innovative applications.

The design clinic is one such design intervention method developed to suit the country's SMEs. It is based on the rich history of experiences gained through working closely with enterprises in these sectors. This unique model of design intervention addresses the critical need of taking design to the doorsteps of these industries, where a conventional model of design consultancy and training would often not be affordable. Design clinics, employing the participatory approach, help SMEs arrive at practical and implementable solutions to improve existing products. They can also guide these businesses in developing new designs. This design clinic model, developed and tested in the field with many small industrial units and clusters, is now being scaled up to be implemented nationally. The Design Clinic Scheme for SMEs (www.designclinicsmsme.org)—launched countrywide by the Government of India and financially supported by the Ministry of Micro, Small and Medium Enterprises—targets about 200 SME clusters throughout the country. With the main objective of seeding design among the SMEs, the scheme provides a platform for constant and continuous interaction between designers and businesses. Products will be designed based on the local context and needs, and one of the expected outcomes will be an increase in employment opportunities. Through systematic design intervention and support, this approach is expected to create a sustainable design ecosystem for the Indian SME sector.

The last five decades of NID's involvement with various sectors of Indian industries and society have helped develop a unique system of education that is particularly suited to the Indian context. This integrated system of design education, design research and design promotion helps the institute stay in touch with industry and society and also provide much-needed exposure and experience to its students, thereby making them aware of the industry's needs and expectations. NID's consultancy wing helps the institute and its faculty members maintain closer and regular contacts with various industry, craft and social sectors. Various sector-specific studios set up at the institute provide opportunities to undertake in-depth research and design intervention projects in specific domain areas, and the real-life experience gained by the institute's faculty members is shared with the students.

The education curriculum is structured around studio- and project-based learning, so as to provide adequate scope and opportunity for experimentation and exploration. Ample opportunities are provided to student designers in order that they face and experience reality. Environmental perception, craft documentation, indigenous innovations and design for special needs are some of the unique course modules developed over the years at NID. These courses help students develop sensitivity and respect for their surroundings and their society, and they also help develop the much-needed empathy and concern for all the stakeholders involved. While building a mutually beneficial relationship with various sectors of Indian industries and society, this model of education helps the institute constantly refine its design methodologies and education curriculum in order to maintain its relevance with the contemporary demands, expectations and aspirations of Indian industries and society at large.

DESIGN FOR SUSTAINABILITY: PROPOSED GUIDELINES

Based on this discussion and with a view to fostering sustainability and social innovations in their various forms to create a sustainable design ecosystem within the country, the following guiding principles are proposed:

- Encourage use of local resources.
- Incorporate ecological aspects of the region and environmentally friendly methods.
- Utilize and develop available skills; avoid de-skilling.
- Help generate new employment opportunities by designing for and encouraging production by masses.
- Create employment opportunities at the doorsteps of the people through constructive and creative utilization and engagement of human resources.
- Design for product affordability by integrating the scope for product customization and adaptability; the product must be affordable to local masses and markets.
- Design for product optimization and refinement, process improvements, product quality and value addition.
- Encourage decentralized fabrication/manufacturing methods.
- Design for technology-intensive but low-capital investment solutions.
- Design for product reparability, serviceability, reusability and recyclability.

- Understand and respect local tradition, culture and the social fabric of the society.
- Encourage services; integrate service component; create opportunities for self-employment.
- Encourage cooperation/sharing and a collaborative approach.
- Encourage a participatory approach to product development.
- Work towards improving the quality of life by adopting people-centric approaches.
- Develop empathetic, holistic and systematic understanding.
- Use design as a catalyst to handhold the entire process linking product development, production, marketing and distribution.
- Take design expertise to the doorsteps of the industries, crafts and social sectors with a view to connecting available/local skills and resources to markets/users.
- Encourage local and indigenous innovations, enterprises and businesses.
- Ensure integrated and continuous education and exposure to sustainability, nature and society.
- Create a platform for the constant and continuous interaction of industries and crafts sectors with designers and experts.

CONCLUSION

Armed with a global outlook and sensitivity to local needs and aspirations, a designer can help industry connect with contemporary markets. It has been acknowledged that design has innovation as its core and can also be a key factor in business success. The design profession can bring in a much-needed empathetic understanding and holistic vision that connects and integrates various efforts towards a positive outcome. A sensitive designer can utilize the unique strengths of the enterprises and industries and help them connect with the user needs.

When the major emphasis is placed on generating newer opportunities that can improve people's standard of living while preserving the values of traditional society, the role and responsibility of the designer assumes greater significance. In this context, the designer has to design products that encourage sustainability in its varied forms. It can be assumed that in India, higher marketability can be attained only by those products that can satisfy the physical and psychological needs of users and incorporate the traditional and ecological aspects of a region. Such products should also have global appeal in terms of product efficiency and performance. In the Indian context, design will have to focus on people, their environment and sociocultural aspects. These factors will determine what type of product will be manufactured and the raw materials and techniques that will be required for manufacturing it.

All these factors highlight the need to focus design efforts towards products that have evolved locally and have succeeded in satisfying the needs of the region in which they are produced. By their very nature of development, any such product innovations will have inbuilt considerations related to the ecological and sustainability aspects. Taking these solutions further, design must primarily focus on value addition by improving the quality and finish of these products and connect these design solutions with the existing skills. Such interventions would improve the marketability of the products and increase the income-generating capacity of the people involved. Though it still has a long way to go, such design interventions can improve the quality of life of the people engaged in a particular industry and also create a strong impact on the sustainable development of both the Indian economy and Indian society as a whole.

REFERENCES

Aravind Eye Clinics (2011), *Managing Innovations: Case Studies*, <http://www.managing-innovation.com> accessed September 10, 2008.

Chakma, J., Masum, H., Perampaladas, K., Heys, J. and Singer, P. A. (2011), 'Indian Vaccine Innovation: The Case of Shantha Biotechnics', *Globalization and Health*, vol. 7: p. 9, <http://www.ncbi.nlm.nih.gov/pmc/articles/PMC3110116/> accessed September 10, 2011.

Eames, C. and Eames, R. (1958), *The India Report*, National Institute of Design: Ahmedabad.

Economic Overview (2006–2007), *The Banyan Tree*, <http://www.thebanyantree.co.in> accessed August 25, 2009.

India's Population (2011), *Population of India*, <http://www.indiaonlinepages.com/population> accessed August 27, 2011.

Jaipurfoot (2007), *Technology—Jaipurfoot History*, <http://www.jaipurfoot.org/03_Technology_history.asp> accessed July 25, 2012.

Mashelkar, R. A. (2010), *A Gandhian Approach to R&D*, <http://www.strategy-business.com> accessed September 3, 2011.

Mashelkar, R. A. (2011), *Gandhian Engineering Is Not Just for the Poor*, <www.bilcare.com> accessed September 3, 2011.

Mehta, S. (2003a), 'Sustainability: The Indian Context', *Design Networks Asia*, vol. 19: p. 7.

Mehta, S. (2003b), 'Services That Sustain', Paper presented at the exhibition *Visions of Possible World*, Milan.

Mehta, S. and Mokashi-Punekar, R. (2005), *Exploring Indigenous Innovations: Ascertaining the Scope for Design Interventions for the Successful Commercialization*, Allemandi Conference Press: Torino.

Platt, J. R. (2010), 'Introducing Gandhian Engineering', *The Institute*, <http://www.ieee.org> accessed September 3, 2011.

Rajvanshi, A. (2004), *Mahatma Gandhi: A Votary for Sustainable Living*, <http://www.boloji.com/index.cfm?md=Content&sd=Articles&ArticleID=922> accessed July 25, 2012.

Rajvanshi, A. (2010), *Sustainable Development—the Gandhian Way*, Nimbkar Agricultural Institute, Phaltan, Maharashtra, India, <http://www.nariphaltan.org/gandhiessay.pdf> accessed July 25, 2012.

Tata Solution (2005), *Tata: Improving the Quality of Life*, <http://www.tataliteracy.com> accessed September 10, 2011.

Vatsyayan, K. (1989), *Leading Lights on Design; 23 Convocation Addresses*, National Institute of Design: Ahmedabad.

willourworld (2012), *Self-Sustainability for Rural India*, <http://willourworld.org/?page_id=399> accessed July 26, 2012.

22

Shè Jì—Change for Sustainable Futures

LOU YONGQI

ESTABLISHING A STRATEGY: THE ORIGINAL MEANING OF SHÈ JÌ IN CHINESE

The original meaning of the Chinese word *shè jì* (design) was 'to establish a strategy'; it originated from military affairs (Yang, 1997, p. 3). The product of shè jì is *jì*, a strategy or solution. Jì contains both goal-setting and process-guiding. Shè jì was dominated by two different classes in ancient China: the literati and the artisans. The former mainly worked on the level of Tao (philosophy, ideology), focusing on military, political, social and cultural purposes in Chinese culture as Tao also has a special significance on the moral/ethical level, and the latter mainly worked on the level of qi (materiality, functionality), covering the fields of technique, arts and crafts.[1]

The dual structure of the Tao and qi is integrated in various aspects of Chinese society and culture. Although this system has been operating successfully in China for thousands of years, the communication between the two levels has been challenging. Furthermore, it had effected the development of the Chinese economy and technology. In the traditional value system of China, the difference between Tao and qi is a common social consensus that the humanities are more important than technology. In China, the humanities were mainly disseminated and inherited by articles and books, while technology was mainly transmitted by personal demonstration and verbal guidance. The strategy of 'stressing agriculture but dampening business' over two thousand years has seriously impeded the development of commerce and industry, marking the foundation and context of the germination and development of contemporary design.

FROM SHÈ JÌ TO DESIGN: THE DEVELOPMENT OF CHINESE CONTEMPORARY DESIGN

The military failures of China's Opium War lit the fuse for the social and cultural revolutions that were to follow. A century of turbulence brought about the crash of traditional culture and social structures. As Westernization and globalization became the catalyst of myriad social changes and developments, fuelled by reformation and the opening of the country starting in 1978, the nation's focus was increasingly on prosperity. As a part of the higher education system, design education in China was based on Western values instead of local traditional values and culture. The introduction and dissemination of modern Western design education and practice theory, from the Beaux-Arts to Bauhaus, provided a shortcut to the development of modern design education and practice in China[2] (Gu, 2007, pp. 5–15). At the same time, however, the efforts to improve China's own contemporary design system were stagnant (Wang, 2008).

From shè jì to design: this phrase sums up the developing processes of China's modern design education and practice. During this development, the traditional notion of shè jì was neglected as it is not sufficiently clear according to the standards of modern disciplines; it was also considered too soft compared with standards in the West. At the same time, craftsmen were seriously marginalized due to a lack of adequate means. This situation was exacerbated due to changes of lifestyle and economic structures. As a result, the traditional notion of shè jì has been increasingly forgotten.

THE RENAISSANCE OF CHINESE SHÈ JÌ

From a contemporary point of view, the core of the Chinese shè jì notion can be described as follows:

- blurred and soft definition: ambiguity with higher applicability, focus on process rather than result, and emphasis on state over material;
- systemic strategy: synthesis of the micro and the macro level, and dual structure of Tao and qi; and
- involvement with decision-makers: collaborative work that functions from the top down; integration with the social system.

The softer Chinese shè jì concept extends the application field of design and also coincides with certain tendencies in today's design fields, such as social design, system design, strategic design and so on (Valtonen, 2007, p. 308). Comparing Chinese shè jì to John Heskett's definition of design, which states, 'design is to design a design that will produce a design' (Heskett, 2002, p. 11), we can easily find a meeting point between East and West.

In the highly organized and government-driven society of China, the renaissance of the traditional shè jì concept can easily gain support from ancestral social structures and decision-making systems. The advantages of China's shè jì notion have become increasingly appropriate in the face of social change. The shè jì towards Tao is precisely the direction of sustainable development. Reinitiation of the notion of shè jì in China has positive significance, but it does not mean that Chinese design will diverge from what is happening in the rest of the world. It is a renaissance, not a restoration. Calling for shè jì means that a design strategy in China can be designed; because it is based on traditional culture, this understanding has an encompassing attitude and resonates more easily with people.

Changing: Problems and Opportunities

China is currently experiencing a rapid transformation. China may also be the most ideal place to develop and realize strategies for change. According to traditional Chinese philosophy, change is embedded in the law of nature. This is important because change is the consequence of gathered energy leading from one state of balance to another. How to take advantage and use this energy to generate sustainable social change is a design issue. First, the discipline of design should change. China's unique context makes it possible to connect design to the paradigm shift, both economically and socially. China is also an ideal test bed for new design. Second, and returning to the original meaning of shè jì, design should intervene to move the world towards a sustainable future in a proactive way.

From Creation to Innovation

With the rise of China's economy, the call for transforming 'made in China' to 'created in China' has become more heated. The difference between creativity and innovation is that the latter is not only based on creativity but also on the shift from creation to implementation. In this process, the selection, development and commercialization of creation are all key factors determining the success of innovation. In a sense, innovation is equivalent to the application and commercialization of creation (Stamm, 2008, p. 1). However, the fact that business and technology have been overlooked in traditional culture hinders the development of innovation in China.

Innovation has three key elements: creativity, technology and business. Only through the integration of these three can innovation be successfully realized. In the industrial sector, the relationship between creativity, technology and business is always linear: from the technical, to the design, and finally to the marketing. In this mode, technology is the sole core of innovation. But the new design-driven innovation mode requires breaking the segregation between these three elements. It can only be realized through in-depth understanding of human beings, culture and socio-economic status.

The commercialization of creation and the impact of the creative industry on society and the economy can be realized in two models: first, the rise and growth of the creative industry has garnered increased importance in the economy and more influence over social life. Second, the creative industry has more impact on the other industries as a special 'producer services industry'.[3] No doubt, the latter not only contributes much more to society and the economy than does the former but also has the potential to change the shape and direction of traditional industry.

Hence, the creative industry should not be limited only to fulfilling the needs of end users, but it should also consider providing services and products for the sustainable innovation of all industries, facilitating the concentration of social resources to advanced industries, and promoting the upgrading of competitive strengths of the sustainable development of the society. In this sense, the creative industry acts as a catalyst in the creation of a new economy, culture and social life. This is the new view of production in an era of knowledge-based economies. For design education, research and practice, new design examples must be generated to catalyse and demonstrate innovative trends.

Changing of Design

In a new era, design must be and is currently being redefined. Socio-economic changes urge designers to think bigger. For the design discipline, expanding roles and tools of design make it more possible than ever to connect and integrate multidisciplinary knowledge on the socio-economic level (Buchanan, 2001, p. 7). Design is now more and more involved in solving strategic and holistic problems in our daily lives. Design thinking, combined with scientific-technological thinking, allows design to explore new frontiers and makes it possible for design to link itself to the future through the balance of desirability, viability and feasibility (Brown, 2009, p. 18).

This new design has raised the bar for knowledge: in depth, breadth and comprehensiveness. Through design, information (concepts) can be turned into results, which can be either physical (e.g., products) or immaterial (e.g., services). An enhanced interdisciplinary identity, the education and training of innovative and T-shape personnel (i.e., depth of expertise combined with ability to collaborate), the exploration into new fields, a change in learning methods and the establishment of new values will be the hallmarks of a new design.

This trend will further influence the business model of design as an industry. It will transform from simply providing design services to providing holistic solutions that have greater social impact and business value. The conventional employment relationship between design and capital will become, in part, more cooperative. The vision has also been expanded from objective and individual efforts to social innovation: to support sustainable ways of living and producing on the basis of a common ethic.

China's Current Context

Advocacy of changing design is faced by the question of national conditions in developing countries like China. In Western society, where material civilization has been highly developed, many hold the view that it is quite natural for physical design to be transformed into immaterial design. In developing countries, however, the quantitative growth of the economy has just started to become qualitative, with society's awareness of the value of design yet to be established. In light of the above, is it premature to talk about changing design in developing countries? Moreover, is the emphasis put on non-material forms of design, such as service system design, going to restrict the development of mainstream design?

These questions cannot be avoided. Actually, in the Chinese context, such kinds of change fit exactly the historical role of shè jì. Furthermore, there are two central questions in the current situation. First, is the transformation possible? Second, is the role of design one of service or guidance? The traditional development approach of developed nations is faced by ever-more critical challenges in a world that is flat, hot and crowded (Friedman, 2008, pp. 63–84). If the resources of the Earth can no longer sustain a future in which developing countries take the same approach to growth as developed ones, then transcendence is not only a possibility but also a necessity. Additionally, it is no longer a topic legitimate only under given stages of development in relation to how design can become an effective tool for advancing the innovation and sustainability of the society. It is time for China to generate a new era of design imbued with traditional culture. Design can likewise transform itself from being driven by the market to providing a role of guidance, which includes supporting new socio-economic modes, integrating design into new business models and providing strategies for solving socio-economic problems creatively.

The rapid development and changing conditions in developing countries like China can make this kind of transformation both more urgent and more achievable than in developed countries. Once these steps are taken, developing countries can similarly make typological contributions to the future of design and social development.

Direction of Changing: Towards Sustainability

The paradigm shift from creation to innovation enlarges the role of design and the creative industry. This will further accelerate the process of change. However, this change may not necessarily be beneficial to humans as if the direction is wrong; it may only accelerate the rate of extinction.

Design has had and still has a huge impact on economic growth. 'Design plays a key role in the creation of high-entropy products, services and infrastructures...None of this productivity, none of this innovation, would happen without input from us: the creative industries, especially designers' (Thackara, 2011, p. 15). In the past decades, design has become an important tool to promote a high consumption–based economy, the same economy that we have now found to be unsustainable. According to the Chinese saying, 'Those who can put the bell around a tiger can also take it off'[4]—that is, the problems caused by design should also be able to be solved by design.

The Chinese Understanding of Sustainability

Today, sustainable development is one of the few universal ethics in the world, but people are realizing that the pursuit of rapid economic changes has only steered our world away from sustainability. In today's highly developed material civilization, we have to admit in shame that our ancestors lived a far more sustainable lifestyle than we currently do.

Nowadays, the whole world is looking for sustainable solutions for its salvation. China is no exception. Sustainability has already become the new criteria for re-evaluating the changes that are happening or have happened in our life and world. We need to pause and rethink our trajectory before taking further steps: to rethink the rationality of modern industrial civilization; to rethink and compare the present physical spaces, social-cultures and lifestyles as compared to what they used to be; to rethink the positions, values, trends and possible social responsibilities of design education, design practice and design research. The fact is that many discarded traditional ways of life are actually consistent with the principles outlined in modern sustainability.

The view of Chinese traditional wisdom on sustainability can be reflected in the ubiquitous phrase 'interaction between human and nature'. This kind of epistemology can be explained as follows:

- Coexistence rather than human-centred: in traditional Chinese ideology, human beings are only a part of the whole world; they live together with and depend on other living organisms.
- Systemic and holistic rather than individual: humans and nature have always been regarded as a whole; the human body and the outside world are both complicated systems sharing many common characteristics. The focus must be on the whole rather than on details.
- Relation-oriented rather than artefact-oriented: this kind of thinking, together with respect and love of nature, led ancient civilizations in pursuit of a world of balance and harmony (the Chinese meaning of 'sustainable') as the highest ideal. The ultimate goal, then, is always towards establishing this holistic relationship over one with physical objects.
- Dynamic rather than static: balance and harmony are always in a state of flux. The strategy changes according to the changing of the context.

Visions of China's Shè Ji

In this era of globalization, Eastern designers have a duty to put forward their views as 'critical regionalists' (Frampton, 1992, pp. 314–27). The quest for a cultural consciousness indicates the opportunity for original Chinese design thinking to flourish.

In the process of realizing the renaissance of the shè jì system, the following trends can indicate the new characters and areas of future Chinese design:

- close relation to major issues of societal and economic change;
- integration with top-down sociopolitical patterns and bottom-up social innovation processes;
- active intervention in political, economic, social and cultural fields;
- use of design through strategic and systematic tools to achieve Chinese social, economic and cultural sustainability;

- focus on folk wisdom with emphasis on a sustainable way of life; and
- redesign of the contemporary Chinese lifestyle without losing cultural essence.

In light of these missions, the rethinking of shè jì is not only needed at the levels of science and technology but also at the systemic and strategic levels. To adapt to the changing of the era, we need to shè (set up) an appropriate jì (vision and strategy) for our future that enables people to live as they like in a sustainable way (Manzini, 2006, p. 14). These goals are not restricted to the design discipline itself but are also for the goal of an inclusive wellness for all of humanity.

SHÈ JÌ: HOMEOPATHY BY DESIGN INTERVENTION

Adjustment Strategy

When discussing the paradigm shift, it should be noted that such kind of change should not be a violent revolution but should be a gradual adjustment process. Compared to Western medical treatment, Chinese medical theory has always emphasized the importance of adaptation. It advocates the use of treatments such as acupuncture and massage, which stimulate the body's resistance, combined with external treatments, in order to heal the human body. This can be seen as a metaphor for proactive design interventions on social problems. It is not only the transformation of the social-economy and its processes but also the communication of this transition that should be redesigned. To achieve a state of 'consuming less, living better', many aspects of today's ways of living and producing (material, non-material) need to be encouraged towards a new direction. In this process, the adjustment strategy is extremely promising, as it can improve the system through proper activation without the risk of collapse.

Enabling Strategy

As the Chinese proverb states, 'Give a man a fish and you feed him for a day; teach a man to fish and you feed him for a lifetime'. When design changes from offering to enabling, then the design approach is changed, but synchronously the subject of design and the value of design are changed. The democratization of innovation characterized by user innovation, popular innovation, open innovation and collaborative innovation is bound to make obsolete the acceptance of a single ideal paradigm adopted by an entire society. Enabling design means not only including those whose lives will be affected by the design when considering of the solution but also means that part of the design will be assumed by the stakeholders. In this process, the autonomy and creativity of design as a specialized way of thinking will be greatly advanced. The value of design will also transcend from fulfilling professional taste towards openness and diversity. The enabling strategy also gives design a much more proactive role to intervene in large-scale social change (Lou, 2010, pp. 23–28).

Collaborative Restoration Strategy

Innovation is not reserved only for designers but exists everywhere in our daily lives and at work, awaiting our discovery. Innovative actions can be differentiated into individual and collective, professional and those of everyday life. Previously, the focus of the design discipline was by and large on individuals and professionals; the difference and barriers between experts and ordinary people were overexaggerated. It seems that whenever we talk about designers, it is automatically related to talents and profession. But we too often ignore the fact that technology is just a tool for problem-solving. In order to use the tool properly, it takes a detailed understanding of the everyday.

The understanding and the wisdom of ordinary people about their own lives should never be underestimated. For example, the poor know much better than most professional designers how to lead decent and sustainable lives with limited resources. In reality, their lives never lack inventions and creations. But due to the absence of professional knowledge, skills and social resources, it is hard for these poor people to refine and promote their knowledge. In this case, designers should utilize their own knowledge to understand, discover, improve and popularize grass-roots innovations that are in line with the ideas of sustainable development, and work with the people to co-design and promote solutions that are more mature, more durable and easier for replication, and thus also further stimulate the creativity of the community. This is called 'social innovation design'. The designer will hopefully discover embryos of new products or service systems from these potential social innovations. Only through the collaborative restoration process can the social changes towards a common sustainable goal be realized.

PROMISING CASES

Shanghai World Expo: Dialogue between Development and Sustainability

One of the biggest changes in China over the past few decades has been the large-scale urbanization that has taken place all over the country. In this context, 'Better City, Better Life', the theme of the 2010 Shanghai Expo, represents the common wish that humans share for better living conditions in future urban environments. Diversity of culture, prosperity of urban economy, innovations, remodelling of communities and interaction between urban and rural areas have been identified as the main topics of this expo. It is clear that all of these topics directly relate to the problems and challenges associated with the process of global sustainable development.

The World Expo in Shanghai achieved many successes. Two are particularly notable. First, sustainable philosophy and technology played an active role in the planning, construction and exhibition of the World Expo. The expo can be seen as a three-dimensional textbook that exhibits sustainable technology, thinking and prototypes to the people in an in-depth yet accessible manner. To give some examples: the Shanghai ideal home, Madrid case, zero-carbon pavilion of Hamburg and Bay Beach Wetland Park. There were many more. As seen by the huge crowd of visitors and media, sustainable technologies and related business are becoming more and more visible and popular. Second, the

Shanghai World Expo was a good example of event-driven urban development, marking a balance of short-term events and long-term sustainable development of the city (see Figure 22.1).

For instance, the Shanghai World Expo accelerated the construction of public transportation, especially the metro system. The level of public services in Shanghai also greatly improved. We cannot say that the expo in and of itself was a sustainable initiative, but it has undoubtedly had significant influence towards the sustainable development of China.

Design Harvests: Strategic Design to Balance the Urban and Rural

Design Harvests—Design for Xian Qiao sustainable rural community in Chongming—is an innovative social collaborative design project of Studio TAO (see Figure 22.2).[5]

One of the main impacts of high-speed economic growth in China is the structure of urbanization and its consequences for the balance between urban and rural areas. Sustainable development in China cannot leave aside the pursuit of a rural-urban balance. This is obviously a complex relationship because the new urbanism affects the rural areas deeply and involves a transformation of the communities. Moreover, design can approach this balance reconstruction process by recognizing the value of both rural

FIGURE 22.1   Master plan of Shanghai World Expo 2010. Courtesy of Tongji University.

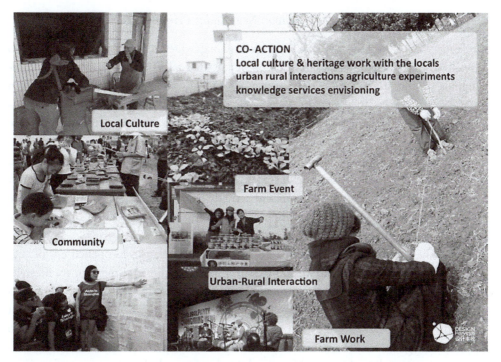

FIGURE 22.2   Design Harvests' social innovation project. Courtesy of Studio TEKTAO.

and urban and enhancing the interaction between them. From a design perspective, we think the local community should be involved in sustainable development strategies with the aim of restoring an urban-rural balance in the area by promoting a dialogue and exchanges between the two entities. The challenge for the designer of systems and services is to stabilize China's growth by fostering ways in which people can sustain themselves economically, environmentally and socially. In meeting this challenge, it will be necessary to involve the intended beneficiaries of the design: only in this way can general principles be adapted to local conditions and proposed solutions be made truly sustainable. The goal of this project is to create prototypes of sustainable rural-urban interaction and development based on the usage of local resources and strengths.

One of the most important proposals is to establish, together with the local community, a network of innovation hubs. Each innovation hub will be a platform for promoting a series of sustainable design solutions for local development. Moreover, each hub will incubate and demonstrate new business models based on the resources of the rural communities and interaction between urban and rural communities. Meanwhile, a systematic network is designed and formed among the hubs to have holistic and systemic impacts throughout the whole territory. The key principles of this project are co-creation and interdiscipline. Social collaboration in this project is not only the cooperation among different stakeholders such as the government, enterprises, designers and communities but also among different disciplines such as economics, sociology, engineering and design (Lou, 2011, p. 107).

A Sustainable School: New Jindai Primary School

In January 2010, the China-U.S. Center for Sustainable Development approached TekTao Design to lead the design and construction of a new sustainable elementary school in Liangping County to replace the one severely damaged in the 2008 earthquake. The design of the school reflects an all-encompassing conception of sustainability: not merely technical but with heavy emphasis on society and culture, and a dynamic integration among the three. The school was designed as growing within the environment (see Figure 22.3).

This goal is composed of four parts: first, that new construction reduce damage to the previous environment as much as possible; second, that new construction interact with the previous scenery in function and activities; third, to achieve harmony with the community and an old temple nearby; and fourth, for the application of sustainable techniques to reduce the ecological footprint.

A 1,000-square-foot (3,000 sq m) tract of agricultural land was opened up for vegetables in the centre of the site to show respect to agriculture and the country lifestyle. At the same time, the farmland provides fresh ingredients for the cafeteria as well as dedicated areas for outdoor farming classrooms. The field is surrounded by a 600-foot (200 m) running track. The design solution places the track at an optimum height to reduce damage to the terrain, not only creating an activity platform from floor to rooftop but also encircling the central farmland. Under the track there is a twenty-four-hour space for transportation and activities.

FIGURE 22.3   New Jindai sustainable primary school. Courtesy of Studio TEKTAO.

The sustainable planning focuses on low-cost, efficient natural conservation, recycling and related comfort strategies tailored to Liangping's humid subtropical climate. The school features an advanced artificial wetland sewage purification system that treats and recycles 4,800 gallons of wastewater and rainwater every day. Buildings are optimally oriented for lighting and ventilation based on an analysis of the local sun path and prevailing wind direction. A range of reclaimed, regional and renewable materials are used throughout.

The entrance is designed as a semi-open community centre. At the gate, the wooden stairs address the topographical difference and also serve as an open grandstand that functions as a terraced classroom during the daytime and a community theatre in the evening, to promote interaction with the villagers. The whole school is deeply rooted in the surrounding context. The design provides the adjacent temple with a viewing platform that visually integrates it throughout the campus. The school was designed as an experiential learning environment, where students become green catalysts, naturally absorbing the lessons from their surroundings and spreading them to their parents and the community to create a bottom-up sustainable society. The users of the school also played an important role in designing and constructing the campus.

FOREVER's Public Bicycle Renting System

Shanghai FOREVER Bicycle is China's foremost bicycle manufacturer. With China's rapid economic development, the car has become more and more popular and as such, bicycle companies like FOREVER are facing huge challenges. However, when faced with the challenge, the company reshaped its business strategy to start a transformation for a better future: from selling products to selling services. First, sustainable transportation was identified, specifically the 'last kilometre' problem (from the public transportation to people's home), as a huge business opportunity. The company worked together with Minhang municipal government of Shanghai to build a pilot project of an urban bicycle rental system (see Figure 22.4).

They developed a mature product and service system: special bikes suitable for outdoor use—all-aluminium alloy frames, solid tires to prevent breakage, Radio Frequency Identification information delivery systems, advanced lock column, chip management rental cards and so on. More importantly, the company has developed a unique community-based service system. Together with the government of Shanghai, FOREVER Bicycle made a plan to popularize the urban bicycle renting system: to build 2,000 to 3,000 renting points in the city of Shanghai, 200 of which are located in the surrounding of metro stations, and the rest located in residential and commercial areas nearby. The total number of public bicycle rentals available is between 150,000 and 200,000. The citizens, the company and the government all benefit from this new business model, and more importantly, this new business is directed towards a more sustainable way of life. The roles of design in this case cover a wide range, including the design of products, services, businesses and ways of living.

FIGURE 22.4   FOREVER's public bicycle renting system. Courtesy of Lou Yongqi.

DESIS-China: The Design Schools' Network

DESIS is a network of schools of design, companies, non-profit organizations and other institutions that are interested in promoting and supporting design for social innovation and sustainability (Manzini, 2010, p. 48). DESIS-China, which was founded in March of 2009, is a sub-network of DESIS-International in China.[6] A defined, basic framework of this network is 'DESIS-International and DESIS-Local'. In fact, every DESIS-Local has its own different local context and network system. Although there is a common vision throughout the network, each sub-network works in quite a different way. DESIS-China is a typical DESIS-Local and was co-founded by six leading design schools in China in collaboration with the Politecnico di Milano in Italy (see Figure 22.5).

DESIS-China actively organizes meetings, seminars, forums and exhibitions in order to promote exchange and collaboration and is often involved in various important events. It consolidates the strategic partnership between its founding members, thus producing effective academic and social impacts both internally and externally. During the 2010 Cumulus conference in Shanghai, the DESIS network organized a forum in

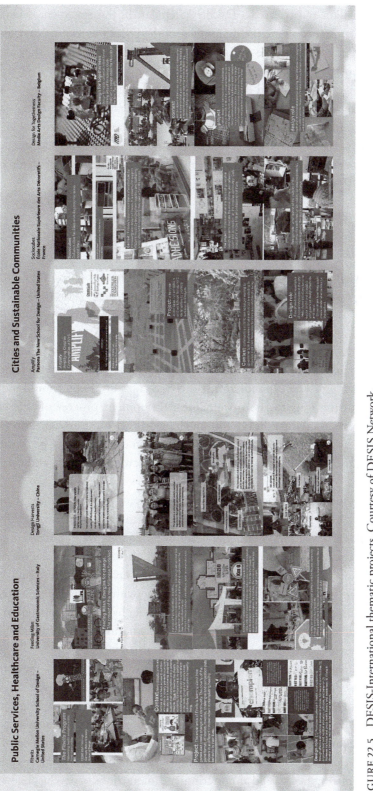

FIGURE 22.5 DESIS-International thematic projects. Courtesy of DESIS Network.

the UN pavilion and released a DESIS statement. In this statement, Manzini empha-sizes that design schools are the main pillar of the DESIS network. Not only are design schools the place to train the next generation of design experts, but they are also active agents for sustainable change.

The design schools could be distributed design agencies that promote social inno-vation (Mulgan, 2006, p. 145). DESIS-China plays an active role to create a network between groups of distributed design schools to promote and contribute to the DESIS research agenda and related projects with a common vision. Using such methods, practi-cal challenges to macro-problems are being addressed, on the path towards a sustainable society (Miaosen and Lou, 2010).

THE NEW MISSION AND CHALLENGE OF DESIGN AND DESIGN EDUCATION

With the change of paradigm towards shè jì, design has become an important tool for creating a 'sustainable', human-centred' and 'creative society' (Sotamaa, 2008, p. 11). In terms of its sphere of influence, design is increasingly providing solutions for some big issues.

On an ethical level, the Tao of shè jì today is the strategic transformation to-wards sustainability, while the qi of shè jì should be the actions and tools that en-able the changes. The expanded missions and roles of design should aid in making greater contributions to the sustainable development process of this era. Human society has been taking a heavy toll on the world with industrialization on a global scale, and, as a result, the crisis of this generation can no longer be ignored. Design and innovation should provide solutions that secure our future and carry out these solutions.

For developing countries, the status of developing is a great asset, which can pro-vide enough energy and space to start a series of sustainable paradigm shifts: reshaping values, rules of action, ways of living, ways of producing, ways of social organizing and ultimately the whole society and economy. It will become one of the major undertak-ings of design to draw inspiration from traditional ways of living and our daily lives: to select visions, proposals and tools that are in line with sustainable principles, improve and popularize them and amplify their social impact by utilizing collaborative networks and the market mechanism (Manzini, 2008). Promoting the traditional shè jì concept in China can greatly help and involve people in this process.

For the design education society, the new missions are already indicated, and the new design ethic, knowledge and education system must be considered and shaped. The university has always had two missions: to create and transfer knowledge and to play a visionary role in society. The change of the design objective and the new requirement for design have presented new challenges that call for the integration of different disciplines. The design-driven interdisciplinary programs should go beyond simply combining dif-ferent disciplines; they should aim to stimulate interactions to develop a new vision, new knowledge, and a new set of tools and skills.

For design education, the second mission is orienting the future direction of social change and development. The task of shè jì in a sustainable future covers a wide range of fields, from aiding communication to directly facilitating transition. If design schools can take advantage of playing a proactive role to connect with the socio-economic issues and work in collaborative ways with the common goal of sustainability, they will become the relevant and unique catalyst to generate sustainable social change.

NOTES

An earlier version of this chapter was the basis of a keynote speech for the Changing the Change Conference held August 2008 in Turin, Italy.

1. For example, the capitals of the empire were always recorded as being designed by the prime minister or even the emperor himself. ChangAn (Xian) City, capital city of Han Dynasty (206 B.C.–220 A.D.), was recorded as being designed by Xiao He, the first prime minister in Han Dynasty. Later it was redesigned by Yuwen Kai, the prime minister in Sui Dynasty (581–618 A.D.), and was the capital of the Sui and later Tang Dynasty (618–907 A.D.). Also, the design concept of most of the Chinese gardens always came from literati while the technical work and detail were finished by the craftsmen. The villages and rural areas were always designed by a feng shui master.

2. As early as in 1930s, a Western arts-and-crafts education system began to influence China because of Chinese students studying in the United States, France, Japan and other countries. Beaux-Arts education became the mainstream in architecture design education from the 1920s and lasted fifty years. In Shanghai, the Bauhaus system of architecture and design education in Tongji University (including St. John's University) was entrenched as early as the 1940s. The Central Academy of Art and Crafts in Beijing, the first technology-based institute of art and crafts, was established in 1956; its focus was dyeing art, ceramics and other applied decorative arts.

3. The producer-service industry plays an intermediary role, which facilitates the production of products and services. These producers mostly use human capital and knowledge capital as the main investment. Producer-service can facilitate the professionalization of production, expand capital and knowledge-intensive production and raise the productivity of labour and other factors of production (see Grubel and Walker, 1989).

4. As recorded in Song Huihong's *Forest Collection* and Mingqu Ruji's *Records of Moon,* a monk named Fayan asked the other monks, 'A golden ring was tied around a tiger. Who could take it off?' Since no one could answer, a Taiqing Master came and said, 'Those who could put it on could put it off'. Today this proverb means that someone who creates a problem can resolve it.

5. Studio TAO is the research unit of TekTao, a Shanghai-based design research and consulting agency. Studio TAO collaborates with a variety of other professionals, universities and organizations focused on common goals. Design Harvests is the flagship research project of Studio TAO. For more information, visit Designharvests.com.

6. The founding members of DESIS-China include Academy of Arts & Design, Tsinghua University (Beijing); School of Design, Hunan University (Changsha); School of Design, Jiangnan University (Wuxi); College of Design and Innovation, Tongji University (Shanghai); College of Design, Guangzhou Academy of Fine Arts (Guangzhou); and School of Design, Hong Kong Polytechnic University (Hong Kong).

REFERENCES

Brown, T. (2009), *Change by Design: How Design Thinking Transforms Organizations and Inspires Innovation,* HarperCollins: New York.

Buchanan, R. (2001), 'Design Research and the New Learning', *Design Issues,* vol. 17, no. 4: pp. 3–23.

Frampton, K. (1992), *Modern Architecture: A Critical History,* Thames and Hudson: London.

Friedman, T. L. (2008), *Hot, Flat, and Crowded,* Penguin Group, Picador/Farrar, Straus and Giroux: New York.

Grubel, H. G. and Walker, M. A. (1989), *Service Industry Growth-Causes and Effects,* Fraser Institute: Vancouver.

Gu, D. (2007), 'The History of China's Beaux-Arts Architectural Education—Transplant, Localization and the Resistance', *ARCHITECT,* vol. 126: pp. 5–15.

Heskett, J. (2002), *Design: A Very Short Introduction,* Oxford University Press: New York.

Lou, Y. (2010), 'Enabling Society: New Design Processes in China: The Case of Chongming', *The Journal of Design Strategies,* vol. 4, no. 1: pp. 23–28.

Lou, Y. (2011), *A Network of Social Collaborative Innovation Hubs,* IASDR 2011 TU Delft Conference Proceedings, Delft University of Technology, Delft, the Netherlands.

Manzini, E. (2006), 'Design, Ethics and Sustainability, Guidelines for a Transition Phase', *Cumulus Working Papers,* vol. 16, no. 6: pp. 9–15.

Manzini, E. (2008), *Design, Visions, Proposals and Tools,* Changing the Change Conference: Turin.

Manzini, E. (2010), 'DESIS Statement', *Creation and Design,* vol. 9, no. 4: p. 48.

Miaosen, G. and Lou, Y. (2010), 'DESIS-China: A Pilot Action on Networking Design Schools in China', in *Asia DesignED Conference Proceedings,* Hong Kong Polytechnic University: Hong Kong, <http://www.sd.polyu.edu.hk/designedconference2010/Proceedings/pdf/DESIS-CHINA.pdf> accessed February 25, 2013.

Mulgan, G. (2006), 'The Process of Social Innovation', *Innovations,* vol. 1, no. 2, spring: pp. 145–62.

Sotamaa, Y. (2008), 'Kyoto Design Declaration 2008', *Cumulus Working Papers,* vol. 20, no. 8: pp. 10–11.

Thackara, J. (2011), *Design for a New Restorative Economy,* Aalto University School of Art and Design Press: Helsinki.

Valtonen, A. (2007), *Redefining Industrial Design-Changes in the Design Practice in Finland,* University of Art and Design Helsinki Press: Helsinki.

von Stamm, B. (2008), *Managing Innovation, Design and Creativity,* 2nd ed., Wiley: Chichester.

Wang, S. (2008), *Criticism of Chinese Design Education,* <http://blog.sina.com.cn/s/blog_4bdabb4901007t5o.html> accessed January 7, 2008.

Yang, Y. (1997), *Design, Art History and Theory,* Garden City Cultural Press: Taipei.

23

Emotionally Sustaining Design

JONATHAN CHAPMAN

TREASURED

I kneel to reach beneath the bed, with outstretched fingers as my eyes; that region of the floor, seldom penetrated by daylight—or the vacuum cleaner nozzle—provides a refuge for treasures of immeasurable value; my dusty fingers spider to the left, and to the right, before falling upon the corner of a small box. I fumble it into my grip before slowly drawing it into the light. Holding the box in both hands, I kneel on the wooden floor for a moment, still, watching the lid as if it were about to blow off, due to power of the meaning locked within. I lift the lid and peel back tinder dry layers of tissue paper to reveal two smooth stones.

These are not diamonds, rubies or emeralds, nor are they Stone Age spearheads or ancient Roman artefacts—to me they are so much more precious than that. They are Sussex flint from a stretch of beach near Worthing; a quiet stretch of shingle beach that must contain over a trillion near-identical stones. But they are not these two stones. My son, Jasper, collected these stones when he was a toddler. He brought them up the beach to me, like a triumphant archaeologist returning from the field, still buzzing with the drug of discovery. Both the size of fat autumn plums, though one noticeably larger than the other, these stones, he said, are 'a Daddy' and 'a Jasper'—ourselves transposed in stone, so to speak.

So I kneel on the wooden floor, with dusty hands, looking into an old shoebox with two stones in it, my mind playing back movies of what has been, and inventing new ones depicting what has yet to be. And so in an experiential sense, I am not really in my bedroom at all. With my mind now awash with memory, I am back on that beach in Sussex, watching my young son scramble his way up the shingle to show me his prize. Arguably my two most treasured possessions, these stones are more powerful than any photograph, or QuickTime file. They remind me that I am a father, and that my son sees me in this way... I felt it. Furthermore, the origin of these rocks is rooted in a slower, geological time, which gives them an enduring permanence. I find this reassuring in a world where nothing stands still.

Now a symbol of our relationship, I begin to superimpose meaning onto the stones that Jasper himself had never intended—the smaller stone is lighter in colour; could this be innocence? The larger stone is bumpier; what could that mean? To me, the stones are a memory container, a totem, a symbol, a time machine, a connection, and they are these things because of the meaningful associations I have with them. To others who do not share these meaningful associations, the stones are, well, just stones... apart from you of course, as you now know the story.

RELATIVITY

As we fumble our way through life, attempting to make sense of it along the way, our need to find explanation leads our minds beyond reason, and into the supernatural. On describing memorabilia and the power of inanimate objects, Bruce Hood, author of *Super Sense* (2009, p. 37), undertook an experiment in which he first hands out a black 1930s fountain pen, which he falsely claimed belonged to Albert Einstein. Everyone in the audience is desperate to hold it and shows great reverence and awe towards the object, as though part of Einstein's soul somehow resided within it. Hood then holds aloft a tattered old cardigan and asks who would be willing to volunteer to wear it. Many offer to do so, until it is revealed that the cardigan belonged to Cromwell Street's notorious serial killer, Fred West. Promptly, almost all volunteers lower their hands.

Hood claims that this change of heart reveals something odd: audience members sitting next to one of those who keep their hand raised, and *are* willing to wear the killer's cardigan, visibly recoil in repulsion of their neighbour's openness to this (Hood, 2009, pp. 40–45). The cardigan is no longer the prime source of repulsion, but more interestingly, the person who feels fine wearing it, or even handling it, must be avoided also.

Conversely, it may also be said that we are drawn towards those who reflect our values, and this need for affiliation can been seen in both human-human, and human-object relations. Moving towards those who share your values inadvertently creates distance between you and those with whom you wish not to be associated. This swarming behaviour is a key factor in our emotional survival—as a society and as individuals. Objects play critical roles in distinguishing us from one another in this way, and there is consensus in social psychology that this form of stereotyping, or group identification, is virtually universal (Brown, 1986, p. 75). Park, who argued that a preference for the familiar and the 'like me' underlay group identification, further explains this universality. He states, we like best those who are familiar and similar to us because we can understand them best and they are generally more predictable (Park, 1950, pp. 65–70). Yet, when we use designed objects—of all scales, from saltshakers to skyscrapers—as a way to communicate our relative position and values to others, each of us must construct our own material world. This world both mirrors and projects meaning, reminding us of who we are whilst mediating the same messages to those around us. And so we no longer share the world, but rather we construct and maintain our own, then compare it with others so that we may better understand ourselves.

In terms of consumer profiling, Whiteley tells us how we design things to 'fit' particular lifestyles: 'traditionalists' or 'mainstreamers' (those who seek the predictable and the reliable, such as branded baked beans and major high street chain stores); 'achievers' (those with wealth and desire to surround themselves with objects which reflect their status); 'aspirers' (consumers who are highly status-conscious and who seek the latest fashionable product); and 'reformers' (consumers with a conscience who buy recycled paper products and avoid aerosols) (Whiteley, 1993, pp. 125–32).

Robotics professor Masahiro Mori describes the uncanny valley hypothesis, in which he states that as the appearance of a robot is made more human, a human observer's emotional response to the robot will become increasingly positive and empathic, until a point is reached beyond which the response quickly becomes that of strong revulsion. However, as the appearance continues to become less distinguishable from a human being, the emotional response becomes positive once more and approaches human-to-human empathy levels (Mori, 1970, p. 34). Explanations as to why the loss of empathy takes place are varied, ranging from pathogen avoidance (the disgust response helps us to avoid potential sources of disease), the violation of human norms (the appearance of the near-human robot challenges a fixed cognitive model of human characteristics) or religious constructions of human identity (near human identity is seen as a threat to some, causing existential anxiety).

Mori's uncanny valley has its critics, and as David Hanson has shown, the uncanny valley could be avoided by adding neotenous, cartoonish features to the entities that had formerly fallen into the valley (Hanson et al., 2005, p. 1729). This design-level intervention is important, as it shows that understanding the conditions that lead people to be either drawn to or repelled from things empowers design thinking.

BELIEF

According to Jasper Morrison, our perception of objects can be broken down as follows: the first encounter may well be based more on an evaluation of the object's cost, the quality of the object relating to the cost, the perceived usefulness of the object to us and the object's desirability. But later on, when it comes to living with an object, we forget all about the cost, and we have in mind the object's usefulness in relation to certain tasks, how much we enjoy using it and how much we appreciate it as a possession. It becomes a part of our lives that we may not think about much, but that nevertheless exists, as witnessed when we move from a house (for example) and may be forced to confront the relationship we have with the object in deciding whether to keep it or not (Fukasawa and Morrison, 2007, pp. 53–54).

In *Super Normal,* we are told how design, which used to be almost unknown as a profession, has become a major source of pollution. Encouraged by glossy lifestyle magazines and marketing departments, it has become a competition to make things as noticeable as possible by means of colour, shape and surprise. Its historic and idealistic purpose, to serve industry and the happy consuming masses at the same time, of conceiving things easier to make and better to live with, seems to have been sidetracked (Fukasawa and Morrison, 2007, pp. 8–10). In the crowded high street, where shop windows are stacked with near-identical mobile phones, sports shoes and table lamps—each a 'just noticeably different' (Norman, 2011, p. 187) version of the other—the idea of a spirit or energy occupying the fabric of an inanimate object such as a pen or a cardigan is clearly not rational. Yet, most of us unconsciously behave in this way, as Hood demonstrated with Fred West's cardigan. For example, if television chef Jamie Oliver were to lend you his favourite knife, would it make you a better—or more *pukka*—cook? Or, if someone were to offer to replace your treasured keepsake with an exact replica, would you accept? Probably not. But why would we reject the offer of a free upgrade to a brand-new product?

In design, we are familiar with seeing the world like this. We understand that objects are so much more than the sum of their parts; they are signs, functions, meanings and styles. Seldom are they discussed purely as inert material entities devoid of character, as this is not their intention—both from the consumers' and the designers' points of view. Furthermore, the superstitious or supernatural beliefs that we map onto objects are powerful and can make the difference between a product being cherished and adored, or resented and discarded in a handful of days. Cynically, waste can be seen as an essential means for us to make way for the new. Not to say that the things we throw out are always broken or dysfunctional, but rather, many are orphaned objects that have been cast aside before their time, to make way for newer, younger models.

In *The Meaning of Things,* the authors describe how, to preserve a breakable object from its destiny, one must pay at least some attention to it, care for it, buffet it from the long arm of chance. Thus, a china cup preserved over a generation is a victory of human purpose over chaos, an accomplishment to be quietly cherished, something to be kind of proud of (Czsiczentmihalyi and Rouchberg-Halton, 1981, p. 83). Paradoxically, this fragility and weakness highlights the strength of these objects in maintaining a visceral connection with their owners and enabling a healthy interaction between a person and their inanimate environment—durability and robustness are not what they might, at first, appear.

According to the director of London's Design Museum, Deyan Sudjic, we live in a world drowning in objects (2008, pp. 5–9); households with a TV set in each room; kitchen cupboards stuffed with waffle makers, bread ovens, blenders and cappuccino whisks; and drawers swollen with a plethora of pocket-sized devices powered by batteries, which themselves are products that take several thousand times more energy to make than they will ever produce. One's material empire—with its aquariums, TV sets, plants, phones, lamps, clocks, scarves, lawnmowers, picture frames, doorknobs, computers, shoes, cameras, bicycles, screwdrivers, jackets, carpets, sinks, cars or anything else for that matter—is made up of stuff, and this stuff defines you, whether you like it or not.

It is important to note that an increase in material possessions is not commensurate with a growth in wellbeing, or happiness—this 'more' is not really giving us 'more'. We live in a time when our relationship with our possessions is undergoing a radical transformation, Sudjic writes. He observes that little in our homes now has to do with basic needs, as might have been described by Maslow. Instead, this excess results from the 'shallow but sharp emotional tug that the manufacture of want exerts on us' (Sudjic, 2008, p. 86).

Each of us shares, to varying degrees, the need for a material world: a world of tangible things to enhance the experiential quality of daily life, such as a faster car, a larger TV or a softer sofa. Beyond their utilitarian affordances, these props are employed to communicate messages to others—whether the part of town we choose to live in, the building we inhabit or the design of the glowing television set within, or that of the armchair and slippers pointing at it. However, beyond basic functionality, each material possession has a far deeper and more personal role to play. Individually, each possession plays its own part; yet together, our material possessions are an aggregate package of information that locates each of us in a custom-built reality.

For the majority of consumers, locating oneself through consumption is reassuring, as it grounds us within social, cultural, economic and political contexts that can be modified and adjusted simply by updating (replacing) certain objects, as one changes, adapts and evolves as an individual. In this scenario, objects that no longer provide accurate representations of who we are must be outcast and replaced with ones that do. Though this may be described as nothing more than a Darwinian process of progress-driven obsolescence, the ecological implications of this practice are grave, leading to the culture of serial discarding and consuming so characteristic of unsustainability in the developed world.

It is clear that the limited ability of material goods to sustain an emotional resonance with their user might present one of the greatest challenges in moving towards sustainable consumption. We must look for more emotionally sustainable solutions if we are to slow the throughput of energy and materials. Recycling, for example, is an important part of the sustainability drive, yet it does not slow throughput of materials and consumes significant quantities of energy via the process of collection, sorting, reprocessing and distribution. Conventionally, industrial activity is based on a crude linear production-consumption flow with inbuilt environmental deterioration at both ends; sustainable design activity over the past forty-five years has made these wasteful and inefficient ends of the scale marginally less wasteful and inefficient. Whether we are talking about life cycle assessment, design for disassembly or grass-roots activism, there is no single big fix. As Fletcher has stated, we do not need mass answers but a mass of answers (2007, pp. 130–5).

LAYERS

Meaning is unstable and is constantly updating itself. For example, in a pet shop, a rat will have a particular meaning associated with it. There will be some variance in this associated meaning due to differences in the way each of us feels about rats as pets, but overall, the meaning is fairly stable. Take that rat out of the pet shop, however, and place it in a restaurant kitchen, and its meaning changes dramatically. The same object—the rat—has transformed instantly before our eyes, simply by changing its context; it has moved from an appropriate to an inappropriate scenario, and as a result we feel repulsion.

This switch in scenarios is common in the designed world. One need only look at electronic devices such as smart phones, where technological up-to-date-ness is the primary value; so long as a given item is the latest, its meaning remains intact. Indeed, placing technological contemporaneousness as the sole value-indicator of a product practically guarantees disappointment, ensuring loss of meaning the moment a newer model hits the shelves (Chapman, 2005, p. 16). In a marketplace of relentless product obsolescence, the notion of consumer satisfaction will continue to remain a tantalizing utopia until product values diversify to incorporate factors beyond technical modernity.

Conventionally, product failure is characterized by blown circuits, stress fractures and a host of other technical and physical glitches; in attending solely to physical ageing, designers overlook numerous invaluable metaphysical renderings of durability. As a creative industry, it is vital that we break away from the physical and begin to understand more about the sustainability of empathy, meaning, desire and other metaphysical factors that influence the duration of product life.

As we drill down into the experiential nature of an object, we reveal layers of meaning, so to speak, some of which are glaringly obvious and readily identifiable, while others lurk much more deeply and are harder to spot. Yet, such inanimate manufactured objects cannot contain meaning, but rather, they can activate meaning within the perceiver; meaning is a construct, and as such there can be no meaning other than that which we create. Like a radio constantly playing in the background, humans are always unconsciously forming judgements about the world around them. These judgements may relate to the quality of an object, the temperament of a stray dog or the wealth of a total stranger. We are often unable to say exactly what it is about them that we are noticing, but the opinions flow like water and shape the nature of our behaviour in powerful ways. Indeed, though these mental processes may seem subtle, even negligible at times, their consequences are profound in shaping our experience of the everyday. As writer and psychologist Sherry Turkle describes, we think with the objects we love; we love the objects we think with (2007, pp. 3–8).

Experience

In *Creed or Chaos*, Dorothy L. Sayers warns that a society in which consumption has to be artificially stimulated in order to keep production going is a society founded on trash and waste, and such a society is a house built upon sand (1999, p. 47). Indeed, marketers play an important role in the construction and manipulation of these experiential levers, as perceived by the end user. However, within the context of product design, both the nature and scope of these designable conditions are not adequately understood. It is also questionable as to whether attachments are actually beneficial in terms of product life extension. For example, Marchand explores detachment from possessions as a way to extend the longevity of objects; in interviews, test subjects revealed that by practicing detachment from objects, they are more predisposed to accept an object's physical age-ing (2003, p. 128).

In *Sein und Zeit* (1927/1986), Heidegger defined two ways in which we experience objects: ready-to-hand and present-to-hand (Verbeek and Kockelkoren, 1998/2010, p. 92). When things are working properly, and we are absorbed in the use of them, they are ready-to-hand, and we experience the world through the object. He gives the much-cited example of the hammer to demonstrate this, telling us how when hammering, our attention is not on the hammer itself but on the nail we are trying to knock into the wall. In this way, we are caught up in the activity, enabled by the hammer. However, should the head of the hammer become loose and wobbly, our attention is drawn away from the nail and the activity of hammering, towards the hammer itself. The hammer, according to Heidegger, is now present-to-hand and must be repaired in order for it to be ready-to-hand once more.

One could describe electricity in a similar way, in that it only becomes noticeable when something goes wrong with it, like a power outage. Importantly, there are connec-tions here between what we expect things to do and what things actually do. Often, we see natural facets of ageing, such as the loosening of the hammer's head, as some kind of disappointing product failure or weakness on the part of the object—disappointment being categorized by a perceivable difference between expectation and reality.

In the case of the hammer with the wobbly head, repair is a fairly straightforward process and may in fact be why so many of us are happy to keep the hammer we have and fix it should it fail, making the return journey from present-to-hand (broken, and visible) to ready-to-hand (working, and transparent). In the case of a more complex product such as a hairdryer, for example, the return journey may be something more complex, and in almost all cases this perceived complexity leads to the discarding of the item.

It is clear that the design for durability paradigm has important implications beyond its conventional interpretation, in which product longevity is considered solely in terms of an object's physical endurance, whether cherished or discarded. Immaterial phenom-ena such as love, desire, fascination, curiosity and trust, for example, can also break and wear out, causing immeasurable quantities of fully functioning objects to be discarded before their time. Understanding the deeper nature of this form of psychological (as op-posed to functional) obsolescence is critical in the search for solutions to the throwaway society.

OBSOLESCENCE

Commercial interest in the lifespans of manufactured objects can be traced back to London's introduction of the term planned obsolescence (1932, p. 1), made popular by Packard in his book *The Waste Makers* (1963, pp. 45–57). Planned obsolescence means designing and producing products in order for them to be considered as 'used up' within a specific time period. More recently referred to as 'designed for the dump' or 'death dating', obsolescence can occur as a result of failed functionality (a refrigerator with a condensing unit that lasts for twenty months) or through failed desirability (those maroon corduroy trousers are no longer on trend). Though informed by the work of London and of Calkins (1932), Packard's dualistic theories of functional obsolescence and psychological obsolescence assert that the deliberate shortening of product lifespans is unethical, both in its profit-focused manipulating of consumer spending and its devastating ecological impact through the nurturing of wasteful purchasing behaviours. He stated that if you are a producer and most families already own your product, you are left with three possibilities for making future sales: you sell replacements; you sell more than one item to each family; or you dream up a new and improved product—or one that at least seems new and improved—that will enchant families that already own an old model of your product. How much more can a toaster or sofa or carpet or sewing machine be improved, really? (Packard, 1963, p. 127). In *Industrial Strength Design,* we hear how Stevens (an opponent of Packard's) defined planned obsolescence simply as instilling in the buyer the desire to own something a little newer, a little better, a little sooner than is necessary (in Adamson, 2003, pp. 129–34)—and Stevens saw nothing wrong with that. Slade explains in his work *Made to Break: Technology and Obsolescence in America* how disposability was in fact a necessary condition for America's rejection of tradition and our acceptance of change and impermanence, yet by choosing to support ever-shorter product lives, Slade argues that we may well be shortening the future of our way of life as well, with perilous implications for the very near future (2007, p. 22). The lesser-known text by Calkins (1932) entitled 'What Consumer Engineering Really Is' may provide a text of equal significance in this context. In consumer engineering, Calkins sees design as a business tool that fashions products to address more closely the changing tastes or needs of the consumer. A broader definition consists of any action that stimulates the consumption of goods; shaping the goods does not mean a simple colour change or more attractive package design. Instead, the process involves changing ordinary goods to modern, distinctive ones; consumer engineering benefits advertisers by supplying them with new product information to reveal in their ads. In turn, the advertisers will be held accountable to these new product claims, thus benefiting the whole of society. In *Emotionally Durable Design* (2005, p. 20), I described how landfills are packed with stratum upon stratum of durable goods that slowly compact and surrender working order beneath a substantial volume of similar scrap. There would, therefore, seem little point in designing physical durability into consumer goods, if consumers lack the desire to keep them. Indeed, durability must no longer be distinguished merely by a product's physical robustness—whether cherished or discarded. One could argue that it is quite easy to design and manufacture an MP3 player that will work without failure for eight years, but it is another thing entirely to design one that people would want to keep for that length of time. Perhaps due to the normalcy of innovation, the made world has adopted an expendable and sacrificial persona. In the majority of cases, the durability of products is characterized simply by specifying resilient materials, fixable technologies and the application of product optimization methodologies that reduce the likelihood of blown circuits, stress fractures and other physical failures. Is this durable product design or simply the designing of durable waste?

DUMPED

The continual churning out of newer and shinier products is an ongoing, evolving discourse about how the world ought to be. At its best, this discourse flexes and warps in response to cultural, social, economic and ecological agendas, making it a compelling critique of what we collectively value and strive for. At its worst, however, we see that this process of continual evolution and adaption leaves behind it a wake of ecological devastation, the enormity of which has yet to be fully understood. Indeed, the complex and thorny nature of our engagement with the designed world directly shapes the ecological impact of our consumption; as designers, as creators of things, we ignore this at our peril.

Today, an edgy sense of instability surrounds the made world, nurtured by continual change to render its offspring fleeting, transient and replaceable orphans of circumstance. Though the need for longer-lasting products is widely recognized, practical working methods, design frameworks and tools that facilitate the development and integration of such emotionally durable characteristics within products are scarce. In this oversaturated world of people and things, durable attachments with objects are seldom witnessed. Most products deliver a predictable monologue of information, which quickly transforms wonder into drudgery; serial disappointments are delivered through nothing more than a product's failure to maintain currency with the evolving values and needs of its user. The volume of waste produced by this cyclic pattern of short-term desire and disappointment is a major problem, not just in terms of space and where to put it but, perhaps more notably, for its toxic corruption of the biosphere. In *Natural Capitalism* (Hawken et al., 1999), we are reminded that the human race was fortunate enough to inherit a 3.8 billion-year-old reserve of natural capital, but at present rates of consumption it is predicted as unlikely that there will be much of it left by the end of this century. Since the mid-eighteenth century, more of nature has been destroyed than in all prior history; in the past fifty years alone, the human race has stripped the world of a quarter of its topsoil and a third of its forest cover. In total, one-third of all the planet's resources have been consumed within the past four decades (Hawken et al., 1999, pp. 3–4). The urgency of this situation is described in 'The Stern Review on the Economics of Climate Change' (Stern, 2006), which states that if no action is taken to reduce emissions, the concentration of greenhouse gases in the atmosphere could reach double its pre-industrial level as early as 2035, virtually committing us to a global average temperature rise of over 2 degrees Celsius. In the longer term, there would be more than a 50 per cent chance that the temperature rise would exceed 5 degrees Celsius. This rise would be very dangerous indeed; it is equivalent to the change in average temperatures from the last ice age to today. Such a radical change in the physical geography of the world must lead to major changes in the human geography—where people live and how they live their lives (Stern, 2006, p. 56).

DESIGN

An empirical study, conducted by the author, examined the relationship behaviours of 2,154 respondents with electronic objects, during the use phase. Through survey research and subsequent focus groups, results from this study demonstrated that within the sample frame, value was perceived due to the presence of one of the following six experiential themes:

- Narrative: users share a unique personal history with the product; this often relates to when, how and from whom the object was acquired.
- Detachment: feel little or no emotional connection to the product; have low expectations and thus perceive it in a favourable way due to a lack of emotional demand or expectation (this also suggests that attachment may actually be counterproductive, as it elevates the level of expectation within the user to a point that is often unattainable).
- Surface: the product is physically ageing well and developing a tangible character through time, use and sometimes misuse.
- Attachment: feel a strong emotional connection to the product due to the service it provides, the information it contains and the meaning it conveys.
- Fiction: are delighted or even enchanted by the product as it is not yet fully understood or known by the user; these are often recently purchased products that are still being explored and discovered by the user.
- Consciousness: the product is perceived as autonomous and in possession of its own free will; it is quirky, often temperamental, and interaction is an acquired skill that can be fully acquired only with practice.

This six-point experiential framework provides distinct conceptual pathways through which to initiate engagement with issues of emotional durability through design, presenting a more expansive, holistic understanding of design for durability—both in terms of the paradigm, and that of the language used to articulate it. The aim of this theoretical architecture is to enable points of entry to the complex and knotty problem of emotionally durable design. It facilitates more structured, focused modes of exploration that could lead to the emergence of a new genre of sustainable design, one that reduces consumption and waste by increasing the durability of relationships established between users and products.

Sustainable design is maturing. In *The Designer's Atlas of Sustainability*, Thorpe refers to this coming of age as the second stage in the debate (2007, pp. 6–7), in which the role of design in economic and social aspects of sustainability is more fully explored, in addition to the already established focus on energy and materials. In examining the actual causes—rather than the symptoms—of our environmental crisis, we begin to understand the deep motivations that fuel the human condition itself. Indeed, the sustainability crisis is a crisis of behaviour and not one simply of technology and production alone. In order to move towards sustainability, we must first recalibrate the parameters of good design in this unsustainable age. Furthermore, to engage on a behavioural level, we must reconsider our creative strategies, tools and languages, exploring new ways of thinking and of designing objects capable of supporting deeper and more meaningful relationships with their users over time. This will call for a dramatic reappraisal of the way in which we design the products, buildings and spaces that constitute the made world.

REFERENCES

Adamson, G. (2003), *Industrial Strength Design: How Brooks Stevens Shaped Your World*, MIT Press: Cambridge, MA.

Brown, R. (1986), *Social Psychology*, 2nd ed., Free Press: New York.

Calkins, E. E. (1932), 'What Consumer Engineering Really Is', in Sheldon, R. and Arens, A. (eds), *Consumer Engineering: A New Technique for Prosperity*, Harper & Brothers: New York. pp. 1–14.

Chapman, J. (2005), *Emotionally Durable Design: Objects, Experiences and Empathy*, Earthscan: London.

Csikszentmihalyi, M. and Rochberg-Halton, E. (1981), *The Meaning of Things: Domestic Symbols and the Self*, Cambridge University Press: Cambridge.

Fletcher, K. (2007), 'Clothes That Count', in Chapman, J. and Gant, N. (eds), *Designers, Visionaries and Other Stories: A Collection of Sustainable Design Essays*, Earthscan: London. pp. 118–132.

Fukasawa, N. and Morrison, J. (2007), *Super Normal: Sensations of the Ordinary*, Lars Muller Publishers: London.

Hanson, D., Olney, A., Pereira I. A. and Zielke, M. (2005), 'Upending the Uncanny Valley', *Proceedings of the National Conference on Artificial Intelligence*, vol. 20: pp. 1728–9.

Hawken, P., Lovins, A. and Hunter Lovins, L. (1999), *Natural Capitalism: Creating the Next Industrial Revolution*, Little, Brown and Co.: Snowmass, CO.

Heidegger, M. (1927/1986), *Sein und Zeit*, Tübingen: Niemeyer.

Hood, B. (2009), *Super Sense: From Superstition to Religion—the Brain Science of Belief*, Constable: London.

London, B. (1932), *Ending the Depression through Planned Obsolescence*. Pamphlet, New York.

Marchand, A. (2003), 'Sustainable Users and the World of Objects Design and Consumerism', in van Hinte, E. (ed.), *Eternally Yours: Time in Design*, 010 Publishers: Rotterdam. pp. 102–31.

Mori, M. (1970), 'The Uncanny Valley', *Energy*, vol. 7, no. 4: pp. 33–35.

Norman, D. A. (2011), *Living with Complexity*, MIT Press: Cambridge, MA.

Packard, V. (1963), *The Waste Makers*, Penguin: Middlesex.

Park, R. E. (1950), *Race and Culture*, Free Press: Glencoe, IL.

Sayers, D. L. (1999), *Creed or Chaos: Why Christians Must Choose Either Dogma or Disaster (Or, Why It Really Does Matter What You Believe)*, Sophia Institute Press: Manchester, NH.

Slade, G. (2007), *Made to Break: Technology and Obsolescence in America*, Harvard University Press: Cambridge, MA.

Stern, N. (2006), 'The Stern Review on the Economics of Climate Change', HM Treasury: London, <http://webarchive.nationalarchives.gov.uk/+/http://www.hm-treasury.gov.uk/

    independent_reviews/stern_review_economics_climate_change/stern_review_report.cfm>
    accessed February 25, 2013.
Sudjic, D. (2008), *The Language of Things,* Allen Lane: London.
Thorpe, A. (2007), *The Designer's Atlas of Sustainability,* Island Press: Washington, DC.
Turkle, S. (ed.) (2007), *Evocative Objects: Things We Think With,* MIT Press: Cambridge, MA.
Verbeek, P. and Kockelkoren, P. (1998/2010) 'The Things That Matter', in Buchanan, R., Door-
    dan, D. and Margolyn, V. (eds), *The Designed World,* Berg: London. pp. 83–94.
Whiteley, N. (1993), *Design for Society,* Reaktion Books: London.

24

I Am a User, Not a Consumer

GIJS BAKKER AND LOUISE SCHOUWENBERG

INTRODUCTION

The word 'sustainability' has become subject to inflation long before its full potential has been realized. At the turn of the twenty-first century, there were countless design symposiums and round-table conferences focusing on the theme. Publications on sustainability followed each other in rapid succession and many design schools were setting up specialist departments focusing explicitly on ecological, economic and social sustainability. If we scan the subjects of the public debates and new publications today, we run into titles such as humanitarian design, democratic design and redesign, but rarely sustainable design. Concepts, too, are subject to trends; predictably, the new names for the same old message will lose their popularity as well. And yet, for now, the message still seems urgent: the spirit of the times demands designers who are ready to take responsibility for the needs of the world. The prosperity and the accompanying consumerism in the West have drawn heavily on the environment and have been maintaining inhumane working conditions in many African and Asian countries. While architects in Europe may have taken the lead in promoting sustainable materials and production techniques, design's close association with consumerism means that designers also have a role to play. It even seems logical to think that designers will take it upon themselves to persuade people of the need for sustainable consumerism. This places a heavy burden on designers; moreover, it is a burden that contains a great number of contradictions. Does this perhaps explain why sustainable products are usually so ugly?

Perhaps there is something wrong with the design mission. When morality becomes the leading factor in the design process, creativity is oppressed even before the first sketch is committed to paper. Perhaps we should do away completely with the word 'sustainability'.

With this chapter, we do not profess to present the final answer to the call for sustainability. Contrary to what many champions of sustainability generally maintain, we believe there is no such thing as a well-rounded story or an all-embracing solution. In the following discussion, we will be ruminating on a set of themes that we believe tie in closely with the sustainability debate. We will be trying to understand why sustainability has failed to become a powerful inspiration for the avant-garde in design; we will be exploring the things we regard as the essence of the design profession; and we will be ruminating on the connection between the different factors featured in the design process. Lastly, but certainly not least, we will be involving beauty in the debate.

I AM A USER

Sustainability is not a subject for design. Naturally, knowledge of (sustainable and non-sustainable) materials and manufacturing techniques should be part of every designer's stock-in-trade. The designer's essential toolkit also includes other elements, such as idealism, intuition, a sense of aesthetics and an awareness of the ever-changing social, cultural, economic and political contexts in which products are born and will function (and all the intervening steps). Each of these elements is relevant in varying degrees according to the assignment, and yet they are inextricably linked. Anyone who isolates sustainability from the entire package and makes it the main objective for a design is obstructing, beforehand, the free space the mind demands to think.

When asked about his views on innovation and creativity in architecture, Canadian American architect Frank Gehry made a few remarkable statements. In his view, architects of mediocre talent use subjects such as sustainability to help them make their point, relegating to the background the thing he believes should be the primary focus—that is, architecture (*Daily Motion*, 2011).

What is sustainable design? To begin with, ideally speaking it would presuppose that all the stakeholders involved are on the same wavelength. Reality has shown, however, that each party struggles with its own agenda or dilemma.

Most governments can be blamed for a discrepancy between their possible intentions, their promises and ultimately their actions. The rules they set up for sustainability to which businesses and consumers have to commit are rarely instigated by higher ideals but all the more often by international pressure. Think, for instance, of the carbon dioxide debate, which has so far been ineffective. Local economic interests and the protectionism of individual states are dominating the agenda.

The rift between the intentions as they are communicated and the actions taken can also be counted against the majority of manufacturers. They will not be easily inclined to seek costly alternatives at their own initiative, unless such alternatives directly improve the company's position on the market. In this respect, Apple provides a telling example. Its products are seen as pioneering in every possible respect, but it is falling behind in its efforts concerning energy-efficient production and non-toxic materials. For instance, the multinational continues to score low marks in the 'Guide to Greener Electronics' created annually by Greenpeace (Carus, 2011). In 2007, Steve Jobs, the former CEO of Apple, tried to give Apple's image a boost with the following message:

> Apple has been criticized by some environmental organizations for not being a leader in removing toxic chemicals from its new products, and for not aggressively or properly recycling its old products. Upon investigating Apple's current practices and progress towards these goals, I was surprised to learn that in many cases Apple is ahead of, or will soon be ahead of, most of its competitors in these areas. Whatever other improvements we need to make, it is certainly clear that we have failed to communicate the things that we are doing well.
>
> It is generally not Apple's policy to trumpet our plans for the future; we tend to talk about the things we have just accomplished. Unfortunately this policy has left our customers, shareholders, employees and the industry in the dark about Apple's desires and plans to become greener. Our stakeholders deserve and expect more from us, and they're right to do so. They want us to be a leader in this area, just as we are in the other areas of our business. So today we're changing our policy. (in Carus, 2011)

They are already doing it, says Jobs. The only thing lacking is a good communication of the facts and the company's plans (in many cases, Apple is ahead of, or will soon be ahead of, most of its competitors in these areas). With this apology, the company, which is widely known for its excellent communications strategies, demonstrates a slow willingness to meet with international regulations.

The thing that governments and manufacturers are sensitive to is consumer pressure; after all, consumers are in charge of demand. The fact that Apple is ahead of the game where attractive, ingenious interfaces are concerned, but not in the field of sustainability, possibly says something about Apple's target group. Most Apple addicts apparently value beauty and smartness over ethical entrepreneurship.

Users are able to exert pressure on businesses and governments, and they do so in a wide range of areas. And yet consumers are still not choosing sustainable products by the masses. This is not due to insufficient knowledge. After all, we are drowned in information on the disastrous effects of overconsumption. This laxness on the part of users may be explained by the implicit appeal to feelings of guilt and a sense of duty that are inherent in the term 'sustainability'. The question arises, for instance, if the environmentalists' moral justification does not cause vexation in the masses, thus acting counterproductively to the things they aim to achieve. Guilt is at odds with the pleasure people can derive from consuming.[1]

How about the designers? A substantial group of designers are emerging as advocates of sustainable materials and production methods, but as with the manufacturers, communication often wins over reality: whenever they see a profitable effect of a green image, they will communicate it in superlatives. Often, sustainability consists of a set of empty gestures 'for the galleries', such as the use of green colours and a thin layer of low-tech, apparently environmentally friendly materials, masking the nastier raw materials.[2] If it is all true, and the ecological footprint of every element in the product's life cycle (material, production, transport, recycling, waste disposal) really is tiny, the product will typically not deserve the beauty prize, nor offer any new perspectives on the profession. The same thing applies even more strongly to products aimed at increasing consumer awareness; the moral message of these products is usually so conspicuous that it smothers any other thought. Apparently, it is not just consumerism and guilt that are incompatible. The creativity of the designer will also suffer from a too conspicuous appeal to moral responsibility.

Sustainability answers the question of how we should address the many ecological and humanitarian crises threatening the world. Sustainability is better than non-sustainability; who would argue against this? But if the answer—the solution—is available beforehand, what are we asking from the designers? Where is their challenge?

In spite of all the commercial slogans to the contrary, it is quite obvious that consumerism can never fulfil the eternal quest for satisfaction of the many human needs. And yet, the famed Cradle-to-Cradle concept,[3] like many other all-encompassing solutions to the sustainability question, has not radically changed the endless increase in objects. The relationship between users and their objects, the single most essential subject for any self-respecting designer, is not explicitly addressed as a subject. This means we are oblivious to the way this relationship has slowly become perverted (McDonough and Braungart, 2002).

The most obvious solution, naturally, is a plea to decrease consumption, primarily appealing to the consumer's sense of responsibility. However, such a plea would ignore economic reality and fall on deaf ears except in a small circle. Designers and businesses have a different agenda. They are not usually out to hamper economic growth and will thus promote better materials and better production methods rather than a decrease in consumption. We suspect there is a third variety: designers and businesses whose focus lies not directly on any sub-aspect such as sustainability but reflects a more fundamental level on the changing relationships between people and their everyday environment, caused by changing developments in society and technology, including globalization and digitalization, but also opposing developments such as a renewed interest in local sourcing and producing and old crafts. This group of designers is concerned with psychological sustainability, in which the focus has shifted from the product to the relationship between people and products, an approach rooted in the idea that enduring relationships will only develop when designers and producers offer a better standard in every sense.[4] They are thus apparently straying from the ideological path of the modernists, who applauded relatively cheap serial manufacturing because it made good design available to the masses. By now we have seen that cheap industrialized manufacturing has gradually led to an overproduction of disposable products without any intrinsic value worth mentioning (and often little functional or aesthetic value)—produced, as it were, for the landfill. Cheap manufacturing has mainly meant more consumption. Many designs that we may call psychologically sustainable are inevitably costly and will therefore not be part of the cycle of mass consumption and mass disposal.

The most essential characteristic of design is functionality—that is, its absolute nature. Usually functionality is interpreted as solving a problem. But this view is too restricted. Crudely speaking, the design world is split into two groups. On one end of the spectrum are those designers who use a set of scientifically quantifiable criteria to find a solution for a precisely formulated problem. They will usually be graduates from a university of technology and as a rule operate anonymously; their products are only marginally distinguishable and are directly in line with market and industry demands. On the other end of the spectrum are those designers, usually graduates of one of the design academies (part of the framework of art education), who act primarily out of a personal fascination with the profession, from a need to relate to the primary question of what is design, from a philosophical, creative, idealist and pragmatic viewpoint. They are author designers, not to be confused with star designers, whose single aim is to spread their reputation. Inherent in their starting point, author designers do not use quantifiable criteria, or only occasionally, but they follow their intuition, senses, imagination and taste, and the way all these ingredients of their talent relate to knowledge and research.

Designers who take a problem-solving approach will always operate within the existing framework of economic laws, social patterns and familiar cultural expressions. They will accept this framework and try to find solutions for sub-aspects in the present, including sustainable materials and manufacturing solutions. Of course, this is an important mission and a necessary one. But we cannot expect these designers to come up with many new views on people's daily interaction with things. Only when a designer is ready to step outside the existing framework can he or she take users along in his or her experimental thoughts on a different, future reality. Stir their imagination. Only the front runners will push back the boundaries of their own profession; only the front runners will not merely instigate technological advances and allow marketing people to do the talking but will change the way in which we experience everyday reality.

The avant-garde in any domain, whether it is visual art, music, architecture, design or science, is primarily interested in questioning their own profession, exploring its boundaries, maximizing its possibilities. The thing that drives the front runners can perhaps be best described as an artistic, or autonomous, quest. Those who choose to take an artistic approach will for instance wonder what the existentialist necessity of a design may be. What is its (added) value? This implies that every avant-garde designer must possess something of the autonomous artist. The artistic quest was what motivated the modernists, the postmodernists and the conceptual designers; it is what motivates the current generation of designers operating in the avant-garde.

> She [Hannah Arendt] has written that the extraordinary thing about mankind is located in people's ability to bring about something new. To create something that was not there before. Art is the ultimate expression of this human quality. In art, creation is not in the service of some function…but in the service of creation itself. (Hilhorst, 2005)

Creating for creativity's sake is a necessity in art. Is creating for creativity's sake possible, or even a necessity, in design as well? Nobody is waiting for the next work of art to appear; the fact that it appears anyway is one of the most powerful characteristics of visual art. Without anyone asking him, without any direct use or gain, the artist feels the need to create his or her view on reality and to communicate it to others. The same applies to the avant-garde designer. Nobody is waiting for the next chair to appear or the next table. The fact that these objects appear regardless and that they testify to the current times is perhaps one of the most important characteristics of avant-garde design. It creates an obligation—not just a moral obligation but an artistic obligation as well. The kinship between art and design lies not so much in the expressions but in the personae of designers, and the extent to which they explore the possibilities of their profession, starting from their own questions. The same attitude can be detected in even the most rigid of sciences, where important turning points and new views are doubtlessly born from a creative, or artistic, attitude.

An autonomous approach to design starts from the existing systems, the essences of the profession, after which the boundaries are pushed back and stretched. Designers, artists, architects or musicians will pass through these systems, make them their own, exhaust them, try to find new possibilities and then create their own sets of laws.

Composer Louis Andriessen: 'I have been trying my whole life to do things I have never done before.'
Interviewer: 'What happens when a writer or a composer, in an attempt at reinventing himself, tries to mess up all his best efforts?'
LA: 'He will probably come out the other end as himself regardless' (Putten, 2011).

One of the main preconditions for a view on design that will do justice to its essential question—what is the relationship between people and their objects?—is 'seeing' people as users. Consumers have a perverted, alienated relationship with objects because they allow aspects to enter their lives that are not essential to their standard of living; they will, for instance, try to build an image through things, harbour an illusory belief in greater happiness or in chasing away boredom by going shopping. When designers approach their target group as consumers, they are in fact reducing people's humanity and degrading them to become unresisting, malleable pawns. When people are approached as users, their humanity remains intact, and the designer can get a grip on the complex relationships people have with their day-to-day context.

The impact of design is greater than people tend to think. Since design deals with the things that are closest to us, with our immediate environment where we experience our humanity, visionary projects are also capable of offering us a new perspective on our humanity.

In the late 1980s and early 1990s, a common approach to the design profession started to emerge among Dutch designers, who began to make a name for themselves as conceptual designers from 1993 onwards, under the common denominator of Droog Design. Contrary to many other movements in design, this was not a stylistic movement; the semi-functional objects made by the Dutch designers displayed an amalgam of stylistic features, which either could or could not be ascribed to the individual designers. The primary focus was the idea, the manifesto on the profession or the story that the participants wanted to express. Everything else—the finishing, the choice of materials, even the functionality—was made subservient to the concept that had to be communicated in a form as pure as possible. Anyone looking at these designs now, nearly twenty years on, will mainly see a portrait of an era. While in the 1980s the international design world was still unquestioningly riding the wave of the economic boom of the preceding years, the first generation of conceptualists was using irony and critical self-reflection to warn about the downside of consumerism. Like a series of materialized mental experiments, the designs created by Tejo Remy, Rody Graumans, Jurgen Bey and many others highlighted the importance of recycling materials, forms and products.

The impact of the Dutch designers' suggestions extended beyond pragmatic solutions for overconsumption. By explicitly naming and materializing the meanings inherent in a product, conceptual design came to mean nothing short of a change in awareness that even changed interpretations of earlier periods in design: contrary to the prevailing notion that implements provided functional answers to questions, the realization dawned that each design contains more stories and meanings, either explicitly or implicitly, than the basic function for which it is apparently designed. Every design says something about the world into which it is born and the world in which it will function. Every design implies a specific use and therefore says something about the relationship between the user and the object; it says something about the state of affairs in technology and about cultural and local characteristics.

Initially, the conceptual objects were mainly 'interpretable' or 'readable' to other designers, who responded with great enthusiasm. Because they were so clear, the messages were soon becoming readable to a wider audience. Indeed, the work appealed directly to the audience and even challenged it. A cupboard consisting of a stack of old drawers bound together (such as the Chest of Drawers, a well-known design by Tejo Remy) does not say, 'This is beautiful', but it says, 'Anyone could have thought of this'. And that is where the strength of the design lies.

Over the course of the years, interpretations of these conceptual products would change, as a result of habituation but also of the path some designers were following. The fact that the Chest of Drawers now fetches $28,000 has even completely reversed its original message: it has become part of the system of consumption that it implicitly criticized. We can imagine what would have happened if Remy had taken his own concept completely seriously and had continued on the mission he set for himself when he started, either consciously or subconsciously: empowering the user. Possibly he would have created a manual explaining how to produce his various objects in a few easy steps. But Remy never did make such a manual. To this day, he, as many others, has continued to create sympathetic designs, by now devoid of social criticism, based on recycling, reuse, redesign or any such word that is used.

The developments at Droog demonstrate that messages can become too easily readable and thus forfeit their importance. Every era needs its own creative visions and unconventional approaches. Every era needs its own avant-garde. Moreover, the developments at Droog demonstrate that every message eventually transforms into a style (with no substance). Epigones will take over its visual vocabulary, ignoring the substance, usually because they fail to understand it. Then the movement loses its original meaning, a phenomenon that is found in every cultural discipline, prompting a re-evaluation of the past time and again.[5]

The first conceptual products, which were virtually without exception produced by hand, lay somewhere between design and craft, thus introducing a new view on the relationship between industry, craft and design. One of the first designers who, from the early 1990s onwards, combined tradition with the present time and reintroduced a focus on the specific qualities of a craftsman-like creative process was Hella Jongerius. Her choice to celebrate the traces of the fallible process of making things by hand, which produced 'misfits' in the end results, was prompted by a desire to infuse products with more soul. After all, only then would they be able to develop a closer relationship with their users. In line with this idea, she has also worked with manufacturers' and museums' archives right from the start of her career, creating reinterpretations of the existing that will do justice to the present.

HJ: 'The fact that my products were the result of what I call the dirty-hands method was certainly not usual at that time. My ideas always emerged directly from the process of making, not vice versa. All the same, my attitude was not completely opposed to the self-reflecting character of the other conceptual designers of that moment. I have always felt a strong affinity with Jurgen Bey, for example, and his special, almost poetic approach to design. I may not have used objets trouvés, but my designs could also be read as a critical comment on the design profession. They were based on ideas, even if I did not understand them all immediately. For instance, I decided intuitively to leave the casting seams of the rubber and porcelain behind on the surface and I punched technical data in relief on the sides of products. It was only later that I realized that those traces did not just say something about the working process, but in fact also worked as decoration. In that early period decoration was a dirty word among designers who focused primarily on concepts or function. But I have gradually experienced that decoration is almost never just ornament, but that, if it is good, it coincides with the function, the form and the content. The decorative traces of the working process in my first products say something about the clash between past and present and about individuality within a serial process of production.'

LS: 'What you did in product design—linking handcrafted production with industrial production—matched what was going on in fashion. [...] You were the precursors of a movement that could no longer be held back and whose voice is heard all over the world at the moment. By the end of the twentieth century it was becoming increasingly difficult to close your eyes to the negative effects that accompanied industrial production. The rapid cycle of buy, use, throw away and buy again has inflicted considerable damage on the environment and has created a great indifference in how we deal with the things around us. When you made BSet, you were concerned with the need for people to cherish the products with which they surround themselves again. You found more testimonies for that vision of design in the old, damaged tableware from grandma's cupboard than in the perfect twelve piece sets of tableware of the present era.' (Schouwenberg, 2010, pp. 125–7)

Many designers have copied Jongerius, and again there is a danger that the followers will scrap the substance, copying only her visual style. However, that does not take away the fact that she set in motion a different view on the relationship of people with their daily things—the essence of design.

The question of what is design, explicitly asked by conceptual designers such as the jewellery designers Emmy van Leersum and Gijs Bakker, co-author of this chapter, and product designers Jurgen Bey, Hella Jongerius and many others, is a fascinating one because it is interpreted differently in every cultural context and in every new era. In the West, for instance, the term 'functionality' has been stretched way beyond its instrumental meaning. In 1936, the German philosopher Heidegger thought the essence of an implement lay in its dependable servitude (Heidegger, 1936/1960). In his view, good objects for everyday use would, as it were, disappear into this servitude, no longer standing out as physical objects. But even during his lifetime, his analysis was not entirely accurate; at the beginning of the twentieth century, objects for everyday use were also drawing more attention to their physical presence, and in the decades that followed this would become increasingly important. Still, Heidegger's view continues to shed light on the differences between works of art and objects for everyday use, and it still explains the inherent tension we find in design that is functional, on the one hand, whereas on the other, it refuses to remain unnoticed. Contemporary design does not disappear into dependable servitude. Its function, paradoxically, lies in its non-functionality. This is how objects for everyday use prove that they inevitably harbour more qualities than mere usefulness.

How far can a designer stray from usefulness? In product design, experimental designs—produced as single copies or in limited editions—offer many designers a necessary licence to experiment with visionary subjects and design strategies such as working in the future, democratizing design, designing the tools, not the end products, co-creation, collaborations with scientists and designing social strategies. They can be compared with haute couture in fashion, which at its best is experimental, makes a statement about the profession and explores the possibilities and the limits of materials, forms and functions. When compared with *prêt à porter* in fashion, industrial products at their best are a translation of earlier experimental and visionary projects.

If taken to excess, limited editions become alienated from any real context, thus losing their relationship with the profession. The moniker 'design-art' is a telling one. Design in its essence harbours a need to relate to its surroundings, its context. The context is a complex one: users, the amalgam of other objects, architecture, the imagined, emotional, spiritual world around it. A table implies a chair, a chair implies a user, and so on; every design implies an almost endless chain of relationships. A product in isolation signifies nothing; this is where things have gone wrong with many of the products that were created under the heading of design-art. Neither art, nor design. Stripped of all contexts. At its worst, it is a money spinner for the speculative art trade that has run amuck; at its best, it is skilfully executed applied arts.

As a logical response to the excesses of design-art, the current generation is feeling a growing need to relate to real and essential questions about the design profession. What is design? What is functionality? Does the world still need design objects? Or should we be trying to find alternative design strategies, scenarios, collaborations? Sustainability is one of the questions the current generation is trying to answer, and also the question if design may lead to an altered awareness in consumers. These are questions that hold a great number of contradictions: a plea for consuming less is at odds with economic reality. A plea for better materials and production methods is not necessarily a good design mission for creative designers whose aim is to make visionary statements about the future. Psychological sustainability is already a step closer to what we may regard as the essence of the profession because its field of research is not sustainability as such but the relationship between users and their day-to-day environment.

One subject has so far not been highlighted, when it is perhaps the most essential aspect of innovative design: beauty. It is abused or disregarded and deemed unimportant by countless idealist design movements and forgotten by many designers who focus on subjects such as ergonomics, sustainability, service design and so on. But it is always the thing that most pressingly strikes us in designs that have stood the test of time. What is the role of beauty? It is the quality lacking in most products that have been designed based on a moral or strictly functional agenda (such as sustainable products and ergonomic tools).

All design movements with an explicit mission, including modernism (form follows function) and conceptual design (the mission to let strong concepts prevail in the design process), have communicated pronounced views on embellishment. The underlying ideas of a design had to be expressed as purely as possible. With the modernists, this led to purism, restraint and minimalism, and, all in all, the same thing can be said about conceptual designs. It was not until the historical and cultural meanings of decoration, materials and techniques became the subject of substantial research for the conceptualists that they let go of their strict minimalism. And yet, even in exuberantly decorated designs such as *Minute Service,* 2003, by Jurgen Bey and *Nymphenburg Sketches,* 2004, and *Non-Temporary,* 2005, by Hella Jongerius, there is not a single unnecessary element added purely and simply for embellishment.[6] The indisputable beauty of these designs must therefore reside somewhere else.

Beauty is not just embellishment. Beauty does not equal decoration. Beauty is not the by-product of a good design; beauty does not sneak in noiselessly once all the other elements are approved. Beauty is not the icing on the cake. Beauty is to be found most of all in the convergence of the underlying story with the external appearance and the intended function. Beauty is inextricably bound to the modernists' decision to discover the essence of functionality. In their urge to strip a form and rid it of all aspects that would draw the focus away from the content, they not only discovered the essence of functionality but also created a new understanding of aesthetics. The conceptualists' decision to appoint a leading role in the design process to critical ideas was a similar quest to get to the essence of design. Like in minimalist art, aesthetics are inherent in the question. The fact that the first conceptualist designs were not immediately received as beautiful in no way detracts from this.

FIGURE 24.1   Stovepipe Necklace, 1967 purple anodized aluminium. Courtesy of Gijs Bakker.

The composer Louis Andriessen, whom we mentioned earlier, believed that every composition centres on this dilemma: 'Failing to get a grip on beauty, this is what it is all about eventually' (Putten, 2011). Beauty comes with all innovation in any profession. A good scientific theory, for instance, merits our saying that it possesses great beauty besides offering new insights. Within product design, the work of the German designer Dieter Rams speaks volumes. He said that the products he created for the Braun company from the 1950s onward should be both beautiful and inconspicuous, as we can read in the ten rules for good design he formulated in the 1980s.[7] His products were restrained, minimalist, and yet they never disappeared into Heidegger's dependable servitude. They have continued to inspire designers to this day because of their clear functionality and timeless beauty.

Perhaps there is something wrong about a design mission like sustainability because the question does not imply any aestheticism.

To close, we turn to the words of Gijs Bakker:

Views on aesthetics expand over time. When I made a necklace out of a piece of stovepipe in 1967 (Stovepipe Necklace) [see Figure 24.1], true enough, it was seen as something exciting, but it was not labeled as beautiful or attractive. In the design process you pass through all kinds of phases. You are familiar with the conventions of your profession, you know the accepted materials and the meanings they carry. And you question all these known entities, you query them, to try and come to some new insight. With the necklace, I was looking for a suitable material that would follow the curves of the neck as closely as possible, and stumbled upon this wonderful half-product that already existed, a pipe that could be bent to fit any curve. The result was not simply a new necklace made of an unusual material, but also a new insight into the question what a piece of jewelry can be. Such a new insight will not be immediately accepted. Only in the course of time, when the impact of an intervention is understood, will a new form of aesthetics arise, as it were; a new appreciation of beauty. When you continue to design using a set of familiar rules, you are denying such a new view on aesthetics a chance. This is the dilemma the avant-garde is faced with: you act, and by acting you are in defiance of accepted opinion. It is what makes the profession of the 'maker' in any creative domain so exciting.[8]

NOTES

1. In this respect, it is interesting to see how retailers who primarily promote their products on grounds of improved taste (for instance the relatively new chain of high-quality products, Marqt, in the Netherlands) have achieved what reform shops have not over the past decades, although they share the same background: sustainable production.

2. 'Playing to the galleries' is a well-known expression in politics; in front of a camera, many politicians will show their ideas in the best possible light compared to reality. With morally charged subjects such as sustainability, there is often also a discrepancy between the good intentions communicated and decisive force. In architecture, where it has become impossible to ignore the demands for sustainable construction, those buildings stand out that have been decked with 'fairy-lights', with rooftops generously scattered with solar panels glittering in the sun, intended to mask all the building's shortcomings such as its high energy consumption during production.

3. The cradle-to-cradle doctrine contains some valuable suggestions, which have mainly inspired young designers (Kane, 2009). Its three key principles are

    *   use solar income;
    *   waste = food; and
    *   respect diversity.

    By now some of these elements have come under fire. Its originators, William McDonough and Michael Braungart, have been accused of disregarding energy consumption during production; they are not known for their opposition to unbridled consumption in the West (Sacks, 2008). It remains to be seen if the doctrine can be applied on a large scale, and its patenting is criticized. After all, failing to make the patent freely available creates obstructions for a broad application of the cradle-to-cradle idea, which is at odds with the ideological motivation.

4. Stressing the product does not necessarily introduce bigger questions in the design process, such as that of what the relevance of specific products are for people's standard of life. Towards the end of the 1980s, the Design Academy Eindhoven (DAE) purposefully changed the names of its design departments, allowing the school to express the idea that it is not the product that should be leading in the design process but the people. Ever since then,

students have been attending bachelor's courses such as man and living, man and leisure, man and public space. The names would soon become corrupted; students now refer to 'living' and 'leisure', but the ambitions have remained: how do people want to live, spend their spare time? How do they want to behave in public space? And what role can creative designers play in meeting and challenging their wishes? This approach to the profession, in which designers work from personal fascinations and a personal involvement with the world, is diametrically opposed to the approach in which pragmatic problem areas are defined by the industry and the market, as known by departments of industrial design in universities of technology (www.designacademy.nl).

5. Since then, some scepticism has arisen among fellow designers about the meaning and impact of the first generation of conceptual products, but nonetheless, they are still receiving ample attention from users globally.

6. Jurgen Bey's *Minute Service* pays tribute to the amount of time the craftsman devotes to each piece, creating awareness in the user of the value of skilled craftsmanship. Hella Jongerius's *Nymphenburg Sketches* displays the many historical treasures of the workplaces, where the skilled craftsmen choose their own images and colours from a vast palette of imagery and colours. Jongerius's *Non-Temporary* is a reinterpretation of a traditional glazing technique; as the pieces are only plunged partially in the glaze, they reveal the bare clay, dug up from the local context of the company Royal Tichelaar Makkum (see http://www.studiomakkinkbey.nl, http://www.jongeriuslab.com and http://www.tichelaar.nl).

7. Dieter Rams's ten commandments of good design are as follows:

Good design is innovative.
Good design makes a product useful.
Good design is aesthetic.
Good design makes a product understandable.
Good design is unobtrusive.
Good design is honest.
Good design is long-lasting.
Good design is thorough, down to the last detail.
Good design is environmentally friendly.
Good design is as little design as possible.

8. From the report of a meeting on the master's courses, held in August 2011: at the start of each school year, the heads of the master's courses debate for a whole day about what is happening in the world and how it might influence our thinking of design. By the end of the day, the themes that will be dealt with during the year are formulated and plans for lectures and the choice of mentors are made.

REFERENCES

Carus, F. (2011), 'Apple Named "Least Green" Tech Company', *The Guardian,* <http://www.guardian.co.uk/environment/2011/apr/21/apple-least-green-tech-company> accessed April 21, 2011.

Daily Motion (2011), 'An Interview of Frank Gehry with Fareed Zakaria', <www.dailymotion.com/video/xkxmno_a-conversation-with-frank-gehry_news> accessed September 7, 2011.

Heidegger, M. (1936/1960), *Der Ursprung des Kunstwerkes*, Reclam Universal-Bibliothek: Stuttgart.

Hilhorst, P. (2005), 'Sublieme verspilling', De Volkskrant: Amsterdam, November 15.

Kane, G. (2009), 'A Discussion of the Pioneers of the Environmental Movement', Green Gurus, <http://www.greengurus.co.uk/2009/06/mcdonough-braungart-cradle-to-cradle.html> accessed June 27, 2009.

McDonough, W. and Braungart, M. (2002), *Cradle to Cradle: Remaking the Way We Make Things*, North Point Press: New York.

Putten, B. (2011), 'Realisme is het laatste waar je aan moet denken. Louis Andriessen over Romantiek, emotie en toch Wagner', *De Groene Amsterdammer*, March 2, <http://www.groene.nl/2011/9/realisme-is-het-laatste-waar-je-aan-moet-denken> accessed February 20, 2013.

Sacks, D. (2008), *Green Guru Gone Wrong: William McDonough*, Fast Company, <http://www.fastcompany.com/magazine/130/the-mortal-messiah.html> accessed November 1, 2008.

Schouwenberg, L. (2010), *Hella Jongerius—Misfit*, Phaidon Press: London.

25

Design Sleepwalking: Critical Inquiry in Design

CRAIG BADKE AND STUART WALKER

INTRODUCTION

People invent new machines and improve existing ones almost unconsciously, rather as a somnambulist will go walking in his sleep.

(Orwell, 1937, p. 191)

The introduction and adoption of new products and technologies often occurs without due consideration of the ways in which they alter our relationships to one another and to the environment. The economic and cultural conditions that surround design practice and often prefigure its actions can engender a kind of perceptual blindness that hinders our ability to explore the profound changes to consumer culture that living in a finite world implies. The implication here is not of evil wrought on the world by unscrupulous designers in the service of industry but of our inability to perceive the consequences of our interventions and the forces defining them. As such, the larger contexts for design intervention can remain vague, assumed, or even unquestioned. Unchallenged, these contexts can have significant implications for judging the appropriateness of our design interventions and the ways in which we conceive them. It becomes necessary, therefore, to critically engage the world of physical objects we live with, not just in terms of design theory but also through design practice. By engaging in such critical design practice, we can seek to understand how we interact with and relate to objects; how designed artifacts embody and reflect our choices and co-shape our moral understandings through their physical presence; and what the implications are for how we consider and create a meaningful material culture.

In this chapter, we will explore the capacities of design as a critical mode of inquiry. To establish a context for this exploration, we begin by looking at the conceptual nature of objects and the inherent criticality at the heart of design. The possibilities that critical design inquiry presents will be further explored and clarified through the work of four designers pursuing critical approaches in sustainability and material culture. Such investigations have important implications, not only for the way we understand and address current concerns over the environment and the pressing contexts of our day but for the ever-renewing cyclical inquiry into what it is to be human in the built world.

CONCEPTUAL NATURE OF OBJECTS

> It is not just ethicists or theologians who answer the question [of 'how to live'].
> The landscape as well as the city are both highly structured and our existence is
> furnished with many different kinds of devices and technological systems. These
> are what instruct people in contemporary societies on 'how to live'.
>
> *(De Vries, 1999/2005, pp. 15–16)*

The images, products, and built environment that constitute our material culture provide the background context of our existence. Artifacts are the intermediaries between nature, ourselves, and other people, and play a significant role in defining our social and economic activities and in determining how we treat the environment (Davison, 2001, p. 97). They inform our everyday practices and, in a very real way, are constitutive of the way we live (Davison, 2001, p. 5). Confronted with the understanding that artifacts help 'shape the way in which people experience their world and organize their existence', we must recognize that they do not exist passively as neutral objects but rather play a significant role as active mediators in our lives (Verbeek, 2005, pp. 11, 216).

Artifacts mediate relations between subject and object, object and nature, subjects and nature. Garments, for example, exist partly in relation to climate (the environment) and partly in relation to social worlds (people); garments mediate between both these things (Dilnot in Badke, 2011). Artifacts are instruments of relation, between people and with their environment.

If artifacts configure our relations, then design is the agent of that configuration. Forty writes of 'design's influence on how we think', and adds that 'it can cast ideas about who we are and how we should behave into permanent and tangible forms' (2002, p. 6). The act of bringing things into the world involves making choices among many possibilities. Those choices set in motion consequences that can have global reach in terms of resource use, transportation, toxicity, safety, labour and wealth distribution, consumption, waste, and how we create identity and social connection. The artifacts of design embody and reflect value systems that are deeply embedded within our culture, values that are often unseen or unacknowledged. Whether designers are conscious of it or not, designed artifacts provide a material answer to questions of how to act and how to live in the world.

Questions of how to live are in essence moral questions. Design is the act of defining the functional, aesthetic, and symbolic nature of things, the implications of which have deep relational consequences in the world—socially, economically, ecologically, and personally (Walker, 2011b, p. 127). The act of designing must therefore also be seen as a moral act (Verbeek, 2005, p. 216). Designed artifacts and the practices they foster can be seen as the material manifestation of our lived morality, deeply reflective of our values, priorities, and choices. However, our consciously held beliefs about ourselves and the values and moral principles most people hold dear can be quite different from those reflected in the objects of consumer society (Shafer, 2003). Easily verbalized values such as equity, peace, justice, and care for others and the environment give way to the lived values reflected in so many of the products we use daily, values that include environmental degradation, questionable labour practices, war over resources, economic and social inequity, and consumeristic notions of self (Fry, 2009, pp. 111–12; Jackson, 2009, p. 387; Hawken, 1999, pp. 2–3; Lansley, 1994; Taylor, 2007, pp. 473–5).

The unsustainability we experience in the world is the direct result of our interaction with the mundane, in our day-to-day activities and the objects we use and surround ourselves with. It arises out of the seemingly simple and innocuous choices we make every day getting dressed, eating, moving around, furnishing our homes, working and entertaining ourselves, communicating with each other, exchanging gifts, attending to our comfort, and making life a little easier. Through our activities and choices, we define what is acceptable practice and behaviour. Whether or not we understand the associations, through our choices and use of objects we tacitly condone and reinforce the conditions of their production and distribution and their environmental and social impacts. Feenberg explains 'that in choosing to use [things] we make many unwitting commitments' (2002, p. 7).

Design acts in the interplay between signs, things, actions, and thoughts (Buchanan 1992, p. 10). It shapes the conceptual nature of objects. Design interventions can either reinforce certain ways of living or propose entirely new ones, not all of which are predictable or controllable. The introduction of new behaviours and new ways of being can alter the way we perceive and relate to the world and each other. Such alterations result from the explicit intentions of those involved in design and production as well as the unforeseen layers of meaning that objects accumulate through their presence and use in the complexity of human environments. Critically untangling these relationships is key if we are to consciously navigate our material culture as citizens or play a meaningful role in its creation as designers.

APPREHENDING POSSIBILITY

Engaging in critical discourse about objects is a way of discerning the propositional character of things, their physicality, and their relational disposition. It allows us to understand how objects exist in the world as well as how we are in the world with them, in terms of the kinds of relations they foster between ourselves and others. Thinking critically about things is a process of discerning the meaning of a situation or object. Through a process of reflection upon the nature of our relationship to an object, and the way it relates to others and the world, we triangulate meaning (Davidson in Malpas,

2010). We bring everything we know to bear on the process, all of our experiences and understandings. Through the sharing of our experiences, we can begin to make judgments as to the appropriateness of such relations. It is a search, not for answers but for a deeper understanding about objects and also about ourselves.

Critical inquiry in design, however, differs from critical discourse in a fundamental way: design is geared toward possibility. Understanding how things are in the world, and how we are with things, is not an end for design. As a creative and generative act, the important and aspirational questions that drive design are how things can be different (Buchanan, 1992, p. 20; Buchanan and Margolin, 1995, p. 25). Design sees what exists as open to transformation (Dilnot, 2011, p. 25). Engagement in design is about apprehending possibility.

This aspirational nature of design inquiry offers a unique opportunity for critical engagement with material culture. The distinct character of the knowledge that critical design inquiry offers us lies in its contextual critique of possibility. As an applied field, the possibility to which design is oriented is always context-specific, having to do with the possibilities arising out of specific situations (Walker, 2011b, p. 2). Ideas, theories, generalizations, and internalized understandings about the human condition are the starting points for design inquiry. Through critique of current practices, design proposes alternatives. Critical design inquiry allows us to move from generalizations about how things could be and how things should be to address the specifics to how things can be. It explores the alternative conditions, contexts, values, and relationships necessary for their existence and exposes the conflicts that arise between them in the process.

As a context-based medium, design grounds philosophical thought in reality by moving from the general toward the specific. Through the design process, political, economic, and technical knowledge, as well as internalized ethical values and social understandings, are synthesized and configured into a new form. Such outcomes should not be seen as solutions, as design outcomes are not definitive but one of many possible configurations among competing and often divergent criteria. Sargent (1994, p. 2) uses the example of car design, which has two key design criteria: to be both fast and safe. These demands are diametrically opposed with no useful points of correspondence. As they are qualitatively different, there is no math that can solve this equation. The fastest car would go 300 miles per hour (500 km/hr) and could not possibly be safe, and the safest car would go 0 miles per hour. Design reconciles such incompatible requirements through negotiation within social contexts (Sargent, 1994, pp. 2–6). With any number of possible outcomes, the design of a car or any other complex thing is entirely a compromise that can only be resolved 'experimentally' and 'imperfectly' (Dilnot via Badke, 2011).

Through negotiation, design possesses the innate ability to navigate complex and emerging subject matter in a way that is nonreductive and avoids generality (Banerjee, 2008). The conditions of design inquiry, 'its subject matter, methods, and purpose', are not fixed, which opens up many worlds of possibility for design (Buchanan and Margolin, 1995, pp. 24–26). Design is free to establish its context in 'open water' through process, allowing it to explore possibilities beyond the conventional contexts of industry and consumerism (Rosenberg, 2000). Designing begets new ideas, generating new perceptions and new possibilities, which can, at once, advance understandings of the current situation and grasp the conditions under which new understandings might emerge. The inspirational potential of the possibility that is offered by design inquiry is not limited to the generation of new approaches to current situations but also encompasses the ability of design to generate entirely new contexts and paradigms. Apprehending these other contexts presents us with theories and principles that can inform further design engagement aimed at shifting the current culture in more informed and preferred directions.

The extent to which these critical capacities of design are not evident or practiced today depends on the environment in which design takes place.

A SPACE FOR THE CRITICAL

> To refuse the understanding [that the critical is the core of design practice] is to offer, against the density, complexity and the dimensions of the capacities that design is capable of touching upon, a merely 'ersatz' version of design, one that is 'fitted', almost exquisitely, to the demands of the market but which is useless for determining our truth in relation to things and thus useless for comprehending the possibilities of design other than in its instrumental roles.
>
> *(Dilnot, 2008, p. 180)*

The distortions and structural weight of the economic and cultural forces that have come to define commercial design practice have suppressed much of design's critical and aspirational nature or, rather, channelled its capacities narrowly toward instrumental concerns of stylistic and functional novelty (Walker, 2011b, pp. 3–4; Chapman, 2005, pp. 16–17; Verbeek, 2005, p. 206). Even when its force is directed at minimizing ecological or social harm, its offerings tend to be in the form of things to buy, neglecting potential avenues of exploration that fall outside the concerns of the market. Further, much of commercial design practice is heavily aligned with technological optimism and the confident assumption that technological progress will render inert the problems it contributes to (Davison, 2001, p. 34). This leaves design's primary role of commercializing new technologies essentially unchallenged and unhindered by critical misgivings or concern for the potential consequences of their introduction into society. All of this weakens design's capacity to play a strong critical and exploratory role in cultural discourses, thus undermining its potential efficacy in confronting and negotiating the economic, cultural, and perceptual barriers that make it difficult for us to view our relationships with objects clearly.

Margolin (2002, p. 99) suggests that a 'crisis of will and imagination' is at the root of design's inability to adequately come to terms with the social and ecological impacts of the service it provides to industry and, in turn, find a substantial voice for itself capable of addressing human welfare both inside and outside the market. By throwing its hands up as powerless to change things in any way other than what the market will allow, design abnegates any such opportunity and closes itself off from its potential as a driving force for positive change.

Dunne says that it is 'not by choice that we [critical designers] find ourselves operating in this space [outside the market], but because of the role for design that we are interested in pursuing' (Dunne and Raby, n.d.). He explains that design, as a 'reflective and critical medium' (Dunne and Raby, n.d.), is at odds with current understandings of commercial design and the demands of marketability and consumption. Time and space for reflection require the luxury of economic independence, something not easily afforded in professional practice and ever-tightening time-to-market cycles of consumer products (Badke, 2011). In open interviews with other leading figures in the design world pursuing critical works and theories, the overwhelming majority identified some form of economic independence as an essential element in being able to explore issues in an open and unbiased manner (Badke, 2011).

Both Walker (2007) and Fuad-Luke (2004) have advocated disconnecting design, at least temporarily, from the context of the market and professional practice to enable exploration of unconventional ideas that might be counter to current understandings; academia is seen as one possible space for open exploration that offers the necessary independence, time, resources, and rigor to pursue reflective critical practice. Others raise concerns that relegation to closed academic circles limits the scope and potential reach of critical design inquiry, and they suggest alternative avenues for critical reflective practice, such as artistic and environmental funding agencies, governmental and private think tanks, academic design labs and outreach programs, local community service, guerrilla interventions, entrepreneurial pursuits, art and design exhibitions, traditional publication, and the wide range of dissemination options that the Internet makes possible (Badke, 2011).

Issues of sustainability are deeply tied to the market, consumption, and technology. By disconnecting critical inquiry from the requirement of commercial success, investigations are free to confront a wider range of issues and possibilities that fall outside the concerns of marketability. Free of the constraints of capital investment and the economic consequences tied to outcome, design inquiry can take on the more challenging aspects of design and sustainability and confront the interplay of economic, environmental, social, and personal issues tied to them. The agility of this model of intervention is such that iteration is inexpensive and nimble, able to change direction and pursue multiple avenues without being locked into one specific direction (Walker, 2007). The iterative nature of design prototyping (conceptual or otherwise) presents a particularly effective mode of inquiry for weeding out unfruitful avenues, developing and testing divergent scenarios, and rapidly advancing concepts within the complexity of real contexts (Banerjee, 2008). Without an expected outcome, interventions can vary greatly in their conception and translation, ranging from the very direct to the highly abstract.

EXPLORING THE OTHER

Sustainability is more than finding ecologically rational methods of production and consumption; it also involves collective judgment on those patterns...As a

normative concept sustainability is a political/ethical issue first and, only deriva-
tively, a technical/economic one second.

(Barry, 1996, p. 116)

Unsustainability has come to light as an issue of ecological destructiveness, but the urgency and force of the issue is misleading as a focus for intervention (Chapman, 2005,
p. 10). Ecological harm can only be adequately addressed if properly understood as an
outcome, as a symptom of unsustainable conduct. The increasing stress on limited natural resources is a manifestation of a relentless drive toward accumulation, founded on
the principle that economic stability can best be achieved through endless growth (Daly,
2008; Hawken, 1999, p. 7; Jackson 2009, p. 49). Ecological degradation is the logical
outcome when continual growth runs up against the ecological limitations of a finite environment. The principle of growth-based prosperity continues as a driving force on the
tenuous grounds that technological solutions will be found to contend with the environmental costs of extraction and accumulation (Davison, 2001, pp. 22–29, 34). A society
that does not account for the true costs of its actions cannot be other than destructive
(Dilnot, 2011). If this is indeed the case, and certainly mounting evidence and analysis
suggests that it is the case (e.g., Leonard, 2010; Nair, 2011), then efforts to improve efficiencies and build upon current green technologies can never amount to more than a
continuation of business as usual, perhaps rendered marginally less destructive, but even
this is not guaranteed within a growth- and consumption-based economic system that is
fundamentally antithetical to sustainable principles. Such efforts fail to consider the full
range of issues that go unaddressed by current practices—precisely, those that perpetuate our society's unsustainable conduct.

Many leading authors in sustainability have suggested that the scale and depth of
changes required to build a more sustaining, more humane, and more meaningful material culture will require considerable systemic transformation at almost every level of
our society (Young, 2008; Dilnot, 2011; Thackara, 2005, p. 18; Wood, 2008). From
this perspective, addressing sustainability beyond eco-efficiency discussions implies a
vast cultural project. Restructuring our relationships with material culture will require
profound economic changes (Jackson, 2009; Daly, 2008; Korten, 2006; Porritt, 2005;
Hawken, 1999), technological reform, and more considered approaches to everyday
practices (Borgmann, 2003, pp. 22, 94; Feenberg, 2002, pp. 13, 184; 2010, pp. X,
76–82, 221–6; Verbeek, 2005, p. 216; Winner 1986, pp. 9, 163), with deep implications for the way we construct our identities, develop meaningful relationships, and understand personal fulfilment and wellbeing (Chapman, 2005, p. 182; Walker, 2011b,
pp. 187–9, 163–79; Mathews 2006, pp. 85–113). Sustainability as a deeply holistic
pursuit calls for a move away from a system of continual economic and material growth,
globalized production and distribution, externalized economic, environmental, and social costs, and monetary and competitive indicators of success and achievement, and
toward a system that recognizes sufficiency, equity, renewal, integration of localized production and distribution, meaningful labour, and internalized costs, and that values
holistic indicators of personal wellbeing, quality of life, satisfaction, and contentment.

For all its exposure, use, and misuse, the concept of sustainability is still an embryonic and contested domain (Davison, 2001, pp. 11–36; Walker, 2006, pp. 15–29). We are far from understanding the full extent of the complexity and interconnectedness of the issues we face, let alone agreeing upon where our efforts should be directed. The process of evolving a fundamentally different path will require us to move past generalities of 'how things ought to be' and to develop the everyday practices and understandings that will change our direction. Many changes will involve government action and economic reform, as well as the strengthening of social movements, but significant changes in the way we design and personally relate to material culture are also required (Fuad-Luke, 2009, p. 193).

Critical inquiry in design offers a way forward to deal with the indeterminate nature of sustainability through open exploration of issues, exploiting the strength that design offers in dealing with complex subject matter and the negotiation of incommensurabilities in context. Design manifests its arguments and deliberations in form, striving for holistic resonance between often divergent and conflicting criteria and possibilities. The transmutation of issues through design can reveal and illuminate practical and conceptual issues, barriers, and conflicts. Such revelations extend our current understandings and help establish appropriate design criteria, values, priorities, and contextual conditions to inform further investigation.

Critical exploration of ideas through design enables us to explore ethical and social issues within the context of daily life, but beyond these critical and investigative capacities, design is also a highly communicative medium of expression. As the embodiment of the deliberations of the designer, design outcomes are visual and tangible manifestations of arguments in form, adept at conveying complexity and ambiguity (Banerjee, 2008). Design outcomes are, in essence, a discursive proposition, where the object as statement opens up reflection as to the nature of its configuration and existence (Dilnot, 1998, pp. 35–36). Confronted with a tangible proposition, we are invited to discern what is happening within the object's configuration and whether or not it is appropriate. Design finds its relevance and power as a medium of familiarity directly related to consumption and the everyday. As Dunne writes, 'Design can shift the discussion from one of abstract generalities separated from our lives to tangible examples grounded in our experiences as members of a consumer society' (Dunne and Raby, 2007).

CRITICAL INQUIRY IN DESIGN

Design is inquiry and experimentation in the activity of making. . . . There is a deep reflexive relation between human character and the character of the human-made: character influences the formation of products and products influence the formation of character in individuals, institutions, and society.

(Buchanan, 1995, p. 30)

In this section, the work of four designers pursuing critical inquiry in design will be discussed. Their work is diverse and their approaches varied, each exploring a different approach to critical inquiry for sustainability. The works provide examples of the kinds of questions and insights that design can bring to light as a medium of critical exploration and communication.

Production: The Toaster Project

Thomas Thwaites began his Toaster Project (Figure 25.1) partly as a reaction to the romantic notion that arises in some ecology dialogues of retreat, of pursuing a more self-sufficient and insular lifestyle. In attempting to produce on a domestic scale what is usually a mass-produced object, the project explores the entire ecosystem of products and the interdependency we have with others for our existence. En route, it questions the sheer scale and implications of the enterprises our society directs at mundane 'benefits'.

Almost everything we have is afforded by a massive global infrastructure of extraction, distribution, and manufacturing. The scale of this infrastructure is the often unacknowledged and unseen background context of consumer culture that belies any notion of inconsequential consumerism. The smooth plastic shells and glossy surfaces of our consumer goods give no hint of their incredible journey and global provenance, nor to the many externalities not accounted for in their retail price. The Arcos brand toaster used as the model for the experiment, which works quite well, costs just £4.99, versus well over £1,100 and two years of labour for the handmade toaster made by Thwaites, which in the end bears little resemblance to the Arcos and barely warms bread.

The Toaster Project represents an open exploration, what Thwaites describes as a 'quest', aimed at discovery. Its outcomes, as such, are not predetermined and do not provide easy answers. The spectacle and the genuineness of Thwaites's commitment, and the considerable logistical and technical challenges that had to be overcome in the project, generate intrigue and engagement in the work. As a search for meaning rather than simple provocation, the toaster becomes an evocative vehicle for a much larger and more complex discussion about consumer society and the conditions of human existence, where everyone is relying on everyone else for their existence.

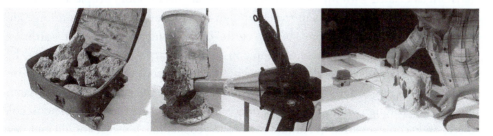

FIGURE 25.1   Thomas Thwaites: Toaster Project (Ore Collecting, Hairdryer Smelter, Toaster). Copyright Thomas Thwaites, 2010.

Thwaites remarks (in Badke, 2011),

> Everything is deeply interconnected, not only extended through space but also extended through time, built completely on very small improvements. Extraction technology improves a fraction, things become a bit cheaper, somebody works out a different way of doing something, and that extends right back to the dawn of the industrial age and probably before.

Thwaites characterizes our position as 'ambiguous', where the scale of industry involved in making an appliance of convenience seems ridiculous, but at the same time the long chain of discoveries and small technological developments that occurred along the way make it entirely reasonable. Thwaites observes that given the level of achievement and development that has preceded it, 'to even have a toaster is quite remarkable,' but the nature of technology is such that 'we get used to things,' and they quickly disappear from plain sight (Thwaites 2010, 2011).

Critical design can be a means of redressing our perceptual blindness when it comes to technology, presenting the everyday in a new way, raising questions through humour and strangeness. The toaster allows us both to see the monstrous footprint of industrial production and to consider its incredible chain of technological development. The Toaster Project as a viable product is unlikely to succeed in the mass market, but that is not its purpose or its value. Its worth lies elsewhere, as a kind of cultural thought experiment, what Dunne refers to as a 'value fiction' (Dunne and Gaver, 1997). Its value comes from trying to understand why the toaster would not work in our current society and from the questions it raises about the priorities of the culture at large.[1]

Consumerism: Product Families

Anne Marchand's work (Figure 25.2) confronts the reciprocal side of design and sustainability, namely consumerism. Through design intervention and qualitative research, her work explores the complex relationships between products and people in consumer culture and investigates notions of responsible consumption. Rather than simply condemning consumerism, Marchand (2011, p. 441) seeks to understand the complex environment in which material acquisition takes place and the 'often noble and positive aspirations' that draw us to objects. Despite the ecological and social degradation associated with mis-consumption and overconsumption, people are drawn to objects because they allow us to travel through time, through cultures, and forge alliances, develop capacities, express beliefs, create identity, and materialize our worth.

Drawing on the experiences of people in the voluntary simplicity movement, her propositional designs explore alternative conceptions of goods that support lighter consumption patterns and ideas of wellbeing that fall outside the consumer cycle (Marchand, 2008). Through minimal appliqué interventions, disparate and valueless household pieces are recontextualized as families of objects, reconciling 'polarities of old and new, valued and unvalued, custom and standard, local and global, diversity within unity' (Marchand and Walker, 2007). The elegance created in these revalued pieces presents

FIGURE 25.2   Anne Marchand: Product Families (Red Handles, Red Dots, Slip Covers). Copyright Anne Marchand 2007, 2008.

a point of tension, challenging our perceptions of newness and the visual languages of uniformity and perfection common in mass production.

As material critiques of consumer drives and aesthetic values, her offerings support a different conception of wellbeing. Central to Marchand's work is the notion that altruism is not incompatible with self-interest, even though they are often presented as such in consumerism dialogs. Marchand's design interventions encourage practices that value sufficiency, contentment, slowness, and quality of life over novelty and material acquisition. They encourage more sustainable practices by appealing to pleasure and personal benefit rather than self-sacrifice.

Emphasis in consumer culture on the aesthetics of novelty give objects an 'aesthetic expiration date', driving premature obsolescence (both fashionable and technological), in turn encouraging fast-paced work-and-spend cycles associated with consumerism (Marchand in Badke, 2011). Sustainability, understood in its fullness, beyond eco-efficiency, will necessarily mean challenging the visual norms and the aesthetic expectations we have for products and how we perceive and value them. Through reuse and revaluation, Marchand's work presents counter-narratives that explore qualitatively different aesthetic experiences and product-user relationships.[2]

Health: Environmental Health Clinic

Prolific and eclectic, Natalie Jeremijenko's work (Figure 25.3) is difficult to pin down. As a political and environmental activist, a conceptual artist with degrees in neuroscience, computer science, and electrical engineering, and an admitted technophile, she is sometimes described as a 'critical interventionist', with her work aimed at determining action and understanding through the transformation of everyday practices and deep engagement with local contexts and environments (Strauss, 2010).

Recognizing external factors such as lifestyle and environmental contamination of our air, water, and food as the leading cause of preventable disease (Trasande et al., 2006), Jeremijenko's Environmental Health Clinic (2010a) inverts the internal biological and genetic medical model of health care and reframes it as an external environmental issue. Playing on the medical model, prescriptions are given by resident designers

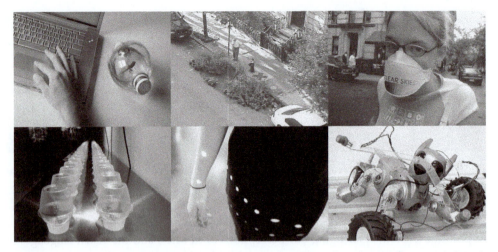

FIGURE 25.3   Natalie Jeremijenko: Environmental Health Clinic 'clinical trials' (from top left: Tadpole Bureaucrat, No-Park, Clear Skies Mask, OneTrees, Solar Awning, Feral Robotic Dogs). Copyright Natalie Jeremijenko, 2002, 2003, 2007.

working within the community, helping 'im-patients' (people impatient with waiting for institutional environmental measures to be legislated and enacted) find ways to participate in their own environmental health. The clinical trials are a diverse mix of green design, engineering, scientific experimentation, and art, involving

- cohabitation and interaction with tadpoles, mice, fish, birds, and other environmentally sensitive species that share our urban environments and stressors
- building and releasing feral robots made from children's toys that sniff out environmental toxins
- cross-species dining
- solar awnings
- chimneys and green lighting that provide tacit and intuitive feedback
- community no-park street gardens
- cloned trees
- home bioengineering projects (Jeremijenko, 2010b)

Underlying Jeremijenko's social and environmental activism is the notion of structures of participation, of redefining who has agency and legitimacy to act, challenging accepted notions of who we consider to be experts. By reframing global issues such as climate change, energy, and pollution so as to be actionable at the local level, the work seeks the creation of headless social movements, of people in situ with intimate knowledge of their environment, empowered, aware, and responsible, negotiating and dealing with each other and their local context. The work is critical practice, not limited to commentary or critique. All projects are implementable and scalable, designed to collect and share data, increasing many-fold the aggregate effects of local action, thus contributing to scientific research and policy making with high standards of evidence for sustainability. Anything one does to improve the air and water quality or biodiversity that affects their health benefits everyone who shares the same air and water.

Rather than seeing social and environmental action in ethical terms, the often playful and discursive lifestyle experiments of Jeremijenko's work are wonder-driven, giving them social salience based on curiosity and intrigue. Through innovative and artistic technological interventions, data collection and experience is made intimately and intuitively relatable. Participation in the work builds tacit knowledge about how individuals and small groups can relate to and affect their local environment through small actions, developing a direct understanding of what does and doesn't work for people in their lives.[3]

Meaning: Wordless Questions

Stuart Walker's work (Figure 25.4) explores merging deeper notions of aesthetics and meaning `cing the overwhelming emphasis on rational and instrumental pursuits with more intuitive and aspirational aspects of our humanity (Walker, 2011a). Walker places together the spiritual with the technical, craft with mass production, the local and regional with the global and ubiquitous, sometimes in resonance, sometimes in uncomfortable juxtaposition.

Scholarly and theoretical, Walker's work, with its often quiet objects, stands in contrast to design for the purpose of provocation. Pursued as an academic mode of research, critical design inquiry is seen as a fundamental aspect of theory development, providing a synthesis of ideas and points of reflection on themes being explored. Research through design offers an opportunity for discovery, often revealing previously unseen or unimagined conflicts, opportunities, and contexts that arise during the design process, spurring

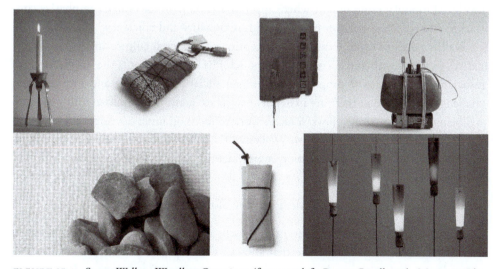

FIGURE 25.4 Stuart Walker: Wordless Questions (from top left, Potato Candlestick, Memoria Olio, Codex Morte, Tempo I, Sustainable Artifact, Pouch Phone, Hanging Lamps). Copyright Stuart Walker, 2006, 2011.

further investigation. In this way, theory nurtures design and vice versa in an iterative, nonlinear process.

Walker's work is informed by a deeply holistic understanding of sustainability, which seeks to incorporate under-addressed and overlooked aspects of design concerning personal meaning and substantive values. In the chapter 'Sermons in Stone', Walker (2011b, pp. 53–83) sets out to imagine what a truly sustainable object might be (ecologically, socially, economically, and personally meaningful) and what conditions, values, and relationship with such objects would be needed to bring them into being and support their existence. In the chapter 'Wrapped Attention', Walker (2011b, pp. 125–61) explores an evolving permanence model for electronics, which similarly would have difficulty existing in our current context but given the right legislation, local industries and infrastructure, consumer values, and aesthetic awareness, could constitute an acceptable and more sustainable alternative to the conventional model of development. Finally, the chapter 'Proximate Objects' (Walker, 2011b, pp. 163–84) explores new opportunities to engage in deeper aesthetic relationships with objects, challenging many of the long-suspect design axioms, such as 'form follows function', which are rendered meaningless in the virtual functionality of electronic objects.

Because our interactions in the world, and the values that drive them, are manifest physically through design, Walker's work is deliberately object-centric, focused on how we might manifest more sustainable conceptions of objects. Rather than using objects purely as a vehicle for social commentary, the work confronts the physical reality of how we make and disseminate objects into the world. Artifacts are considered from within alternate economic models that support local economies and wealth distribution, meaningful employment, local traditions, skills, and aesthetic sensibilities. Material sourcing involves a combination of largely unprocessed materials in their raw state, which can be easily returned to the Earth, reuse, and local reclamation, alongside regionally mass-produced modular components where appropriate. As well, his designs emphasize considered and reflective use over maximizing functionality and efficiency.

Walker's designs explore different conceptions of material culture and present alternatives to the growth and accumulation model. His work confronts the implications of associating technological progress with human social development and meaning and challenges the idea that there are material answers to questions of human fulfilment and wellbeing. This departure allows Walker's work to focus on inner development, contentment, considered use, and reflection (Walker, 2012), rather than the values of accumulation, increase, novelty, and distraction so prevalent in contemporary consumer culture.[4]

Critical Inquiry Summary

These examples of critical design inquiry present a very different mode of engagement with sustainable design issues, one that allows us to step outside of eco-efficiency and green design discussions and pursue a much wider range of questions and avenues of intervention concerning material culture. Such work can often be quite challenging and require thought, reflection, and investment on the part of the viewer, but the outcomes of such engagement are distinguished by their potential to inspire and illuminate our culture in profound ways.

Thomas Thwaites's work confronts our perceptual blindness concerning the scale of globalized extraction and industrial production that we take for granted every time we make a purchase. It raises awareness as to the complexity of the environment we operate and exist in as designers and the impact of our choices as consumers. The Toaster Project makes us less naive as to the impact our actions have in the world. It does not offer answers or easy solutions, only insight, laying bare the context hidden in plain sight in all its ambiguity and complexity for our consideration and reflection.

Anne Marchand's work allows us to feel what a different relationship with consumerism might be like, challenging many of our aesthetic preconceptions about what we desire and value. Her projects challenge the way we construct self-image, bringing into closer alignment notions of altruism and self-interest. Her interventions allow us to consider how we as consumers might live better with values of sufficiency and contentment, demonstrating how design can support different relational conceptions with material culture.

The participatory interventions of Natalie Jeremijenko nurture empowerment and deep tacit understanding as to the kinds of influence we as citizens can have over our environmental and social health. Her work recasts people as experts and stewards of their local contexts. Profoundly democratic, her lifestyle interventions are aimed at action, laying the foundation for scalable aggregate effects through individual daily habits and practices.

Stuart Walker's rich holistic approach to product design attempts reconciliation between efficiency and rational considerations and the more intuitive, aspirational, and spiritual aspects of our humanity. Engaged at the conceptual level of objects, Walker's propositions present alternatives to the way we currently conceive, make, relate to, and connect with our material culture. They represent a radical departure from current norms, based on a deep understanding of sustainability in line with notions of equality, equity, fairness, charity, personal development, and wellbeing incorporated into all levels of a product's inception, manufacture, distribution, use, and post-life.

These examples present a diversity of approaches and outcomes that take advantage of the strengths of design practice as a relational, critical, generative, and communicative medium. Taken together, they illuminate the potential of design to stimulate and contribute to a broad and substantial cultural dialog about contemporary society's relationship to material culture and the consequences of consumerism.

CONCLUSIONS

The interesting puzzle in our times is that we so willingly sleepwalk through the process of reconstituting the conditions of human existence.

(Winner, 1986, p. 10)

Critical design inquiry allows us to get at the very heart of the challenges that confront us in setting out to build a more humane, sustaining, and nurturing world. It has a number of attributes that facilitate this:

- design is relational: in defining the conceptual nature of objects, design co-shapes our relationships toward each other, to things, and to the world.
- design is critical: critical inquiry in design provides a means of investigating, critiquing, and discussing our relationship with material culture.
- design is generative: design is geared to possibility and provides us with means of generating alternatives.
- design is communicative: as a highly evocative means of communication tied to the everyday culture of consumerism, design is a relatable, engaging, and persuasive medium providing us with a means of disseminating understandings and raising awareness.

Building a more sustainable world is a project without end, one that challenges us to critically understand and navigate how we live in the world with objects, essentially the source of our unsustainability. Critical inquiry through design provides a means to meet these challenges, which allow us to do the following:

- question the values and assumptions that prefigure current practices in the production and consumption of material culture
- understand the conceptual nature of objects and how they co-shape our ways of acting toward each other and the world
- debate the ethical tenets of current and emerging economic, social, ecological, and technological paths
- explore and establish appropriate design criteria, values, priorities, and contextual conditions to inform further investigation
- design the intermediary steps to move us from our current context to one more conducive to sustainability
- address essential and underexplored issues, such as personal meaning and substantive notions of wellbeing, which are often overlooked both in consumer culture and the more pragmatic approaches to sustainability
- explore alternative conceptions of material culture and practices in context

Designed artifacts provide material answers to questions of how to live, forming the background context of our existence, which influence the ways we interact with each other and the environment. This is the conceptual nature of objects. The quality and character of our built environment is a reflection of the lived values and priorities of our society. Too often we find the values of fairness, equity, and concern for the environment that most people share are not always found in that reflection. Critical inquiry in design is presented as a means of bringing our lived values into closer alignment with our internal beliefs. Rather than seeing its outcomes as definitive solutions, the propositional explorations of critical in-quiry reflect an inherently imperfect exploration of possibility, which represent our current understandings. Such exploration is part of a project without end to navigate our material culture and deal with the ever-changing contexts of human existence.

NOTES

1. The Toaster Project, 2011, Princeton, www.thetoasterproject.org/.
2. Projects available at www.detnk.com/node/1495; www.idsa.org/connecting-through-time.
3. Projects available at www.environmentalhealthclinic.net/; www.nyu.edu/projects/xdesign.
4. Projects published in *The Spirit of Design*, 2011, Earthscan, http://imagination.lancs.ac.uk/people/Stuart_Walker.

REFERENCES

Badke, C. (2011), 'Design Sleepwalking: Developing New Approaches to Electronic Objects', unpublished PhD thesis, University of Calgary, Alberta, Canada.

Banerjee, B. (2008), 'Design as an Agent of Change: A Vision for Catalyzing Rapid Change', Proceedings of the Changing the Change Conference, Turin, July 10–12, <http://emma.polimi.it/emma/showEvent.do?idEvent=23> accessed July 28, 2008.

Barry, J. (1996), 'Sustainability, Political Judgement and Citizenship: Connecting Green Poli-tics and Democracy', in Doherty, B. and de Geus, M. (eds), *Democracy and Green Political Thought: Sustainability Rights and Citizenship*, Routledge: London, pp. 113–30.

Borgmann, A. (2003), *Power Failure: Christianity in the Culture of Technology*, Brazos: Grand Rapids, MI.

Buchanan, R. (1992), 'Wicked Problems in Design Thinking', *Design Issues*, vol. 8, no. 2., spring: pp. 5–21.

Buchanan, R. and Margolin, V. (1995), *Discovering Design: Explorations in Design Studies*, University of Chicago Press: Chicago.

Chapman, J. (2005), *Emotionally Durable Design: Objects, Experiences and Empathy*, Earthscan: London.

Daly, H. (2008), 'A Steady State Economy', Sustainable Development Commission, April 24, <www.theoildrum.come/node/3951> accessed September 30, 2008.

Davison, A. (2001), *Technology and the Contested Meanings of Sustainability*, SUNY: New York.

De Vries, G. (1999/2005), Zepplins: *over filosofie, technologie en cultuur*, Van Gennep: Amsterdam.

Dilnot, C. (1998), 'The Science of Uncertainty: The Potential Contribution of Design to Knowledge', Doctoral Education in Design Conference, Ohio State University, <https://www.jiscmail.ac.uk/cgi-bin/filearea.cgi?LMGT1=PHD-DESIGN&a=get&f=/dilnot.rtf> accessed August 24, 2011.

Dilnot, C. (2008), 'The Critical in Design (Part One)', *Journal of Writing in Creative Practice*, vol. 1, no. 2, June 9, pp. 177–89.

Dilnot, C. (2011), 'Sustainability and Unsustainability in a World become Artificial', *Design Philosophy Papers*, no. 2, <http://www.desphilosophy.com/dpp/dpp_journal/paper4a/body.html> accessed August 20, 2011.

Dunne, A. and Gaver, W. (1997), 'The Pillow: Artist-Designers in the Digital Age', CHI 97 Electronic Publications, <http://www.sigchi.org/chi97/proceedings/short-talk/wwg.htm> accessed May 25, 2009.

Dunne, A. and Raby, F. (2007), *Critical Design FAQ*, <http://www.dunneandraby.co.uk/content/bydandr/13/0> accessed September 25, 2011.

Dunne, A. and Raby, F. (n.d.) <http://www.dunneandraby.co.uk/content/bydandr/465/0> accessed February 26, 2013.

Feenberg, A. (2002), *Transforming Technology: A Critical Theory Revised*, Oxford University Press: Oxford.

Feenberg, A. (2010), *Between Reason and Experience: Essays in Technology and Modernity*, MIT Press: London.

Forty, A. (2002), *Objects of Desire: Design and Society Since 1750*, Thames and Hudson: London.

Fry, T. (2009), *Design Futuring: Sustainability, Ethics and New Practice*, Berg Publishers: Oxford.

Fuad-Luke, A. (2004), 'Slow Design', Section 2.2, Slow Theory, <http://www.slowdesign.org/> accessed May 8, 2007.

Fuad-Luke, A. (2009), *Design Activism: Beautiful Strangeness for a Sustainable World*, Earthscan: London.

Hawken, P. (1999), *Natural Capitalism: Creating the Next Industrial Revolution*, Back Bay: New York.

Jackson, T. (2009), *Prosperity without Growth: Economics for a Finite Planet*, Earthscan: London.

Jeremijenko, N. (2010a), xDesign Environmental Health Clinic, <www.environmental healthclinic.net/> accessed May 1, 2010.

Jeremijenko, N. (2010b), *xDesign Environmental Health Clinic Project Hub*, <http://www.nyu.edu/projects/xdesign/> accessed May 1, 2010.

Korten, D. (2006), *The Great Turning: From Empire to Earth Community*, Berrett-Koehler: San Francisco.

Lansley, S. (1994), *After the Gold Rush: The Trouble With Affluence*, Century: London.

Leonard, A. (2010), *The Story of Stuff*, Constable: London.

Malpas, J. (2010), 'Donald Davidson', in Zalta, E. N. (ed.), *The Stanford Encyclopedia of Philosophy*, fall, <http://plato.stanford.edu/archives/fall2010/entries/davidson/> accessed August 1, 2011.

Marchand, A. (2008), 'Responsible Consumption and Design for Sustainability', PhD thesis, University of Calgary.

Marchand, A. (2011), 'Sustainability and the Weakness of the Will', Cumulus Conference International Association of Universities and Colleges of Art, Design and Media, Shanghai, September 7–10, 2010.

Marchand, A. and Walker, S. (2007), 'Connecting through Time', Connecting '07 IDSA Education Symposium, ICSID/IDSA World Design Congress, San Francisco, October.

Margolin, V. (2002), *The Politics of the Artificial: Essays on Design and Design Studies*, University of Chicago Press: Chicago.

Mathews, F. (2006), 'Beyond Modernity and Tradition: A Third Way for Development', *Ethics & the Environment*, vol. 11, no. 2: pp. 85–114.

Nair, C. (2011), *Consumptionomics: Asia's Role in Reshaping Capitalism and Saving the Planet*, Infinite Ideas: Oxford.

Orwell, G. (1937), *Road to Wigan Pier: The Complete Works of George Orwell*, vol. 5. Secker & Walburg: London.

Porritt, J. (2005), *Capitalism as if the World Mattered*, Earthscan: London.

Rosenberg, T. (2000), '"The Reservoir": Towards a Poetic Model of Research in Design', *Working Papers in Art and Design 1,* <http://sitem.herts.ac.uk/artdes_research/papers/wpades/vol1/rosenberg2.html> accessed August 18, 2011.

Sargent, P. (1994), 'A Non-Scientific Theory of Design', *Design Studies,* vol. 15, no. 4: pp. 389–402.

Shafer, M. (2003), 'In the Eye of the Beholder: Looking Good, Being Good', University of Minnesota, <http://cla.umn.edu/news/claToday/summer2003/eaton.php> accessed December 5, 2009.

Strauss, C. (2010), 'Slow Lab > People: Natalie Jeremijenko', <http://slowlab.net/natalie%20jeremijenko.html> accessed October 2, 2010.

Taylor, C. (2007), *A Secular Age,* Belknap: London.

Thackara, J. (2005), *In the Bubble,* MIT Press: Cambridge, MA.

Thwaites, T. (2010), 'Interview with Thomas Thwaites', June 30, 2009, Royal College of Art, London.

Thwaites, T. (2011), *The Toaster Project: Or an Attempt to Build a Simple Electric Appliance from Scratch,* Princeton Architectural Press: New York.

Trasande, L., Balk, S. J., Boscarino, J., Carpenter, D., Dunkel, G., Falk, R., Forman, J., Frumkin, H., Galvez, M., Geslani, J., Graber, N., Kaplan-Liss, E., Korfmacher, K., Landrigan, P., Laraque, D., Miller, R. K., Moline, J. and Schechter, C. (2006), 'The Environment in Pediatric Practice: A Study of New York Pediatricians' Attitudes, Beliefs, and Practices towards Children's Environmental Health', *Journal of Urban Health,* vol. 83, no. 4, <http://www.ncbi.nlm.nih.gov/pmc/articles/PMC2430476/?tool=pmcentrez&rendertype=abstract> accessed October 2, 2010.

Verbeek, P. (2005), *What Things Do: Philosophical Reflections on Technology, Agency, and Design,* Penn State University Press: Philadelphia.

Walker, S. (2006), *Sustainable by Design: Explorations in Theory and Practice,* Earthscan: London.

Walker, S. (2007), *Disconnecting Design from the Bottom Line,* Sustainable Innovation 07 Conference, Farnham Castle, Farnham, UK, October 29–30.

Walker, S. (2011a), 'Proximate Objects for Sustainability Practice-Based Research in the Physical, the Virtual and the Meaningful', Design Principles and Practices Conference, Sapienza University, Rome, February 2–4.

Walker, S. (2011b), *The Spirit of Design,* Earthscan: London.

Walker, S. (2012), 'Design on a Darkling Plain: Transcending Utility through Questions in Form', *The Design Journal,* vol. 15, no. 3: pp. 347–72.

Winner, L. (1986), *The Whale and the Reactor,* University of Chicago Press: Chicago.

Wood, J. (2008), 'Changing the Change: A Fractal Framework for Metadesign', *Proceedings of the Changing the Change Conference,* Turin, July 10–12, <http://emma.polimi.it/emma/showEvent.do?idEvent=23> accessed July 28, 2008.

Young, R. A. (2008), 'A Taxonomy of the Changing World of Design Practice', Proceedings of the Changing the Change Conference, Turin, July 10–12, <http://emma.polimi.it/emma/showEvent.do?idEvent=23> accessed July 28, 2008.

26

Critical Agendas: Designing for Sustainability from Products to Systems

CHRIS RYAN

INTRODUCTION

It is as impossible for anyone now to describe the world that could evolve from a sustainability revolution as it would have been for... an English coal miner of 1750 to imagine a Toyota assembly line. The most anyone can say is that, like the other great revolutions, a sustainability revolution could lead to enormous gains and losses. It could change the face of the land and the foundations of human self-definitions, institutions and cultures. Like other revolutions, it will take centuries to develop fully.

(Meadows, Meadows, and Randers, 1992, p. 222)

The next twenty-five years will see a fundamental transformation of design for sustainability; it will be transformed in its knowledge base, in its skills, and in its practice as it turns from (re)constructing the world of goods and services and buildings, to 'reinventing' the systems of provision[1] that make human life and the economy possible. This is no wild speculation (nor, as the quote from Meadows, Meadows, and Randers makes clear, is it particularly new); it is a logical consequence of the coming transition of the global economy out of the carbonaceous period of human development—around two centuries of civilization built on the exploitation of a vast, cheap, and accessible store of millions of years of long buried animals and plants, the fossils we turned into fuels.

The general shape of the next period of human development is reasonably clear; it will change both the 'face of the land' and the 'foundations' of our existence. Economies and the lives of people over the coming decades will be based on an increasing use of diverse sources of renewable energy, a decreasing per capita consumption of critical resources (particularly energy), and the reconfiguration of infrastructure systems to provide resilience to changing weather conditions and extreme climate events.

This revolutionary change will be every bit as significant in human history as was the Industrial Revolution (to which the coming period is a long-gestating reaction). As with that revolution, this one will involve the development of new technologies as well as new uses for existing technologies, but it will not be a technological revolution per se, for it will involve major changes in social organization, lifestyles, worldviews, and human values, governance and power relations. Whether this future unfolds as a peaceful transition or as a period of great turbulence and hardship (and this is certainly where predictions break down), it will see a disruptive change to long-established regimes of practice and the economic paradigms that have defined progress and prosperity in the world we have constructed.

How do we understand design for sustainability in this context of change? How can designers begin to build their conceptual and practical skills and knowledge and orient their best creative energies for this next era of human history? In this chapter, we will look for the answers to those questions through a brief reflection on the history of design for sustainability (DfS) and current thinking about the likely future impacts of past patterns of development. However, we argue that the most valuable insights for DfS come from responses to the early experience of climate shifts and extreme weather events in countries where existing systems of provision (e.g., energy, water, and food) have proven brittle (leaving communities to deal with a new vulnerability in the face of changing conditions). This suggests that future DfS will evolve from thinking about distributed systems, resilience, and systems biomimicry.

A BRIEF REFLECTION ON THE HISTORY OF DESIGN FOR SUSTAINABILITY

Following the considerable success of cleaner production through the 1970s and 1980s (the concept of redesigning production processes to eliminate unwanted pollution and unnecessary resource consumption [UNEP, 2002]), the 1990s saw the growing application of the redesign approach to the products of our production processes, to reduce life cycle environmental impacts (inputs and outputs). 'DfS', 'eco-design', and 'life cycle design' were various terms used to describe this product-focused work. In large government-funded programs in Australia and the Netherlands in the early 1990s, teams of academic and professional designers worked with manufacturers to understand the life cycle impacts of those manufacturers' leading products and to design approaches for reducing those impacts, whilst improving market success (Gertsakis et al., 1996; Brezet and van Hemel, 1997; Tischner et al., 2000). Those design-action research projects delivered around thirty eco-designed products to the market, covering almost as many sectors (from packaging of flowers and cosmetics, to white-goods and kitchen appliances, office furniture, dispensing machines, and so on). With parallel growth in eco-design projects within leading global manufacturers, product-DfS quickly developed into sophisticated design methodologies[2] (Ryan, 1996).

The Win-Win Idea

DfS, like cleaner production before it, was one expression of a mode of thinking that has shaped business strategy and investment, government policy formation, and private and public sector research across the industrialized world since the last decades of the twentieth century. Categorized under various labels[3] and working at different scales within the economy, this underlying orientation to the problematic of sustainability is most commonly expressed as win-win: that it is possible to find pathways for the future that avoid an oppositional relationship between the environment and the economy, pathways that would (ultimately) bring natural and financial capital into alignment (Schmidheiny, 1992; Hawken, Lovins, and Lovins, 1999). DfS reinforced the idea of win-win; there were so many products where superior environmental performance was achieved without any reduction in quality or significant increase in price, seeming to confirm the idea of a sustainable future in which the economy could grow through expanding the market for ever greener products. By the turn of the century, however, developments in DfS practice and theory were raising significant questions about the win-win potential of product-focused eco-design.

The Limits to Product Improvement as
a Win-Win Strategy

The proposition that sustainable economic growth is possible as long as there is significant and ongoing reduction in the (life cycle) environmental impacts of its goods and services requires that the rate of reduction in the impact of those goods and services is greater than the rate of growth of overall consumption.[4] Figures of 60 to 80 percent reductions in product (life cycle) impact, achieved across the range of products in the Australian and The Netherlands programs, seemed at first to be a positive affirmation of the win-win scenario (Ryan, 2003). However, extrapolating those individual product gains to the economy as a whole is problematic on three counts: first, large impact reductions are often one off as past (environmental) inefficiencies in design are corrected, with further iterations of eco-design showing increasingly marginal improvement; second, growth in consumption for many products in most markets has easily outpaced unit efficiency improvements, so that the net result is an overall deterioration in conditions (Ryan, 2002; UNEP, 2011); finally, there are complex 'rebound' effects in which improvements in the efficiency of products become a stimulus for increased consumption in another area (Jevons, 1866; Greening, Green, Difiglio, 2000).

Thinking about Product-Systems

Whilst DfS methodologies made much use of life cycle analysis (LCA)[5] to quantify eco-design objectives, it is life cycle thinking (LCT) that has probably had the greatest impact on ideas of where and how to focus design to achieve a sustainable future. LCT brings the wider product system into focus, shifting attention from the product-as-object to the system of production-distribution-consumption that gives the product its utility and value. This product system is fundamentally socio-technical in nature; it includes established regimes[6] of resource provision (the infrastructure for delivery of materials, energy, water, and so on); patterns of living that define forms of consumption (either as structurally imposed[7] or as a social or cultural norm); information networks (including advertising and media); forms of ownership or access (private possession, leasing, sharing); end-of-life reuse or recycling processes; regulations and standards—and so on.

Products, and the socio-technical systems in which they are embedded, evolve in tandem as mutually supporting elements. The history of the development of major products generally illustrates the complexity of this evolution. In her classic technology history How the Refrigerator Got Its Hum', Ruth Schwartz Cowan (1985) charts the course to market supremacy of the 'noisy' form of home refrigerator (based on the electric compressor) against the 'silent' version (based on gas-absorption technology). The now-dominant noisy refrigerator did not succeed because of its superior technical efficiency; in fact, the lack of moving parts for the absorption technology made it more reliable (at least in theory). Instead, the compressor technology emerged as the successful form of domestic cooling unit in a protracted market struggle between different companies with competing technologies—a struggle that favored powerful, well-capitalized companies like General Electric, Kelvinator, and Westinghouse. Competing refrigerator technologies depended on different energy sources and distribution networks (gas for the absorption and electricity for the compressor), making the role of General Electric critical because its core business was the manufacture of equipment for all aspects of the electricity network.[8] The home refrigerator and the electricity network evolved in a codependent way, in turn supporting the progressive expansion of a system of a food production and distribution that is (at least in developed countries) now functionally dependent on the existence of home-refrigerated storage to extend the life of perishable foods.

Services and Radical Systems Redesign

The transformative potential of product-focused DfS seems to be greatly compromised by the issues discussed above. Clearly, continuing the incremental improvement in individual products (including buildings) is essential; we are a long way from saturating the (global) market with green(est) products (Ryan, 1998a, 1998b). Every successful eco-designed product contributes to a reduction in the rate of growth of resource use and pollution (if we can mitigate rebound effects, a big 'if'). However, from a societal point of view, slowing the rate of environmental damage is a viable strategy only if it provides time for other more truly transformative processes to be developed and implemented.

Many designers and researchers see great prospect in shifting the focus of DfS from products to product-service systems (PSS). The design of appropriate services to enhance the lower-consumption attributes of a product (its efficient operation, its upgradability, its availability as a shared resource, and so on), or to replace a material product completely (dematerialization)[9], has become a growing domain of DfS and business research and development (Tukker and Tischner, 2006; Vezzoli, Tischner, and Ryan, 2009). However, reflecting on the significant challenges to win-win eco-design, Brezet and van Helmel (1997) predicted that overall environmental improvement (from a societal perspective) would require a transition from product redesign to product-concept innovation, including PSS (already underway), and then, ultimately, to system innovation (a transition expected to take many decades).

We are just beginning to see what design for system innovation might entail.

OIL, CLIMATE CHANGE, WEATHER, AND VULNERABILITY

There is overwhelming evidence that the patterns of development of the last century and a half (since the Industrial Revolution) have been unsustainable for far too long and now threaten human life and future survival. After more than a half-century of scientific investigation, the effect of the release into the atmosphere of a vast amount of previously locked-up carbon, through the burning of fossil fuels, is clear and unequivocal. That the biosphere is heating as a result of the rising level of carbon dioxide (and other gasses, particularly methane) in the atmosphere since the Industrial Revolution is beyond doubt. We are currently adding around a million years' worth of previously buried carbon to the atmosphere every year.

What will happen as a result of the extra heat circulating in the system is difficult to predict with precision and certainty; all the advances in science and computer modeling and sensing technology still only give us probabilities of effects over time. Yet the overall picture of the likely impacts of global heating[10] is so disturbing that the necessity to act is beyond precautionary; we understand that in something like a quarter of the time that it took us to burn all that fossil fuel, we have to change to a carbon-free energy system and adopt processes that will suck carbon back out of the atmosphere and lock it up.

Over the last decade or so, researchers, national governments, international agencies, cities, consulting firms, and open source professional communities have been producing plans for such a transition (see, for an overview, Wiseman and Edwards, 2012). There are (as to be expected) differences in priorities across those plans, yet the broad pattern of change seems reasonably consistent and clear. Table 26.1 (items 1–8) summarizes the common elements of post-carbon transition plans. Such changes are proposed or have already commenced in many economies over the last decade or so. Even so, the International Energy Agency (IEA) in its 'World Energy Outlook' (IEA, 2011) warned that actual change has been much too slow and that 'urgent' and 'radical' policy changes are required before 2015 to avoid global temperature rises of 3.5 degrees or higher.

Clearly the transition out of the carbonaceous era, even in the face of projected calamity, is not easy for the global community to negotiate, and a quick reflection on the elements in Table 26.1 explains why. We are immersed in a world that has evolved around the release of fossil fuels, a world of products, systems of provision, and constructed habitat that locks in our dependence on large continuous flows of carbonaceous

TABLE 26.1   THE OBJECTIVES OF A POST-CARBONACEOUS TRANSITION

1. A steady, possibly rapid, decline in the contribution of fossil fuels to global energy consumption, with a steep rise in fossil fuel costs, particularly for oil (from supply-demand effects and carbon pricing).

2. Rapid growth in renewable energy (from diverse sources) largely focused on electricity production feeding into an enhanced grid (but including a mix of liquid fuels)

3. A dramatic reduction in per capita energy (and other resource) consumption over time, even with economic growth (reductions deriving from huge energy-efficiency improvements, changes in life-styles, including the consumption of material goods, travel, and so on, as well as from the design of goods and services.)

4. Diverse forms of storage, connected into the electricity grid (including, for example, batteries in new products, like electric cars).

5. A significant shift in transport and mobility toward public transport, walking, and cycling, and replacement of liquid-fuel vehicles with electric ones.

6. A realignment of land-use for carbon sequestration (biomass) and nonanimal-based food production.

7. Higher density urban living incorporating urban forests and urban agriculture.

8. A significant reduction in the materials intensity (in materials flows) of the economy and a growing replacement of energy-intensive materials by organic (carbon-based) materials such as timber (as a form of carbon sequestration in situations where the durability of materials is high).

9. The reconfiguration of the physical infrastructure of urban existence to provide resilience in the face of changed weather patterns, extreme weather events, and the escalating cost of oil.

10. The progressive development of a physical and cultural world that provides for an immersive reconnection with natural ecosystems and an appreciation of the evolution of life on Earth.

Source: Ryan, 2011.

energy. As the IEA (2011) report emphasizes, the need for action is urgent; the longer we delay, the more difficult it will be to adapt to the heating world. Programs of action are already expanding from mitigation to consider adaptation, to address the issues of our vulnerability in the face of changing climate conditions.

Vulnerability and the Potential of Infrastructure Breakdown

Knowledge and experience of the climate has directly shaped the process of forming the world we inhabit. Throughout history, cities and towns have located where conditions—rainfall, ground water, temperatures, sunlight, and soil—supported the formation of livable communities. Livability depended on the provision of shelter, food, water, energy, transport, and the safe disposal of waste. As those systems of provision have evolved in different contexts, they have been attuned to average weather patterns (as well as the expected range of variability around that average[11]).

With global heating already raising the temperature of the Earth around a degree since the Industrial Revolution, past patterns of weather are no longer a reliable guide to future conditions. Not only will average weather conditions shift over time[12] but variability and extremes will change as well. Current projections of the Intergovernmental Panel on Climate Change (IPCC) are for an intensification of extreme weather events in different combinations in different parts of the world: droughts, heavy rainfall, extreme hot or cold days, more intense tropical cyclones/hurricanes, ocean storm surges, and so on. The recent publication of the IPCC-SREX (2011) on the risks of extreme events contained enough of the medium- and high-confidence projections[13] to have generated global policy concerns about a future of new extremes. The critical message of the IPCC-SREX work is the importance of exposure and vulnerability to new extremes; experience of weather events, particularly in highly urbanized settlements, can quickly demonstrate the brittleness of infrastructure designed for past conditions. Those climate-related vulnerabilities are occurring at the same time as an escalating rise in the cost of oil, as supplies peak,[14] providing another challenge for life in conditions dependent on high flows of oil. The critical uncertainty for the coming transformation is how rapidly these challenges to our fossil fuel, weather-dependent existence will occur and how rapidly our constructed world can adapt. Regardless of the rate of change, it is clear that Table 26.1 would be incomplete without reference to resilience—considered as the capacity of a system to regain essential functions after being severely disrupted (e.g., by floods or fires).

One other critical issue has also to be considered: the last five years have seen a surge in analysis focused on understanding why the mounting evidence of global heating has not translated into appropriate action. Clearly an important dynamic in the social response to climate change is our embedded dependence on the very resources that are generating the problem (Ryan, 2011). However, that dependence is both physical and cultural, involving historically constituted relationships to the weather, science, economic growth, and the structures of power (Hume, 2009; Jasanoff, 2010; Rommetveit, Funtowicxz, and Strand, 2010; Swyngedouw, 2010; Wynne, 2010). One recurring theme in the examination of those cultural roots is that the form of our constructed world—the structure of our institutions and the social practices and routines of daily life—have created an enduring disconnect in our relationships to, and experience of, nature, engendering a profound ignorance of ecosystems, geological history, evolution, and symbiosis (Hamilton, 2010; McCright and Dunlap, 2010; Shove, 2010; Ernstson et al., 2010). This is the thinking that underpins item 10 in Table 26.1.

SYSTEMS BIOMIMICRY FOR A RESILIENT NON-CARBONACEOUS WORLD—TOWARD A NEW FRAMEWORK FOR DFS

'Complex adaptive systems' such as the climate, the economy and ecosystems, do not change gradually when highly stressed. They have a range... of conditions within which change is relatively predictable. As human impacts push systems close to these thresholds of stability, they can behave unpredictably—with small changes having big and often surprising results... the kinds of 'high impact, low probability' events that planners, engineers, insurers find extremely hard to prepare for.

(Biggs et al., 2010, p. 5)

A closer look at patterns of response to climate challenges and the vulnerability of our constructed world where those challenges are already evident suggest an emerging new paradigm—a new resilience architecture—for those fundamental systems that underpin the way that our world functions. This new paradigm appears to have both a creative and practical power for reconceptualizing DfS to meet the objectives in Table 26.1; it suggests that there is a rich inspirational field for all areas of DfS emerging from new models that align the designed world more closely with natural systems. This could be called 'systems biomimicry'.

Over the last decade, biomimicry ('asking nature')[15] (Benyus, 1997) has grown as an important creative source for the design of innovative products inspired by elements of the natural world. A biomimicry taxonomy has developed that provides a classification of natural processes able to inspire design solutions—learning from the way that animals, plants, and microbes have solved problems that now confront us as designers.[16] Yet the focus on species as inspiration for new products may be much less profound and relevant to the transformative challenges of the future than a biomimicry focus on the characteristics of the systems that have sustained those species. A closer look at places under challenge from extreme events can bring this into focus.

Some Inspiration from Australia

There are lines of a 1904 poem by poet Dorothea MacKellar[17] that are a part of cultural memory for most citizens of Australia; lines that are likely to come to mind whenever Australians encounter what she described as 'the beauty and the terror' of their 'sunburnt country'. Talking of the land with its 'droughts and flooding rains', its 'floods and fire and famine', MacKellar's poem portrays Australia as a 'willful, lavish land' with 'a pitiless blue sky'. Her poem evokes life on a land that most Australians adopt as part of their identity, yet seldom experience: the outback, with its vast thirsty paddocks, where cattle live or die at the mercy of the variable rainfall. The reality is that most Australians live a very urban existence; today 90 percent of the twenty-three million inhabitants of Australia live in cities strung out along the coast, where the oceans moderate the harsh climate.

In the last few of decades, the willful nature of Australia has hit the population with an intense period of droughts, floods, fires, severe storms, and record temperatures. The impact of some of these ferocious events has been so devastating, in terms of the economy and loss of life and property, that they are ever-present in the minds of the population, with disaster remembrance ceremonies, new programs to deal with public (disaster) trauma, high-profile judicial and parliamentary enquiries, new research-funding streams for disaster resilience, and increased support for new and old (formal and voluntary) organizations that deal with natural disasters. The relationship of these events to global heating is part of a protracted national debate. Table 26.2 summarizes some of the most recent events.

Of course none of the examples in Table 26.2 describe something unique to Australia; globally, the number and cost of natural disasters is spiraling (estimated at $360 billion in 2011)[18]. However, the way that Australia is responding to a future with these events is

TABLE 26.2   A SNAPSHOT OF SOME RECENT EXTREME CLIMATE EVENTS IN AUSTRALIA

OF DROUGHTS

Australia has the lowest annual rainfall of all continents, with the greatest variability of all continents, although its coastal cities have on average better rainfall than many European capitals. The country has relied on large storage dams to supply the cities through the periodic variation in supply; many cities have more than a five-year supply held in storage. However, Australia has amongst the highest per capita freshwater consumption, and the lowest water pricing, in the Organisation for Economic Co-Operation and Development (OECD).

From 1997 to 2010, the southern regions of Australia experienced severe and prolonged drought. Melbourne, in the south of the country (a city of over four million people), found that the inflow of rainfall into its dams that had been, on average 615 gallons per year was now 385 gallons per year. During this period, water storage for the city, designed to be at 60 to 75 percent capacity entering the summer period, was progressively reduced to less than 30 percent (in spite of water restrictions and very successful social campaigns that saw a 25 percent reduction in per capita consumption).

AND FLOODING RAINS

Models by research institutions predict a long-term decline in rainfall in many critical areas of the country (urban areas and agricultural lands). That decline in rainfall is associated with an increase in high(er) temperature days but also, paradoxically, with an expected increase in the number of above average rainfall days or periods.[1] In December 2010 and January 2011, much of Eastern Australia was affected by torrential rain and storms affecting three states and their capitals—Brisbane, Sydney, and Melbourne. An area of land over three hundred thousand square miles (more than half a million square kilometers)—larger than France and Germany—were submerged by floodwater across Queensland, New South Wales, and Victoria. An estimated eight billion tons of water crashed down on southeastern Queensland, spreading out to flash floods along rivers and valleys; a rural town was destroyed by what was described as an inland tsunami; 14,000 properties in the capital city of Brisbane were affected; roads and infrastructure were severely disrupted with 150,000 residents in Queensland being without power for many days; more than 100,000 hectares (250 acres) of crops destroyed; 80 percent of coal mines in Queensland were affected, some catastrophically, by excess water. This is recorded as one of the worst natural disasters in Australian history—a 'one in one-hundred year' event.[2] Yet, one year later, these extreme events were repeated with some of the same regions and towns in Queensland, Victoria, and New South Wales hit again; the largest evacuation of population in Queensland history (2,200 people) was necessary for the town of St George.

SUNBURNT

On the February 7, 2009, Melbourne recorded is hottest day on record—46.40 degrees Celsius (115.50 degrees Fahrenheit)–after three successive days over 43 degrees Celsius (109.0 degrees Fahrenheit). Public transport systems collapsed due to buckling of rail lines and the inability of air-conditioning systems to cope with internal temperatures. Peak electricity loads from household and commercial cooling demands caused an overload and large-scale blackouts. Then came the fires in a region close to the city's water storage dams, an area with dense forest coverage usually damp and cool even in the summer months. The fire was the hottest ever recorded; described as more of a travelling fireball, apparently causing pyrolysis of vegetation as the front moved with high velocity. Over two thousand houses were destroyed on that day in what became known as the Black Saturday Bushfires, which resulted in the deaths of 173 people.

---

[1] Particularly associated with two apposing—quasi-periodic—oscillations in the surface temperatures of the Pacific Ocean known as El Niño and La Niña that have opposite impacts on the weather patterns for Australia (as well as the United States, New Zealand, Chile, and Peru).

[2] The National Geographic Chanel captured these events in an evocative and alarming film called *Australia's Great Flood* (2012), by Sally. Ingleton, largely based on material documented by those affected using phone and other cameras. (Ironically a similar film could have been made again one year later.)

worthy of attention, if only because it seems to concentrate in one place changes that are discernible in many other contexts where dealing with a changed and changing climate is also becoming an imperative. In Australia these responses begin with water—coping with both too much and too little.

Water: Everywhere is a Catchment

Water is a distributed resource. It arrives (when it does) as rain falling over the ground (and over the sea). It flows into creeks, drains, gutters, underground aquifers, lakes, and rivers, and finally to the ocean. In the past, this resource has been divided into (broadly) three classes: freshwater (collected in natural catchment areas, from rivers and dams), storm water, and wastewater (particularly sewerage). Brilliant engineering systems have been developed for each of these classes of water, forming a critical part of the history of public health.[19] This three-tiered classification of classes of water (and the three distinct engineering systems developed to keep them separate) has worked well for most of history, when freshwater (as rain) has been plentiful and consumption demands relatively low (compared to stocks available).

In situations of drought, when a city such as Melbourne, with over four million people, can be left with less than 30 percent of its freshwater storage going into summer, there is a clear and pressing need to rethink the architecture of water systems. Confronted with the impacts of the prolonged drought on parks and gardens and street trees[20] (already identified as a critical dimension of the city's repeated standing amongst the top three of the worlds 'most livable cities'),[21] Melbourne developed a new program for its water management. The paradigm shift in thinking was evident from its title: the City as Catchment.[22] Mapping water flows through the city, it was found that almost as much water is discharged via its storm-water drains as is consumed from the freshwater supply, even in times of drought. An ambitious plan to collect, store, and use storm water was announced—involving aboveground and underground storage of water collected from streets and roofs; new permeable surfaces to replace previously impermeable parts of footpaths and road gutters (to increase flow to underground aquifers); rain gardens (small, wet landscapes filled periodically by heavy rain), and so on. The city's plans included support for blackwater mining: extraction of water from the sewerage system to be cleaned and used as recycled water (for toilet supply in buildings, for cooling towers of air-conditioners, and to supply parks and gardens).[23] New residential buildings are encouraged to install grey water[24] recycling systems and to adopt more differentiated metering of consumption.

The City as Catchment program is a high-profile reflection of a much wider societal change that sees different classes of water being used (even at residential scale) to replace inappropriate use of freshwater (for toilets, car washing, and for watering parks, gardens, sporting arenas, and so on). Rainwater tanks installed in urban gardens have attracted small subsidies from the government; tanks and grey water recycling systems have rapidly become a new industry and a new domain for innovative design and business.

The logic of consuming water as close as possible to where it is produced (because of its high energy cost to move around) has generated experiments with decentralized neighborhood recycling and sewerage systems (including urine-separating toilets),[25] neighborhood-scale rainwater storage systems, industries using combinations of recycled water and rainwater from their roofs, new commercial buildings incorporating rainwater retention tanks, and so on. A new standard for the plumbing of recycled water has seen the introduction of third pipe systems (with purple color used for pipes and fittings to help prevent inappropriate plumbing connections or water use). There are low-tech natural systems with reed beds and worm colonies (for sewerage recycling) and high-tech systems with reverse-osmosis filters and smart sensors for systems monitoring.

This physical reconfiguration of water systems has been accompanied by significant changes in social practices and cultural values. Water is harvested in the home as a precious resource for gardens. Where diversion and collection of grey water is difficult because of existing house plumbing, it has become common to find buckets being used for the collection of wasted water (from showers for example), another area for new design.[26] Four-minute showers became a badge of water responsibility, with some subcultures adopting other practices such as only showering every second day or not flushing toilets of urine.[27] Feedback about consumption patterns has become important; water companies provide comparative graphs of household consumption (with monthly consumption back over a year, as well as relative consumption compared to other comparable households); social media and online consumption blogs and tools appeared (with some competitive ranking of low- and high-consumption neighborhoods).

Energy and Food—in the New Distributed Architecture

The transformation underway in the systems of provision for water is significant for our investigation of the future of DfS because it has similar characteristics to changes evident in other systems. The most obvious equivalent is the provision of renewable energy, where a new paradigm has emerged driven by a number of economic and technological factors (including resilience) but essentially shaped by the need to exploit renewable sources of energy. The emerging model for this new energy infrastructure is considered to be Germany,[28] where investment in solar energy,[29] principally from photovoltaic panels on residential roofs, has become an icon of the decarbonization of the economy and of the transformation of energy systems that that will involve.

The emerging paradigm for energy (and water) infrastructure can described as distributed, with distributed production (and consumption) systems replacing the pattern of development established through the carbonaceous era (based on ever-larger-scale production units, a decreasing range of productive sources and longer and longer linear, 'unidirectional' distribution systems to consumers [Ryan, 2008, 2009a; Biggs et al., 2010]).

As it is with water and energy, so it seems it will be for food. There appears to be a rapidly growing social movement in most developed economies directed at changing the infrastructural arrangements for the provision of food toward a more distributed model, with a diversity of urban food production,[30] creating, in effect, a distributed farm.

Distributed systems of resource provision are growing wherever technical, physical, and social factors make this more viable—and reliable—than traditional linear systems. Renewable energy (solar, wind, geothermal, biomass), water (rain), and food (actually 'land and sun') are naturally distributed resources, so it makes sense to exploit them through a system based on dispersed, localized supply. Distributed systems do not replace all aspects of the old linear systems; for example, the supply infrastructure (the electricity grid, the water reticulation system) can perform an essential network function of evening out supply-and-demand patterns (balancing excess and deficiency) across multilocal systems of production and consumption.[31] In the German solar roof-top example, a house will consume up to the amount that their photovoltaic system is producing and then take the rest from the grid; if a household produces more than is needed, the excess is available through the grid for their neighbors (next door, down the street, across town, or across the country).

The new infrastructure for water and food is not an exact equivalent to that for energy; there is no grid through which to transport units back and forth, for example, but the morphology is very similar. Local production of water or food displaces demand from the larger-scale, linear production-distribution system; consumption from that system is replaced by local consumption of local recycled water, vegetables, fruit, and so on. Old infrastructures of supply (gas-fired electricity generation, dams, fields of wheat, and so on) do not disappear, but their contribution to overall provision is progressively reduced.

Systems Biomimicry, Distributed Resilience

Interest in bringing knowledge from ecosystems science into processes of management and design of the human-constructed world has grown with understanding of the implications of climate change (Ernstson et al., 2010), particularly in relation to learning from the characteristics of ecosystems that confer resilience (the ability of systems to recover from exogenous disturbances or to evolve to thrive in new conditions). Critics of economic systems have long argued that such systems are disconnected from the biophysical realities of the natural world, even though it is those biophysical systems that provide the natural capital (or ecosystem services) that we exploit for prosperity (Hawken, Lovins, and Lovins, 1999). Endless economic growth implies endless supply of resources and endless sinks for waste, whereas in the real world both are finite; also, in nature, resource systems are cyclic; to use the early aphorism of ecologists, in nature 'waste equals food' (Commoner, 1972; Hawken, Lovins, and Lovins, 1999; McDonough and Braungart, 2002). Similar disconnections from ecosystem services may apply to the structure and function of the constructed world more generally, and planners, designers, sociologists, and ecologists are thinking about urban resilience and resilient cities, considering cities as social-ecological systems (see for example, Newman, Beatley, and Boyer, 2009).[32]

Research in terrestrial (and aquatic) ecosystems has identified two critical features that are essential for resilience, which can be a basis for design thinking about resilient cities: response diversity and ecological memory (Bengtsson et al., 2003; Elmqvist et al., 2003). Response diversity defines the different ways that species and organisms in an ecosystem react to a disturbance or shock. If the response diversity is high, then it can be expected that enough organisms will be either positively affected, or unaffected, so that ecosystem functions are sustained. Ecological memory refers to processes of renewal that allow ecosystems to return following a shock that destroys whole populations. Generally, ecological memory requires some form of redundancy—reserves that can be called on to restore lost species—and functional links though which seeds and live organisms can be transported (e.g., winds, birds, and larger animals). In a direct way, the ecosystem services of cities (for example, their landscapes, parks, water, and agricultural supplies) need to be constructed to ensure response diversity and ecological memory in the face of anticipated climate events.

Ernstson et al. (2010) build on the idea of cities as social-ecological systems, arguing that resilience in cities depends critically on their ability to harness social networks of innovation to sustain ecosystem services. The city as a social engine of creativity and innovation, facilitating (even forcing) social interaction, is increasingly seen as its greatest positive contribution to human wellbeing (Glaeser, 2011). The morphology of cities, their size and diversity has significant impacts on innovation outputs (Bettencourt et al., 2007) as does governance. Ostrom and Folke have shown that social and ecological resilience may be better protected in polycentric—networked—governance, where power is shared between local and central levels (Ostrom, 1999; Folke et al., 2003; Ostrom, Janssen, and Anderies, 2007).[33] Ernstson et al. (2010) acknowledge that this devolution of power and potential weakening of control by governments is bound to meet 'stiff resistance'.

As the history of DfS suggests (and as Ernstson et al. [2010] confirm), our constructed world (cities) involves multiple interdependencies across different scales of the social-technical-ecological networks and systems that design has helped embed in the physical world. The distributed infrastructure paradigm brings the technical sphere

TABLE 26.3   DESIGN OBJECTIVES FOR DISTRIBUTED ECO-SYSTEMS BIOMIMICRY

FOR THE TECHNO-SPHERE:

- Maximize the diversity of sources or forms of resource supply (energy, water, food).
- Localize production and consumption, recognizing the heterogeneity of local conditions and solutions.
- Build in redundancy (for failure recovery).
- Localize the reuse of waste.
- Create strong interconnected networks of flow, or load-sharing (including storage—stocks, not only flows).

FOR THE SOCIO-SPHERE:

- Support polycentric governance (recognizing that spatial and cultural diversity require some local rules and differing priorities).
- Allow for citizens to become 'prosumers' (move from passive consumers to a closer engagement in production, as well as consumption).
- Build or strengthen diverse local economies (and economic networks).
- Strengthen knowledge systems that value local social capital and that recognize reciprocal relationships between the local, regional, and global ecosystems.
- Increase the frequency of diverse social interaction.
- Value innovation.

FOR THE INFORMATION-SPHERE:

- Use Information and Communication technology (ICT) to provide visible feedback on production and consumption levels (stocks and flows).

- Configure ICT to provide for centralized monitoring and service of physically distributed systems (so that the status of system components can be efficiently monitored, with localized service provided as a response to problems).

- Provide for social networking to build and share local knowledge (including design experimentation) and to integrate diverse data streams in polycentric governance for resilience and disaster management.[1]

---

[1] See, for example, www.hardenup.org.au or www.bushfireconnect.org.

into the resilient ecosystem model, treating goods and services and infrastructures of provision as essential elements of a human-constructed industrial ecology[34] that shapes the flow of energy, water, food, and information. If we take this expanded human-ecosystem perspective, then a distributed systems biomimicry could be guided by the design principles in Table 26.3, derived from the resilience literature and various programs exploring design for a resilient future (briefly introduced in the final section).

CONCLUSION: START WITH THE SYSTEM; DESIGN FOR REINVENTION FOLLOWS

> We will not transition successfully to a restorative economy until systems thinking becomes as natural, for millions of people, as riding a bike.
>
> *(Thackara, 2011)*[35]

There are professional design practices that regularly begin their projects with an analysis of ecological principles and the environmental history of the site of their design intervention. There are community bottom-up movements, such as Transitions Towns,[36] that have spread around the world bringing communities and systems thinking to the project of reinventing post–fossil fuel societies; many of those towns are attracting young designers eager to explore the role of DfS in a process of post-carbon transition. Whilst national governments and international agencies have struggled to find consensus for action on climate change, cities and communities appear more able to take a lead, and the spirit of that engagement seems explicitly or implicitly to accept the idea of the city as a complex adaptive (socio-technical-ecological) system. According to the Carbon Disclosure Project, 92 percent of cities report the involvement of senior leadership in tacking climate change,[37] confirming 'the local' as a force for transformation. Those cities have formed networks (the C40 cities for example)[38] sharing design and policy initiatives that frequently emphasize the success of small-scale mosaic developments in transport, water, food, and energy. Long-established organizations that have focused on the greening of business and industry are shifting their focus to systems innovation, with the Forum for The Future, for example, recently redefining its objective as 'transforming the systems which serve our vital needs' and only engaging with businesses that accept the need for systems change.[39] There are rapidly growing programs in many countries that bring professional designers and design students together with communities to explore the creative potential of design to deliver a resilient post-carbonaceous future, beginning with the exploration of radical systems change. In the distributed networks of VEIL[40] (the Victorian Eco-Innovation lab) and DESIS[41] (Design for Social Innovation and Sustainability), for example, we can see the next generation of designers building their conceptual and practical skills and knowledge for the future that they will help transform.

NOTES

1. Systems of provision refers to

    all those processes and infrastructures through which goods and services are made available for consumption…the combination of established industry processes and business practices, accumulated physical production and delivery infrastructure and the corresponding social and cultural practices, which together define the ways in which life-styles and particular sets of products and services become mutually supporting structures. This includes…the design, production, distribution and disposal of products and services…[and] the shared set of expectations and established practices of consumption that affirm particular categories of products and services as 'necessary' for daily lifestyles to function. (Ryan, 2002, p. 41)

2. Eco-design was often represented as a set of rules of thumb, such as use recycled materials; use less materials; use biodegradable materials; reduce energy consumption in use; and so on. However, those rules do not provide guidance for tackling a specific product; some were mutually contradictory; they also took no account of the actual life-cycle impacts that needed to be addressed. Simplified approaches were possible by developing rules of thumb about the canonical shape of life-cycle impacts for different categories of products and select design approaches accordingly (see, for example, Ryan, 2009b).

3. There are close theoretical and practical linkages between the concepts of eco-design and eco-efficiency (WBCSD, 2001; for 'eco-innovation', Fussler and James, 1996; Ryan, 1998b; Ryan, 2004; for 'ecological modernization', Mol and Sonnenfeld, 2000).

4. Of course, it also depends on population growth. An equation often used to relate the determinants of environmental impact says that $I = P \times A \times T$, where I is total environmental impact; A (affluence) is the level of consumption by the population; and T (technology) is a measure of the efficiency of the transformation of resources into goods and services. The equation grew out of a debate between Barry Commoner (1972) and Paul R. Ehrlich (1972) about the relative importance of population growth and technology in creation of environmental problems.

5. For a brief overview of LCA and design, see Crul, Diehl, and Ryan, 2009.

6. The term *regime* is used throughout this chapter with the meaning given in the literature on revolutionary transitions in technologies; regimes are typically described as those sets of artifacts, production systems and distribution infrastructure, institutional and professional structures, cultures and practices (including corporate structures, finance systems, governance, regulations, planning, and so on) that provide a framework for stable trajectories of innovation and development (e.g., Geels and Schot, 2007).

7. Tukker and Tischner (2006) use the term *obligatory consumption* for this part of individual consumption patterns. *Structural consumption* is perhaps a more transparent term, emphasizing that there are patterns of consumption that are imposed by our physically constructed world (e.g., car dependence, the consumption of energy necessitated by the heating or cooling of buildings to provide acceptable living or working conditions). Deliberate, planned obsolescence with goods constructed to have a finite life or engineered to fail also fits into this category (like the so-called Phoebus cartel, 1927, to limit incandescent light bulb life to a thousand hours, organized by General Electric [Reich, 1992]).

8. General Electric moved into the domestic appliance market to build demand for electricity, and the refrigerator was a significant twenty-four-hour-a-day electricity-consuming device.

9. Frequently illustrated by the substitution of physical storage media for music—vinyl, CDs, and so on—by digital information.

10. *Global heating* is the term preferred by James Lovelock, who is concerned to ensure that we pay attention to the amount of additional heat the Earth has absorbed from the sun. As he says, 'The global mean temperature is like the current account balance which varies from day to day; the total heat absorbed is an indication of the reserves' (Lovelock, 2010).

11. With the creation of reliable records, variability could encompass consideration of the probability of outlier events, such as 'one-in-one-hundred year' floods.

12. With (most likely) the tropics getting wetter, high latitudes getting warmer and wetter, and the zones in between getting drier and expanding toward the poles.

13. With the only low-confidence conclusion being attached to increases in tropical cyclone activity (intensity, frequency, duration)—though this conclusion was accompanied by a warning that low confidence does not imply low possibility of change, only that data reliability and noise in existing data make any conclusions difficult.

14. *Peaking* refers to the point at which demand for a resource is greater than available supply.

15. See http://biomimicry.net/, accessed February 26, 2013.

16. See http://www.asknature.org, accessed February 26, 2013.

17. The poem is 'My Country' (see http://allpoetry.com/poem/8526595-My_Country-by-Dorothea_Mackellar).

18. According to the annual recording of such events by the insurance company Munich Re (accessible from www.munichre.com).

19. A high proportion of fresh water is for direct, and indirect, human ingestion; health and quality control are vital. Runoff (storm water) from human settlements is often contaminated, from air pollution, waste, animal feces, the breakdown products of tires, paint, and so on. Human sewerage poses a considerable threat for human health, and its separation and treatment is often considered as the most important advance in delivering public health outcomes.

20. Potable water use for landscape purposes (gardens, street trees) was around 1.2 million liters (317,000 gallons) per year in 2008; the city water plan committed to reducing that by 60 percent in three years.

21. The global Livable Cities Index (www.eiu.com/).

22. See http://www.melbourne.vic.gov.au.

23. First demonstrated in the new Melbourne City Council offices, known as CH2 (see http://www.melbourne.vic.gov.au/Environment/CH2/Pages/CH2Ourgreenbuilding.aspx).

24. Waste-water from baths, showers, clothes washing, and so on—effectively all waste-water apart from sewerage.

25. See current sustainability report: Yarra Valley Water (www.yvw.com.au).

26. Many people unscrewed the trap from under kitchen sinks letting water flow into buckets. Public media swapped ideas for water saving and ways of avoiding back problems from carrying water to the garden. Awards were won for the design of collapsible buckets, for tanks, and so on. See, for example, www.rainwaterharvest.com.au/; www.fulltank.com.au/; www.needarainwatertank.com.au/tanks.html.

27. A note can be found above many household toilets: 'If its brown flush it down; if its yellow let it mellow' (Australians are very poetic as well as practical).

28. Although it is likely that China, India, and Japan will quickly outpace Germany for this leading role.

29. Amounting to twenty-five gigawatts in 2010.

30. From community gardens to productive horticulture in parks, fruit trees in streets, roof-top gardens, tower (or vertical) farms, aquaculture businesses, and so on. See www.verticalfarms.com for an updated resource on urban farming, or www.cityfarmer.info/; www.urbanfoodpolicy.com/; www.ruaf.org/; www.agdevjournal.com/.

31. This is what makes large networks of renewable energy (from, say wind and sun) into a reliable supply—deficient production in one place (because it is cloudy or still) is compensated by excess from another place (when the sun shines and the wind blows).

32. For a database of such thinking, see the urban social-ecological research section of the Stockholm Resilience Centre (http://www.stockholmresilience.org/research/researchthemes/urbansocialecologicalsystems.html).

33. This stands in contrast to the idea of command and control, previously considered the only solution to the essential conflict between individual and collective interests in the management of common resources (often referred to as 'the tragedy of the commons', after Hardin, 1968).

34. There is a significant literature on industrial ecology—on the design of industrial systems using ecosystem principles. See, for instance, the *Journal of Industrial Ecology* (http://www.yale.edu/jie/).

35. From http://changeobserver.designobserver.com/feature/how-to-make-systems-thinking-sexy/28518/ (also see www.doorsofperception.com/) (for an overview of systems thinking, see Meadows, 2008).

36. See www.transitionnetwork.org/.

37. See www.cdproject.net.

38. See http://live.c40cities.org/.

39. See http://www.forumforthefuture.org/.

40. See www.ecoinnovationlab.com.

41. See www.desis-network.org.

REFERENCES

Bengtsson, J., Angelstam, P., Elmqvist, T., Emanuelsson, U., Folke, C., Ihse, M., Moberg, F., and Nyström, M. (2003), 'Resilience and Dynamic Landscapes', *AMBIO*, vol. 32, no. 6: pp. 389–96.

Benyus, J. (1997), *Biomimicry: Innovation Inspired by Nature*, Harper Collins: New York.

Bettencourt, L.M.A., Lobo, J., Helbing, D., Kühnert, C., and West, G. B. (2007), 'Growth, Innovation, Scaling and the Pace of Life in Cities', *Proceedings of the National Academy of Sciences of the United States of America,* vol. 194, no. 17: pp. 7301–6.

Biggs, C., Ryan, C., and Wiseman, J. (2010), 'Distributed Systems: A Design Model for Sustainable and Resilient Infrastructure', University of Melbourne, <http://www.ecoinnovationlab. com/briefing-notes/318-distributed-systems-research-paper> accessed July 25, 2012.

Brezet, J. C., and van Hemel, C. G. (1997), *EcoDesign: A Promising Approach to Sustainable Production and Consumption,* United Nations Environment Program: Paris.

Commoner, B. (1972), *The Closing Circle,* Random House: New York.

Cowan, R. S. (1985), 'How the Refrigerator Got Its Hum', in MacKenzie, D. and Wajcman, J. (eds), *The Social Shaping of Technology,* Open University Press: Milton Keynes. pp. 202–16.

Crul, M., Diehl, J. C., and Ryan, C. (eds) (2009), *Design for Sustainability (D4S): A Step-By-Step Approach,* United Nations Environment Program: Paris.

Ehrlich, P. R. (1972), *The Population Bomb,* Buccaneer Books: New York.

Elmqvist, T., Folke, C., Nyström, M., Peterson, G., Bengtsson, J., Walker, B., and Norberg, J. (2003), 'Response Diversity, Ecosystem Change and Resilience', *Frontiers of Ecological Environment,* vol. 1, no. 9: pp. 488–94.

Ernstson, H., van der Leeuw, S., Redman, C. L., Meffert, D. J., Davis, G., Alfsen, C., and Elmqvist, T. (2010), 'Urban Transitions: On Urban Resilience and Human Dominated Ecosystems', in *AMBIO,* vol. 39: pp. 531–45.

Folke, C., Colding, J., and Berkes, F. (2003), 'Synthesis: Building Resilience and Adaptive Capacity in Social-Ecological Systems', in Berkes, F., Colding, J. and Folke, C. (eds), *Navigating Social-Ecological Systems: Building Resilience for Complexity and Change,* Cambridge University Press: Cambridge, pp. 352–87.

Fussler, C., and James, P. (1996), *Driving Eco-Innovation: A Breakthrough Discipline for Innovation and Sustainability,* Pitman Publishing: London.

Geels, F., and Schot, J. (2007), 'Typology of Sociotechnical Transition Pathways', *Research Policy,* vol. 36: pp. 399–417.

Gertsakis, J., Lewis, H., and Ryan, C. (1996), *A Guide to EcoReDesign,* RMIT University Press: Melbourne.

Glaeser, E. (2011), *Triumph of the City: How Our Greatest Invention Makes Us Richer, Smarter, Greener, Healthier and Happier,* Penguin Press: New York.

Greening, L. A., Green, D. L., and Difiglio, C. (2000), 'Energy Efficiency and Consumption— The Rebound Effect. A Survey', *Energy Policy,* vol. 6, no. 7: pp. 389–401.

Hamilton, C. (2010), *Requiem for a Species: Why We Resist the Truth about Climate Change,* Earthscan: London.

Hardin, G. (1968), 'The Tragedy of the Commons', *Science* vol. 162: pp. 1243–8.

Hawken, P., Lovins, A., and Lovins, L. H. (1999), *Natural Capitalism—The Next Industrial Revolution,* Little, Brown and Co.: Boston.

Hume, M. (2009), *Why We Disagree about Climate Change. Understanding Controversy, Inaction and Opportunity,* Cambridge University Press: Cambridge.

IEA (2011), *World Energy Outlook,* International Energy Agency: Paris.

IPCC-SREX (2011), *Managing the Risks of Extreme Events and Disasters to Advance Climate Change Adaptation* (SREX), <ipcc-wg2.gov/SREX/> accessed February 26, 2013.

Jasanoff, S. (2010), 'A New Climate for Society', *Theory Culture & Society,* vol. 27, nos. 2–3: pp. 233–53.

Jevons, W. S. (1866), *The Coal Question; An Inquiry Concerning the Progress of the Nation and the Probable Exhaustion of Our Coal Mines,* Macmillan: London.

Lovelock, J. (2010), *The Vanishing Face of Gaia,* Penguin Books: London.

McCright, A., and Dunlap, R. (2010), 'Anti-Reflexivity: The American Conservative Movement's Success in Undermining Climate Science and Policy', *Theory Culture & Society,* vol. 27, nos. 2–3: pp. 100–33.

McDonough, W., and Braungart, M. (2002), *Cradle to Cradle: Remaking the Way We Make Things,* North Point Press: New York.

Meadows, D. H. (2008), *Thinking in Systems,* Chelsea Green Books: Vermont.

Meadows, D. H., Meadows, D. L., and Randers, J. (1992), *Beyond the Limits: Global Collapse or a Sustainable Future,* Earthscan: London.

Mol, A. P., and Sonnenfeld, D. (eds) (2000), *Ecological Modenisation Around the World: Perspectives and Critical Debates,* Frank Cass: London.

Newman, P., Beatley, T., and Boyer, H. (2009), *Resilient Cities: Responding to Peak Oil and Climate Change,* Island Press: Washington, D.C.

Ostrom, E. (1999), 'Coping with Tragedies of the Commons', *Annual Review of Political Science,* vol. 2, no. 1: pp. 493–535.

Ostrom, E., Janssen, M., and Anderies, J. M. (2007), 'Going beyond Panaceas', *Proceedings of the National Academy of Sciences (PNAS),* vol. 104, no. 39: pp. 15176–8.

Reich, L. (1992), 'General Electric and the World Cartelization of Electric Lamps', in Kudo, A. and Hara, T. (eds), *International Cartels in Business History: International Conference of Business History 18,* University of Tokyo Press: Tokyo. pp. 213–31.

Rommetveit, K., Funtowicxz, S., and Strand, R. (2010), 'Knowledge Democracy and Action in Response to Climate Change', in Bhaskar, R., Frank, C., Höyer, K. G. and Parker, J. (eds), *Interdisciplinarity and Climate Change,* Routledge: London, pp. 149–63.

Ryan, C. (1996), 'A Review of EcoDesign', in Roy, R. (ed.), *Innovation, Environment and Strategy,* Open University Press: Milton Keynes, UK.

Ryan, C. (1998a), 'Moving Beyond the Low-Hanging Fruit in Design for Environment', *Journal of Industrial Ecology,* vol. 1, no. 3: pp. 1–5.

Ryan, C. (1998b), 'Designing for Factor 20 Improvements', *Journal of Industrial Ecology,* vol. 2, no. 2: pp. 3–6.

Ryan, C. (2002), 'Global Status Report,UN Johannesburg Summit: Sustainable Consumption', United Nations Environment Program (Division of Technology, Industry and Economics): Paris.

Ryan, C. (2003), 'Learning from a Decade (or So) of Eco-Design Experience, (Pt One)', *Journal of Industrial Ecology,* vol. 7, no. 2: pp. 10–12.

Ryan, C. (2004), 'Learning from a Decade (or So) of Eco-Design Experience (Pt Two)', *Journal of Industrial Ecology,* vol. 8, no. 4.

Ryan, C. (2008), 'Climate Change and Ecodesign: Part I: The Focus Shifts to Systems', *Journal of Industrial Ecology,* vol. 12, no. 2: pp. 140–3.

Ryan, C. (2009a), 'Climate Change and Ecodesign, Part II: Exploring Distributed Systems', *Journal of Industrial Ecology,* vol. 13, no. 3: pp. 350–3.

Ryan, C. (2009b), 'A Quick Start Approach to Design for Sustainability', in Crul, M., Diehl, J. C. and Ryan, C. (eds), *Design for Sustainability (D4S): A Step-By-Step Approach,* United Nations Environment Program (UNEP): Paris.

Ryan, C. (2011), *Eco-Acupuncture: Designing Future Transitions for Urban Communities for a Resilient Low-Carbon Future,* Proceeding of the State of Australian Cities Conference, Melbourne, <http://www.soac2011.com.au/> accessed July 25, 2012.

Schmidheiny, S. (1992), *Changing Course: A Global Business Perspective on Development and the Environment,* MIT Press: Boston.

Shove, E. (2010), 'Social Theory and Climate Change: Questions Often, Sometimes and Not Yet Asked', *Theory, Culture & Society,* vol. 27, nos. 2–3: pp. 277–88.

Swyngedouw, E. (2010), 'Apocalypse Forever? Post-Political Populism and the Spectre of Climate Change', *Theory, Culture & Society,* vol. 27, nos. 2–3: pp. 213–32.

Thackara, J. (2011), Keynote at the Buckminster Fuller Challenge awards in New York, NY, June 8, 2011.

Tischner, U., Prosler, M., Rubik, F., and Schminke, E. (2000), *How to Do EcoDesign?* Verlag Form Praxis: Frankfurt.

Tukker, A., and Tischner, U. (eds) (2006), *New Business for Old Europe,* Greenleaf: Sheffield, UK.

UNEP (2002), 'Cleaner Production', *Industry and Environment,* vol. 25: pp. 3–4.

UNEP (2011), 'Decoupling Natural Resource Use and Environmental Impacts from Economic Growth', Report of the Working Group on Decoupling to the International Resource Panel, Paris.

Vezzoli, C., Tischner, U., and Ryan, C. (2009), 'Product Service Systems', in Crul, M., Diehl, J. C. and Ryan, C. (eds), *Design for Sustainability (D4S): A Step-By-Step Approach,* United Nations Environment Program: Paris, pp. 94–101.

WBCSD (2001), *Sustainability Through the Market,* World Business Council for Sustainable Development: Geneva.

Wiseman, J., and Edwards, T. (2012), 'Post Carbon Pathways: Reviewing Postcarbon Economy Transitions Strategies', *CPD Occasional Papers,* vol. 17: p. 132.

Wynne, B. (2010), 'Strange Weather Again', *Theory, Culture & Society,* vol. 27, nos. 2–3: pp. 298–305.

27

Meta-Designing Paradigm Change: An Ecomimetic, Language-Centred Approach

JOHN WOOD

INTRODUCTION

While design for sustainability is very important, it has yet to make us safe from catastrophic climate changes or from an accelerating decline in biodiversity. The world needs a paradigmatic transformation at the level of behaviours and lifestyles; however, this is very unlikely to come out of piecemeal innovation or discrete problem-solving exercises. Paradigms resist change partly because of the vested interests that maintain the economic, political, and social order. In order to succeed, designers may need to work, at a higher strategic level, alongside scientists, and politicians. This means reforming design practice to make it more coherent, joined-up, integrated and holistic. This chapter outlines a framework for development, referring to it as 'meta-design'. Where, traditionally, designers are trained to create deliverables for the future, meta-designers would, also, cocreate opportunities in a shared series of 'present tenses' or 'presents' (Wood, 1998, pp. 88–101). They would seek to complement fact-based or evidence-based approaches used by governments. The purpose of this is to find, and to benefit from, hitherto unnoticed opportunities. We see our development of metadesign as a way to develop 'design thinking', while acknowledging that the traditional idea of design as a system of predictive control is unrealistic when applied to complex communities or ecological habitats.

TERMINOLOGY

As the term 'meta-design' can be characterized as the (re)design of design within a situated context, a meta-design team should be ready to think beyond fixed meanings. This would help meta-designers to harvest more possibilities than those that might be obvious to the specialist designer. In looking for a more symbiotic (i.e., synergistic) mode of design practice, the chapter uses the term 'ecomimetic' (Fairclough, 2005, p. 42) instead of 'biomimicry' (c.f. Benyus, 1997). This term was intended to allude to the living world as a whole. However, it is more commonly used in copying the functionality, or capability, of individual organisms or their parts. This reflects a Westernized, corporate worldview in which the quest for competitive advantage has led to policies of technological 'disruption', rather than ecological adaption. This mind-set is probably at its most alarming in relation to bioengineered products that are designed to become part of a living ecosystem, yet are sometimes described in either a cozy, Disney-esque way or in a more Newtonian language of certainty and control. Nature is ineffable and emergent, and it defies clear definition (Wood, 2011, pp. 27–32). Nonetheless, words are vital within meta-design because they shape our realities and, therefore, guide our actions. When describing how living organisms sustain themselves, Maturana and Varela used the word 'language' as a verb (1992, p. 211). While this may seem grammatically strange to English speakers, it helps us to understand the dynamic process they call 'autopoiesis' (literally, 'self-creation'). This describes how living systems survive by maintaining a necessary equilibrium between their internal and external identities. This is not only a theory about the seamlessness of interplay between action and theory (e.g., Searle, 1970, p. 17), it is also a practical way for design teams to cocreate their survival as whole, living systems. However, this active, radical, consensual reframing of meaning means that, in theory, the participant's perceived reality will change. As this change would be both shared and self-reflexive, the self-identity of the teams would change with it (von Foerster, 2003). This process is a kind of collective version of Freud's early notion of 'polymorphous perversity' (Freud, 1905/1991, p. 191), which describes how an infant steers its habits and identities by making situated choices based on its personal experience of gratification or displeasure. These habits may later be guided by the values and responses of the society, mediated by the framework of language that the infant will, in theory, be free to cocreate as a member of that society. In terms of our metad-esign methodology, increasing ecological diversity may be attainable but hard to imagine and foresee. This is partly because the language we use to enframe nature is inadequate to the task. It may also be that there is insufficient creative optimism, or opportunism, within the meta-design team. This also has useful implications for democracy in general, as empowering the collective imagination is far more powerful than counting individual choices.

In seeking to change the paradigm, it is necessary to challenge some of the terms of reference that we commonly use to discuss sustainable design. Paradoxically, one of them is the term 'sustainable design', which evolved from Brundtland's notion of 'sustainable development' (1987). Harry Truman's use of the term 'development' in 1949 reflected a widespread assumption that there should be capital investments and a transfer of knowledge from the 'developed' to the so-called underdeveloped world (Sachs, 2010, p. xvi). Variations on the idea of sustainable development became increasingly popular after 1987, when politicians needed a new environmentalist creed that would reassure the markets while appearing to be scientifically credible. Unfortunately, the term is so presumptuous and confused as to be counterproductive. What is meant by unsustainable might be considered something that it is not resilient enough to continue by itself. Alternatively, it may refer to something that it is not appealing enough to warrant approval. The chapter therefore uses the term 'co-sustainment' instead of 'sustainability', as it accentuates the reciprocal dependency of all living systems (Wood, 2002, p. 4). While the logic of co-sustainment may seem strangely circular from within the traditional logic of design it is a fundamental principle of meta-design. The root verb 'to sustain' usually denotes a continuation over time but can also be applied in the nontemporal sense of something holding together. No organism enjoys longevity because of an a priori moral right or evolutionary purpose. In order to endure—that is, to remain a viable part of the whole—it must always adapt to its changing habitat. This means adjusting its actions and identities.

DESIGN EVOLUTION

What we would currently recognize as design emerged in the 1880s from an industrial revolution that was managed in order to attain a more enlightened, prosperous, and harmonious society. This integration of the creative arts and technology was, in many ways, an extremely successful venture, even though what we now understand as design has remained as a set of rather narrow specialist practices. The corporations did not see this as a problem. Indeed, the lowly status and disconnectedness of the design professions better enabled them to focus on the limited agenda of commercial profit. Most designers are still trained as lowly integrators of form and function. Many seem happy to act as hidden persuaders or to work on smart widgets and myopic, technical fixes. However, these are symptoms of the paradigm that is killing us. They are a by-product of a culture of division, solipsism, fragmentation, and specialization. To be fair, not all designers unthinkingly accepted their role as mercenary catalysts of consumption. In the 1960s and 1970s, some were trying to reconnect community, food, and energy production, transport and shelter within a single vision. However, the spirit of radical idealism that impelled this quest had lost much of its momentum by the late 1980s when, crudely speaking, the collapse of the Soviet Union's political power base reduced the number of dominant ideologies from two to one. After this seismic event, a more pragmatic compromise emerged. This was based on the belief that idealism had failed and that our only option was to reform industrial capitalism by improving its products and services. Terms such as 'alternative energy' or 'alternative technology' gave way to notions of 'sustainable consumption' and the 'green consumer'. As a result, many design educators defaulted to a less troublesome role as teachers of industry-friendly skills. This has helped to perpetuate a cycle of collective dysfunction in which altruistic, noncommercial design visions became risible, invisible, and, ultimately, unconceivable. It is fortunate that digital, networked systems are making the sharing of big, controversial ideas seem, perhaps for the first time in history, for many, both rewarding and safe.

It is difficult to predict the forthcoming changes within design because of movements such as open source innovation, social networking, and online activism. These have already begun to challenge the professional sanctity of design and inspire new genres of design thinking. These developments are affecting both designers and citizens, albeit in different ways. How might we synchronize 'bottom-up' and 'top-down' approaches in a way that enables the 'creative city' (Landry, 2000, p. xxxii) to become the context for what, in 1939, Dewey envisaged as the rise of a 'creative democracy' (1939/1976). If we see the continued upsurge of movements like permaculture or 'Transition Towns', will designers play a small, supporting role or one that is centre stage? Is it possible that the design professions would slowly be absorbed into a bigger, more emancipatory picture? We need some big visions that embody the unique benefits of design thinking. Richard Buckminster Fuller and John Chris Jones come to mind, here, as they exemplify different attempts to see beyond the narrow boundaries of professional specialism that epitomized professional design in the twentieth century. Fuller believed that designers should reflect upon the whole cosmos, then upon our place on the planet, before deciding how to address the design task immediately in front of them. His call for a 'comprehensive anticipatory design science' (1969, p. 9) is, therefore, a serious one. It is almost unique in forecasting the key issues of the twenty-first century from a designer's perspective, despite his abstract mode of description and his, apparently arcane, techno-centric concerns. By contrast, John Chris Jones adopted a more modest, human, and personal standpoint from which to embark upon the redesigning of designing (c.f. Jones, 1992, 2012). He is one of many who reflected on the range of options and methods that designers might use, extrapolating this quest into the possibilities for 'creative democracy' (1998). He conceived designing as a manifold array of activities that may include the devising of whole systems or environments, the involvement of the public in the decision-making process; design as open source creativity, and design as a synergistic fusion of art and science that may transcend both. His notion of 'designing without a product, as a process or way of living in itself' (1992, p. ix) is especially important, as it conflates the classical distinctions between designer and client, present and future, action and thing. However, some might find the styles and approaches of Fuller and Jones so different as to be incommensurate. Fortunately, as synergy emerges from difference, I believe they could be combined in a way that would help us to develop meta-designing as a framework for action.

ECONOMY VERSUS ECOLOGY

One of the obstacles to formulating a large-scale, optimistic ecological design agenda in the twenty-first century is the growth-cantered, economic mind-set that contaminates all new visions of the possible. While designers may have the capability to bring about a new ecological paradigm, their efforts are routinely subverted by what Harvey calls the 'creative-destructive tendencies inherent in capitalism' (2010, p. 46). Typically, although the 2005 'Cox Report' on creativity in business was important as a consciousness-raising exercise, it totally ignored its environmental implications (e.g., Cox and Dayan, 2005, p. 7). The dominant view of the world as an economic entity, rather than an ecological one, has meant that designers tend to be valued for their ability to maintain a competitive advantage for employers or economies, rather than for cultivating abundance for all. This is why many worthy initiatives, such as green design, eco-design, design for sustainability, and service design have, unwittingly, fortified the market forces they hoped to reform. As if this were not enough, markets dogmas have also shaped government policies that influence the way that designers are regarded, whether as learners or as professionals. Even if a positive paradigm change were easy to achieve, our old habits of thinking would probably make it seem elusive or obtuse. For example, while they know that the current economic system is causing massive environmental damage (c.f. Giddens, 2009), governments persist with what Douthwaite called the 'growth illusion' (1992, pp. 6–7), even though they know it fails to deliver lasting happiness (c.f. Easterlin, 1974; Layard, 2005) or wellbeing (c.f. Veblen, 1902; Oswald, 1997). While their attempts to address the problems, say, of climate change are often laudable, governments are too weak to change paradigms. This is because they lack imaginative coherence. Fiscal policies, targets, and legislative measures are too oversimplified, abstract, bureaucratic, and indirect to be effective (Meadows, 1999, pp. 163–4). This is why, in the United Kingdom, economist Nicholas Stern's views (2006) were taken more seriously than previous warnings by ecologists. The fiscal case in the Stern Report was that, while spending one per cent of GDP per annum on green infrastructure may seem costly, it would save us from having to spend 5 per cent of GDP if we ignore the problem (Stern, 2006, p. vi). However, this kind of top-down approach is based on truth-based assumptions rather than what some call 'designerly ways of knowing' (Cross, 2010, p. 5) or 'design thinking' (Rowe, 1987, p. 1), which tend to be more creative, opportunistic, and contingent

META-DESIGN

This chapter asserts that, if design as we know it were able to reinvent the fundamentals of the way we live—for example, to rethink our systems of production and consumption in a more integrated and coherent way—we might avert the threat of extinction. My interest in meta-design (c.f. Maturana, 1997) began in 1989, when we founded of the Department of Design at Goldsmiths, University of London. It grew from our attempts to challenge the customary methods of teaching designers as specialists. In 2002, the Higher Education Academy funded our exploration of the value of purpose-defined writing within/for the practice of art and design and helped us establish the international Writing-PAD Network in 2002 (Lockheart et al. 2004, pp. 89–102). After 2005, the Arts and Humanities Research Council (AHRC) and the Engineering and Physical Sciences Research Council (EPSRC) funded our more specific inquiries into meta-design. Since then we have conducted metadesign experiments and given public lectures in the United Kingdom, Germany, Portugal, Norway, Sweden, Switzerland, Korea, Japan, China, and Thailand. Our work also owes much to the previous insights of many others including Maturana (1997), Jones (1992), and Giaccardi (2005), who inspired the launch of the Meta-Designers Network. However, as most designers are trained for a relatively well-defined context or to limit their angle of vision to discrete products and services, we still have a great deal of work ahead before we can be confident that we can change paradigms or design miracles.

Because our agenda is complex and self-reflexive, we decided to redefine the purpose and meaning of design. When Aristotle described design as a 'final cause', he was expressing the ancient belief that the universe is defined by an ultimate, future purpose (Tarnas, 1991, pp. 60–62). Orthodox design is therefore a singular act that gains its raison d'être from the future. In today's rational, humanist terms, we might say that it is the designer's mind that anticipates, and strives to attain, a preferred state of affairs (Simon, 1969, p. 111). But Aristotle's theory reflected an era before anyone had conceived the idea of independent human creativity. For this reason, design was seen as a process of emulating nature in terms of an ultimate purpose. In short, it pictured the universe in a linear time frame. However, when we think of design in this way, we see two timescales, rather than one. The first is that of a local, short-term future that we might, for example, find in a project deadline. The second, much longer, timescale would be exemplified, perhaps, by the outcome of a project that is completed within its deadline. For designers, the second timescale might be interpreted as the scale of ecological damage that derives from the way consumers use, modify, or misuse their design once it is ready for use. Where Taylorism ignored these issues, it is increasingly important to reconcile short-term and long-term costs. These days, we must balance the benefits of journey and destination. Meta-designers would, therefore, seek to steer events for the present, as well as for the future. This process would be guided by feedback from both modes of future. Its complexity brings conditions that make it qualitatively different from Aristotle's model. In our version of meta-design, we explicitly resist the creation of desire for the future. This subverts the consumer paradigm. It makes it less of a discrete, predictive process and more of a collective seeding activity (Ascott in Giaccardi, 2005, pp. 342–9) that highlights opportunities that may have been unforeseen or, even, unforeseeable. Today, focusing on the traditional, short-term, purpose-based mode of design is easy because the consumer is accustomed to judging the success of a design by the aesthetics of its form and function. However, to achieve success within the second timescale, the designer must continue to redesign, or to manage, the 'design affordances' (Norman, 1988, p. 82) that are deemed to be immediately useful to consumers and other stakeholders. These always have unpredictable consequences that are a mixture of beneficial and harmful outcomes. The design of a more environmentally sustainable car is a good example. Despite its obvious environmental benefits at the local, short-term level, it may, nevertheless, attract more drivers away from public or human-powered transport systems and back onto the roads (Illich, 1975, p. 18). Where the classical Aristotelian designer would have designed mainly at the level of the product or service, the meta-designers seek to regulate many affordances and outcomes as they unfold over time. Managing this process ethically calls for a comprehensive, long-term approach that is beyond the capacity of any one individual, however gifted and well-informed she or he may be. We have, therefore, taken license to define meta-designing as a loose superset of any, or all, known design methods, plus other relevant expertise from elsewhere. The following list is offered as a working summary of some key attributes of metadesign (see Table 27.1).

A distinctive characteristic of meta-designing is its focus on synergy as a principal indicator of success, where synergy is defined as the 'behavior of integral, aggregate, whole

TABLE 27.1   TEN ATTRIBUTES OF THE META-DESIGN FRAMEWORK

METADESIGN FEATURE	PURPOSE
A new paradigm is needed	Piecemeal reform is not enough
'Languages' new realities	Paradigms exist partly in the mind
Eco-mimetic	Seeks inspiration from Nature
Seeks a synergy-of-synergies	Synergy is Nature's unique, free bonus
Comprehensive.	We need to join up all the parts
Adaptable and interoperable	Needs to be developed and applied by all
Collaborative	We must work alongside other experts
Present oriented	It is too complex to be predictive
Seeks fractal outcomes	We need to find our way around systems
Radically optimistic	We need to think beyond the possible

systems unpredicted by behaviors of any of their components or subassemblies of their components taken separately from the whole' (Fuller, 1979, p. 78). In practical terms, whenever we identify at least two different entities we may be able to combine them in order to get something extra, without requiring additional resources. As the term 'resources' is merely a subjective descriptor for aspects of the world that we find beneficial to our lifestyle, we may prefer to bring together problems, or even different points of view, in order to create beneficial synergies. In practical terms, this process is limitless (Simon, 1969, p. 166), which means that synergies can be combined to create an ultimate 'synergy-of-synergies' (c.f. Fuller, 1979; Wood, 2007c). Although this is ambitious, it is achievable, provided suitable resources are wisely combined. As synergies are elusive, meta-design teams would seek to map them by looking for anything that might help to locate, recreate, adapt, and orchestrate them. For example, consider the following:

1. imaginable, desirable synergies that do not yet exist
2. things that are complementary to one another (i.e., known compatibilities)
3. relative balance of ingredients to create affinities (e.g., precise culinary compatibilities)
4. synergistic relations that exist but that can produce additional benefits
5. possible synergies that do not yet exist and that may emerge from experiment
6. existing synergies that derive from a combination of other synergies
7. new synergies that might emerge by combining existing synergies

Although synergies may commonly exist at many levels, they may be hard to pinpoint. For example, they may adjoin one another or nest, imperceptibly, within one another (Corning, 2003, p. 298) and, therefore, defy easy description. Indeed, working with small teams, we found that some synergies exist on the intangible boundaries between emotions, ideas, people, actions, and objects. This creates a paradox, methodologically speaking. Unless you have clear definitions of the agent roles in a system of this complexity, you must rely on intuitive feelings that may be difficult to share with others outside your team. On the other hand, any attempt to define and classify roles will inevitably create precedents and assumptions that might blind you to latent synergies that have yet to be identified and named. Synergy is hard to harness (Goold and Campbell, 1998), as it is necessary to acknowledge the ineffable nature of many types of synergy. A systemic and eco-mimetic approach is useful, therefore, because it may inspire a less reductionist approach.

While, for example, fixed hierarchies are rare in nature, it is customary for business to create a hierarchy of roles in order to find economies of scale. By contrast, a meta-design approach evokes the idea of ecologies of scale rather than economies of scale. Ashby's 'Law of Requisite Variety' (1956, p. 207) implies that the self-management of an organization is preferable to micromanagement from the outside. When industrial organizations grow, they fragment into large, many-tiered hierarchies. This reduces what we call 'team consciousness', defined as the ratio of direct to indirect relations within the system. Another way to say this is that, de facto, a higher proportion of members become outsiders to the activities of their colleagues. When this happens, it becomes more difficult to orchestrate a 'synergy-of-synergies' (Backwell and Wood, 2011, p. 36). In our research, we avoided big hierarchies by developing small, heterogeneous, leaderless codesign teams. We also adapted management methods (e.g., Belbin, 2010, p. 120) to suit the purposes of meta-designing. In order to establish a basis for adaptable working relations, team members learn to diagnose their own interests, capabilities, and potentials, and to create possible roles within self-assembled teams. Unlike a commercial context, in which professional roles are usually predefined, a meta-design system would need to manage more intangible values, processes, and shared experiences in its own way. Participants would need to reflect upon and, perhaps, revise the assumptions, purposes, and terms of reference that brought them together. This includes learning how to orchestrate and co-steer a shared sense of wellbeing within a community of codesigners and stakeholders. A possible use for these methods is for acting as a creative bridge between the different discourses, say, of governments and grassroots activists.

PARADIGM CHANGING

It is very difficult to reform behaviour without also changing the paradigm that sustains it. Some readers may be confused by the word 'paradigm', as the ancient Greek word *paradeigma* (παράδειγμα) was long used to refer to patterns, models or exemplars, such as factory 'display models' used by managers and buyers. This had a more static meaning than we find in the twenty-first century sense of the word. Plato's understanding of a paradigm was based on his interest in the perfect uniqueness of ideas, models, and prototypes that he saw as being more true to the generality, or typology, of a vase or bed than to the actual (i.e., less perfect) production copy that reaches the street. In the early twentieth century, the linguistics theorist de Saussure expanded the word to describe a cluster of adjacent meanings and signs that constitute the structure, rather than the content, of what is said. When we substitute particular words in a sentence for other words, we may change the meaning without changing its structural paradigm (c.f. de Saussure, 1974). The later idea of semiotic paradigms meant that designers were not limited to words but could also use any other signs, such as sounds, smells, or gestures. This allows us to harness more senses and experiences in the thinking process and, thus, to create more imaginative possibilities.

In 1962, Kuhn published his research on the phenomenon of 'paradigm shift' (in Preston, 1995, p. 39), which is helpful in a metadesign context. He explored the idea of belief systems within science, noting that scientific academies and establishments fiercely resist change for inordinate lengths of time. Although this sense of the word still alludes to previous meanings, it is far more complex because it also acknowledges the systemic role of vested interests and other strong forces. Each paradigmatic discourse is upheld, in part, by particular experiments, theories, and vocabularies that have come to seem natural to proponents. According to Kuhn, scientific paradigms change only as a result of a full-scale revolution, in which the belief system in question is finally defeated by a huge weight of evidence and political pressure. Alternatively, the paradigm may perish when the generation that created it retires from power and gives way to a younger generation with different viewpoints. Kuhn's idea of paradigm change helps to explain why previous versions of sustainable design were too weak and fragmented to work. The old, Platonic idea of the paradigm assumed a singular, static identity and therefore was relatively easy to work with. By contrast, Kuhn's paradigms operate more like living organisms and are, therefore, extremely hard to compare with one another. To make things even more difficult, Feyerabend has pointed out that conventional research methods may also be inapplicable or incommensurate with them (1975, pp. 224–5; Wood, 2011, pp. 27–32). In the paradigm of urban architecture, for example, architects strive to create unique, individual styles, yet few challenge the use of concrete, steel, and glass, each of which has a massive energy, water, and carbon footprint. Ironically, while glass is excellent for harnessing solar energy, this design paradigm produces an embarrassing surplus. This means we need an additional source of energy to throw it away. In short, instead of refining the design of office blocks, what is needed is a better paradigm (Wood, 2007c). But this is not a trivial quest. At the systems level, paradigms are hard to change because of internal and external forces. Internally, they co-sustain one another. Externally, they also co-sustain other paradigms. Where, in eco-mimetic terms, these synergies are akin to symbiotic relations, in ethical, sociopolitical terms we might see them as expedient, vested interests. In the social example, this would probably need to be re-languaged in a way that sounds more affirmative.

How might we apply the modern notion of a paradigm within a meta-design project? We could start with the example of the private automobile. Here, instead of seeing cars as individual artifacts, we might try to see them as part of a larger, Taylorist paradigm (c.f. Fleischman, 2000, pp. 597–624). We could do so by describing the success of the automobile in eco-mimetic terms (Kauffman, 1995, p. 240).

At this systemic level, although the vehicle at the centre of Figure 27.1 is a 1912 Model T Ford, it could be substituted for a sustainable electric car or a gas guzzling SUV, as each

rapid response
hospital services

flat roads   roads
(tarmac)   **taxation**

accident   commuter belt
insurance   **housing estates**

epidemic   traffic news
strategies   **radio stations**

borderless   out-of-town
currencies   **supermarkets**

gas station   fast food
shopping   **industries**

weight-loss
therapies

FIGURE 27.1   Early mass-produced automobile, mapped onto codependent paradigms.

one is merely a different version of the same paradigm. Each requires the same infrastructure to co-sustain the way we shop, go to work, meet friends, or visit other places. This picture shows twelve systems that co-sustain the automobile. In addition to their co-sustainment with the automobile, each paradigm also has a relationship with the others. However, these are not weak, abstract relationships. They are codependent affinities that afford enduring habits of exchange. Maturana and Varela refer to this phenomenon as 'structural coupling' (1980, p. xxi), where the conduct of a given player is also a function of the conduct of the others in the system. As if this were not complex enough, Figure 27.2 offers a bigger snapshot of the whole paradigm. Each of the sixteen systems paradigms shown is, to a greater or lesser extent, structurally coupled to each of the others, as represented by a simple line. In practical terms, each line represents a complex amalgam of habits, beliefs, policies, and practices. In eco-mimetic terms, each organism will value and defend its own interests. This highly simplified diagram helps us to identify, and explore, a total of 120 structural couplings across the whole system. The combined force of these couplings illustrates the scale of difficulty we encounter when seeking to change the paradigm.

This amounts to a comprehensive set of changes that require simultaneous intervention at many locations within the paradigm. The mapping method used enables us to set up a detailed future-possible model that offers new benefits to all. Mapping the vested interests may enable us to broker multi-stakeholder deals that attract fundamental change by offering clear benefits to all concerned. In principle, redefining the agreed purpose of a paradigm should make it easy to change (Meadows, 1999, p. 18). However, social inertia

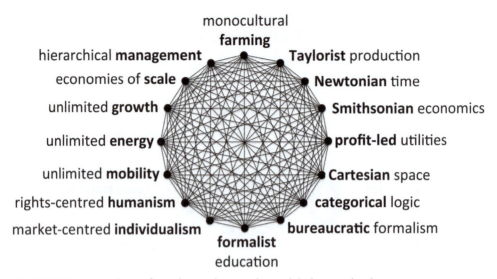

FIGURE 27.2   A paradigm-of-paradigms, showing that each links to each other.

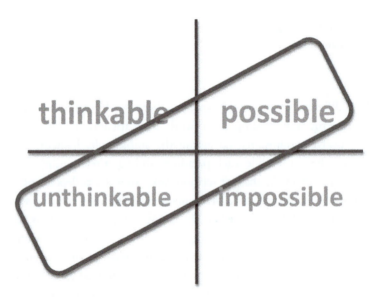

FIGURE 27.3   Mapping beyond the thinkable.

is co-sustained by the language and customs of the old paradigm, and these tend to mask opportunities, making them seem difficult, unthinkable, or impossible. Figure 27.3 illustrates one of the arguments meta-designers use in seeking to redraw the boundaries of professional practice. I use it to remind designers that many important innovations would have seemed miraculous or impossible to our ancestors. We may, therefore, need to look for new configurations that are 'unthinkable' but possible (Wood, 2007b).

If behaviour is normal, it is invisible to everyone, except outsiders to the culture, who may find it baffling or crazy. In social terms, paradigms are part of the unthought habits of the silent majority. Like many human habits perpetuated by subjective belief, there is a whole network of products, services, habits, and myths of language that sustain them. Our metadesign approach is based on the idea that, given the right team of experts, these could be re-languaged and/or redesigned.

LANGUAGING NEW PARADIGMS

The old idea that language co-sustains our reality by setting the boundaries for thought (c.f. Whorf, 1956; Lakoff and Johnson, 1980) is also implicit in von Uexküll's term 'Umwelt' (Ingold, 2011, p. 64), which sought to map the phenomenological boundaries that precondition a given living creature's worldview. This notion underpins the psychological and ecological notions of 'affordance' (e.g., Gibson, 1986, p. 16) that extends to the way that language operates. At the political level, re-languaging the status quo has proved very powerful as, for example, when Lemkin coined the term 'genocide' (McDonnell and Moses, 2005, pp. 501–29). Although his previous petitions to the United Nations had proved unsuccessful, the creation of this new word was enough to inspire a new international law. A similar approach was recently tested in a UK court, to ascertain whether 'ecocide' should be recognized as an international crime against species (Higgins, 2010, p. 61; Carrington, 2011). While, in design terms, the purpose of biological diversity is to maintain homeostasis for all life forms, diversity is in sharp decline. The COP10 meeting in Nagoya estimated that ecocidal damage by the world's top corporations cost the equivalent of $4 trillion in 2009 (Higgins, 2010, p. 65). Unfortunately, the methods used to confront the problem seem shockingly dysfunctional, perhaps because bureaucracy seeks to work with objective parameters by oversimplifying and rigidifying (c.f. Wood, 2011) its terms of engagement. But, if language plays such an important role in shaping and negotiating our perceived reality, it may be surprising that the role of writing and speaking has been so undervalued within the act of designing. This may have been caused by anti-theory sentiments (Wood, 2000, p. 1). At the social (e.g., codesign) level, Wittgenstein's idea of 'language games' illustrates the way that certain entities (words, or beliefs) gain favour in a consensual way (Brenner, 1999, p. 16). Some of our coauthorship approaches emulate ecological conditions by trying to ignore the conventional rational distinctions between knowledge, location, and team. We used the term 'sympoiesis' to show that the more profound stages of coauthorship are important within team building and in maintaining symbiotic relations (Nieuwenhuijze and Wood, 2006, pp. 87–102).

These approaches offer a discursive framework that refrains from critical or oppositional statements, that focuses on actions, opportunities, and outcomes, rather than on explanations, consistencies, truths, or taxonomies. Some of these methods invoke what I call 'auspicious reasoning' (Wood, 2009, pp. 315–27), which seeks to think outside the design box. They are inspired by the Darwinian logic behind the theory of Gaia (Lovelock, 1979, p. x; Margulis, 1998, p. 5), which depicts planet Earth as a vast, symbiotic, self-maintaining system. The Gaia theory's lack of distinction between living and inanimate offers a useful step toward re-languaging the design agenda at a high level. In nature, it is the variety, or diversity, of forms and conditions that enable the planet, as a whole, to regulate its own conditions for survival. When a given species cannot perceive and re-language new, emerging conditions that suit its habitat, it may die (Maturana and Varela, 1980, p. xvi). Extinctions are, therefore, normal and useful because they create a niche in the whole system that affords new, more appropriate patterns to emerge.

How might designers support the difficult task of government? Government representatives are powerful, but they are only type of agent within a set of participants. While individuals do their best to achieve the most favourable outcome, the combined process resembles a trading situation rather than a prudent act of collective reasoning. The process involves the use of scientific evidence to plot past, present, and future levels using an arithmetical language. Rather than radically rethinking the way we design our cities, economies, and food and energy chains, the international response by politicians and scientists seems to focus on making lists and setting targets and timelines. In 2010—the Year of International Biological Diversity—the 2010 Nagoya World Biodiversity Summit was successful in setting some targets, although few experts believe we will meet them (Gross and Williams, 2010, pp. 496–7). Missing targets is a common occurrence that adds to the task because it tends to create apathy and to discourage unanimous compliance with agreements. One of the problems in the current system is a fundamental ignorance about ecosystems. The traditional role of science is to provide sound, verifiable data upon which nations can audit what they do, then frame their strategies accordingly. In this case, however, the framing of policies based on sound evidence seems unlikely when 86 per cent of land species and 91 per cent of sea species remain undiscovered or unclassified (c.f. Mora et al., 2011). In order to encourage an increase in biodiversity, the Nagoya agreement designated large areas of land and sea as regions of wilderness. While this goes further than the largely bureaucratic requirements of the 1992 Convention on Biological Diversity—that is, making targets, inventories, taxonomies, budgets, timelines, and so on—it will not work because the natural replenishment of species in the areas chosen is too low (Harrop, 2011, pp. 117–28). Whether formal classification follows Linnaean, Darwinian, or other approaches, it need not and, indeed, should not, obscure the dynamic relationships among species. This is because the fluidity of relations among living creatures is an important aspect of how biodiversity arises and evolves through 'natural inclusion' as the 'fluid-dynamic, cocreative transformation of all through all in receptive spatial context' (Rayner, 2012, p. 6).

What might meta-designers and business leaders learn from the way that biological diversity co-sustains ecosystems? For one thing, it is important to manage creativities, diversities, and complexities at appropriate (i.e., local) levels within the industrial business context, allowing corporate hierarchies of immense size to simulate their appearance for PR purposes. This may mean asking governments to reward smaller-scale, cocreative endeavours for their ability to manage complexity. In theory, adding complexity to business could make it more profitable in the long-term but also more difficult. It means, for example, introducing parallel innovations that will intermesh with one another to create many layers of synergy. These might be sets of 'long-tail' enterprises (Anderson, 2006) that intersect in exquisitely ingenious ways over a long period. Single-product businesses will come to be frowned upon or even outlawed by governments as cash crop adventures that lack vision and, thus, are likely to be squandering common resources and opportunities. What is needed is a redesign of the fishing paradigm (i.e., a more selective system instead of one that exhausts limited stocks) by incorporating many more modes of business into existing practices. These should offer a greater variety of synergies and abundances to many more recipients.

SOME PRACTICAL IMPLICATIONS

The European Union has admitted that standard procedures have failed to manage the crisis of overfishing. It has failed to protect stocks, to provide a sustainable food source, and to help fishing communities to be profitable (c.f. Brown, 2011). One reason for this is that the players—for example, ship builders, fishing fleets, supermarkets, shoppers, and politicians—all see their primary task as securing a local, competitive economic advantage, rather than finding shareable synergies. All do their best, but the outcome is a disaster. For example, scientists give predictive data to politicians, knowing that the data may be manipulated before being used to set quotas for how many fish can be harvested. Fishermen do not want to throw dead fish back into the sea but have no alternative if they cannot fully control the type of fish they net. One answer is to introduce a meta-design approach in place of the targets, legal, and fiscal measures. Although we have sophisticated digital instruments for locating fish in the sea, the design of fishing nets has improved very little over thousands of years. A more entrepreneurial, eco-mimetic approach might look for a more selective trawl system that would only catch mature fish of known species and age. This is not offered as a smarter way to sustain business as usual in the fishing industries but, rather, a way to encourage more complex business systems that glean more value from each step in a long cycle of eco-friendly processes. Complementary clusters (c.f. Wood, 2007a) of business opportunities, such as maritime travels for a variety of interconnected reasons might include transport, marine biology cruises, or weekend breaks that include classes in, for example, filmmaking or cooking. One well-established approach is to turn the current linear, competitive, GDP-targeted system into a circular economy based on zero-waste or cradle-to-cradle models of business (e.g., Hawken et al., 1999, p. 9; McDonough and Braungart, 2002). More design-led approaches are already being developed by innovative service designers and by high-profile organizations, such as IDEO, McDonough and Braungart Design Chemistry (MBDC), the Young Foundation, and Participle. In an ideal scenario, this new breed of designers would be paid to work primarily on behalf of society and the biosphere, rather than for the vested interest and profit of individual organizations, which compete, rather than synergize with one another. The best way to achieve this would be for governments to ask designers to help deliver a more democratic, effective, and eco-cantered governance.

Many of the problems we face are caused by the paradigm of economic growth and a collective failure to imagine the world in a more coherent, joined-up way. Another way to put this is to say that we need to synchronize parallel innovations within 'networks of innovation' (Bussracumpakorn and Wood, 2010). This means understanding self-interest as a more relational, imaginative, long-term, and collective process. Our meta-design approach therefore seeks to replace the quest for objective data with more imaginative, shareable 'futures' that make sense within a cocreative presence, or 'presents' (Wood, 1998, pp. 88–101). How might meta-designers apply these ideas in a practical way? Let us start by seeking to synergize several problems into a new paradigm. For example, what are the hidden opportunities of connecting the water and energy utilities, clothing fashion, and cars? We might answer this question with a provocative riddle: what is the carbon footprint of rain? This may remind us that, in many developed countries, when it rains we prefer to drive short distances instead of walking. This behaviour is sustained, not by necessities of health or safety but by a shared assumption that masquerades as an aesthetic truth. Fortunately, the idea that rain is dangerous or unpleasant is subjective and therefore compliant to suggestion. In the United Kingdom, for example, it is sustained by the infectious habit of greeting others by maligning the rain. However, in Scandinavia they say, 'There is no such thing as bad weather, only bad'. This suggests that the fashion industry might enable us to gain more enjoyment from the rain without getting wet. While energy suppliers or water utility companies are not renowned for their inventive spirit, fashion designers are. Yet, despite their much-vaunted creativity, few fashion designers are taught how to innovate at an entrepreneurial business level. As one of our researchers put it, the fashion industry 'thrives on innovation' but 'resists change' (c.f. Tham, 2008). Here, what Barthes called the 'fashion system' (1983, p. 39) may also be thought of as a 'paradigm', in the sense that it consists of a network of agents whose ability to co-sustain one another is what creates resilience within the whole system. For example, if one rethinks the notion of clothing outside the fashion silo it might overlap with transport (e.g., wheelies), packaging (e.g., pockets), architecture (e.g., hoods), and energy creation (e.g., electrodynamic shoes or photovoltaic textiles) and so on, but these should then be integrated with other innovations, to create additional levels of synergy. These could be orchestrated to create an ultimate synergy-of-synergies.

REFERENCES

Anderson, C. (2006), *The Long Tail: Why the Future of Business is Selling Less of More,* Hyperion: New York.

Ashby, W. R. (1956), *Introduction to Cybernetics,* Chapman & Hall: London.

Backwell, J. and Wood, J., (2011), 'Catalysing Network Consciousness in Leaderless Groups: A Metadesign Tool', in Ascott, R. and Girão, L. M. (eds), *Consciousness Reframed 12, Art, Identity and the Technology of the Transformation,* University of Aveiro: Portugal, pp. 36–41.

Barthes, R. (1983), *The Fashion System,* trans. M. Ward and R. Howard, Hill & Wang: New York.

Belbin, R. M. (2010), *Team Roles at Work,* Butterworth-Heinemann: Oxford.

Benyus, J. (1997), *Innovation Inspired by Nature: Biomimicry,* William Morrow & Co.: New York.

Brenner, W. H. (1999), *Wittgenstein's Philosophical Investigations,* State University of New York, Series in Philosophy: New York.

Brown, P. (2011), 'UK Cod Collapse Due to Overfishing and Political Failure, Says Fisheries Expert', *Guardian,* <http://www.guardian.co.uk/environment/2011/sep/30/uk-cod-collapse-overfishing?> accessed September 30, 2011.

Brundtland, E. (1987), 'Our Common Future', Report of the World Commission on Environment and Development, <http://www.un-documents.net/wced-ocf.htm> accessed March 18, 2012.

Bussracumpakorn, C. and Wood, J. (2010), *Design Innovation Networks, Critical Factors that Can Contribute to Successful Collaborative Development of Innovative Products,* Lambert Academic Publishing: Saarbrücken, Germany.

Carrington, D. (2011), 'Trial Tests Whether "'Ecocide" Could Join Genocide as Global Crime', *The Guardian,* October 1, <http://www.guardian.co.uk/environment/damian-carrington-blog/2011/sep/29/ecocide-oil-criminal-court?CMP> accessed October 1, 2011.

Corning, P. (2003), *Nature's Magic: Synergy in Evolution and the Fate of Humankind,* Cambridge University Press: Cambridge.

Cox, G. and Dayan, Z. (2005), *Cox Review of Creativity in Business: Building on the UK's Strengths,* TSO: Norwich.

Cross, N. (2010), *Designerly Ways of Knowing,* Springer-Verlag: London.

de Saussure, F. (1974), *Course in General Linguistics,* Open Court Publishing: Peru, IL.

Dewey, J. (1939/1976), 'Creative Democracy: The Task before Us', in Boydston, J. (ed.), *John Dewey: The Later Works, 1925–1953,* vol. 14, Southern Illinois University Press: Carbondale. pp. 224–30.

Douthwaite, R. (1992), *The Growth Illusion,* Green Books: Dublin.

Easterlin, R. (1974), *Does Economic Growth Improve the Human Lot? Some Empirical Evidence',* in Nations and Households in Economic Growth: Essays in Honour of Moses Abramowitz, Academic Press: New York, London.

Fairclough, K, (2005), 'Ecozen', in Jones, H. (ed.), *Agents of Change: A Decade of MA Design Futures,* Goldsmiths College: London. p. 42.

Feyerabend, P. (1975), *Against Method,* Verso: London.

Fleischman, R. K. (2000), 'Completing the Triangle: Taylorism and the Paradigms', *Accounting, Auditing & Accountability Journal,* vol. 13, no. 5: pp. 597–624.

Freud, S. (1905/1991), *On Sexuality: Three Essays on the Theory of Sexuality and Other Works,* Penguin: Harmondsworth, UK.

Fuller, R. B. (1969), *Operating Manual for Spaceship Earth,* Southern Illinois University Press: Carbondale.

Fuller, R. B. (1979), *Synergetics: Explorations in the Geometry of Thinking,* Macmillan Publishing: New York.

Giaccardi, E. (2005), 'Metadesign as an Emergent Design Culture', *Leonardo,* vol. 38, no. 4: pp. 342–9.

Gibson, J. (1986), *The Ecological Approach to Visual Perception,* Lawrence Erlbaum Associates: New York.

Giddens, A. (2009), *The Politics of Climate Change,* Polity: London.

Goold, M. and Campbell, A. (1998), 'Desperately Seeking Synergy', *Harvard Business Review,* vol. 76, no. 5: pp. 130–43.

Gross, M. and Williams, N. (2010), 'Missed Targets', *Current Biology,* vol. 20, no. 12: pp. R496–R497.

Harrop, S. (2011), '"Living In Harmony with Nature?" Outcomes of the 2010 Nagoya Conference of the Convention on Biological Diversity', *Journal of Environmental Law,* vol. 23, no. 1: pp. 117–28.

Harvey, D. (2010), *The Enigma of Capitalism and the Crises of Capitalism,* Profile Books: London.

Hawken, P., Lovins, A. and Lovins, H. L. (1999), *Natural Capitalism,* Little, Brown and Company: New York.

Higgins, P., (2010), *Eradicating Ecocide: Exposing the Corporate and Political Practices Destroying the Planet and Proposing the Laws Needed to Eradicate Ecocide,* Shepheard-Walwyn: London.

Illich, I. (1975), *Tools for Conviviality,* Harper & Row: New York.

Ingold, T. (2011), *Being Alive; Essays on Movement and Description,* Routledge: New York.

Jones, J. C. (1992), *Design Methods,* 2nd ed., John Wiley & Sons: London.

Jones, J. C. (1998), Creative Democracy, with Extended Footnotes to the Future, *Futures,* vol. 30, no. 5: pp. 475–9.

Jones, J. C. (2012), 'Softopia', <http://www.softopia.demon.co.uk/2.2/designmethodsforeveryone.html> accessed March 12, 2012.

Kauffman, S. (1995), *At Home in the Universe, the Search for the Laws of Self-Organization,* Oxford University Press: New York.

Lakoff, G. and Johnson, M. (1980), *Metaphors We Live By,* University of Chicago: Chicago, London.

Landry, C. (2000), *The Creative City: A Toolkit for Urban Innovators,* Earthscan: London, Sterling, VA.

Layard, R. (2005), *Happiness. Lessons from a New Science,* Allen Lane: London.

Lockheart, J., Edwards, H., Raein, M. and Raatz, C. (2004), 'Writing Purposefully in Art and Design (Writing-PAD)', *Art, Design and Communication in Higher Education,* vol. 3, no. 2: pp. 89–102.

Lovelock, J. (1979), *Gaia: A New Look at Life on Earth,* Oxford University Press: Oxford.

Margulis, L. (1998), *Symbiotic Planet: A New Look at Evolution,* Basic Books: New York.

Maturana, H. R. (1997), 'Metadesign', <http://www.inteco.cl/articulos/metadesign.htm, Instituto de Terapia Cognitiva> accessed May 4, 2009.

Maturana, H. and Varela, F. (1980), *Autopoiesis and Cognition: The Realisation of the Living,* Boston Studies in Philosophy of Science, Cohen, R.S. and Wartofsky, M. W., (eds), Reidel: Boston, Vol. 42.

Maturana, H. and Varela, F. (1992), *The Tree of Knowledge: Biological Roots of Understanding,* Shambhala: Boston.

McDonnell, M. and Moses, D. (2005), 'Raphael Lemkin: The "Founder of the United Nation's Genocide Convention" as a Historian of Mass Violence', *Journal of Genocide Research,* vol. 7, no. 4: pp. 447–52.

McDonough, W. and Braungart, M. (2002), *Cradle to Cradle: Remaking the Way We Make Things,* North Point Press: New York.

Meadows, D., (1999), 'Leverage Points; places to intervene in a system', The Sustainability Institute, available at http://www.sustainer.org/pubs/Leverage_Points.pdf, accessed 14 August, 2009.

Mora, C., Tittensor D. P., Adl, S., Simpson, A.G.B. and Worm, B. (2011), 'How Many Species Are There on Earth and in the Ocean?' *PLoS Biol,* vol. 9, no. 8: pp. 100–27, <http://www.plosbiology.org/article/info%3Adoi%2F10.1371%2Fjournal.pbio.1001127> accessed April 1, 2012.

Nieuwenhuijze, O. and Wood, J. (2006), 'Synergy and Sympoiesis, Writing of Joint Papers; Anticipation with/in Imagination', *International Journal of Computing Anticipatory Systems,* vol. 10: pp. 87–102.

Norman, D. A. (1988), *The Design of Everyday Things,* Doubleday: New York.

Oswald, A. (1997), 'Happiness and Economic Performance', *The Economic Journal,* vol. 107, no. 445: pp. 1815–31.

Preston, J. (1995), 'Kuhn's The Structure of Scientific Revolutions Revisited', *Journal for General Philosophy of Science,* vol. 26, no. 1: pp. 75–92.

Rayner, A. (2012), *NaturesScope,* O Books: Winchester, UK.

Rowe, G. (1987), *Design Thinking,* MIT Press: Cambridge, MA.

Sachs, W. (2010), *The Development Dictionary: A Guide to Knowledge as Power,* Zed Books: New York.

Searle, J. (1970), *Speech Acts: An Essay in the Philosophy of Language,* Cambridge University Press: Cambridge.

Simon, H., (1969), *The Sciences of the Artificial,* 3rd ed., MIT Press: Cambridge, MA.

Stern, N. (2006), 'Summary of Conclusions', Stern Review Report on the Economics of Climate Change, <http://www.hm-treasury.gov.uk/d/CLOSED_SHORT_executive_summary.pdf> accessed March 1, 2012.

Tarnas, R. (1991), *The Passion of the Western Mind,* Pimlico: London.

Tham, M. (2008), 'Systems for Sustainable Fashion Moments. Mode, Tid och Ekologi: System för hållbara modeögonblick', in Bertilsson, C. and Hellmark, M. (eds), *Grön Design,* Natur-skyddsföreningen: Stockholm.

Veblen, T. (1902), *The Theory of the Leisure Class: An Economic Study of Institutions,* MacMillan: New York.

von Foerster, H. (2003), *Understanding Understanding: Essays on Cybernetics and Cognition,* Springer-Verlag: New York.

Whorf, B. L. (1956), *Language, Thought and Reality: Selected Writings of Benjamin Lee Whorf,* MIT Press: Cambridge, MA.

Wood, J. (1998) (ed.), *The Virtual Embodied; Presence, Practice, Technology,* Routledge: London, New York.

Wood, J. (2000), 'The *Culture of* Academic *Rigour:* Does Design Research Really Need It?' *Design Journal,* vol. 3, no. 1: pp. 44–57.

Wood, J. (2002), '(Un)managing the Butterfly: Co-Sustainment and the Grammar of Self', *International Review of Sociology: Revue Internationale de Sociologie,* vol. 12, no. 2: p. 1.

Wood, J. (2007a), 'Win-Win-Win-Win: Synergy Tools for Metadesigners', in Inns, T. (ed.), *Designing for the 21st Century, Interdisciplinary Questions and Insights,* Gower Publishing: London, pp. 114–28.

Wood, J. (2007b), *Design for Micro-Utopias; Thinking beyond the Possible,* Farnham, UK: Ashgate.

Wood, J. (2007c), 'Synergy City; Planning for a High Density, Super-Symbiotic Society', *Landscape and Urban Planning,* vol. 83, no. 1: pp. 77–83.

Wood, J. (2009), 'Auspicious Reasoning; Can Metadesign Become a Mode of Governance?' *Journal of Postcolonial Studies,* vol. 12, no. 3: pp. 315–27.

Wood, J. (2011), 'Languaging Change from Within; Can We Metadesign Biodiversity?' *Journal of Science and Innovation,* vol. 1, no. 3: pp. 27–32.

28

Imagination's Promise: Practice-Based Design Research for Sustainability

STUART WALKER

INTRODUCTION

The divorce of art from industry is the consequence of the divorce of business from morals, from ethics, from metaphysics, from any kind of wisdom, from goodness, from beauty.

(Gill, 1942, p. 75)

Perhaps the most important role for design today is to explore ways of reuniting our material world with a world of meaning—with ethics, inner growth, and spiritual well-being. Currently, we are far removed from such a conception of design, implicated as it is in an aggressively competitive, profit-centred corporate system that not only seems to have lost its moral compass but is also severely affecting the natural systems of the planet. In this world of unrestrained, consumer-based capitalism, material beauty has become merely the façade of technological progress, which is the dynamo of corporate growth. This superficial version of beauty conceals a ruinous path. It is a shallow, de-based beauty divorced from notions of goodness and right action; the outer aspect of a world of things alienated from perennial truths.

Within such a system, it is virtually impossible for the discipline of design to effectively and substantially address the interrelated issues of environmental responsibility, social obligation, and personal meaning. A quite different arena is needed, one in which new directions can be explored and more beneficent conceptions of material culture developed; conceptions that are more comprehensively considered in terms of nature, society, and self. This arena requires profit and other such motives to be set aside in order to encourage and value freedom of thought. It becomes necessary to explore an alternative path, one that contests a century or more of manufacturing and marketing conventions that are propped up by an increasingly untenable ideology. This is the ideology of progress and growth, which in reality tends to mean technological progress and growth in profits, with attendant growth in production, consumption, resource depletion, waste, pollution, and exploitation. Consequently, it is unrealistic to think we can formulate immediate solutions that would be either commercially feasible or pragmatically admissible within this existing production complex, not least because the norms and expectations of its ideology are still prevalent, powerful, and proving resistant to change. Instead, there is a need for creative exploration and the development of propositions that respond to the principles and ethos of sustainability. And such propositions require reflection and debate to ensure emerging directions are both substantive and robust.

In this context, for design to contribute in a significant way, we have to consider the role of design practice, which represents the creative core of the discipline. More specifically, we have to consider the role and place of design practice within design research and scholarship, and its potential contribution to knowledge advancement.

Design has relatively little history of academic research, and when we consider the role of practice, the term 'research' becomes somewhat problematic. Research is generally understood to mean the collection of information about and the systematic inquiry into a subject in order to discover facts and principles. Now, it is certainly true that design practice can be used to delve into a subject, to learn about process and material possibilities, and to probe areas of interest. However, the creative methods employed are rarely systematic, the collection of information may support but is not core to the activity, and facts are rarely discovered via this process—although it can lead to the development of principles and understandings about relationships. One cannot collect information and systematically inquire into and discover facts and principles about that which does not yet exist. This is a critical difference between traditional notions of research and the processes that are characteristic of the arts, including the applied arts. The essential core of creative design is not concerned with investigating what already exists but with envisioning what could be. It calls not on the power of rationalization and methodical examination but on the power of human imagination and open-minded exploration.

Nevertheless, the term 'design research' is widely used, and it will be used here—but with the understanding that it refers to a process that includes design practice as a creative mode of exploration, expression, and learning, coupled with learning from literature, debate, writing, and publication, and with critical thinking and reflection. Also, as with other practice-based disciplines, dedicated practice and the accumulation of experience can enhance accomplishment and contribution. Such a process might be better described by terms such as 'design scholarship' or 'scholarly research', both of which imply academic learning and attainment but without such strong connotations of systematic method and primary data acquisition. For the discipline of design, creative practice is a primary mode of discovery and a significant facet of the learning process, but, as we shall see, its contingent nature tends to defy systematization.

In this discussion, based on more than two decades of engaging in academic design practice, I describe how the activity of designing, as a component of the research methodology, can be a powerful way of probing, developing, and illustrating ideas and arguments. I explain the basis for creating propositional objects, and show that when such objects are developed within a fundamental design research agenda, they can be an effective means of challenging conventions, positing questions, and offering directions for reform. And, of course, any such reform must more effectively and more substantially align design practices with notions of material culture that conform to an ethos of sustainability. Therefore, I will consider in some detail how the creative and inherently unpredictable design process can further our understandings of a sustainable material culture by integrating disparate, often diverging, priorities into a unified whole. This aspect of the discussion is complemented by a series of exploratory objects, which serve to demonstrate the relationship between issues raised by sustainability and the design of functional artifacts. These examples also begin to indicate the potential of propositional design to advance knowledge.

PROPOSITIONAL DESIGN'S CONTRIBUTION
TO DESIGN RESEARCH

It is incumbent on design to develop discipline-appropriate research modes that can confront the challenges raised by sustainability, advance knowledge, and contribute to new understandings. For the reasons indicated above, it may not be able to do this effectively within professional practice. However, it can do so within academic, research-based practice. In this context, design engagement has to be included as an essential ingredient of the research methodology because without it we are not being true to the discipline and its particular modes of thinking and doing. These modes are vital to the development of creative ideas and insights, and to the development of design knowledge, whether explicit or tacit. Moreover, as an element of a research methodology whose purpose is primarily exploratory and conceptual, the activity of designing should be regarded less as a problem-solving activity and more as a question-asking activity. By bringing together a variety of ideas and, through creative practice, translating them into tangible form, questions can be raised about the nature of material culture in relation to sustainability or, indeed, in relation to any other issue of concern. The resulting artifacts, which are effectively questions-in-form, exist within a continual process of exploration, debate, and knowledge development.

To include designing as a bona fide constituent of an academic research methodology, we must be clear about its purpose, its mode of progression, and its potential contribution within a comprehensive research process.

Many forms of academic inquiry adopt a procedure that includes breaking down the topic into its constituent elements, categorization, investigation, and prioritization. This is an analytical approach to research. Designing, however, is concerned less with analysis than with synthesis. It composes, organizes and constructs, and resolves and integrates disparate factors. It is concerned with the entirety and seeks articulation by sensitive consideration of the whole, taking into account factors such as function, aesthetics, and materials. In the process, the designer is realizing, discerning, becoming aware of hitherto unknown or unrecognized relationships and connections, and discovering through a symbiotic, creative process of thinking and doing.

As an element of design research, the role of designing is to manifest the implications of abstract arguments through the creative process—through imagination and postulation—by combining particular elements and materials into specific forms and expressions, based on rigorously developed general theses and criteria. The results of such work are not design solutions but design propositions that ask us to consider if this or that synthesis is a useful contribution to our developing understandings of where design could and, more importantly, should be heading. Such propositions can enable us to see things in new ways, to question our assumptions, to grasp new possibilities and directions. They constitute a holistic, nontextual form of expression that encompasses and conveys ideas, arguments, and possibilities. Hence, this kind of noncommercial, academic, research-based designing, together with its outcomes, can be termed propositional design.

The purpose of propositional design is to pose questions about our material culture, to challenge industry conventions and disciplinary norms, and, importantly, to offer constructive possibilities that begin to tease out a different path. Such propositions can probe, stimulate debate, and begin to open up new design directions. As such, propositional design has a dual function—first, it offers critique of the existing condition, and second, it poses questions-in-form as to how these criticisms might be constructively addressed. It is a key element of a research approach that also includes theoretical discussion and advancement through reasoned argument, together with continual reflection on the relationship between general, theoretical, abstract ideas and specific, tangible design outcomes.

This type of propositional design is similar in several respects to what Dunne refers to as 'critical design' (Dunne, 2005, p. 63). These kinds of practice, which are characteristically conceptual, are used to explore alternative notions of material culture. They can address a wide variety of issues and concerns, and they might employ a range of approaches. Dunne and Raby, for example, focus on the 'social, cultural and ethical implications of existing and emerging technologies' by employing satire, extrapolating trends, sounding a cautionary note about possible futures, and blurring 'the boundaries between the real and the fictional' (Dunne and Raby, 2011; Dunne, 2005, p. 84).

The approach taken in this present discussion, of propositional design within a research agenda centred on sustainability, employs a rather different process and has a distinctive emphasis and tenor. Its focus is the (ever-changing) present, rather than possible technological futures. And it emphasizes enduring notions of human meaning through quiet interventions that aim to achieve a harmony between our material culture and nature, society, and self. In doing so, it draws on contemporary sources as well as long-standing philosophical and spiritual traditions. While it tends not to employ satire or fiction, it does centre on advancing design knowledge through the researcher's direct engagement in the creative thinking-and-doing design process. As a significant aspect of a larger research approach, in which design artifacts emerge from and contribute to theory, particular emphasis is placed on the interplay among theorizing, designing. and reflecting (Figure 28.1) (see Walker, 2011, pp. 125–41):

- Theorizing: developing sound theoretical positions through reasoned argument and analysis, articulating the potential implications of these arguments for material culture, and developing intentions and criteria for design engagement. This aspect of the research process requires contextualization and extensive reading, writing, and thinking, all of which are carried out in conjunction with designing and reflecting on emerging outcomes.
- Designing: the transmutation of the theoretical implications and criteria into design propositions that encompass and express ideas, and which ask if these discrete manifestations offer cogent and constructive contributions or directions forward. This phase utilizes design and visualization skills involving materials, sketching, making, and manifesting.

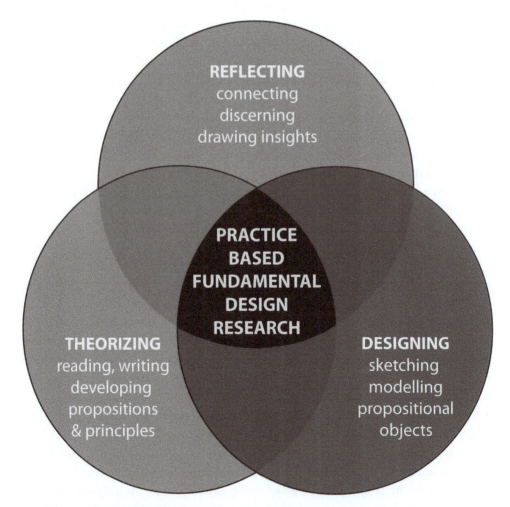

FIGURE 28.1   Practice-based fundamental design research.

- Reflecting: pervading the whole process, contemplation of the theoretical ideas and criteria, and reflecting on the propositional outcomes can connect up and synthesise the endeavour and act as a springboard for subsequent phases of research. Reflecting on the readings, writings, and design propositions involves periods of contemplation where seemingly nothing is being done. However, valuing and giving time to reflection can yield spontaneous, intuitive awarenesses and sudden insights in which discontinuities and discordances become unified and harmonies are found. Reflection is critical to the process and, like the activity of designing, it is also a practice-based activity, which benefits from discipline, persistence, and experience.

This creative, propositional ingredient enables design research to encompass the full span of the discipline and comprehensively address its various aspects, from the logical and the diagnostic to the emotional and the aesthetic. For this reason, designing can be seen as an essential ingredient of an holistic design research approach that combines the following:

- rational analysis, cognitive knowledge, and explanation with intuitive decision-making, tacit knowledge, and expression; and
- theory and general principles with discrete, case-specific syntheses.

Within this approach, critique of the existing condition is inevitable, while also being urgently necessary if the relationship between the design of our material culture and the principles of sustainability is to be confronted. However, design is also a creative discipline and tends to be inherently constructive and optimistic. The development of propositional objects within practice-based research remains true to this hopeful, positive spirit. It is a phase of the process that requires the researcher to wrestle with current shortcomings and new opportunities through imaginative practice. And it results in discipline-appropriate outcomes that articulate the implications of arguments and provide a focus for discussion and further development.

Through such means, design research can offer alternative conceptions of material culture that rest on a firm footing of reasoned argument and scholarly inquiry. Moreover, within academia, design has the freedom to embrace arenas of human apprehension that have long been excluded from conventional, too-narrowly defined notions of product.

For these reasons, propositional design, together with other forms of critical design that may emphasize rather different priorities and processes, can be viewed as essential elements of design research that seeks to advance ideas and knowledge about the practices, products, and potential of design.

These forms of academic designing are so essential to design research because when we engage in the creative process of designing we are dealing with the intimate relationships between materials, form, aesthetics, and intention as we strive to find synthetic resolution within the particularities of specific propositions. Without this creative engagement, any implications, findings, or recommendations from theoretical arguments remain untransmuted, untested, and uninformed by the tacit knowledge, intuitive decision-making, and expressive sensitivity that designing can bestow. The doing of design can inform the knowing about and knowing from design; one learns and apprehends significance through the process of doing. Without the doing, this knowledge remains unrecognized and unrealized. As we engage in the process of designing, we move from one sphere and scale of expression to another—from general theory and abstract ideas to specific manifestation and concrete expression. Yet, despite this change in mode of expression, we are still attempting to articulate ideas and conclusions that emerge from academic inquiry, reasoned argument, and creative exploration.

It becomes clear that the role of the propositional object within academic design research can be quite different from that which we normally associate with product design. It is not an overture for a stand-alone product intended for use by a third party. In commercially oriented or applied design research, object concepts and product proposals are commonly used to gauge people's responses—through focus groups, surveys, or observational studies. This kind of qualitative data acquisition is not necessarily appropriate for propositional objects that explore and express theoretical ideas within an academic research agenda; this is a form of fundamental or pure design research rather than applied. By way of comparison, we would not normally gather qualitative data to gauge people's responses to a set of findings from a research paper. Instead, such conclusions are disseminated via conference presentations, journal papers, and books, and the validity and value of the conclusions are assessed by an informed audience of peers. Propositional objects, as an element of fundamental design research, can be treated in the same way (see later).

Propositional Design in Fundamental, Rather than Applied, Design Research

When the design researcher engages in propositional design practice within an agenda of fundamental design research, the aim is to develop an ongoing series of probes—each new creative exploration building on the insights and reflections stimulated by preceding design explorations, literature reviews, and research papers, together with new ideas and information from additional sources. In this way, propositional design becomes an essential contributing element within an integrated and cumulative process of inquiry, learning, and knowledge advancement.

Hence, academically based propositional design practice differs in purpose and outcome from commercial design practice. Each designed artifact is

- a provisional resolution of continually evolving issues, insights, and considerations;
- incomplete in itself—it is always supplemented with theoretical arguments, and so on;
- intimately linked to the preceding and the following theses and design explorations; and
- regarded as a question or propositional query rather than a conclusion or solution.

In addition, over time, a succession of sketches and object propositions is accumulated and this too can be revealing and contribute to knowledge. The twists, turns, and developments—when reviewed *in totum*—can yield further insights, which may have gone unrecognized while immersed in each of the incremental stages of the work.

And as I hope to demonstrate, by incorporating creative work within a broader design research process that focuses on sustainability, the discipline can begin to demonstrate how functional objects might become more comprehensive and more substantive expressions of human meaning and purpose.

PROPOSITIONAL DESIGN'S CONTRIBUTION TO KNOWLEDGE

We see that propositional design practice can be part of a comprehensive design research process that comprises theorizing—designing—reflecting. However, for such design practice to be considered a legitimate element of research, it has to contribute in some way to the advancement of knowledge and the development of understanding. Therefore, let us consider three interrelated sources of potential knowledge that are specifically associated with the creative activity of designing:

1. knowledge attained from the creative designing process
2. knowledge attained from the artifacts of the designing process
3. knowledge attained from a body of work

1. Knowledge Attained from the Creative Designing Process

The design process, like any creative activity, is open-ended and unpredictable (Rust et al., 2007, 13). It follows its own path and its own pace. It cannot be hurried, and it is often rather uncomfortable, for the very reason that one does not know where it is going or, indeed, if it is going anywhere. There is an inherent and unavoidable element of risk; it requires ways of working that cannot be planned in detail. One is following one's nose, as it were, allowing the process to unfold. One proposition leads to another, one reading or piece of writing leads to sketches or three-dimensional studies that, in turn, generate more writing, reading, drawing, and making. The path is characterized by twists, turns, backtracks, sidetracks, and dead-ends (Figure 28.2). To identify its potential contribution to research and scholarship, knowledge that may be acquired from this process must be distinguished from existing knowledge that we may bring to the process. We must also try to identify any discipline-specific contributions to knowledge that may not be acquired by other, nondesign means.

Existing knowledge can include procedural knowledge (knowing how to do something), declarative knowledge (rules and methods to be applied), and heuristic knowledge (rules of thumb) (Rogers and Clarkson, 1998). Engagement in the process of designing will often incrementally add to these kinds of knowledge. Additionally, in the research context, when we refer to knowledge it is common to think of facts or data obtained by applying investigative methods that separate out information about a subject

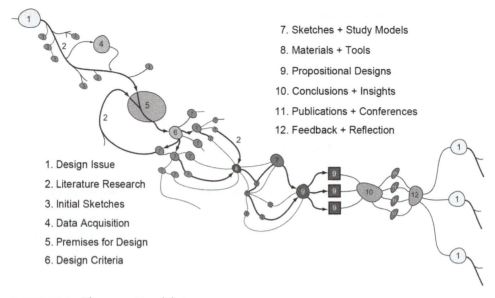

7. Sketches + Study Models

8. Materials + Tools

9. Propositional Designs

10. Conclusions + Insights

11. Publications + Conferences

12. Feedback + Reflection

1. Design Issue

2. Literature Research

3. Initial Sketches

4. Data Acquisition

5. Premises for Design

6. Design Criteria

FIGURE 28.2 The propositional design process.

into its constituent elements. This type of explicit knowledge is acquired by employing analytical techniques. Such methods and techniques, which may precede or interpose the creative designing process, are used in many other disciplines, and therefore the kinds of knowledge they may yield are not distinctive to the activity of designing. Such procedures can just as easily be implemented, and the resulting information and knowledge acquired, without recourse to design expertise.

The types of knowledge to be gained from the creative process of designing tend to be less dependent on analytical techniques and are often less explicit; in fact, they are usually rather difficult to articulate. They include knowledge gained from immersing oneself deeply in the process, familiarizing oneself with a variety issues and considerations pertinent to the inquiry, and then exploring possibilities through expressive means by externalizing and visualizing ideas. The process is one in which relationships are spontaneously recognized between previously unconnected ideas, resonances occur, and discoveries are made. It is also a process that includes serendipity. The designer is continually generating ideas, making connections, and attempting to separate out the wheat from the chaff to effectively express the essence of the issues under consideration. In identifying and clarifying the crux of the matter being addressed, there are periods of discernment and points of realization. Through such means, new insights are gained, new ideas emerge, and new knowledge is developed. One aspect of this is a knowledge of congruities and harmonious composition, rather than a detailed knowledge of separate parts. During the process, the designer gains a new awareness, a new comprehension of possibilities. Associations are revealed and connections are made that are intuitively regarded as appropriate or right in the context of the project. Hence, engagement in designing enables learning and discovery through doing. In this way, design practice cultivates and incrementally adds to knowing how as well as to knowing what, and we can also know from doing design because the process allows us to make new realizations that would otherwise remain unacknowledged.

The difference between the kinds of knowledge attained from analysis (breaking apart, separating out) and from synthesis (bringing together, working in unison) is exemplified in other activities that, like design, require a combination of practice and creative sensitivity. For example, we can explain to someone how to play a musical instrument. We can describe in minute detail the principles involved, the physical actions required, and the musical notation. They may be able to accept and understand all these things intellectually, but they will only be able to play the instrument with any degree of proficiency once they have spent long hours practicing and learning through direct experience—in other words, once they know how to do as well as know what to do. However, they will only be able to make an original, creative contribution if they use that proficiency to challenge conventions and probe and explore new directions. They have to be not only technically proficient but also sufficiently experienced, sensitive, and motivated if they are to employ their know-how in creative, expressive ways that add to our understandings through an originality of expression or contribution. The same is true of the creative design process, which includes the designer's skills and experience in combination with an informed basis for challenging conventions and exploring new areas. These aspects of the designer's particular knowledge partly reside in knowing what (intellectual understandings) and knowing how (practical techniques and skills) but also include knowing from doing design—that is, learning, understanding, and developing knowledge during the use of intellectual knowledge and practical skills and techniques in the process of designing. As such, these creative, expressive knowing-from-doing aspects of the discipline represent vital ingredients of 'designerly ways of knowing' (Cross, 2001).

It becomes apparent that, when propositional design is included as a significant element of design research, a number of important contributions are assimilated into the research procedure that would be difficult or impossible to incorporate by other means. In moving from theory to the activity of designing, a shift is made from explicit knowledge in the form of text-based explanations and descriptions, data analysis, and intellectual arguments to form-based manifestations, aesthetic harmonization, and intuitive knowledge. Rationalized lines of reasoning, objectivity, and cognitive ways of knowing become complemented by experiential knowledge, spontaneous insight, and direct discernment in the expressive exploration and development of a unified whole through the implementation of practical techniques and skills. Linear, logical thinking takes second place to integrative thinking and contemplation. Hence, by incorporating creative design practice in the research process, explicit intellectual knowledge is combined, via practical knowledge or know-how, with implicit tacit knowledge. Tacit knowledge is not learned via rational, logical means but is developed through practice, experience, perception, and feeling during the unifying process of designing. It is informally acquired; one may not even be aware of it or its process of acquisition (Blackler et al., 2010). Synthesis of ideas into a unified propositional artifact is an outcome of engaging in designing in order to develop knowledge. Polanyi, a key authority on tacit ways of knowing, regards this process of integration as the critical contribution of the tacit dimension and the basis of all knowledge development and advancement (Polanyi, 1966, p. 7).

The aim of practice-based design research for sustainability is to probe and delineate key issues and to explore new directions for material culture. In this process, the creation of propositional artifacts requires aesthetic (sense-based) judgments. Consequently, human emotions (feelings about the emerging object) will play some part in determining the artifact's expressive qualities. In many respects, this is entirely appropriate because one requirement of sustainability is that we take a more comprehensive approach to our endeavours. Within the designing process, emotions can influence the particularities of expression and will be an ingredient in determining the essential nature of the object; I expand on this later.

Hence, the design process can be understood as a way of becoming intimately familiar with and knowing about an area of concern. The designer builds this familiarity by engaging in the creative process of thinking and doing, and in this way new knowledge and insights are gained. We might refer to these as 'the knowledge and insights of synthesis'; they encompass a comprehension of the issues together with a clear or deep perception about how they might be combined into a unified whole. If they are to be useful and be open to scrutiny, these insights and knowledge, which include tacit ways of knowing that may not be expressible in words, have to be articulated in some manner. And the most appropriate mode of articulation is the designed artifact itself.

2. Knowledge Attained from the Artifacts of the Designing Process

It is important to recognize that the meanings of creative works are not explicit but are open to interpretation, and to misinterpretation. However, unlike creative works in a gallery or on a store shelf, in the context of design research creative propositional works are elements within a broader research process. They are complemented by arguments and explanations, not necessarily of the work itself but of the ideas underlying and being addressed in the creative work. In this way, the explicit and the tacit, the analytical and the synthetic, and the intellectual and the intuitive—which represent different ways of encountering the world, different ways of understanding, and different aspects of being human—contribute to the advancement of knowledge.

The artifacts that emerge from the designing process represent attempts to encompass and express ideas and areas of concern via a unified form. As elements of fundamental design research, such propositions must be considered and critiqued in a rather different way from the artifacts of applied design. The factors relevant to commercial projects, such as economic viability, manufacturability, market appeal, positioning, brand recognition, and ergonomics, are of little import here. Instead, the concern is with the conceptual nature of material culture.

In the context of this present discussion, such design work can aim to offer original insights about existing products in relation to sustainability, or about how new products might be created so as to be in closer accord with sustainability. In contemplating the work, we might ask if it enables us to see and understand the issues from fresh perspectives and in ways that are useful and valuable. If so, we can consider how it is doing this and what is the nature of those insights and understandings. For instance, the propositional design work might suggest the following:

- a way of seeing older, unwanted products anew, and revaluing them;
- a beneficial approach to how we view or use materials and how, or indeed if, we process materials for use in products;
- a new language of design that has implications for how we conceive of products;
- how localization, an important aspect of sustainability, can be integrated into a globalized manufacturing system; and
- how deeper notions of human meaning—the communal, the compassionate, the ethical, and the spiritual—might be inculcated into our material culture.

Hence, propositional artifacts can enable us to become deeply familiar with the ways in which design can contribute to sustainability. Knowledge is gained from looking at, using, and interacting with the artifacts—reflecting on their presence, their qualities of articulation, their meanings, intentions, and intimations. If the work encapsulates and manifests ideas in creative ways, then it will make us aware—enable us to know—of new possibilities. It may demonstrate new ways of addressing the issues, or represent an entirely different, more sustainable system for making material culture.

Any contributions to knowledge are encompassed in the particular objects under scrutiny, and the conventional way of determining the merit and contribution of such knowledge is through a process of informed critique and review.

3. Knowledge Attained from a Body of Work

As we have seen, in this kind of creative research one idea or development tends to follow on from what has gone before in an unpredictable manner. When immersed in a particular practice-based project or stage of exploration, the researcher might be unaware of the changes that are occurring over time. Therefore, potentially, there are new understandings, insights, and knowledge to be acquired by examining a body of work developed over an extended period. Key changes, points of departure, or stages of realization may be identified. Hitherto unrecognized insights may be perceived and, in the process, new knowledge is acquired. This kind of knowledge might not be evident if we examine just one instance of design practice, one artifact, or even a limited range of artifacts. But by standing back and reviewing a body of work, we may become aware of significant transformations, or see a gradual emergence of qualitative differences in approach, materials, form, or modes of expression. Then we can consider what these observations might mean, what they signify, and what they might suggest for taking the work forward.

Hence, design knowledge can be attained from a longitudinal examination of the propositional artifacts emerging from practice-based research. Along with the agendas attached to the specific artifacts, it may be possible to build up a comprehensive under-standing of the factors that can affect, and the possibilities for, design for sustainability.

Critique and Modes of Evaluation

Normally, when a particular stage of academic research reaches a natural endpoint, one or more scholarly papers are developed that describe the issues, methods, and findings. And recommendations are made that may provide a basis for the next stage of the re-search. Implicitly, such findings and recommendations ask questions of the reader, who in the first instance would usually be a peer reviewer—that is, a person qualified to judge its merits and contribution. For example, do the findings hold water? Are they reason-able, given the accompanying explanation, arguments, and method? Are they valid? Are they original and/or significant? And are the recommendations reasonable given the findings?

The propositional object within practice-based design research can have exactly the same function. The mode of expression is different, and it necessarily encompasses as-pects that are particular and essential to the discipline but that lie beyond rational, ana-lytical explanation. Even so, the propositional object is a form of research finding; it is an expressive encapsulation of reasoned arguments and criteria that address a particu-lar set of issues. As such, the propositional object can provide a basis for the next stage of the research, and it asks questions of the reader/viewer. Does this proposition hold water? Is it reasonable, given the accompanying explanation, arguments, and design cri-teria? Is it a valid synthesis and expression of the issues being addressed? Does such a synthesis offer an original or useful contribution to our understandings?

The usual procedure for obtaining peer review is via papers submitted to academic conferences or, particularly, scholarly journals. It may be possible to obtain peer review by other means, such as through exhibition, but this can be more problematic because such forms of review do not generally fit so readily into established academic norms. Moreover, this kind of propositional design work is only part of a research process that also includes development of theory, and reflection. Propositional artifacts in the aca-demic context are not stand-alone items. Therefore, all these elements need to be articu-lated if the peer reviewers are to properly evaluate the soundness and significance of the work. This integration of propositional artifacts via designing combined with theoreti-cal development and discussion via writing is a distinctive characteristic of the research process. However, it is an approach that is not widely recognized, even in discussions of practice-led research (Rust et al., 2007), nor does it fit comfortably into Frayling's three categories of research into, through, or for design (Frayling, 1993/1994).

Depending on the particular issues being addressed and the methods used, appraisal of the propositional artifacts would refer to some or all of the following considerations:

- the qualities of its language, its ambience, the nature of its essential condition as a thing;
- the precision and clarity of its articulation with respect to the intentions;

- the qualities of the materials and the making and their appropriateness with respect to the intentions;
- the composition, harmony of the form, and aesthetic qualities of the whole;
- the originality, and the value and significance of this originality with respect to the intentions; and
- the overall contribution to our understandings through and of design.

In other words, we must ask if the designed artifact, in conjunction with the accompanying arguments and intentions, is effective in encompassing, demonstrating, and furthering our understandings and knowledge of the issues under scrutiny. In this regard, it is important to recognize that a designed artifact asserts both its own existence and the ideas and values that it embodies, and together these can be a persuasive means of expressing arguments, scholarly findings, and original directions forward. Buchanan has referred to this as 'declaration by design', which he describes as a form of 'epideictic or demonstrative rhetoric'—a form of argument that stems from norms and materials of the past and suggests possibilities for the future but is, nevertheless, primarily addressing attitudes and approaches of the present (Buchanan, 1989).

Hence, within the field of design scholarship, propositional artifacts can provide a means of embodying issues of concern and reflecting on their implications. In turn, this can foster additional lines of inquiry, generate further readings and fresh arguments, and lead to new avenues of creative exploration. Significantly, because propositional artifacts are capable of embodying intuitive decision-making and modes of expression together with emotional and tacit ways of knowing, in addition to more explicit ways of knowing, they can make an original and discipline-appropriate contribution to the advancement of design knowledge. Such knowledge cannot be acquired solely through conventional intellectual and analytical methodologies.

PRACTICE-BASED DESIGN RESEARCH FOR SUSTAINABILITY

Let us now consider more specifically how the creative research process can be applied to the area of sustainability and what it might tell us about our conceptions of material culture.

We have seen over the course of the last few decades various developments that in some manner have addressed design for sustainability, including design for human ecology and social change (Papanek, 1971/1985), green design (Burrall, 1991), ecological design (Van der Ryn and Cowan, 1996; Fuad-Luke, 2002/2006), and sustainable design (Datschefski, 2001), to name but a few. These have been accompanied by a host of procedures for designing differently, many of which, in one way or another, consider the whole life cycle of products. These developments in design have helped raise understandings and awareness, and have generated a host of examples and innovative possibilities.

Today, there is a wide variety of products being produced that attempt to respond to the challenges posed by sustainability. These include solar-powered and hand-cranked products that avoid use of disposable batteries; electric cars that reduce distributed exhaust emissions, products made from recycled materials, and products that replace other, less sustainable products—such as cloth grocery bags instead of disposable carriers. While these kinds of commercially available products can incrementally ameliorate certain aspects of our ways of living, we must be cautious of directions that seem to suggest that we can consume our way to sustainability. In this respect, within the existing paradigm, many greener products can actually be counterproductive because they tend to support rather than challenge consumption-based ways of living that are fundamentally, and often grossly, unsustainable.

In addition to incremental changes, we have to look beyond current ways of living, accepted ideas of material goods, and traditional notions of design. Practice-based academic inquiry represents an important and germane way of doing this because it endorses the creative process and gives rein to human imagination. Given the scales of social inequity and environmental damage associated with contemporary consumption-based lifestyles, academic research in design for sustainability is duty bound to explore radically different possibilities. Directions must be developed that challenge the ideologies, ways of understanding the world, and notions of human purpose that permeate contemporary culture, all of which are intimately tied to our inherently unsustainable ways of living. Such explorations involve environmental considerations, social concerns, and economic issues, and bring to the fore ideas about socioeconomic justice, localization, and design for and from place, and product-service relationships.

Also, as I have previously argued, in common with a number of other authors, deeper notions of human meaning, inner development, and spiritual wellbeing are vital to a more comprehensive understanding of sustainability. The inadequacies of our current approaches are linked to a lack of appreciation of these deeper issues and the development of the inner self (Schumacher, 1973, pp. 44–51; Papanek, 1995, pp. 49–74; Orr, 2003; Senge et al., 2005, p. 66; Walker, 2011). Our most profound notions of human meaning defy rationalistic understandings and lie beyond, but are not incompatible with, reason, and they resist analysis. They therefore lie outside the scope of scientific inquiry and philosophical positions that give credence only to naturalistic materialism, as well as the constraints imposed by evidence-based research methodologies. Nevertheless, they have always been vital ingredients of human understanding and wellbeing and are critical aspects of the world's most enduring philosophies, worldviews, and spiritual traditions. They represent vital aspects of being human and, therefore, must be included as significant, if not critical, ingredients of any comprehensive notion of sustainability.

It is here that the intuitive, tacit, creative design process can make an important contribution to understandings and knowledge. Through engagement in the design process, propositional objects can be developed that grapple with these ideas, transmute their implications, and begin to express inherently ineffable notions and apprehensions through visualization, manifestation, and form. Such artifacts can encapsulate and synthesize ideas and indicate new possibilities and new realizations through nonverbal, visual means. As such, they can be a powerful means of demonstrating alternative ways of thinking about the world and can point in directions that are more holistic and, potentially, more fundamentally sustainable in their ethos. In this way, through the continual development of intellectual understandings in conjunction with creative design propositions and probes, design knowledge for sustainability can be advanced. Moreover, it can be advanced in a manner that embraces the human imagination and is more comprehensively representative of human understandings and potential than is possible if we restrict our notions of research to intellectual approaches, rationalistic arguments, and evidence-based criteria.

Indeed, if inner development and spiritual growth are key to deeper understandings of sustainability, these aspects simply cannot be effectively addressed or expressed via techniques that rely solely on intellectual argument, data acquisition, and analysis. Outer knowledge that is concerned with utilitarian needs and acting in the world has to be complemented with inner knowledge, and being rather than doing or having. As in the creative process itself, apprehension of these inner ways of knowing is also tacit, experiential, and intuitive—and inner progress is critically dependent on individual discipline and practice. Understandings of inner development, which in all cultures has been long associated with our most profound notions of meaning, are traditionally expressed in symbolic rather than literal forms because such apprehension is intuitively recognized but lies beyond description or explanation.

While these deeper aspects of human awareness and knowledge, and their potential relationship to sustainable forms of material culture, cannot be effectively or wholly addressed via conventional research methodologies, they do lend themselves to creative, expressive modes. For this reason, design for sustainability research that adopts a practice-based approach is well placed to tackle and find ways of manifesting and communicating these vital aspects of the human condition. In doing so, it will be exploring the relationship of these issues to the creation of a more sustainable and a more meaningful material culture, and its production, use, and disposal.

In pursuing such a direction, it is important to recognize the role of human emotions. Our feelings about the things we create represent the connection between the inner and the outer person; they connect an inner sense of meaning with our outer actions. This connection between inner and outer, through the emotions and human feeling, is related to the idea of meaningful actions, and it is precisely here that reflection becomes such a vital ingredient of thoughtful, practice-based research and scholarship. It behoves us to reflect on the emotions invoked by objects and their creation. We must consider our feelings about the design decisions we make and the kinds of objects we are creating, and we must consider the kinds of emotions designed artifacts are intended to invoke in others. We must beware of seeking to develop designs that cultivate feelings of exclusivity, rivalry, vanity, or pride—either in ourselves during the creative process, or in others once the designs are completed. Such emotions are at odds with notions of social equity and compassion that are fundamental to an ethos of sustainability in which deeper aspects of human meaning and the importance of spiritual growth are fully recognized.

PROPOSITIONAL DESIGNS FOR SUSTAINABILITY: EXAMPLES

For illustrative purposes, a number of propositional objects created within my own scholarly practice are included in Figure 28.3. Each of the objects shown is one of a series developed within a particular phase of research that examined a specific aspect of design for sustainability (Walker, 2011). As an individual thing, each object is merely an inquiring probe, a minor vignette, a question in form. The value of each lies in its role as a contributor in the development of ideas, as a manifestation of a particular stage of understanding, and as a focus for reflection and for spurring on the next stage of exploration. Hence, these artifacts are not conclusions or design solutions but merely points of synthesis along the way.

'**Replay**' (top left) is an example from a series that focused on how unfashionable, discarded, but still working electrical products could be seen anew and revalued with little or no modification to the product itself. It comprises a white wall panel with shelf onto which is mounted an old cassette stereo linked to an MP3 player. The panel reframes the out-of-date stereo, thereby separating it from its surroundings. In this way, a valueless product becomes a key constituent within a larger composition. This enframing panel decontextualizes the older product and presents it anew within a larger composition. In doing so, its old-fashioned

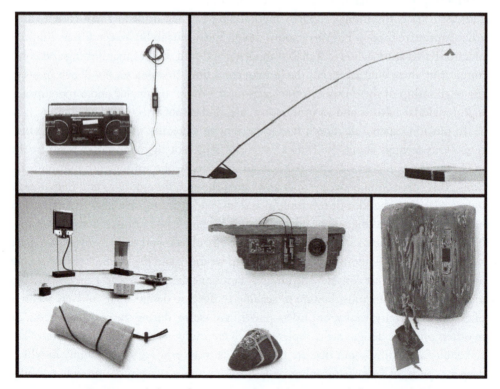

FIGURE 28.3   Propositional objects from practice-based design research for sustainability.

styling, its obsolete cassette drawer, and its scars of age all become important features of a new functional work. Hence, this direction questions conventions of newness and the short-lived aesthetics of perfection that characterize today's unsustainable notions of product.

'**Bamboo and Stone II**' (top right) combines unprocessed natural materials with off-the-shelf lighting technology in a small desk lamp concept. The product being off the shelf means the technological components can be easily repaired or replaced, and because these elements were not designed for this specific object, when the lamp is no longer wanted they can be readily reused in other applications. The unprocessed elements can be returned to the natural environment with no ill effect. This proposition points to a system that brings together large-scale mass-production with local materials, and combines product manufacture with local parts supply and maintenance. Within such a system, the use of raw and generic elements eliminates or significantly minimizes product waste and reduces shipping and packaging. The inclusion of natural, locally available elements also begins to create a material culture that has an aesthetic identity linked to place.

'**Wrapped Attention**' (bottom left) is a propositional object that explores mobile communication products in ways that challenge assumptions about convenience, and address concerns, emerging from various areas of research, related to multitasking and distracted use patterns. This mobile phone concept aims to discourage impromptu use and facilitate focused, single-pointed attention. In addition, because it is volumetrically unconstrained, future replacement parts can be integrated with old, which over a series of upgrades could reduce e-waste by roughly 80 per cent. Products that rely on rapidly advancing technologies quickly become obsolete, discarded, and replaced. This proposition explores product as a thing that is capable of continual evolution, rather than as a fixed, short-lived commodity.

'**Lagan Bell**' (bottom middle) combines aspects of the previous two propositions and includes symbolic references about history and identity. Found elements are brought together with new, mass-produced circuitry and silk fabric, the silk industry once being a significant part of the local economy. The object exposes rather than encloses—revealing circuitry and batteries that are normally hidden. This adds a level of comprehension to things and discloses—and therefore raises questions about—common practices, such as the use of nonrechargeable batteries.

'**Memoria Humanus**' (bottom right) introduces figurative symbolism, with references to time, memory, and meaning, evoked through worn surfaces, marks, and insignia. The primitive form serves as a keeper, a physical location for a detachable memory device in the form of a USB card. This exploration is concerned with development of form that is expressive and symbolic of deeper human stirrings, aspects of being human that reach beyond utility and materialistic explanation. Physical and virtual memory come together in an attempt to create an aesthetic harmony between the technological and the natural, the archaic and the contemporary, the useful and the meaningful.

The Body of Work: in reviewing the body of work, represented here through five examples, we see a transformation through time. 'Replay', for all its benefits in terms of sustainability, represents an outmoded, modernist notion of material culture—one characterized by an aesthetic of functional minimalism with clean lines and pristine surfaces. It is an aesthetic that is anonymous and unlocated. Through these examples, we travel from an homogeneous, mass-produced aesthetic to a material culture whose heterogeneous aesthetic emerges from and reflects place, cultural identity, and local needs. We travel from a notion of product as primarily something to be produced, sold, and forgotten to a product/service combination in which localization of maintenance, repair, parts replacements, upgrade, and reuse become fundamental to the essential nature of the object. In turn, this can reduce disposal, waste, and consumption, create local employment, and contribute to a more distributed and more equitable economy, and result in a less profligate, more intelligible and more intelligent version of material culture. Finally, over the course of these developments, culminating here with 'Memoria Humanus', we travel from a notion of product that is primarily concerned with worldly utility to an object that combines utility with deeper notions of human meaning—the mythical, the meaningful, the symbolic, and the spiritual.

CONCLUSIONS

In this discussion, I have attempted to demonstrate the critical importance of including practice-based modes of inquiry in our approaches to design research and scholarship for sustainability. Through such means, it becomes possible to address those very things that are too often omitted or are incapable of being dealt with via conventional analytical, evidence-based modes. The aesthetic and the emotional, when aligned with deeper notions of beauty and goodness, become linked to understandings of profound meaning and spiritual growth, which many regard as essential to any comprehensive notion of sustainability. Thus, these aspects can be seen as vital considerations in our attempts to develop a material culture that is more equitable, more moderate, more sustainable, and more nourishing. Practice-based modes of inquiry can yield new understandings of material culture, new approaches to design, and new knowledge about process and product. There is great potential, great opportunity, and an urgent need for the design disciplines to take on these challenges and develop discipline-appropriate modes of research. Recalling the words of Eric Gill quoted at the beginning of this chapter, such an approach to the design of our material culture would begin to reunite industry with art, and business with ethics, wisdom, goodness, and beauty.

REFERENCES

Blackler, A., Popovic, V. and Mahar, D. (2010), 'Investigating Users' Intuitive Interaction with Complex Artefacts', *Applied Ergonomics,* vol. 41: pp. 72–92.

Buchanan, R. (1989), 'Declaration by Design: Rhetoric, Argument, and Demonstration in Design Practice', in Margolin, V. (ed.), *Design Discourse: History, Theory, Criticism,* University of Chicago Press: Chicago. pp. 91–109.

Burrall, P. (1991), *Green Design,* Design Council: London.

Cross, N. (2001), 'Designerly Ways of Knowing: Design Discipline versus Design Science', *Design Issues,* vol. 17, no. 3, summer: pp. 49–55.

Datschefski, E. (2001), *The Total Beauty of Sustainable Products,* Rotovision: Hove, UK.

Dunne, A. (2005), *Hertzian Tales—Electronic Products, Aesthetic Experience, and Critical Design,* MIT Press: Cambridge, MA.

Dunne, A. and Raby, F. (2011), *Critical Design FAQ,* <http://www.dunneandraby.co.uk/content/bydandr/13/0> accessed June 13, 2011.

Frayling, C. (1993/1994), *Research in Art and Design,* Royal College of Art Research Papers, Royal College of Art: London, vol. 1, no 1.

Fuad-Luke (2002/2006), *Eco-Design: The Sourcebook,* Chronicle Books: San Francisco.

Orr, D. W. (2003), *Four Challenges of Sustainability,* School of Natural Sciences, University of Vermont, <http://www.ratical.org/co-globalize/4CofS.html> accessed July 12, 2011.

Papanek, V. (1971/1985), *Design for the Real World,* 2nd ed., Thames & Hudson: London.

Papanek, V. (1995), *The Green Imperative: Natural Design for the Real World,* Thames & Hudson: New York.

Polanyi, M. (1966), *The Tacit Dimension,* Anchor Books, Doubleday & Co.: New York.

Rogers, P. A. and Clarkson, P. J. (1998), 'An Investigation and Review of the Knowledge Needs of Designers in SMEs', *The Design Journal,* vol. 1, no. 3: pp. 16–29.

Rust, C., Mottram, J. and Till, J. (2007), *AHRC Research Review: Practice-led Research in Art, Design and Architecture,* Arts and Humanities Research Council: London.

Schumacher, E. F. (1973), *Small is Beautiful: Economics as if People Mattered, Buddhist Economics,* Penguin Books: London.

Senge, P., Scharmer, C. O., Jaworski, J. and Flowers, B. S. (2005), *Presence; Exploring Profound Change in People, Organizations and Society,* Nicholas Brealey Publishing: London.

Van der Ryn, S. and Cowan, S. (1996), *Ecological Design,* Island Press: Washington, D.C.

Walker, S. (2011), *The Spirit of Design: Objects, Environment and Meaning,* Earthscan/Routledge: London.

29

Design Activism: Challenging the Paradigm by Dissensus, Consensus, and Transitional Practices

ALASTAIR FUAD-LUKE

INTRODUCTION

Design activism carries an ambiguity with tensions that ripple out to designers, activists, and citizens. There is an ongoing dialogue to define the territory, language, and syntax of design activism that is challenging. First, because the term 'design' is notoriously difficult to define as it permeates contemporary human cultures, societies, and environments in different ways, while simultaneously being applied by diverse professionals in very precise ways (Erloff and Marshall, 2008, p. 104). Second, to design is to be human (Papanek, 1974, p. 17), and design is a common human behaviour to change an existing situation into a preferred one (Simon, 1969/1996, p. 130). Similarly, 'activism' is a tricky term to define, although it too implies changing, or trying to change, what already exists. Activism is invoked by those championing causes taken up by social, environmental, political, and artistic or creative movements that strive for alternative visions, utopias, and the reorganization of society (Parker et al., 2007). To be an activist covers a broad spectrum of behaviour from seeking political transformation, possibly involving extremist actions (Scruton, 2007, p. 6), to everyday gestures and actions at the personal level (Norton, 2007, pp. 26–43). Ennis Carter, founder and director of Design for Social Impact in the United States, simply sees activism 'as engaged practice of living where actions reflect core values and the results are beneficial' (quoted in Chick and Micklethwaite, 2011, p. 70). I have previously defined activism as 'taking actions to catalyze, encourage or bring about change to elicit social, cultural and/or political transformation. It can also involve transformation of the individual activists' (Fuad-Luke, 2009, p. 6).

The history of design is also the history of design activism. It is not a new phenomenon. The story of the individuals, groups, and movements is rich, varied, and passionate (Jané, 2011a; Fuad-Luke, 2009, pp. 33–52; Thorpe, 2008–2012). The voices of design activists are often heard during periods of rapid social change or unrest. They comprise luminaries in design history, such as William Morris, a key social reformer and proponent of the British Arts and Crafts Movement of the late nineteenth century; Hannes Meyer, director of the Bauhaus in the late 1920s; Richard Buckminster Fuller, a maverick polymath of the mid-twentieth century famous for his Dymaxion houses, geodesic domes, and being founder of the World Resources Institute; various radical design and antidesign-groups in Italy in the 1960s to early 1970s, including Superstudio, Archizoom, Gruppo Strum, and later, Studio Alchemia; graphic designer Ken Garland for his 1964 First Things First Manifesto; Victor Papanek with his seminal book, *Design for the Real World*, in 1972; numerous postmodern ecologists including Ian McHarg, Sim Van der Ryn, Sterling Bunnell, Hassan Fathy, Christopher Day, Nancy Jack Todd, and John Todd, to name a few. To these we can add a growing roll call of lesser-known design activists from history whose works are currently being reappraised. For example, Frederick Ward in Australia for his postwar Patterncraft paper furniture patterns encouraging affordable DIY making (Carter, 2011); architect and spatial theoretician Yona Friedman's work around 'simple technologies' and 'self-help manuals' through the 1970s and 1980s (Hunter, 2011); numerous examples from the Spanish-speaking world in Spain and South America (Argentina, Brazil, Chile, and Mexico), including two remarkable women, Clara Porset and Lina Bo Bardi in the 1930s and 1940s (Flores, 2011).

This timeline of design activists is the backdrop to resurgent interest in design activism that has gathered significant momentum over the last decade. Practitioners, academics, and writers have addressed activism in specific design disciplines, including architecture (Bell, 2004; Architecture for Humanity, 2006;), graphic design and design communication (Heller and Vienne, 2003; Lasn, 2006), and design for emerging or developing countries (Smith and Cooper-Hewitt Museum, 2007; Brown, 2009, pp. 203–25; Pilloton, 2009), while others have explored multidisciplinary perspectives framed within the sustainability agenda (Manzini and Jegou, 2003; Thackara, 2005; Walker, 2006; Thorpe, 2008–2012, 2012; Chick and Micklethwaite, 2011), the sociopolitical agenda (Julier, 2011b, 2011c; Thorpe, 2008–2012, 2012), or both agendas from a philosophical perspective (Fry, 2008, 2011; Oosterling 2011). Yet others have focused on specific design approaches whose aim is to activate stakeholders and citizens, such as transformation design (Cottam and Leadbeater, 2004), codesign (Mattelmäki and Sleeswijk Visser, 2011; Sanders, 2000), slow design (Fuad-Luke, 2002; Strauss and Fuad-Luke, 2008), meta-design (Giaccardi and Fischer, 2005; Wood, 2008), and open design (van Abel et al., 2011). The debate is in good health, but such a range of perspectives also presents a challenge for those trying to make sense of design activism.

EMERGENT DEFINITIONS OF DESIGN ACTIVISM

While a growing body of literature explores design activism, it is clear that there is not, presently, a universally accepted definition. Nonetheless, here are some of those recently published:

> Design activism arises anywhere—from within advocacy groups, businesses or public agencies. Design activists use artifacts and design processes to influence change by disrupting the status quo and revealing better visions for society. (Thorpe, 2008–2012)

> Design activism encompasses a wide range of real-life, socially and environmentally engaged actions. It includes innovative forms of creative practices, and provides models by which designers might work, or challenge existing conventions of design knowledge. (Leeds Festival of Design Activism, 2009)

> Design activism is 'design thinking, imagination and practice applied knowingly or unknowingly to create a counter-narrative aimed at generating and balancing positive social, institutional, environmental and/or economic change.' (Fuad-Luke, 2009, p. 27)

> Design activism is characterised both by its clear intent (the social or ecological cause being pursued) and the often radical nature of its practice (how design is used, and by whom). (Chick and Micklethwaite, 2011, p. 59)

> Generally, design activism is defined as representing the idea of design playing a central role in (i) promoting social change, in (ii) raising awareness about values and beliefs (climate change, sustainability, etc) or in (iii) questioning the constraints of mass production and consumerism on people's everyday life. (Markussen, 2011, p. 102)

The common ground for these definitions centres around design practices that inculcate positive social and ecological change by creating real-life counter-narratives, raising awareness, and catalyzing those targeted to take action and/or change their behaviour. Implicit too is the notion that the design practices applied might also challenge conventional design knowledge and approaches. Design activism therefore sets out to address sociocultural and ecological change by activating people while simultaneously aspiring to change the culture of design itself. What specifically differentiates design activism from everyday design activities? I have previously attempted to differentiate between design-orientated activism, design supporting an existing activist organization, and design-led activism, where the designers themselves set the agenda, the focal issues, and their intentions—that is, design is the strategy and means to implement the activism (2009, pp. 25–26). In the urban environment, in public space, Markussen sees activism as a 'disruptive aesthetic practice' creating a dissensus, an unsettling of the status quo (2011, p. 104–106). Thorpe has been consistent in her blog, designactivism.net, envisaging activism as forms of action to bring about intentional change, often in relation to a contentious issue (e.g., how could we stabilize the climate) or on behalf of a 'wronged, excluded or deprived group' (2008–2012). Critical to all these perspectives is a clear articulation of the chosen sociocultural, environmental, political, institutional, and/or economic issue or problem space that the design activism sets out to address, and the subsequent activation of people to respond to that issue in order that *they* might become the change. Design activism is intended to be catalytic, enabling, and/or transformative, though Lees-Maffei queries whether there is a difference between design activism and design reform and cites Polly Cantlon's notion that the collective is about '"design humanism" (the exercise of design activities for social purposes)' (Lees-Maffei, 2012, p. 92).

What distinguishes design activism from design altruism? Altruism, a form of mutual support, is defined by James Ozinga as 'behaviour benefitting someone else at some cost to oneself, while selfishness is behaviour that benefits oneself at some cost to others' (1999, p. 9). Chick and Micklethwaite (2011, p. 67) consider design altruism as 'design practice and theory that is principally motivated by a commitment to benefitting the genuine needs of others, without the mediation and distortion of those needed by markets.' Design altruism is also seen as a subset of design activism by Thorpe (Chick and Mickelthwaite, 2011, p. 73)—as a philanthropic design methodology of benefit to underprivileged communities or societies (Stairs, 2005)—and is perhaps typified by the notion of pro bono design work. The motivation for those to undertake design altruism projects at one end of the spectrum links directly to the historical legacy of Papanek's ethical stance on design and Design for Need made in the 1970s (1974), while at the other end of the spectrum it can have a thin veneer of altruism and a heavy dose of Corporate Social Responsibility.[1] Although altruism is integral to certain expressions of design activism, the challenge for those engaging in design altruism is to empower the beneficiaries without the (unintended) effect of offering external inputs that might be construed as culturally unhelpful, or at worst, patronizing.

EMERGENT FRAMEWORKS AND APPROACHES

At the first ever international conference specifically naming and addressing design activism, entitled 'Design Activism Social Change', organized by the Design History Society and held in Barcelona, September 2011, the territory was revealed as diverse and eclectic (Jané, 2011a). There is healthy discourse about the most effective way of framing and evolving the best approaches. This conference arose out of earlier events, such as The Leeds Festival of Design Activism in 2008, 2009, and 2010, initiated by Guy Julier, colleagues at Leeds Metropolitan University, and other creatives from the city. Indeed, since 2008 there has been a significant and growing interest in design activism (Brown, 2009; Chick and Micklethwaite, 2011; DiSalvo, 2010; Julier, 2011b; Thorpe, 2008–2012, 2012; Markussen, 2011). Thorpe allies design activism with sociological approaches to activism, proposing a 'typology of actions' (2008, pp. 1532–3) and later expanding this sociological position by embracing steady-state economics and politics (Thorpe, 2012). Elsewhere, I have outlined the problem spaces for design activism

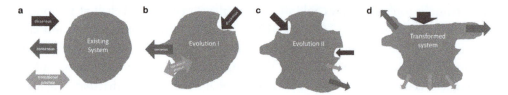

FIGURE 29.1   Transforming the existing system by dissensus, consensus, and transitional practice.

within a sustainability agenda focused on the environmental and sociocultural, with reference to a framework of ten 'capitals' that the activist can protect, regenerate, nourish, and/or grow (Fuad-Luke, 2009). Markussen rejects both these frameworks in favour of design activism as a 'disruptive aesthetic practice' of revelation, contest, and dissensus (2011, p. 104). Analysis of the complexity of the agendas, approaches, methods, and tools at the Design Activism Social Change conference indicates that there might be a meta-framework to accommodate current theoretical variance. This meta-framework works within, on the edge of, and without (outside) the existing system paradigm (Figure 29.1). Each way of working holds validity since it is the collective impact of these ways that challenges then transforms the existing paradigm.

Markussen's notion of design activism as 'aesthetic dissensus', stimulated by Steven Corcoran's *Dissensus: On Politics and Aesthetics* (2010), could be perceived as actions outside and oppositional to the [existing] paradigm. This type of action fits certain categories of Thorpe's typology, such as 'demonstration' artifacts and 'protest' artifacts (Thorpe, 2012, p. 138), and Walker's 'propositional' artifacts (2008). An iconic example of aesthetic dissensus is Rakowitz's PARAsite project for homeless people (Fuad-Luke, 2009, p. 128) and the artifacts of critical design practice (see, for example, Dunne and Raby, 2001). And, it embraces what Gaspar Mallol refers to as 'F(r)ictions, design as a cultural form of micro-situations of dissent where design fictions (understood as projections) and frictions (considered as irritations) help "re-fabulate the commonplace"' (Gaspar Mallol, 2011, p. 1). Dissensus is a central strategy of raising awareness about issues and contesting hegemonic socioeconomic and political systems that has a rich history in graphic design and design communications (Heller and Vienne, 2003) and includes Adbusters' culture jamming (Lasn, 2006). The ability to apply design tactics and strategies from outside the paradigm can offer significant jolts to sociocultural and political discourse.

It is clear that design activism is also working within or inside the (existing) paradigm, especially where designers have chosen to work closely with social communities and groups (Thorpe 2008–2012; Design Council 2007, 2011) or are engaged in altruistic or pro bono work (Architecture for Humanity, 2006; Pilloton, 2009) and, as recently noted by Julier, to help local government develop social innovation or new social services in the face of fiscal challenges (Julier, 2011c). An expanding social design agenda, including the notion of 'creative communities' (Meroni, 2007); the underlying nature of cross-disciplinary, interdisciplinary, and transdisciplinary ways of meta-designing (Wood, 2008); and codesign or cocreative practice (Mattelmäki and Visser, 2011), all indicate creative ways of working with people *within* the (existing) paradigm.

Lastly, design activism acts on the edge of the (existing) paradigm through the redirection of individual and collective design practice. On the edge because such changes in practice necessitate a gradual transition from the practice within the paradigm to practice in the emergent paradigm. These actions stem from individuals choosing to practice differently: for example, by 'quiet activism' through craft practice (Hackney, 2011), 'craftivism' as slowing down (Patel, 2011), codesigning as making (Neuberg and Bowles, 2011), and by opening up so design is or becomes configurable as in 'open design' (Klaassen and Neicu, 2011, p. 73; van Abel et al., 2011).

Oosterling suggests that, potentially, the default position of design activism is that we are all invoked, that the (design) activism is about 'being in between', an ontological 'inter-esse'; it is always 'we' first and 'I' later. Design activism is 'eco-social inter-esse' (Oosterling, 2011 pp. 7, 8, 10) working on and in the existing paradigm.

Emergent Approaches

This leads to the suggestion of an emergent meta-framework, where design activism within the paradigm adopts a consensus over dissensus approach, while outside the paradigm the approach is one of dissensus over consensus. The edge of the paradigm is where consensus and dissensus meet, either in individual and/or collective transitional practices.

We can also ask how design activism acts on our anthropocentric condition. This condition can be expressed in the form of social, human, and cultural capital, as follows:

Social capital...concerns connections between and within social networks that encourage civic engagement, engender trust, create mutual support, establish norms, contribute to communal health, cement shared interests, facilitate individual or collective action, and generate reciprocity between individuals and between individuals and a community. (Fuad-Luke, 2009, p. 7)

Human capital is...'any one individual's physical, intellectual, emotional and spiritual capacities.' (Porritt, 2007, p. 163)

Cultural capital...is a mercurial and complex form of capital that Bourdieu recognized as existing in several inter-connected states: individuals as an embodied state (an inherited or acquired set of properties conferring certain social relations); an objectified state (material and symbolic goods); an institutionalized state (being conferred on institutions to individuals). Cultural capital is in a constant state of flux as individuals move within and between different social units or networks where their cultural capital will be perceived as having significant, moderate or no value. (Fuad-Luke, 2009, p. 8)

Actions within the (existing) paradigm tend to focus on building new social capital, actions on the edge of the (existing) paradigm tend to develop individual human

TABLE 29.1   AN EMERGENT META-FRAMEWORK FOR DESIGN ACTIVISM.

RELATION TO EXISTING PARADIGM	WITHIN THE PARADIGM	EDGE OF THE PARADIGM	OUTSIDE THE PARADIGM
Orientation	Consensus over dissensus	Consensus and dissensus– transitonal practice	Dissensus over consensus
Tendency to Act Predominantly on...	social capital	human capital	cultural capital
Typical Design Approaches	co-design craftivism meta-design open design participatory design social design user-centred design	craftivism eco-design hacktivism open design slow design social design sustainable design	craftivism critical design design interventions design propositions hacktivism open design slow design

capital, and actions outside the (existing) paradigm tend to contest current constructs of cultural capital, although it is acknowledged that these capitals are relational and the boundaries can be fuzzy.

The meta-framework offers a means by which it is possible to understand how different design approaches are being applied (Table 29.1). Building social capital requires participatory modes of design practice—this involves processes of engagement, facilitation, building relations, collective intelligence, and sense making, new value creation, democratization. Growing human capital requires a building up of individual skills or exchange of skills and learning often found in more open, sharing forms of practice—this involves seeking new livelihoods and testing alternative ways of designing and making. Contesting existing forms of cultural capital requires critical, frictional, and interventionalist modes of practice—this involves disruptions, provocations, dissent, intentional actions, frictions, fictions. Some modes of practice, such as craftivism, hactivism, open design, and slow design, have a tendency to act on more than one form of anthropocentric capital.

THE EMERGENT POLITICAL CONDITION
OF DESIGN ACTIVISM

Design activism is contesting the paradigm, from within, outside, or on the edge. Where, therefore, does design activism sit within the political arena? DiSalvo specifically notes that in the discourses of agonistic pluralism,[2] 'politics are *the means* by which a state organization or other social order is held together, politics are the structures and mechanisms that enable governing,' whereas the 'political is a *condition* of society. It is a condition of ongoing opposition and contest' (DiSalvo, 2010, p. 2–3). Yet design occupies a rubric that consists of the apolitical, the politics of the state or institutional authorities, and the political everyday social-cultural milieu. Design and designers' ability to be neutral to deliver, for example, functionality and utility for everyday use, can be regarded as apolitical as the intention, in these circumstances, is not to challenge or affect the institutions through which power is exercised, although the existence of a truly apolitical condition is contested, too.[3] Bonsieppe suggests that every design act is a political act if one construes design as part of social discourse, if design is asking, 'In what sort of a society do members of that society wish to live?' (Bonsieppe, 1997) This is acknowledged by Neutra's observation that 'Design, never a harmless play with forms and colours, changes outer life as well as our inner balances' (Neutra, 1954, p. 318).

The meta-framework previously outlined suggests that the intentionality and purpose of design activism is varied and that it embraces a spectrum of sociopoliticized activities. The political ambitions of design activism are clearly invoked by DiSalvo's 'design for agonistic pluralism', Fry's 'design as politics', Thorpe's sociological typology of design actions and 'patterns of power', and my 'mootspace' for anticipatory democracy (DiSalvo, 2010; Fry, 2011; Thorpe, 2008, 2012, p. 28; Fuad-Luke, 2009, pp. 196–200). The way that design activism levers political change depends upon whether the design approaches set about to encourage dissensus, consensus, or both. Arguably, it is a potent mix of all three approaches that effectively invokes transformative change.

Contentious new political ambitions for design were laid down in Fry's *Design as Politics* (2011). This can be seen as a work of powerful dissensus aimed squarely at design culture (designers, design researchers, and academics), although it clearly also reaches out to political, sociological, and philosophical audiences. Developing his early treatises on how design 'de-futures', precluding options for future generations and further defining 'Sustainment' as the overcoming of the unsustainable (Fry, 2008), Fry notes that current models of representative democracy are inadequate, suggesting that only a 'dictatorship of the imperative of Sustainment' will deliver the needed change (2011, p. 123–4). Of concern is that much of this argument is made, to quote Fry, 'In the Shadow of Carl Schmitt's Politics', a philosopher noted for focusing on the weak points of liberal and democratic theory while failing to critique reactionary fascist and nationalistic ideology to the extent of being seen as an apologist for such ideologies (Mautner, 2000, p. 507). What is clear is that *Design as Politics* has made an upward gear shift in the political debate around design activism. This was amply demonstrated at the Design Activism Social Change Conference in Barcelona in September 2011 when Fry's advocates and doubters met (Julier, 2011d).

Markussen's design activism as 'disruptive aesthetic practice' (2011, p. 104) is a form of dissensus observed throughout the history of design. It is a strategy that might appeal to the 'maverick solo designer' (Fuad-Luke, 2009, p. 195) or the hactivist (von Busch, 2008) but can require careful pitching to its intended audience because acts of design dissensus potentially posit the designer(s) as part of an 'avant-garde'. As Pogglioli noted, being part of the avant-garde is to negotiate a fine line between being bourgeois and popular culture (1968), and therefore one's ability to affect social change. The 'reveal, contest and dissensus' of Markussen's design activism framework is clearly 'political' rather than 'politics'. Some of the examples he cites, such as Santiago Cirugeda's Recetas Urbanas, downloadable designs for built interventions for the urban environment, and Laura Kurgan's Million Dollar Blocks remapping of crime and prison-related data, avoid the avant-garde tag in that they are freely available or visible via the Internet. Perhaps the real value of these design acts of dissensus is the reframing or exposing of the real *problematique* in a different way to existing conventions of (the) politics.

Those seeking a more consensus-driven approach to design activism embrace design approaches that involve multiple actors, stakeholders, communities of practice, interest, and/or place while encouraging participation, inclusion, and openness about how the design processes are applied. Inherent is a common attitude to democratizing the design decision-making based upon shared understandings, perceptions, and framings of the problem spaces. As governments face mounting challenges over managing fiscal futures, there is a surge of interest as to how design can encourage social innovation and new enterprises within communities and municipalities. For example, the National Endowment for Sciences, Technology, and Arts (NESTA) Public Services Lab in the United Kingdom has encouraged a number of design-inspired initiatives involving established service and social design agencies creating social innovation labs, intergenerational enterprises, and other social initiatives (NESTA, 2011). To what extent such socially orientated service design activates, or is activist, is not yet clear, nor is its role in positive social change. Designers need to maintain a political awareness as to the original intentionality and effectiveness of the design outcomes. Recent examples from the United Kingdom, where design activism creates social enterprises or results in the 'agentification' of public sector services, reveal 'an uneasy coalition with neo-liberalist arrangements' (Julier, 2011c). Consensus modes of design activism might have the potentiality to be readily absorbed by the existing paradigm.

Where do consensus and dissensus meet and what are the political agendas here? The conjoining of these, apparently, oppositional positions is to be found in the following design approaches: open design (van Abel et al., 2011; Klaassen and Neicu, 2011), slow design (Fuad-Luke, 2002; Strauss and Fuad-Luke, 2008), craftivism (Greer, 2008), fashion hactivism (von Busch, 2008), quiet activism (Hackney, 2011), and the broader domains of eco-design, social design, and sustainable design.[4] It involves the designer 'taking a position' on how to express the consensus-dissensus tensions in the forms, directionality, and ethics that are embodied in their practice. Open design, where the underlying tenet is to allow free distribution, documentation, and permitted modifications or variations of the original designs (van Abel et al., 2011, p. 11), seems capable of ranging from hactivism to collaborative design, from dissensus to consensus, from within to outside or on the edge of the paradigm. In this sense, it is the most politically heterogeneous of the design activism approaches able to operate at micro-, medial-, and meta-levels in systems. It is synergistic with the digital open source movement but has found tangible expression more recently through all facets of the design field. It embraces cocreation, creative commons, crowdsourcing, downloadable designs, grassroots invention, hacking, and the publication of manifestoes. Its potency is in its savvy ability to use the social democracy of the Internet and digital technologies to disseminate its activities. Open design is politically mercurial, difficult to contain, and has potential to operate effectively on the political.

So, the political terrain of design activism is gaining some detail, but how does design activism manifest itself, what processes are deployed, how are people activated, and what are the outcomes?

ACTIVATING PEOPLE IN SOCIAL SPACES

A further development of the meta-framework is necessary to help understand the diverse variance of expression manifest by design activism. In human society, all space is social, involving appropriated places for social relations (Lefebvre, 1991, pp. 186–7). Design activism has to operate in these social spaces to affect change. However, social spaces are complex, real, virtual, and conceptual (intellectual and mental). In real, tangible spaces, they vary from the personal to private, semiprivate, semipublic, and public. Within these real social spaces, it is recognized that culturally held notions of individual space also exist—for example 'personal space' (proxemics), and 'intimate space' (Hall, 1966). Manuel Castells differentiates between real social spaces as a 'space of places' and contrasts them with the virtual social spaces of the digital age society, an abstraction of space, time, and dynamic interactions, which he named the 'space of flows' (Castells, 2004). There is strong evidence that certain design activism approaches, for example open design, need to occupy the space of flows *and* space of places to be manifest. It is also necessary to consider conceptual (intellectual or mental) space as visualizing and bringing visions to life that currently do not yet exist. This is a space central to the development of design research, 'Design Culture' (as defined by Julier, 2008), and its expressions include drawing, sketching, CAD renders, storyboarding, prototyping, critical design(s), scenario development, and other techniques.

Emblematic examples of design activism can now be posited in an expanded meta-framework that links the design to acting in specific social spaces (Table 29.2) using the following categorization:

Space of Places

Personal—that is, the individual human

Private—for example, home shared with partner, family, friends

Semiprivate—for example, communal housing, gardens, laundry; members' club

Semipublic—for example, community centres, libraries, shops, cafés and bars, universities

Public—for example, footpaths, squares, civic amenities, public access areas in the countryside

Space of Flows

Technological space—for example, digital technological devices and digital environments

Space of Concepts

Intellectual and mental space—for example, visualizations of potential, but not yet existing design(s) that are, largely, within the discourse of Design Culture

TABLE 29.2 LOCATING SELECTED DESIGN ACTIVISM CASE STUDIES IN AN EXPANDED META-FRAMEWORK OF SOCIAL SPACES.

RELATION TO EXISTING PARADIGM	WITHIN THE PARADIGM	EDGE OF THE PARADIGM	OUTSIDE THE PARADIGM
Orientation	Consensus over dissensus	Consensus and dissensus—transitonal practice	Dissensus over consensus
Tendency to Act Predominantly on...	social capital	human capital	cultural capital
personal space	*Note: not relevant category–personal space is associated with one person*	**P1 Encouraging new skills and/or perceptions** CASE STUDIES *Sasa Clock* by Thorunn Arnadottir	*Note: not relevant category–personal space is associated with one person*
private space	**P2 Introducing artefacts for social group health and wellbeing** CASE STUDIES *Watercone* by Stephan Augustin	**P3 Sharing processes, blueprints** CASE STUDIES *Instructables* by everyone *Shades of Wood* by Jorn van Eck and Overtreders-W	**P4 Signalling the ethical, technological and/or temporal** CASE STUDIES *Tyranny of the Plug* by Dick van Hoff
semi-private spaces	**P5 Gathering or sharing knowledge** CASE STUDIES *Lunchbox Laboratory* by Future Farmers	**P6 Learning and sharing new skills** CASE STUDIES *Play Rethink* by Lili de Larratea *Hacking IKEA* by Premsela Foundation	**P7 Challenging the ethical, technological and/or temporal** CASE STUDIES *Suburban Ark* by Ton Matton
semi-public space	**P8 Gathering or sharing knowledge** CASE STUDIES *MetaboliCity* byLoop pH	**P9 Learning and sharing new skills** CASE STUDIES *Fab Labs* by MIT *The People's Print* by Emma Neuberg and Melanie Bowles	**P10 Challenging the ethical, technological and/or temporal** CASE STUDIES *The Eco-cathedral* by Louis Le Roy
public space	**P11 Gathering or sharing knowledge in places** CASE STUDIES *Green Route Todmorden* by Liam Hinshelwood and Tom White, Pi-Studio, Goldsmiths *EcoBox* by Atelier d'architecture autogérée (aaa)	**P12 Learning and sharing new skills in places** CASE STUDIES *Urban Farming Project Dott07* by the Design Council *Project-H* by Emily Pilloton	**P13 Challenging the ethical, technological and/or temporal in places** CASE STUDIES *No Shop* by Thomas Matthews *PARAsite* by Michael Rachowitz *Recetas Urbanas* by Santiago Cirugeda *Recycled Soundscape* by Karmen Franinovic *EcoBox* by Atelier d'architecture autogérée (aaa)[1]

Space of Places- Real Space

Space of Flows— Technological spaces	forms of spatial arrangements in synchronous, real time interaction though digital and technological means	**F1 Open source source knowledge gathering, sharing, and learning in virtual spaces** CASE STUDIES *c,mm,n* open source sustainable mobility by Natuur en Milieu	**F2 Open source, DIY, DIT skills and learning in virtual spaces** CASE STUDIES *Cell System, Dendrite, and Radiolaria*by Nervous System *Repair Manifesto* and *(Un)limited Design Competition* by Premsela Foundation	**F3 Raising awareness and challenging perspectives or re-framing problems/issues in virtual spaces** CASE STUDIES *Changing Habits* by Giraffe Innovation *Million Dollar Blocks* by Laura Kurgan *iSEE-map* by Institute for Applied Autonomy *Worldmapper* by University of Sheffield, UK and University of Michigan, USA
Conceptual or Mental Space	ideas, sketches, digital renders, scenarios and storyboards research prototypes	**C1 Challenging perspectives and offering processes or re-framing problems/issues in the spaces of Design Culture** CASE STUDIES *Sustainable Everyday* and *Creative Communities* by INDACO, Politechnico Milano	**C2 Offering processes, tools or re-framing problems/issues in the spaces of Design Culture** CASE STUDIES*Grow Fur* by Cay Green *Three White Canvas Clocks* by Stuart Walker *Living with Things* by Monica Hoinkis	**C3 Challenging perspectives or re-framing problems/issues in the spaces of Design Culture** CASE STUDIES *Fab Tree Hab* by Mitchell Joachim, MIT Smart Cities *Placebo Project* by Anthony Dunne and Fiona Raby

[1] EcoBox by Atelier d'architecture can be perceived as generating consensus by encouraging people to come together to maintain and nurture the garden, and as dissensus in its role in reclaiming public space.
Sources: All case studies taken from Fuad-Luke (2009) with the exception of the following, all accessed on July 5, 2012: Instructables, http://www.instructables.com/index; *Shades of Wood* by Jorn van Eck and Overtreders-W, http://unlimiteddesigncontest.org/product/shades-wood-0; *Play Rethink* by Lili de Larratea, http://www.playrethink.com/; *Hacking IKEA* by Premsela Foundation, http://www.platform21.nl/page/3293/en; *Suburban Ark* by Ton Matton, http://www.mattonoffice.org/MO/projects/Seiten/Suburban_Ark._Rotterdam_Architecture_Biennale.html#25; *MetaboliCity* by Loop pH, http://loop.ph/bin/view/Loop/MetaboliCity; *Fab Labs* by MIT, http://fab.cba.mit.edu/; *The People's Print* by Emma Neuberg and Melanie Bowles, http://thepeoplesprint.blogspot.com/2011/11/peoples-print-on-film.html; *Green Route Todmorden* by Liam Hinshelwood and Tom White, Pi-Studio, Goldsmiths; *EcoBox* by Atelier d'architecture autogérée (aaa), http://www.urbantactics.org/home.html; *Project-H* by Emily Pilloton, http://www.projecthdesign.org/; *Recetas Urbanas* by Santiago Cirugeda, http://www.recetasurbanas.net/; *Recycled Soundscape* by Karmen Franinovic, http://www.zero-th.org/RS/FraninovicVisellSoundDesign04.pdf; *Cell System, Dendrite, and Radiolaria* by Nervous System, http://n-e-r-v-o-u-s.com/; *Repair Manifesto* and *(Un)limited Design Competition* by Premsela Foundation, Platform21 http://www.platform21.nl/page/4315/en and http://unlimiteddesigncontest.org/; *Million Dollar Blocks* by Laura Kurgan, http://l00k.org/; *iSEE-map* by Institute for Applied Autonomy, http://www.worldchanging.com/archives/006970.html.

DESIGN ACTIVISM AS REORIENTATING THE INDIVIDUAL AND THE COLLECTIVE

The space of places, space of flows, and space of concepts coincide with three key but relational audiences: the general public, the online networked public, and the individuals and communities of Design Culture.[5] As such, the influence and affect of the act of design activism are circumscribed by these audiences and their habitus.[6] How much each case study is able to trigger system change and to shift the paradigm is clearly influenced by the scale of the social space and the influence of these socialized activities.

Not all the case studies in Table 29.2 can be considered in detail, but it is clear that design activism is intent on reorientating the personal, the private (home), and the individual within the collective. It also seems to be reorientating the focus of design activities—that is, what design should apply itself to.

Reorientating the Personal

Given the importance of everyday activism and personal transformation, Saga Clock by Arnadottir, taking a slow design approach, asks the wearer to learn a new skill, to tell the time differently, to set a new rhythm for his or her daily life (Figure 29.2). A string of beads turns on the electric cogwheel of a clock. Each blue bead represents five minutes, red and orange hour points, gold and silver beads for noon and midnight. When owners

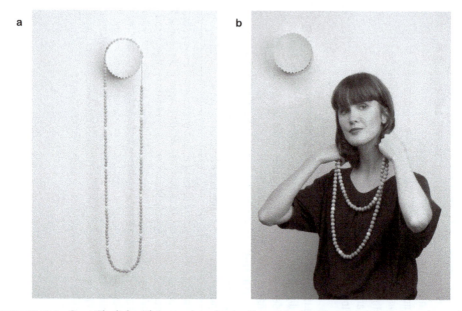

FIGURE 29.2   Sasa Clock by Thorunn Arnadottir. Copyright by Thorunn Arnadottir, photos by Matthew Booth.

want free time, they remove the string of beads from the cogwheel and adorn their body with the necklace of beads, returning them to the cogwheel when clock time is required again. Saga Clock is consensus and dissensus, challenging the hegemony of 365–24–7, time as a commodity, time as a metric. There is an opportunity for designers to undertake more design activism projects in personal space.

Reorientating the Private (Home)

In the quiet of the private space of the home, design activism encourages new perceptions, experiences, aesthetics, and meanings that challenge the primacy of mass-produced objects and the systems that they represent. A common feature of the case studies is an encouragement for the user/consumer/person to become active, to reject the passivity often associated with things or services of the marketplace. Watercone helps deal with the harsh reality of intermittent and unsafe water systems by giving people the means to use solar distillation to create their own potable water. The Hacking IKEA project encourages people to reconfigure what already exists into something with a new use function. Jorn Van Eck and Overtreders-W won Premsela's (Un)limited design competition with their downloadable standard lamp design, Shades of Wood, whose blueprint enables distinctive high quality DIY design (Figure 29.3). The Tyranny of the Plug

FIGURE 29.3 Shades of Wood by Jorn van Eck and Overtreders-W.
© Jorn van Eck.

encourages users to unhook from the (dependency) of the (national) electricity supply networks by creating efficient human-powered mechanisms to replace energy hungry gizmos. Self-reliance is also suggested in Premsela's Repair Manifesto, while Instructables allows P2P (person to person) design with uploading and downloading of designs, encouraging people to make for themselves and others. The design enterprise Nervous System gives people an opportunity to design their own digital prototypes for displaying or wearing after fabricating with a professional rapid prototype. Reorientation by design focuses on activating citizens within their habitus.

Reorientating in the Semiprivate to Public Space of Places and Flows

Many of the artifacts and interventions featured in semiprivate, semipublic, public, or digital environments engage us through a consensual shared activity, be it around growing food (Ecobox, Urban Farming Dott07, MetaboliCity), playing creative games (Rethink), making digital things (FabLabs), codesigning digital textile prints (The People's Print [Figure 29.4]), open source designing and prototyping (c,mm,n hydrogen car), hand-making (yarn-bombing), making buildings (Project-H, Architecture for Humanity, Rural Studio), and, even, making semiautonomous floating farms (Suburban Ark). Individual skills are gifted and shared in a process of mutual reorientation.

In contrast, many design interventions in semipublic or public space seek to reorientate by contesting meaning, by challenging our perceptions. They raise our awareness beyond 'the cage of aesthetic convention' (Walker, 2002, p. 3) and, in doing so, disrupt the code of our habitus, reshaping our cognitive/emotive filters, contesting the usual 'aesthetic sign function' (Vihma, 1995). This is exemplified by Louis le Roy's

FIGURE 29.4   The People's Print, 'Born to be Wild swatch book', by Emma Neuberg, Melanie Bowles, and codesigners. Copyright Melanie Bowles.

FIGURE 29.5 *Recetas Urbanas* by Santiago Cirugeda.

Ecocathedral, Michael Rachowitz's PARAsite, and Santiago Cirugeda's *Recetas Urbanas* (Figure 29.5).

In the space of flows, reconfiguring and revisualizing digital information is deployed to dramatic effect in Changing Habbits by Giraffe Innovation (algorithm display of personal carbon footprint data); Million Dollar Blocks by Laura Kurgan (data about American prisoners transposed to the city blocks from which they originate, suggesting a significantly different problem space to that seen by the prison authorities); iSEE (a website for finding routes that avoid ubiquitous CCTV cameras in cities); and Worldmapper (cartograms showing the new shape of a standard world map projection according to different metrics applied to each national territory).

Whether in the spaces of places or spaces of flows, these aesthetic disruptions challenge the default paradigmatic meanings held by individuals or social groups and so generate counter-narratives, counter-dialogues.

Reorientating the Focus of Design Activities

Less visible in the public realm and, perhaps, even within the design industry are the activities of design researchers contesting the modus operandi of design itself.[7] These activities lever change on design culture as 'an object of study' and Design Culture as an 'academic discipline' (Julier, 2008, pp. 3–11).

Under the broad banner of collaborative sustainability design, the work of IND-ACO, Politechnico di Milano is well-known, with projects over the last decade including Sustainable Everyday (Manzini and Jegou, 2003), Creative Communities (Meroni, 2007), and, since 2010, several projects around collaborative services (Meroni and Sangiorgi, 2011). Design for Sustainability, scenario-building, concept design, service design, codesign, and design communication are just a few of the approaches and tools applied to create sustainable scenarios, amplify promising real-life cases, and encourage enabling solutions. Envisioning sustainable ways of living is also driven by generating conceptual CAD designs such as those from the MIT Smart Cities project—for example, Fab Tree Hab by Mitchell Joachim and his team. These challenge our capacity to imagine and set visions. Other researchers embrace critical design, challenging the relationships we have with the objects that surround us or raising contentious social issues. Monica Hoinkis's Living With Things reminds us of the objects we take for granted, and Stuart Walker's Three White Canvas Clocks, which can be reconfigured by the owner to his or her own aesthetic preference, suggest new modes of (more) sustainable coproduction. Antony Dunne and Fiona Raby's Placebo Project focused attention on electromagnetic radiation from electronic gadgets in the home using a series of objects or probes, some of which had embedded functionality triggered by electromagnetism; others were neutral (placebos). The primary purpose of these interventions was to stimulate social and academic discourse on a neglected, and important, issue. Standing slightly aside from the previous research work of 'design as the message' is a project by Cay Green called Grow Fur, which is a booklet containing various design tools and processes to enable people to design their own ways of reducing energy use in the home. This is 'design as the means'. It empowers individuals by giving them their own design processes to fix problems.

The potential of this design research work to lever positive change is significant if it can move beyond the confines of academic discourse, scale up, and find mutually interested partners for these projects to capture the popular imagination.

CONCLUDING REMARKS

Design activism is currently resurgent and divergent, testing ways that design can challenge the existing paradigm through consensus, dissensus, or both. The design activists embrace diverse actors, stakeholders, and communities of interest and practice. They include facilitators and enablers (empowering people, communities), researchers (foraging for new knowledge), quiet activists (knitters, 'yarn bombers'), hactivists (open source hackers of existing designs), transitional practitioners (redirecting their practice), and diverse others who believe in design's power to lever positive change. They apply their skills in the terrain of the political, and hence in the aesthetics and ethics of the societal. They insist in applying design in a way that has a 'lucid critical consciousness (both sociological and ecological)' that tries to address 'contingent reality' (Maldonado, 1972, p. 50). They deploy a wide range of design approaches depending upon the chosen context—audience, social space (from private to public), and type of space (places, flows, conceptual)—either within, on the edge of, or from outside the existing paradigm. They aim to effect changes in human, social, and/or cultural capital and thus to be an agency of transformative positive change. Less clear, at this present juncture, is how effective the design activists are, and can be, at challenging the existing paradigm. Design activism is a concurrent dialogue alongside Design(ing) for Sustainability, seeking transition toward more sustainable realities and ways of thinking, living, working, and playing. It is evident is that the design activists are growing and getting more vociferous.

NOTES

1. The global design agency IDEO was criticized by David Stairs, Designers without Borders, as commercializing altruism for its marketability (Chick and Micklethwaite, 2011, p. 69). Certainly, IDEO's CEO Tim Brown takes a broad brush approach to design activism in his book *Change by Design* (Brown, 2009, pp. 203–25), taking examples of social entrepreneurs, recent initiatives by the UK Design Council, the Dott 07 project, and fresh educational approaches, but this sits in isolation amongst the pitch toward commerce about applying design thinking. However, a genuine act of altruism is IDEO's Human-Centred Design (HCD) Toolkit, an innovation guide for social enterprises and nongovernmental organizations (NGOs).
2. DiSalvo defines 'agonistic pluralism' as 'a model of democracy grounded in productive conflict or contest' (DiSalvo, 2010, p. 2).
3. See Roger Scruton's definition of apolitical: 'A stance is called apolitical if it does not have, as part of its main purpose, intentions regarding the political order: i.e. regarding the institutions through which power is exercised' (2007, p. 31). However, he recognizes that anything that affects social change might have an effect on those institutions, and therefore a truly apolitical position might be hard to interpret.
4. The body of literature is extensive for eco-design, social design, and sustainable design; the reader is referred to the other chapters in this handbook. It is sufficient to note that the aforementioned design approaches are still not regarded as conventional everyday design practice and might still be considered as a minority of practice. As such, these practitioners

offer dissensus from normative practices in industry, but as they typically work within the paradigm, their actions often originate in a consensual, participatory mode of practice.

5. Guy Julier defines 'Design Culture' as identifiable alongside Visual Culture, Material Culture. It is to be distinguished from design culture 'as an object of study', which is about processes, tools, and so on (Julier, 2008, pp. 3–11).

6. I define habitus here as socially acquired ways of living that are taken for granted as an accepted set of principles, sensibilities, dispositions, and tastes.

7. The premise of this book, *The Handbook of Design for Sustainability,* contests 'design as usual'.

REFERENCES

Architecture for Humanity (ed.) (2006), *Design Like You Give A Damn,* Thames & Hudson: London.

Bell, B. (ed.) (2004), *Good Deeds, Good Design: Community Service through Architecture,* Princeton Press: New York.

Bonsieppe, G. (1997), 'Design—the Blind Spot of Theory, or, Theory—the Blind Spot of Design', Conference text for a semi-public event of the Jan van Eyk Academy, Maastrict, April.

Brown, T. (2009) *Change by Design: How Design Thinking Transforms Organizations and Inspires Innovation,* Harper Business: New York.

Carter, N. (2011), 'Blueprint to Patterncraft: DIY Furniture Patterns and Packs in Post-War Australia', in Jané, C. (ed.), *Design Activism and Social Change,* Design History Society Annual Conference, Barcelona, September 7–10, Book of Abstracts, p. 33, <http://www.historiadeldisseny.org/congres/pdf/7%20Carter,%20Nanette%20%20BLUEPRINT%20TO%20PATTERNCRAFT%20DIY%20FURNITURE%20PATTERNS%20AND%20PACKS%20IN%20POST-WAR%20AUSTRALIA.pdf> accessed June 29, 2012.

Castells, M. (2004), *The Rise of the Network. The Information Age: Economy, Society and Culture,* vol. 1, Blackwell: Oxford.

Chick, A. and Micklethwaite, P. (2011), *Design for Sustainable Change. How Design and Designers Can Drive the Sustainability Agenda,* AVA Publishing: Lausanne.

Corcoran, S. (2010), 'Editor's Introduction', in *Dissensus: On Politics and Aesthetics,* Continuum International Publishing Press: London, New York. pp. 1–24.

Cottam, H. and Leadbeater, C. W. (2004), *Red Paper 101 Health: Co-Creating Services,* Design Council: London.

Design Council (2007), 'Design of the Times', Dott07, <http://www.designcouncil.org.uk/our-work/challenges/Communities/Dott-07/> accessed June 29, 2012.

Design Council (2011), 'Co-designing Ways to Improve How We Live, Work and Play: Dott Cornwall', <http://www.designcouncil.org.uk/our-work/challenges/Communities/Dott-Cornwall1/> accessed June 29, 2012.

DiSalvo, C. (2010), 'Design, Democracy and Agonistic Pluralism', Proceedings of the Design Research Society International Conference, July 7–9, Université de Montréal.

Dunne, A. and Raby, F. (2001), *Design Noir: The Secret Life of Electronic Objects,* Birkhäuser: Basel.

Erloff, M. and Marshall, T. (eds) (2008), *Design Dictionary: Perspectives on Design Terminology,* Birkhäuser: Basel.

Flores, O.S. (2011), 'Design Pioneers in Latin America', in Jané, C. (ed.), *Design Activism and Social Change,* Design History Society Annual Conference, Barcelona, September 7–10, Book of Abstracts, p. 109.

Fry, T. (2008), *Design Futuring. Sustainability, Ethics and New Practice,* Berg Publishers: Oxford, New York.

Fry, T. (2011), *Design as Politics,* Berg Publishers: Oxford.

Fuad-Luke, A (2002), '"Slow Design": A Paradigm Shift in Design Philosophy?', Development by Design Conference, Shristi School of Art & Design, Bangalore, India, December 1–2.

Fuad-Luke, A. (2009), *Design Activism: Beautiful Strangeness for a Sustainable World,* Earthscan: London.

Gaspar Mallol, M. (2011), 'F(r)ictions. Design as Cultural Form of Dissent', in Jané, C. (ed.), *Design Activism and Social Change,* Design History Society Annual Conference, Barcelona, September 7–10, Book of Abstracts, p. 60, <http://www.historiadeldisseny.org/congres/pdf/38%20Gaspar%20Mallol,%20Monica%20FRICTIONS%20DESIGN%20AS%20CULTURAL%20FORM%20OF%20DISSENT.pdf, p1> accessed June 29, 2012.

Giaccardi, E. and Fischer, G. (2005), 'Creativity and Evolution: A Metadesign Perspective', Sixth International Conference of the European Academy of Design (EAD06) on Design>System>Evolution, University of the Arts, Bremen, March.

Greer, B. (2008), *Knitting for Good!, A Guide to Creating Personal, Social and Political Change, Stitch by Stitch,* Trumpeter Books: Boston.

Hackney, F. (2011), 'Under the Pavement the Antimacassar: Quiet Activism and Radical Domestic Crafts', in Jané, C. (ed.), *Design Activism and Social Change,* Design History Society Annual Conference, Barcelona, September 7–10, Book of Abstracts, p. 65.

Hall, E. T. (1966), *The Hidden Dimension,* Doubleday/Anchor: Boston.

Heller, S. and Vienne, V. (eds) (2003), *Citizen Designer. Perspectives on Design Responsibility,* Allworth Press: New York.

Hunter, P. (2011), 'Communication and Self-Construction: Yona Friedman's "Immediate Education for Survival",' in Jané, C. (ed.), *Design Activism and Social Change,* Design History Society Annual Conference, Barcelona, September 7–10, Book of Abstracts, p. 67.

Jané, C. (ed.) (2011), *Design Activism and Social Change,* Design History Society Annual Conference, Barcelona, September 7–10, Book of Abstracts.

Julier, G. (2011a), 'Political Economics of Design Activism and the Public Sector', Nordes '11: The 4th Nordic Design Research Conference, Making Design Matter!, School of Art and Design, Aalto University, Helsinki, May 29–31, pp. 77–84, <http://www.nordes.org> accessed June 29, 2012.

Julier, G. (2011b), 'An Uneasy Coalition of Economies: Design Activism and the End of the Welfare State', in Jané, C. (ed.), *Design Activism and Social Change,* Design History Society Annual Conference, Barcelona, September 7–10, Book of Abstracts, p. 70.

Julier, G. (2011c), 'Day 4: Reflections, Comments and More', Design Activism Social Change Conference blog, <http://designactivismconference.wordpress.com/> accessed June 29, 2012.

Julier, G. (2008), *The Culture of Design,* 2nd ed., Sage Publications: London.

Klaassen, R. and Neicu, M. (2011), 'CTRL-ALT-Design', in Jané, C. (ed.), *Design Activism and Social Change,* Design History Society Annual Conference, Barcelona, September 7–10, Book of Abstracts, p. 73.

Lasn, K. (2006), *Design Anarchy,* Adbusters Media Foundation: Vancouver.

Leeds Festival of Design Activism (2009), <http://www.designactivism.org> accessed June 29, 2012.

Lees-Maffei, G. (2012), 'Reflections on Design Activism and Social Change', *Design Issues:* vol. 28, no. 2, spring: pp. 90–92.

Lefebvre, H. (1991), *The Production of Space,* Blackwell: Oxford.

Maldonado, T. (1972), *Design, Nature and Revolution: Toward a Critical Ecology,* trans. by Mario Domandi, Harper and Row: New York.

Manzini, E. and Jegou, F. (2003), *Sustainable Everyday: Scenarios of urban Life,* Edizione Ambiente: Milan.

Markussen, T. (2011), 'The Disruptive Aesthetics of Design Activism: Enacting Design Between Art and Politics', in *Nordes '11: the 4th Nordic Design Research Conference,* Making Design Matter!, School of Art and Design, Aalto University, Helsinki, May 29–31, pp. 102–10, <www.nordes.org> accessed June 29, 2012.

Mattelmäki, T. and Sleeswijk Visser, F. (2011), 'Lost in Co-X. Interpretations of Co-Design and Co-Creation', in Roozenburg, N.R.M., Chen, L. L. and Stappers, P. J. (eds), *Diversity and Unity, Proceedings of IASDR2011, the 4th World Conference on Design Research,* Delft, The Netherlands, October 31–November 4.

Mautner, T. (2000), *The Penguin Dictionary of Philosophy,* Penguin Books: London.

Meroni, A. (ed.) (2007), *Creative Communities: People Inventing Sustainable Ways of Living,* POLI design: Milan.

Meroni, A. and Sangiorgi, D. (2011), *Design for Services,* Gower Publishing: Farnham.

NESTA (2011), National Endowment for Sciences Technology and Arts, Public Services Lab, <http://www.nesta.org.uk/areas_of_work/public_services_lab> accessed June 29, 2012.

Neuberg, E. and M. Bowles (2011), '"Born to be Wild" Swatch Book Reality!', *The People's Print,* December 3, <http://thepeoplesprint.blogspot.com/2011/12/born-to-be-wild-swatch-book-reality.html> accessed June 29, 2012.

Neutra, R. (1954), *Survival through Design,* Oxford University Press: Oxford.

Norton, M. (2007), *The Everyday Activist,* Boxtree in collaboration with Unlimited: London.

Oosterling, H. (2011), 'Designature. On the Eco-Relational Paradigm', Design Activism and Social Change, Design History Society Annual Conference, Barcelona, September 7–10, <http://www.historiadeldisseny.org/congres/pdf/35%20Oosterling,%20Henk%20DESIGNATURE%20ON%20THE%20ECO-RELATIONAL%20PARADIGM.pdf> accessed June 29, 2012.

Ozinga, J. R. (1999), *Altruism,* Praeger Books/Greenwood: Santa Barbara, CA.

Papanek, V. (1974), *Design for the Real World: Human Ecology and Social Change,* Paladin: St Albans.

Parker, M., Fournier, V. and Reedy, P. (2007), *The Dictionary of Alternatives: Utopianism and Organisation,* ZED Books: London.

Patel, U. (2011), 'Crafting Culture: In(ter)vention and Women Artisans in Kundera, Rajasthan', in Jané, C. (ed.), *Design Activism and Social Change,* Design History Society Annual Conference, Barcelona, September 7–10, p. 93.

Pilloton, E. (2009), *Design Revolution: 100 Products That Are Changing People's Lives,* Thames & Hudson: London.

Pogglioli, R. (1968), *The Theory of the Avant Garde,* trans. by G. Fitzgerald, Belknap Press: Cambridge, MA.

Porritt, J. (2007), *Capitalism as if the World Matters,* Earthscan: London.

Sanders, E.B.N. (2000), 'Generative Tools for Codesigning', in Scrivener, S. A. R., Ball, L. J., and Woodcock, A. (eds), *Collaborative Design,* Springer Verlag: London, pp. 3–14.

Scruton, R. (2007), *The Palgrave MacMillan Dictionary of Political Thought,* 3rd ed., Palgrave Macmillan: Basingstoke.

Simon, H. (1969/1996), *The Sciences of the Artificial*, MIT Press: Cambridge, MA.

Smith, C. E. and Cooper-Hewitt Museum (2007), *Design for the Other 90%*, Editions Assouline: Paris.

Stairs, D. (2005), 'Altruism as Design Methodology', *Design Issues*, vol. 21, no. 2 spring: pp. 3–12.

Strauss, C. and Fuad-Luke, A. (2008), 'The Slow Design Principles: A New Interrogative and Reflexive Tool for Design Research and Practice', in Peruccio, C. and Peruccio, P. (eds), *Changing the Change Proceedings*, Turin, Italy, June, pp. 1440–50, <http://www.changingthechange.org/papers/ctc.pdf> accessed June 29, 2012.

Thackara, J. (2005), *In the Bubble: Designing in a Complex World*, MIT Press: Cambridge, MA.

Thorpe, A. (2008), 'Design as Activism: A conceptual tool', in Peruccio, C. and Peruccio, P. (eds), *Changing the Change Proceedings*, Turin, Italy, June 2008, pp. 1523–35, <http://www.changingthechange.org/papers/ctc.pdf> accessed June 29, 2012.

Thorpe, A. (2008–2012), 'Design Activism', <http://www.designactivism.net> accessed June 29, 2012.

Thorpe, A. (2012), *Architecture & Design versus Consumerism. How Design Activism Confronts Growth*, Earthscan: Abingdon, Oxford.

van Abel, B., Evers, L. Klaassen, R. and Troxler, P. (2011), *Open Design Now. Why Design Cannot Remain Exclusive*, BIS Publishers: Amsterdam.

Vihma, S (1995), *Products as Representations*, University of Art and Design: Helsinki.

von Busch, O. (2008), 'Fashion-Able. Hactivism and Engaged Fashion Design', PhD thesis, University of Goteburg, Sweden.

Walker, S. (2002), 'The Cage of Aesthetic Convention. Stasis in Industrial Design and the Necessity of the Avant-Garde', *The Design Journal*, vol. 5, no. 2: pp. 3–7.

Walker, S. (2006), *Sustainable by Design: Explorations of Theory and Practice*, Earthscan: London.

Walker, S. (2008), 'Following Will-o-the-Wisps and Chasing Ghosts: Design-Centered Studies and Design Exploration', *The Design Journal*, vol. 11, no. 1: pp. 51–64.

Wood, J. (2008), 'Changing the Change: A Fractal Framework for Metadesign', in Peruccio, C. and Peruccio, P. (eds), *Changing the Change Proceedings*, Turin, Italy, 2008, pp. 1698–1705, <http://www.changingthechange.org/papers/ctc.pdf> accessed June 29, 2012.

30

Design for Cyber-Sustainability: Toward a Sustainable Digital Future

BRAN KNOWLES, STUART WALKER
AND LYNNE BLAIR

INTRODUCTION

In this chapter, we present the concept of cyber-sustainability as a necessary dimension of any sustainability discussion in our highly digitized world. We begin by clarifying the terminology of cyberspace—as distinct from the Internet and the Web—in order to differentiate the digital realm from the physical infrastructure that supports it. Such delineations are necessary to more clearly recognize the real and negative effects our engagements with the Web are having on the planet. Next we discuss the direction in which Web development seems to be heading and the degree to which this trajectory may be at odds with the principles of sustainability.

Rather than focusing on sustainability as a question of our continued ability to exist, we instead derive the premises of cyber-sustainability from the tradition of design for sustainability and the different levels of human meaning that need to be satisfied if we are to experience a fulfilling existence. We argue that cyber-sustainability, therefore, must deal with considerations about environmental, social, and spiritual issues, while also acknowledging the economic dimension currently functioning as a barrier to change. This serves to take the sustainability discussion beyond the still prevalent materialistic metaphysic to include issues of ethics and personal, inner growth (Taylor, 2007; Mathews, 2006; Smith, 2001).

We describe cyber-sustainability not simply as a goal but as a direction. We argue that extricating ourselves from destructive (i.e., unsustainable) patterns of technological development requires a plan for change. In the final section, we present antipatterns as a tool for diagnosis, and its antithesis, patterns, as building blocks in the development of this plan. A handful of antipattern/pattern couplets are suggested as examples of this methodology, and we challenge readers to pick up the torch and identify further building blocks toward realizing a cyber-sustainable future.

INTERNET, WORLD WIDE WEB, AND CYBERSPACE

People commonly use the word 'cyberspace' as a poetic synonym for the 'Internet' or the 'World Wide Web'. The distinction between these terms is, however, significant:

- Internet refers to a standardized mechanism of packet switching and hierarchical routing—a means of sharing data over a network of linked computers—which was initially developed for defensive purposes as ARPANET in 1969. This has evolved over time into the TCP/IP protocol that today's computers use to connect to the global computer network (Comer, 2007).
- The World Wide Web (aka the Web) is a hypertext (HTTP) protocol for linking documents, and we use browsers (e.g., Internet Explorer, Firefox, etc.) as interfaces for viewing and searching these documents (Web 1.0). But often when we speak of the Web today, we are referring to Web 2.0, a recent tendency of Web applications to support participation (user-generated content), communication, and collaboration—for example, social media such as Facebook, Blogger, and YouTube.
- Cyberspace: the fact that the Internet enabled the sending of data between computers inadvertently facilitated our consideration of a dimension lying between these computers through which the data travels, and thus the concept of cyberspace emerged. Gibson first popularized this term in his science fiction novel *Neuromancer* (1984, p. 69), where he famously describes it as 'a consensual hallucination experienced daily by billions of legitimate operators.' Insofar as our ability to understand and experience cyberspace involves a shift in perception—one facilitated by the technological apparatus of the Internet—it is aptly characterized as a hallucination, and insofar as we can enter this space via the Internet, and experience the sensation of being online, the hallucination is indeed consensual and realistic.

As a philosophical construct, cyberspace allows us to differentiate between two qualitatively distinct yet simultaneously coexisting realities—the physical world and the digital world. Wertheim explains:

> In a very profound sense, this new digital space is 'beyond' the space that physics describes, for the cyber-realm is not made up of physical particles and forces, but of bits and bytes. These packets of data are the ontological foundation of cyberspace, the seeds from which the global phenomena 'emerges' … Because cyberspace is not ontologically rooted in these physical phenomena [of particles and forces], it is not subject to the laws of physics, and hence it is not bound by the limitations of those laws. (1999, p. 226)

Yet there are potentially serious consequences of imagining cyberspace as separate from our physical existence. This seeming duality makes it easy to forget that because cyberspace is mediated through material technology, our digital activity can have significant implications in the physical world. Separating the digital from the physical opens the door to the conceiving of digital technologies in vacuo by externalizing (and therefore conveniently, if incorrectly, ignoring) the very real physical costs associated with a given design decision.

We should concede, however, that even if this duality has spurred a particular kind of technological development, it is perhaps inaccurate to claim that we actively experience two distinct realms of being. Most of us—and especially the Web-savvy and those born into the era of the Web (aka digital natives)—navigate fluidly between the digital and our real lives. We now live digital lives, whereby Web technologies and devices that enable access to the Web are overlaid upon our experience of our physical environments. Ironically, however, instead of rectifying the mental disconnect between our cyber activity and its physical consequences, this conflation of the physical with cyberspace has made us that much hungrier for digital technologies. Indeed, our apparently insatiable appetite for cyber activities ostensibly serves to justify increasing environmental—and also, therefore, human—costs. What we seem to forget is that cyberspace is not a thing, like the Internet or the Web. Instead, it represents potential. Although we have exploited one particular use of cyberspace, there are any number of alternative uses that have not yet been considered—some of which could, potentially, enhance our lives beyond our wildest imaginings for the future of the Web, and do so without threatening our real lives.

EMERGING TRENDS

When we speak of the damage our Web technologies may be having, it is important to look not only at what they are doing now but more importantly at the direction they appear to be heading.

Most conspicuously, the Web is on a trajectory of rapid growth. Today, the number of digital 'atoms' (1s and 0s) in cyberspace is 'already bigger than the number of stars in the universe' and growing tenfold every five years (Gantz et al., 2008). This expansion is partly the result of the explosion of user-generated content—otherwise referred to as our growing digital footprints. For example, every month 2.5 billion photos are uploaded to Facebook (Pingdom, 2010); every minute, twenty-four hours of video are uploaded to YouTube (YouTube, 2011); and every six months, the quantity of content in the blogosphere doubles (Dube, 2006). We see a simultaneous growth in our digital shadows—the unconsciously generated accumulation of what is said and done about us in cyberspace, combined with all of our metadata, or the data about our data (Gantz et al., 2008; Harper et al., 2008b). If each person takes up roughly forty-five gigabytes of space pertaining to them, less than half of this is user-generated (Gantz et al., 2008). The remainder—that is, the proportion that makes up one's digital shadow as opposed to one's digital footprint—is produced by categories such as the following:

- CCTV cameras (Gantz et al., 2008)
- records of financial transactions (Gantz et al., 2008)

- data multiplication—that is, copies made to protect data loss from corruption or inadvertent deletion, which collectively accounts for about 75 per cent of the data in cyberspace (Gantz et al., 2008)
- GPS-enabled devices, which collate large amounts of location data (Gantz et al., 2008)
- analytics software, which gathers information on who is using webpages and how they are using them, which is in turn used to improve the targeting of advertisements to likely consumers (Simons and Pras, 2010)

Other, and likely more significant, components of the expansion of cyberspace include the following:

- cloud computing, which transfers personal data storage burdens to the Web—that is, to the world's data centres—and is growing in popularity; and
- ubiquitous computing, a term that refers to embedded technologies that record vast quantities of sensing data, whether environmental, governmental, societal, and so on.

Web access is also rapidly expanding; this has been especially marked since wireless access became more prevalent. In the past, people would access the Web via a modem connected to their desktop PC. Today, many connect via phones and smart phones, especially in regions of the world that lack the infrastructure for broadband. So whereas the Internet began as a network of connected computers, we are witnessing the emergence of 'the One Machine' (Kelly, 2007), or what some call 'the cloud', and the proliferation of mobile devices that serve as portals into that machine, such as laptops, netbooks, smart phones, and tablets.

In addition, over the last few years, influential thinkers have suggested that we are on the brink of the next evolutionary phase of the Web, notionally referred to as Web 3.0. While this term has been variously defined, two important trends seem to be emerging:

- The Semantic Web—this is fundamentally a technological transition from linked documents (Web 1.0 and Web 2.0) to linked data, which will, at least theoretically, improve our abilities to find relevant information and discover new connections. To work optimally, it requires the sharing of as much data as possible, and already many have already begun to upload raw data (Berners-Lee, 2009) to the Web for others to draw upon (e.g., BBC Backstage, http://backstage.bbc.co.uk/). Related to this is the use of the Web for ostensibly humanitarian archival purposes, so that all kinds of media can be explored by anyone with Internet access. Examples include Google Book Search, which aims to digitize and make searchable every book in the world (about 129 million) (Taycher, 2010), and Internet Archive, which aims to provide 'universal access to all knowledge': all books, music, film, television, historical Web content, and software (Kahle, 2007). While the aim of the Semantic Web is to help us manage (i.e., sift through) the ocean of data in cyberspace, it purports to be solving a problem that it is in practice exacerbating; namely, that it encourages users to increase their digital footprints, and it will vastly increase our digital shadows by adding huge amounts of metadata in the form of data tags to facilitate searching.

- The Internet of Things—this second Web 3.0 trend would allow us to connect directly to any object in the world through the Web. The concept is simple enough: every physical object would obtain a digital identification, against which data would be stored. Realizing this concept is far more complex, though recent strides have been made with platforms such as Pachube (https://pachube.com/), a data infrastructure to support the Internet of Things, which allows users to share and connect data streams from various objects. However, by enabling us to capture information about objects that would not previously have been associated with information at all—objects that would not only produce digital footprints but also digital shadows—the Internet of Things will place unprecedented strains on our capacity to store information.

It is no surprise, therefore, that there has been growing concern recently about the world's data centres. Data centres account for a significant portion of the total energy bill of the Internet. Altogether, data centres have been estimated to be responsible for 1 to 5 per cent of the world's total electricity usage (respectively, Renzenbrink, 2011; Kelly, 2007)—notably doubling from 2000 to 2005 (Gigaom, 2009)—and they are estimated to emit 130 million tonnes of CO_2e into our atmosphere per year (Berners-Lee, 2010, pp. 161–2). These figures are likely to rise considerably as cyberspace expands. Furthermore, currently the Internet and the Web are heavily reliant on the coal, uranium, and natural gas used to generate electricity—transmitted over grids that, in many cases, are already overtaxed (Heinberg, 2009, p. 204). Moreover, all these fuels are nonrenewable and all produce harmful by-products in their use. Furthermore, oil is used in the construction, maintenance, and distribution of the necessary machinery to enable access to the Web. As resources become scarcer, not only is the Web unlikely to remain free (i.e., in terms of direct monetary cost to users) but even simple activities such as a Web search may become prohibitively expensive in aggregate (see Berners-Lee, 2010, pp. 12–14, for current CO_2e costs per individual), at which point the entire cyberspace project would be compromised.

What seems clear is that as seductive as our Web ambitions may be, they are directly at odds with the practicalities of providing future resources to make them a reality. As we embark on Web 3.0, we do so from the privileged position of a culture that has not (yet) had to face the consequences of our planetary destruction.

CYBER-SUSTAINABILITY

We recently introduced the concept of cyber-sustainability as a means of discussing the ways in which current Web development may be incompatible with the principles of sustainable design (Richards et al., 2011). The concept recognizes that Web development impacts not only the viability of cyberspace as a metaphorically habitable dwelling but also the habitability of our real-world environments. So far we have discussed the fact that production and consumption of digital content has the unintended and very often unappreciated effects of the following:

1. contributing to the production of greenhouse gasses (CO_2e);
2. exploiting virgin and nonrenewable resources that are fast depleting; and
3. leaving us with unmanageable quantities of electronic waste.

Together, these threaten what Maslow terms our physiological needs. We need a hospitable climate; we need energy resources to allow us to continue providing necessities such as food; we need our water free from contaminants—such as those that might arise from electronic waste seeping into water tables (Panorama, 2011). In short, our health directly depends on the health of our environments, and the extent to which digital activity threatens this health puts it at odds with our most basic, fundamental human needs.

Admittedly, compared to some of the other ways we are damaging our environment, the Internet has a relatively minimal impact. And fortunately, there is a growing interest in developing green IT. Very public efforts are being made by companies such as Google, Facebook, Apple, and Yahoo to make data centres more efficient (respectively, Zelman, 2011; Bosker, 2011; Smalley, 2011; Treacy, 2009) and to power them by alternative energy (e.g., solar, hydroelectric, wind); meanwhile, others approach green IT from the perspective of aiming to make the manufacturing and disposal of these technologies more environmentally friendly (Murugesan, 2008).

The greening of our Web technologies represents a positive step toward not only reducing the negative impact of our digital activity on our environment but also raising public awareness about the issue. Yet unless these technological advancements are coupled with—or perhaps inspire—moderation of our production and consumption of data, we will likely continue to see a growing environmental cost of the Web, not to mention a soaring monetary cost of maintaining the Web as rising energy demands meet the world's dwindling resource supplies.

Meanwhile, it is heartening to see the emergence of sustainable HCI (Human-Computer Interaction) and its growing popularity since its inception in 2007 (DiSalvo et al., 2010). Researchers in this area emphasize a range of environmental issues surrounding computer technology, including increasing the product life cycle and slowing obsolescence cycles to cut down on waste (Blevis, 2007; Mankoff et al., 2007), minimizing the harmful effects of both hardware and software, such as finding ways to reduce their energy use (Mankoff et al., 2007), and making users aware of the environmental impact of digital activity through various feedback mechanisms (Cardenas-Tamayo et al., 2009; Foth et al., 2009; Reitberger et al., 2008).

There is no doubt that such efforts are a necessary step in improving the environmental sustainability of Web-related technologies. But missing from this discussion is an awareness of the other components required for true sustainability. Traditionally, sustainability is defined as the ability to meet our current environmental, social, and economic needs without compromising the ability of future generations to meet theirs (paraphrased from

Our Common Future, World Commission on Environment and Development, 1987). These considerations are the basis of the so-called triple bottom line of sustainability, and while these criteria help us in formulating instrumental goals for ensuring the continuance of human society (Mathews, 2006), they stop short of addressing the existential questions about why we might want to be sustained—that is, what ought to be sustained to make our continued existence meaningful and fulfilling (Orr, 2003).

To arrive at an understanding of what meaningful sustainability would be, it is necessary to begin with a holistic understanding of the human condition and our unique propensity for making meaning. Schumacher argued that science (a product of materialism) reduces man to an animal and in doing so neglects a basic condition of being human, namely to be self-conscious (1978, pp. 24–35). This self-consciousness is what causes us to question who we are and what our role in this world might be, and it is from questioning that we develop the meanings that inform our behaviours and worldviews. It is also possible to identify different levels of meaning employed in various contexts and in conjunction with one another. Hick (1989) articulates three such levels of human meaning, which closely parallel Maslow's hierarchy of needs:

Physical/Natural—this emphasizes our condition as biological organisms and our relation to our physical world. As physical beings, we have needs related to basic survival, such as food, water, shelter, clothing, and so on. At this survival level, for our activities to be meaningful, we have to correctly interpret the natural world and respond appropriately.

Socio-Ethical—this recognizes that we are social beings, and as such, we negotiate relationships with an awareness of what is socially acceptable and morally right.

Religious/Spiritual—this reflects a human need to find some higher order and significance to our existence, such as a striving to understand what Hick calls 'the ultimately Real'.

In an effort to account for these meaning-seeking needs, Walker (2011) has reconfigured the traditional model of sustainability by incorporating these different meanings, suggesting that the elements of sustainability that are necessary conditions of being human include the environmental, the social, and the personal/spiritual, and that the economic, which is a human construct rather than a condition of being human, mediates and affects our ability to satisfy these other needs. In other words, design for sustainability would necessarily address our current and future needs with respect to environmental, social, spiritual, and economic considerations (see Figure 30.1).

Bearing this in mind, an understanding of cyber-sustainability ought to include more than just the environmental impact of technologies for cyberspace. We should also be asking questions about how well the Web satisfies our uniquely human needs in facilitating fulfilling social engagements—for example, friendships and communities defined by human rather computing understandings of these terms—and in helping us flourish and achieve our human potential. Thus, Web-based activities should enable the

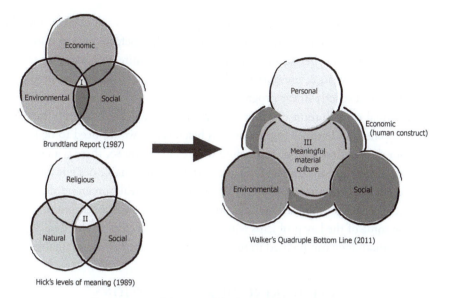

FIGURE 30.1   Comparison of the Brundtland Report model (Our Common Future, 1987) of sustainable development (I = sustainable development), Hick's levels of meaning (II = fully satisfied human), and Walker's Quadruple Bottom Line for design for sustainability (III = meaningful material culture).

development of meaningful social relationships as well as offering conditions and ways of interaction that are conducive to inner development rather than conditions and activities that may be detrimental to it. It could be argued that Web technology that does not meet these standards is unsustainable from a human-user perspective—that is, that users will eventually reject the technology—either due to inherent incompatibility with real social needs or due to their disenchantment with digital life whereby it comes to be regarded as being inconsistent with deeper notions of what constitutes a meaningful life.

To this point, in the development of cyberspace, people overwhelmingly do not reject technology for these reasons—perhaps to their own detriment. As prominent critics such as Carr (2010, 2008), Lanier (2010), and Turkle (2011) argue, developers of Web technology are not dealing effectively enough with social and spiritual issues. Yet, we adopt these technologies to satisfy immediate and instrumental needs, resulting in the overall diminishing of our health, happiness, and potential. So, indeed, the greater threat to our ability to live fulfilling social and spiritual lives is the likelihood that we will be so mesmerized by the parade of new technologies that we are unable to recognize just what it is that we are losing. Therefore cyber-sustainability, in contrast to the triple bottom line or sustainable HCI, is concerned not simply with our continued ability to maintain our technologies for cyberspace but instead with how and the degree to which cyberspace may factor into living full and fully human lives.

As will become clearer in next section, Web development and our thinking about what cyberspace affords have already started to become 'locked in' (Lanier, 2010, p. 3) to a particular way of doing that is highly integrated. This means that in order to realize cyber-sustainability without plunging our digitized society into chaos, we need to plan and execute a logical sequence of design interventions (what we later describe in the terminology of 'patterns' and a 'pattern language'), such that each change could be co-opted by other interdependent technologies and stabilize before moving onto the next change. This notion of cyber-sustainability consisting of a direction and plan for change is captured by Figure 30.2, presented with the proviso that the diagram should not be read as implying a strictly linear progression.

The eventual contribution of cyber-sustainability would be to identify exactly what these development milestones (represented as black rings) would need to be in order to arrive at our desired destination. But before we are able to do so, there is a need to identify the flawed assumptions that underlie the current unsustainable designs for cyberspace and how these assumptions prevent us from satisfying our real human needs. In the next section, we discuss the implications of a small number of such assumptions as a means of exposing some of the key problems with the current trajectory of the Web and explore how this methodology can be used to reveal implications for cyber-sustainable design.

RETHINKING OUR ASSUMPTIONS

Current unsustainable models for cyberspace development have taken hold because it is part of a larger human story that has been evolving over centuries. Cyberspace is one node in a highly integrated (economically, socially, culturally, and philosophically)—and thus mutually reinforcing and self-perpetuating—constellation of meaning. In other words, the reason we live unsustainably is because it makes a certain sense to us. Therefore, what is required for achieving cyber-sustainability is a radical shift in our thinking. This shift will either be thrust upon us by imminent crisis, or it will come about in a more gradual and graceful way, beginning with us identifying and naming the assumptions that have led us to this place.

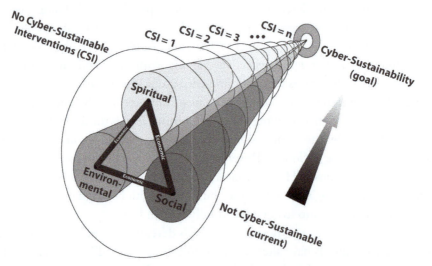

FIGURE 30.2 Cyber-sustainability as the confluence of environmental, social, and spiritual issues, and requiring a plan for change toward realizing a sustainable future.

In this section, we examine the metaphysical premises that guide our understanding of the world, the ways in which these have shaped the way we relate to the world (our modality) (Mathews, 2006), and how it has given rise to our current, particular manifestation of cyberspace.

To address these issues, we employ a technique called pattern language, initially used in the field of architecture (Alexander et al., 1977) and subsequently appropriated by computer programmers (Gamma et al., 1995). Specifically, we draw upon a variation on this technique, known as antipatterns (Brown et al., 1998). Our approach is structured using the template shown in Figure 30.3.

#. AntiPattern: '(name of AntiPattern)' – this is the flawed assumption we are challenging.

'(Insert illustrative quote or image)'

Forces: a) *(name of force);*

b) *(name of force); etc.*

(these are the factors that drive us to our flawed assumptions)

Scenario – description of the situation.

a) *(force #1)*

(Description of how the force acts on our thinking)

b) *(force #2)*

(Description of how the force acts on our thinking)

Sub-assumptions [optional]

(Scenario continued – introduction to Sub-assumptions)

Sub-assumption # - (name of sub-assumption) [optional] –

(these are key beliefs subsumed within this larger flawed assumption.)

Conclusions

(justification of the AntiPattern, and suggestion for alternative Pattern.)

Un-Sustainable Assumption (AntiPattern): *Name of AntiPattern.*

Cyber-Sustainable Assumption (Pattern): *Name of Pattern.*

(This is a healthier assumption for realizing sustainable cyberspace development.)

(Conclusions continued – final remarks)

FIGURE 30.3   AntiPattern Template

The goal of this section is to begin to develop a language to speak about unsustainable design decisions (antipatterns), to present a series of initial guidelines for more cyber-sustainable development (patterns), and to formalize a structure that may be adopted by others wishing to contribute to the project of developing this pattern language for cyber-sustainability. The following four sections exemplify use of the above method and template to address the following flawed assumptions:

1. AntiPattern: Cyberspace is infinite.
2. AntiPattern: Humans are inferior machines.
3. AntiPattern: Technology is neutral.
4. AntiPattern: The Web is invincible.

1. AntiPattern: Cyberspace Is Infinite

The Web is in some sense a black hole that's sucking up everything into it.

(Kelly, 2007)

Forces

a. the ideology of progress
b. externalization of costs
c. disincentives for digital accountability

Scenario: In our daily use of the Web, it certainly feels as if cyberspace will expand indefinitely. We can upload as much content as we like at no direct monetary cost to the individual but with externalized costs absorbed elsewhere, and cyberspace simply absorbs it. But what we perceive as limitlessness is in reality the externalization of limiting factors and their transference elsewhere. In practice, cyberspace is constrained by server capacity—that is, physical hardware and the finite raw materials we use to produce them—and the energy required to power the physical hardware. In fact, we may already be approaching the limits to its growth. For the first time since its inception, we are finding that 'we couldn't store all the information we create even if we wanted to,' and rather than generating vast new quantities of data, we need to 'develop strategies for storing, retaining, and purging information on a regular basis' (Gantz et al., 2008). Importantly, however, the average users are not aware of the need to prioritize cyberspace, nor are they encouraged to use it responsibly.

a. The Ideology of Progress: Our technological optimism in the face of what are likely very real practical limitations is a consequence of our deeply ingrained ideology of progress, which sustains the belief that 'all of human history is a grand tale of human improvement' (Greer, 2008, p. 37). Moreover, in practice—and part and parcel of the too-narrowly framed worldview of modernity, which is firmly based in a philosophy of materialism—this ideology has tended to mean progress is understanding and commanding the natural environment and in accelerating technological advancement. Yet we have seen in the last forty to fifty years that there are limits to technological and scientific ability, energy production, physical production, and even our ingenuity (cf. Homer-Dixon, 2000). In other words, the modernist outlook, which emphasizes continuous, step-wise progress as our primary avenue to meaning, is outmoded. This means that the assumption that Web progress, in the form of growth, improvement, and increased complexity, would be an inherently meaningful contribution to society must also be challenged.

b. Externalization of Costs: Although digital content is growing exponentially, many argue that this trend will be offset by the increased efficiency of our IT equipment (Koomey et al., 2010). What they fail to recognize is that continually increasing efficiency comes at a cost. The total amount of resources needed to continually upgrade our IT infrastructure as technological capabilities improve will increase over time while material (i.e., environmental) resources deplete. We are likely to see further diminishing returns (less improvement for greater investment) as we approach the limits to IT efficiency.

That said, cost as measured in terms of raw materials and energy is an insufficient metric as it is currently construed. Corporations routinely externalize many of the costs associated with production in order to ensure profit maximization for the organization and its shareholders. This serves as a major disincentive for digital accountability. Associated with this is the underpricing of resources—the true costs of which, in terms of resource denudation, pollution, infrastructure maintenance such as roads used in resource transportation, and so on, are excluded from the economic models. The costs are paid for by the taxpayer or ignored and therefore effectively act as subsidies for corporate growth and profit agendas. To determine the true cost of this continual technological treadmill, these social and environmental factors have to become internalized within the corporate accounting models. As suggested by Pigou (1920) and Schumacher (1973/2011), we need to cultivate a sensibility whereby human and environmental costs are treated with the same frugality that we treat economic capital. Only then can we assure that our health and happiness are weighed appropriately with respect to any technological decisions.

c. Disincentives for Digital Accountability: Currently, far from an ethos of frugality, there are incentives for unrestrained, indeed exorbitant, data accumulation. There are many inducements for individuals and businesses to transfer data from personal hard drives to the cloud, including not having to run and maintain the IT needed for storage, as well as the high availability and security provided by cloud services. This translates into massive cost savings, while enabling the increased production of data. We might characterize this relationship—greater environmental cost yielding financial savings for users—as a disincentive for digital accountability and therefore as a force in opposition to realizing cyber-sustainability.

Conclusions: Questions of whether our ingenuity will enable us to develop effective limits to cyberspace growth or when we will hit a wall is a very difficult—and potentially foolish—to try to predict. The subtler and more important point to be made here with respect to cyber-sustainability, however, is not about the possibility that we can continue to support a constantly swelling cyberspace but rather why this would be a meaningful project. Although an ever-expanding cyberspace would contribute to meaning in the sense that it would be an affirmation of an instrumentalist modality, we suggest that bending the world to our whims is far less fulfilling than experiencing life as flourishing participants in a more profound story that integrally intertwines us with nature and the meaningful limits it poses.

Our challenge is to delineate new metrics of meaning in our cyberspace endeavours. In order to begin down this path, we would need to adopt a new assumption that can serve as the foundation for a cyber-sustainable future:

- from the unsustainable assumption (antipattern): cyberspace is infinite
- to cyber-sustainable assumption (pattern): cyberspace represents infinite possibility

When we start to think of cyberspace in terms of infinite potential, we can begin to envision more humanly satisfying uses of this opportunity that do not require unrestrained growth. Furthermore, linking cyberspace to social and spiritual meaning may increase our reverence for it and encourage us to consider and use it more mindfully, thereby prescribing a new cyber-sustainable ethos of moderation that will in turn allow us to continue cyberspace well into the future.

2. AntiPattern: Humans are Inferior Machines

The Singularity will allow us to transcend these limitations of our biological bodies and brains.

(Kurzweil, 2006, p. 9)

Human beings are ashamed to have been born instead of made.

(Anders in Carr, 2010, p. 173)

Forces

- a. Web's 'unreasonable effectiveness' in contemporary society
- b. idolization of technology
- c. scientific rationalism
- d. informationism

Scenario: Eugene Wigner once commented that mathematics is an 'unreasonably effective' lens through which to view the world (Wigner in Wertheim, 1999, p. 219), a feature that has enshrined mathematics as a valued way of knowing. Similarly, the fantastic successes of the computer at performing specific operations has elevated computer-like thinking to the status of a human ideal, consequently subordinating our uniquely human ways of thinking. As some have noted, the sovereignty of the Web is invoked through the ways in which it seems intellectually superior to us (Postman, 1993; Carr,

2010). 'If we are lucky', quips Marvin Minksy (in Postman, 1993, p. 111), 'they [computers] will keep us as pets.'

a. Web's Unreasonable Effectiveness in Contemporary Society: We are in something of a chicken-and-egg situation with respect to our Web technologies. They help us negotiate the additional burdens that they are partly responsible for creating, such as '*continuous coordination* of communications, social networks and the mobile self' (Elliot and Urry, 2010, p. 31). Additionally, with each engagement with the Web our brains become increasingly hardwired to think in machine-like ways (Small et al. in Carr, 2010, pp. 120–1). So while the Web 'gives us powerful new tools for expressing ourselves, and conversing with others… [it] also turns us into lab rats constantly pressing levers to get tiny pellets of social or intellectual nourishment' (Carr, 2010, p. 117).

At the very least, what we could say of the Web is that its effectiveness is hardly surprising, given that it is a condition of the nature of contemporary society, which it has helped to shape.

b. Idolization of Technology: It is important to point out that the Web is only intellectually superior to us when measured in terms of speed of retrieval, quantity of retention, and accuracy of recall and calculation. Practically, this means that it is relatively inefficient to use our brains to store information (Suderman in Carr, 2010, p. 181). But in this assessment, we are quick to dismiss our natural human competencies, such as depth of contemplation, quality of retention (the layered and multimodal complexity of our memories), creativity, and comprehension, not to mention the importance of forgetting (Harper et al., 2008a). The devaluation of these natural skills is a consequence of our modern idolatry (Fromm, 1997; Schumacher, 1973/2011; Ellul, 1964)—that is, our exclusive valuation of the product of our own hands. In other words, the human capabilities we are born with are less enchanting to us than the human capabilities we can acquire through our technological ingenuity.

c. Scientific Rationalism: It has been said that 'what Taylor [F.W. Taylor of 'Taylorism'] did for the work of the hand, Google is doing for the work of the mind' (Carr, 2010, p. 150), which is to say that the Google strives to eliminate the inefficiencies of our human minds by augmenting them with technology that does thinking faster. This is extremely rational, particularly given the ways in which knowledge is linked to economic capital (e.g., Lesser and Prusak, 2004), but it neglects other subjective measures of progress. For example, a tradeoff of faster processing can be shallower processing (Carr, 2010).

d. Informationism: The premise of Web 3.0 is that we need more information in order to be better humans (i.e., better at understanding our world, better at solving problems). Indeed, our significant social and economic investment in the Web thus far fosters the notion that our most serious problems will be solved by inventing technology that provides 'fast access to information otherwise unavailable' (Postman, 1993, p. 119), and in turn, we have adopted information 'as both the means and the end of human creativity' (Postman, 1993, p. 61). This has been criticized by some as the digital age's cult of informationism—that is, 'a non-discerning, vacuous faith in the collection and dissemination of information as a route to social progress and personal happiness' (Schultze, 2002, p. 26).

By conceding our inferiority to machines, we tacitly accept that what technology can do well is what people need in order to be better people. And in mistaking technological aims as our own, we subject ourselves to domination by an entity that is 'indifferen[t] to empirical, real human projects and happiness' (Ellul in Szerszynski, 2005, p. 62). As a result of this misjudgement, we now see in our augmented population soaring rates of anxiety, depression, and addiction-like behaviour (Schor, 2004; Kasser, 2002; Niemz et al., 2005; Holmgren, 2002), along with declining empathy, compassion, and tolerance (Naish, 2009). In short, we see the diminution of the qualities that ethical and spiritual traditions have long cherished as pathways to human flourishing, which correlates (unsurprisingly) to negative effects on wellbeing.

Yet despite the reality borne out by our experiences, our Web ambitions continue to be rooted in the belief that Web augmentation will help us achieve our human potential. The reason for this logical disconnect arises from two deeply ingrained sub-assumptions.

Sub-Assumption 1: The mind operates like a machine. This assumption is the legacy of the Enlightenment, which sought to understand the world in mechanical terms and so dismissed the immaterial and developed a worldview based on naturalistic materialism. Today we still seek to explain the mind in terms of biological and chemical processes, occurring specifically in the brain. While this might be useful for addressing psychological imbalances and explaining behaviour, it does little to provide us with a spiritually satisfying explanation of what it means to be human.

Sub-Assumption 2: The machine is like a mind. If our minds can be understood as machines, we often draw the false syllogism that machines are therefore equivalent to minds. And although computers are (at least currently) incapable of replicating human social forms of intelligence, we have seen the emergence of new and supposedly innovative forms of human socialization through computer models of friendship and community. These computational socializations are fundamentally reductionist, yet, intertwined as they are in the rhetoric of progress, they have been welcomed as plausible and acceptable surrogates for deeply meaningful human interactions (Turkle, 2011, p. 87).

But clearly online friendships are qualitatively different to real-world friendships; online communities lack real communion. Because we now have access to new forms of socialization, many suggest that we need to broaden our definitions of these terms to account for their emerging colloquial usage. The danger, however, is that in doing so we strip these words of their traditional human meanings (Turkle, 2011, p. 238; Lanier, 2010, p. 53), which is to say we relinquish human ways of knowing the world and replace them with Web-like ways of knowing—a substitution unlikely to contribute to human fulfilment.

This same danger lies at the heart of the Semantic Web project, which seeks to model meaning in order to help us weed out irrelevant information and provide us with only the information we really need. But as Lanier points out, our technical abilities to model meaning are deeply insufficient: 'So instead we make this pseudo-filter, like a search engine keyword thing, and then you're supposed to pretend that it understands you, and therefore you make yourself into a moron to make the software look good' (*The Guardian*, 2010). In other words, in accepting computer-modelled meaning as comparable to human meaning, we lose precisely that which makes us intellectually superior to the Web.

Conclusions: We argue that this erosion of human values (i.e., both the valuing of humans and the qualities we cherish in life) is unsustainable according to our definition of cyber-sustainability. Given that the Web currently does not satisfy our human needs (see Cyber-Sustainability section above)—indeed it tends to make it harder for us to differentiate these from technological progress—its increasingly prominent role in society is a threat to our continued ability to live fulfilling lives. For this reason, we need to correct our assumption in a way that is more likely to enable us to thrive.

- from the unsustainable assumption: humans are inferior machines
- to the cyber-sustainable assumption: machines are fundamentally dissimilar to and are relatively simplistic constructs of humans

The benefit of consciously inverting and restating this hierarchy is that it prevents us from falling into the trap of being led by what we can do from a technological perspective rather than by what we need as humans. And once we recognize the meaningful ways in which machines are inferior to us—that is, with respect to what it is that makes life worth living—we will recognize our misguided dependence on simulated socialization (e.g., Facebook) and meaning (e.g., Semantic Web) and the unacceptability of offering these as substitutes for human ways of doing and being in the world. Adopting this humanistic assumption as one of the pillars of new cyber-sustainable development will mean, instead, that we will focus our efforts on imagining more humanly satisfying uses of cyberspace.

3. AntiPattern: Technology Is Neutral

I think that technologies are morally neutral until we apply them. It's only when we use them for good or for evil that they become good or evil.

(Gibson in Josefsson, 1995)

Forces

- a. net neutrality
- b. Western/capitalistic ideals
- c. instrumentalism

Scenario: Recently there has been a great deal of criticism about the Web and the effect it is having on us, including the following:

- the ways in which we are beginning to think like computers (Carr, 2010; Lanier, 2010);
- the negative effect it is having on our character and mental wellbeing (Elsner, 2010);
- its erosion of spiritual values (Schultze, 2002); and
- its contribution to our loss of substantive notions of meaning (Lanier, 2010).

But the response to such critiques is invariably—But the Web does so much *good* too!—followed by the enumeration of all the ways in which various apps have made our lives easier, the joys of cheap and easy communication across long distances, the power of democratization of information for global social justice, and any number of philanthropic activities supported by the Web. Debate is usually brought to stalemate with a seemingly judicious assessment: there will always be bad people who use any technology for bad purposes, but most people are good and will use it to do good.

The problem with acquiescing to this counterargument is that the purpose for which people are using the Web is not the cause of the changes we see in ourselves. As McLuhan (1964) so aptly commented, 'The medium is the message'—which is to say that every new medium changes us by changing our means of expression and thereby influencing how we think and act.

Whether the benefits of the Web outweigh the disadvantages is a purely subjective calculation, but they do not cancel each other out to the extent that combined they yield the Web a neutral influence. The Web, like all technologies, has affected and will continue to affect us in significant and unexpected ways. And yet there are understandable reasons—albeit reasons we challenge—why our assumption of its neutrality persists.

a. Net Neutrality: Net neutrality is one of the main tenets of the Web and is fiercely protected not only by prominent Web proponents (e.g., Berners-Lee in Wade, 2011) but by legislation (Smith, 2011). This, at least nominal, neutrality is ensured by treating all data the same, meaning that content is not to be censored, access is not to be denied, and services, platforms, and different media are not to be given weighted priorities.

b. Western/Capitalistic Ideals: Clearly the rules for the treatment of data (net neutrality) are philosophically intertwined with Western free market values, as well as with notions of the rightness of democracy. And in a sense this makes the idea of neutrality itself non-neutral, as it is loaded with positively connoted meanings within a predominant worldview, based in naturalistic materialism, that values and prioritizes a version of progress that is principally enacted via scientific and technological advancement, democracy, and free market capitalism.

That neutrality has become synonymous with freedom and democracy in discussions about the Web obfuscates the other meaning of neutrality—that is, whether the Web influences society in a particular direction.

c. Instrumentalism: Another implicit, if not explicit, feature of net neutrality is that the Web makes information available to all. Therefore, given our modality of instrumentalism, whereby we 're-make the world in accordance with human ends' (Mathews, 2006), we are obligated by our sense of morality to bring this gift to every person on the planet irrespective of their race, socioeconomic condition, education, and so on. 'Imagine the cultural impact,' says Google's Eric Schmidt about the Google Book Project, 'of putting tens of millions of previously inaccessible volumes into one vast index, every word of which is searchable by anyone, rich or poor, urban or rural, First World or Third, *en toute langue*—and all, of course, entirely for free' (in Carr, 2010, p. 162).

We, of course, forget (or deem overwhelmingly positive) that part of the package of this gift is a specifically Western worldview. One of the characteristics of this is the belief that humans are categorically distinct from nature, hence enabling us to use the natural environment as a resource to serve our own ends—regardless of the costs. But there are other cultures that do not make such a distinction and see themselves as playing an integral 'environmental and spiritual role in the web of life' (Margolin, 2004, p. 72), therefore prescribing a very different ethos that encourages ecological stewardship and engenders human-nature harmony. While global access to the Web might be viewed as morally just, this homogenization threatens to eradicate equally valid—and often far more sustainable—orientations to the world.

Conclusions: As Postman so bluntly put it, 'To be unaware that a technology comes equipped with a programme for social change, to maintain that technology is neutral, to make the assumption that technology is always a friend to culture is, at this late hour, stupidity plain and simple' (1987, p. 162). This naivety is dangerous from a cyber-sustainability perspective because it blinds us to the environmental, social, and spiritual impacts of our technologies for cyberspace. To overcome this wholly inadequate, unsophisticated, and inherently risky view, we have to consciously adopt a new way of thinking about our technology.

- from the unsustainable assumption: technology is neutral
- to the cyber-sustainable assumption: technology reinforces the worldview that produced it

Once we recognize this, it not only gives us an appreciation of our influence, it also allows us to leverage this influence in a direction that is necessary to ensure sustainability. We can, for example, design cyberspace technology upon a foundation of respect for nature and for the things that make life worthwhile, and engagements with these technologies are more likely, in turn, to reinforce these sustainable values.

4. AntiPattern: The Web Is Invincible

[In the year 2100, I predict] the Internet will be in your contact lens. Imagine blinking, and then instantly going on line, accessing your home office, or home entertainment system anywhere or anytime. We will be able to download any movie, song, Web site, or piece of information off the Internet directly onto our Internet-enabled contact lenses. These lenses will also be able to identify people's faces, translate their comments and provide subtitles, so that we will always know exactly with whom we are speaking and what they are saying in any language. We will live in a cross between 'The Matrix' and real life.

(Kaku, 2011)

Forces

  a. Technological trend toward mythic status

Scenario: When we look around us, enormous efforts are being made to lay the foundation for a digital future. For example, in President Obama's 2011 State of the Union address, he urged the nation to invest in infrastructure which would bring high-speed broadband service to 98 per cent of Americans by 2016 (Trawick, 2011), the rationale being that the Digital Age is upon us and that a competitive edge will be gained by preparing for that eventuality.

And the proliferation of Web technologies would certainly seem to suggest that the Digital Age is upon us. But is the Digital Age forever? Several forces and assumptions blind us to the very real possibility that the Digital Age may be but a brief moment in human history.

a. Technological Trend Toward Mythic Status: Particularly for the generation of digital natives, the digital seems part of the natural order of the world. We expect and, in many cases demand, the Web, as if it is a God-given human right, even as it is evolving (what might be described by Postman, borrowing Barthes's definition, as the achievement of 'mythic' status) (Postman, 1998). For example, in 2009, Finland was the first country to rule Internet access as a legal right for its citizens (Ahmed, 2009), followed quickly by Estonia (BBC News, 2010), and in 2011 the United Nations declared Internet access a basic human right (Rufino, 2011). In short, although it has only come to prominence in the last twenty years, the Web has become so deeply ingrained into society—economically, culturally, and psychologically—that we can no longer imagine life without it.

Sub-Assumption 1: The Web is resilient. Historically the Internet has proven highly resilient, and therefore much of the business that makes society function has been integrated into the cloud in the belief that the Internet will always be up and running. But recent (2007) cyber-attacks in Estonia call into question this supposed resilience (Traynor, 2007). The attacks, which caused one of Europe's most wired societies to shut down during the period of temporary network disruption, demonstrate that the growing interdependence of Web businesses and applications is a very real threat to the Web's resilience.

Sub-Assumption 2: The Web is exempt from the forces of collapse. As Greer notes, 'At the core of the modern world's identity is the conviction that our civilization is exempt from the slow trajectories of rise and fall that defined all of human history before the industrial revolution' (2008, p. x). And yet, belief in our historical exceptionality does little to protect us from the probability that we are not, in fact, exempt from peril. The painful lesson we may be about to learn is that expansion and contraction (toward a lower state of complexity) is the nature of all systems (Holmgren, 2002; Tainter, 1988), and the Digital Age is subject to these same forces. The challenge for us is not how to prevent the end of the Digital Age, but how to plan for a graceful transition to whatever is next (Orr, 2003).

The fact is, at present we need to believe that the Web will last forever because we have put all our eggs in this basket. We have shaped our cultures and societies around what the Web currently enables us to do. But choosing to take the Internet's invincibility on faith—no matter how desperately we wish it were true—might very well amount to what Greer (2008) calls 'perilous optimism'.

Conclusions: In believing that the Web is going to be around forever, we have allowed ourselves to become dangerously dependent on it as a means of 'doing' our lives, but there are several reasons why this dependence is unsustainable:

- First, if something were to happen to the Web, society would be thrust into chaos. In other words, we are not designing a future that will ensure our continued thriving.
- Second, we seem to be conceding that from now on, humans will forever live in symbiosis with Web technology, and this concession prevents us from asking important questions about the meaningfulness of this relationship—that is, whether it is truly desirable.
- Third, our dependence prevents us from extricating ourselves from this technology if and when we decide that it does not meet our human needs. We are bound not only by force of habit and the organization of our society around digital ways of doing and being but further (arguably most immediately and pressingly) by the economic forces that are interwoven into the project of technological progress that propel us further down the route of digitization.

Although we recognize how threatening it is to our cultural mythology, we suggest that the assumption that our Web-enabled lives can continue forever on our current trajectory needs to be rejected for the benefit of our human wellbeing.

- from the unsustainable assumption: the Web is invincible
- to the cyber-sustainable assumption: the Web is a temporary gift

If we choose to assume, instead, that the Web may disappear at any moment, we will begin in earnest to build an infrastructure that prepares businesses, governments, and us to become less dependent on the Web. The truth is, the longer we wait, the more dependent we become, so we need to act swiftly to make infrastructural change. Although this might be viewed as anti-modernization (according to traditional metrics of progress), we suggest that future-safing our world could become a more meaningful direction for development—that is, the kind of meaningful alternative to predominant interpretations of progress that we are so desperate for.

And finally, adjusting our assumption prevents us from taking cyberspace for granted. It may just inspire us to ask important questions, such as, What do we really want to do with the limited time we have to develop in cyberspace? The key is recognizing that the

Web as it exists and is heading now is merely one possible use of the massive potential that is cyberspace. We need to stop thinking that our two choices are: having the Web and all of the wonders it affords, and having nothing, effectively turning back the clocks to the 1960s. We have a third option: to develop an alternative Web. So, ironically, instead of asking how we are going to save the planet, perhaps we should begin by asking how we are going to save cyberspace (Hawken, 2010, p. 20).

CONCLUSION

In this chapter, we have referred to human fulfilment and more profound notions of human flourishing as reasons for attending to questions of meaning within the realm of cyberspace. In this regard particularly, continuance of the Web as we know it is not a necessary condition of Cyber-sustainability. By definition, cyber-sustainability is concerned not with the continuance of cyberspace but with the contribution of cyberspace to conditions necessary for human thriving. However, we do not take it as given that cyberspace and digital technologies need play any part in human thriving.

That said, we recognize the significant and growing influence of the digital technologies sector on the global economy, which functions as the driving force behind our continued investment in the Web as is. However, it is this very investment in—and hence vested interest in—the Web as is that seems to preclude the take-up of more sustainable and, potentially, more meaningful alternatives; this is exactly what Lanier refers to in his discussion of locked-in technologies (Lanier, 2010, p. 3). We have only just begun, here, to identify the building blocks—highly conceptual though they may be at this stage—that we can implement in developing a real and viable alternative to our current unsustainable digital technologies. The next step is to identify further antipatterns/patterns, some of which must necessarily address the complicated economical issues associated with becoming truly sustainable (cf. Schumacher, 1973/2011; Jackson, 2009; Daly, 1997), and we invite others to take up our challenge to contribute to the building of this cyber-sustainability pattern language.

Let us conclude by emphasizing the importance of the issue of cyber-sustainability. As Smith has written, 'To test the strength of a trouser belt, a hard yank is enough, for the consequence would be minimal if the belt broke. Where lives are at stake, however, the situation changes, thus the strength of parachute ropes must be precisely calibrated' (2001, p. 40). He concludes that the question of what is at stake will inform us how seriously we ought to regard the evidence for or against something. We have argued here that there is something even greater at stake with the issue of cyber-sustainability than whether humans are going to survive long into the future—for it seems that life is resilient enough to continue in one form or another in even the most extreme conditions. What is potentially being eroded with our technological pursuits is the potential to flourish as human beings—in a full and meaningful sense.

Any development in cyberspace ought to be concerned, therefore, with how it enables us to be fully human, not how it enables us to live optimally in a world that presupposes a set of distinctly modern values (e.g., efficiency, technological progress, growth). To quote the preeminent voice of sustainability, E. F. Schumacher,

> Our ordinary mind always tries to persuade us that we are nothing but acorns and that our greatest happiness will be to become bigger, fatter, shinier acorns; but that is of interest only to pigs. Our faith gives us knowledge of something better: that we can become oak trees. (1978, p. 155)

With respect to the Web, we have to wonder whether its evolution toward Web 3.0 is more akin to improving our 'acorn-ness' than actually helping us become 'oak trees'. The message of cyber-sustainability is that if we deliberately address human meaning as the springboard for the design process of development in cyberspace, we are more likely to contribute a design that satisfies our environmental, social, and spiritual needs. And in the end, if we are disciplined enough in our design process, perhaps by employing the technique of Pattern Language, we may find that cyberspace represents a unique opportunity to maximize what really matters for life—not profit, efficiency, or intelligence, but human potential.

REFERENCES

Ahmed, S. (2009), 'Fast Internet Access becomes a Legal Right in Finland', *CNN Tech*, October 15, <http://articles.cnn.com/2009–10–15/tech/finland.internet.rights_ 1_internet-access-fast-internet-megabit?_s = PM:TECH> accessed October 28, 2011.

Alexander, C., Ishikawa, S, Silverstein, M., Jacobson, M., Fiksdahl-King, I. and Angel, S. (1977), *A Pattern Language: Towns, Buildings, Construction*, Oxford University Press: New York.

BBC News (2010), 'Internet Access Is "A Fundamental Right",' *BBC News*, March 8, <http://news.bbc.co.uk/1/hi/8548190.stm> accessed October 27, 2011.

Berners-Lee, M. (2010), *How Bad Are Bananas?* Profile Books: London.

Berners-Lee, T. (2009), 'Tim Berners-Lee on the Next Web', <http://www.ted. com/talks/tim_berners_lee_on_the_next_web.html> accessed February 12, 2011.

Blevis, E. (2007), 'Sustainable Interaction Design: Invention & Disposal, Renewal & Reuse', CHI '07 Proceedings of the SIGCHI conference on Human Factors in Computing Systems, San Jose, CA, April 28–May 3: pp. 503–12.

Bosker, B. (2011), 'The Open Compute Project: Why Facebook Is Giving Away the Goods', *The Huffington Post*, April 8, <http://www.huffingtonpost.com/2011/04/08/facebook-open-compute-project_n_846925.html> accessed April 22, 2011.

Brown, W. H., Malveau, R. C., McCormick, H. W. and Mowbray, T. J. (1998), *AntiPatterns*, John Wiley & Sons: Hoboken, NJ.

Cardenas-Tamayo, R. A., García-Macías, J. A., Miller, T. M., Rich, P., Davis, J., Albesa, J., Gasulla, M., Higuera, J., Penella, M. T., Garcia, J., Fernández-Montes, A., Grado-Caffaro, M., Kappel, K., Grechenig, T., Umut, L., Uçar, E., Wall, J. and Ward, J. (2009), 'Pervasive Computing Approaches to Environmental Sustainability', *IEEE Pervasive Computing*, vol. 8, no. 1: pp. 54–57.

Carr, N. (2008), *The Big Switch*, W. W. Norton & Co.: New York.

Carr, N. (2010), *The Shallows,* W. W. Norton & Co.: New York.

Comer, D. (2007), *The Internet Book,* Prentice Hall: Upper Saddle River, NJ.

Daly, H. (1997), *Beyond Growth,* Beacon Press: Boston.

DiSalvo, C., Sengers, P. and Brynjarsdóttir, H. (2010), 'Mapping the Landscape of Sustainable HCI', CHI '10 Proceedings of the 28th International Conference on Human Factors in Computing Systems, Atlanta, April 10–15: pp. 1975–84.

Dube, J. (2006), 'How Many Blogs Are There? 50 Million and Counting', *CyberJournalist.Net,* August 7, <http://www.cyberjournalist.net/news/003674.php> accessed February 12, 2011.

Elliot, A. and Urry, J. (2010), *Mobile Lives,* Routledge: Oxon.

Ellul, J. (1964) *The Technological Society,* Knopf: New York.

Elsner, A. (2010), 'Is Social Media a New Addiction?' *Retrevo Blog,* March 15, <http://www.retrevo.com/content/blog/2010/03/social-media-new-addiction%3F> accessed February 4, 2011.

Foth, M., Paulos, E., Satchell, C., and Dourish, P. (2009), 'Pervasive Computing and Environmental Sustainability: Two Conference Workshops', *IEEE, Pervasive Computing,* vol. 8, no. 1: pp. 78–81.

Fromm, E. (1997), *On Being Human,* Continuum International Publishing Group: New York.

Gamma, E., Helm, R., Johnson, R. and Vlissides, J. (1995), *Design Patterns,* Addison-Wesley Longman Publishing Co.: Boston.

Gantz, J.F., Chute, C., Manfrediz, A., Minton, S., Reinsel, D., Schlichting, W., and Toncheva, A. (2008), 'The Digital and Exploding Digital Universe', <http://www.emc.com/collateral/analyst-reports/diverse-exploding-digital-universe.pdf> accessed April 17, 2011.

Gibson, W. (1984), *Neuromancer,* Ace Books: New York.

Gigaom (2009), 'Jonathan Koomey at Green:Net 09: The Environmental Cost Of Cloud Computing', <http://www.youtube.com/watch?v = GP4SOiqMFX8> accessed August 3, 2011.

Greer, J. M. (2008), *The Long Descent,* New Society Publishers: Gabriola Island.

Harper, R., Randall, D., Smyth, N., Evans, C., Heledd, L. and Moore, R. (2008), 'The Past is a Different Place: They Do Things Differently There', *Proc. ACM on DIS '08:* pp. 271–80.

Harper, R., Rodden, T., Rogers, Y. and Sellen, A. (2008), *Being Human,* Microsoft Research: Cambridge, MA.

Hawken, P. (2010), *The Ecology of Commerce, Revised Edition,* Harper Business: New York.

Heinberg, R. (2009), *The Party's Over,* Clairview Books: East Sussex.

Hick, J. (1989), *An Interpretation of Religion,* Yale University Press: New Haven, CT.

Holmgren, D. (2002), *Permaculture,* Permanent Publications: East Meon, Hampshire.

Homer-Dixon, T. (2000), *The Ingenuity Gap,* Knopf: New York.

Jackson, T. (2009), *Prosperity without Growth,* Earthscan: London.

Josefsson, D. (1995) 'An Interview with William Gibson (by Dan Josefsson)', <http://josefsson.net/gibson/> accessed November 14, 2011.

Kahle, B. (2007), 'Brewster Kahle Builds a Free Digital Library', <http://www.ted.com/talks/lang/eng/brewster_kahle_builds_a_free_digital_library.html> accessed February 11, 2011.

Kaku, M. (2011), 'The World in 2100', *New York Post,* March 19, <http://www.nypost.com/p/news/opinion/opedcolumnists/the_world_in_GZUFMdV7uCsp8Z4QleuujN> accessed November 1, 2011.

Kasser, T. (2002), *The High Price of Materialism,* MIT Press: Cambridge, MA.

Kelly, K. (2007), 'Kevin Kelly on the Next 5,000 Days of the Web', <http://www.ted.com/talks/kevin_kelly_on_the_next_5_000_days_of_the_web.html> accessed February 12, 2011.

Koomey, J. G., Berard, S., Sanchez, M. and Wong, H. (2010), 'Implications of Historical Trends in the Electrical Efficiency of Computing', *IEEE Annals of the History of Computing*, vol. 33, no. 3: pp. 46–54.

Kurzweil, R. (2006), *The Singularity Is Near*, Penguin: New York.

Lanier, J. (2010), *You Are Not A Gadget: A Manifesto*, Allen Lane: London.

Lesser, E. and Prusak, L. (eds) (2004), *Creating Value with Knowledge*, Oxford University Press, Inc.: New York.

Mankoff, J. C., Blevis, E., Borning, A., Friedman, B., Fussell, S. R., Hasbrouck, J., Woodruff, A. and Sengers, P. (2007), 'Environmental Sustainability and Interaction', *CHI '07 Extended Abstracts on Human Factors in Computing Systems*, San Jose, April 28–May 3: pp. 2121–4.

Margolin, M. (2004), 'The Human-Nature Dance: People as a Keystone Species', in Ausubel, K. and Harpignies, J. P. (eds), *Nature's Operating Instructions*, Sierra Club Books: San Francisco.

Mathews, F. (2006), 'Beyond Modernity and Tradition: A Third Way for Development', *Ethics & the Environment*, vol. 11, no. 2: pp. 85–113.

McLuhan, M. (1964), *Understanding Media*, McGraw-Hill: New York.

Murugesan, S. (2008), 'Harnessing Green IT: Principles and Practices', *IEEE IT Professional*, January–February: pp. 24–33.

Naish, J. (2009), 'Warning: Brain Overload', *The Times*, June 2, <http://women.timesonline.co.uk/tol/life_and_style/women/the_way_we_live/article6409208.ece> accessed February 2, 2011.

Niemz, K., Griffiths, M. and Banyard, P. (2005), 'Prevalence of Pathological Internet Use among University Students and Correlations with Self-Esteem, the General Health Questionnaire (GHQ), and Disinhibition', *CyberPsychology & Behaviour*, vol. 8, no. 6: pp. 562–70.

Orr, D. (2003), 'Four Challenges of Sustainability', *Conservation Biology*, vol. 16, no. 6, pp. 1457–60.

Panorama (2011), *Track My Trash*, BBC1 television, May 16.

Pigou, A. C. (1920), *The Economics of Welfare*, Macmillan & Co.: London.

Pingdom (2010), 'Internet 2009 in Numbers', *Royal Pingdom*, January 22, <http://royal.pingdom.com/2010/01/22/internet-2009-in-numbers/> accessed February 9, 2011.

Postman, N. (1987), *Amusing Ourselves to Death*, Methuen Publishing: London.

Postman, N. (1993), *Technopoly*, Vintage Books: New York.

Postman, N. (1998), 'Neil Postman: Five Things We Need to Know about Technological Change', *The New Technologies and the Human Person: Communicating the Faith in the New Millennium*, Denver, Colorado, March 27.

Reitberger, W., Tscheligi, M., de Ruyter, B. and Markopoulos, P. (2008), 'Surrounded by Ambient Persuasion', *Proc CHI '08*: pp. 3989–92.

Renzenbrink, T. (2011), 'Data Centres Use 1.3% of World's Total Electricity. A Decline in growth', *Tech the Future*, August 2, <http://www.techthefuture.com/energy/data-centres-use-1-3-of-worlds-total-electricity-a-decline-in-growth/> accessed October 28, 2011.

Richards, B., Walker, S. and Blair, L. (2011), 'Cyber-Sustainability: Leaving a Lasting Legacy of Human Wellbeing', *Proc. alt. HCI*, Nottingham, July.

Rufino, P. (2011), 'UN Declares Web Access As Human Right', *FutureGov*, June 13, <http://www.futuregov.asia/articles/2011/jun/13/un-declares-web-access-human-right/> accessed June 21, 2011.

Schor, J. B. (2004), *Born To Buy*, Scribner: New York.

Schultze, Q. (2002), *Habits of the High-Tech Heart,* Revell: Grand Rapids, MI.

Schumacher, E. F. (1973/2011), *Small Is Beautiful,* Vintage Digital: New York.

Schumacher, E. F. (1978), *A Guide For The Perplexed,* Abacus: New York.

Simons, R.J.G and Pras, A. (2010) 'The Hidden Energy Cost of Web Advertising', Technical Report TR-CTIT-10–24, Centre for Telematics and Information Technology University of Twente, Enschede, <http://eprints.eemcs.utwente.nl/18066/> accessed March 15, 2011.

Smalley, E. (2011), 'Apple Pumps Sunlight Into iCloud Data Centre', *Wired Enterprise,* October 26, <http://www.wired.com/wiredenterprise/2011/10/apple-pumps-sunlight-into-icloud-data-centre/> accessed October 28, 2011.

Smith, H. (2001), *Why Religion Matters,* HarperSanFrancisco: San Francisco.

Smith, J. (2011), 'House Republicans: Net Neutrality Rules Aren't Common Sense', *Tech Daily Dose,* October 27, <http://techdailydose.nationaljournal.com/2011/10/house-republicans-net-neutrali.php> accessed October 28, 2011.

Szerszynski, B. (2005), *Nature, Technology and the Sacred,* Blackwell Publishing: Oxford.

Tainter, J. (1988), *The Collapse of Complex Societies,* Cambridge University Press: Cambridge.

Taycher, L. (2010), 'Books of the World, Stand Up and Be Counted! All 129,864,880 of You', *Inside Google Books,* August 5, <http://booksearch.blogspot.com/2010/08/books-of-world-stand-up-and-be-counted.html> accessed September 15, 2011.

Taylor, C. (2007), *A Secular Age,* Harvard University Press: Cambridge, MA.

The Guardian (2010), 'Jaron Lanier Talks about the Failure of Web2.0 with Aleks Krotoski', <http://www.youtube.com/watch?v = aIwikI7IVYs> accessed February 17, 2011.

Trawick, T. (2011), 'Obama Wants High-Speed Wireless for 98 Percent of Americans by 2016', *Geekosystem,* January 26, <http://www.geekosystem.com/obama-high-speed-wireless-98-percent-americans/> accessed October 28, 2011.

Traynor, I. (2007), 'Russia Accused of Unleashing Cyberwar to Disable Estonia', *The Guardian,* May 17, <http://www.guardian.co.uk/world/2007/may/17/topstories3.russia> accessed May 1, 2011.

Treacy, M. (2009), 'Yahoo! Data Centre Will Be Powered by Niagara Falls', *Yahoo! Green,* July 2, <http://green.yahoo.com/blog/ecogeek/1125/yahoo-data-centre-will-be-powered-by-niagara-falls.html> accessed August 6, 2011.

Turkle, S. (2011), *Alone Together,* Basic Books: New York.

Wade, A. (2011), 'Net Neutrality: Online, We're All Equal—But For How Much Longer?' *The Guardian,* October 3, <http://www.guardian.co.uk/media-tech-law/ netneutrality-business-democracy-usa?newsfeed = true> accessed October 28, 2011.

Walker, S. (2011), *The Spirit of Design,* Earthscan/Routledge: London.

Wertheim, M. (1999), *The Pearly Gates of Cyberspace,* Virago Press: London.

World Commission on Environment and Development (1987), *Our Common Future,* Oxford University Press: New York.

YouTube (2011), 'YouTube Fact Sheet', <http://www.youtube.com/t/fact_sheet> accessed February 9, 2011.

Zelman, J. (2011), 'Transphorm, Google-Backed Startup, Claims Major Breakthrough In Energy Technology', *The Huffington Post,* February 25, <http://www.huffingtonpost.com/2011/02/25/transphorm-google_n_828427.html> accessed February 25, 2011.

31

Emerging Directions

TONY FRY

INTRODUCTION

What is to hand with(in) a handbook? Is it merely an invitation and a means to take practical action? Certainly a handbook can be viewed as a purely pragmatic object guiding practical action. Yet if we are to act futurally and thoughtfully, if we are to engage in a praxis, if we are to take responsibility for how and what our actions inform and direct, then such a book has to be far more than an object of instruction. It needs to assist us in thinking about the strategic forms our action should take, what they should engage, their directional consequences, and the nature of the conditions that direct them.

We often act without sufficient thought by limiting our horizon of consideration to the immediate problem at hand. But if our intent is to advance the ability to sustain, then we have to think ahead, and thereafter carefully, about every design action we will take and then, how all subsequent ongoing design outputs will continue to design. Whatever we bring into being by design is always, by degree, elemental to defuturing or futuring by design—either taking the time of our finitudinal being away or extending it. It needs to be constantly asserted that the product of design is never a closure, never finished—the agency of the designed is never contained by the design object. The implication is that the designer has to exist in a condition of continuous questioning of how things are as 'they appear to be to'. Things are not positioned as *Zuhandenheit* (readiness-to-hand); neither do they necessarily reveal what they really are, and thus we cannot assume that what appears as *Vorhandenheit* (present-at-hand) is actually a reality.

Brought to the issue of identifying and responding to emergent directions, such questioning requires that we, in our difference, critically examine our actual situation and thereafter consider what thinking should be made integral to our praxis.

WHITHER WHAT?

On what basis can emergent directions be reported? Certainly one familiar approach would simply be to undertake a literature review, but this implies a time lag and often a conservative representation of what was actually happening, as action always goes ahead of reflection. In contrast, and to begin with, what will be presented here is an account of an event that took place in Brisbane in July 2011. It brought together a selected group of fifty change agents to work toward an open program of action based on rethinking considering the relation between 'Design Action, Leadership, and the Future.'[1] The participants were educators and practitioners critical of the status quo, not least in their working lives. They came from the Asia Pacific countries, Europe, South Africa, and the Americas. Most had adopted design futures methods—all left open to them. They all came in response to this invitation:

> Design practice (in all its disciplines, including architecture) is at a crossroads.
>   Notwithstanding the introduction of 'sustainability' in design education and in commerce, design dominantly still serves the unsustainable. To move towards
>   'Sustainment' as project and process, radical and effective action is needed.
>   For this to happen a dynamic, global change community of focused thinkers, activists and leaders has to be created.

The people who attended were representative of an emergent global constituency that recognizes the inappropriateness and inadequacy of most design education to meet challenges of the age. The direction that emerged from the event was based on acknowledging the limitations of the university as the primary generator of the new kinds of knowledge that would underpin the radical changes needed to establish sustain-ability.[2]

The event sharpened the recognition that another type of university is needed—one liberated from upholding the status quo. The existing instrumentalized institution was seen as operating, in significant part, as a service provider to an economy that either feeds the unsustainable or, at its most progressive, sustains the unsustainable. The new institution, named as the Urmadic University[3] began to be understood as one based on a dispersed learning and a growing change community (Fry, 2011, p. 58). It was conceptualized as a university without a place that would not be under the direction of the managerialism of what was once called the 'professional managerial class' (Walker, 1979, pp. 5–44). This proto-institution was seen as more than just another network, not least because it would have a common direction, shared projects, and a highly developed means to exchange intellectual labour. Moreover, it would be able to gather knowledge from its radical antecedents and create new knowledge out of a confrontation with the contemporary forces of defuturing. The ranks of this university without a place would come from the margins and marginalized, the disempowered and alienated members of the university of the status quo (that is, from the kind of people who attended the event). This event marked the start of the process of bringing this university into being. The cadre created by the event is developing an agenda of strategic action with the potential to engage, inform, reform, deform, and re-form how design (in its broadest sense) could be thought about and taught (see theodessey.org). The modern university was a product of the earliest universities appropriating new knowledge, especially during the fifteenth century. As a result of this process, the university's theological centre of gravity became overwhelmed by the establishment and rule of secular knowledge.

In the lacuna within which the modern university exists, the project of the Urmadic University could have the potential to repeat such a process of transformation via appropriation. While the modern university has been responsible for creating the vast amount of the knowledge that made the modern world, it is now showing itself to be incapable of bringing into being what needs to be known in order to deal with this world. The university has degenerated into a role of servicing the status quo it helped create. As a consequence, instrumental knowledge and vocational training are displacing more fundamental modes of learning. In this educational environment, the humanities, which in truth begged revitalization, are dying. It is hard to know how long it will take for a process of transformation to gain real momentum. If geo-environmental circumstances permit, it may take several decades, or perhaps even a century or two.

Thinking of the university without a place puts design in a far more significant position—a position with directive importance far beyond the way the current design community understands it in the broadest sense. Design, in this placement, is the world of human fabrication in every respect. In contrast, the more designers and design thinkers continue to focus on material and immaterial design objects, the less the nature of design is grasped and the more its actual ontologically transformative power is overlooked.

Taking design beyond design, to expose what it could be, will be done in the six conceptual moves that follow. While these moves aim to set a very wide and long-term developmental direction, they are nonetheless able to inform and influence immediate understanding and action. In this respect, they are handy moves and in fact invite being seen as the basis for a futural praxis (which is to say, they invite a thinking to be embedded in transformative action). The stakes here are of course much higher than the transformation of the agency of design and the nature of the university. Put baldly, unless we can learn to think what we do—rigorously, reflectively, and over time—so as to create the material conditions that in turn create an ontological shift in what we are (and thus does not depend on thinking), then we are have but a bleak prospect.

MOVE 1: THINKING DESIGN IN TIME

We human beings are frightened of time: our ability to sustain our self, and all we depend upon, is delimited by our illusions of permanence (Magnus, 1978, pp. 190–5). In most cases, we do not think of time beyond our own interests and the immediate past or future decades. An expressed concern for future generations here folds into an unconscious expression of human centredness and a horizon delimited by one's children and grandchildren. Locked as we are in the ever-present now, we neither look backward nor forward into deep time, nor develop the conceptual means to attempt to do this. For the most part, we live as momentary beings. Yet unless we learn to think and act in time, we are fated—this implies both acting with urgency and acting in the medium of time.[4] Likewise, it means moving beyond a preoccupation with design in space. It means designing in time. But what does it mean to design in time?

Essentially everything designed has a being-in-time and as such has continued design agency, and thus is an ongoing designing. Amid the sum of things, a house, mobile phone, pair of shoes, chair, railway station are all examples of objects that have their own time (Heidegger, 1996, p. 383; 1972, p. 3). We misread time as the measurement of duration. For, in truth, time is change, and all that comes into being does not change in, or at, the same time. Our invented time is singular, whereas real time (ontic time as change occurs) is plural. To engage with design in time not only acknowledges this but takes it into account. It does this by seeking to discover via reflection and research what a designed entity will encounter over time, what it will have to withstand (but without any illusion of true disclosure). This information is then employed directively toward changing what a design practice and process brings into being. The anticipatory character of design in time de facto alters the nature of the designer's responsibility, taking it beyond the delivery of a product, its performance and safety. The issue becomes one of efficacy, affect and care beyond the thing itself, considered over time as the thing brought into being by design goes on designing. Imperfect as this method might be, it can deliver much better results than the myopia of object-focused design practice.

MOVE 2: UNDERSTANDING THE WORLD MADE HUMAN BEYOND INSTRUMENTALISM AND THE RHETORIC OF SUSTAINABILITY

It is not possible to design for sustain-ability without understanding what is being designed against. This means having in place a clear understanding of the unsustainable prior to any attempt at designing to overcome it. Yet dominantly, the unsustainable is taken as given and reduced to a litany of identified impacts or characterized as symptomatic problems such as waste, overconsumption, resource stress, or climate change. Obviously these are all real problems, but they are not the primary causes of unsustainability, or its essence. The real, the fundamental, problem is us, our ontology, our anthropocentric mode of being-in-the-world as it is (being) globalized. In our self-centring of interests, as the most dangerous of animals we have become derelationized, disconnected, and inequitable. Effectively, and by design, we have constructed a world in mind and matter at odds with that upon which we depend. So while the consequences of this have to be dealt with, the primary task is to design against our continuing disposition to act as we do. This requires a shift into designing what designs us so that we may be ontologically designed to be in another way (this totally reconfigures how we think and create all that is brought into being by design). To clarify this point, two dominant meta-historical conditions of our ontological designing can be registered.

The first was the ontological condition of being nomadic. For around 150,000 of the 160,000 years of its planetary existence *Homo sapiens* was nomadic. This mode of earthly dwelling, wherein the world was our home, took varied forms according to climate and environment. Above all, the story of nomadism was a story of survival in the face of often severe climatic changes that make at least the foreseeable projected prospects of global warming pale into insignificance. At the depth of the Ice Age, the human species was reduced to a few thousand. Over the totality of this vast period, the world was our home (Fagan, 2004, pp. 12–96).

The second was the condition of settlement. This started in the Fertile Crescent of the Middle East about ten thousand years ago. Prior to this, the climate had warmed, cooled, and rewarmed, the West remained cold and the East dry, but in the Fertile Crescent food was abundant with cereals, fruits, nuts, and edible roots (Fagan, 2004, pp. 12–96) Slowly, agricultural practices arrived and with them the conditions that were to lead to the first small settlements and the production of surpluses—and with them, what was to become the basis of economic exchange. Uruk, the first city, was established 7,500 years ago, and the path to urbanism and economically centred societies was set. These developments were part of an ever-larger transformation: the creation of a world-within-the-world that amplified a fundamental characteristic of our species: creation (prefigured making—design) without sufficient recognition of what is destroyed in the process. Here then is the seed of unsustainability—inherent in our very becoming, amplified by numbers, and advanced by technology to blossom into the danger that now threatens. We still hardly glimpse this danger and its extension via our education in error as it sustains the unsustainable status quo. Yet events are beginning to occur that disturb this picture.

In fact, geophysical climate events are starting to collide with a discourse that enfolds the expression of unsustainability (including climate change) in symptomatic terms. Effectively, this is shifting the way events are understood irrespective of their actual causality (which is often indeterminate). What is arriving is a feeling of unsettlement, that, while often centred on a traumatic event that directly unsettles the people affected (cyclones, floods, earthquakes, etc.), actually generates a wider unsettling effect within and beyond any particular locality or nation. For example, the horrific earthquake and tsunami in Japan in 2011, and the associated rhetoric, made it apparent that as the global population increases and as cities become larger and denser, natural disasters, even if their frequency and level remain the same, will have increasing impacts on populations. This is to say that with a growing number of extreme weather events, unsettlement will become a more widespread and ubiquitous psychological condition of being-in-the-world, globally, for increasing numbers of people who feel continually more vulnerable. It can be said with some certainty that this condition will deepen as the impacts of climate change intensify over coming decades and beyond.

What this situation tells us is not only that there is a physical and cultural dimension to unsettlement but that the telos of human development has ended, for a very long time or maybe forever. We have no developmental destiny, no assured prospect of progress or certainty that the fabric that holds civilizations together will remain intact. Uncertainty unsettles. Indeed, around 30 per cent of the global population already lives encased in the condition we fear, wherein the ability to sustain is reduced to getting from one day to the next.

As clusters of thinkers around the world are now starting to realize (and produce evidence through projects), we may be at the edge of a third age of human habitation, an urmadic age—an age partly urban and partly nomadic. Why? The answer is simply that many of us will have to move as climate and conditions change and direct. Yet we cannot revert to nomadism nor totally abandon the nature of urban life. Thus some kind of synthesis between the two will be forged. An opening into learning at the dawn of the third epoch of human habitation has already commenced (Fry, 2011, pp. 4–8). Such learning has to face the propensity of developed and developing humanity to defuture, to act in ways that negate time. The counter-measure—futuring—thus begs to be the emergent design paradigm. There are signs that this process has started (as the already discussed Brisbane event and its dispersed arrival in design education suggest).

MOVE 3: ENGAGING ANTHROPOCENTRISM AND THE DIALECTIC OF SUSTAINMENT

Anthropocentrism is an inherent feature of *Homo sapiens,* and this trait, it seems, has been with us from our inception, as is suggested by our suspected elimination of other hominoid competitors (in particular Neanderthals) (Fry, 2012). Certainly the trait is seen in the imposition of the human will upon other beings (especially those animals that humans have domesticated), as well as in the way the natural world has come to be treated as a resource—which we gave ourselves a total right to exploit. This is how we came to be, and we cannot be and not be so. Yet everything changes once we know this. For once we know what and how we are, it becomes possible to take responsibility.

So framed, and in the sphere of practicality, everything also changes once the dialectic of sustainment is recognized. At its simplest, this names the indivisible relation between creation and destruction, and once recognized, it carries with it an ethical imperative that travels with design as it prefigures making and/or unmaking. Cities, roads, buildings, all manufactured products, the rural and urban landscape—in sum, the entire world-within-the-world of human creation—arrive out of the destruction of the form of matter of the given world: action that is most crudely exemplified by the extractive industries and all modes of harvesting. Our coming into life in human settlement took the anthropocentric disposition (the imposition of our will to be on the world around us) and amplified it. As time passed, our numbers grew, and our disposition became extended via technology; thus our ability to make and unmake was further amplified to its current and ongoing monstrous proportions. As the relation between what we needed to sustain ourselves and our acquisitive desires divided, and the dialectic of sustainment got its head, we, especially us moderns (the nonpoor), were unknowingly propelled toward the current condition, which is characterized by a truly massive disjuncture between what we need and what we take. Mostly, we remain oblivious to what we make and what we destroy—to our unsustainability. In this imbalance between creation and destruction, making and unmaking, needing and taking, all that travels under the heading of sustainability is a deflection, a deception, insofar as it is deployed to support and extend what we are and do.

Sustainable development captures the irrationality of the seeming reasonableness of sustainability, not only as it sustains the unsustainable but as it directs us away from finding ways to establish fundamental conditions of the project and process of sustainment. This requires discovering ways to bring a measure of what we can reasonably be said to need into alignment with what we actually take from the world. So considered, material modesty equates to survival (of our species).

MOVE 4: ACKNOWLEDGING RAMPANT PRODUCTIVISM AS ELEMENTAL TO STRUCTURAL UNSUSTAINABILITY

Productivism arrived as an ancient thinking from the Greeks that grasped structural connections and, in so doing, expanded the perception of what it was possible to make. Productivism provided the conceptual foundation for the practical attainments that brought the material fabric of the things of the modern world into being. Yet it also naturalized the unchecked production of destruction as integral to what we now call development. It was thus the means by which the dialectic of sustainment (which is how the indivisible relation between creation and destruction can be understood) was perverted and allowed to transmute into a material means of absolute nihilism (a giving way to unchecked unsustainability by simply thinking and acting on the basis of being helpless in the face of 'that is how the world is').

To acknowledge productivism is a move toward the unmaking and the elimination of much that defutures—that which productivism helped to create. Making this move shifts the way the world is seen. It opens into recognizing an urgent need to deal with a great deal of what already exists by its destruction or material or immaterial redirection. As such, this move prioritizes dealing with what is over making more and the new.

MOVE 5: GOING BEYOND INSTRUMENTALISM

Going beyond instrumentalism is going beyond productivism as an unconsidered thinking and acting. Together with the ever-rising dominance of instrumental education, humanity is being taken, by its enduring relation to technology (wherein the nature of technology itself is indivisible from our very being), toward an even-greater condition of unreflective instrumentalism. What this means is unknowingly giving way to practices that underscore the material extension of structural unsustainability. To counter this situation, it is essential to create a form of praxis embedded in sustainment. This involves developing an understanding of sustainment as a directional project and process that needs to be created on a huge scale, able to redirect the making of the world within the world so that it acts to future rather than defuture. It means acting against compliant instrumental action (including under the banner of sustainability); it means putting yourself in a position where you know what you are actually doing. It does not follow that one shouldn't employ instrumental action—in fact it is vital. But such action has to be intellectually directed and subordinated to the appropriate end: sustainment.

Such thinking directly opposes all thinking that suggests it is possible to engineer humanity into sustainability. Techno-salvationalism cannot be but hyper-productivism. The problem of the unsustainable cannot just be solved instrumentally; it cannot deliver the values, modes of being, and sensibilities that future. In so saying, it is not to say that we can cease to be technological being, for we have always been so (Fry, 2012).

MOVE 6: RESPONDING TO THE IMPERATIVES OF SUSTAINMENT

In a world made unsustainable and unsettled (by that anthropocentric species that we are, as we formed a world within the world acting against the foundational world that is), what does it mean to respond to the imperatives of sustainment? Sustainment needs more qualification in order to help expose some imperatives.

So exactly what is (the) sustainment? It has already been named as a project and process—but what is the project and what is the process?

The project is of epochal significance and can be equated in scale and perhaps time to the Enlightenment. But whereas the Enlightenment brought the modern world into existence (the modernization of the world within the world), the sustainment becomes the intellectual means—the creator of the knowledge, culture, and institutional constructs—the means to redirect and reconfigure the world made modern (in its inequitable unevenness) so that human actions can become orientated toward making time for the species rather than continuing to take it away. By implication, the reconfigurations of the sustainment would have to set out to transform law, the state, the subject, scientific and cultural knowledge, politics, the economy, and the culture of everyday life. At the moment, all that can be enunciated are openings into the process (but recognizing that some have started—earlier reference to the Brisbane Hot House being just one indicator). Four openings into a critical view can be brought to this move to advance it.

Opening one recognizes our education in error. From infancy and throughout our life, we are educated in error—we do not become unsustainable by accident. Immersed in structural unsustainability, unsustainability is something we learn as we learn to be producers of the modern world—but at Bruno Latour pointed out some time ago, 'We have never been modern'; we have never arrived at what modernity/the modern university set out to make us become (Latour, 1993, pp. 46–48). This is to say that we are taught how to be unsustainable, and we are inculcated into it. The unsustainable frames our perceptions; it is inscribed into the language we learn, how we are visually inducted into seeing the world, and how we behave—it is the mark and measure of our failure to become modern. Of course, this is never an overt declarative process; rather it arrives as the world is made ready to hand for us—objectified in forms able to be learnt, appropriated, purchased, made our own, used, discarded, imposed upon, aestheticized, and destroyed. In essence, such an education is the normalized gaining of the sense of ourselves and how to act in relation to the myriad ways in which the world exists for us. Whatever, and however, we make in this world is equally a making for ourselves (even when couched as worldly conservation). In sum, our education in error in its essence validates the unknowingness of our being anthropocentric as a mode of being.

Opening two responds to opening one by comprehending that a project is needed so as to learn to be another way. This again is a vast project that enfolds formal and informal education at all levels, and that will have to turn on material modesty in difference as something to be given shape as a desire, as the basis of a remade design that designs, and as the basis of another kind of education institution. The first moves toward this creation, this learning, have begun and are expressed in the form of a dispersed university—an institution without a place—centred on developing redirective and reconfigurative knowledge in and over time—an Urmadic University.

Opening three confronts the recognition implicit in the project of sustainment—which is a need to make a mode of being in the world wherein we humans cease making a world within the world that is destructive of the world of our, and other living beings', dependence. This opening implies exposing the scale of the transformation required to move from what we are to what we need to do (if we are to continue to be). While the Brisbane Hot House affirmed there was already a cohort of pathfinders starting to work toward this end, it is realized that the scale of the transformation is again one that will require the efforts of many over an extensive period of time.

Opening four makes clear there is an imperative to act ethically. Ethics is seen here in materialist terms at their most fundamental—it is what things affirmatively do. As a consequence, it is liberated from morality. The opening is enacted through the consequence of what we make and do as these actions draw the line between creation and destruction; futuring and defuturing; sustain-ability and unsustainability; making time and negating it. Decision in such a context rests with the emergent thinking that holds itself accountable to sustainment and the formation of a culture able to help bring it, as project and process, into being.

CONCLUSION

For many people, the response to the situation of the symptomatic problems of the unsustainable is to be pragmatic. This is the easiest thing to do and the most therapeutic form of action to hand. But it cannot solve the causal problem of the unsustainable. More fundamentally, this choice of action almost always adds up to a have-our-cake-and-eat-it position that sustains the unsustainable status quo. Advancing sustainment is a much longer and infinitely harder task that exceeds the reach of any lifetime. Yet it is the only choice if the problem is seen in time. The choices are stark—there is no middle ground. Sustaining the status quo cannot but serve the negation of our time (it defutures). At the very best, this action may buy some time. But it offers little in the face of the coming global population of ten billion plus, of whom 80 per cent are likely to be locked into unsustainable consumption; the need for this population to be fed; the environmental challenges of a changing climate; and the threats of conflict arising from the effects of a changing climate, such as water shortages, movement of populations, and more. In contrast, the enormously difficult task of moving toward sustainment opens into the third age of human earthy habitation—the urmadic. This project is not utopian; it does not offer the good life; rather it is futuring writ large and as such it is the future to make. Obviously, it is still an idea in an amorphous state. Certainly it demands so much that is currently beyond us. Yet as the psychology of unsettlement deepens, there will be significant numbers of thinkers and makers who will start to grasp that there is no other option. By implication, the immediate task is thinking how to bring it to hand.

NOTES

1. 'Design, Action, Leadership and the Future', http://www.theodessey.org/?p=601, accessed February 22, 2013.
2. The term "sustain-ability" is used not only as an alternative to "sustainability" (and "sustain-able") but in opposition to them. This is because the usage of "sustainability" has become debased: it is a signifier with multiplicities of contradictory significations. In contrast, although meaning can never be fully secured, "sustain-ability" (and "sustain-able") are more specific and declarative qualifiers.
3. The term "urmadic" means ur(ban no)madic.
4. We talk, for example, as if global warming were a problem that with the right mix of economics, policy, and technology could be fixed, whereas it will now exist for a very long time no matter what we do. One significant research project indicates that it is irreversible for at least a thousand years (see Susan Solomon, U.S. National Oceanic and Atmospheric Administration, who has shown in her research that surface temperatures, rainfall, and sea levels are largely irreversible for more than a thousand years after carbon dioxide emissions have stopped [http://www.noaanews.noaa.gov/stories2009/20090 126_climate.html]).

REFERENCES

Fagan, B. (2004), *The Long Summer,* Basic Books: New York.

Fry, T. (ed.) (2011), *The Urmadic City: The Idea and the Image,* Queensland College of Art: Brisbane.

Fry, T. (2012), *Becoming Human by Design,* Berg: Oxford

Heidegger, M. (1927/1996), *Being and Time,* trans. by Joan Stambaugh, SUNY UP: New York.

Heidegger, M. (1969/1972), *On Time and Being,* trans. by Joan Stambaugh, Harper and Row: New York.

Latour, B. (1993), *We Have Never Been Modern,* trans. by Catherine Porter, Harvard University Press: Cambridge, MA.

Magnus, B. (1978), *Nietzsche's Existential Imperative,* Indiana University Press: Bloomington.

Walker, P. (ed.) (1979), *Between Labor and Capital,* Harvester Press: Brighton.

32

Literature and the Environment

JOHN RALSTON SAUL

The icebergs are melting, grizzly bears are wandering ever farther north and mating with polar bears, and the Arctic Ocean ice is opening up bit by bit, retreating from its inaccessible mystery. The temperature is rising. None of this is very complicated. In fact, if you tell the story in this way it comes to resemble a desperate, romantic novel by Jules Verne. Why would an approaching catastrophe of planetary proportions resemble an adventure story—a good quality adventure story—designed for boys, or perhaps for men who want to be boys? It has always been difficult to turn enormous human disasters into great fiction for the simple reason that great fiction prefers a local story, that, through the genius of the writer, becomes universal.

Global warming presents a particularly difficult literary problem because it is so diffuse in its causes and villains and errant knights. The result may be concrete, but the process is a complex, drawn-out story in which the individual characters play only passing roles.

Let me go at this in another way. Why is this melting of ice, mating of bears, opening of mysterious regions, rising of temperatures taking place? There are a multitude of explanations. Certain are more probable than others. For example, those that involve a continuous intensifying of human industrial activity stand a good chance of being at least partially true. But of course there is no absolute scientific proof that they are. The more precise we attempt to be, the more problematic the argument becomes. Which causal action is responsible for what part of the crisis cannot be proved. Or rather, if we take a scientific approach, and gather information until all the facts are in, it will almost certainly be too late to do anything about our findings—which means it will be too late to do anything about our existence or loss of it.

What we are faced with is not a scientific problem or a scientific conundrum or even a test. Science has a role to play, but it is only of secondary or tertiary importance. When it comes to the environment, literature and other forms of public language are probably much more important and relevant than science. Yet literature—and we who create this language of the imagination—have so far failed to find our words—that is, our role—in today's most important drama.

For thirty years I have been flying about the Arctic in small airplanes. They are called Twin Otters—the workhorse of the North. In an era when most airplanes are computer driven and most air travel relates to cattle trucks, the Twin Otter remains deeply mechanical, practical, and somehow romantic. There it is again, that irrational word: romantic. The plane is so straightforward that anyone of us could imagine ourselves flying one. A Twin Otter can land on an ice flow or squeeze down a deep canyon. When it crashes, you may well live. We often fly around at between 600 and 1,600 feet (200 and 500 m). In this way, I have drifted over most of the glaciers in the Canadian Arctic. They often resemble fat, white spiders. The gigantic body lies in a high mountain bowl, while its legs of ice stretch down the various surrounding valleys, narrow and long. At the bottom, on the edge of the Arctic Ocean, the spider's feet look like great chessboards as the ice breaks up into skyscraper-sized pieces, which then fall over into the water and float away as icebergs.

Specialists have been taking pictures of these glaciers for at least fifty years. The pictures are perfectly clear. Fifty years ago, even thirty years ago, the legs stretched all the way down to the water's edge, and so thousands of icebergs were created. Now, when you fly over, you see that the legs have melted back up the mountain valleys, 300 feet (100 m), 1,500 feet (500 m), 3,000 feet (1,000 m). There is nothing to be discussed or debated. Nothing to be argued about. The old photographs are perfectly clear. Today's situation is perfectly clear. It isn't a matter of science. It is a matter of simple comparison. It does not require literature in order to see and understand what any child could see and understand. The glaciers are melting. And that simple fact of observation should be enough.

If the glaciers are melting, the implications for the planet and for all of us on it are enormous. If there is any possibility that any of the causes are produced by us, we must urgently remove that possibility. It is a question of strategy. What do you do when faced by a life-or-death scenario? You act fast to save your life. The first thing you don't do is take the time to establish proof. And yet we are moving, if at all, at what one would have called in the past a glacial pace. We are moving slower than today's glaciers are melting, as if there is no urgency, as if a less than glacial pace is rational or dignified or respects a scientific process. As if that is what matters.

Why? Here we do have the utilitarian answers: there are short-term commercial interests; short-term national interests; short-term job concerns. All around us, specialists in silos are arguing about the meaning of proof and proposing narrow, highly complex technical possibilities; these are solutions that respect the narrowness of their silos. There are elections to be won or lost. There are sadly isolated economists, shut up in their university departments, talking among themselves in a micro manner, so micro in fact that they cannot conceive that the environment is anything other than a source of commercial exploitation or, failing that, a cost to the taxpayers, a cost we cannot afford.

They cannot imagine a change in their intellectual construct that would reinvent the saving of the environment, for example, as an investment, a way to create new wealth.

But all of these are merely utilitarian explanations. I feel that if we look as writers at our civilizations, we will see that we are responding to this crisis in the manner of a classic—standard—literary figure. Many of the greatest novels and plays are about characters who can see disaster looming up on them. They can see that this disaster is largely self-created and self-imposed. And yet they cannot change. They cannot control themselves. They are deeply passive. They cannot act to save themselves. In other words, they must destroy themselves. That is their destiny—or rather, that is their fate. Anna Karenina. Madame Bovary. Captain Ahab. In most cases we come to understand these characters as symbols of ourselves, of our civilizations or some part of them.

Asian writing seems perhaps even more focused on such characters. The professor in Natsume Soseki's *Sanshiro*. Lu Xun's *The True Story of Ah Q*. I wonder if Yi Kwang-Su's *Mujong / The Heartless* doesn't fall into this category. Or today, Young-ha Kim's *I Have the Right to Destroy Myself*. The industrialized world and those who seek to imitate the industrialized world seem to be playing out Ah Q's drama, except that highly sophisticated education has become the modern world's equivalent of Ah Q's uneducated form of ignorance and passivity. Our excuse for passivity is that we know so much. We know so much and are so obsessed by knowing more that we feel increasingly ignorant and somehow unable to act for fear that we will upset our complex system of specialist experts. That was one of the messages I was attempting to deliver seventeen years ago when I wrote *Voltaire's Bastards; the Dictatorship of Reason in the West*.

We could say that our societies, faced by the environment, have an almost Macbeth-like quality to them. We kill the king—in our case, the king is the place upon which we depend for life—and so must die. And so Burnham Woods must move.

One of the most curious things about our situation is the role of literature and indeed film and other creative languages. Why have we been unable, so far, to create the words, phrases, characters that in turn will create the sense of reality—the real reality—that allows citizens to make change happen? Why are we still stuck in the Unreal City? We know that great changes rarely come. And there are very few ways to bring about change. Even catastrophes rarely bring movement. Witness the collapse of the Manchu empire, from one disaster to another, stretched out over a century. Or look at the economic events of the last four years. Every sign tells us that much of the economic system in place is deeply flawed and caused the disaster. Yet here we are, alternately spending trillions of kick-start dollars or starving the system through austerity, while making no real changes.

What are the few ways to provoke rapid change—which is what we need? It may come in the wake of violence. But the experience in the West has been that, provoked in this way, change usually careens onto an uncontrolled path of actions and reactions and more reactions. Change can also come with extraordinary speed when language changes. When the language is right, humans can express what they want to do, what they know must be done. When the language is right, it can change human relations. Words are the primary way we imagine ourselves. Language produces the multiple concepts by which we act or do not act. If we get the language right, we can act. We will need to act. And while some languages may be more powerful than others, because of population numbers and geographical size, the breakthrough to these essential new understandings of words may as easily, perhaps more easily, come from less powerful languages. They have less to sell, less need to justify their role beyond their own communities. And so they may be driven by a greater sense of how to use language to effect change. I personally feel that my two languages, English and French, are doing miserably at responding to the environmental crisis. English in particular has allowed the language of the environment to be captured by the sort of specialist obscurantism, which prevents citizens from feeling that they can be directly involved, except in the most populist of ways. Those who are employed to save the planet are often far more specialist and obscure and lost in a dialect than those who are in denial of our reality.

Indeed, for the last three decades, the two dominant languages around the world could hardly be described as languages. They certainly have not been English or French or Spanish or Chinese. The first has been and remains the specialist dialect of economics. Second, there is the language of the managers, which could best be described as an anti-language. In such a situation, politics in its broadest sense—that is, the shaping of the public good—has been expressed through two false means of communications. Put another way, the eye of the needle through which we try to see ourselves has been shaped by two deeply anti-literature languages or anti-literary languages. Perhaps this is one of the explanations for the difficulty we as writers continue to have in dealing with a reality like the environment. Not only is the dominant relevant language pitifully irrelevant, it is not even language.

Economists pretend to be above languages. After all, any real language is filled with doubts, debates, choices, and ethical parameters. What they tell us, which is meant to be value-free, is presented as no more than numbers and truth. Their concepts are therefore presented as scientific expressions of reality, so natural and true that they can trump more mundane factors such as human dignity or ethics or freedom of speech. It is difficult to keep on reminding ourselves that economics is no more than one of the many social science professions—the silo professions—to emerge over the last century. Even the idea that this is a profession is dubious. It is an area of constant speculation, not of truth. And in the hands of real theoreticians, economics has always had more to do with philosophy than with science, let alone with inevitability. That is a healthy approach because it establishes economics as a literate force—one that offers choices. For the last thirty years, economics has been an illiterate force.

The language of management is even more troubling. It is built upon a dialect designed to obscure meaning and prevent change. Because of the constant breakthroughs in knowledge over the last century, our societies have come to be dominated by a multitude of narrow, specialist dialects, all operating in closed silos. These silos may do wonderful things—such as switch your heart for another or build a bridge—but they prevent communication. Managerial leadership has arisen as a way to hold the silos together, to manage them. Put another way, the power of managers lies in their maintenance of noncommunication between the silos. And so the manager lives upon his or her capacity to prevent communications, to deny the force of real language, which can produce the power for change.

Confucius was the original theorist of social and governmental organization. The opinions of today's management consultants are usually forgotten not long after they are given. Two-and-a-half thousand years later, Confucius is still relevant. When asked what he would do first if he were given power, he said he would rectify the names. I cannot read the original text, but I have looked at a multitude of translations into English and French, and I believe what he meant by rectifying the names was that he would reexamine the terms and concepts through which people talk to each other. And he would rectify the conceptual language to make it accurate. He went on, 'If the names aren't right, what you say will sound unreasonable. If what you say is unreasonable, what you try to do will fail' (Lau, 1992, p. 121).

This strikes me as a convincing explanation of the situation we find ourselves in. If our language cannot express reality in a way that empowers us to act, well then, the names need to be rectified. If we do not do this, which we have not, we become the victims of ideology. After all, what are ideologies but the kidnappers of concepts? They kidnap names, and once under their control, they use these concepts to their own purposes. And so we find that terms, which ought to empower us to deal with something like the environmental crisis, have no traction.

Western languages have taken ideas such as reason and defined them in such a way that efficiency trumps ethics. In other words, reason has been reduced to a utilitarian tool, which then favours, for example, profit over the public good. I increasingly feel that Western languages will not be able to escape the linear logic of false reason unless there is a radical change in our linguistic and creative sources of language. Today, even when we write and speak against the deforming forces of this false reason, we find ourselves reduced to the parameters of the theoretically rational argument.

I cannot know what the implications of these arguments are in other languages. But I do know that many of these definitions of names coming out of economics and management have developed equivalent forms around the world. And our incapacity to talk about the environment in a way that leads to action—rather than specialist negotiations that produce complex but minor changes, such as the agreement in Kyoto—seems to be shared in all of our languages. In other words, what I feel increasingly about the Western languages is that we will only be able to rectify the names if we walk away from the Western or European tradition. We need to walk away from the increasingly narrow and linear approaches that dominate in our ways of writing and, in effect, of not communicating.

We need to introduce other approaches to language, which come from outside. In Canada, we still have over fifty Aboriginal languages, with a growing and increasingly powerful indigenous population. Many of these languages are at risk of disappearing; some are not. I raise this because these languages take a very different approach to the relationship between people and place. Aboriginal languages do not use the Western, theoretically rational, device, which separates people from place in order to establish that humans can be levitated above the rest and therefore have the right to do what they wish to their physical surroundings. It is this rational conceit that lies at the heart of our environmental crisis. And our literature has not successfully challenged the deep assumptions of the last half millennium, which put us so firmly in charge of the planet because we are above it. Our interests can therefore be seen intellectually as separate from those of the planet.

The Aboriginal languages take a quite different approach. In their literature, their great poetic sagas, their philosophy, they see humans as an integrated piece of the whole. Theirs is not a romantic idea or an old-fashioned idea. Theirs are ideas that are reemerging today as perfectly modem and adapted to our time. I can think of a few perfectly clear concepts that make sense of where we are. There is a Cree concept called *witaskewin,* which focuses on how humans must live within the place. Or there is a Pacific Coast idea—*Tsawalk*—in which the worldview is that everything is one (Atleo, 2004).

A few years ago I saw a Korean equivalent of this in a valley near the old royal capital of Kyongju. Indeed, I wrote about what I saw there in *The Unconscious Civilization.* It is the house that the great Confucian teacher Yi On-chock built for himself in 1516. What I remember is the seamless, perfect integration between a great man's dwelling and the place in which he had imagined and built it.

To go back to the Aboriginal languages, one of their strengths is that they are still driven by the oral, rather than the written. It is the written that has been so effectively kidnapped by the linear and the narrow specialist dialects. This is particularly troubling for so many of us who are the voices of written literature. We are trapped within a world where that same written form has become the tool of systems that cannot deal with the environmental reality. I believe that within these oral languages and oral civilizations lie the forces that could help us to break out of the silos and the false languages, which dominate when we attempt to deal with crises as present and as threatening as global warming.

What this means in literature is a need to turn away from the linear process, which can confuse being modern with a sophisticated but powerless response to our overly written society. I feel that there is a great power to be released within us, one that reestablishes the concept that all is one—that we are perfectly capable of acting according to reality because we are part of that reality and not above it.

NOTE

An earlier version of this document was presented at the 16th International Literary Symposium, Korean PEN, Seoul, September 17, 2009.

REFERENCES

Atleo, E. R. (2004), *Tsawalk; A Nuu-chah-nulth Worldview,* UBC Press: Vancouver.

Lau, D. C. (trans.) (1992), *The Analects by Confucius,* book XIII, Chinese University Press: Hong Kong.

INDEX

Note: Page numbers followed by italicized letters indicate material found in figures (*f*), notes (*n*) or tables (*t*).

physical rationality of design, 274
physical/natural level of meaning, 494
pick-your-own produce, 248
pictures, memory and, 329
Pigou, A. C., 499
Placebo Project (Dunne and Raby), 482
place-mood, 215
plan simplification, 225–6
planetary boundaries, 60–1
planned obsolescence, 141–3, 304, 369–71, 423n7
Plater-Zyberk, E., 231
Plato, 435
'playing to the galleries', 386n2
pleasure, as human choice, 328
The Pleasures and Sorrows of Work (de Button), 51–2
pluralism, of liberal-modern societies, 32
plurality, human condition and, 332
Pogglioli, R., 473
Polanyi, M., 455–6
Policy Reform scenario, 266
political condition, of design activism, 472–5
Politics of Nature (Latour), 48
pollution (external/intrinsic), 82
Pollution Prevention Pays initiative, 308
'polymorphous perversity', 429
population, in first/third world, 82
population growth, 422n4
Porset, Clara, 467
Positive Development (PD), 74, 86–8
possibility, apprehending, 391–3
post-carbon pathways, 317
post-carbonaceous transition, objectives of, 413t
Postman, N., 505
post-materialism, 33–5
poverty, urban, 274
  see also recyclable collectors
practical needs for living, 5–6
practice-based design research, 450f, 459–61
Pratt Institute, 130
preferences vs. reason, 82–3
Preliminary Teaching Manual for Sustainable Design Education (IDEC), 126–7
prematerialism, 28–9
premodern wisdom, 63

Premsela, 480
'presencing', 64–5
present-to-hand objects, 369, 512
Princen, T., 162
private open space, 230
pro bono design work, 469, 470
problems, dealing with, 24
produce, 'pick-your-own', 248
producer-service industry, 361n3
product failure/longevity, 369
product families, 398–9, 399f
product improvement limits, 410
product life-cycle phases, 110f
product lifespans, 370
product model, rethinking, 306–8
Product Responsibility initiative, 310
production technique optimization, 112t
production-focused approach, 289
productive chain of recycling, 281n1
productivism, 519
products vs. process, 238–9
product-service systems (PSS), 2, 107, 115–16, 411–12
product-systems, 410–11
progress
  belief in, 17
  ideology of, 498–9
  linear view of, 75
propositional artefacts, 456, 457–9, 470
propositional design
  contribution to design research, 448–53
  contribution to knowledge, 453–9
  process of, 454f
propositional objects, examples of, 462–4, 462f
prosthetic limbs, 340
psychoactive world, 37
psychological obsolescence, 370
public bicycle renting system, 357, 358f
public language, 319, 525–8
public open space, 230
Punk Metal product range, 193f

Quammen, D., 256
Quartier Jardin
  dwellings design, 233–4, 234f
  project description, 231–2